REPORTING FOR THE
MEDIA

REPORTING FOR THE MEDIA

Sixth Edition

FRED FEDLER
University of Central Florida

JOHN R. BENDER
University of Nebraska

LUCINDA DAVENPORT
Michigan State University

PAUL E. KOSTYU
Ohio Wesleyan University

Harcourt Brace College Publishers

Fort Worth   Philadelphia   San Diego   New York   Orlando   Austin   San Antonio
Toronto   Montreal   London   Sydney   Tokyo

Publisher	Christopher P. Klein
Senior Acquisitions Editor	Carol Wada
Developmental Editor	Cathlynn Richard
Project Editors	steve Norder/Andrea Wright
Production Manager	Melinda Esco
Senior Art Director	David A. Day

Library of Congress Catalog Card Number: 96-78071

Some material in this work previously appeared in REPORTING FOR THE MEDIA, Instructor's Manual, Fifth Edition, copyright © 1993, 1989, 1984, 1979, 1973 by Harcourt Brace & Company.

Harcourt Brace College Publishers may provide complimentary instructional aids and supplements or supplement packages to those adopters qualified under our adoption policy. Please contact your sales representative for more information. If as an adopter or potential user you receive supplements you do not need, please return them to your sales representative or send them to: Attn: Returns Department, Troy Warehouse, 465 Lincoln Drive, Troy, MO 63379.

Although for mechanical reasons all pages of this publication are perforated, only those pages imprinted with Harcourt Brace & Company are intended for removal.

Address for orders:
Harcourt Brace & Company
6277 Sea Harbor Drive, Orlando, FL 32887-6777
1-800-782-4479 or 1-800-433-0001 (in Florida).

Address for editorial correspondence:
Harcourt Brace College Publishers
301 Commerce Street, Suite 3700, Fort Worth, TX 76102

ISBN: 0-15-503724-2

Printed in the United States of America

6 7 8 9 0 1 2 3 4 5 066 9 8 7 6 5 4 3 2 1

Preface

Each new edition of this book has contained significant changes. This sixth edition continues that tradition. Its most obvious changes include (1) the addition of three co-authors, (2) two new chapters, (3) an expanded "Introduction for Students" and (4) a shortened title.

The co-authors add breadth, expertise and experience. Together, all four authors have a total of 33 years of full-time media experience and 49 years of full-time teaching experience. Moreover, they continue to work for the media: consulting, freelancing and spending an occasional summer in a newsroom.

This book was a massive undertaking for a single individual. Typically, about a third of each new edition was rewritten, and the work required 18 months, including time to help with the production: proofreading, obtaining illustrations and permissions and completing the Instructor's Manual.

Now each co-author can focus on his or her specific areas of expertise. For example, one of the new co-authors, John Bender, covered local government and politics as a reporter. He has rewritten this edition's chapter on Public Affairs Reporting, adding more introductory information that explains how police, local governments and courts work.

A growing number of schools require all their students, including those in broadcasting, advertising and public relations, to complete a basic or "core" writing course. To serve those students, this edition provides a new chapter on writing for public relations (chapter 17) and a new chapter on writing for the broadcast media (chapter 18). Another of the new co-authors, Lucinda Davenport, wrote these chapters. Because of their inclusion, the book's old title, "Reporting for the Print Media," no longer seemed appropriate. Thus, the word "Print" has been dropped. Similarly, references within each chapter have been broadened to include all the media.

To provide space for the new chapters, the entire book has been tightened, and some duplicate exercises eliminated. In addition, a chapter on statistical material has been combined with chapter 20 (Advanced Reporting).

The four authors have made thousands of other changes, from improving the wording of some sentences to adding new sections in many of the chapters. Some of the most significant changes include:

- For easy reference, journalism's standard copy editing symbols are printed on the inside of the front cover.

- New, up-to-date examples include references to the Unabomber, O. J. Simpson case, the William Kennedy Smith trial and Lorena and John Bobbitt, for example.

- Chapter 4 (Selecting and Reporting the News) includes a new section on Public/Civic Journalism written by the third of the new co-authors, Paul E. Kostyu.

- Chapter 12 (Communication Law) has been totally rewritten, emphasizing libel and privacy. The chapter also discusses problems of newsgathering, the protection of confidential sources and the free press/fair trial controversy.

- Chapter 20 (Advanced Reporting) includes a discussion of computer-assisted reporting (CAR) and several CAR exercises.

- A new appendix discusses common writing problems.

The book's primary emphasis has not changed, however. "Reporting for the Media" continues to provide both the instructions and exercises needed to help students become better writers.

The book also continues to reflect the belief that students learn to write by writing: that students should be given as much practice as possible and that the practice should be as realistic as possible. Thus, many of the assignments in this book are genuine: actual laws, interviews, speeches, police reports and news releases.

Other Features of Particular Interest to Faculty Members

Answer Keys

After reading the chapters and working on their exercises, some students will want more practice. They can complete the extra exercises marked "Answer Key Provided," then correct their own work. The answers to those exercises appear in Appendix D.

Appendices

"Reporting for the Media" provides five appendices: (A) a city directory, (B) a summary of The Associated Press Stylebook and Libel Manual, (C) rules for forming possessives, (D) answer keys for some exercises and (E) a discussion of common writing problems. Appendix E is new.

Checklists and Other End-of-Chapter Materials

A variety of supplemental teaching materials appears at the end of each chapter. The materials include expanded checklists that review and reinforce each chapter's primary instructions. Other materials vary from chapter to chapter, but typically include (1) lists of readings, (2) discussion questions, (3) suggested projects, (4) newsroom bulletins and (5) ombudsmen's commentaries.

This edition reprints a half-dozen bulletins titled "Write & Wrong" and prepared for the staff of the St. Louis Post-Dispatch. The bulletins discuss common errors and provide additional examples of good and bad writing. To teach students more about problems involving ethics and good taste, this book also reprints several columns written by newspapers' writing coaches and ombudsmen (the journalists hired to answer reader complaints).

Flexibility

"Reporting for the Media" is flexible. Teachers can assign its chapters in almost any order. Moreover, there are enough exercises so that faculty members can assign their favorites, then assign extra exercises for students who need more help in an area. Some teachers use the book for two semesters: for their schools' basic and advanced reporting classes. There are enough exercises for both terms.

Faculty members who prefer the book's traditional emphasis on the print media can assign the new chapters (writing for public relations and broadcasting) as optional readings. Both chapters appear at the end of the book.

Hundreds of Examples

"Reporting for the Media" contains hundreds of examples, some written by students and some by professionals. While introducing a new topic or discussing an error, this book typically shows students two or three examples then shows students how they can avoid or correct the error.

Some examples have been written by prize-winning professionals, and students can use their stories as models. An example from The Milwaukee Journal shows students how an entire story can be written in chronological order. Similarly, many journalists consider Jim Nicholson of the Philadelphia Daily News the nation's best obituary writer, and he is quoted extensively in chapter 15 (Writing Obituaries).

Realistic and Often Genuine Exercises

This book contains a multitude of exercises, and teachers can select the ones most appropriate for their students. Many are real. Exercises in chapter 9 (Interviews and Polls) contain verbatim accounts of actual interviews conducted especially for this book. Chapter 17 (Speeches and Meetings) includes President Bill Clinton's address at a memorial service for victims of the Oklahoma City bombing. Other exercises, although fictionalized, involve topics recently in the news: stories involving a dentist with AIDS, predictions of an earthquake along the New Madrid Fault, and a debate over the controversial exhibits funded by the National Endowment for the Arts.

To add to the realism, many of the exercises contain ethical problems: four-letter words, sexist comments, the names of rape victims, bloody details and other material that many editors would be reluctant to publish. Students completing those exercises will have to deal with the problems, and their decisions are likely to provoke lively discussions.

Instructor's Manual

The authors provide a detailed Instructor's Manual: about 150 pages of ideas, recommendations, answers and quizzes. The manual's introductory sections discuss accuracy, grades and suggested policies and assignments. Those sections are followed by sample course outlines and lists of the exercises that contain ethical dilemmas and sexist remarks. Other lists tell you which exercises can be localized: which mention your city, state or school. Later sections provide answers for many of the exercises. There are also tests covering style, vocabulary, attribution and spelling, as well as true/false questions for most chapters. (If you would like your city or school mentioned in an exercise in the next edition, contact any of the authors.)

Computer Software

Faculty members with access to Macintosh computers can use this book with "MediaWriter: Computerized Lessons in News Reporting," also written by Fred Fedler and co-authored by Lucinda Davenport of Michigan State University. The software, sold separately or with the textbook, provides 32 interactive exercises for the students in reporting classes. The first exercise emphasizes the fundamentals of news writing: spelling, style, accuracy and objectivity. Other exercises teach students how to write more clearly and concisely, with practice in writing leads and complete news stories. All exercises are designed to test student judgment and ethics.

Practical Approach

Like previous editions, this sixth is concrete, not abstract or theoretical. Its tone is both practical and realistic. Its language is readable: clear, concise, simple and direct. Because of the book's realism, students will encounter the types of problems and assignments they are likely to find when they graduate and begin work at entry-level jobs with the media.

Pro Challenge

Several exercises in the chapters about leads and the body of news stories are subtitled "Pro Challenge." Professionals have completed the exercises so students assigned the same exercises can compare their work to that of the professionals.

A Single Volume

By combining everything students need in a single volume, "Reporting for the Media" provides a convenient package at a reasonable price. Like earlier editions, this sixth edition includes both the instructions and examples that students need to learn to write more effectively. It also includes a multitude of exercises and a summary of The Associated Press Stylebook. Thus, students do not have to buy a separate style manual or workbook.

A Note of Thanks

Journalists are wonderful people: enthusiastic, interesting and helpful. While working on this book, we wrote to dozens of them. Reporters, photographers and editors from Salt Lake City to Philadelphia, from Miami to New York, answered our letters and provided advice and samples of their work.

We would especially like to thank the many professionals who gave us permission to quote their work: Donald L. Barlett and James B. Steele of The Philadelphia Inquirer; Roy P. Clark of the Poynter Institute for Media Studies; Lucille S. deView, writing coach for The Orange County (Calif.) Register; Harry Levins, writing coach for the St. Louis Post-Dispatch; Henry McNulty, a former reader representative for The Hartford (Conn.) Courant; Jim Nicholson, an obituary writer for the Philadelphia Daily News; Debbie M. Price, former executive editor of the Fort Worth Star Telegram; and Neil J. Rosini, an attorney whose work originally appeared in the IRE Journal.

Four colleagues also gave us permission to quote their work: Eugene Goodwin, a retired journalist, professor and author of "Groping for Ethics in Journalism"; M. Timothy O'Keefe, a professor and freelance writer; Jay Rosen, a professor and proponent of public journalism; and Frank R. Stansberry, a local professional of The Miami Herald who contributed a column on careers in public relations.

Numerous publications and news services gave us permission to quote their stories or republish their photographs: the Ann Arbor (Mich.) News, The Arizona Daily Star in Tucson, The Associated Press, The Deseret News in Salt Lake City, The Detroit News, Knight-Ridder, The Miami Herald, The Milwaukee Journal, The New York Times and Long Island's Newsday.

The following organizations also allowed us to quote their material: the American Society of Newspaper Editors, the Society of Professional Journalists and the National Victim Center.

Several professionals, all former students, completed the exercises titled "Pro Challenge": Eric Dentel, Dana Eagles, Geoffrey M. Giordano, Mike Griffin, Lisa Lochridge and Loraine O'Connell. Another former student, Barry Bradley, gave us permission to quote his account of an exceptional front-page story about a mugging in a nursing home.

We would also like to thank another colleague, Pat Mills of the Department of Journalism at Ball State University, for her help during a previous edition in revising and improving the chapter on feature stories.

For their insightful comments and useful suggestions during the development process, thanks go to Jeff Brody, California State University-Fullerton; Roberta Kelly, Washington State University; Harry Kloman, University of Pittsburgh; Linda Levin, University of Rhode Island; Robert McClory, Northwestern University; Donna Munde, Mercer County Community College; David Nelson, Southwest Texas State University; Carl Sessions Stepp, University of Maryland-College Park.

We would also like to thank the staff at Harcourt Brace—Carol Wada, senior acquisitions editor; Cathlynn Richard, developmental editor; steve Norder, project editor; David A. Day, senior art director; and Melinda Esco, production manager—for their part in the publication of this new edition of "Reporting for the Media."

The Authors

Fred Fedler received his bachelor's degree from the University of Wisconsin in Madison, then worked as a newspaper reporter in Dubuque and Davenport, Iowa, and as a copy editor in Sacramento, Calif. He received his master's degree from the University of Kentucky and doctorate from the University of Minnesota. Since 1971, Fedler has taught at the University of Central Florida in Orlando, and heads the School of Communication's News/Editorial Division. He regularly conducts research in the field of journalism but also continues to freelance for popular publications. Fedler's other books include "Introduction to the Mass Media" and "Media Hoaxes." In addition, Fedler serves on numerous committees concerned with journalism education. Because of his book about hoaxes, you may hear Fedler on radio or see him on television. When a new hoax appears in the news, he is sometimes asked to serve as a guest commentator.

John R. Bender is an assistant professor in the College of Journalism and Mass Communications at the University of Nebraska at Lincoln. Bender worked for six years as a reporter at the Pittsburgh Morning Sun in southeast Kansas, covering local government and politics. He became the paper's assignment editor, news editor, then managing editor. During his term as managing editor, the Morning Sun won awards for farm coverage, photography and editorial writing. Bender has taught at the college or university level for 10 years. He was a journalism instructor at Culver-Stockton College in Canton, Mo., for five years and joined the faculty at the University of Nebraska in 1990. His teaching and research areas include news reporting and writing, communication law, media history and controls of information. As an undergraduate, Bender majored in sociology at Westminster College in Fulton, Mo. He holds a master's degree in journalism from the University of Kansas and a doctorate in journalism from the University of Missouri at Columbia.

Lucinda Davenport is an associate professor in the School of Journalism at Michigan State University and also serves as the school's assistant director. As an undergraduate at Baylor University, Davenport double majored in journalism and radio/TV/film (today called "telecommunications"). She received a master's degree in journalism from the University of Iowa and a doctorate in mass media from Ohio University, where she was named "Outstanding Doctoral Student." Davenport has taught and worked in several areas, including public relations and newspaper and broadcast reporting. At Michigan State, she teaches, conducts professional workshops and publishes research in the areas of media ethics and computer-assisted reporting. She has developed interactive software and recently completed a multi-media CD-ROM for newswriting and reporting classes.

Paul E. Kostyu is an associate professor in the Department of Journalism at Ohio Wesleyan University. He graduated with a bachelor's degree in English and biology from Heidelberg College in 1973 and began his journalism career with the Tiffin (Ohio) Advertiser-Tribune. While working as a reporter, photographer and area editor, Kostyu completed a master's degree in popular culture at Bowling Green State University. In 1978, he joined the Greensboro Daily News (later the News & Record) as a bureau reporter. In 1981, Kostyu received a Rotary International Foundation Journalism Award that allowed him to study in Bangor, Wales, for a year. He returned to Greensboro as a layout editor and was named chief of the paper's largest bureau. In 1985, Kostyu became editor of the faculty/staff newspaper at Bowling Green State University, beginning his doctoral work at the same time. He began teaching full-time in 1986. He teaches in a variety of areas, including reporting and writing, media law and journalism history. Kostyu recently spent a summer helping The Ann Arbor (Mich.) News establish a computer-assisted reporting program.

Finally, dozens of students and teachers have written to us, telling us what they like and dislike about this book and suggesting new features. We have adopted many of their ideas, and we would like to hear from you. If you have a suggestion or comment, please write to any of us:

Fred Fedler
School of Communication
University of Central Florida
Orlando, Fla. 32816-1344

John Bender
College of Journalism
University of Nebraska
Lincoln, Neb. 68588-0127

Lucinda Davenport
School of Journalism
Michigan State University
East Lansing, Mich. 48824-1212

Paul E. Kostyu
Department of Journalism
Ohio Wesleyan University
Delaware, Ohio 43015

☆☆☆☆☆

Contents

INTRODUCTION

This is an exciting time for people entering the field of journalism, a time of challenge and change. Students majoring in journalism will enjoy unprecedented opportunities. Many will work for traditional media: for newspapers, radio and television stations, and advertising and public relations agencies. But others will find new opportunities, perhaps with cable, telephone or computer companies—or with conglomerates that run several of the companies.

Information is traveling at the speed of light, and the new information superhighway is forcing companies into new partnerships and mergers. The companies are investing billions of dollars in entertainment and information systems that will transform everyone's lives, but especially journalists'.

The stakes are enormous. There are 92 million households in the United States, and virtually all of them have a television set and telephone. Daily newspapers and cable television reach about 60 percent of the nation's households, and about 27 percent have personal computers. The companies that control those systems will control a huge new market. Americans already spend $12 billion a year on video rentals and $70 billion on catalog shopping, for example, and the information superhighway may take over both industries, along with countless others.

There will be hundreds of new television channels, with most catering to more specialized interests. At the same time, more and more programming—news and entertainment—will be delivered on demand from giant computer disks, so viewers may be able to watch any movie, weather report or college class at any time.

To strengthen their position, traditional rivals are merging. They want to control two major elements: (1) the means of transmitting digitized signals into homes, and (2) the system's programming or content. Time Warner, an entertainment and publishing giant, has formed an alliance with a telephone company. Microsoft is working with NBC on a cable and Internet news service. Through a merger, Disney gained control of the ABC television network. By acquiring broadcast and cable properties, Disney obtained a distribution system for its movies and television programs.

Older media are adjusting to the competition, a never-ending process. Existing media have already adjusted to a myriad of new competitors. The newspaper, radio and magazine industries adjusted to the introduction of television. The television industry adjusted to the introduction of cable, and the movie industry adjusted to the introduction of VCR's and video rentals. Moreover, many of the older media profit from their new rivals. Television producers earn more when cable systems rebroadcast their programs. Hollywood studios earn more when people buy or rent videos of their movies.

Newspapers are experimenting with a multitude of new ventures, including news delivery by radio, television, cable and fax. Some newspapers encourage readers to call and listen to personal ads, sports scores, and movie and restaurant reviews. Readers in other cities can request faxes of recent restaurant reviews. Readers with computers can also converse with newspaper staffs, enjoying two-way conversations with reporters and editors.

The potential is enormous. In the past, a newspaper's size was limited by its publication costs. As a result, a typical newspaper printed only 10 percent of the information it received each day, discarding the other 90 percent. In a few years, that 90 percent may become available online. Readers will be able to turn on a computer (or perhaps a television screen that functions like

Harcourt Brace & Company

a computer) and move to a menu with labels such as "Local News," "National News," "Business," "Sports" and "Entertainment." Readers will be able to select any box and browse through it, perhaps to obtain more in-depth information about a story in that day's paper. Or, readers may request the full text of a speech, more photographs or more comics. Other readers may request minor stories that larger dailies have never had the space to report: the time of church services, bus and airline schedules, the hours of shopping malls, or a daily list of crimes committed in their neighborhood.

Readers interested in a specialized topic, such as birds, swimming, dancing or mathematics, may program their computers so they automatically display more stories about the topics. If they want, those readers will also be able to print every story.

Some experts predict that, eventually, newspapers will no longer need printing presses and carriers. Rather, people will receive an electronic paper: "a digitized blend of text, graphics, color photos, sound and full-motion video dancing across a book-sized portable computer." The computer will be wireless, so you will be able to take it anywhere. That may not happen in our lifetimes. Even when it does, some readers may prefer their traditional daily.

In many cities, you can already receive portions of your local daily online. Increasingly, dailies are also creating message boards and sponsoring daily chat rooms about topics that range from politics to dating.

One of the most innovative organizations, the Chicago Tribune Co., established ChicagoLand TV, a 24-hour cable news channel that reaches 90 percent of the homes with cable in the Chicago metropolitan area. The newspaper's staff helps gather and present news on the channel, using mini television studios set up in Tribune newsrooms. More than 140 of the Tribune's staffers appeared on ChicagoLand TV during its first year, reaching more people with their stories.

Tribune readers with computers and modems can use Chicago Online, another new service, to obtain electronic versions of the Tribune's stories and classified advertisements. Or, readers can send messages to the Tribune's staff.

The Chicago Tribune Co. also owns more than a dozen television stations; produces news and entertainment programs for those stations; owns six radio stations; and bought a large stake in America Online, the fastest growing of the major online services.

The fields of advertising and public relations are also changing. Practitioners in both fields can use the information superhighway to communicate directly with the public. Because their messages are no longer filtered through reporters and editors, the practitioners retain total control over the messages' content. But like journalists, the practitioners must learn new skills.

Changes in the media are changing Americans' lives. More and more Americans are studying, shopping and working at home, a trend certain to continue. With E-mail, it is also becoming easier for Americans to communicate with one another. Homes may eventually be equipped with video phones, so callers will be able to both see and talk to one another. Or, families may transmit videos directly to a relative's home.

Merchants envision a burgeoning market. While sitting in your living room, you will be able to stroll through your favorite mall, decide what stores to enter, inspect their merchandise and request more information about items you like. Then, you will be able to order the items, charging them to a credit card.

But important questions remain unanswered. The most important is how companies will profit from the information superhighway. Many, afraid of being left behind, are experimenting with the system, but earn little or no money from it. For example: people rarely pay anything when they look at a newspaper online. Newspapers cover some costs by establishing 900 numbers, so readers are charged for calls that request a sports score or that answer a personal ad. Or, newspapers may receive a fee each time someone uses their system to buy an airline ticket or to reserve a hotel room. But to earn a significant profit, the field's pioneers will have to learn how they can use the system to deliver content so valuable that millions of people will be willing to pay for it.

Other important questions include:

Harcourt Brace & Company

- How soon will the information superhighway become available to most Americans?

- How much will consumers be willing to pay for the necessary equipment and fees?

- How will the system protect Americans' privacy? (Increasingly, computers maintain your school, financial and medical records; driving and employment histories; information and entertainment preferences; shopping habits; and more.)

- Will every American be able to afford and understand how to use the information superhighway? And will it be available in even poor and remote areas? If not, the system may divide Americans into classes of "haves" and "have-nots."

- How will government regulate the system?

Other changes in journalism are occurring simultaneously. At first, those changes may seem confusing, or even overwhelming. But the changes are exciting, and reflect the field's diversity and potential. Because of the protection provided by the First Amendment, journalists enjoy an unusual degree of freedom, and different journalists reach different—even opposite—conclusions about the best way to respond to the changes. Employers will not expect you to agree with them on every issue, but may expect you to be aware of the issues (and be prepared to deal with them).

Briefly, the following pages introduce you to a few of the major issues in journalism today: trends discussed in more depth later in this book. Those trends include changes in the field's ethics, reporters' relationships with their audiences, ownership and boundaries.

In 1994, only 13 percent of the nation's adults expressed a great deal of confidence in the media, down from 29 percent in 1966. That is not unusual, however. The public seems to be unhappy with every major institution. In 1994, only 8 percent of the nation's adults expressed a great deal of confidence in Congress, down from 42 percent in 1966. Similarly, the public's confidence in major companies dropped from 55 to 19 percent, in colleges and universities from 61 to 25 percent, and in medicine from 73 to 23 percent.

Partly because of the public's dissatisfaction, journalists are improving their ethical standards. Journalists hope the improvement will help them regain the public's confidence—and that, as more people learn to respect the media, more will patronize them. As part of the process, editors are adopting codes of ethics, and some want their codes to be so specific that employees will understand what is expected of them in every situation.

Most codes are similar. They declare that journalists must be honest, accurate, fair, courteous, compassionate and objective. Many add that journalists should correct their errors and avoid deception and trickery of any kind: impersonations and hidden cameras, for example. Journalists cannot accept anything of value from people they write about, and must also avoid other conflicts, such as an involvement in politics.

Some journalists dislike the codes. They warn that no code can anticipate every problem and specify the proper behavior in every situation. Skeptics explain that problems change over time, and are rarely black-and-white. There may be exceptions to some rules, and skeptics want their staffs to think for themselves: to be able to decide what is best in a particular situation. Skeptics also warn that the codes' value is exaggerated: that codes of ethics are unlikely to change people's behavior—or the public's opinion of the media.

Other journalists worry that the codes will be used against them. People suing the media for libel may win more easily if they can show that an organization has a code, and that an employee violated it.

The following examples, all real, demonstrate the complexity of the issues that confront journalists—and the difficulty of writing a code that specifies the proper response to every problem:

- If you learn that a candidate for president is having an affair, would you report the story? Is the affair a public or private matter? If you publish the story, the candidate is likely to be defeated. Yet popular presidents, such as Franklin D. Roosevelt and

Harcourt Brace & Company

John F. Kennedy, apparently had affairs even while in office. Would the country have benefited from their defeat?

- Imagine that the Unabomber mailed you a 35,000-word manifesto—a 62-page, single-spaced article—that assailed the industrialized world. The Unabomber was responsible for three deaths and 23 injuries. Now, he promises to stop the bombings if you publish his entire manifesto. Would you publish it? If so, how would you respond to people who said you submitted to the Unabomber's blackmail? If you refused, how would you respond to the victims' families when the Unabomber struck again, killing more innocent victims?

- If you managed a television station in Waco, Texas, and learned that the Bureau of Alcohol, Tobacco and Firearms planned a raid on the compound occupied by David Koresh and his followers, would you broadcast the raid live? Would you continue your live coverage during negotiations after the raid, and later show the compound being engulfed in flames? If so, how would you respond to critics who said your coverage encouraged Koresh to extend the confrontation, satisfying his hunger for attention.

Those issues, like many others, do not have answers that are clearly right or wrong. And no matter what you decide—or how ethically you try to act—your decisions will be controversial: certain to offend a portion of your audience.

To better serve the public, other journalists are trying an idea called "public journalism." The idea's proponents want journalists to listen more closely to their audiences and to play a more active role in their communities. They believe that journalists should care about their communities and do more to help improve them.

Thus, journalists in some cities are becoming catalysts for change. Instead of remaining objective and detached, they promote reforms and ask the public to help decide which stories they should cover and how they should cover them. To learn what their readers want, the journalists invite focus groups to discuss issues that concern them. Or, journalists conduct surveys and arrange town meetings.

The trend may be most evident on editorial pages. Some newspapers publish fewer syndicated columnists and use the space to publish more of their readers' opinions: more letters, cartoons, essays and call-in comments. Activists hope the policy will do more than improve their communities. They hope it will also strengthen the bond between newspapers and the public.

But again, journalists are divided. Skeptics consider public journalism a threat. They say their colleagues are too involved in the news, and that their involvement creates conflicts that hurt everyone's credibility. If the media promote as well as report, journalists will have to cover reforms that their own employers support.

Skeptics also worry that the media will become more hesitant to express unpopular ideas. Yet some unpopular ideas have been courageous and right: editorials opposed to segregation in the South and to the demagoguery of Wisconsin Sen. Joseph McCarthy, as well as editorials about Watergate and about the war in Vietnam, for example. Or, the media may emphasize more frivolous topics, giving the public more entertainment rather than news. That fear reflects an issue that journalists have debated for years: Should they give the public what it wants, or should they give the public what they think it needs?

The third change involves the media's ownership. For years, many of the media were small, family-run ventures. Since World War II, the media have become bigger, more profitable and more valuable. Most have been sold to larger companies, often conglomerates (organizations that own different types of companies and that often sell their stock to the public). Journalists complain about new financial pressures, especially a greater emphasis on profits, and many blame the media's new owners.

The newspaper industry typifies the trend. At their peak, more than 2,200 daily newspapers were published in the United States. Many large cities had 8 or 10 dailies, including some published in foreign languages. As recently as 1946, the United States had 1,763 dailies, compared to about 1,540 today. What's happened is simple—and creates a misleading impression of the industry's health.

Only 33 cities still have two or more dailies owned by different companies: dailies that truly compete with one another. Another 30 cities have two dailies owned by the same company. Thus, in all but a handful of cities, only the strongest daily—usually the daily with the largest circulation—has survived. Although many smaller dailies have failed, the surviving, or monopoly, papers tend to be extraordinarily profitable.

A typical supermarket has a profit margin of 1 to 2 percent. The average for retailers in the United States is 6 to 7 percent. For years, monopoly dailies had a profit margin of 20 percent or more. Some dailies had a profit margin as high as 40 percent. Newspapers continued to earn high profits even as their circulations declined. In 1946, publishers sold 382 daily papers per 1,000 population. Today, publishers sell about 60 million daily papers, but only 233 per 1,000 population. Fortunately for the industry, newspapers reach the type of people that advertisers like: the wealthy and well educated.

Newspapers are sensitive to business cycles and were hurt by a recession during the early 1990s, when advertisers cut back on their accounts. Since then, newspapers have been hurt by the rising cost of newsprint and intense competition from other media. Some have laid off employees, closed bureaus and begun to publish fewer pages. Newspapers will survive those and other problems, but may never be as profitable as in the past.

Radio and television stations have experienced similar trends. Many have been taken over by larger companies, and those companies often merge or acquire other companies, until a single conglomerate owns a multitude of newspapers, magazines, radio and television stations, cable systems, and more.

Some journalists feel a nostalgia for the past. They fear that journalism is losing its glamour and romance, and becoming just another business. Yet other fields are being affected by similar pressures and some, such as medicine, are experiencing even more difficult and revolutionary changes. Moreover, there is little or no evidence that the media owned by today's conglomerates are, on average, any better or worse than the older family-run ventures. Some of today's newspaper groups have a reputation for excellence: Knight-Ridder Inc.; The Times Mirror Co.; The New York Times Co.; Dow Jones & Co. Inc.; the Chicago Tribune Co.; and the McClatchy Newspapers, for example. Unfortunately, others do not.

Finally, new technologies are blurring the boundaries between different fields. When sent out to cover a story, the reporters at some newspapers bring video cameras, then broadcast the video over their newspaper's news channel. Other reporters discuss the news on local radio or television stations.

Other evidence of journalism's converging technologies include the following trends:

- Newspapers have become almost totally electronic. Reporters write their stories on computers, and editors use computers to polish the stories, arrange them on pages and transmit them over the Internet.

- Television stations work with newspapers, radio stations and cable systems.

- Some cable systems also offer their subscribers telephone service. Soon, a single company—perhaps a telephone or cable company—will offer local, long-distance, cellular, paging and cable services.

- Initially, movies are shown on film, but may be edited for television and rented on videos.

- People in advertising use computers and other electronic equipment to prepare messages that appear in every medium.

What does all that mean for you?

Harcourt Brace & Company

The information superhighway is primarily a communications system that offers new opportunities and rewards for the field's pioneers.

Although journalism's technology is changing, its primary attraction for students is not. Jobs in the field are exciting, important, creative and varied. As a journalist, you will have an opportunity to write, to serve the public and to experience something new every day. Moreover, talented young people can move ahead quickly in the field.

As the information superhighway expands, there are also likely to be more jobs for journalists. To place information online, the media will need more writers, editors and technicians to prepare information, converting it into a form the public can use.

Journalism majors have traditionally been given a broad liberal arts education. Today, some editors want journalism majors to take more business courses, so they can move into management. Other editors want journalism majors to take more courses in computer science. That advice may or may not be the best. To succeed, you will still have to be well informed about the world. Increasingly, you will also have to be flexible. Thus, despite the changes, a broad liberal arts education may still be the best for journalism majors.

Academia, too, is adjusting to the new technologies. That is one of the reasons why more students are enrolled in writing and reporting courses such as yours. Schools are reviewing their requirements, and some are establishing a basic core for all their students.

Many schools now require every journalism major to enroll in a reporting class and to use a book like this one. Why? Because the skills emphasized in reporting classes are needed by the professionals in every area of journalism, including those in broadcasting, advertising and public relations.

Before writing anything, everyone has to first gather, understand and organize all the necessary information. If you want the media to use the information, you will also have to understand their definitions of news. The media are unlikely to use even the most well-written story if it contains no news: nothing of interest or importance to the public. Finally—but most important—you will also have to be a good writer.

BECOMING A GOOD WRITER

Many Americans seem to believe that writing is an easy, glamorous job. The people who think that, says author Elizabeth Lane, "have probably never written anything longer than a check." Lane explains that writing hurts. There is, however, a simple formula for success. "It's this," Lane says. "Fanny on the chair. Elbows on the desk. Fingers on the keyboard. For however long it takes to finish the job."

Like other writers, Lane sometimes asks herself why she got into the business and why she continues to write. "I'm hooked," she answers. "I have a hundred stories in my head and this driving compulsion to put them on paper to read."[1]

Lane is not a journalist. She is a romance writer who has published 10 books. It doesn't matter. Most writers, regardless of their specialty, agree with Lane.

Journalists, too, get hooked. They enjoy the challenge of uncovering important stories and the thrill of being there to watch the stories unfold. Journalists also enjoy the challenge of writing stories quickly, under deadline pressure, and of putting words together in a way that will interest readers. However, their greatest rewards come when they finish a piece: when it appears in print, they see their byline and hear from people who like their work.

Elizabeth Lane adds that writers must also be diligent. Most students realize that athletes and musicians must practice hours a day. Many fail to realize that writers, too, must practice regularly and systematically. Author Sheila Hailey explains:

---

[1] Elizabeth Lane. "Writing Romance." *WordPerfect Magazine,* August 1989, p. 70.

The one thing all professional writers have in common . . . is that they get down to it and write. They don't just talk about it, they don't wait for inspiration, they don't wish they had time to write. They make time and press on. Oh, there's often some pencil-sharpening and desk-tidying that goes on first. But sooner or later, they write, though never knowing with certainty if they are at work on a masterpiece or a disaster.[2]

Other writers agree with Lane's assertion that writing is hard work—not the result of inspiration, luck or good assignments. G. Wayne Miller, a prize-winning writer for the Providence Journal-Bulletin, adds:

. . . despite whatever level of talent an individual may have, a lot of the creative process is discipline. It's actually doing it. It's work, hard work. You just have to remain at the top of your craft, and the way you do that is not by having brilliant inspirational bursts every couple of months. You get down and you just do it every day.[3]

Columnist James J. Kilpatrick explained:

Our task is deceptively simple. It is as deceptively simple as the task of carpenters, who begin by nailing one board to another board. Then other boards are nailed to other boards, and lo, we have a house. Just so, as writers we put one word after another word, and we connect those words to other words, and lo, we have a news story or an editorial or if it goes badly, a plate of spaghetti.[4]

To avoid a plate of spaghetti, you need a good editor or teacher: someone who cares about you and who will spend the time needed to critically evaluate your work. For most students, that criticism is the hardest part of all. When they submit a story to a teacher, most students want praise and an "A." Not a critical analysis of their work. Not a dozen corrections. Not a note saying they will have to rewrite the entire piece.

If you are serious about becoming a good writer, you will have to learn to accept, even welcome, criticism of your work. However painful, that is how you learn. Too many students fail to realize that. Rather than appreciating their editor's or instructor's criticism, students resent it. Worse, some take it personally, failing to study and learn from it.

For as long as you write, you will have an editor. For the moment, that editor will be your instructor. And a good instructor will do everything possible to improve your work, whether it is a news story, advertisement or news release. Be grateful, never thin-skinned and resentful.

Prize-winning writers have recognized and praised their editors' help. One of those prize-winners, Colin Nickerson, began his career as the only reporter at a small weekly. Four years later, Nickerson became a reporter for The Boston Globe, quickly becoming one of that paper's foreign correspondents. Nickerson says:

I learned that writing was a lot tougher than I'd ever expected it to be. I learned that writing takes a lot of thought and a lot of effort. That the whole difference between a bad newspaper story and a good newspaper story has nothing to do with what the story's about. . . . The difference is usually the amount of thought and effort that the reporter, and then later his or her editors, are willing to put into it.[5]

This book, too, will help you learn to write. Its assignments have been made as realistic as possible. While completing them, you will be expected to perform like a professional: to be accurate; to write under deadline pressures; and to produce copy so clear, concise and interesting that your audience will be able, even eager, to read every word.

---

[2] Sheila Hailey. *I Married a Best Seller*. Garden City, NY: Doubleday, 1978, p. 95.

[3] Karen F. Brown, ed. *Best Newspaper Writing 1992 (Winner: The American Society of Newspaper Editors Competition)*. St. Petersburg, FL: The Poynter Institute for Media Studies, 1992. Interview with author G. Wayne Miller, p. 86.

[4] James J. Kilpatrick. "The Art Of The Craft." The Red Smith Lecture in Journalism. University of Notre Dame, Department of American Studies. Notre Dame, IN: August 1985. Reprinted in pamphlet form, p. 2.

[5] Karen F. Brown, ed. *Best Newspaper Writing 1992*. Interview with writer Colin Nickerson, p. 149.

This book will also teach you more about the media: about how journalists define news, handle news releases, avoid libel suits and cope with a multitude of other problems.

Because journalists often encounter problems that involve ethics and good taste, exercises throughout this book will challenge your judgment in those areas as well. You will have to decide whether you should use the information provided by anonymous sources; report some bloody details and four-letter words; quote sexist comments; and identify innocent victims, including the victims of rape.

Early chapters emphasize fundamentals, providing basic, introductory exercises for people with no experience in journalism. They deal with news stories' basic format and style, and with spelling, grammar and vocabulary. Exercises in the following chapters give you a few facts and ask you to summarize them in acceptable newswriting style. Later exercises are more complex and require more sophisticated writing techniques. Still others will send you out of your classroom to gather information firsthand.

Many of the exercises are intentionally disorganized and poorly worded so that you will have to make extensive revisions. You will, for example, have to develop the habit of critically examining every sentence before using it. That will be part of your job in journalism: to decide what is most newsworthy, to emphasize those points and to remember your audience—always writing for it, not yourself.

To add to the realism, your teacher is likely to impose deadlines that require you to finish your stories by a specified time. Because writing a story in longhand first takes a great deal of time, you may be required to compose your stories on a typewriter or computer.

Mistakenly, students who spend hours working on their first take-home assignments worry about their slowness. As you begin to write, accuracy and clarity are more important than speed. Through practice, you will develop speed naturally, over time.

Also remember that few first drafts are so perfect that they cannot be improved. You will need to develop the habit of editing and rewriting your own work, sometimes a dozen times or more.

Here are some additional guidelines to follow while using this book:

- Unless it mentions another location, assume that every story in this book occurred on your campus or in your community. Also assume that every story will be published by a newspaper in your community.

- Good writing requires good thinking. Do not automatically begin a story with the first information you are given. Rather, critically examine all the information and begin with the most newsworthy. Similarly, do not automatically repeat a source's wording. If you can improve a source's wording—if you can express an idea more clearly, simply or concisely—do so.

- Use only the facts that you are given or are able to obtain or verify from other sources. Newswriting is based on fact. Never make any assumptions, and certainly never make up any facts.

- Verify the spelling of names that appear in the exercises by consulting the city directory in Appendix A. So that you get in the habit of checking the spelling of every name, some names in the exercises are deliberately misspelled, sometimes two or three different ways. Only the spellings in the city directory are correct. People's position in their community is also important. While consulting the city directory, you may find that someone charged with a crime is a police officer, or that someone who died played a prominent role in the community (a role that your obituary should mention).

- To achieve a consistent style of abbreviations, capitalization, punctuation and so forth, follow the guidelines suggested by The Associated Press Stylebook and Libel Manual. This style is used throughout "Reporting For The Media," and a summary of the stylebook's most commonly used rules appears in Appendix B. Most newspapers in the United States follow the guidelines recommended by The Associated Press. Copies of the entire stylebook are available at most bookstores.

Harcourt Brace & Company

CHAPTER 1

THE BASICS: FORMAT, SPELLING AND AP STYLE

If you wish to be a writer, write.

(Epictetus, Greek philosopher)

More changes than ever are being made in newsrooms. Up to 20 years ago, reporters typed their stories on sheets of paper, then used a pencil to correct their errors before giving the paper to an editor. The editor would often make further changes on the paper before giving the reporter's story to a typesetter. Starting in the 1970s, media organizations have experienced a period of rapid technological change. Most journalists now type their stories on computers or word processors. As the stories are typed, they appear on screens above the terminals' keyboards, and journalists can use the keyboards to correct all their errors. When the journalists finish their work, their stories are stored in a computer until an editor is ready to view them on another terminal. Finally, the edited stories are transmitted to other machines, which set them in type. Everything is done electronically, and the system can save a single news organization millions of dollars a year by eliminating its need for typesetters, other skilled workers and all their old equipment.

Few typewriters are found in today's newsrooms. Reporting students, however, must still learn the traditional format and copy-editing symbols. Reporters and editors handle some typed copy from free-lance writers, public relations agencies and a variety of other sources. Also, the traditional format and copy-editing symbols are helpful in some college classes.

Journalism departments at most colleges now have computers, but few require their students to use the computers for every assignment in every class. Although many assignments must be typed, not all students have access to networked computers for homework assignments that their instructors can receive and grade electronically. Instead, some students continue to use typewriters, and the traditional format and copy-editing symbols, especially for homework assignments. Others, even after using a computer, may notice an error in their work moments before an assignment is due. In making corrections, they are expected to use the proper format and copy-editing symbols. These are the same format, editing and style guidelines that journalists across the country use when editing on paper. Accordingly, we review these guidelines in this chapter.

NEWS STORY FORMAT

Reporters have developed a unique format for their stories, and each story you write should follow the guidelines suggested here. Although minor variations exist from one news organization to another, most publications are remarkably consistent in their adherence to these rules.

Type each news story on one side only of separate 8½- by 11-inch sheets of paper. Avoid onionskin and other types of glossy or erasable bond paper because it is more difficult to write corrections on such paper.

Type your name as the journalist, the date you've written the story and a slugline describing the story on the upper left-hand corner of the first page:

Fred Fedler

Jan. 12, 1999

Highway Plans

Editors use sluglines to help them identify and keep track of stories that are being prepared for publication. Sluglines also provide a quick summary of each story's topic. A story that reports a speech by your city's mayor might be slugged "Mayor's Speech"; a story about a fire at an elementary school might be slugged "School Fire." Sluglines should not exceed three words and should be as specific as possible. Vague sluglines, such as "Speech" or "Fire," might be used on more than one story; and the stories, their headlines and their placement in the paper might then become mixed up with one another.

In devising a slugline, you should avoid jokes, sarcasm, insensitivity and statements of opinion that would cause embarrassment if the slugline were accidentally published, as sometimes happens. A reporter in Texas was irritated when she was told to cover a story at the local high school. It was about a talk given by a 22-year-old high school dropout urging others to complete their schooling. The reporter thought the story was unimportant and uninteresting. Angrily, she slugged it, "Wannabe Whines." She was almost fired when the slugline inadvertently appeared in print. Similarly, a writer in Michigan wrote a story about a man who had kept his dead mother in a lifelike position in the house for several years. Another employee thought the writer's slugline was the headline—and an accurate one. It was set in type, and the story the next morning bore the insensitive headline "Mommie's a Mummy."

Begin each story about one-third of the way down the first page. When you write for a news organization, the space at the top of the first page provides room for your byline, a headline and special instructions to production workers. In class, the space provides room for your instructor to evaluate your work.

Leave a one-inch margin on each side and at the bottom of every page. Standard margins help editors and production workers gauge the length of each story. Your instructor will use this space to write comments.

Indent five spaces at the beginning of each paragraph. Type and double-space each story so that it is neat, uniform and easy to read. Do not leave any extra space between paragraphs.

To save time, you will have to learn to type the first draft of every story you write. You will miss deadlines and waste effort if you write news stories in longhand first. If you are a slow typist, you should practice until you can manage at least 30 words per minute.

Traditionally, journalists never divided a word at the end of a line because typesetters might mistakenly assume that the hyphen was part of the word and set it in type. Today, if you use a computer, it will automatically move an entire word to the next line rather than hyphenate it. If you use a typewriter, you will be expected to put the entire word on the next line yourself.

Also traditionally, journalists never divided a paragraph between pages. A story would often go to the production department in pages (or "takes"). If a news reporter broke a paragraph between pages, then the production staff would be delayed in its attempt to move the story through the production process. A student using a computer can insert a page break between paragraphs. Sometimes a page break is not necessary because production processes are electronic and not print. Students who use a typewriter and do not have room to complete a paragraph on the same page will have to scratch it out and start anew on the second page.

Harcourt Brace & Company

If a story is continued on a second page, type the word "more" centered at the bottom of the first page to indicate to the editor and production staff that the story does not end here; more information is on an additional page.

Begin the second page and all later pages about 1 inch from the top of the page. Type your last name, the page number of the story and the slugline in the upper left-hand corner:

Fedler

Highway Plans

Page 2

At the end of your story, type an end mark to show that you are finished. Traditional end marks to Linotype operators were "-30-" or three pound signs ("###"). Today, reporters usually type or write "#" or their initials.

And you are finished with formatting your story!

Be aware that news organizations use different terms to mean the same thing. Instead of using the word "paragraph," some journalists shorten it to "graph." Similarly, instead of using the word "page," other journalists use "add" or "take." And, instead of using "story" to mean the written version, many journalists use the term "copy." Also, some editors ask their reporters to triple-space rather than double-space their stories.

News organizations also vary on the use of datelines, which indicate a story's geographical source. When beginning a story, some organizations require journalists to place a dateline at the beginning of the first line of each story. Datelines normally include the name of the city, printed entirely in capital letters and followed by a comma, the abbreviation for the state in upper/lower case and a dash (for example: LEXINGTON, Ky.— or PORTLAND, Ore.—). Names of major cities that most readers will immediately recognize (such as Boston, Chicago, Miami and Houston) are used alone, without their state. Most news organizations do not use datelines for stories that originate within their own communities, and they use only the names of other cities within their own state, omitting the name of the state.

COPY-EDITING SYMBOLS

Reporters are expected to edit their stories and correct all their errors before giving the final version to an editor. If the editor finds a problem, the story is often returned to the reporter for revisions. Almost all journalists correct their work using a standard method. Correcting stories is called editing; symbols used to edit are called copy-editing symbols.

Most stories written for your reporting classes will not have to be typed perfectly, but should be neat and easy to read. If you want to edit a story after typing it, use a pencil to insert the copy-editing symbols shown in the paragraphs below.

If you have several errors within one word, draw one line through the word and place the correct spelling above it. If several major errors appear in a paragraph or section of a story, retype that section. If your corrections become too numerous and messy, retype the entire story so that it is easy to read. The following is an example of copy-editing for print and public relations publications. Copy-editing symbols for broadcast are discussed more thoroughly in Chapter 18.

Double-space your story. Indent every paragraph in a news story, and mark the beginning of each paragraph with the proper copy-editing symbol: ⌐_____ If you want to mark a paragraph to be divided into two shorter paragraphs, you can use either the same copy-editing symbol or this one: ¶ .

If you indent a line and then decide that you do not want to start a new paragraph, link the lines together with a pencil, as shown here.

The same symbol is used to link the remaining parts of a sentence or paragraph after a major deletion, ~~involving the elimination of a great many words and more than one line of type, or even a complete sentence or two,~~ as shown here.

Always use a pencil, not a pen, to correct any errors that appear in your stories. If you make a mistake in correcting your story with a pen, the correction will be difficult to change.

Write "OK" above facts or spellings that are so unusual that your editors are likely to question their accuracy, and circle the letters. (For example, you might need to check again the spelling of Suzanne Schlovitkowitz, when writing that she became a millionaire at the age of 13.) The notation "OK" indicates that the information is correct, regardless of how odd, unlikely or bizarre it may appear to be.

If you accidentally type an extra word or letter, cross out with one line the word or ~~or~~ letter, then draw an arc above it to link the remaining portions of the sentence. An arc drawn above a deletion indicates that the remaining segments of the sentence or paragraph should be moved closer together, but a space should be left between them. To eliminate a space within a word, draw an arc both above and below i t. To eliminate an unnecessary let-ter, draw an arc both above and below i t, plus a *vertical* line through it. To delete a letter or punctuation at the end of a word, you can draw a symbol through it like this.

When two words or letters are inverted, use symbol this to indicate that they should be transposed. If you want to move an entire paragraph, retype that portion of the story. Particularly if the transposed paragraphs are on different pages, several er-rors are likely to occur if you fail to retype them.

draw three lines under a letter to indicate that it should be capitalized. If a letter is capitalized, but should not be, draw a *slanted* line through it. If two words are incorrectly run to-gether, draw a *straight*, vertical line between them to indicate that a space should be added.

If you make a correction and then decide that the correction is unnecessary or mistaken, write the word "stet" (from the Latin word "stare," meaning "let it stand") alongside the correction to indicate that you want to retain the original version.

If you want to add or change a letter, word or phrase, write or type the change above the line, then use a caret to indicate where it fits into the sentence. Many punctuation marks, includ-ing colons, semicolons, exclamation points and question marks, are added in the same manner (for example: When will he have din-ner ready). Make certain that your caret is legible by insert-ing it in the space above or below the text line.

To add a comma, draw a comma in the proper place and put a

caret *over* it (for example: The dog is big black and furry.). If

you add an apostrophe or quotation mark, place a caret *under* it

(for example: He said, "Im going to the store."). To add a pe-

riod, draw either a dot or a small "x" and circle it. A hyphen is

indicated by the symbol=, and a dash by the symbol)—(.

Never type or write over a letter or word. Also, place all

corrections above (never below) the typed line and error. Other-

wise, an editor won't know if your correction goes with the line

above or below it.

As you examine various newspapers, you will see that they

never underline ~~because typesetters do not have a key to under-~~

~~line.~~ However, you can use the symbol shown here to indicate that

a word needs to be set in italics, and you can use the symbol

shown here to indicate that a word needs to be set in boldface.

You can use this symbol to center a line on the page:

]By Gordon Elliott[

This symbol means flush left. This symbol means flush

right.

Spell out most numbers below 10 and use numerals for the num-

ber 10 and most larger numbers. Consult The Associated Press

Stylebook and Libel Manual for more exact guidelines. If you type

a numeral, but want it spelled out, circle it (for example: She

has ④ dogs.). If you spell out a number, but want to use the nu-

meral, circle it (for example: She has (twelve) horses.). Simi-

larly, circle words that are spelled out, but should be

abbreviated (for example: He is from Madison, (Wisconsin)), and

words that are abbreviated but should be spelled out (for exam-

Harcourt Brace & Company

```
ple:  Her dad is from Tex .  Do not use a circle to indicate that

a letter should or should not be capitalized.

    Below the last line of each news story, in the center of the

page, place one of these "end marks":

                              -30-

                              ###
```

As a reporter, you will not normally be expected to write headlines for any of the stories you write, nor put your own byline on the stories. Editors write the headlines after they determine the headlines' size and decide where to place the stories in their papers. Editors also control the use of bylines.

THE ASSOCIATED PRESS
STYLEBOOK AND LIBEL MANUAL

Most news organizations have adopted The Associated Press Stylebook and Libel Manual. The stylebook lists thousands of rules, presented in alphabetical order, for abbreviations, capitalization, punctuation, grammar, spelling and word usage. A summary of the stylebook appears in Appendix B of this book, and you will be expected to study and learn all its rules. If you want to buy a copy of the complete stylebook, it is available at most campus and community bookstores.

The stylebook helps reporters to be more accurate by helping them to avoid misspellings and errors in grammar and word usage. In addition, the stylebook saves journalists time since, in a single volume, it answers most of the questions they are likely to ask about the proper use of the language. Thus, journalists seldom must search through several reference books or interrupt more experienced colleagues to ask them. Further, news organizations have found it less expensive and much easier to follow the style of a nationally accepted stylebook.

Large news organizations employ dozens, even hundreds, of journalists. By specifying a single set of rules for everyone to follow, The Associated Press Stylebook also encourages consistency. Without a single set of rules, news organizations would publish more errors, which could be both costly and embarrassing. Four or five reporters might use the same word in front-page stories, and each reporter might use a different style. For example: one reporter might spell "percent" as one word ("17 percent"), another might use two words ("17 per cent"), a third might use the percentage sign ("17%"), and a fourth might spell out the number 17 ("seventeen percent"). The first version (17 percent) is correct. If the page had already been prepared for publication, it would be expensive for an editor who noticed the inconsistencies to correct all the stories and order a new printing plate.

In addition to its other uses, the stylebook helps students prepare for their first jobs. If you learn the book's basic rules while you are enrolled in college, it will be easier for you to begin writing for the media—and to move from one employer to another. Because most news organizations have adopted The Associated Press Stylebook, you will not have to learn a new set of rules each time you move to another newsroom.

A few large newspapers, such as The New York Times and The Washington Post, have published stylebooks of their own. Other large news organizations publish brief supplements that specify the rules for handling unusual stylistic problems that arise in their communities. Similarly, some college newspapers publish supplements that specify a standardized set of rules for common usage on their campuses.

Harcourt Brace & Company

ACCURACY OF FACTS AND SPELLING

Responsible editors (and instructors) do not tolerate sloppiness of any kind, and they are particularly critical of spelling errors, because there is rarely any excuse for them.

Be especially careful to check the spelling of people's names. Most misspellings are the result of carelessness, and they anger two sets of people—those who were intended to be named as well as those who are inadvertently named. Most editors require their reporters to consult a second source, usually a telephone book or a city directory, to verify the way names are spelled.

Use the city directory that appears in Appendix A to verify the spelling of names used in this book's exercises, and place a box around the names to show that you have checked their spelling and that they are accurate (for example: Mayor Sabrina Datolli has resigned). To avoid inconsistent spellings, check and box a name every time it appears in a news story, not just the first time it is used. Some names in later exercises have deliberately been altered, and you will misspell them if you fail to use the city directory.

Like other city directories, the directory in this book does not list people who live in other parts of the country. Thus, if a story mentions that someone lives in another city, you can assume that the person's name is spelled correctly. Because the name will not be listed in the city directory, it will be impossible to check.

You will want to complete the exercises involving commonly misspelled words at the end of this chapter. Common phrases such as "a lot" and "all right" are frequently misspelled. Five other words that students often misspell are: "criteria," "data," "graffiti," "media" and "phenomena." All five are plural forms. The singular forms are: "criterion," "datum," "graffito," "medium" and "phenomenon." Thus, it would be correct to say, "The four criteria are adequate" or "The datum is lost," but not, "The media is inaccurate" or "The phenomenon are unusual."

A final point on spelling: Journalists are usually formal in their spelling. For example, they normally use "until" rather than "till" and "although" rather than "though." They also avoid slang.

Journalists understand the importance of double-checking the accuracy of every fact in every news story. Any factual error will damage a news organization's reputation and may seriously harm people mentioned in the stories. Because of the serious consequences of inaccuracies, your instructor is likely to lower your grade significantly whenever you make a factual error. You will also be penalized for errors in diction, grammar and style. If your instructor accepts late assignments (many do not), your grades on them may be lowered because you missed your deadline. All media organizations must meet rigid deadlines, and editors expect work to be turned in on time.

COPY PREPARATION CHECKLIST

During this course, as you finish writing each of your news stories, consult the following checklist.

1. Devise a slugline (no more than three words) that specifically describes your story's content.
2. Start typing your story one-third of the way down the first page and 1 inch from the top of all following pages.
3. Double-space each story, with only one story on a page.
4. Indent each paragraph.
5. Use a pencil and the proper copy-editing symbols to correct your errors.
6. Make certain that no words are divided and hyphenated at the end of a line, and that no paragraphs are divided between pages.

7. If the story continues on a second page, type "more" at the bottom of the first page; type your name, page number and slugline at the top of the second page; and type an end mark at the end of the story.
8. If the story originated outside your community, add the proper dateline.
9. Use the city directory to verify the spelling of all names used in the story; check and draw a box around those names every time they are used.

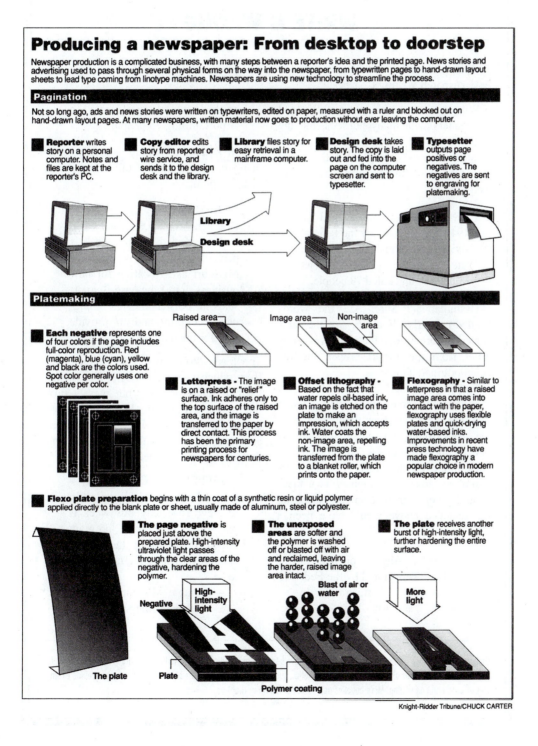

Producing a newspaper: From desktop to doorstep

Newspaper production is a complicated business, with many steps between a reporter's idea and the printed page. News stories and advertising used to pass through several physical forms on the way into the newspaper, from typewritten pages to hand-drawn layout sheets to lead type coming from linotype machines. Newspapers are using new technology to streamline the process.

Pagination

Not so long ago, ads and news stories were written on typewriters, edited on paper, measured with a ruler and blocked out on hand-drawn layout pages. At many newspapers, written material now goes to production without ever leaving the computer.

Reporter writes story on a personal computer. Notes and files are kept at the reporter's PC.

Copy editor edits story from reporter or wire service, and sends it to the design desk and the library.

Library files story for easy retrieval in a mainframe computer.

Design desk takes story. The copy is laid out and fed into the page on the computer screen and sent to typesetter.

Typesetter outputs page positives or negatives. The negatives are sent to engraving for platemaking.

Library

Design desk

Platemaking

Each negative represents one of four colors if the page includes full-color reproduction. Red (magenta), blue (cyan), yellow and black are the colors used. Spot color generally uses one negative per color.

Raised area

Image area — Non-image area

Letterpress - The image is on a raised or "relief" surface. Ink adheres only to the top surface of the raised area, and the image is transferred to the paper by direct contact. This process has been the primary printing process for newspapers for centuries.

Offset lithography - Based on the fact that water repels oil-based ink, an image is etched on the plate to make an impression, which accepts ink. Water coats the non-image area, repelling ink. The image is transferred from the plate to a blanket roller, which prints onto the paper.

Flexography - Similar to letterpress in that a raised image area comes into contact with the paper, flexography uses flexible plates and quick-drying water-based inks. Improvements in recent press technology have made flexography a popular choice in modern newspaper production.

Flexo plate preparation begins with a thin coat of a synthetic resin or liquid polymer applied directly to the blank plate or sheet, usually made of aluminum, steel or polyester.

The page negative is placed just above the prepared plate. High-intensity ultraviolet light passes through the clear areas of the negative, hardening the polymer.

The unexposed areas are softer and the polymer is washed off or blasted off with air and reclaimed, leaving the harder, raised image area intact.

The plate receives another burst of high-intensity light, further hardening the entire surface.

High-intensity light

Blast of air or water

More light

Negative

The plate

Plate

Polymer coating

Knight-Ridder Tribune/CHUCK CARTER

Harcourt Brace & Company

St. Louis Post-Dispatch

WRITE & WRONG

By **Harry Levins**
Post-Dispatch Writing Coach

Who says wind is weightless? We load our readers with many burdens, but the heaviest may be windy sentences. Here's an all-too-typical example. It fell short of springing the scale but was needlessly weighty:

> National Airport, opened in 1941 and operated by the Federal Aviation Administration, was the site of a crash by an Air Florida jet in January that killed 78 people.

Grammatical? Sure. Are the words spelled properly? You bet. Are the facts correct? More or less; the crash was a few miles from the airport proper, but the flight originated there.

So what's wrong?

Simple: the sentence meanders through two separate and distinct thoughts. One is the background on when the airport opened and who runs it. The other is the background on the crash. The ideal remains one idea per sentence. Two ideas should get one sentence apiece. Repairing the sentence above would have been a simple matter:

> National Airport opened in 1941 and is operated by the Federal Aviation Administration. In January, an Air Florida jet

crashed after taking off from the airport, killing 78 people.

Here's another windy sentence, one that gets tangled up in detail before it can make its point:

> JEFFERSON CITY (UPI)— Gov. Christopher S. Bond's trip to New York City this week is part of a program to promote Missouri as a location for new business, to increase export sales, to bolster the state's stagnant economy and to provide jobs for unemployed workers.

Too many "to" verbs. The sentence has four, which suggests trouble. The writer tried to tell everything but merely produced an eye-glazer. We could have spared the reader by giving him one-idea sentences, leading with the general and then describing the specific:

> JEFFERSON CITY (UPI)— Gov. Christopher S. Bond's trip to New York City this week is part of a three-point program aimed at boosting the state's economy. The governor hopes to:
>
> —Promote Missouri as a site for new businesses.

Daily newspapers such as the St. Louis Post-Dispatch have begun to hire writing coaches to help reporters improve their writing. Many of the coaches also prepare in-house bulletins, such as this one, that discuss common problems and provide examples of good and bad writing. More bulletins appear in the following chapters.

Harcourt Brace & Company

—Increase exports of Missouri's goods.

—Provide more jobs.

At times, we go out of our way to complicate sentences. Here's an example from The New York Times News Service, a mother lode of complicated sentences:

WASHINGTON—John W. Hinckley Jr., complaining of restrictions placed by St. Elizabeth's Hospital on his contacts with reporters, has asked the American Civil Liberties Union for help.

The reader dips his toe in—and promptly loses it to the teeth of a nonrestrictive clause. Nonrestrictive clauses (phrases set off by commas) constitute one of the biggest roadblocks to readability. They interrupt the reader's train of thought, sidetracking him into a second idea that may or may not be crucial at that point.

At times, we're forced to use such clauses. But The Coach remains convinced that the nonrestrictive clause often represents a crutch for a writer who lacks the time, talent or inclination to recast his stuff. Sometimes, the sentence can be broken into two, each with its own idea. Sometimes, the information in the clause can be shifted deeper in the story, preferably in a sentence of its own.

And every so often, a two-idea sentence can be recast into something that more nearly meets the ideal of one idea per sentence. For example, that Hinckley lede could have read this way:

WASHINGTON—John W. Hinckley Jr. wants the American Civil Liberties Union to help him fight what he says are restrictions by St. Elizabeth's Hospital on his contacts with reporters.

Ah, well—at least The Times held itself to a two-idea sentence. Here's a locally produced sentence with *three* ideas:

Mayor Vincent C. Schoemehl Jr., who asked Hohman to come to St. Louis, said the study would not be directly related to Homer G. Phillips Center, which the mayor is trying to reopen as a full-service hospital.

Try diagramming *that*. The result looks like the genealogy of a family that practices incest. The writer overloaded the sentence with two nonrestrictive clauses—the ones beginning with "who" and "which." And all of those editors dumped it untouched onto the readers.

Somewhere, somebody could have broken off the first part as a single sentence:

Mayor Vincent C. Schoemehl Jr. invited Hohman to St. Louis.

One down, two to go:

The mayor said Hohman's study would not be directly related to Homer G. Phillips Center, an emergency room and clinic on the city's North Side.

Okay, that sentence has 1.6 ideas. Still, we're four-tenths of a point ahead. And now, Strike Three.

Schoemehl has been trying to re-establish Phillips as a full-service hospital.

But at times, the cure can be as vexing as the ailment. Here's a paragraph that The Coach suspects started life as one sentence:

The ILO's Committee on Freedom of Association will take up the case when it meets in Geneva, Switzerland, on Nov. 8 and 9, according to Stu Smith. He is executive director of the Capitol Employees Organizing Group.

Somebody deserves praise for making the effort. But somebody also deserves admonishment for doing it so clumsily. The last sentence reads like an afterthought. A

(continued on next page)

bit more work would have made the transition smoother.

. . . meets in Geneva, Switzerland, on Nov. 8 and 9. The announcement was made by Stu Smith, executive director . . .

***

At least once a week, The Coach runs across a sentence like this:

Smith, 38, lives in rural Belleville.

What is "rural Belleville"? Or "rural Kirksville" or all the other "rurals" we write about? Presumably, we mean "outside Belleville" or "in a rural area near Kirksville." If so, we ought to say it that way. Otherwise, we are calling Belleville a bucolic village—a description to which 41,000 people might take exception.

***

Some parting shots on words:

Ceremonies. This word almost always appears as a plural; it almost always should be singular. "The awards are to be presented in ceremonies in the rotunda of City Hall." Sorry, but *a ceremony* is all that's planned.

Jobless, joblessness. Here's more headlinese that has crept into copy. The word "jobless" is bad enough in a headline, but a copy editor can plead tight space. No such excuse extends to people who use "jobless" and "joblessness" in copy as substitutes for "unemployed" and "unemployment." We're better off repeating a good word than substituting something from the junkpile of journalese just for the sake of variety.

Plague. Early in the history of journalism, some clever writer seized upon the word as a synonym for "vex," "bother," "trouble," "annoy," "anger," "harass," etc. Very shortly thereafter in the history of journalism, everybody else started using it. They turned the verb "plague" into a punchless piece of journalese. Let's retire it.

SUGGESTED READINGS

Born, Roscoe C. *The Suspended Sentence: A Guide for Writers*. Ames, IA: Iowa State University Press, 1993.

Botts, Jack. *The Language of News: A Journalist's Pocket Reference*. Ames, IA: Iowa State University Press, 1994.

Goldstein, Norm, ed. *Associated Press Stylebook and Libel Manual*. Reading, MA: Addison-Wesley, 1994.

Kessler, Lauren, and Duncan McDonald. *When Words Collide: A Media Writer's Guide to Grammar and Style*, 3rd ed. Belmont, CA: Wadsworth, 1992.

Lippman, Thomas W., ed. *The Washington Post Deskbook on Style*, 2nd ed. New York: McGraw-Hill, 1989.

MacDowell, Ian, compiler. *Reuters Handbook for Journalists*. London: Butterworth-Heinemann, 1992.

UPI Stylebook, 3rd ed. Lincolnwood, IL: NTC Business Books, 1992.

Harcourt Brace & Company

Name ——————————————————— Class ———————————— Date ————————

E X E R C I S E　1

FORMAT AND COPY-EDITING SYMBOLS

INSTRUCTIONS: Using the proper copy-editing symbols, correct the errors in the following stories. If necessary, refer to the reference chart for copy-editing symbols on the inside of the front and back covers.

Except for some obvious errors, the stories' style (the abbreviations, punctuation and spelling, for example) is correct. There is one exception, however: You will have to form all the possessives. If you need help, see Appendix C, "Rules for Forming Possessives."

1. GIRL SCOUTS

the countys Girl Scout Council no loonger will acept any checks during its annual cookie sale-a-thon.

During its last sale-a-thon, the council lost $4,284 due to worthlesschecks.

"That may not sound like a lot, but its a serious loss for us," said Linda Goree, the Girl Scoust county executive. "It cuts into our profits, but al so wastes too many hours of our timme."

Next year, Goree said, thecountys Girl Scouts will accept only cash

Two factors agravated the prov problem during the scouts last sale-a-thon, Goree continued. first, more pepople paid by check. Second, a larger percentage of the checks teh Girl Scouts received bounced.

"Some people pay by check because they don't have the cash," Goree said. "Or, they want to place a large order. We have people who place orders for $100 or more, and thosse poeple are especially likely to pay by check. we also receive checks for a little as one or two dollars." Scout leaders call people who signed the checks that bounce and, in most cases,ask them to mail neW checks to the cty. office. The scout leadesr are unable to reach everyone, however. Smoe People have moved. Other s do not have telephones — or do not seem to answer their tele phones.

"usually its an honest mistake, ad andpeople are embarrassed when we call them."

Goree said. "THey want to take care of the problem right away. Other people say they want

to pay but dont have the money, and

we can usually work something out with them. Unfortunately, there are other people who

get mad at us, like its our fault or something, and refuse to pay. Or, they write new checks

that also bounce. It puts our leadess in a terrible situation. A Girl Scout leadershouldn't

have to deal with problems like that. Also, its not a good situation or example for our girls,

and that's the reason for our ne w policy, why we'll no longer accept any checks."

###

2. MEN'S LONGEVITY

Being a middle-aged man and single can be deadly, too sociologists at your college

warned today

The sociologists, Margo Matos and LeeAnne verkler, found that middle-aged men who

remain single double their chances of dying.

For 10 years, Matos and verkler tracked one thoussand men in the state. All of the men

were 40 old years at the start of the study, and half were married. Matos and Verkler fuond

that 11.7 percent of the men who remained unmarried died before their 50th birthday, com-

pared to only 5.9 percent of themen who remained married.

Some of the maried men were divorced or widowed during the study, and 7.1 percent of

those who remainedd alone for at least half the period also died.

"We arent sure of all the reasons," verkler said. "That's what we'll look at next. WE

think poor diet plays a role. Also the use of alcohol, smoking, a lack of exercise and low

incomes. Men who live by themselves seem to do more drinking and smoking, and many

don't PREprepare good meals when theirs only one to cooke for instead of tow. Plus

there's the absence of social support. It ehlps to have someone to talk with, someone who

shpares your li fe and is there to provide help when you need it."

Harcourt Brace & Company

Matos and Verkler found that men also live longer if they have a roommate. "It doesn't matter who the persn is, a parent, child orfreind," Verkler said. "We've found, however,that none of the alternatives are as conducive to a long life as a stable marriage. those are the man who live the longest, the men who are happily married."

###

3. HEROIC GIRL

while walking to school this moningmorning, an 11-year-old girl noticed a person with a gun robbuing two clerkS in a convenence store on Colonial Drive

The girl, Kathryn Kunze of94 Jamestown Drive, raran to a nearby telephone, dialed 911, then returned to the store and noticed an empty car par ked naearby withits motor running. she reachedd inside, shut off the cars motor and took the keys.

"Imagine what the rober thought when he ran out of the storee, jumped into HIS car and realized the keys weregone," said Sgt. Tammy Dow. "she was one smart girl, and Brave, too."

The gunman went bavck into the stoer and asked the clerks there for the keys to there cars. Bothclerks, however, said that they had walked to work and did not own a car.

The gunman then walked to a near,by park, and the police Aarrested a man there five minutse later.

William j. Chuey, 27, of 5710 michigan Ave was charrged with armed robbery.

Polic e officers later questioned the girl at school. "I saw this man with a gun, just like on telivision" she said. "Then I saw thecar. It was running, and I just figured it was the robbers, so I took his keys and ran here."

Kathryn's mother, said she was p' ' 'proud—and frightened—by her daughters actions. "I'Mm proud she thought so quickly," Mrs. Lauren Kunze said. "But I don't wnat her to trfy anything like that ever again."

###

4. REPOSSESSING CARS

Police Chief Barry Kopperud Wants to ebgin seizing t he cars driven by drunken drivers.

While testifyingbefore a legislative committee in the state capital this morning, Kopperud said police oficers in the state need the authority to to seize the vehicles used by motorists convicted three or more times of drunken driving. Kopperuds pproposal would al so apply to motorists convicted of driving with a license suspended or revoked because of drunken drving—and to motorists convicted of driving undre the Influence of drugs.

"Were runninng across too many repeat offjenders," kopperud said. "They ignore the laws now in eff ect, and its time to do something about it. It doesn't do any good to just take away their lcenses. They'll drivewithout one."

Kopperud said some motorists in the statehave been convicted of drunken driving more than a dozentimes . "Weve gott peopel who've served a year in jail, some who've served five years," Kopperud said. "It doesn't seemtodo any good. weather they have a liense or not, they star"t to drink and drive again as soon as they get out. If wetake away their cars, they'll havetostop. U nless they're ultra-rich, there's a limit to howmany cars they can afford to buy."

###

Name _____ Class _____ Date _____

E X E R C I S E   2
SPELLING

INSTRUCTIONS: The dozen words listed below are the ones that journalism students misspell most frequently. Some of the words are spelled correctly here, but most are misspelled. Use the proper copy-editing symbols to correct all the misspelled words. If several spellings are normally permissible, use the one recommended by The Associated Press Stylebook.

---

1. alot

2. ammendment

3. criticised

4. definately

5. develop

6. explaination

7. it's (possessive)

8. judgement

9. occured

10. recieve

11. seperate

12. teenager

Here are 25 more words that journalism students frequently misspell. Use the proper copy-editing symbols to correct the words that are misspelled.

1. accidently

2. adviser

3. alledgedly

4. among

5. apparantly

6. arguement

7. broadcasted

8. calendar (for dates)

9. catagorized

10. cemetary

11. conscious

12. fourty

13. lightning

14. liscense

15. magizines

16. medias

17. occasionally

18. opportunity

19. payed

20. practise

21. priviledge

22. reguardless

23. sophmore

24. suing

25. thier

Harcourt Brace & Company

Name _____ Class _____ Date _____

E X E R C I S E   3
SPELLING

INSTRUCTIONS: The following list contains 60 words that college students frequently misspell. Some of the words are spelled correctly here, but most are misspelled. Use the proper copy-editing symbols to correct all the misspelled words. If several letters in a single word need to be corrected, rewrite the entire word. If several spellings are normally permissible, use the one recommended by The Associated Press Stylebook.

1. admited	21. equipted	41. lieutenant
2. attendants	22. exagerate	42. likelyhood
3. baby-sit	23. existance	43. liveable
4. believeable	24. expeled	44. ninety
5. besiege	25. favortism	45. patroled
6. changeable	26. foreigner	46. picknicing
7. chauffeur	27. fraternitys (plural)	47. pneumonia
8. controled	28. fulfill	48. questionaire
9. cryed	29. goodbye	49. quizes
10. delirius	30. harrassment	50. respondent
11. descended	31. heros	51. singuler
12. descrimination	32. inaugurate	52. sizeable
13. disasterous	33. indispensible	53. summerize
14. dormitories	34. innoculate	54. tenative
15. drunkeness	35. irrate	55. terrace
16. elete	36. irregardless	56. towards
17. eligable	37. itinerary	57. trys
18. embarrass	38. ketchup	58. useable
19. emphacize	39. kindergarden	59. victum
20. employe	40. leisure	60. worrys

Harcourt Brace & Company

Name _____ Class _____ Date _____

E X E R C I S E   4
SPELLING

INSTRUCTIONS: The following list contains 60 words that college students frequently misspell. Some of the words are spelled correctly here, but most are misspelled. Use the proper copy-editing symbols to correct all the misspelled words. If several letters need to be corrected in a single word, rewrite the entire word. If several spellings are normally permissible, use the one recommended by The Associated Press Stylebook.

1. accommodate	21. grammer	41. poisonous
2. advertizing	22. illegitimate	42. populer
3. alright	23. imposter	43. proceded
4. ambulence	24. indorsed	44. protestor
5. brocoli	25. infered	45. pryed
6. bureaucracy	26. janiter	46. pursued
7. casulties	27. likeable	47. realised
8. cautious	28. maintinance	48. recyling
9. committed	29. massacre	49. refered
10. congradulations	30. mileage	50. repetative
11. contraversial	31. miraculous	51. resturant
12. convenient	32. mispell	52. rhythm
13. defendant	33. mosquitos	53. saleries
14. delagates	34. necessary	54. sandals
15. desireable	35. negligence	55. sargeant
16. deviding	36. noticeable	56. skillfull
17. dilemas	37. occurence	57. transfered
18. dispise	38. paniced	58. vaccuum
19. forsee	39. parallel	59. visability
20. govermental	40. phenomenon (plural)	60. wreckless

Name _____ Class _____ Date _____

E X E R C I S E   5

AP STYLE

INSTRUCTIONS: After studying The Associated Press Stylebook in Appendix B, use the proper copy-editing symbols to correct the mechanical, spelling and stylistic errors in the following sentences. Remember that none of the possessives have been formed for you. If you need help in forming the possessives, see the guidelines in Appendix C.

1. The girl, Anne Stockdale, age nine, was carrying 2 small boxes, five cents, and a can of mace.

2. At 12 noon yesterday, the Priest gave the 7 year old girl from Eugene Oregon a bible and five dollars.

3. Forecasters in northern Illinois say the temperature will fall from 0 to -15 by 12 midnight tomorrow evening.

4. The teenager, who lives on Erie Av., is 5′, 6″ tall, weighs 140 pds., and likes both oreos and french fries.

5. During the 20th century, the Federal Govt. spent 4,840,000 million dollars to protect wildlife in the Calif. park.

6. Seven persons, including Mrs. Richard Miehe, will meet the Realtor at 12 noon at the Sherer Realty Company on King Dr.

7. The boy, age seven, was sipping a coke and carrying $0.25 as he walked north on Jamestown Blvd. at 8:20 a.m. yesterday.

8. The Governor, a member of the democratic party, said his son earned a Ph.D. in the department of history during the 1980s.

9. The temperature in the Midwest fell below 0 at 12 midnight, then climbed to the 30s as the wind continued to blow from the north.

10. Leaning backwards, the baby sitter in Reno Nevada said he saves 50 percent of his earnings, or about one hundred dollars a month.

Harcourt Brace & Company

11. Ms. Andrea Maye works as a reporter in the southwest and, eleven years ago, won a pulitzer prize for a book entitled Tragedy.

12. At 10:00 AM this morning, the Vice-President of the U.S. will meet with three persons, including Rev. Juanita Hernandez of Toledo Ohio.

13. The presidential aide said the odds are five to four that the Porsche driven by Movie Star Paul Newman will exceed two hundred miles an hour.

14. She was a member of the Kansas legislature, then the U.S. Senate, and says it will cost from $7 to $9 million dollars to seek re-election.

15. They arrived at 11:00 pm yesterday and, afterwards, revealed that Mrs. Samuel Swauger of 4987 Huron Dr. won the election by a vote of 18732-14011

16. The F.B.I. agent, who lives at 410 East Lake Dr. in Fort Worth Texas drove South on Austin Blvd., then stopped at the Targill Corporation on Bell Av.

17. The vice-president and two of his advisers said afterwards that they invited 5 outstanding teenagers from Wis. to visit the U.S. Capital Bldg. next Fall.

18. The President, Pope, and other dignitaries will meet in the oval office of the white house at 10:00 a.m. tomorrow, then move to room 312 of the senate office bldg.

19. Reverend Alice Caruna held a bible in one hand and a copy of the U.S. constitution in the other as she spoke to members of the Georgia Alumni Assn. yesterday afternoon.

20. While visiting the President in the Oval Office, Senator Edward Whitewing, a Democrat from Montana, warned that the Social Security system will go bankrupt during the 21st Century.

Name _____ Class _____ Date _____

E X E R C I S E   6

AP STYLE

INSTRUCTIONS: After studying The Associated Press Stylebook in Appendix B, use the proper copy-editing symbols to correct the mechanical, spelling and stylistic errors in the following sentences.

1. The girl, age nine, said her Mother is a democrat and a capt. in the United States Army.

2. The basketball player is a high school Junior, 17 years old, and six ft., three inches tall.

3. By a vote of 387-322, employes at Wilson Brothers Bakery on Crawford St. rejected the Union.

4. The teenager, Tommy Morningdove of Bowling Green Ohio, said the building will cost $880 thousand.

5. Prof. Lara Ruffenach, a member of the department of english, said her office is in room 311 of the Humanities Bldg.

6. Irregardless of the danger, two Seniors from Colonial High School tackled the theif as she ran South on Colonial Dr.

7. He was born on March 1 1974 in Pittsburgh Pennsylvania, attended high school in Mich., then moved to the northwest.

8. It was fathers day, and the 8 yr. old girl, Deborah Nunziata of 1410 1st Avenue, said she had four dollars to buy some flowers.

9. On Oct. 31, 1996 the eleven executives met at 500 West Robinson Street and voted 9-4 to pay the bill which totals 1128 dollars.

10. The girl, who is in her early 20's, died at 7:00 p.m. yesterday evening after receiving severe burns in a fire at her home at 2106 North Ninth St.

11. On January 3, the American Federal Insurance Company filed for bankruptcy in Hartford Connecticut, listing debts of 12,640,000 dollars.

12. Afterwards, Andrew A. Vornholt Senior of 10 East Lake Rd. said his number one choice for the position of Mayor is a democrat who works as a realtor.

13. Atty. Pat Keegan Junior works for the Federal Govt. and estimates that, in the next ten years, 3/4 of the states doctors will be sued for malpractice.

14. The boy, age 19, said he enjoys reading USA Today and time magazine, but also enjoys watching 3 television programs: Murphy Brown, Frazier, and 60 Minutes.

15. Karen McGorwan, President of the Kansas Alumni Assn., said the Fall meeting will be held at 5:00 p.m. Monday October 14th in the Clayton Bldg. at 210 Packwood Drive.

16. Prof. Allison DiLorento, an Associate Prof. who teaches Political Science and, 3 years ago, won a Pulitzer Prize, interviewed former Tex. governor Anne Richards at 2 PM yesterday.

17. Irregardless of the controversy, Asst. Dist. Atty. Leo Friedman said the book, entitled Hope, is protected by the 1st amendment to the United States constitution.

18. The thirty year old Okla. man said he paid 26,000 dollars for the toyota and was driving south at about 45 m.p.h. when the accident occured at the intersection of Packwood and Erie Streets.

19. Executives at Creative Computers Incorporated, the number one company in the field, predict that the United States congress will buy 40000 of the new computers for the United States army, navy, and air force.

20. The temperature fell from 0 to −12, yet fifty-two % of the citys voters turned out for the election.

Name _____ Class _____ Date _____

E X E R C I S E   7

Answer Key Provided: See Appendix D

AP STYLE

INSTRUCTIONS: After studying The Associated Press Stylebook in Appendix B, use the proper copy-editing symbols to correct the mechanical, spelling and stylistic errors in the following sentences.

1. The consultant was given $125,000 on Feb ruary 7th, 1996 in aust in texas

2. The temperature feyll to −14 aftre a blizzzard struck Denver colorado in december 1992.

3. Tom Becker, a black born in the south during the 1950s was elected Mayor of the Cit.y

4. a senior who will graduate next Spring said "history and english are my favoite subjects".

5. Susan Woo, age eleven, is five ft. tall and weighs eighty-seven lbs.

6. the caddccident Occurred on Interstate 80, about twleve miles West of Reno Nevada.

7. Atty. Martha Dilla, forgmerly liglived at 4062 South EastlanD DRIVE andworks fo r the Westinghouse coporation

8. the companys presidnet said her firm willProvide more than $100,000,000 dollars to develoxpe an electric car able to travel sixty miles per hour.

9. The yout,h a high School Sophomore, said the temperture in Idaho often falls below 0 during the WIntsr.

10. 50 women who met yesterday morning at 11 am said there children are entitled to use the new park on Vallrath Avenue.

11. The 5-member city council wantxxs ot canvass the towns voters to determene weather a large group favors the establishment ov a Civic Orchestra.

12. Mrs. Marie Hyde, Asst. Supt. for Public Educatioon for the City, said the 16 year old girls were raised in athens georgia

13. The lady earned her beachelors degree from te university of Kentucky and her masters degr ee froum Indiana Univertiy during the 1960s.

14. The suspects were arested at 1602 North Highland Avenue, 64 East Wilshire Drive, and 3492 3rd Street.

15. Chris Repanski, of pocatello idaho will enrolled in the college as a Sophmore nxt fall and hopes to become an Attorney

16. The man, whose i n his mid 30s, joined the F.B.I. after Recieving a Ph.D. in Computer Science.

17. Reverand Andrew Cisneros estimated that ⅓ of his parishioners contribute att leeast five per cent of their annuall income to the churchs general revenue fund.

18. The cops arrested four kids dirvng North on Michigan Ave. minutes atfer the restaurant was robed of $1640.83 last Friday.

19. the bill of rights was added to the unites states constitution durign the eightheenth century.

20. Since the 1960s, Marty Whitedeer has livedin five States Ws., Ken., Mass., N.Y., & Ca.

CHAPTER 2

NEWSWRITING STYLE

Simplicity is the surest route to clarity.

(Jack Hart, writing coach at *The Oregonian*)

A sign in the administration building at Valparaiso University stated:

> An oleaginous resin coating has recently been applied to nearby surfaces and is still in an incomplete state of oxidation.
>
> Contact with aforementioned surfaces will cause pigment transference to skin or clothing, compromise the decorative integrity of the coating and invoke ire.

Never write like that! Newswriters are expected to use plain, simple terms that everyone can understand. A good newswriter could replace the 42 words in that sign with five: "Wet paint. Do not touch."

News media serve a mass audience, and the members of that audience possess diverse capabilities and interests. To communicate effectively—to convey information to a mass audience—newswriters must learn to present information as interestingly and simply as possible so that almost everyone will want to read and be able to understand it.

Good writing, however, is more than the use of short, simple words. It also involves choosing the correct word, composing the right sentence and picking the appropriate pace of writing. The secret to writing, according to writing coaches Don Fry and Roy Peter Clark, is "to start writing for readers, not for our own convenience." Writing is also thinking. According to editor Bob Giles, writing is done with the mind. "The inner game of writing involves creativity, imagination, willingness to take risks, structure and discipline." The keys, Giles said, are the three Ds: "detail, discipline and deadlines."

News organizations have developed a distinctive style of writing, and every element of that style serves a specific purpose. Together, the elements enable the news media to convey information to their readers, listeners and viewers clearly, concisely and impartially. At first the style may seem difficult and perhaps even awkward. It may also dismay some students because of its emphasis on facts; but newswriters are reporters, not creative writers.

As a first step, reporters must learn to avoid excessive formality. Beginning writers are often too formal, and their articles are awkward and pompous. A good writer should be able to present even the most complicated and important ideas simply—in clear, plain language. Writing, according to one journalism professor, is the marriage of craft and thought. The best writing informs readers and touches their hearts. It is also visual. The more specific a story is, the more visual it is. The more visual a story is, the easier it is to understand.

Test your stories by reading them aloud to yourself or to a friend. If your sentences sound awkward, or if you would not use them in a conversation with friends, they may have to be rewritten. Be particularly careful to avoid complex phrases and long, awkward sentences.

Harcourt Brace & Company

SIMPLIFY WORDS, SENTENCES AND PARAGRAPHS

George Orwell, in his classic commentary "Politics and the English Language," complained that simple verbs and appropriate nouns are too often replaced by complicated phrases.

To simplify stories, avoid long, unfamiliar words. Whenever possible, substitute shorter and simpler words that convey the same meaning. Use the word "about" rather than "approximately," "build" rather than "construct," "call" rather than "summon" and "home" rather than "residence."

Commentator and author Andy Rooney says he is suspicious of writers who use the words "launder" when they mean "wash," "inexpensive" when they mean "cheap," "perspiration" when they mean "sweat" and "wealthy" when they mean "rich." Rooney also complains: "People often replace the simple word 'now' with something that sounds fancier to them. I don't know why they aren't satisfied with just plain 'now.' They say 'currently,' 'presently' or 'at this point in time.'"

Also use short sentences and short paragraphs. Very long or awkward sentences should be rewritten and divided into shorter units that are easier to read and understand. Research has consistently found a strong correlation between readability and sentence length: the longer a sentence is, the more difficult it is to understand. One survey found that 75 percent of the people shown sentences containing an average of 20 words were able to understand them, but the percentage dropped rapidly as the sentences became longer.

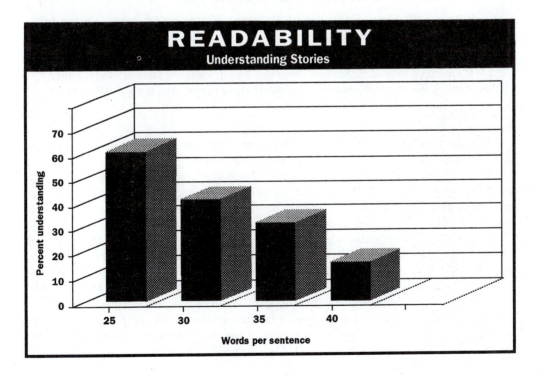

This does not mean all stories should have nothing but short sentences. Earl H. McDaniel, writing coach for the York (Pa.) Daily Record, comments, "Long sentences, properly constructed, can be just as clear as the sacred 25 words or fewer." The secret, he says, is to write for the ear, keeping a rhythm, and to write for the eye, showing vivid pictures in tight snapshots. If you can do that readers will follow, whether your sentences are long or short. But McDaniel cautions writers to use unusually long sentences "only for a good reason, just as you would unusually short sentences."

Because of the strong correlation between readability and sentence length, publications quite obviously cater to their intended audiences. The sentences in comics contain an average of about eight words, whereas the sentences in publications for the general public contain an average of 15 to 20 words. Publications containing 20 to 30 words per sentence are much more difficult to understand, and they appeal to more specialized and better-educated audiences. These publications include such magazines as Harper's and The Atlantic, and scholarly, scientific and professional journals.

Similarly, paragraph length varies from publication to publication. A paragraph should demonstrate relationships between ideas. It is a means of making complicated material clear. Paragraphs should not combine unrelated ideas. But ideas that are related or belong together should not be artificially separated just to create shorter paragraphs. If you needlessly separate ideas, you risk producing choppy writing. The introduction to a quote, for example, belongs in the same paragraph as the quote so the logic of the sequence is not disrupted. According to Jack Hart, senior editor and writing coach at The (Portland) Oregonian, "A skilled writer who makes full use of various paragraph structures can create something that goes beyond making a single point of emphasis, grouping related material or connecting ideas in logical sequence."

For some reason, college students tend to write sentences that are much too long. Students are more likely to write sentences containing 40 or 50 words than sentences containing four or five. Yet short sentences are clearer and more forceful. A forceful sentence rests on the subject, verb and object. Notice, for example, the clarity and impact of the following sentences:

> The rain poured. Lightning flashed, and their car stalled.

> Robinson, 40, never studied English in college. He never took writing classes. In fact, this jack-of-all-trades had never shown any interest in writing until 1993.
> That's when he was paralyzed.

> The wounds were deep. Students were suspended, President Donald Morris retired, the dean of students and academics resigned. Many people wondered if things would ever get back to normal at the college.
> They haven't.

To make their newspapers more readable, many editors are demanding shorter stories and simpler writing, including shorter sentences and simpler words.

Some critics have charged that newspapers' emphasis on simplicity makes their stories dull, yet the exact opposite is true. When stories are well-written, simplicity makes them clearer and more interesting. Well-written stories contain no distracting clutter; instead, they emphasize the most important facts and report those facts in a clear, forceful manner.

Jerry Ballune, a California editor, has pointed out: "Our goal is to write . . . in short, understandable sentences. We talk in short sentences. Unless we're Einsteins, we think in short sentences. Readers understand our writing in short sentences. Even Einstein, who had less need for it than most of us, advised: 'Keep it simple.'"

There's another important reason for using short sentences and short paragraphs in news stories. Newspapers are printed in small type, with narrow columns, on cheap paper. Long paragraphs—large, gray blocks of type—discourage readers. So reporters do well to divide stories into bite-sized chunks that are easy to read. Also, the white space left at the ends of paragraphs helps brighten each page.

Edna Buchanan, a Pulitzer Prize-winning police reporter for The Miami Herald, wrote in her best-selling book "The Corpse Had a Familiar Face":

> Dozens of fires erupted at intersections. Firefighters were forced back by gunfire. Businesses and stores burned unchecked. "It's absolutely unreal," said Miami Fire Inspector George Bilberry. "They're burning down the whole north end of town."
> Late Sunday, 15 major blazes still raged out of control. Snipers fired rifles at rescue helicopters. The looting and burning went on for three days. Public schools were closed, and an 8 p.m.-6 a.m. curfew was established.

Harcourt Brace & Company

There are only 8.1 words in Buchanan's average sentence. Several of her sentences contain only five or six words. The longest contains 11.

Compare Buchanan's work with the following sentence taken from William L. Shirer's book "Gandhi: A Memoir":

> Clever lawyer that he was, Jinnah took the independence that Gandhi had wrestled for India from the British by rousing the masses to non-violent struggle and used it to set up his own independent but shaky Moslem nation of Pakistan, destined, I believed then, to break up, as shortly happened when the eastern Bengali part, separated from the western part by a thousand miles of India's territory, broke away to form Bangladesh; destined eventually, I believed, to simply disappear.

Because of its length and complexity, this sentence is much more difficult to understand. It contains 80 words.

To succeed as a newswriter, you will have to do more than write short sentences, however. You will also have to write simple sentences, using the normal word order: subject, verb and direct object. Notice how much clearer and more concise the following sentence becomes when it uses this normal word order:

> Voting will take place on Nov. 8 in the General Election.
> REVISED: The election is Nov. 8.

Also be certain the ideas in each sentence are related. If they are not, even short sentences can become too complicated and unreadable:

> Appointed editor of the student newspaper, she likes to swim.

> Born in New York on Dec. 21, 1971, he was seriously injured when his car overturned.

Using too many clauses, particularly at the beginning of a sentence, makes the sentence more difficult to understand. The clauses overload sentences, so their main points fail to receive enough emphasis; instead, they are buried amid the clutter:

> Left paralyzed on the left side of his body after brain surgery last summer, the 22-year-old is suing his doctor for $6 million.
> REVISED: The 22-year-old is suing his doctor for $6 million. He has been paralyzed on his left side since brain surgery last summer.

Sometimes beginners pack too many ideas into a single sentence:

> She said that just when the new technology is placing greater demands than ever upon journalists to become proficient in grammar, punctuation and spelling, many young people seeking careers in news, advertising, public relations and other communication fields find themselves severely handicapped by today's educational system, which places its priorities elsewhere.
> REVISED: She said the new technology is placing greater demands than ever upon journalists. They must be proficient in grammar, punctuation and spelling. Today's educational system severely handicaps young people seeking careers in news, advertising, public relations and other communication fields. The system's priorities are placed elsewhere.

WRITE CLEARLY AND SIMPLY ABOUT EVEN COMPLEX TOPICS

News stories about even the most complex topics, such as the federal budget, can be written clearly and simply. Read the opening paragraphs of this example, written by Donald L. Barlett and James B. Steele of The Philadelphia Inquirer:

Harcourt Brace & Company

PHILADELPHIA—A key provision in the federal budget act passed three weeks ago was hailed by Congress as increasing taxes of the country's highest-income individuals and families.

It does not.

In fact, it extends at least one tax benefit to some wealthy households that did not have it before.

Congress boasted that the change would raise $10.8 billion in new tax revenue.

It will not.

In fact, it may raise only $2 billion or $3 billion—if that. In addition, that money would come from the upper middle-income group, not the wealthy.

An analysis of the deficit-reduction package by The Philadelphia Inquirer revealed that the provision won't increase taxes one penny for most of the 650,000 individuals and families with incomes of more than $250,000 a year.

How is that possible?

Analyze the story's sentence structure:

- How many words are in the average sentence?

- How many words are in the longest and shortest sentences?

- Are the three- and four-word sentences effective?

Writing is a process that involves five steps, according to Pulitzer Prize winner Don Murray—selecting, reporting, organizing, drafting and clarifying. The process writers take with complex stories is particularly important. Don't expect to get it right the first time. Experienced writers sometimes organize and focus their stories in their heads before typing the first word. But that takes practice. Beginners should remember that "each point grows from the previous point and leads to the next."

A rough draft of a story is important. It should be done quickly, without regard to what the finished product will be. Writing coach Don Fry suggests that drafting allows the writer to avoid getting bogged down with the lead. Instead, the writer can focus on getting information down. This approach prevents the writer from tiring midway through the story, which causes the story to tire as well. When all the information in a complex story is written down in rough-draft form, the reporter can better understand the story and organize its main components.

The clarifying stage allows the writer to self-edit and polish. Clarifying should come after a short break which creates an emotional distance from the story. Writers should read the story aloud, looking at each word, to test for clarity.

ELIMINATE UNNECESSARY WORDS

Newswriters must learn to be concise—to avoid using unnecessary words. However, newswriters must also be specific and detailed enough to make their stories informative.

Most news organizations can publish or air only a fraction of the information they receive each day; for example, an editor for The New York Times once estimated The Times received 1.25 to 1.5 million words every day but had enough space to publish only one-tenth of that material. By writing concisely, reporters present as much information to readers as possible. Brevity also helps readers to grasp quickly the main idea conveyed by each story, because it eliminates the need to spend time reading unnecessary words. Writers who use two or more words when only one is necessary waste time and space. Some words are almost always unnecessary: "that," "then," "currently," "now" and "presently," for example. Because the proper verb form, and often the noun, tells when an action occurred—in the past, present or future—it is redundant to add a second word reiterating the time, such as *past* history," "is *now*" and "*future* plans."

Harcourt Brace & Company

QUIZ

Are you ready for a quiz? Do not rewrite the following redundant sentences; simply cross out the unnecessary words.

1. She was in a quick hurry and warned that, in the future, she will seek out textbooks that are sexist and demand that they be totally banned.
2. As it now stands, three separate members of the committee said they will try to prevent the city from closing down the park during the winter months.
3. His convertible was totally destroyed and, in order to obtain the money necessary to buy a new car, he now plans to ask a personal friend for a loan to help him along.
4. After police found the lifeless body, the medical doctor conducted an autopsy to determine the cause of death and concluded that the youth had been strangled to death.
5. In the past, he often met up with the students at the computer lab and, because of their future potential, invited them to attend the convention.
6. Based upon her previous experience as an architect, she warned the committee members that constructing the new hospital facility will be pretty expensive and suggested that they step in and seek out more donors.
7. The two men were hunting in a wooded forest a total of 12 miles away from the nearest hospital in the region when both suffered severe bodily injuries.
8. Based upon several studies conducted in the past, he firmly believes that, when first started next year, the two programs should be very selective, similar in nature and conducted only in the morning hours.

Now count the number of words you eliminated—and your score. If you need help, the answers appear in Appendix D.

0–30:	Amateur.	Were you really trying?
31–40:	Copy kid.	Time to enroll in Newswriting 101.
41–50:	Cub.	You've still got a lot to learn.
51–60:	Pro.	You're getting there, but can do even better.
61 +:	Expert.	Time to ask your boss for a raise or your teacher for an "A."

Notice how easily several unnecessary words can be deleted from the following sentences without changing their meaning:

> She was able to persuade him to leave.
> REVISED: She persuaded him to leave.

> At the present time the restaurant opens for business at 6 a.m. every morning of the week.
> REVISED: The restaurant opens at 6 every morning.

Be especially careful to avoid phrases and sentences that are redundant—that unnecessarily repeat the same idea. The following phrases contain only two or three words, yet at least one—the word in italics—is unnecessary:

Harcourt Brace & Company

bodily injuries	*lone* gunman
dropped *downward*	*new* innovation
end result	*now* serves
free *of charge*	*past* experience
helped *along*	*physical* pain

Improving some redundant sentences requires more thought and effort:

Deaths are extremely rare, with only one fatality occurring in every 663,000 cases.
REVISED: One death occurs in every 663,000 cases.

The problem often arises because writers introduce a topic, then present some specific information about it. In most cases, only the more specific information is needed:

In an attempt to put out the fire, two men tried to smother it with a blanket.
REVISED: Two men tried to smother the fire with a blanket.

Repetition is even more common in longer passages involving several sentences. Sentences appearing near the end of a paragraph should not repeat facts implied or mentioned earlier:

This is not the first time she has been held up. She has been robbed three times in the past eight months.
REVISED: She has been robbed three times in the past eight months.

REMAIN OBJECTIVE

During the Revolutionary War, American newspapers were journals of opinion and frequently propagandized for or against the British. A colonial editor named Isaiah Thomas joined the militia that fired on British troops at Lexington, then reported the battle in his paper, the Massachusetts Spy. His May 3, 1775, story began:

AMERICANS! forever bear in mind the BATTLE OF LEXINGTON! where British troops, unmolested and unprovoked, wantonly and in a most inhuman manner, fired upon and killed a number of our countrymen, then robbed, ransacked, and burnt their houses! nor could the tears of defenseless women, some of whom were in the pains of childbirth, the cries of helpless babes, nor the prayers of old age, confined to beds of sickness, appease their thirst for blood!—or divert them from their DESIGN of MURDER and robbery!

Some publications, such as Time magazine, continue to use a similar—though usually less inflammatory—style of writing. In addition to reporting the news, Time interprets it. When the Dow Jones industrial average plunged 508 points in a single day, news media dubbed it "Black Monday." Time explained it as a failure of the Reagan administration: "What crashed was more than just the market. It was the Reagan Illusion: the idea that there could be a defense buildup and tax cuts without a price, that the country could live beyond its means indefinitely."

Today, most journalists strive to be as impartial or "objective" as possible. Editors and other newspaper employees can express their opinions in editorials and columns, but not in news stories. Newspaper reporters are expected to be neutral observers, not advocates or participants. Reporters should not discriminate against any ideas nor tell their readers what to think. Stories should, however, tell people what to think about—what's important.

Assume your readers are intelligent and capable of reaching their own conclusions about issues in the news. Your job as a reporter is to gather and report facts your readers need to make wise judgments—not to make the judgments for them. Avoid adjectives and labels reflecting your opinions. Avoid loaded words, such as "demagogue," "extremist," "radical," "racist," "segregationist" and "zealot." They are unnecessary, may be inaccurate and may unnecessarily infuriate readers who have opposite views.

In addition to being unnecessary, most expressions of opinion state the obvious: that an argument was "heated," a rape "violent" or a death "unfortunate." Reporters can eliminate the opinions in some sentences by deleting a single word: "*alert* witness," "*famous* author," "*gala* reception," "*thoughtful* reply." Here are two more examples:

> The tickets will cost only $19.
> REVISED: The tickets will cost $19.

> He drives an expensive car.
> REVISED: He drives a $52,000 Mercedes.

To avoid the problem, report factual details as clearly and thoroughly as possible. Avoid labels and avoid drawing any conclusions about the facts. Entire sentences sometimes convey opinions rather than facts. In most cases, the opinions are expressed as trite generalities, unsupported by facts. Good editors (and instructors) will eliminate those sentences. Often, deletion is the only way to correct the problem. Here are two examples:

> The findings look favorable.

> He is a hero to everyone in the city.

As a newswriter, you can report the opinions expressed by other people, but must clearly attribute those opinions to their source. If you fail to provide the proper attribution, readers may think you are expressing your own opinions or agreeing with your source:

> The family filed a lawsuit because the doctor failed to notice the injury.
> REVISED: The family's lawsuit charges the doctor failed to notice the injury.

A single word expressing an opinion can infuriate readers. When a college student was raped, a news story reported she suffered cuts on her arms and hands but "was not seriously injured." An irate reader asked, "Since when are rape and attempted sodomy, at knifepoint, not enough violence to constitute serious injury?"

AVOID SEXUAL STEREOTYPES

In the past, news stories mentioning women seemed to emphasize their roles as wives, mothers, cooks, seamstresses, housekeepers and sex objects. During the 1960s and 1970s, women began to complain such stereotypes are false and demeaning because women are human beings, not primarily housewives and sex objects.

Fawn Vraze, a writer for The Philadelphia Inquirer, noted, "These are bewildering times for males, especially those who think that old phrases, terms of endearment or jokes—the very ones that women might have shrugged off or smiled at years ago—are still acceptable today." Women are offended when phrases appear in print that assume they are inferior to men.

When you write for the media, you are expected to avoid demeaning comments and sexist stereotypes that will offend your readers. Yet it is difficult for some writers to break old ways of thinking, especially the stereotypes they developed in childhood.

As a first step, avoid occupational terms that exclude women: "fireman," "mailman," "policeman" and "workman," for example. Journalists substitute "firefighter," "mail carrier," "police officer" and "worker." Similarly, use the words "reporter" and "journalist" instead of "newsman."

Although some groups favor their use, The Associated Press Stylebook recommends journalists avoid awkward or contrived words, such as "chairperson" and "spokesperson." Instead,

Harcourt Brace & Company

the stylebook advises using "chairman" or "spokesman" when referring to a man or to the office in general, and using "chairwoman" or "spokeswoman" when referring to a woman. When appropriate, reporters can use a neutral word such as "leader" or "representative."

Also avoid using the words "female" and "woman" in places where you would not use the words "male" or "man" (for example: "woman doctor" or "female general"). Similarly, use unisex substitutes for words such as "authoress" (author), "actress" (actor), "aviatrix" (aviator) and "coed" (student).

Women object to being called "gals," "girls" or "ladies," and to being referred to by their first names. News stories do not call men "boys" and usually refer to them by their last names, rarely their first.

Other unacceptable practices include:

• Suggesting homemaking is not work.

• Identifying a woman solely by her relationship with a man—for example, as a man's wife, daughter or secretary—unless a woman insists upon the use of her husband's name.

• Describing a woman's physical characteristics—her hair, dress, voice or figure—when her appearance is irrelevant to a story.

• Mentioning a woman's marital status, especially if she is divorced, unless it is clearly relevant to your story. Even when a woman's marital status is relevant, it seldom belongs in the lead.

To avoid problems, ask yourself, "Under the same circumstances, would I describe a man's physical characteristics or marital status?"

Never assume everyone involved in a story is male, all people holding prestigious jobs are male, or most women are full-time homemakers. Be especially careful to avoid using the pronouns "he," "his" and "him" while referring to a typical American or average person. Some readers will mistakenly assume that you are referring exclusively to men.

A headline announced, "Woman Exec Slain in Waldorf-Astoria." Critics said the slain person's sex was irrelevant to the story, and few journalists would have written, "Male Exec Slain." A headline in The Washington Post said, "School Job May Go to Woman Educator." Critics asked editors at The Post why they used the term "woman educator," because they would never use the term "man educator." Moreover, the headline's wording suggested it is unusual for a woman to achieve a position of importance.

A story in The New York Times reported a secretary "wore a full-length blue-tweed coat, leather boots and gold bangle bracelets." Critics responded that the secretary's clothing was neither unusual nor relevant to her involvement in the news. Moreover, the reporter would not have described the attire of a man in the same position.

A story published by a campus newspaper referred to women as "chicks." Several female students and faculty members were outraged. They complained the word implies women are cute, little, fluffy and helpless.

Some advertisements still contain sexual stereotypes. Radio advertisements have urged women to ask their husbands for money so they could shop at a certain clothing store. Another advertisement urged mothers (not fathers) to take their children to a certain amusement park.

Also avoid the cumbersome and repetitive "he/she" or "he and she." The effort to rid the language of male bias should never become so strained that it distracts readers. There are several techniques you can use to avoid those cumbersome terms:

1. Avoid titles that exclude women: for example, titles that begin or end with the word "man."

Most newsmen are college graduates.
REVISED: Most reporters are college graduates.

Harcourt Brace & Company

DON'T WRITE LIKE THIS

Here are examples of bad writing that came from statements made on insurance forms. Car drivers attempted to summarize the details of their accidents in the fewest words possible.

- Coming home, I drove into the wrong house and collided with a tree I don't have.

- The other car collided with mine without giving warning of its intentions.

- I thought my window was down, but I found out it was up when I put my head through it.

- I collided with a stationary truck coming the other way.

- A truck backed through my windshield into my wife's face.

- The guy was all over the road. I had to swerve a number of times before I hit him.

- I pulled away from the side of the road, glanced at my mother-in-law and headed over the embankment.

- In my attempt to kill a fly, I drove into a telephone pole.

- I had been shopping for plants all day and was on my way home. As I reached an intersection, a hedge sprang up, obscuring my vision and I did not see the other car.

- I was on my way to the doctor with rear-end trouble when my universal joint gave way causing me to have engine trouble.

- I had been driving for 40 years when I fell asleep at the wheel and had an accident.

- My car was legally parked as it backed into another vehicle.

- The pedestrian had no idea which way to run, so I ran over him.

- A pedestrian hit me and went under my car.

- As I approached the intersection, a sign suddenly appeared in a place where no stop sign ever appeared before. I was unable to stop in time to avoid the accident.

- I was sure the old fellow would never make it to the other side of the road when I struck him.

- I saw a slow-moving, sad-faced old gentleman as he bounced off the roof of my car.

- I told the police that I was not injured, but on removing my hat, I found that I had a fractured skull.

- An invisible car came out of nowhere, struck my car and vanished.

- The indirect cause of the accident was a little guy in a small car with a big mouth.

- I was thrown from my car as it left the road. I was later found in a ditch by some stray cows.

- The telephone pole was approaching. I was attempting to swerve out if its way when it struck the front end.

- To avoid hitting the bumper on the car in front, I hit a pedestrian.

2. Substitute an article for the male pronouns "he" and "his."

> To succeed, a gardener must fertilize his crop.
> REVISED: To succeed, a gardener must fertilize the crop.

3. Substitute plural nouns and pronouns for male nouns and pronouns.

> A reporter must cultivate his sources.
> REVISED: Reporters must cultivate their sources.

4. Substitute names, descriptions or job titles for male nouns and pronouns.

> A spokesman for the 300 workmen said they expect a strike.
> REVISED: Union leader Marla McKinney said the 300 truck drivers expect a strike.

5. Use a woman's own name, not just her husband's.

> Mrs. Samuel Rothberg received the award.
> REVISED: Carla Rothberg received the award.

AVOID STEREOTYPES OF OTHER GROUPS

Journalists are expected to avoid stereotypes of all groups: blacks, Asians, Native Americans, the disabled and the elderly, for example.

Journalists mention a person's race, religion or ethnic background only when that fact is clearly relevant to a story. Typically, employees at The New York Times are told: "The writer—or the characters quoted in the story—must demonstrate the relevance of ethnic background or religion. It isn't enough to assume that readers will find the fact interesting or evocative; experience shows that many will find it offensive and suspect us of relying on stereotypes."

Both students and professionals often report that a "black" or "Hispanic" committed a crime, even in instances when the criminal's race is irrelevant to the story. A story may fail to describe a specific individual whom readers might identify for the police, thereby casting suspicion upon every member of the race. Henry McNulty of The Hartford (Conn.) Courant explained that paper's policy in this regard:

> A long-standing Courant policy states that race and sex alone do not constitute an adequate description. For instance, if the only thing a witness tells police is that a "white woman" or "black man" committed the crime, the Courant will not use any description. Only when such things as height, weight, hair length, scars, clothing and so forth are given will the newspaper print the information.

Follow that policy in the stories you write. If you are writing about a crime, for example, mention a person's race only while describing a specific individual whom some of your readers might be able to identify. For example:

> Witnesses said the bank robber was a white male, about 50 years old and 6 feet tall. He weighed about 250 pounds, was wearing a blue suit and escaped on a Honda motorcycle.

Veterans' organizations have accused the media of portraying the men and women who served in Vietnam as violent and unstable. The media, critics explain, sometimes report that a person charged with a serious crime is "a Vietnam veteran," regardless of the fact's relevance.

Other stories demean Native Americans. Avoid such obviously stereotyped words as "wampum," "warpath," "powwow," "tepee," "brave" and "squaw" and such offensive terms as "drunk," "irresponsible," "lazy" and "savage" in stories about Native Americans.

Harcourt Brace & Company

The terms "disabled" and "challenged" have replaced "handicapped." More acceptable is "person with a disability" or "person who is blind" or "person who has mental retardation" and so forth. Such phrasing emphasizes the individual before the condition.

Most stereotypes of the elderly are negative, suggesting older Americans are all alike: lonely, inactive, unproductive, poor, passive, weak and sick. In fact, most are still active, and some are quite wealthy. When asked to describe their health, a majority respond "good" to "excellent." Yet television programs often portray the elderly as eccentric, foolish, forgetful, sick and unproductive. Similarly, news stories express surprise when older people buy a sports car; fall in love; or remain alert, healthy, innovative and productive.

ARE YOU A SEXIST?

Do you:

- Mention the marital status of women, but not men?

- Describe women in greater physical detail than the men you write about?

- Refer to adult women as "girls," "gals" or "ladies" but to males as "men"?

- Use the words "female," "lady" and "woman" as occupational modifiers, as in "female doctor," "lady carpenter" and "woman architect"?

- Call women by their first names and men by their last names in similar contexts?

- Call women by their husbands' names (for example: "Mrs. Kevin Voll")?

- Identify women as "wives" when you do not refer to men as "husbands" in similar contexts?

- Exclude women from occupational categories by using words ending in "man" (business*man*, congress*man*, repair*man*)?

CHECKLIST FOR NEWSWRITING STYLE

As you begin to write news stories, check to make sure you follow these guidelines.

1. Use short, familiar words.
2. Use short sentences and short paragraphs.
3. Eliminate unnecessary words.
4. Avoid statements of opinion.
5. Avoid overloading sentences with unrelated ideas.
6. Use relatively simple sentences, with the normal word order: subject, verb, direct object.

SUGGESTED READINGS

Bazerman, Charles. *The Informed Writer*, 4th ed. Boston: Houghton Mifflin, 1992.
Browne, Neil M., and Stuart M. Keeley. *Asking the Right Questions, A Guide to Critical Thinking*. Englewood Cliffs, NJ: Prentice-Hall, 1986.
Burack, Sylvia K., ed. *The Writer's Handbook*, 5th ed. Boston: The Writer, 1986.

Harcourt Brace & Company

Cheney, Theodore A. *Getting the Words Right: How to Revise, Edit and Rewrite*. Cincinnati: Writer's Digest Books, 1983.

Clark, Roy Peter. *The American Conversation and the Language of Journalism*. St. Petersburg, FL: Poynter Institute for Media Studies, 1994.

Flocke, Lynne, Dona Hayes and Anna L. Babic. *Journalism and the Aging Population*. Syracuse, NY: Syracuse University Series in Gerontology Education, Center for Instructional Development, Syracuse University, 1990.

Gibson, Martin L. *The Writer's Friend*. Ames, IA: Iowa State University Press, 1989.

Hohenberg, John. *Concise Newswriting*. New York: Hastings House, 1987.

Kilpatrick, James J. *The Writer's Art*. New York: Andrews, McMeel and Parker, 1984.

Moss, Andrew, and Carol Holder. *Improving Student Writing*. Pomona, CA: California State Polytechnic University, 1988.

Murray, Donald M. *Write to Learn*. 4th ed. New York: Harcourt Brace Jovanovich, 1993.

———. *Writing for Your Readers*. Chester, CT: Globe Pequot Press, 1983.

Plotnik, Arthur. *The Elements of Editing: A Modern Guide for Editors and Journalists*. New York: Macmillan, 1984.

Rooney, Andrew A. *Word for Word*. New York: Berkley Books, 1987.

Reporting on People with Disabilities. Washington, DC: Disabilities Committee of the American Society of Newspaper Editors, American Society of Newspaper Editors, 1990.

Yates, Edward D. *The Writing Craft*, 2nd ed. Raleigh, NC: Contemporary, 1985.

Zinsser, William. *On Writing Well: An Informal Guide to Writing Nonfiction*, 4th ed. New York: Perennial Library, 1990.

CORRECTING WORDY PHRASES

Journalist Lou Bate and his colleagues on the city desk of The Deseret News in Salt Lake City compiled these examples of wordy phrases which appeared in their newspaper, along with more concise equivalents:

held a meeting	should be trimmed to **met**
was a winner of	should be trimmed to **won**
voted to appoint	should be trimmed to **appointed**
was the recipient of	should be trimmed to **received**
is presently studying	should be trimmed to **is studying**
made a denouncement of	should be trimmed to **denounced**
will give a lecture on	should be trimmed to **will lecture on**
made a $10,000 donation	should be trimmed to **donated $10,000**
conduct an evaluation of	should be trimmed to **evaluate**
have come to a compromise	should be trimmed to **have compromised**
come into compliance with	should be trimmed to **comply with**
gave its tentative approval	should be trimmed to **tentatively approved**
several members of the public	should be trimmed to **several people**

Name _____ Class _____ Date _____

E X E R C I S E   1

NEWSWRITING STYLE

DISCUSSION QUESTIONS

1. Imagine that you have just been named editor of your city's daily newspaper. Formulate a policy that specifies when your staff can report that a person is "adopted," "illegitimate," "receiving welfare," "gay" or an "ex-convict."

2. Imagine that your city's new mayor, elected today, had never met his father and did not even know his identity. He was raised by his mother, who never married. Would you report that fact while describing the new mayor? Why?

3. If a bank in your city today named a woman as its president, and she became the first woman to head a bank in your city, should your local daily publish a story about her promotion? Why? Would you publish stories when the first women are named to head a local college, a local hospital and a local police department?

4. If you interviewed the coach of a women's basketball team at your school, and the coach referred to his players as "my girls," would you use the term in your story? Would it matter whether you used the term in a direct quotation?

5. Can you think of any satisfactory substitutes for these words that begin or end with "man"?
   a. Fisherman
   b. Freshman
   c. Gunman
   d. Manhole
   e. Sportsman

6. Think of your favorite television programs. What percentage of the characters on the programs are elderly, and how are they portrayed—favorably or unfavorably?

7. For one week, examine every story published on the front page of your local daily. What percentage of the stories' bylines are men's, and what percentage are women's? Do you notice any differences in men's and women's assignments?

8. For one week, examine every story published on the front page of your local daily. Circle the name of every person mentioned in the stories. What percentage of the people are men, and what percentage are women? Explain your findings.

9. For one week, examine every photograph published on the front page of your local daily. What percentage of the photographs show a woman? Also, what percentage of the photographs show a man by himself, and what percentage of the photographs show a woman by herself? What other differences do you notice in the way the photographs portray men and women?

Name _____ Class _____ Date _____

EXERCISE 2

NEWSWRITING STYLE

SEXISM

SECTION I: AVOIDING SEXIST TITLES AND TERMS

Replace these titles with words that include both men and women.

1. businessman	6. fatherly	11. paperboy
2. chairman	7. founding fathers	12. repairman
3. congressman	8. man	13. salesman
4. craftsman	9. mankind	14. statesman
5. fatherland	10. man-sized	15. workman

SECTION II: AVOIDING EXCLUSIVELY MALE NOUNS AND PRONOUNS

Rewrite the following sentences, eliminating their use of male nouns and pronouns.

1. A reporter is expected to protect his sources.

2. A good athlete often jogs to build his endurance.

3. Normally, every auto mechanic buys his own tools.

4. No one knows which of the nation's congressmen leaked the details to his wife and friends.

5. If a patient is clearly dying of cancer, doctors may give him enough drugs to ease his pain, and perhaps even enough to hasten his death.

SECTION III: AVOIDING STEREOTYPES

Rewrite the following sentences, avoiding sexist language and comments.

1. Randy Ortiz married his wife seven years ago.

2. Tom Yapengco and his wife urged their son, James, to act like a man.

3. A male nurse, Richard Diaz, and his wife, an authoress, arrived today.

Harcourt Brace & Company

4. Lois Zarrinfar, who never married, is 73 and the daughter of a famous poetess.

5. The bank's chairman said that the average depositor has $3,248 in his savings account.

6. The two married ladies, both trim red-heads, are serving as the programs co-chairmen.

7. The city fathers announced that 10 men and 4 females, all clergymen, will serve on the board.

8. The store sells toys of all types, from guns and chemistry sets for boys to dolls and beauty kits for girls.

9. Although a wife and the mother of four, Mrs. Henry Conaho, a slender blonde, is also president of the community college.

10. A spokesman for the company announced that it has reached a gentlemans agreement with the sportsmen on their use of the woods.

Harcourt Brace & Company

Name _____ Class _____ Date _____

E X E R C I S E   3

NEWSWRITING STYLE

BEING CONCISE

SECTION I: USING SIMPLE WORDS

Substitute simpler and more common words for each of these words.

1. altercation	7. expenditure	13. reimburse
2. assistance	8. incarcerate	14. relocate
3. apprehend	9. indicate	15. request
4. apprehensive	10. intoxicated	16. residence
5. commence	11. lacerations	
6. community	12. purchase	

SECTION II: AVOIDING REDUNDANT PHRASES

The following phrases do not have to be rewritten; simply cross off their unnecessary words.

1. abolish altogether	7. end result	13. is presently
2. are currently	8. free gift	14. sum total
3. are in need of	9. future plans	15. totally destroyed
4. at a later date	10. head up	16. whether or not
5. brilliant genius	11. honest truth	
6. crisis situation	12. hung down from	

SECTION III: AVOIDING WORDY PHRASES

Use a single word to replace each of these phrases.

1. are in agreement	4. caused damage to	7. gave their approval
2. at present	5. caused injuries to	8. get underway
3. came to a halt	6. gave chase to	9. in the course of

Harcourt Brace & Company

10. is hopeful that

11. is in need of

12. made a contribution

13. made a decision

14. made the ruling

15. made their escape

16. made their exit

17. posed a question

18. proceeded to leave

19. thunderstorm activity

20. were aware of

SECTION IV: ELIMINATING UNNECESSARY WORDS

Eliminate the unnecessary words from the following sentences. The sentences do not have to be rewritten; simply cross off the words that are not needed.

1. Anyone may participate if they would like to.

2. Before the robbers left, they also took some liquor.

3. At the present time, about 100 students participate.

4. The results showed that only 31 percent passed the test.

5. Firefighters reached the scene and extinguished the blaze.

SECTION V: REWRITING WORDY SENTENCES

Rewrite the following sentences, eliminating as many words as possible.

1. He said the cost of putting on the program will be about $500.

2. The police officer opened fire, shooting six times at the suspect.

3. Sanchez was taken to Memorial Hospital and is in fair condition there.

4. They told the midwife that there was not much time left before the baby was due.

5. Of the 10 stock car drivers interviewed, eight felt like it is inevitable that you are going to have some injuries and deaths among the people participating in their races.

SECTION VI: SIMPLIFYING OVERLOADED SENTENCES

The following sentences are too long and complicated. Divide them into simpler, more concise sentences.

1. Two high school students, Joan Harnish and Sara Courhesne, were driving north on Carpenter Road at 10:20 p.m. when they came around a sharp curve in the road and noticed a wrecked motorcycle and, about 25 feet away, a man, about 20 years of age—apparently seriously injured—sprawled near a telephone pole.

2. In a 122-page report, the Department of Health and Human Services stated that drunken driving causes 28,000 traffic deaths a year, costing the nation $45 billion, and that nearly 9 million persons suffer from alcoholism or lesser drinking problems, a number that represents 10 percent of the U.S. workforce.

3. The injured boy was taken to Mercy Hospital where a spokesman said the youth, who is from Seattle Washington, was in serious condition with a gunshot wound to the chest accidentally fired by a friend with a .22 caliber revolver they found in a box.

4. The man, described by witnesses as about 30, slender, white, and bald, leaped from a blue Ford car at about 3 p.m., grabbed a vinyl bag being carried by Max Butler, then shot him three times, fatally wounding him, before escaping with the bag that contained an estimated $10,000 that Butler, a courier for the First National Bank, had picked up from a Realtor.

5. The chase, which reached speeds of 80 miles an hour, ended when the Pontiac struck two other cars on Holton Drive, where the police arrested the Pontiacs driver, identified as Lynn R. Pryor, and charged her with armed robbery, reckless driving and fleeing to elude capture following an incident in which a convenience store on Mercy Dr. was robbed of less than $20 shortly after 6 a.m. this morning.

Name _____ Class _____ Date _____

EXERCISE 4
NEWSWRITING STYLE

TESTING ALL YOUR SKILLS

SECTION I: AVOIDING REDUNDANT PHRASES

The following phrases are redundant. They do not have to be rewritten; simply cross off the unnecessary words.

1. brand new	6. jail facility	11. right now
2. combine together	7. join together	12. small in size
3. continue on	8. new discovery	13. sent away for
4. set a new record	9. sum of $600	14. unpaid debt
5. they both agreed	10. personal friend	15. won a victory

SECTION II: AVOIDING SEXUAL STEREOTYPES

Rewrite the following sentences, avoiding sexist language and comments.

1. A California man and his wife attended the reunion.

2. While the girls were playing tennis, their husbands were playing golf.

3. While her husband works, Valerie Dawkins raises their children and dabbles in politics.

4. Mrs. John Favata is a widow, 56 years old and a petite grandmother but still plays tennis five days a week and, today, won the citys Senior Women's Tournament.

5. Councilman Alice Cycler, the attractive wife of a lawyer and mother of eight girls, is fighting to improve the citys parks.

SECTION III: REMAINING OBJECTIVE

The following sentences do not have to be rewritten; simply cross off the opinionated words and phrases.

1. Only 7 of the 94 people aboard the ill-fated plane were killed.

2. The boys grief-stricken father says he intends to sue the prestigious school.

3. In an important speech Monday, the governor said the state must adopt needed laws to protect the unfortunate victims.

4. Eight-six students miraculously escaped injury when an alert pedestrian noticed the flames and quickly warned them to leave.

5. One of the most interesting facts he revealed was that the Chinese replace each barrel of oil with one barrel of water to ensure that all their oil is pumped out of the ground.

SECTION IV: ELIMINATING UNNECESSARY WORDS

Eliminate the unnecessary words from the following sentences. The sentences do not have to be rewritten; simply cross off the words that are not needed.

1. Since the inception of the program it has saved three lives.

2. The boy was submerged under the water for about five minutes.

3. He was pinned in the car for 40 minutes before he could be removed.

4. The engineer said that, in her opinion, relatively few people actually use the road.

5. The center will have a total of eight separate offices for different ministers to occupy.

SECTION V: AVOIDING WORDY PHRASES

Substitute a single word for the wordy phrases in the following sentences.

1. The gunman made off with about $700.

2. Her medical bills are in excess of $35,000.

3. The operation left him in a state of paralysis.

4. The new law will no longer allow tinted car windows.

5. Margaret Van Den Shruck addressed her speech to the Rotary Club.

SECTION VI: SIMPLIFYING SENTENCES

Rewrite the following sentences more simply and clearly.

1. He was the recipient of numerous awards and honors.

2. The police were then summoned to the park by a girl.

3. She said that their farm is in close proximity to the park.

4. Snow removal vehicles are undertaking a cleanup of the city.

5. They said that a visit to their grandmothers was where they were going.

SECTION VII: TESTING ALL YOUR SKILLS

Rewrite the following sentences, correcting all their errors.

1. They reached a settlement of the debt.

2. Applications must be submitted on or before the deadline date of March 1.

3. A total of eight qualified persons, four men and four females, served on the important committee.

4. The mayor said that, at the present time, she is favorably disposed towards the passage of the important new law.

5. When questioned by the police, the suspect, an unidentified juvenile, maintained that he had been drinking and had no recollection at all of the events that transpired on that tragic Saturday night in question.

Name _____ Class _____ Date _____

E X E R C I S E 5

Answer Key Provided: See Appendix D

NEWSWRITING STYLE

REVIEW

SECTION I: REMAINING OBJECTIVE

Rewrite the following sentences, eliminating all their statements of opinion and other errors.

1. Students may find it worth their time to attend the 15th annual Pre-Law Day scheduled for Nov. 3 at the Student Center.

2. Speaking with great confidence, the attractive young woman did not hesitate to tell the crowd that she favors abortions.

3. The famous school, established 10 years ago, has scheduled a lavish banquet to celebrate its first decade of success.

4. His provocative speech was well received, as he was interrupted 17 times by applause.

5. Another important concept is the authors startling idea that it does not matter whether children begin to read before they are 10 years old.

SECTION II: AVOIDING REDUNDANT PHRASES

The following phrases are redundant. They do not have to be rewritten; simply cross off the unnecessary words.

1. actual facts	6. free gifts	11. right here
2. close down	7. in order to	12. tracked down
3. dead bodies	8. new innovation	13. very unique
4. dropped downward	9. past history	14. winter months
5. first began	10. revert back to	15. young child

SECTION III: AVOIDING WORDY PHRASES

Substitute a single word for each of the following phrases.

1. came to a stop
2. did not pay attention to
3. due to the fact that
4. in advance of
5. in the near future

6. in the vicinity of
7. is in possession of
8. made an investigation of
9. took under consideration
10. united in holy matrimony

SECTION IV: AVOIDING UNNECESSARY WORDS

The following sentences do not have to be rewritten; simply cross off the unnecessary words.

1. The city council voted to go ahead and sue the builders.

2. The accident occurred when a pickup truck collided with a car.

3. There is a possibility that the sign may be installed sometime later this month.

4. When the police arrived at the scene, they found only an empty box, not a bomb.

5. Police responding to the call found that the assailants had kicked him in the face, head and neck.

SECTION V: TESTING ALL YOUR SKILLS

Rewrite the following sentences, correcting all their errors.

1. He suffered the loss of his right eye.

2. The debt was then not nearly so large as it is today.

3. He criticized the president, calling him inconsistent and unrealistic.

4. The politician extended his appreciation to those who had supported him.

5. The purpose of this article will be to examine the problems of migrant workers.

6. Before a young child reaches the age of 18, he will see a total of 20,000 acts of violence on the tube.

7. The consensus of opinion among participants in the workshop is that it should be up to the governor to decide how to expend the funds.

8. It was brought out at the conference that the terms of the agreement are not in accordance with the desires of the people of Israel.

9. The 62-year-old spinster, the daughter of retired judge Myron Hanson, does not look the part but has become an expert on criminal law.

10. At a party given in her honor on the day of her retirement, co-workers celebrated the occasion by presenting the librarian with a trip to Paris.

11. Mike Deacosta, his wife and their two children, Mark and Amy, served as the hosts.

12. An attractive young blonde, Elaine Gardepe, seems to be an unlikely person to write a book about the topic, yet her book about auto mechanics has become a best seller.

CHAPTER 3

WORDS

"Some lucky stiffs, whom you will learn to envy if you're not one of them, have the facility for swift, painless writing. Others, the majority I believe—and you may count me in—find writing a labored agony of mental sweat. They figuratively have to flog themselves into starting, and they love it only for the satisfaction of having done it, never for any joy in doing it."

(From the book "Newspaperman" by Morton Sontheimer)

Adults chuckle at the writing errors young students make. The errors often occur because students are still developing their vocabularies and use the wrong word. Consider the following sentences, written by high school students:

Socrates died from an overdose of wedlock.

A horse divided against itself cannot stand.

Floods can be prevented by putting dames in the river.

The following errors are similar but were written by college students:

Gothic architecture is distinguished by flying buttocks.

Another method of getting rid of trash is incarceration.

The players returned to the court when the buzzard sounded.

Other errors, as in the following examples, arise because students fail to think and to express their ideas clearly and precisely. As a result, some of their sentences state the obvious (or impossible). Others may have unintended, often comical, meanings:

Rural life is found mostly in the country.

Ask the dead man if it matters as to what killed him. See what he says. I do not think he will care.

That summer I finally got my leg operated on, and what a relief! It had been hanging over my head for years.

Theodore Roosevelt was saddened when his young wife died and went to a ranch in the Dakotas.

People expect more of college students—and especially of journalism students, who must master the English language. Teachers also fear that students who develop bad habits in college will continue to make mistakes while working for the media after graduation.

The men and women who devote their lives to journalism develop a respect for the language. They value prose that is clear, concise and accurate. They strive to select the exact word needed to convey an idea, use the word properly and place it in a sentence that is grammatically correct.

When professional journalists hire a new reporter, they look for someone who understands and respects the language, knows spelling and grammar, possesses an extensive vocabulary and writes in a clear and interesting manner.

Journalists know their readers, viewers and listeners expect the media to be accurate and to use the language properly. Inevitably, mistakes are made, and thousands of people notice and

Harcourt Brace & Company

laugh at them. If the errors become too numerous, they may damage a news organization's credibility and force it to print or broadcast costly and embarrassing corrections. To avoid the problem, many news organizations test job applicants on spelling, vocabulary and writing, and hire only those who produce the best work.

BE PRECISE

To communicate effectively, reporters must be precise, particularly in their selection of words. Mark Twain wrote, "The difference between the right word and the almost right word is the difference between lightning and the lightning bug." The perfect choice makes a sentence forceful and interesting; imprecision creates confusion and misunderstanding.

Some words are simply inappropriate for use in news stories. Few editors or news directors permit the use of words such as "cop" or "kid" (unless you are referring to a goat), or derogatory terms about a person's race or religion. News executives allow profanity only when it is essential to a story's meaning and, even then, refuse to publish the most offensive terms. They prefer the word "woman" to the archaic "lady." Many ban the use of contractions, except in direct quotations. Professional journalists also object to nouns used as verbs. They would not allow you to report that someone "authored" a book, "detailed" a plan, "hosted" a party, "headquartered" a company, "impacted" a community or "gunned" an enemy. Nor would they allow you to report that food prices were "upped," plans "finalized" or children "parented."

Some errors occur because the reporter is unaware of a word's exact meaning. Few journalists would report that a car "collided" with a tree, that a "funeral service" was held, that a gunman "executed" his victim or that a child "was drowned" in a lake. Why? Two objects collide only if both are moving; thus, a car can strike a tree, but never "collide" with one. The term "funeral service" is redundant. "Executed" means put to death in accordance with a legally imposed sentence; therefore, only a state—never a murderer—can execute anyone. A report that a child "was drowned" would imply that someone held the child's head underwater until the victim died.

Such considerations are not trivial. Journalists who do not use words correctly may confuse or irritate their audience. Thus, your instructors will object if your use of the language is sloppy and inaccurate, as in these examples:

> Wallace grew up around the fossil beds of Volmer County.

> The youth produced a pistol and threatened the cashier.

> Paramedics took the victim to a hospital with minor cuts and bruises.

"Around" means surrounding or encircling; Wallace could not have been "around" the fossil beds as he grew up, but he was "among," "amid" or "near" them. A robber may "draw" or "display" a pistol but is unlikely to produce (to manufacture) one in the midst of a robbery. Only a victim—not the hospital—can suffer cuts and bruises.

Sentences and paragraphs become awkward and even nonsensical when writers fail to express their ideas with clarity and precision. The worst examples are not only garbled but inaccurate. Fortunately, that type of error is easy to correct:

> She received a limp.
> REVISED: She suffered a broken leg and now walks with a limp.
>
> The campus police are open 24 hours a day.
> REVISED: The campus police station is open 24 hours a day.
>
> The kitchen of a local restaurant caught fire Tuesday but caused little damage.
> REVISED: A fire in the kitchen of a local restaurant Tuesday caused little damage.

Before it was rewritten, the third sentence suggested that the kitchen, not the fire, caused the damage.

When reporters fail to express their ideas clearly and precisely, audiences derive a different meaning from the one intended. The unintended meaning may be difficult for the writer to detect. Double meanings in the following headlines, all of which actually appeared in newspapers, illustrate the problem:

> Squad Helps Dog Bite Victim
>
> Milk Drinkers Turn to Powder
>
> Juvenile Court to Try Shooting Defendant
>
> Mayors Marry More Often Than You Might Think
>
> Police Say Man Hid Crack in Buttocks
>
> Astronauts Practice Landing on Laptops
>
> Prosecutors Say Simpson Had an Hour to Kill

Readers often consider the double meanings humorous. Few editors or news directors, however, are amused when the errors appear in their newspapers or news broadcasts. Yet even the best news organizations occasionally make mistakes. Here is an example from The New York Times:

> The State Health Department is surveying hospitals around the state to ascertain whether women patients are being given Pap tests to determine if they have uterine cancer as required by law.

Confusion often arises because words look or sound alike. For example: a recent story reported, "About 40 years ago, she left her native Cypress for New York City and set up a bakery on Ninth Avenue near 40th Street." Few people are born in trees, and an editor wondered, "Could that have been 'Cyprus'"?

College students are more likely to confuse words such as "buses" and "busses," "naval" and "navel," and "reckless" and "wreckless." The word "busses" refers to kisses, not the vehicles people ride in. A "navel" is a belly button, and some motorists drive "wrecks," but are convicted of "reckless" driving.

Are you ready for a quiz? Can you find the errors of imprecision in the following sentences? (If you need help, look at the explanations at the bottom of the following page.)

1. The attorney admitted that his client had an intoxicated driving record.
2. She was given one year in jail, probation and a $1,000 fine.
3. The fire department responded to the call about a small fire, checked it and drove away.

Harcourt Brace & Company

4. Once inside the house, a shotgun and some coins were stolen by the swindler.
5. Although two fire trucks, a rescue squad and a police car arrived within minutes, they were unable to extinguish the flames before the home was destroyed.

USE STRONG VERBS

Verbs can transform a drab sentence into an interesting—or even a horrifying—one. Notice the impact of "stopped," "evaporated" and "turned" in the first example, from a New York Times story about how Americans learned of the verdict in the O.J. Simpson trial, and "danced" in the second, published by the Minneapolis Star Tribune:

> At the Barnett Bank branch on Biscayne Boulevard in Miami, tellers stopped counting bills and the lines of customers evaporated as everyone turned tantalized to the television on the wall.

> While searchlights danced in the sky, thousands of fun-seekers converged on the Mississippi riverfront Wednesday night to mark the beginning of a new year.

Strong verbs like these help readers or listeners envision the events described in the stories. The following sentences are also colorful, interesting and vivid. Why? Because the college students who wrote them used descriptive verbs:

> A cargo door *popped* open, *tearing* a hole in the plane's side. Eleven passengers *sucked* out of the hole *plunged* 30,000 feet to their deaths.

> A gunman *jumped* behind the customer service counter of a department store Monday, *grabbed* a handful of money—then *fled* on a bicycle.

By comparison, the following sentences are weak and bland, yet it is easy to improve them. Simply add a strong verb:

> The suspect was gone before police arrived.
> REVISED: The suspect fled before police arrived.

> A man with a gun told her to give him all her money.
> REVISED: A gunman demanded all her money.

Notice that, in addition to making sentences more interesting, active verbs make them more concise:

> There is about $20 in the cash register.   (8 words)
> REVISED: The cash register contains about $20.   (6 words)

> It is speculated by police that the boy ran away.   (10 words)
> REVISED: Police speculate that the boy ran away.   (7 words)

Strong verbs describe one specific action. Weak verbs cover a number of different actions. The first sentence below is vague and bland because it uses a weak verb. The last three use specific, descriptive verbs and are more interesting—and informative:

> His brother *got* a personal computer.
> His brother *bought* a personal computer.
> His brother *won* a personal computer.
> His brother *stole* a personal computer.

---

1. The attorney may have admitted that his client had a record of driving while intoxicated; few records, however, can become intoxicated. 2. Judges order criminals to pay fines; they do not give criminals a fine. 3. Firefighters are expected to extinguish fires; they do not drive away after simply checking them. Also, change "the fire department" to "firefighters." 4. A criminal, not the shotgun and coins, entered the house. Also, houses are robbed by burglars, not swindlers. 5. Firefighters, rescue workers and police officers may extinguish a fire. Cars and trucks cannot.

Harcourt Brace & Company

Avoid the repeated use of forms of the verb "to be," such as "is," "are," "was" and "were." These verbs are overused, weak and dull. Again, notice that sentences using passive verbs are also wordy:

> The protest was filed by a history teacher.   (8 words)
> REVISED: A history teacher filed the protest.   (6 words)

> A sharp criticism of the plan was voiced by the mayor.   (11 words)
> REVISED: The mayor sharply criticized the plan.   (6 words)

> Police officers were summoned to the scene by a neighbor.   (10 words)
> REVISED: A neighbor called the police.   (5 words)

Tips from a Pro

FRESH VERBS SPICE UP STORIES

By **Lucille S. deView**
Writing Coach
The Orange County Register

Check the verbs in these stories by Francis X. Clines of The New York Times:

> An Air Florida jetliner taking off from National Airport in a snowstorm crashed into a crowded bridge this afternoon and broke as it plunged into the Potomac River, leaving at least 10 persons dead and more than 40 missing, according to unofficial police estimates.
> The twin-engine plane suddenly appeared out of the swirling snow over the 14th Street Bridge at the height of an early commuter exodus and sheared open a truck and at least four automobiles, then caromed in pieces into the frigid river.

> The voices of Richard M. Nixon and his inner sanctum people leaked out from the 32 sets of earphones, making the library buzz and burble metallically like the American summer at Locust Pine.

Crashed, broke, plunged, appeared, sheared, caromed. Leaked, buzz, burble.

Fresh, strong, active verbs are a specialty of this talented writer, who switches gracefully from hard news to features, to profiles, to essays. His verbs help the reader envision the scene; they coax tears or smiles.

Alas, as we churn out stories on deadline it becomes all too easy to lean on the same few, vapid verbs. What, we wonder, happened to those rich words we once prized? What, indeed.

If your copy suffers from verb stagnation, try this remedy:

• Flag your verbs: Before submitting your story, cruise through the copy on your computer and highlight the verbs in bold. Study them.

• Substitute vigorous verbs for weaklings: Consult the dictionary, reference books, colleagues. Jolt your thinking. Get out of that rut.

(continued on next page)

- Use the active voice: Consult "Elements of Style" by William Strunk Jr. and E.B. White, who extoll the active voice as "usually more direct and vigorous than the passive."

    Examples: Passive—"There were a great number of dead leaves lying on the ground." Active—"Dead leaves covered the ground." Passive—"The reason he left college was that his health became impaired." Active—"Failing health compelled him to leave college."

- Eliminate "there is," "there are": This inevitably paves the way for descriptive verbs.

    Examples: "There is a deserted house beside the narrow highway." Try: "A deserted house looms above the narrow highway." "There is a lace curtain blowing inside a broken window." Try: "A lace curtain flutters inside a broken window."

- Shorten, tighten your copy: The stronger the verbs, the fewer the words needed to tell the story.

- Keep a verb list: As you read good fiction, non-fiction and poetry, jot down verbs you admire. Keep a running list for future use. The goal is never to be obscure or show off, but to employ the rich vocabulary of verbs at the writer's disposal.

To praise Clines' writing is to praise those who handle his copy, preserving as they do the clarity and power of his carefully chosen verbs. Astute editors and copy editors protect verbs that are simple and clear and do not arbitrarily suppress verbs that are slightly less familiar, so long as they suit the situation.

The gifted editor or copy editor, like the gifted writer, is not above taking a chance. Risk is the name of the good writing game. Risk it. Strengthen those verbs.

WORDS TO AVOID

Adjectives and Adverbs

Newswriters avoid adverbs and adjectives, since they tend to be less forceful, specific and objective than nouns and verbs. William Strunk Jr. and E.B. White, authors of the influential book "The Elements of Style," wrote, "The adjective hasn't been built that can pull a weak or inaccurate noun out of a tight place." Along the same lines, Mark Twain warned, "When you catch an adjective, kill it."

Most adverbs and adjectives are unnecessary. They waste space by stating the obvious, and they may unintentionally inject a reporter's opinion into the story. If you write about a child's funeral, you do not have to comment that the mourners were "sad-faced," the scene "grim" and the parents "grief-stricken." Nor is there reason to report that an author is "famous," a witness "alert" or an accident "tragic."

Typically, the adverbs and adjectives in the following sentences editorialize. Rather than simply reporting facts, they comment on those facts:

It was not until 9 p.m. that the police were finally able to find the child.
REVISED: Police found the child at 9 p.m.

After receiving the frightening report, the mayor made it quite clear that she is concerned about the program's outrageous costs.

REVISED: After receiving the report, the mayor said she is concerned about the program's costs.

The word "finally" in the first sentence suggests that the police were negligent and should have found the child sooner. Similarly, if you report the facts in the second story clearly and concisely, you should not have to add that the report was "frightening" and the costs "outrageous." Also avoid concluding that the mayor made anything "clear."

Clichés

Because they eliminate the need for thought, clichés have been called the greatest labor-saving devices ever invented. Clichés are words or phrases that writers have heard and copied over and over. Many are 200 or 300 years old: so old and so overused that they have lost their original impact and meaning. Clichés no longer startle, amuse or interest the public.

The news media can take a fresh phrase and overuse it so that it quickly becomes a cliché. Presidential candidate H. Ross Perot opposed the North American Free Trade Agreement on the grounds that it would eliminate American jobs. He said the migration of jobs to Mexico would create a "giant sucking sound." The phrase was fresh and effective when Perot first said it in a presidential debate, but journalists and others soon nearly wore it out. The American Journalism Review counted seven appearances of the phrase in different major publications over a five-day period several months later. Other phrases that have become clichés, according to the American Journalism Review, are "comfort level," "wake-up call" and "sea change."

Journalists employ clichés when they lack the time (or talent) to find words more specific, descriptive or original. So a reporter under the pressure of a deadline may say that a fire "swept through" a building, that an explosion "rocked" a city, that police officers gave a suspect a "spirited chase" or that protesters were an "angry mob."

Other clichés exaggerate. Few people are really "blind as a bat," "cool as a cucumber," "light as a feather," "neat as a pin," "straight as an arrow," "thin as a rail" or "white as a sheet."

Political reporting is especially susceptible to clichés. It seems as though candidates always are nominated in "smoke-filled rooms" or "test the waters" before "tossing their hats into the ring." Other candidates launch "whirlwind campaigns" and "hammer away" at their opponents, or they employ "spin doctors" to try to control unfavorable news. Some candidates "straddle the fence" on the "burning issues of the day." However, few "give up without a fight."

You are likely to be so familiar with the clichés that you can complete them after seeing just the first few words. Want to try? The final word is missing from the following clichés, yet you are likely to complete all 10:

a close brush with _____	has a nose for _____
a step in the right _____	last but not _____
could not believe her _____	left holding the _____
evidence of foul _____	lived to a ripe old _____
fell into the wrong _____	lying in a pool of _____

Some clichés are so closely associated with newswriting that they are called "journalese." The term identifies phrases reporters use to dramatize, exaggerate and, often, distort the events they describe. In news stories, fires "rage," temperatures "soar," earthquakes "rumble" and people "vow." Rivers "go on a rampage." Third World countries are often "war-torn" or "much-troubled." Sometimes they are "oil-rich." Politicians who get in trouble are "scandal-plagued," and if the scandal lasts long enough, reporters will create a name for it by tacking the suffix "-scam" or "-gate" to an appropriate noun, as in "Abscam" and "Koreagate."

Journalese is especially common on sports pages. Sports reporters fear overusing the word "won" to describe the outcomes of contests. Instead (especially in headlines) they report that one team "ambushed," "bombed," "flattened," "nipped," "outlasted," "scorched," "stunned," "thrashed" or "walloped" another.

Sometimes a cliché can be twisted into a fresh expression or used in a surprising way, as in this sentence from a New York Times story about a National Basketball Association championship series between the New York Knicks and the Houston Rockets: "It is the city that never sleeps versus the city that never wins." Such opportunities for the effective use of clichés are rare.

Clichés that journalists should recognize and avoid appear in the box on the following page.

Slang

Journalists avoid slang, which tends to be more faddish than clichés. Some words that started out as slang have won acceptance as standard English. "Blizzard," "flabbergast" and "GI" (for soldier) are among such terms. Most slang never makes this transition, however.

Feature stories and personality profiles sometimes employ slang effectively, but it is inappropriate in straight news stories because it is too informal and annoying. Moreover, slang may baffle readers who are not of the right age or ethnic group to understand it.

Slang rapidly becomes dated, so that a term used in a story may already be obsolete. During the 1970s and 1980s, young people overused such terms as "cool," "freaked out," "heavy," "gnarly" and "radical." Young people complained that they were unable to "get it together." They also wanted to go "where the action is" but admired people who were "mellow" or "laid back." By the 1990s, young people found a whole new set of "slammin'" slang terms and "dissed" anyone still using the slang of the 1980s as a "Melvin."

Harcourt Brace & Company

CLICHÉS

There are thousands of clichés and slang phrases that reporters must learn to recognize and avoid. Some of the most common are listed here.

a keen mind
ambulance rushed
around the clock
arrived at the scene
at long last
at this point in time
baptism of fire
bare minimum
beginning a new life
behind the wheel
benefit of the doubt
bigger and better
blanket of snow
blessing in disguise
called to the scene
calm before the storm
came to their rescue
came to rest
came under attack
came under fire
cast aside
caught red-handed
clear-cut issue
colorful scene
complete stranger
complete success
coveted title
crystal clear
dead and buried
decide the fate
devoured by flames
dime a dozen
doomed to failure
dread disease
dream come true
drop in the bucket
dying breed
erupted in violence
escaped death
exchanged gunfire
faced an uphill battle
fell on deaf ears

few and far between
foreseeable future
gained ground
gave it their blessing
get a good look
go to the polls
got off to a good start
grief-stricken
ground to a halt
hail of bullets
heated argument
heed the warning
high-speed chase
hits the spot
in his new position
in the wake of
landed the job
last but not least
last-ditch stand
left their mark
leveled an attack
limped into port
line of fire
lingering illness
lodge a complaint
lucky to be alive
made off with
made their escape
made their way home
miraculous escape
Mother Nature
necessary evil
never a dull moment
no relief in sight
notified next of kin
once in a lifetime
one step closer
only time will tell
opened fire
paved the way
pillar of strength
pinpointed the cause

pitched battle
police dragnet
pose a challenge
proud parents
proves conclusively
pushed for legislation
quick thinking
real challenge
reign of terror
see-saw battle
set to work
smell a rat
sped to the scene
spread like wildfire
start their mission
still at large
stranger than fiction
strike a nerve
sudden death
sweep under the rug
take it easy
talk is cheap
tempers flared
time will tell
tip of the iceberg
tipped the scales
took its toll
too late to turn back
tower of strength
tracked down
traveled the globe
tried their luck
under siege
under their noses
undertaking a study
up in the air
view with alarm
went to great lengths
won a reputation
word of caution
words of wisdom
word to the wise

Slang also conveys meanings journalists may want to avoid. John Algeo, a professor of English at the University of Georgia, believes people invent slang to give a name to something that will express their attitude toward the thing. Thus, slang terms such as "flaky," "ego trip" and "flatfoot" convey evaluations of the things described. Reporters, however, should leave to editorial writers or readers and viewers the job of making evaluations.

Technical Language and Jargon

Nearly every trade or profession develops its own technical language or jargon. When professionals use the jargon to impress or mislead the public, critics call it gobbledygook, bafflegab, doublespeak or bureaucratese. Most jargon is abstract, wordy, repetitious and confusing. For example, a government agency warned, "There exists at the intersection a traffic condition which constitutes an intolerable, dangerous hazard to the health and safety of property and persons utilizing such intersection for pedestrian and vehicular movement." That sentence contains 31 words. A good journalist could summarize it in four: "The intersection is dangerous."

Many of the sources reporters routinely use—doctors, lawyers, business people, press releases, technical reports, and police and court records—speak in jargon. Journalists must translate that jargon into plain English. Here are three examples:

JARGON: Identification of the victims is being withheld pending notification of their next of kin.
REVISED: The victims' names are being withheld until their families are notified.

JARGON: Dr. Stewart McKay said, "Ethnic groups that subsist on a vegetarian diet and practically no meat products seem to have a much lower level of serum cholesterol and a very low incidence of ischemic diseases arising from atherosclerotic disease."
REVISED: Dr. Stewart McKay said races that eat little meat have low rates of coronary heart disease and related illnesses.

JARGON: When the prosecutor asked the plaintiff to describe her first sexual encounter with the defendant, she bowed her head and began to cry.
REVISED: When Smith asked the 13-year-old girl to describe her first sexual encounter with her stepfather, she bowed her head and began to cry. (This example also illustrates how jargon can confuse reporters. There are no plaintiffs in criminal prosecutions; the proper term is "victim.")

Americans expect teachers to set a good example for their students by writing clearly and accurately, but even teachers succumb to jargon. Some call themselves "educators" or "instructional units." Desks have become "pupil work stations," libraries have become "instructional resource centers," hallways have become "behavior-transition corridors" and schools have become "attendance centers." A principal in Houston sent this note home to parents:

Our school's cross-graded, multi-ethnic, individual learning program is designed to enhance the concept of an open-ended learning program with emphasis on a continuum of multi-ethnic, academically enriched learning using the identified intellectually gifted child as the agent or director of his own learning.

This passage translates as, "Our curriculum lets the gifted student learn at her or his own pace." Why do people use jargon unnecessarily? Probably they want to make themselves and everything they say seem more important.

Readers usually can decipher the jargon's meaning, but not easily. Sometimes jargon is almost impossible to understand:

The semiotic perspective promotes a reflective mode of thinking that requires attention to specific contextual clues and relates them to one's understanding of the world

Harcourt Brace & Company

with a kind of "informed skepticism" that the authors believe is fundamental to critical thinking.

This kind of technical language may be appropriate in some specialized publications written for the experts in a particular field. It is not appropriate in newspapers written for a mass audience.

Euphemisms

Euphemisms are vague expressions used in place of harsher, more offensive terms. Judith Martin, who writes the syndicated column "Miss Manners," has said, "Etiquette cannot do without euphemisms," which disguise what people mean. Prudishly, Americans often say that a woman is "expecting" rather than "pregnant," and that they have to "go to the washroom" rather than "go to the toilet." Other examples of euphemisms preferred by Americans are "donkey" for "ass," "intestinal fortitude" for "guts" and "affirmative action" for "minority hiring."

Whatever value euphemisms have for etiquette, they detract from good news writing, in which clarity and precision are the most important goals. Geneva Overholser, ombudsman at The Washington Post, has said journalists need to realize that they sometimes hurt or offend people when they report incidents involving sexist and racist speech. Nevertheless, she said, the fear of giving offense should not interfere with the journalist's obligation to report facts and situations readers need to know. The (New Orleans) Times-Picayune put that principle into practice recently when it covered the Louisiana gubernatorial campaign of David Duke, who had a history of involvement in the Ku Klux Klan. When Duke urged a return to "neighborhood schools," the Times-Picayune reported that Duke was using the phrase as a euphemism for "segregated schools."

Some incidents test the willingness of journalists to be blunt. An example is the case of Lorena Bobbitt, who used a kitchen knife to cut off her husband's penis after he allegedly raped her.[2] The word "penis" rarely had appeared in news stories, and some news organizations were squeamish about using it, especially in headlines. Euphemisms like "member," "organ" or "offending organ" appeared instead. The widespread coverage the Bobbitt case received apparently diminished journalistic sensitivity to the word. A computer search found more than 1,000 news stories that used the word "penis" in the six months after the Bobbitt story broke, compared to only 20 mentions in the previous six months.

Other uses of euphemisms have proved more durable. From 1933 to 1941, "Cactus Jack" Garner of Texas served as vice president under Franklin D. Roosevelt. Contrary to legend, Garner never said the office of vice president is "not worth a pitcher of warm spit." What he actually said was that the vice presidency is "not worth a pitcher of warm piss." Most publishers, even publishers of history textbooks, still prefer the euphemism.

Americans use many euphemisms while talking about death. They say that a friend or relative "passed on" or is "no longer with us," not that their friend or relative has died and been buried. Hospitals report a "negative patient outcome," not that a patient died. Funeral directors object to being called "morticians"—a word which itself was originally a euphemism for "undertakers."

During a recession, major companies lay off thousands of their employees. Few admit it, however. Instead, corporate executives say they are "restructuring" their companies, "downsizing" (or "rightsizing") them to get rid of "excess workers." Some executives insist that through such "reductions in force," they are offering their employees "career enhancement opportunities."

The prestigious titles that some Americans give their jobs are euphemisms. Garbagemen call themselves "sanitation workers," prison guards have become "corrections officers," and dogcatchers have become "animal welfare officers."

---

[2]The husband, John Wayne Bobbitt, was charged with marital sexual assault but was acquitted. Lorena Bobbitt was prosecuted for malicious wounding but was found innocent by reason of temporary insanity.

Harcourt Brace & Company

War spawns some of the most grotesque euphemisms, perhaps, as some critics say, to hide the human pain and suffering every war causes. Killing the enemy has become "servicing the target." Airplanes no longer bomb enemy soldiers; instead, they "visit a site." And if, while bombing enemy troops, some civilians are killed, that is "collateral damage." The United States calls the largest of its land-based nuclear missiles "Peacekeepers." During the war against Iraq, the U.S. military rarely admitted that the American soldiers captured by Iraqi troops were tortured. Instead, briefing officers said, "Allied personnel being forcibly detained appear to be under considerable duress." Finally, modern armies no longer retreat. Instead, they "move to the rear," "engage in a strategic withdrawal" or "occupy new territory in accordance with plan."

THAT, WHICH, WHO AND WHOM

"That" and "which" are little words, but they can make big differences in the meaning of sentences. The late John B. Bremner, a copy-editing teacher and expert on the language, used the following sentences to illustrate how changing "that" to "which" changes the meaning of a sentence:

> Go to the third house that has green drapes.

> Go to the third house which has green drapes.

In the first sentence, the clause introduced by "that" is essential to the meaning of the sentence. It tells you to count not the number of houses, but the number of houses with green drapes and go to the third. In the second sentence, the clause introduced by "which" is not essential. You are told simply to go to the third house. It is helpful, but not necessary, that you know the color of the drapes.

Here's a rule that can help you decide between "that" and "which": If you can read the sentence without the subordinate clause and the meaning does not change, the word you should use to introduce the clause is "which." Otherwise, use "that."

"That" and "which" introduce clauses that refer to ideas, inanimate objects or animals without names. "Who" and "whom" begin clauses that refer to people and animals with names.

The distinction between "who" and "whom" causes problems for some writers. "Who" is used as the subject of a clause; "whom" is used as the object of a verb or a preposition. Whether a word is a subject or an object may not always be clear in relative clauses or questions, either of which may depart from normal word order.

Either "who" or "whom" may appear as the first word in a question, but which you should use depends on its grammatical relationship to the rest of the sentence. These two sentences illustrate the difference:

> Who gave you the scarf?

> Whom do you prefer as student body president?

In the first, "who" is the subject of the clause, the initiator of the action "gave." In the second, "whom" is the object of the verb "prefer."

Native speakers of English rarely use "whom" to begin a question when they should use "who." They do use "who," however, when they should use "whom." Here is an example:

> Who did you speak to?

Because the question asks about the object of the action—speaking—"whom" is correct.

A similar confusion arises in relative clauses, which qualify a noun or pronoun that appeared earlier in the sentence. For example:

> The report names the man whom the police believe caused the child's death.

The author of this sentence used "whom" thinking it was the object of the verb "believe." Actually, it is the subject of the relative clause "caused the child's death." Therefore, "who" should be

Harcourt Brace & Company

used. The confusion arises from the insertion of "police believe," which attributes the suspicions about the man to the police. Because the attribution separates the subject of the relative clause from the verb, the writer can become confused about whether the relative pronoun is a subject or an object.

One way to avoid or reduce confusion over "who" and "whom" is to replace them with a personal pronoun. If "he" or "she" sounds right, then use "who." If "him" or "her" would be more natural, use "whom." If you do that in the following sentence, you realize immediately that "whom" is wrong:

> The candidates argued about whom was responsible for the tax increase.

At first the relative pronoun appears to be the object of the preposition "about," but when you substitute personal pronouns you realize that the relative pronoun is the subject of the clause "was responsible for the tax increase." No one would say "her was responsible . . ." But "she was responsible . . ." makes sense. The relative pronoun you want to use here is "who."

KEEP RELATED WORDS TOGETHER

Once a reporter has selected the right word, she or he must put that word in the proper place in the sentence. Related words and ideas should stand as close together as possible. For example, keep modifiers close to the words they modify. If the words are separated, the sentences containing them will become more difficult to understand. The sentences' meaning also may change, sometimes comically:

> The gunmen tied the victim and left him with his hands and feet taped and lying on the back seat.
> REVISED: The gunmen tied the victim, taped his hands and feet and left him lying on the back seat.

> He is making a list of the empty lots in the neighborhood so he can track down their owners and ask if he can plant them next summer.
> REVISED: He wants to plant the empty lots in the neighborhood next summer and is making a list of them so he can find their owners.

Placement errors are particularly common in the first paragraph in news stories, and often involve modifiers of time and place, as in the following examples:

> A 62-year-old woman was convicted Monday of embezzling $143,000 in Circuit Court.

> After spending seven months in jail, Neil Lefforge was taken before Judge Samuel McGregor and sentenced to life in prison for the possession and sale of cocaine Tuesday.

In the first example, the 62-year-old woman was convicted in Circuit Court; she did not embezzle the money there. The defendant mentioned in the second example was sentenced Tuesday; he did not sell the cocaine then.

Here are other examples of the problem. The related words appear in italics and, in the revisions, are moved together:

> The police found a broken *bottle* in the back seat *that* was apparently thrown through the windshield.
> REVISED: The police found a broken *bottle that* was apparently thrown through the windshield. It was on the back seat.

> "I like the idea," *said* Concetta Ciulla of the University of Kansas *in a speech* Tuesday.
> REVISED: "I like the idea," Concetta Ciulla of the University of Kansas *said in a speech* Tuesday.

Harcourt Brace & Company

Chris Brown *charges that* as a result of the accident which occurred last summer at the intersection of Star Road and Power Drive *she suffered* a broken leg.

REVISED: Chris Brown *charges that she suffered* a broken leg in the accident which occurred last summer at the intersection of Star Road and Power Drive.

CHECKLIST

1. Choose words that convey your meaning as precisely as possible.
2. Use active verbs and vivid nouns.
3. Prune adjectives and adverbs from your sentences.
4. Avoid clichés, journalese, slang and euphemisms.
5. Rewrite technical language and jargon in plain English.
6. Observe the proper usage of "that" and "which," "who" and "whom."
7. Keep related words together.

St. Louis Post-Dispatch

WRITE & WRONG

By **Harry Levins**
Post-Dispatch Writing Coach

Good writing draws a clear picture in the writer's mind. When a reader can see a sharp image in his mind, the writing comes alive.

But vague writing blurs the image, throwing it out of focus. Writers who rely on adjectives often blur their images. True, an adjective can evoke a specific image in the *writer's* mind. After all, the writer was on the scene; when he writes of a "giant ice-cream cone," as one reporter recently did, the word "giant" recalls to the writer the three-scoop diet-buster (or whatever it was) that somebody was eating.

But the reader was elsewhere; the reader never *saw* the ice-cream cone in question. As a result, the reader must grapple with a vague word: "giant." How giant is giant? One reader's "giant" ice-cream cone is another's appetizer.

Here's a lede in which the writer made an effort to fix a sharp image in the reader's mind:

Laurie Ann Oilar of Kahoka, Mo., was a large, red-haired woman who liked to fix autos, tend farm animals and play with her baby daughter.

It worked, except for one word—"large."

What does "large" mean?

Does it mean that Ms. Oilar was fat?

Does it mean that Ms. Oilar was tall?

Does it mean that Ms. Oilar was buxom?

Does it mean that Ms. Oilar was Junoesque?

"Large" could fit any number of attributes. In this case, nobody knows which

Harcourt Brace & Company

one—except for the writer (and, of course, Ms. Oilar's acquaintances, who needed no word pictures). We would have served the reader better with precision:

> Laurie Ann Oilar of Kahoka, Mo., was a 325-pound, red-haired woman who . . .

Or:

> Laurie Ann Oilar of Kahoka, Mo., was a 6-foot, 2-inch woman who . . .

Or whatever fits in the context. Even such relatively vague adjectives as "heavy-set" or "plump" or "tall" would have been more precise than "large." Moral: make sure that the picture in *your* mind can be developed in the reader's mind as well.

Sometimes, we're vague because we assume that the reader knows as much as we do—always a dangerous assumption. Here's an example, from a political story in which mayoral contenders were talking about appointing blacks to high-level city jobs:

> Bosley said the number of blacks in such positions should be proportionate to the city's black population.
>
> Jackson would not put a specific number on the percentage of blacks he would place in such posts . . .

And neither would the writer, which was unfortunate. Blacks make up about 47 percent of the city's population. Had we used that figure and the number of jobs in question, the reader would have had some idea of how many blacks Bosley was talking about.

Similarly, a story on the recovery by the police of some stolen goods ended with this paragraph:

> Sgt. Stewart said many of the stolen goods had been sold at tremendous discounts. "For example, we learned that they were

selling cigarettes at $30 a case," he said.

But unless we know the retail value of a case of cigarettes, this information is worthless. How much of a discount does $30 represent? Fifty percent? Ninety percent? Who knows? The Coach has few equals as a consumer of cigarettes, but even he has no idea how many packages or cartons of cigarettes make up a case.

At times we're vague through a poor choice of words. A recent lede provides an example:

> A number of major road construction projects in the St. Louis area have been affected by the strike of Teamsters union truck drivers against the Material Dealers Association.

What is "a number of"? Answer: anything from one to infinity. What does "have been affected" mean? Some effects are good, some are neutral, some are bad. Some effects are slight, some are moderate, some are severe. What information did this lede convey? That from one to countless road projects is or are being affected in some way or other to some sort of degree. Conclusion: mush.

On the other hand, the sort of information that readers need was contained in (or perhaps was edited into) a recent AP story on asbestos exposure. The story said current government regulations limited asbestos at places of work "to two fibers for each cubic centimeter of air." Then it added:

> That volume is about the size of a small sugar cube.

Most Americans know little about the metric system. So the sentence about the sugar cube took a hard fact and put it into terms that readers can understand.

Martha Shirk took the same extra step in a story about the sales tax increase

(continued on next page)

proposed in the city. After noting that the increase would add three-eighths of a cent to the tax, she wrote:

> The sales tax increase would add $18.75 to the price of a $5,000 automobile and 37½ cents to the cost of a $100 suit.

She needed only a moment to calculate the figures and a few words to convey them. But the beneficial impact can be way out of proportion to the effort. Numbers are abstractions; cars and suits are real.

***

TO BE OR NOT TO BE

Here's an all-too-common sort of sentence:

> Mrs. Clark's problem is that a city ordinance forced her to run as an independent in a special election last month.

A purist might note that Mrs. Clark ran by choice, not because a city ordinance forced her to. But The Coach had more problems with the writer's use of the verb "is."

Verbs represent the strongest words in English. Verbs propel a sentence. But among English verbs, "to be" in any of its forms is the weakest. With "to be," nothing *happens*; things merely *are*. Nothing *moves*; things merely *exist*.

Naturally, some sentences require "to be." But in many instances, we can replace "to be" with a more active verb:

> Mrs. Clark's problem stems from a city ordinance that barred her from running as a Democrat in a special election last month.

Another example:

> . . . for Tammy Beckham, 16, of St. Louis, who is in need of a liver transplant operation.

The solution:

> . . . for Tammy Beckham, 16, of St. Louis, who needs . . .

SUGGESTED READINGS

Bernstein, Theodore M. *The Careful Writer: A Modern Guide to English Usage*. New York: Atheneum, 1965.

Bremner, John B. *Words on Words: A Dictionary for Writers and Others Who Care About Words*. New York: Columbia University Press, 1980.

Brooks, Brian S., and James L. Pinson. *Working With Words: A Concise Guide for Media Editors and Writers*. New York: St. Martin's Press, 1989.

Cooper, Gloria, ed. *Red Tape Holds Up New Bridge: And More Flubs from the Nation's Press*. New York: Perigee, 1987.

Hayakawa, S.I. *The Use and Misuse of Language*. Greenwich, CT: Fawcett, 1962.

Kessler, Lauren, and Duncan McDonald. *When Words Collide: A Media Writer's Guide to Grammar and Style*, 4th ed. Belmont, CA: Wadsworth, 1996.

Lewin, Esther, and Albert E. Lewin. *The Thesaurus of Slang*. New York: Facts on File, 1988.

Lutz, William. *Doublespeak*. New York: Harper & Row, 1989.

Neaman, Judith, and Carole G. Silver. *Kind Words: A Thesaurus of Euphemisms*, Expanded and rev. ed. New York: McGraw-Hill, 1990.

Safire, William. *On Language*. New York: Times Books, 1990.

Strunk, William Jr., and E. B. White. *The Elements of Style*, 3rd ed. New York: Macmillan, 1979.

Urdang, Laurence. *The Dictionary of Confusable Words*. New York: Facts on File, 1988.

Van Dijk, Teun A. *Communicating Racism: Ethnic Prejudice in Thought and Talk*. Newbury Park, CA: Sage, 1987.

Harcourt Brace & Company

Name _____ Class _____ Date _____

EXERCISE 1
VOCABULARY

INSTRUCTIONS: The following pairs or groups of words often cause confusion because, although they may look or sound similar, their meanings differ. In the space provided, define each of the words and explain how its usage differs from that of the other word or words. If necessary, use additional sheets of paper for your answers.

1. above/more than/over _____

    _____

2. affect/effect _____

    _____

3. as/like _____

    _____

4. average/mean/median/mode _____

    _____

5. bloc/block _____

    _____

6. blond/blonde _____

    _____

7. burglar/robber/swindler/thief _____

    _____

8. capital/capitol _____

    _____

9. censor/censure _____

    _____

10. cite/sight/site _____

    _____

11. complement/compliment _____

    _____

12. compose/comprise _____

    _____

13. convince/persuade _____

    _____

14. elusive/illusive _____

    _____

15. entitled/titled _____

    _____

16. fewer/less _____

    _____

17. fiance/fiancee _____

    _____

18. fourth/forth _____

    _____

19. hanged/hung _____

    _____

20. imply/infer _____

    _____

21. incite/insight _____

    _____

22. lay/lie _____

    _____

23. marshal/marshall _____

    _____

Harcourt Brace & Company

24. moral/morale _____

_____

25. nauseated/nauseous _____

_____

26. principal/principle _____

_____

27. ravage/ravish _____

_____

28. reign/rein _____

_____

29. role/roll _____

_____

30. than/then _____

_____

31. trustee/trusty _____

_____

32. who's/whose _____

_____

Name _____ Class _____ Date _____

E X E R C I S E   2
VOCABULARY

INSTRUCTIONS: Words with different meanings often look or sound similar. As a journalist, you should be familiar with the words and use them correctly. Cross out the wrong words from the following sentences, leaving only the correct ones. Also correct errors in style and use of the possessive. If you need help, the rules for forming possessives appear in Appendix C.

1. Three women, all (alumnae/alumni/alumnus) of the college, (adviced/advised) the officials to (altar/alter) (their/there/they're) plans.

2. The (principal/principle) said her (role/roll) in maintaining school discipline is (miner/minor).

3. (Fewer/less) than a dozen (statues/statutes) were erected at the (cite/sight/site).

4. Attorneys warned that the city (ordinance/ordnance) is (liable/libel) to cause more (decent/descent/dissent).

5. (Irregardless/Regardless) of (weather/whether) the (phenomena/phenomenon) is unusual, the firms stockholders want to protect (their/there/they're) investment.

6. The mass media (are/is) likely to (affect/effect) the teams (moral/morale).

7. The play, (entitled/titled) "Never, Never," was banned by Soviet (censors/censures) until the author (altared/altered) a controversial scene.

8. The mayors (aid/aide) favors the plan but warned that (its/it's) likely (to/too) seem (bazaar/bizarre).

9. A (burglar/robber/swindler/thief) broke into the (principals/principles) garage and took a (canvas/canvass) tent.

10. Each year, thousands of (people/persons) (emigrate/immigrate) (to/too) the United States.

11. The banks (trustee/trusty) said he wants to (ensure/insure) its success (because/since) thousands of (people/persons) depend upon (its/it's) services.

12. They are (confidant/confident) that the enemys (naval/navel) forces will (loose/lose) the battle.

13. A (marshal/marshall) predicted that the evidence will (ensure/insure) the mans conviction for (liable/libel).

14. They want (to/too) know (who's/whose) public opinion (pole/poll) is most reliable.

15. The (forth/fourth) person to (decent/descent/dissent) said he lives in the state (capital/capitol) and objects (to/too) (its/it's) new (ordinance/ordnance).

16. He (hanged/hung) the painting in his home but said (its/it's) larger (than/then) he expected.

17. The student is not (adapt/adept/adopt) at mathematics, and his adviser (implied/inferred) that he is (liable/libel) to fail.

18. He wants to (lay/lie) down for a few minutes, (than/then) address the 1,000 (envelopes/envelops).

19. He accused the schools (trustee/trusty) of (inciting/insighting) a riot among (its/it's) thousands of (alumnae/alumni/alumnus).

20. Seventeen (people/persons) obtained copies of the (calendar/calender) before anyone noticed (its/it's) (miner/minor) errors.

Name _____ Class _____ Date _____

E X E R C I S E   3

SPELLING AND VOCABULARY

INSTRUCTIONS: Some words in the following sentences have been placed in parentheses. The words often cause confusion because they look or sound like other words. Decide which of the words is correct here and circle it. Cross out all the other words.

The sentences also contain possessives that need correcting. If you need help, the rules for forming possessives appear in Appendix C.

1. The school (principal/principle) criticized the teachers (aid/aide).

2. The story (implies/infers) that the girl (hanged/hung) herself.

3. He (adviced/advised) the city to find another (cite/sight/site).

4. She asked (who's/whose) jacket is (laying/lying) on the floor.

5. His (fiance/fiancee) said (its/it's) unlikely to succeed.

6. They asked (who's/whose) (role/roll) she will be given.

7. He said the (data/datum) eliminated by the (censor/censure) was mistaken.

8. They wondered why (your/you're) being so (elusive/illusive) about the issue.

9. He said the (statue/statute) is likely (to/too) be declared unconstitutional.

10. He is trying to raise more (capital/capitol) to (insure/ensure) the store's success.

11. They (complemented/complimented) the architect but want (fewer/less) windows.

12. He is (confidant/confident) that the movie, (titled/entitled) "Romance," will succeed.

13. They want to (altar/alter) the plans so the buildings are (farther/further) apart.

14. (Their/There/They're) inheritance will total (over/more than) $7 million.

15. The committee (composes/comprises) 14 nurses, and they addressed all 5,000 (envelops/envelopes).

16. They (canvased/canvassed) the neighborhood and learned that the problem is (miner/minor).

17. A (loose/lose) wheel (that/which) broke off the trailer caused the accident.

Harcourt Brace & Company

18. Representatives from one (media/medium) said the criteria (is/are) too strict.

19. The (blond/blonde) said that (burglars/robbers/swindlers/thieves) broke into his house.

20. Thousands of the schools (alumnae/alumni/alumnus) voiced their (decent/descent/dissent).

21. The banks (trustee/trusty) said she was unable to (affect/effect) the decision.

22. The (trail/trial) began three months after he was charged with (inciting/insighting) the riot.

Name _____ Class _____ Date _____

E X E R C I S E   4
VERBS

SECTION I: AVOIDING USE OF NOUNS AS VERBS

Rewrite the following sentences, eliminating the use of nouns as verbs.

1. She doctored her own illness.

2. They were helicoptered to the site.

3. They are dialoguing with their teacher.

4. They trucked a load of furniture to their new home.

5. They were shotgunned to death, and their bodies will be autopsied Friday.

SECTION II: USING STRONGER VERBS

List three stronger, more active and more descriptive verbs that could replace the verbs in the following sentences.

1. They got a pool for their home. _____

2. About 800 students are in the school. _____

3. The family's scrapbook has many photographs. _____

4. The book should have more information about tennis. _____

5. The editor did a study of newsroom computerization. _____

SECTION III: USING STRONGER VERBS

Rewrite the following sentences, using stronger verbs. Also use normal word order (subject, verb, direct object).

1. The club is in need of more members.

2. Kathy Tijoriwali is the owner of the hot dog stand.

3. Miller testified that she was visited by Paddock on three occasions.

4. The teacher got a lemon meringue pie thrown in her face by a student.

5. The summer recreation program is set up so that the costs are paid by the city.

Harcourt Brace & Company

6. To obtain more money, she has three college students renting rooms in her house.

7. To make a story interesting a good use of verbs can be extremely effective.

8. A short circuit in the electrical wiring at the church was the cause of the fire.

9. One problem cited in the report was that the mechanic failed to inspect the airplanes engine.

10. It is recommended by the article that the appointment should be temporary, lasting only one year.

Name _____ Class _____ Date _____

EXERCISE 5

AVOIDING COMMON ERRORS

SECTION I: AVOIDING GRAMMATICAL AND VOCABULARY ERRORS

Rewrite the following sentences, correcting their wording.

1. Rapists usually attack women that are vulnerable and alone.

2. The school board asked their attorney to help all the students that lost money.

3. Speaking for the highway patrol, Lucas said they would like larger and faster cars.

4. There is not much a student can do to prevent cheating except cover their exam papers.

5. The five men and three ladies that serve on the board predicted that the amount of people seeking help at the clinic will grow to around 500 a month.

SECTION II: KEEPING RELATED WORDS AND IDEAS TOGETHER

Rewrite these sentences, improving the word placement.

1. The girl was taken to a hospital for observation by her parents.

2. Twenty-one students were honored by the high school teachers, two of whom were freshmen.

3. The school board voted to ban seven books from the schools which contain racist statements.

4. A suspect in the burglary case was arrested after a high-speed chase involving two lawnmowers stolen from a hardware store.

5. Robert Allen Wiese was placed on probation after pleading guilty to violating probation by Circuit Court Judge Samuel McGregor.

SECTION III: AVOIDING IMPRECISION

Rewrite the following sentences, making them as precise as possible.

1. Smaller grocery stores usually know their customers.

2. After paying a $325 fine, the dog was free to go home with its owner.

Harcourt Brace & Company

3. A car stopped to help the accident victims, then called the police.

4. A police officer saw a man fitting the description of the suspect he had been given.

5. Minutes after the man left the bar, he collided with a car that totally destroyed his pickup truck.

Harcourt Brace & Company

Name _____ Class _____ Date _____

E X E R C I S E   6

Answer Key Provided: See Appendix D

REVIEW

SECTION I: AVOIDING SLANG AND CLICHÉS

Rewrite the following sentences, eliminating their slang and clichés.

1. The club president said he plans to call it quits.

2. She said the student has a long way to go before he can graduate.

3. The mayor painted a rosy picture of the city's financial situation.

4. The bank vice president admitted coming up $43,000 short in her accounts.

5. The exercise trail is geared toward the average adult citizen who is serious about getting

   into good shape.

SECTION II: IMPROVING VERBS AND SENTENCE STRUCTURE

Rewrite the following sentences, using stronger verbs and normal word order (subject, verb, direct object).

1. The governor's goal is to raise teachers salaries.

2. The woman had her purse snatched by a boy, about 16.

3. The bike path is used by other people as an exercise track.

4. Their lawsuit complains that the bottle had an insect in it.

5. The cost of the chapel is estimated by church officials to be $320,000.

SECTION III: KEEPING RELATED WORDS AND IDEAS TOGETHER

Rewrite the following sentences, moving the related words and ideas as close together as possible.

1. He was charged with shooting his girlfriend, Saundra Marrston, 33, a waitress at

   Freddy's Inn, 410 Lakemont Ave., in the throat.

2. She married her high school sweetheart, David Garner, in Greenville, North Carolina,

   on Jan. 3, 1985, who works as a tennis instructor.

Harcourt Brace & Company

3. To help the crippled children, she begged her parents and other responsible adults in a speech at the church to donate the money they need for medical care Sunday evening.

4. The good samaritan, described by witnesses as a white male, approximately 35 years old, 5 feet 8 inches tall, with black hair, brown eyes and a bandage on his forehead, was driving a honda civic.

5. She said that if a student fails two or more subjects, is frequently absent, has discipline problems, and shows signs of low self esteem, loneliness or stress, that youngster is at high risk for dropping out of high school.

SECTION IV: TESTING ALL YOUR SKILLS

Rewrite the following sentences, correcting all their errors.

1. He said the book is a good read.

2. The plan was deemed illegal by the city attorney.

3. The teacher does not get her ideas across very well.

4. The council chairman cast a strong no vote against the proposal.

5. The purpose of the new program is to provide medical services to the indigent.

6. The plan of the youths was never to tell their parents about how they obtained the money.

7. It was stated in the report that water skiing is a sport that can be enjoyed by anyone regardless of their age.

8. The consensus of opinion among participants in the workshop is that a pay raise of 15 to 20 percent should be received by the nurses.

SECTION V: AVOIDING JOURNALESE

Rewrite the following sentences, eliminating their slang and journalese.

1. She racked up $30,000 in medical expenses.

2. He gave an OK to spending the $26,000 figure for a car.

3. The program is geared toward helping high school students.

Harcourt Brace & Company

4. The new building will carry a price tag of about $6 million.

5. The proposal met with opposition from three council members.

SECTION VI: AVOIDING JARGON

Rewrite the following sentences, eliminating their jargon.

1. He wants to show teachers how to utilize computers as an instructional tool in their classrooms.

2. The university president said he is looking to the private sector for funds with which to construct the cafeteria.

3. Teresea Phillips, a/k/a Marie Phillips, testified that she entered the store and helped the defendant steal an unknown quantity of jewelry from the premises on or about the 9th day of last month.

4. Brown's lawsuit charges that, as a result of the auto accident, he suffered from bodily injury, disability, disfigurement and mental anguish. Browns lawsuit also charges that he has lost his ability to earn a living and that the accident aggravated a previous condition.

Name _____ Class _____ Date _____

E X E R C I S E   7

Answer Key Provided: See Appendix D

SPELLING AND VOCABULARY

INSTRUCTIONS: Correct all the errors in the following sentences, which contain a number of words that cause confusion because they look or sound like other words. You were asked to define many of the words in Exercise 1.

 The sentences also contain possessives that need correcting. If you need help, the rules for forming possessives appear in Appendix C.

1. He adviced the city to adopt the ordinance.

2. The concept was to illusive to insure success.

3. Its rules were altered, but the affects were minor.

4. The blonds fiance said there new home was robbed.

5. Who's statue was laying near you're construction cite?

6. Rather than dissenting, he agreed to study their advise.

7. The alumnae, all men, said the dissent became to violent.

8. He censured the aides behavior and ignored their descent.

9. A prison trustee said its two miles further down the road.

10. The council was confidant that his advice would insure success.

11. The data was placed in envelops and sent to all the news medias.

12. The governors two aids were given offices in the capitol building.

13. The man was hung because he insited a riot which caused three deaths.

14. The portrait hung in his brother-in-laws office in the state capital building.

15. Six of the schools alumnus said there childrens curriculum should be altered.

16. The principle is liable to lose his students respect if he blocks their proposal.

17. The phenomenon were unusual and affected their son-in-laws roll in the family.

18. The board is composed of seven alumnus rather than seven students or teachers.

19. He sited three precedents and implied that the councils decision could be altered.

20. Thomas Alvarez, a tall blonde from California, said the governments data is false.

21. The councilor was confidant of victory but said his roll in the matter was minor.

22. The church alter lay on its side, less than a dozen feet from the broken statutes.

23. His insight, conscience and high principles ensured an excellent performance.

24. The schools principle threatened too censure the newspaper if it tries to publish an article advicing students on how to obtain an abortion.

25. Merchants, fearing that they would lose thousands of dollars, complained that the governments criteria is to difficult to implement.

CHAPTER 4

SELECTING AND REPORTING THE NEWS

Give 'em a show, laughs, tears, wonders, thrills, tragedy, comedy, love and hate.

(Harry Tammen, *The Denver Post*)

"The press is the ultimate guarantor of the people's right to know," says John Wallach, a former New York Times, CNN and National Public Radio journalist. Yet deciding what the public should know is a difficult daily struggle for editors and reporters. News organizations do not have enough reporters, time or space to report everything that happens. Also, not even all the journalists in one newsroom will agree on what to use, what to hold for another day and what to ignore. Moreover, subscribers, viewers and listeners could not afford to pay for all the news and would not have enough time or interest to read or watch it.

Instead, journalists serve as filters, or "gatekeepers." They evaluate potential news stories, then decide their fate. If journalists consider a story newsworthy, they may open the gates, allowing the story to flow into the nation's news channels and reach the public. If journalists consider a story unimportant, however, they may cut or kill it.

To be effective gatekeepers, journalists must listen to what readers and viewers want. They want interesting and important stories. Stories should focus on their communities and the people readers can identify with in those communities. Stories should explain the world that readers and viewers have to cope with, and they should interpret events so readers and viewers can assess their meaning. Audiences also want information that is easy to find and understand.

The selection process is subjective: an art, not a science. Journalists do not have any scientific tests or measurements to help them judge a story's newsworthiness. Instead, they rely on their instincts, experience and professional judgment. For most journalists, the process becomes automatic. They look at a story and instantly know whether it is news.

If you asked journalists to define the term "news," many would be unable to respond. Some might say definitions are unimportant. Others might say news is impossible to define because almost anything can become news. Faced with a similar dilemma, Supreme Court Justice Potter Stewart once confessed he could not define "obscenity" but added, "I know it when I see it."

Journalists have tried to define news, but no single definition has won widespread acceptance. Also, no definition acknowledges all the factors affecting the selection process. Here are some definitions:

What protrudes from the ordinary . . . a picture of reality on which [people] can act.

(*Walter Lippmann*, columnist)

The departure from the normal.

(*Leo Rosten*, political scientist and author)

Things that people don't want to be known.

(*Nicolas Tomalin*, journalist)

What I say it is. It's something worth knowing by my standards.

(*David Brinkley*, ABC commentator)

Harcourt Brace & Company

91

Other writers use a variety of definitions. Some journalists call news the reporting of (or an account of) an event; the gathering of information by trained reporters; or information that serves the reader, listener or viewer. News could be what an editor decides belongs in the paper or on the air. It becomes what he or she thinks readers or viewers want to know or that they did not know yesterday. News may be a current idea, current event or current problem—anything timely. News is also tomorrow's history. It may be something that interests the reader or viewer, something people are talking about. News may also be something that will help newspapers sell their product or newscasts attract more viewers so their advertisers will be happier.

Photographs taken for The Associated Press show President Ronald Reagan as he was struck by a bullet while walking to his limousine just three months after taking office. The second photograph shows Reagan glancing toward his assailant, and the third shows him being shoved into the limousine. Doctors who saved his life at the George Washington University Hospital in Washington, D.C., found that the bullet struck Reagan under his left arm, then tore a 3-inch furrow through his lung.

THE CHARACTERISTICS OF NEWS

While news organizations cannot use all stories because of space, time or staff limitations, a journalist has failed if he or she cannot recognize a good story. Jack Hart, writing coach for The (Portland) Oregonian, says a good story should have the following characteristics: (1) an interesting central character who (2) faces a challenge or is caught up in a conflict and (3) whose situation changes as (4) action takes place in (5) an engaging setting.

Good stories also contain most or all of the following characteristics:

Timeliness

Journalists stress current information—stories occurring today or yesterday, not several days or weeks ago. Moreover, journalists try to report the stories ahead of their competitors. Obviously, print journalists are at a disadvantage when competing with the electronic media. If a story occurred even one or two days earlier, journalists will look for a new angle or development to emphasize in their leads. If some background information is necessary, they usually keep it to a minimum and weave it throughout a story.

Importance

Reporters stress important information: stories that affect, involve or interest thousands of readers. A plane crash that kills 180 people is more newsworthy than an automobile accident that kills two. Similarly, an increase in your city's property taxes is more newsworthy than an increase in the license fees for barbers and beauticians because the former affects many more residents of your city.

As you evaluate potential news stories, consider their importance or magnitude. Ask yourself whether a story is about a *severe* storm, a *damaging* fire, a *deadly* accident, a *major* speech or an *interesting* organization. Also, you should usually consider stories with serious consequences more newsworthy than stories about more frivolous topics.

Prominence

Stories about prominent individuals, such as a mayor, governor, school administrator or business leader, are newsworthy because of the role those people have in civic affairs. Almost everything the president does is news because he is the nation's leader. The president may veto a bill, fly to Europe, play golf, jog or seek a divorce. Because of his prominence, the media would report all five stories. Yet, while covering the prominent we shouldn't ignore less important people who also play a role in community affairs.

You may object to journalists' emphasis on celebrities, but the American public seems to have an insatiable appetite for information about them. People magazine, for example, is phenomenally successful because it fills its pages with facts and photographs about the lives of famous people.

Proximity

Journalists consider local stories more newsworthy than stories that occur in distant places. Editors explain that readers are most interested in stories about their own communities. Readers are more likely to be affected by those stories. Also, they may know the people, places or issues mentioned in them.

Henry Coble, a former editor with the Greensboro (N.C.) News & Record, often evaluated a story's proximity by its closeness to the Haw River, which flows through central North Carolina. When a story's dateline was distant, Coble was fond of saying, "It's a long way from Haw River." He meant News & Record readers would be less interested in a story the farther away it was from the Haw.

Proximity may be psychological. Two individuals who share a characteristic or an interest may want to know more about each other although thousands of miles separate them. An American mother may sympathize with the problems of a mother in a distant country. American college students are likely to be interested in the concerns of college students elsewhere.

Oddities

Deviations from the normal—unexpected or unusual events, conflicts or controversies, drama or change—are more newsworthy than the commonplace. The fact that two people died in an automobile accident is more newsworthy than the fact that thousands of other commuters reached their destinations safely. Similarly, the fact that your mayor is squabbling with another city official is more newsworthy than the fact that two other officials are good friends.

Journalists must be alert for unusual twists in otherwise mundane stories. Few newspapers will report a minor auto accident, but if a 6-year-old girl, a robot or a police chief was driving the car, the story could become front-page news.

The Ann Arbor (Mich.) News published a front-page story about a birthday party. The host and guests were dogs—eight of them. Each dog received party favors and dined on ice cream.

Critics charge that the media's emphasis on the unusual gives their audiences a distorted view of the world. They say that the media fail to portray the lives of normal people on a typical day in a typical community. Editors respond that, because there is too much news to allow them to report everything, they report problems requiring the public's attention. Also, routine events are less important, and therefore of less interest, to the public. However, reporters should write stories about things that work in a community: organizations that help a community improve its education or health care, programs that defeat youth or domestic violence, efforts to reduce teen drinking or pregnancy.

Other Characteristics

Dozens of other factors affect journalists' selection of news. However, most definitions of news acknowledge only a few of those factors. Reporters look for humorous stories—anything that will make their readers laugh. They also report straightforward events—fires, storms, earthquakes and assassinations—partly because such dramatic events are easier to recognize and report. Journalists are less adept at reporting complex phenomena: for example, the causes and consequences of crime, poverty, inflation, unemployment and racial discrimination. Journalists also have difficulty reporting stories that never culminate in obvious events.

That is changing, however. New technology and the increased use of computers have allowed journalists to analyze information that in the past was difficult to gather and compare. Stories that report, analyze and explain are becoming the norm at larger news organizations. Even small organizations attempt such projects. While technology has helped, editors still face the prospect of getting a paper out or a broadcast aired every day. Smaller budgets and reduced staffs prevent news organizations, particularly small ones, from hiring the staff necessary to spend time on such projects.

Just as there are many definitions of news within one medium, the definition varies between media. Daily newspapers emphasize events occurring in their communities during the last 24 hours. Weekly newsmagazines report events of national interest, often in more depth, and try to explain the events' significance. Television reports headline news: a few details about the day's major stories. Former CBS news anchor Walter Cronkite observed, "In an entire half-hour news broadcast, we speak only as many words as there are on two-thirds of one page of a standard newspaper." Television journalists also look for visual stories: colorful stories filled with action, drama and excitement.

A news organization's size and the size of the community it serves affect the selection of news. A newspaper in a small town may report every local traffic accident; a newspaper in a medium-sized city may report only the accidents that cause serious injury; and a newspaper in a large city may have enough space to report only the accidents that result in death. Similarly, newspapers in small cities often publish all wedding announcements and obituaries, whereas newspapers in larger cities publish only those of prominent citizens. Death announcements in some papers appear not as news stories, but as advertisements paid for by families.

The day of the week on which news occurs is important. Newspapers publish more advertisements on Wednesdays, Thursdays and Sundays and consequently have more space for news stories on those three days. Most newspapers attempt to maintain a specific ratio of advertisements to news, often about 65 percent advertisements to 35 percent news. So on the days they publish more advertisements, newspapers also publish more news.

News organizations are most likely to use the types of stories they have traditionally published. The New York Post traditionally emphasizes crime, sex, sports and photographs. The New York Times, which appeals to a more sophisticated audience, places a greater emphasis on political, business and foreign news. Similarly, some newspapers diligently investigate the problems in their communities, whereas others hesitate to publish stories that might offend their readers or their advertisers.

Few publishers or station managers admit they favor any individuals or organizations. Yet, most develop certain "do's and don'ts" that reporters call "policies" or "sacred cows." Sacred cows reflect the interests of an organization's executives. Unfortunately, some publishers use their power to distort the news. Those deeply involved in politics, for example, sometimes order their staffs to report only positive stories about their favorite candidates, political parties, causes or organizations.

TYPES OF NEWS

There are two major types of news: "hard" and "soft." The term "hard news" usually refers to serious and timely stories about important topics. The stories may describe a major crime, fire, accident, speech, labor dispute or political campaign. Journalists call hard news "spot news" or "straight news." "Breaking news," a similar label, refers to events occurring, or "breaking," now.

The term "soft news" usually refers to feature or human-interest stories. Soft news entertains and informs, and may appeal to its readers' emotions. Such stories may make readers laugh or cry, love or hate, envy or pity. While still newsworthy, soft news often is less timely than breaking news. Consequently, editors can delay soft stories to make room for more timely stories. Soft stories may also use a less formal style of writing, with more anecdotes, quotations and descriptions.

Many Americans are more familiar with the terms "good" and "bad" news. Critics frequently charge that the media report too much bad news. Spiro T. Agnew, vice president to Richard Nixon, once called journalists "nattering nabobs of negativism." More recently, Dee Dee Myers, former press secretary to President Bill Clinton, said some reporters have the philosophy that "good news is no news."

David Brinkley of ABC News has criticized local newscasts for their emphasis on bad news. Brinkley complained:

> There's a tired old cliché that news is about a man biting a dog. That's silly. News is something worth knowing, something you didn't know already. I don't look at local news much. I'm tired of seeing stories about crime on the sidewalk: blood, knives, guns, death and destruction. I don't like the stories about bodies on sidewalks. It's of no interest except, of course, to the family of that body on the sidewalk.

Al Neuharth, former chief executive officer of Gannett Co., which owns USA Today and is the largest news chain in the United States, agrees that too much news is negative. He adds that too many editors practice a "journalism of despair." They are skeptics, Neuharth says. They believe that "their mission is to indict and convict rather than inform and educate." He suggests that, instead, reporters provide the public with "journalism of hope."

Systematic studies have found most readers exaggerate the amount of crime and violence reported by the media. Dozens of studies have examined the issue and found individual newspapers devote 2 percent to 35 percent of their space to violence. On average, one-tenth of newspaper content concerns violence.

Television offers a visual view of violence. There has been a continuing debate about violence in the media and its effect on people, particularly children. However, this complaint usually pertains to the entertainment media—television shows, movies, music—not the news media.

Because of the public's complaints, journalists have tried to report more good news, but without much success. A Miami paper once tried to eliminate all the violence from its editions for one day. It didn't publish a single violent feature. The paper deleted three comics, and news stories about armed robberies, a bloody campus riot and a boxing match. The newspaper's editors almost abandoned the experiment when a shootout involving the police that morning resulted in the capture of a fugitive sought for murdering a police officer. Instead, the paper's front page featured a strike by garbage workers and a waiter awarded $3 million.

One of the newspaper's editors wrote a front-page explanation that concluded, "De-emphasis of violence for this one day may demonstrate that we, as readers, would not receive from our paper an accurate and complete picture of the world around us if the paper practiced such deliberate selectivity every day and tried to shield us from reality."

Nevertheless, the criticisms continue. The Ronald Reagan administration accused the media of prolonging a recession by constantly reporting bad news about the nation's unemployment rate. Journalists responded that it was absurd to believe that news stories could affect anything so complex and massive as the nation's economy. President Reagan urged the television networks to devote a week to good news; "then, if the ratings go down, they can go back to the bad news." CBS news anchor Dan Rather responded that Reagan was blaming his administration's difficulties on "the people who call attention to the problems." Reagan was not unusual in that regard. Many people—politicians, ministers, business people and others—blame the media for life's problems.

PUBLIC/CIVIC JOURNALISM

A new movement finding its way into newsrooms—about 200 around the country—affects how journalists define news. Proponents call it public or civic journalism. Professor Jay Rosen, a leading supporter of public journalism, defines it as at least three things.

First, it's an argument about the proper task of the press. Second, it's a set of practices that are slowly spreading through American journalism. Third, it's a movement of people and institutions.

What the argument says is this: Journalism cannot remain valuable unless public life remains viable. If public life is in trouble in the United States, then journalism is in trouble. Therefore, journalists should do what they can to support public life. The press should help citizens participate and take them seriously when they do. It should nourish or create the sort of public

Harcourt Brace & Company

talk that might get us somewhere, what some of us would call a deliberative dialogue. The press should change its focus on the public world so that citizens aren't reduced to spectators in a drama dominated by professionals and technicians. Most important, perhaps, journalists must learn to see hope as an essential resource that they cannot deplete indefinitely without tremendous costs to us and them.

Supporters base public journalism on a fundamental concept of democracy espoused by James Madison—that by participating in the governing of themselves, people preserve democracy. To have the kind of democracy envisioned by Madison, the press must be a participant because a democracy needs an informed citizenry.

Americans have grown tired of the press because they are tired of the sameness of the news. They are busy and suspicious of the media. They believe the news is not entertaining and is biased. In a Times-Mirror poll, 71 percent of Americans said the press makes it more difficult for the nation to solve its problems.

Another survey asked respondents about their level of confidence in what they see and read in the news. Over a five-year period, the percentage of people who said they had a great deal of confidence in television news dropped from 55 to 35 percent, in newsmagazines from 38 to 12 percent, and in newspapers from 50 to 20 percent. Recently, at least among newspapers, the confidence rating edged up to 24 percent, due in part to the success of public journalism.

Proponents say the news media must be more involved in their communities. Eight of every 10 editors responding to a University of Kansas survey said their newspapers should be among their communities' most active and most involved institutions. Public journalism provides information to help people tackle problems, and even offers potential solutions. News organizations sponsor public meetings, suggest ways for people to get involved, and campaign in news columns to encourage people to vote.

Public journalism occurs in a variety of forms. In political coverage, news organizations turn away from the horse-race aspect of coverage—who's ahead, who's behind. Instead, journalists conduct extensive interviews, polls and public forums with voters to find out what issues concern them. This process allows the public to decide what is important. Other newspapers assign staff members to report on divisive issues like racial conflict.

Francie Latour, a reporter in Norfolk, Va., says journalists cannot live in a vacuum as neutral outside observers. Latour says public journalism uses the same characteristics found in the advocacy journalism of muckrakers—painstaking reporting, moral outrage and optimism. She advises students to listen to citizens; listen to all voices, not just the loudest; and listen particularly to those people in the middle. She suggests that the routine 5Ws and H questions (who, what, where, when, why and how) work well but may not be the only ones that work. In public journalism, we should ask:

- **Who**—cares, is affected, needs to be included, has a stake, is missing from this discussion?

- **What**—are the consequences, does it mean to citizens, would this accomplish, values are at work?

- **When**—were things different, can things be different, should dialogue lead to action?

- **Where**—are we headed, is the common ground, should debate take place, is the best entry point for citizens?

- **Why**—is this happening, do we need discussion, are things not happening, should we care?

- **How**—does it affect civic life, did the community do, does my story encourage action or help the public decide?

The Knight-Ridder chain surveyed more than 16,300 readers and nonreaders in the 26 communities where it publishes newspapers. The survey found that people with a real sense of connection to their communities are almost twice as likely to be regular readers of newspapers.

While this result was not surprising, it was a message about what papers need to do. "Newspapers that immerse themselves in the lives of their communities, large or small, have the best prospects for success in the years ahead," said James K. Batten, the late president of Knight-Ridder. "And they have the best chance of drawing people in from the apathetic periphery to the vibrant center of community life. That will be good for the communities, and good for the newspapers."

THE CONCEPT OF OBJECTIVITY

A previous chapter noted that news stories must be objective, or free of bias. Journalists gather information and then report that information as factually as possible. They should not comment, interpret or evaluate. If an issue is controversial, journalists interview representatives of all the sides involved, then include as many opinions as possible. Some representatives may make mistakes, and some may lie, but journalists cannot call their statements lies.

On Feb. 17, 1898, a single story filled the front page of William Randolph Hearst's New York Journal. The story reported that the USS Maine had been destroyed and 260 seamen killed. Hearst wanted the United States to declare war against Spain and immediately suggested the Spaniards were responsible for the explosion. A Navy Court of Inquiry found that the explosion was caused by something outside the ship—but was unable to determine who was responsible for it.

Journalists traditionally assumed, perhaps mistakenly, that if they reported all the information, their readers would think about the conflicting opinions and then decide which were most important and truthful. Because that has not always worked, newspapers now publish separate stories analyzing major issues in the news. The stories, labeled "commentary" or "analysis," critically evaluate the news to help readers better understand it.

No human can be totally objective, but "you have to remain as objective and impartial as possible," says journalist John Wallach. Like everyone else, reporters are influenced by their families, educations, personal interests and religious and political beliefs. Nevertheless, editors believe objectivity is a worthwhile goal and journalists can be taught to be more objective.

News stories rarely are the work of a single individual. Normally, an editor assigns a story and a reporter writes it. Several other editors may then evaluate and change it. Each serves as a check on the others. If one expresses an opinion in a story, another has a chance to detect and eliminate that bias.

DETAILS NEWSPAPERS ARE RELUCTANT TO PUBLISH

Reporters must learn to recognize the types of information that are not considered newsworthy and that news organizations rarely use. News organizations rarely mention routine procedures, such as the fact that a city council met in a city hall and began its meeting with the Pledge of Allegiance. Reporters delete the obvious and the irrelevant: the fact that police officers rushed to the scene of a traffic accident, and that an ambulance carried the injured to a hospital.

News organizations must often decide whether to use information about a crisis or threat. The so-called Unabomber, whose decades-long series of terror bombings baffled law enforcement authorities, sent a lengthy manifesto to The New York Times and The Washington Post. He promised that his killings would stop if the papers published his manifesto. The newspapers' executives decided to publish, knowing that the bomber might make good on his threat to continue bombing. Not all journalists agreed with that decision.

The Problem of Good Taste

Generally, editors omit material that is obscene or in poor taste, usually on the grounds their newspapers or broadcasts reach children as well as adults. What would be the point, for example, of using gruesome photographs or video, particularly when the material lacked significance? Normally, news organizations avoid specifics about sexual assaults. They report accidents, but not all their bloody details.

Reporters provide enough detail so readers or viewers know what happened. Different news organizations adopt different policies about what kinds of information they will use. Journalists must understand their employers' policies.

The Problem of Sensationalism

Most news organizations avoid sensationalism, but not sensational stories. Historically, the word "sensationalism" has described an emphasis on or exaggeration of stories dealing with crime, sex, oddities, disasters and sports. However, some stories are inherently sensational: stories about presidential assassinations, wars and other disasters. The media do not make those stories sensational. Because of their importance, such stories must be reported.

A 13-year-old boy in Lakeland, Fla., was electrocuted while climbing a tree. The boy lost his footing, reached out and grabbed a high-voltage electric line. A Lakeland newspaper, The Ledger, published this photograph showing the victim's body being lowered from the tree, with his legs visible over the side of the bucket. Another photograph showed the boy's mother weeping and embracing a friend.

The Ledger's executive editor, Louis M. "Skip" Perez, defended the photos—but wondered how the mother felt. "Nothing you did made me angry," she told Perez. Nor was she offended by the photos. "I appreciate having them now," she said. "They are the only photos I have of that day. You really couldn't see my son's face."

Journalists evaluating a potentially scandalous or sensational story must weigh several conflicting considerations and may ask themselves:

- How seriously will this story harm the people it mentions?
- How will readers react to the information?
- Is the story newsworthy?
- Does the public need and have a right to this information?

In the O.J. Simpson trial, for example, newspapers and television news reported graphically how Nicole Brown Simpson and Ronald Goldman died. In the case of John Bobbitt, news organizations had to say that Lorena Bobbitt cut off her husband's penis to accurately describe the event.

Avoiding anything tasteless or sensational can make it more difficult for journalists to report the news. A federal judge's ruling that the lyrics of a 2 Live Crew song were obscene contributed to a national furor about censorship and sexually graphic music. Ironically, it was impossible for most readers to decide for themselves whether the lyrics were offensive and obscene because newspapers refused to print the lyrics. The lyrics called women "bitches" and mentioned forcing anal sex on a woman, forcing a woman to lick feces and "busting" the walls of a vagina. John Leo, a columnist for U.S. News & World Report, commented, "The general tone of coverage was: Censorship is stupid, but we can't show or tell you what it is that we think shouldn't be censored."

Another controversy involved the work of photographer Robert Mapplethorpe. News organizations reported that some people objected to exhibits of Mapplethorpe's photographs because some were "homoerotic." Editors were hesitant to report that one photograph showed a man urinating into another man's mouth, that another photograph showed a finger inserted into a penis, and that three other photographs showed men with various objects inserted in their rectums.

Now news organizations find themselves reporting stories about obscene words and images used on the Internet. Again, editors must decide what language to use to accurately report messages coming through cyberspace without offending readers and viewers.

There are no right or wrong answers to these problems; each is a matter of individual judgment. The examples, however, reflect journalists' dilemma. Journalists are reluctant to report graphic details likely to offend the public. Yet readers denied those details may consider them important and be unable to understand some stories.

Newspapers are becoming less squeamish about the use of four-letter words. For years, newspapers referred to syphilis and gonorrhea as "social diseases" and used the terms "streetwalker" for "prostitute" and "operation" for "abortion." Editors also changed "damn" to "darn" or deleted it entirely. As society became more candid, editors began to use previously objectionable words, provided readers needed them in order to understand an event or a person's character.

Rumors

News organizations are reluctant to report rumors, especially harmful ones. Yet the failure to report some rumors may confuse, frighten or alienate the public. As a rumor spreads through a community, more people are likely to become interested in it and to believe it. More people are also likely to believe that journalists are deliberately suppressing the story.

Some rumors involve important issues, such as racial problems, and therefore cause widespread anxiety. Normally, responsible editors investigate the rumors and, if they find no evidence the rumors are true, conclude there is no story. Editors will consider the rumors' effects upon the community, and especially upon innocent people. Editors may decide a story exposing a harmful rumor will be more helpful than their news organizations' continued silence. For example, a story exposing a rumor may help clear the subject's reputation.

In the wake of Hurricane Andrew in Florida, The Orlando (Fla.) Sentinel exposed many rumors. "Thirty-six days after Hurricane Andrew roared through South Dade [County]," a reporter wrote, "the rumor mill is working as hard as disaster relief crews, passing wild tales across the state about the conspiracy to hide a mounting death toll." Among the rumors: bodies were loaded into refrigerated trucks in the dark of night, U.S. Navy submarines fired corpses into the ocean through torpedo tubes, the dead were stockpiled at Homestead Air Force Base, and countless bodies were burned along with hurricane debris. The story explained away each rumor with facts.

Rape

Most news organizations refuse to identify the victims of rape, even when they have a legal right to do so. Reporters should become familiar with their company's policy regarding the use of

Harcourt Brace & Company

such information. Some journalists believe that publishing the names of victims may discourage women from reporting the crime.

To help the media deal with issues concerning victims and survivors of rape and other violent crimes, the National Victim Center (NVC) in Arlington, Va., established several voluntary guidelines:

- Give the public factual, objective information concerning the type of crime, the community where the crime occurred, the name or description of the alleged offender if appropriate, and significant facts that may prevent other crimes.

- Present a balanced view of the crime by ensuring the victim's and the criminal's perspectives are given equal coverage when possible.

- Advise the victim and survivors that they may be interviewed "off the record" or "on the record" or not at all.

- Quote victims, families and friends fairly and in context.

- Avoid photographing or filming crime scene details or follow-up activities such as remains of bodies or brutality, instruments of torture, disposal of bodies.

- Notify and ask permission from victims and their families before using pictures or photographs for documentaries or other news features.

The NVC suggests the media not:

- Publish unverified or ambiguous facts about the victims, their demeanor, background or relationship to the offender.

- Publish lurid or graphic details of the crime.

- Promote sensationalism in reporting the crime or court proceedings.

"I think my most important message [to the media]," said Anne Seymour of the NVC, "is that sensitive media coverage of victims' stories will get you a better story in the long run."

Other Details Reporters Avoid

News organizations constantly search for humorous stories, but few make fun of another person's misfortune. Also, the news media generally do not identify juveniles accused or found guilty of a crime, unless they are tried as adults for a serious offense like murder.

Newspapers rarely mention lotteries because the U.S. Postal Service can refuse to deliver any publication that advertises or promotes them. A lottery is any contest involving a prize awarded by chance in exchange for a financial consideration, such as the price of a ticket. Newspapers seldom report that a charitable organization will raffle off a television set or that the winning ticketholder will receive a new car at a county fair. However, newspapers can mention a lottery after it becomes newsworthy—for example, if a local teacher wins $50,000 in some sweepstakes or if a state legislature debates the establishment of a government lottery to raise money for education.

Some editors hesitate to mention trade names, because they think publication of trade names is unnecessary and provides free advertising for the products. But detail is important to a story, and the use of specific names can add to that detail. However, if a reporter is unsure of the brand, then a generic term should be used. "Soft drink" is an acceptable generic term if a reporter does not know if a subject was drinking a "Coke" or a "Pepsi." Similarly, a journalist may report that someone used a "tissue" rather than a "Kleenex" or made a "photocopy" rather than a "Xerox copy."

Manufacturers encourage journalists to use trade names properly. They place advertisements in magazines read by journalists to remind them to capitalize all trade names. Manufacturers want journalists to use their trade names to describe the products made by their companies, not similar products made by competitors. If the public begins to use a trade name to describe every product within a certain category, the manufacturer will eventually lose its exclusive right to use that trade name.

If carried to an extreme, the media's policy of avoiding trade names can have unfortunate results. When a small airplane crashed during a snowstorm in a mountainous area of California, a family aboard the plane survived for three days by drinking melted snow and eating boxes of Cracker Jack. In reporting the family's ordeal and rescue, some newspapers pointlessly substituted the term "candied popcorn" for Cracker Jack. Similarly, a copy editor became disgusted because his paper refused to allow him to use the trade name "Jeep" in a story about several hundred people who had formed a caravan of Jeeps for a weekend camping trip (called a "Jeep Jamboree"). He substituted the phrase "small truck-type four-wheel-drive vehicles of various manufacture." He did not expect his newspaper to print this circumlocution, but it did.

Common sense should dictate whether a reporter uses a trade name. If you believe a trade name is pertinent, include it in your story.

Some trade names have become generic terms. Manufacturers lost the right to the words' exclusive use because the public repeatedly used the words to describe similar products. Examples include:

aspirin	escalator	raisin bran
brassiere	kerosene	shredded wheat
cola	lanolin	tollhouse cookies
corn flakes	linoleum	trampoline
cube steak	mimeograph	yo-yo
dry ice	nylon	zipper

THE IMPORTANCE OF ACCURACY

When Mark Twain began his career as a reporter, an editor told him never to state as fact anything he could not personally verify. Here is his account of a gala social event: "A woman giving the name of Mrs. James Jones, who is reported to be one of the society leaders of the city, is said to have given what purported to be a party yesterday to a number of alleged ladies. The hostess claims to be the wife of a reputed attorney."

Reporters should avoid taking the advice given to Twain as literally as he did, but accuracy is important. Errors affect the public's perception of the media.

Accuracy in Facts

The information appearing in newspapers and on television news is more accurate than most Americans believe. Professionals who manage news organizations do their best to report the news as fairly and as accurately as possible. Journalists, however, are not always able to convince the public of that fact. When reporters Bob Woodward and Carl Bernstein of The Washington Post investigated the Watergate scandal, their editors required that they confirm every important fact with at least two sources. This policy is not uncommon. Editors insist on accuracy.

"Accuracy is imperative in journalism," says Jim Underwood, a longtime Ohio journalist. "If you don't get it right the first time, there are no second chances after those presses start to roll or you're standing in front of that camera attempting a broadcast report. Inaccuracy and misquoting someone are the most grievous of errors in journalism."

Debbie Price, former executive editor of the Fort Worth (Texas) Star-Telegram, says that it is critical to get things right: names, streets, time—everything, even the most obscure detail. A mistake hurts the reputation of the journalist and his or her news organization. As a result, journalists have to be willing to admit and correct their mistakes.

Unfortunately, errors still occur, and some have been stupendous. In the rush to be first with a story, several news organizations reported that the bombing of a federal office building in Oklahoma City was the work of Middle Eastern terrorists. As a result, some angry people threatened Arab-Americans, their businesses and mosques. As an investigation later proved, foreign terrorists were not involved at all.

Other factual errors are embarrassing. A daily newspaper in Iowa was forced to publish a correction after one of its reporters mistakenly quoted a dead sheriff. The reporter had called the sheriff's office to obtain information about an accident and assumed the man who answered the telephone was the sheriff. He was the sheriff, but a new one; his predecessor had died a few weeks earlier. In writing a story about the accident, the reporter—who failed to ask the sheriff his name—attributed all the information to his dead predecessor.

Carelessness causes most factual errors, like those just described. After finishing a news story, reporters must learn to recheck their notes to be certain the story is accurate. If reporters lack some information, they should consult their sources again. If the sources are unavailable or are unable to provide the information, reporters may have to delete portions of the story or, in extreme cases, kill the entire story. Reporters should never guess or make any assumptions about the facts; they are too likely to make an error.

Reporters must also be certain they understand a topic before they begin to write about it. Too often, when asked about a fuzzy sentence or paragraph, beginners respond, "I really didn't understand that myself." Never try to write about a topic you do not understand. Instead, go back to your source and ask for a better explanation. If that source is unable to help, find another.

Good, accurate writing requires specifics instead of generalities. Getting specifics requires more effort, but in the end the story will be better and more accurate. Readers or viewers will appreciate it more. The trick is to double-check, even triple-check, all the information, to ask for specifics, to ask for spellings, to ask whether the information you have is correct. Improving accuracy improves credibility.

Accuracy and Credibility

In times of stagnant growth in newspaper readership, improved credibility also means improved circulation. "The No. 1 killer of our credibility is inaccuracy," Price says. "Our credibility is all we have." The basics of credibility are accuracy, honesty, fairness and decency.

Price describes credibility issues in terms of crimes:

- Capital cases—fabricated quotes, sources and facts; plagiarism (a firing offense at the Star-Telegram); profiteering (bribery, insider trading, etc.); dishonesty; selective quoting (not reporting all that is known).

- Felony offenses—misspelled names and places, bias, careless and otherwise gross errors; conflicts of interest (sleeping with sources, promoting personal causes, failure to reveal personal interests, involvement in political causes); laziness.

- Sins of commission—one-sided reporting, cynicism, negativism, slanted reporting and writing, extreme interest in molehills (Hillary Clinton's hairstyle, for example), pack journalism, reliance on labels and clichés.

- Sins of omission—superficial reporting; overlooked stories, trends and issues; reluctance to report positive news (things that are working); failure to report all sides of a story; failure to ask how, why and what.

Journalists anxious to meet their deadlines—and to beat their rivals—sometimes guess at a story's outcome. In 1948, editors at the Chicago Tribune were certain that Thomas Dewey would defeat President Harry Truman. They rushed copies of this early—and mistaken—edition to the city's newsstands.

Accuracy in Names

News organizations are particularly careful in their handling of names. Spelling errors damage a paper's reputation and infuriate its readers, particularly when the misspelled names appear in wedding announcements, obituaries and other stories readers will save. Consequently, many newspapers require reporters to verify the spelling of every name that appears in local news stories. They can do so by consulting a second source, usually a telephone book or city directory.

Other errors arise because of a reporter's carelessness. A source may say his name is "Karl" and a reporter may mistakenly assume his name is spelled with a "C" rather than with a "K." Dozens of other common American names have two or more spellings including, for example: Ann (Anne), Cathy (Cathie, Kathy), Fredric (Fredrick, Frederic, Frederick), Gail (Gayle), John (Jon), Linda (Lynda) and Susie (Suzy).

Obstacles to Accuracy

Some errors may be inevitable. Because of the need to meet strict deadlines, reporters must work quickly and often lack the time needed to perfect their stories. Reporters are also vulnerable to misinformation. They obtain much of their information from people who may not know all the facts, and reporters may unknowingly report their misstatements. If a prominent person discusses a matter important to the public, that discussion is news and must be reported, despite any doubts journalists might have about the comments' validity. This definition of news required journalists to report President Lyndon Johnson's claims of victory in Vietnam and President Richard Nixon's claims of innocence in Watergate. Other news stories written by journalists questioned the accuracy and even the truthfulness of both presidents. Yet, not everyone read those stories, and they lacked the impact of the presidential speech or proclamation.

Historians can often be more accurate than journalists because they see more of a story before they begin to write. Journalists deal with isolated fragments; they obtain stories piece by piece and cannot always predict their outcome or ultimate significance. Reporters sometimes will revisit a story at a key moment to put events into perspective and give them meaning. Such stories allow readers to get a complete picture of events that originally came in piecemeal fashion.

Some news organizations check their stories' accuracy. About 50 daily newspapers employ a proofreading affiliate in Lakeland, Fla. Employees there read each newspaper twice a year to find factual and grammatical errors. In 10 years the error rate has gone from an average of four per page to 2.5. Some papers assign staff members to monitor whether stories are factual. Some papers send sources copies of their stories, with letters asking for reactions. Others require copy editors to double-check reporters' math by calculating percentages and statistics in stories. Many errors occur because reporters fail to check their stories' internal consistency. For example:

> Of the 10 men and women who were interviewed, five favored the proposal, three opposed it and three said they had not reached any decision.

Journalists might eliminate even more errors by giving the people named in news stories an opportunity to read and correct those stories before papers publish them. The idea has been discussed most seriously by science writers and other journalists who deal with complex issues and have more time to write in-depth articles. However, most editors prohibit the practice. They fear that it would consume too much time and that sources might try to change all the statements they disagreed with, not just factual errors.

Researchers who have analyzed sources' corrections have found that sources believe about half the stories they are shown contain an error. However, many perceived errors are judgmental rather than factual. Sources may interpret some facts differently from reporters or want to include, emphasize or de-emphasize different facts. Sources also may complain a story misquotes them or a headline distorts a story. Only about one-third of the errors that sources point out are typographical or factual errors. Most involve misspelled names and inaccurate times, dates, numbers, addresses, locations and titles.

Most journalists agree a correction should appear in a paper or on the air as quickly as possible. Some believe it is healthy to go through the catharsis of admitting an error. By correcting an error, journalists show their willingness to respond to public concerns, to improve their relationship with the public and to improve their credibility. Others argue that admitting all errors, including the most trivial, harms a news organization's credibility. According to Henry McNulty, a former reader representative of The Hartford (Conn.) Courant, the paper runs about 100 corrections a month and is "very picky, down to the middle initials" of people in stories.

Some news organizations identify the reporter or editor who made a mistake. Others believe public humiliation does not solve the problem nor help an individual improve. Many news organizations fire journalists who consistently make errors, because errors affect the integrity of the organization.

APPLYING THE PRINCIPLES OF NEWS SELECTION

How can you find a good topic? Ken Fuson, an award-winning reporter for The Des Moines (Iowa) Register, suggests: "Whenever you find yourself laughing at a situation, shaking your

Harcourt Brace & Company

Things You Should Know About Readers

- About 54 percent of the nation's adults say they read a newspaper daily, compared to 74 percent who say they watch television news regularly.

- While 28 percent of the nation's adults read a magazine, only about 5 percent read a news magazine regularly.

The typical newspaper reader:
Spends an average of 26 minutes a day reading a paper.
Is about 35 years old.
Attended college.
Has a white–collar job.
Has a household income of $50,000 or more.
Is registered to vote.
Lives in an urban area.

Most popular news stories:
Wars, crime, disasters, weather, human interest, consumer information and scientific discoveries.

Least popular news stories:
Business, agriculture, religion, minor crimes, state government, art, music and literature.

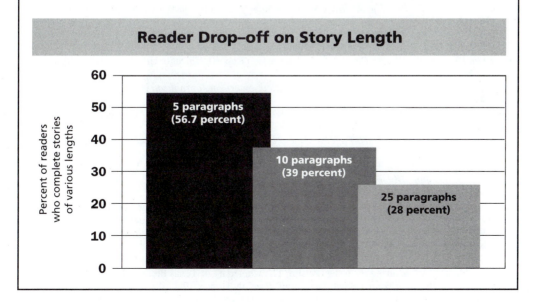

Reader Drop–off on Story Length

Percent of readers who complete stories of various lengths

- 5 paragraphs (56.7 percent)
- 10 paragraphs (39 percent)
- 25 paragraphs (28 percent)

head or saying to someone 'Listen to this,' you've probably got a story." Fuson adds, if your idea for a story is not a good one, "no amount of solid reporting or pretty writing can salvage it."

Think about your own experiences. What on your campus is new? What is scheduled for next week, next month or next year? What are your campus' needs? What do you like? What do you dislike? What interests you and your friends? What puzzles or troubles you and your friends? Who is your most interesting friend or faculty member? If something is new, needed, interesting, troubling or confusing, it may be worth a story.

Also, approach other people. Ask them about ideas for stories that are new, different, interesting and important. You may have to approach a dozen friends, secretaries, faculty members and other people before finding a good topic. That type of digging is part of a reporter's job, perhaps the most important part.

AUDIENCES' RESPONSES TO THE NEWS

Researchers have found an "all-or-none principle": Adults who use one source of news are likely also to use several others. One study revealed that 75 percent of the adults who watched a television news program on a particular day also read a newspaper. By comparison, only 59 percent of the adults who did not watch a television news program read a newspaper that day.

Journalists should not expect every story they write to interest every reader or viewer. Many people are in a hurry and read their papers on the run: while riding a bus, eating lunch, watching television or talking with friends. They skim each page, looking for stories of particular interest. They may pause to read a headline or lead. If they encounter an obstacle—a dull or confusing paragraph—they quickly move on to another story.

A typical man looks at 20 percent of all the items published by a newspaper. Younger men read fewer items, about 15 percent. Women read almost the same number of items as men and generally enjoy reading the same types of stories, except sports. Five percent more men than women are likely to read a daily paper.

SUGGESTED READINGS

Abel, Eli, ed. *What's News: The Media in American Society*. San Francisco: Institute for Contemporary Studies, 1981.

Adam, G. Stuart. *Notes Towards a Definition of Journalism: Understanding an Old Craft as an Art Form*. St. Petersburg, FL: Poynter Institute for Media Studies, 1993.

A Free and Responsible Press (The Hutchins Commission Report). Chicago: University of Chicago Press, 1947.

Bates, Stephen. *If No News, Send Rumors: Anecdotes of American Journalism*. New York: Henry Holt, 1991.

Bogart, Leo. *Press and Public: Who Reads What, Where, and Why in American Newspapers*, 2nd ed. Hillsdale, NJ: Erlbaum, 1989.

Broder, David S. *Behind the Front Page: A Candid Look at How the News Is Made*. New York: Simon & Schuster, 1987.

Brunvand, Jan. *The Choking Doberman and Other "New" Urban Legends*. New York: Norton, 1984.

———. *The Vanishing Hitchhiker: American Urban Legends and Their Meaning*. New York: Norton, 1981.

Carey, James. "A Republic if You Can Keep It: Liberty and Public Life in an Age of Glasnost," in Raymond Arsenault, ed., *Crucible of Liberty: 200 Years of the Bill of Rights*. New York: Free Press, 1991.

Charity, Arthur. *Doing Public Journalism*. New York: Guilford, 1995.

Clark, Roy Peter. *A Call to Leadership*. St. Petersburg, FL: Poynter Institute for Media Studies, 1992.

Fishman, Mark. *Manufacturing the News*. Austin, TX: University of Texas Press, 1980.

Gans, Herbert J. *Deciding What's News*. New York: Random House, 1980.

Gaunt, Philip. *Choosing the News: The Profit Factor in News Selection*. Westport, CT: Greenwood Press, 1990.

Harcourt Brace & Company

Hausman, Carl. *The Decision-Making Process in Journalism*. Chicago: Nelson-Hall, 1990.

Jensen, Carl. *Censored: The News That Didn't Make the News—and Why*. Chapel Hill, NC: Shelburne Press, 1993. (Published annually since 1976)

Kaniss, Phyllis. *Making Local News*. Chicago: University of Chicago Press, 1991.

Manoff, Robert Karl, and Michael Schudson, eds. *Reading the News*. New York: Pantheon, 1987.

Mayer, Martin. *Making News*. Garden City, NY: Doubleday, 1987.

Making Sense of the News. St. Petersburg, FL: Poynter Institute for Media Studies, 1983.

Merritt, Davis. *Public Journalism & Public Life, Why Telling the News Is Not Enough*. Hillsdale, NJ: Erlbaum, 1995.

Miller, Edward D. *The Charlotte Project: Helping Citizens Take Back Democracy*. St. Petersburg, FL: Poynter Institute for Media Studies, 1994.

Neuharth, Al. *Confessions of an S.O.B.* Garden City, NY: Doubleday, 1989.

Rose, Tom. *Freeing the Whale: How the Media Created the World's Greatest Non-Event*. New York: Birch Lane Press, 1989.

Rosen, Jay. *Community Connectedness: Passwords for Public Journalism*. The Poynter Papers: No. 3. St. Petersburg, FL: Poynter Institute for Media Studies, 1993.

———. *Politics, Vision and the Press: Toward a Public Agenda for Journalism*. New York: Twentieth Century Fund, 1992.

Seib, Philip. *Who's in Charge? How the Media Shape News and Politicians Win Votes*. Dallas: Taylor, 1987.

Stephens, Mitchell. *A History of News: From the Drum to the Satellite*. New York: Viking, 1988.

The Harwood Group. *Timeless Values, Staying True to Journalistic Principles in the Age of New Media*. Reston, VA: American Society of Newspaper Editors, 1995.

Weinberg, Steve. *Trade Secrets of Washington Journalists*. Washington, DC: Acropolis Books, 1981.

An Ombudsman's Report

CASE STUDY NO. 1

By **Henry McNulty**
Former Reader Representative
The Hartford (Conn.) Courant

Imagine this scene:

You are a newspaper editor. One afternoon, leaving the newspaper office, you meet one of the paper's photographers, and you both stand chatting on the street. All of a sudden, a friend rushes up to you and says, "Come home quickly! Your child has just been killed in a terrible plane crash."

You are stunned. For a few seconds you can't move—you can't even think. But the photographer quickly raises a camera and snaps off several frames—pictures that show clearly the panic and agony on your face.

The photos are news, the photographer says. They tell the human story, and report reaction to an event of importance.

Would you, the editor, want these used in your newspaper? If it were in your power to stop publication of them, would you permit them to be used? I have asked a number of editors these questions many times over the years. Not even one has answered, "Yes, I would want them used." Most have told me that the moment was too private—too personal, intimate and shattering to share with the reading public.

Yet newspapers run photos like this all the time.

After Pan Am Flight 103 was blown up over Lockerbie, Scotland, The Record of Hackensack, N.J., printed a photograph of a grief-stricken mother lying on the ground

(continued on next page)

Harcourt Brace & Company

at New York's JFK International Airport clutching a rosary. The National Press Photographers Association elected it as one of the "Pictures of the Month." (Interestingly, the photographer said her editors were "squeamish" about putting the photo on Page 1, so it went on Page A16.)

At my newspaper, we occasionally poll readers about how they would have handled tricky ethical situations. Once, we asked readers what they would do with a photo of a man who had just been told his son died in a fire.

About three-quarters of the readers answering the question said such a picture should not be printed. At the same time, the newspaper's editors were asked whether they would print the picture. A majority said they would.

In the face of overwhelming public sentiment against these tragedy-reaction shots, and in light of editors' statements that they wouldn't want themselves to be the subjects of such photos, why do they keep being used?

The most common answer is that these pictures fulfill the public's right to know. This answer, in my opinion, doesn't hold up well.

There's no question the First Amendment gives newspapers the *right* to print this type of picture. But photographs are not needed to fully inform the public, or to fulfill the right-to-know doctrine. For nearly 150 years, my newspaper informed its readers without using a single photograph. Saying "the mother fell to the floor when she heard her child was dead" may not be elegant, but *it tells the news*.

Of course, it's obvious that photos tell the news in a way that even the most carefully crafted words cannot. Pictures have an immediacy, an intimacy and an impact far beyond that of text. But how related are such matters to the public's right to know? To inform is one thing, but do newspapers have an obligation to let the public *feel* the news, as well as to know it?

Another common answer to the question "Why run this photo?" is that pictures of this type can be a valuable teaching tool. They can, for instance, warn about playing with matches, or leaving your children unattended for even a minute or going swimming with no lifeguard.

There are several problems with this answer. One is the question of whether there's any lasting teaching effect. Many people can recall the so-called "scare films" that were shown in schools at the time teen-agers were getting their driver's licenses. I'm unconvinced that these had any meaningful impact on the teen-age car-crash statistics of any generation.

Another problem is whether newspapers really have a commitment to such teaching or whether editors simply haul out this answer to defend using an intrusive photo. Would the paper be willing to devote news space on a regular basis to teaching its readers about auto, plane, fire and boat safety? I'd say not, but newspapers frequently open up space for photos of grieving relatives after crashes, fires or drownings.

Perhaps the most common reason for using such pictures is what I call "the reality argument."

Every day, photographers and editors have to deal with what are basically setup shots. From the well-known ribbon-cuttings, proclamation-signings, check-passings and trophy-receptions to portraits, press conferences and parades, lots of what photographers deal with is posed. It is "set up" for them to shoot.

And when it isn't, it's likely to be impersonal: car crashes, sports action shots, driving-in-a-snowstorm, and so forth.

Real life, so to speak, seldom plays a part.

Harcourt Brace & Company

But occasionally, there is a moment when all pretense and posing are swept away and the naked emotion is revealed. To the photographer, this is the rare time when reality and truth are present, with no formality, no time to say "cheese." It is what photographers dream of.

Is this a compelling argument for using intrusive photos? Perhaps, except it speaks too much of the newspaper's needs, not the needs of readers.

I find myself frequently asking photographers, on behalf of readers, why this photo, or that photo, was taken. Quite often, the answer has been "because it was something different." In many cases, I think what this really means is "because I'm so bored taking pictures of smiling mayors, beauty queens and politicians."

Journalists should have a problem with turning our boredom into an excuse for violating someone's basic right to privacy.

Harcourt Brace & Company

EXERCISE 1

SELECTING AND REPORTING THE NEWS

DISCUSSION QUESTIONS

1. What do you think is "news"? Devise a good definition of the term.

2. David Brinkley of ABC News said he does not watch much local television news because he is tired of seeing stories about blood, knives, guns, death and destruction. Al Neuharth made similar statements.

    a. Do you think Brinkley and Neuharth are right in saying local newscasts devote too much time to crime and violence?
    b. If so, why do you think local newscasts devote so much time to that type of story?
    c. Is the public inconsistent? Many Americans complain that the media report too much bad news. Would television stations broadcast that type of story if it didn't boost ratings?

3. If you edited your local daily, would you have printed the controversial lyrics sung by 2 Live Crew? Why?

4. If you edited your local daily, how would you have handled the Mapplethorpe controversy? Specifically, how would you have described the photographs?

5. Should newspapers devote more space to worthwhile causes and organizations in their communities, recognizing and promoting their good work? Is that the type of story you and your friends like to read?

6. Should journalists help communities solve their problems as advocated by supporters of public (or civic) journalism?

7. Do you believe journalists are objective? Why?

8. Do you read your local daily? Why?

    a. If you don't, is there anything that its editor could do to improve the paper so you would read it?
    b. If you (or a classmate) said you do not have time to read a daily newspaper, do you also lack the time to watch television? Why?
    c. If editors fail to interest young adults in reading newspapers, will that generation of Americans ever begin to read a paper? If not, how can newspapers survive?

9. A recent study concluded young adults "know less and care less about news and public affairs than any past generation of Americans." Do you believe that conclusion is an accurate one? Why?

10. Do you agree that newspapers are obsolete and that reading newspapers is an old person's habit? Why?

Harcourt Brace & Company

11. Normally, newspapers report every birth, death, marriage, divorce and bankruptcy in their community.

    a. Do you agree with that policy? Why?
    b. As editor, would you include announcements of births to unwed mothers? Why?
    c. As editor, would you include the "weddings" of gay couples? Why?
    d. As editor, would you report every local suicide? Why?

12. Assume your governor has often criticized the state's welfare system and the fact that some recipients are able-bodied adults without children. If you learned your governor's 27-year-old son (who does not live at home) was broke because of a business failure and had applied for welfare, would you publish the story?

13. Assume three local high school students, each 15 years old, have been charged with arson; they started a fire that caused $80,000 in damage at their high school, closing it for a day.

    a. If you obtained the students' names, and it was legal to do so, would you identify them in your story?
    b. Before publishing the story, would you call and warn (or interview) the students or their parents?

14. Reporters are forced to make difficult decisions about which elements of a story are most newsworthy. Assume two men robbed a local restaurant and shot a customer earlier today. Then, during a high-speed chase through the city, a police car skidded out of control and struck a pedestrian, a 34-year-old nurse. Both the customer and the pedestrian were hospitalized in serious condition. Which element would you emphasize in your lead: the customer shot by two robbers, or the pedestrian struck by police chasing the robbers?

15. If a member of the American Nazi Party spoke in your community and criticized blacks, Jews and immigrants, would you report the story? How would you justify the story's publication or suppression?

16. Imagine a member of your city council, a Democrat, offered to give you information proving that store personnel had caught your mayor, a Republican, shoplifting. The store's owner has declined to prosecute. Moreover, the Democrat insists that you never identify him as your source. The Democrat is a potential candidate for mayor and an obvious rival of the current mayor. Yet the information is genuine. How would you respond?

17. Assume a local woman today announced her candidacy for mayor. Which—if any—of the following facts about her personal life would you include in a story about her candidacy?

    a. She is 57 years old.
    b. She is a millionaire.
    c. She's the mother of four children.
    d. She is 5 feet, 1 inch tall, has gray hair and weighs 180 pounds.
    e. Her first husband died, and she divorced her second.
    f. Her first husband committed suicide two years after their marriage.
    g. After her husband's death, she transformed a small restaurant they established into one of the largest and finest in the city.

h. She now lives with a bank executive.
i. The bank executive is 36 years old.
j. One of her sons is a high school teacher. Two help her in the restaurant. The fourth is in prison, convicted of selling cocaine.

18. Which of the details you want to publish about the candidate described in question 17 would affect her performance if she were elected mayor?

   a. If some details about her private life would not affect her performance as mayor, how can you justify their publication?
   b. Would you publish the same details about a male candidate?

19. How would you localize the following AP story for the local newspaper where you attend school? For a paper in New Hampshire? In Louisiana?

> LAWRENCE, Kan.—One of the smallest states in the union is also the most livable, according to an analysis of 42 factors ranging from the crime rate to the percentage of sunny days.
>
> New Hampshire won the year's "Most Livable State" award for the second straight year, said Scott Morgan, president of Morgan Quitno Press, a publishing company that specializes in analyzing state statistics.
>
> "New Hampshire certainly is not perfect, but it comes closer than 49 other states," Morgan said this week.
>
> On the opposite end of the rankings, Louisiana kept its last-place finish on the livability scale.
>
> The award, which was begun four years ago, considers statistics including median household income, high school graduation rates, divorce rates and highway fatality rates.
>
> Rounding out the top five states were Wisconsin, Iowa, Minnesota and Kansas. Preceding Louisiana in the bottom of the rankings were Alabama in 49th, West Virginia in 48th, Kentucky in 47th and Mississippi in 46th.

(Note: Accompanying the story was a state-by-state list by rank with the previous year's ranking.)

CHAPTER 5

BASIC NEWS LEADS

There is a great disposition in some quarters to say that the newspapers ought to limit the amount of news they print; that certain kinds of news ought not to be published. I do not know how that is. I am not prepared to maintain any abstract position on that line; but I have always felt that whatever the divine Providence permitted to occur, I was not too proud to report.

(Charles A. Dana, a 19th-century newspaper editor)

The first paragraph or two in a news story is called the "lead." The lead (some people spell it "lede") is the most important part of a story—and the most difficult part to write. It is the part of the story that attracts the reader and, if it is well-written, arouses a reader's interest. It should tell the reader the point of the story, not hide the subject with unnecessary or misleading words and phrases.

A summary lead—one that summarizes the main points of the story—allows skimmers who glance from one story to another to pick stories that interest them. If a lead fails to interest readers—if it is confusing or dull—readers will move on to another story.

Before reporters can write an effective lead, they must learn to recognize what is news. Leads that fail to emphasize the news—the most interesting and important details—cannot be used, regardless of how well they are written. After deciding which facts are most newsworthy, a reporter must summarize those facts in sharp, clear sentences, giving a simple, straightforward account of what happened. Examine these leads, which provide clear, concise summaries of momentous events in the nation's history:

> DALLAS, Nov. 22—A sniper armed with a high-powered rifle assassinated President Kennedy today. Barely two hours after Mr. Kennedy's death, Vice President Johnson took the oath of office as the thirty-sixth President of the United States.
>
> *(The Associated Press)*

> WASHINGTON, D.C.—Richard Milhous Nixon announced his resignation last night as President of the United States, the first chief executive to resign in the Republic's 198-year history.
>
> *(San Francisco Chronicle)*

> CAPE CANAVERAL—Space shuttle Challenger exploded into a fireball moments after liftoff today, apparently killing all seven crew members, including schoolteacher Christa McAuliffe.
>
> *(The Associated Press)*

THE QUESTIONS A LEAD SHOULD ANSWER

In the past, every lead was expected to answer six questions: *Who? How? Where? Why? When?* and *What?* Newspapers have abandoned that rigid style because leads that answered all six

Harcourt Brace & Company

questions tended to be too long and complex. Also, answers to all the questions were not always important. Because few readers in large cities know people involved in routine stories, the names of those people do not have to appear in leads. The exact time and place at which a story occurred may also be unimportant.

Today, leads emphasize answers only to the most important of the six questions, and they vary from one story to another. The following example, although exaggerated, is a traditional lead that attempts to answer all six questions. Its revision, following the currently preferred style, answers only the most important questions:

> Brian Earl Taylor, 22, of Ypsilanti was pronounced dead at St. Joseph Mercy Hospital and his 20-year-old companion is hospitalized following a drive-by shooting at 9:30 p.m. Sunday in which an unknown number of gunmen shot into a crowd gathered along Second Avenue in front of the Forrest Knoll public housing complex on the city's south side.
>
> REVISED: A 22-year-old Ypsilanti man is dead and his 20-year-old companion hospitalized following a drive-by shooting Sunday evening. An unknown number of gunmen shot into a crowd gathered along Second Avenue.

To determine which questions are most important for a story, consider the following points:

1. What is the most important information? What is the story's main point or topic?
2. What was said or done about the topic? What happened or what action was taken?
3. What are the most recent developments? What happened today or yesterday?
4. Which facts are most likely to affect or interest your readers?
5. Which facts are most unusual?

Each of the following leads emphasizes the answer to only one of the six basic questions—the question that seems most important for that particular story:

> **WHO:** One of the alleged leaders of Colombia's Cali cocaine cartel surrendered Saturday, the fifth kingpin of the world's biggest drug gang to wind up in jail in less than a month.

> **HOW:** A 22-year postal worker punched his boss in the back of the head, then pulled a gun from a paper bag and shot him to death, authorities said.

> **WHERE:** Turkish troops clashed with Kurdish rebels in northern Iraq on Saturday.

> **WHY:** Her lawyers are expected to argue that Susan Smith has been the victim of destructive relationships and influences since she was born.
>
> *(The New York Times)*

> **WHEN:** SEOUL, South Korea—Days after rescuers all but gave up hope, a man trapped for 9½ days was pulled from the rubble of a collapsed department store.

> **WHAT:** An estimated 1.3 million Americans were victims of gun-related crimes last year, the Justice Department reported Sunday. While the handgun was the most commonly used weapon among criminals of all ages, assault weapons were often the firearm of choice among juveniles.
>
> *(Los Angeles Times)*

SENTENCE STRUCTURE IN LEADS

Most leads consist of a single sentence, and that sentence must follow all the normal rules for punctuation, grammar, word usage and verb tense. If an event occurred in the past, the lead must

Harcourt Brace & Company

use the past tense, not the present. Leads must be complete sentences and should include all the necessary articles—the words "a," "an" and "the."

Some problems with sentence structure arise because beginners confuse a story's lead with its headline. The lead is the first paragraph of a news story. The headline is a brief summary that appears in larger type above the story. To save space, editors use only a few key words in each headline. However, that style of writing is not appropriate for leads:

> HEADLINE: Serbs attack 'safe area'

> LEAD: SARAJEVO—Rebel Serbs fired a barrage of tank shells and launched an infantry assault on the outskirts of an eastern Bosnian enclave Saturday.

> *(The Associated Press)*

While writing leads, reporters use a relatively simple sentence structure. Most leads begin with the subject, which is closely followed by an active verb and then by the object of the verb. Reporters deviate from that style only when they want to emphasize some other element of a story. Leads that begin with long qualifying clauses and phrases lack the clarity of simpler, more direct sentences. Long introductory clauses also clutter leads, burying the news amid a jumble of less significant details. Paula LaRocque, assistant managing editor of The Dallas Morning News, calls these "backed-into leads." She describes them as "one of the most pervasive and uninviting habits a writer can fall into":

> According to police, two men robbed the Domino's Pizza store at 1200 Packard Road, after they pulled a handgun, demanded money from employees and walked out with $300 shortly after midnight last Wednesday.
> REVISED: Two men robbed a pizza store on Packard Road Wednesday night.

Before it was revised, the lead delayed the news—information about the robbery—until its 13th word, and it unnecessarily put the attribution first.

GUIDELINES FOR WRITING EFFECTIVE LEADS

Be Concise

Newspapers' concise style of writing makes it easier for the public to read and understand leads, but more difficult for reporters to write them. "Readers want a quick hit on most news stories," says Jack Hart, writing coach at The (Portland) Oregonian. "They need an overview that gets them oriented to the topic without immediately bogging them down in detail."

Two- or three-sentence leads often become wordy, repetitious and choppy, particularly when all the sentences are very short. Like most multi-sentence leads, the following example can be made more concise as a single sentence:

> Two women robbed a shopper in a local supermarket Tuesday. One woman distracted the shopper and the second woman grabbed her purse which contained about $50.
> REVISED: Two women stole a purse containing $50 from a shopper in a local supermarket Tuesday.

The original lead was redundant. It reported two women robbed a shopper, then described the robbery.

Reporters use two-sentence leads only when the need to do so is compelling. Often, the second sentence is used to emphasize an interesting or unusual fact of secondary importance. It may also be impossible to summarize all the necessary information about a complex topic in a single sentence. The following example from The Ann Arbor (Mich.) News uses a second sentence to illustrate the first:

Duck hunting is an important part of family life for Chuck Brezeale. Last year, he and his daughter, Shannon, shot more than 40 ducks during the October to November season.

Sometimes professionals do a poor job of keeping their leads concise. A recent study found the average number of words in leads from different sources was: The Washington Post, 39; Los Angeles Times, 34.6; The New York Times, 33; United Press International, 30.5; The Associated Press, 30; and Scripps Howard News Service, 25.5. A 25-word lead was considered "difficult" and a 29-word lead "very difficult." A better average would be 18 to 20 words. Examine your leads critically to determine whether they are wordy or repetitious, or contain facts that could be shifted to a later paragraph.

Reporters shorten leads by eliminating unnecessary background information—dates, names, locations—or the description of routine procedures. Leads should not contain too many names, particularly names that readers are unlikely to recognize, or the names of people who played minor or routine roles in a story. If you include someone's name in a lead, you may also have to identify that person, and the identification will take up even more space. Substitute descriptive phrases for names. Similarly, a story's precise time and location could be reported in a later paragraph. A lead should report a story's highlights as concisely as possible, not all its minor details:

A former Roxbury woman, who has eluded federal law enforcement authorities since she allegedly hijacked a flight from San Juan to Cuba using a plastic flare gun in 1983, was arrested yesterday as she stood alone on Union Street in Boston, according to the Federal Bureau of Investigation.

REVISED: The FBI arrested a former Roxbury woman who has eluded authorities since 1983.

Likewise, there is no *minimum* length for leads. An effective lead may contain only four, five or six words: "The president is dead" or "Americans landed on the moon" or "There's new hope for couch potatoes."

Be Specific

Good leads contain interesting details and are so specific that readers can visualize the events they describe. As you read the following lead from The Tampa (Fla.) Tribune, you should be able to imagine the dramatic scene it describes:

At 59, she'd never touched a gun—until someone held one to her head.

The following lead is less interesting because it is abstract and contains vague generalities. Reporters can easily transform such leads into more interesting ones by adding more specific details:

Delaware County's Council for Older Adults has received a clean audit verification for its last fiscal year.

REVISED: The Council for Older Adults moved into a new facility, paid off its debt and helped more people than ever before last year. The council passed its annual financial inspection by state auditors.

Some leads use worn-out clichés—a lazy way of summarizing a story. Avoid saying that "a step has been taken" or that someone has moved "one step closer" to a goal. Present specific details:

A step has been taken toward banning parking along the south side of Liberty Street to improve traffic flow.

REVISED: The City Council wanted traffic to move better on Liberty Street. So members voted Monday to ban parking on the street's south side.

Harcourt Brace & Company

Avoid "iffy" leads. In addition to being too vague, "iffy" leads are too abstract, tentative and qualified. Avoid reporting that one thing may happen if another happens. Report the story's more immediate and concrete details.

Use Strong, Active Verbs

A single word—a descriptive verb—can transform a routine lead into a dramatic one. As you read the following lead, for example, you may be able to picture what happened:

> Charlene Heydrich's last act wasn't pretty.
> On an August night last year, she staggered into the bathroom of a Daytona Beach motel room and threw up in the sink.
> Then she tucked herself back into bed and died.
> It was exactly what she wanted.
>
> *(The Orlando [Fla.] Sentinel)*

The following lead contains several colorful verbs, and they make the lead more interesting, even exciting:

> BUDAPEST, Hungary—Thousands of East German refugees—cheering, laughing and crying—poured into the West today after Hungary agreed to let them flee across its border with Austria.
>
> *(USA Today)*

Avoid weaker nondescriptive verbs, especially forms of the verb "to be"—such as "is," "are," "was" and "were"—used in passive constructions. Strong, active verbs are more colorful, interesting and dramatic:

> One person *was killed* and four others *were injured* Sunday morning when their car, which *was traveling* west on Interstate 80, *hit* a cement bridge pillar and *was engulfed* in flames.
> REVISED: A car *traveling* west on Interstate 80 *swerved* across two eastbound lanes, *slammed* into a cement bridge pillar and *burst* into flames, *killing* one person and *injuring* four others Sunday morning.

If you write a passive lead, you can easily convert it to the active voice. Simply rearrange the words, so you begin by reporting: (1) who . . . (2) did what . . . (3) to whom. Instead of reporting: "Rocks and bottles were thrown at firefighters," report: "Rioters threw rocks and bottles at firefighters."

Emphasize the Magnitude of the Story

If a story is important, reporters emphasize its magnitude in the lead, often by revealing the number of dollars, buildings or other objects it involves. When describing a storm, reporters may emphasize the amount of rain or snow that fell. When describing a major fire, they may emphasize the amount of damage, the number of people left homeless or the number of injuries:

> NEW YORK (AP)—Secondhand cigarette smoke will cause an estimated 47,000 deaths and about 150,000 non-fatal heart attacks in U.S. nonsmokers this year, a study says. That's as much as 50 percent higher than previous estimates.

Most good leads emphasize the impact stories have on people.

Harcourt Brace & Company

Stress the Unusual

Leads also emphasize the unusual. By definition, news involves deviations from the norm. Consider this lead from a story about a woman who had had multiple miscarriages:

> On Tuesday, Donna and Richard Hergenroeder will celebrate the birth of their ninth baby.
> None of the others were cause for celebration.
> This baby, when—and Donna adds, if—it comes, is the longest of long shots. This is the baby they'd ached for, sacrificed for, lost so many times and finally given up on.
>
> *(The Ann Arbor [Mich.] News)*

Leads about a board of education meeting should not report the board met at 8 p.m. at a local school and began its meeting with the Pledge of Allegiance. Those facts are routine and consequently not newsworthy. Most school boards meet every couple of weeks, usually at the same time and place, and many begin all their meetings with the Pledge of Allegiance. Leads should emphasize the unique—the action that follows those routine formalities.

Bank robberies are so common in big cities that newspapers normally devote only a few paragraphs to them. Yet a robbery at the Burlington National Bank in Columbus, Ohio, became a front-page story, published by newspapers throughout the United States. A story transmitted by The Associated Press explained:

> A 61-year-old man says he robbed an Ohio bank with a toy gun—he even told the FBI ahead of time when and where—because he wants to spend his golden years in federal prison.

After his arrest, the bank robber insisted he did not want a lawyer. Instead, he wanted to immediately "plead guilty to anything." The man explained he recently was divorced, had no family ties and was disabled with arthritis. He had spent time in at least three federal prisons and wanted to return to one of them. "I knew what I was doing," he insisted. "I wanted to get arrested, and I proceeded about it the best way I knew how."

Reporters must learn to recognize and emphasize a story's unusual details:

> MIAMI (AP)—Nineteen-year-old Jose Pico thought he was doing a good deed when he chased down a hit-and-run driver and held him at gunpoint until police arrived.
> He still can't understand why he was arrested and the driver was set free.

Localize and Update Your Lead

Reporters are trained to localize and update their leads whenever possible by emphasizing their communities' involvement in stories. Readers are most interested in stories affecting their own lives and the lives of other people they know.

Reporters also try to localize stories that arise in other parts of the world. When a bomb exploded in a Pan Am plane over Lockerbie, Scotland, newspapers across the United States not only ran the story of the bombing, but localized the story on the basis of where the passengers had lived. The Gazette in Delaware, Ohio, focused on the death of a student from Ohio Wesleyan University, which is located in the town. Similarly, when the FBI reports on the number of violent crimes committed in the United States, reporters stress the statistics for their communities:

> The FBI reported today that the number of violent crimes in the United States rose 8.3 percent during the last year.
> LOCALIZED: The number of violent crimes committed in the city last year rose 5.4 percent, compared to a national average of 8.3 percent, the FBI reported today.

Harcourt Brace & Company

Reporters update a lead by stressing the latest developments in the story. If a breaking story appears in an early edition of a newspaper, a reporter will gather new information and rewrite the story for later editions. The same thing happens with a television news broadcast. Instead of reporting that a fire destroyed a local store the previous day, reporters may stress that authorities have since learned the fire's cause, identified the victims, arrested an arsonist or estimated the monetary loss. Stories are updated so they offer the public something new—facts not already reported by other newspapers or by local radio or television stations. Major stories about such topics as economic trends, natural disasters, wars and political upheavals often remain in the news for months and must regularly be updated.

Not every lead can be updated or localized. If a story has no new or local angles, report it in a simple, straightforward manner. Do not distort the story in any way or fabricate any new or local angles.

Be Objective and Attribute Opinions

The leads of news stories, like their bodies, must be objective. Reporters are expected to gather and convey facts to their readers, not to comment, interpret or advocate. To avoid infuriating or offending your readers, never express your opinion in stories.

There is rarely any justification for calling the people involved in news stories "alert," "heroic" or "quick-thinking," or for describing facts as "interesting" or "startling." These comments, when they are accurate, usually state the obvious. Leads that include opinion or interpretation must be rewritten to provide more factual accounts of the news:

> Speaking to the Downtown Rotary Club last night, Emil Plambeck, superintendent of the City Park Commission, discussed a topic of concern to all of us—the city's park system.
>
> REVISED: Emil Plambeck, superintendent of the City Park Commission, wants developers to set aside 5 percent of the land in new subdivisions for parks.

The original lead is weak because it refers to "a topic of concern to all of us." The reporter does not identify "us" and is wrong to assert that any topic concerns everyone.

Here are other examples of leads that state an opinion or conclusion:

> Adult entertainment establishments have fallen victim to another attempt at censorship.

> Recycling does not pay, at least not economically. However, the environmental benefits make the city's new recycling program worthwhile at any cost.

To demonstrate that both leads are statements of opinion, ask your friends and classmates about them:

- Do *all* your friends and classmates agree that the regulation of adult entertainment establishments is "censorship"?

- Do *all* your friends and classmates agree that recycling programs are "worthwhile at any cost"?

Although reporters cannot express their own opinions in stories, they often include the opinions of people involved in the news. A lead containing a statement of opinion must be attributed so readers clearly understand the opinion is not the reporter's.

Reporters often use "blind leads" that do not specifically name their source. Details are held back so the reporter can get to the central theme of the article more quickly. Beginners should not misinterpret the terminology. A blind lead does not hide the focus of the story, only information that the reader does not have to know immediately. Writing coach Jack Hart of The (Portland) Oregonian calls blind leads "absolutely central to straight news reporting, because they're the most immediate way of answering the question central to every straight news story: 'What's this about?'"

Hart lists other advantages to blind leads:

- They serve readers.

- They get readers oriented toward the story.

- They boil wording down to a more readable, short, punchy form.

- They force the writer to think hard about the central point of the story.

- They help organize the rest of the story.

Such leads are followed by a "catchall graf" that briefly identifies sources and answers questions created by the lead. Missing details can be placed in subsequent paragraphs:

> BOSTON (AP)—A study published today concludes that lactose intolerance is probably not responsible for bouts of intestinal mayhem that people often blame on milk.

In its second paragraph, the article defined "lactose intolerance" and in the third paragraph identified the source of the study as the New England Journal of Medicine.

A lead containing an obvious fact or a fact the reporter has witnessed, or can verify by some other means, generally does not require attribution. An editor at The New York Times, instructing reporters to "make the lead of a story as brief and clear as possible," noted: "One thing that obstructs that aim is the inclusion of an unnecessary source of attribution. . . . If the lead is controversial, an attribution is imperative. But if the lead is innocuous, forget it." Thus, if a lead states a fact that no one is likely to question, you can place the attribution in a later paragraph because none is necessary in the lead:

> Sidney Baylis, a 38-year-old musician who grew up in Ann Arbor, was killed Friday in a freak traffic crash on a Nebraska expressway.
>
> *(The Ann Arbor [Mich.] News)*

Strive for Simplicity

Every lead you write should be clear, simple and to the point. Here is an example:

> PHILADELPHIA—She kept saying "no."
> She said it when Robert Berkowitz lifted her shirt and bra. She said it when he pushed her on the bed and took off her underwear.
> She didn't try to escape. She didn't try to fight. He didn't use force.
>
> *(The Associated Press)*

Jack Hart gives this example of a lead that suffers from far too much detail:

> Officials of the city and the Gladstone School District are breathing sighs of relief following the Clackamas County Housing Authority's decision to pull out of a plan to build an apartment complex for moderate-income people on 11 acres of land between Southeast Oatfield and Webster roads.

The lead could be rewritten any number of ways. The reporter must decide what the important point is. Here are two versions of a simple blind lead for the same story:

Harcourt Brace & Company

Several officials applauded the county's decision to scrap plans for a subsidized housing complex.

A new subsidized housing complex will not be built, and officials are relieved.

AVOIDING SOME COMMON ERRORS

The following pages discuss the errors that appear most often as students begin to write leads.

Begin with the News

Be particularly careful to avoid beginning with an attribution. Names and titles are dull and seldom important. Moreover, if every lead begins with the attribution, all leads will sound too much alike. Place attribution at the beginning of a lead only when it is unusual, significant or deserves that emphasis:

At a press conference in Washington, D.C., today, Neil A. Schuster, spokesperson for the U.S. Bureau of Labor Statistics, announced that last month the cost of living rose 2.83 percent, a record high.

REVISED: The cost of living rose 2.83 percent last month, a record high, the U.S. Bureau of Labor Statistics reported today.

Originally, the lead devoted more space to the attribution than to the news. As revised, it emphasizes the news—the information revealed by the Bureau of Labor Statistics. The attribution has been condensed and can be reported more fully in a later paragraph.

Emphasize the News

Chronological order rarely works in a news story. By definition, news is what just happened. The first events in a sequence rarely are the most newsworthy. Decide which facts are most interesting and important, then write a lead that emphasizes these facts regardless of whether they occurred first, last or in the middle of the story:

The O.J. Simpson trial started with the selection of jurors, which was a long and arduous process. After opening arguments by the prosecution and defense, the prosecutors began calling their witnesses and started building their case against the former football star. After months of legal maneuvering and bickering, prosecutors rested their case.

Now O.J. Simpson's attorneys plan to call their first witness Monday morning. The next few weeks promise a lineup of Simpson's friends, family and golf chums testifying about his demeanor before and after the murder.

REVISED: Now O.J. Simpson has the ball.

With the prosecution case finished after five months of testimony, Simpson's lawyers are about to begin presenting his side of the story.

(The Associated Press)

The City Council started by approving the minutes of its last meeting, accepting a budget report and examining a list of proposed ordinances.

REVISED: Cats will no longer roam the city. The City Council approved a leash law to rein in wayward felines.

Harcourt Brace & Company

Other leads place too much emphasis on the time and place at which stories occurred:

> Last weekend the women's volleyball team participated in the regional playoffs.
> REVISED: The women's volleyball team won five of its seven games and placed second in the regional playoffs last weekend.

Until it was revised, the lead emphasized the story's time rather than the outcome of the team's efforts.

Look for a story's action or consequences. That's what should be emphasized in a lead. The following lead, as revised, stresses the consequences of the accident:

> A 15-year-old boy learning to drive his family's new car struck a gasoline pump in a service station on Hall Road late Tuesday afternoon.
> REVISED: A 15-year-old boy learning to drive created a fireball Tuesday. The family car he was driving struck a gasoline pump at a Hall Road service station, blocking traffic for three hours while firefighters extinguished the blaze.

Avoid "Label" Leads

An introductory paragraph that fails to report the news—that mentions a topic but fails to reveal what was said or done about that topic—is called a "label" lead. Leads should report the substance of a story, not just its topic. A good lead does more than report that a group met, held a press conference, issued a report or listened to someone speak. The lead reveals what the group did at its meeting or what was said at the press conference, in the report or during the speech.

Label leads are easy to recognize and avoid because they use similar words and phrases, such as "was the subject of," "the main topic of discussion," "spoke about," "delivered a speech about" or "interviewed about." Here are two examples:

> The City Council last night discussed ways of regulating a new topless club in the city.

> Faculty and staff members and other experts today proposed strategies to recruit more minority students.

The first lead should summarize the city council's discussion, clearly explaining how the council plans to regulate the topless club. The second lead should summarize the experts' strategies for recruiting more minority students.

Avoid Lists

Avoid placing any lists in leads. Most lists, like names, are dull. If a list must be used, place an explanation before it, never after it. If a lead begins with a list, readers will not immediately understand its significance. If an explanation is placed before a list, readers can immediately understand its meaning:

> The company that made it, the store that sold it and the friend who lent it to him are being sued by a 24-year-old man whose spine was severed when a motorcycle overturned.
> REVISED: A 24-year-old man whose spine was severed when a motorcycle overturned is suing the company that made the motorcycle, the store that sold it and the friend who lent it to him.

Avoid Stating the Obvious

Avoid stating the obvious, and avoid emphasizing routine procedures in leads. If you are writing about a crime, do not begin by reporting police "were called to the scene" or ambulances "rushed" the victims to a hospital "for treatment of their injuries." This problem is particularly common on sports pages, where many leads have become clichés. For example, most coaches and players express optimism at the beginning of every season; news stories then report the obvious: The coaches and players want to win most of their games.

The following lead, before its revision, is ineffective for the same reason:

It can be a frightening experience to wake up and find an armed intruder in your bedroom. Just ask 20-year-old Stacy Hidde. It happened to her Tuesday.
REVISED: A 20-year-old college student woke at 2 a.m. Tuesday and saw a prowler, with a knife in one hand, searching her bedroom.

Avoid the Negative

When writing a lead, report what happened—not what failed to happen or what does not exist:

Americans over the age of 65 say that crime is not their greatest fear, two sociologists reported today.
REVISED: Americans over the age of 65 say their greatest fears are poor health and poverty, two sociologists reported today.

Avoid Exaggeration

Never exaggerate in a lead. If a story is weak, exaggeration is likely to make it weaker, not stronger. A simple summary of the facts can be more interesting (and shocking) than anything that might be contrived:

A 78-year-old woman left $3.2 million to the Salvation Army and 2 cents to her son.

A restaurant did not serve a dead rat in a loaf of bread to an out-of-town couple, a jury today ruled.

Avoid Misleading Readers

Every lead must be accurate and truthful. Never sensationalize, belittle or mislead. A lead must also set a story's tone—accurately revealing, for example, whether the story that follows will be serious or whimsical:

The party went to the dogs early—as it should have.
Parents who host parties for their children can understand the chill going up Susan Ulroy's spine. She was determined guests wouldn't be racing over her clean carpeting with their wet feet. "This could be a real free-for-all," she said.
Even though only seven guests were invited, eight counting the host, that made 32 feet to worry about.
This was a birthday party for Sandi, the Ulroys' dog.

(The Ann Arbor [Mich.] News)

Harcourt Brace & Company

Breaking the Rules

Occasionally, it pays to use your imagination, to try something a little different, perhaps reporting the facts more cleverly than the competition.

Edna Buchanan, who won a Pulitzer Prize for her police reporting at The Miami Herald, was consistently able to make routine stories interesting. Here's a lead she reported with some imagination. Notice the active verbs and description she incorporates into her writing:

> Gary Robinson died hungry.
>
> He wanted fried chicken, the three-piece box for $2.19. Drunk, loud and obnoxious, he pushed ahead of seven customers in line at a fast-food chicken outlet. The counter girl told him that his behavior was impolite. She calmed him down with sweet talk, and he agreed to step to the end of the line. His turn came just before closing time, just after the fried chicken ran out.
>
> He punched the counter girl so hard her ears rang, and a security guard shot him—three times.

Remembering Your Readers

While writing every lead, remember your readers: the general public. If you want people to read your work, you will have to be clear and interesting. The following lead, until revised, fails both tests:

> Two policy resolutions will come before the Student Senate this week.
>
> REVISED: Two proposals before the Student Senate this week would raise your parking and athletic fees by more than $100 a year.

Did the original lead interest you? Why not? It emphasized the number of resolutions the student senate was scheduled to consider. Yet almost no one would care about the number of resolutions or, from the lead, would understand their significance: the fact that they would affect every student at your school.

Rewriting Leads

Finally, critically examine every lead, and rewrite it as often as necessary. First drafts are rarely so perfect that they cannot be improved. Even experienced professionals often rewrite their leads three or more times.

APPLYING THE GUIDELINES TO OTHER KINDS OF LEADS

The guidelines in this chapter are for effective writing of all kinds of openings, not just leads for news stories. Good writing does not vary from one medium to another. You may want to work in public relations, to write for a radio or television station, to become a columnist or to write a book. Regardless of your goal, the guidelines will help you achieve it.

Begin to analyze everything you read. You are likely to find some surprising similarities among books, magazines and newspapers. Also watch the opening scenes in movies and on television. Most, like a good lead, begin with a detail (or a story or scene) likely to capture your attention.

Harcourt Brace & Company

These, for example, are the opening sentences of two newspaper columns:

On Feb. 11, Terry Shapiro put "Bambi" on the VCR, picked up a pistol and fired five bullets into her sleeping husband's body.

(Kathleen Parker)

'Twas the night before Christmas when Gerald Williams shot his wife, Alice, in the head.

(Clarence Page)

Similarly, these are the opening sentences in two books:

The small boys came early to the hanging.

(Ken Follett, "The Pillars of the Earth")

On the 26th of July, my best friend decided he wanted to kill me.

(Wyatt Wyatt, "Deep in the Heart")

CHECKLIST FOR WRITING LEADS

Use the following checklist to evaluate all the leads you write:

1. Be specific rather than vague and abstract.
2. Avoid stating the obvious or the negative.
3. Emphasize your story's most unusual or unexpected developments.
4. Emphasize your story's most interesting and important developments.
5. Emphasize your story's magnitude and its impact on its participants and readers.
6. Use complete sentences, the proper tense and all the necessary articles—"a," "an" and "the."
7. Be concise. If it exceeds three typed lines, examine a lead critically to determine whether it is wordy or repetitious or contains some unnecessary details. If so, rewrite it.
8. Avoid writing a label lead that reports your story's topic but not what was said or done about it.
9. Begin your lead with the news—the main point of the story. If you began with attribution or the time and place your story occurred, rewrite it.
10. Use a relatively simple sentence structure, exercising particular care to avoid beginning the lead with a long phrase or clause.
11. Use strong, active and descriptive verbs rather than passive "to be" verbs such as "is," "are," "was" and "were."
12. Make sure every name that appears in the lead is essential. Avoid using in your lead unfamiliar names and names requiring lengthy identification that could be reported in a later paragraph.
13. Attribute any quotation or statement of opinion appearing in the lead.
14. Localize the lead, and emphasize the latest developments, preferably what happened today or yesterday.
15. Eliminate statements of opinion, including one-word labels such as "interesting" and "alert."
16. Justify the use of a two-sentence lead if you used one. Check to be certain it is concise and nonrepetitive.
17. Remember your readers. Write a lead that is clear, concise and interesting, and that emphasizes the details most likely to affect and interest your readers.
18. Read the lead aloud to be certain that it is clear, concise and easy to understand.

Harcourt Brace & Company

St. Louis Post-Dispatch

WRITE & WRONG

By **Harry Levins**
Post-Dispatch Writing Coach

Ledes are the make-or-break part of the story that determines so often whether a reader will stay with the rest. A few samples of note, and the reasons why:

> **Specific nouns:** ST. CLAIR, Mo.—It was the kind of heat that could fry a piece of bologna on the hood of a Buick.
>
> *(Bill Smith)*

Not just any kind of food (especially not the egg of cliché), but "a piece of bologna." Not just any kind of car, but "a Buick," an especially massive, solid and square car. Specific nouns focus the images in the reader's mind.

> **Vivid verbs:** Higher education officials sighed with relief this week when the Missouri Legislature approved higher taxes to stave off deep budget cuts for colleges and universities.
>
> *(Virginia Hick)*

Face it: A story on education budgets can easily turn into what Ben Bradlee calls "a real room-emptier." But Hick's lede used bright verbs to help the reader over the hump of abstraction.

> **Perfect quote:** JOPLIN, Mo.—Johnny Lee Wilson, described by his lawyer as a person who "was not dealt the proper cards in life," went to court Tuesday in a bid to end his life prison term.
>
> *(Jim Mosley)*

Rather than bog the reader down up front about the specifics of Johnny Lee Wilson's case, Mosley used a quote that cuts to the heart of things, giving the reader a keen sense of what this story is going to be about without snagging the reader in needless detail. Not all stories offer this kind of quote—but when they do, the smart writer grabs them.

> **Straight-to-the-point English:** Creston Austin says it was his life or hers when he shot to death a graduate student at Lindenwood College on a secluded parking lot in the West Port Plaza area.
>
> *(Bill Lhotka)*

"It was his life or hers . . ." Lhotka translated the abstract concept of self defense into the simple Anglo-Saxon English that real people use in real life.

> **Key detail:** A car taking a 12-year-old girl to meet her grandparents for a summer visit was struck broadside by a pickup Tuesday night at a highway intersection in St. Charles County, killing the girl and her 8-year-old cousin.
>
> *(Kim Bell)*

Bell's inclusion of the victim's plans for a summer visit to her grandparents lifted this lede above mere news by adding a poignantly human touch.

The human touch: Barbara Moore figures that what she doesn't know might hurt her.

The Aug. 8 ballot carries eight proposals to increase fees for various St. Louis County services, but the ballots don't say what the new fees would be.

So Moore, a retired teacher from Creve Coeur, said that if she had to vote on what she saw earlier this week on a sample ballot, she would vote no.

(Virgil Tipton)

A reader heading into a typical election advance finds tough going—a swamp of facts, figures and government officials speaking in bureaubabble. But here, Tipton introduced the reader to a kindred soul, pondering the election issue in the terms that real people use.

Clear compression: Missouri has started filling its excess prison space by renting beds to Illinois and Colorado. It hopes to make $10 million to $13 million a year until its own prisoners fill the space.

(Fred Lindecke)

In the paper, this lede came out as five lines of clear, simple English in which the reader learns (a) what's happening, (b) why it's happening, and (c) how long it will last. Lindecke wasted nary a word but still conveyed his information smoothly.

Clever word play: Beverly Hotchner ended her discussion on s-e-x with a four-letter word: "T-a-l-k."

(Lorraine Kee Montre)

That sort of lede grabs a reader's attention, but Montre refused to tease the reader for more than one brief sentence. Having grabbed the reader with a brief flash, she went on in the next graf to the substance of the story, leading the reader in gently by repeating the last word from her lede:

Talk to your children about the pleasurable and not-so-pleasurable aspects of sex, Hotchner, a sex therapist, told a group of about 20 people at a Parenting Fair seminar.

Maximum use of the facts: FREDERICKTOWN, Mo.—Cindy Box jumped anxiously each time her telephone rang Monday evening, hoping that someone had spotted her little girl.

No one had—not since 10:30 p.m. Saturday, when 13-year-old Gina Dawn Brooks disappeared just six blocks from her modest clapboard house.

(Dan Browning)

That's a second-day story about a day in which, in hard-news terms, nothing happened. But staying strictly within the facts, Browning found a touch of drama that made a compelling lede.

In a class by itself: Enough already on title-insurance offices and concrete plazas. Clayton wants some snazzy storefronts.

(Sue Brown)

That lede came out of—get this—*a zoning hearing*, the dullest of possible events.

Harcourt Brace & Company

SUGGESTED READINGS

Brooks, Brian S., George Kennedy, Daryl R. Moen and Don Ranley. *News Reporting and Writing*, 4th ed. New York: St. Martin's Press, 1992.

Buchanan, Edna. *The Corpse Had a Familiar Face*. New York: Random House, 1989.

Cappon, Rene J. *Associated Press Guide to News Writing*. New York: The Associated Press, 1991.

Garrison, Bruce. *Professional News Writing*. Hillsdale, NJ: Erlbaum, 1990.

Harriss, Julian, and B. Kelly Leiter. *The Complete Reporter*, 6th ed. New York: Macmillan, 1991.

Hohenberg, John. *The Professional Journalist*, 5th ed. New York: Holt, Rinehart and Winston, 1983.

Hough, George A. *News Writing*, 4th ed. Boston: Houghton Mifflin, 1988.

Izard, Ralph S., Hugh M. Culbertson and Donald A. Lambert. *Fundamentals of News Reporting*, 6th ed. Dubuque, IA: Kendall/Hunt, 1994.

Metz, William. *Newswriting: From Lead to "30,"* 3rd ed. Englewood Cliffs, NJ: Prentice-Hall, 1990.

Metzler, Ken. *Newsgathering*, 2nd ed. Englewood Cliffs, NJ: Prentice-Hall, 1986.

Stephens, Mitchell, and Gerald Lanson. *Writing & Reporting the News*. New York: Holt, Rinehart and Winston, 1986.

Ward, Hiley H. *Professional Newswriting*. San Diego: Harcourt Brace Jovanovich, 1985.

Harcourt Brace & Company

E X E R C I S E   1

LEADS

EVALUATING GOOD AND BAD LEADS

INSTRUCTIONS: Critically evaluate the following leads. Select the best leads and explain why they are effective. In addition, point out the flaws in the remaining leads. As you evaluate the leads, look for lessons—"do's and don'ts"—that you can apply to your own work.

1. Even after 34 years on the police force, 63-year-old Chief Barry Kopperud has not lost sight of his goal to "protect and serve."
2. The city's public schools have come under fire since it was revealed that student test scores are declining. Now, the superintendent of schools has responded to the criticism.
3. The school board will offer a $30,000 settlement in exchange for the resignation of a teacher acquitted of sexually molesting two fifth-grade girls.
4. A new health insurance plan will pay city employees for staying well.
5. A man who admitted slashing his neighbor with an 8-inch kitchen knife was acquitted today of aggravated assault. A jury decided the man acted in self-defense.
6. Local schools have a lot of holiday activities planned for their youngsters.
7. A college student was left bound and gagged in her dormitory room last night after being robbed by a man who answered her advertisement in the campus newspaper.
8. A motorcyclist involved in an accident at about 5 p.m. Sunday suffered multiple injuries.
9. Carbon monoxide sucked into an air conditioning duct spread through a house at 105 Crown Point Drive early today, killing a couple and their five children.
10. The School Board has voted to give Greg Hubbard a 12 percent raise and to extend his contract as superintendent of schools for another three years.
11. Two people remain hospitalized after a collision on State Route 419 at 2:30 a.m. Thursday.
12. After 25 years as an undercover agent, retiring Drug Enforcement Administration agent Daniel Sweers is speaking out against the way the government is fighting the drug war.
13. A local man was beaten and robbed Monday, losing both his pants and wallet.
14. A 32-year-old man described Tuesday how he and another man robbed a tavern.
15. Transfer students often have problems adjusting to their first semester here. There are ways to make it easier.
16. The university's president, Amy Clayton, told the Alumni Association that she is proud of what her administration has already accomplished, "but no one can afford to relax."
17. It's the sort of thing many a beleaguered bill payer has probably dreamed of doing: getting a gun and making the electric company turn the power back on.
18. Toxic waste chemicals at the university are going down the drain—literally.

Harcourt Brace & Company

E X E R C I S E 2

LEADS

WRITING LEADS

SECTION I: CONDENSING LENGTHY LEADS

Condense each of these leads to no more than two typed lines, or about 20 words.

1. Maggie Baile, 28, of 810 N. Ontario Ave., an employee at the Halstini Manufacturing Plant, 810 Hall Road, suffered second and third degree burns at 2:15 p.m. yesterday when sparks from her welders torch started a fire that quickly spread through the factory, causing nearly $1 million in damage and totally destroying the facility.

2. During a regularly scheduled meeting that began in its chambers at 8 p.m. last night, the City Council voted 5 to 2, after nearly 3 hours of debate, in favor of a proposal which, for the convenience of pedestrians, will require developers to construct a sidewalk in front of every new home and subdivision in the city.

SECTION II: USING THE PROPER SENTENCE STRUCTURE

Rewrite the following leads, using the normal word order: subject, verb, direct object. Avoid starting the leads with a long clause or phrase. You may want to divide some of the leads into several sentences or paragraphs.

1. Saying that he had concluded that no benefit would come to anyone from the imprisonment of a 51-year-old woman who killed two teenagers while driving while intoxicated last summer, Circuit Court Judge Bruce R. Levine today suspended the womans drivers license for five years and sentenced her to one year in the county jail, then suspended her jail sentence on the conditions that she seek professional help for her chronic alcoholism and pay all the teenagers medical and funeral expenses.

2. Because the victim contributed in large measure to his own death by refusing medical attention that might have saved his life after the incident, James K. Arico, the 47-year-old man accused of stabbing him in the chest during an argument seven months ago, was allowed to plead guilty to assault today and was sentenced to six months in the county jail. He had been charged with murder.

SECTION III: EMPHASIZING THE NEWS

Rewrite the following leads, emphasizing the news, not the attribution. Limit the attributions to a few words and place them at the end, not the beginning, of the leads.

1. During a meeting in her office in Washington, D.C., today, the secretary of Health and Human Services told a group of health care specialists that American men and women who practice "wellness," a program of health promotion and disease prevention, can expect to live 11 years longer than people who neglect their health.

2. Tracy Tibitts, Lisa Drolshagen and Dorothy Brayton, all members of the Delta Delta Delta sorority at Iowa State University, appeared in a local courtroom this morning and

testified that the defendant, Steven House, appeared drunk when he got into his car to leave the party moments before he struck and killed the pedestrian.

SECTION IV: COMBINING MULTISENTENCE LEADS

Rewrite each of the following leads in a single sentence.

1. Acting on a tip, four detectives staked out a restaurant at 12:50 a.m. this morning and foiled an armed robbery. While posing as customers and employees, they observed two men with guns approach a cashier. The detectives captured both men.
2. Two city officials resigned today. Both had been criticized for abusing their positions. Mechanics at the city garage complained that both officials had them repair and wash and wax their cars. One of the city officials was the mayor. The other was her assistant. They never paid for any of the services.

SECTION V: STRESSING THE UNUSUAL

Write only the lead for each of the following stories.

1. Daniel J. Silverbach is a policeman in your community. Last year, because of his heroic rescue of seven persons held at gunpoint during a robbery, Police Chief Barry Kopperud named him the departments Police Officer of the Year. Kopperud fired Silverbach when he reported for duty at 7 a.m. today. The department adopted certain grooming standards, and Kopperud said Silverbachs mustache was a quarter inch too long and his sideburns a half inch too long, and he refused to trim them. Kopperud added that he warned Silverbach a month ago to trim his hair, then ordered him to do so at the first of last week. He fired him for failing to obey the order of a superior officer.

2. Terri Snow of 3418 Hazel St. is a nurse at Mercy Hospital. She is married to Dale Snow, a former eighth-grade science teacher at Mays Junior High School. Snow was crippled after a diving accident three years ago, when his arms and legs were paralyzed. He met his wife at the hospital, where he was a patient, and they were married last month. Now state officials have suggested that they get a divorce. Before his marriage, Snow received $345 a month from the states Department of Social Services and a monthly $792 federal Supplemental Security Income payment. Because of his wifes income, he is no longer eligible for the payments, and the couple says without the payments they cannot afford to pay for Snows continuing medical treatments and special diet. State officials have advised them that Snow will again become eligible for the aid if they get a divorce. The officials refused to talk to reporters, however.

3. Cremation is rising in popularity. Nearly 30 percent of the people who die in your state are now cremated. The Funeral Directors Association in your state met at noon yesterday and discussed a growing problem. The ashes of nearly 50 percent of those people they cremate are never claimed by family members, friends or anyone else, so they are stored in the funeral homes, and the directors want to dispose of them but are uncertain of their legal right to do so. They voted to ask the state legislature to pass a bill that spells out disposal procedures. The bill they propose would require funeral homes to make every effort to settle with the family of the deceased the desired disposal method. Families would have up to 90 days to pick up the remains or to specify what they want done with them. After 90 days, the funeral homes would be free to get rid of them either by burying them, even in a common container (in a properly designated cemetery) or by scattering them at sea or in a garden, forest or pond.

Harcourt Brace & Company

4. A home at 2481 Santana Avenue was burglarized between the hours of 1 p.m. and 4 p.m. yesterday afternoon. The owner of the home is Dorothy R. Elam, a sixth-grade teacher at Madison Elementary School. She said no one was home at the time. Neighbors said they saw a truck parked in the driveway but thought some repairmen were working at the home. The total loss is estimated at in excess of $8,000. The items stolen from the home include a color television, a videocassette recorder, stereo, sewing machine, computer, 2 pistols and many small kitchen appliances. Also, a stamp collection valued at about $1,000, some clothes, silverware and lawn tools were taken. Roger A. Elam, Mrs. Elams husband, died 2 days ago. The robbery occurred while she was attending his funeral at 2:30 p.m. yesterday at the Powell Funeral Chapel, 620 North Park Avenue. Elam died of cancer after a long illness.

5. Gladys Anne Riggs is 81 years old. Her husband, George, died 10 years ago. She is retired and normally receives about $800 a month in Social Security benefits. She complains she has not received her benefits for the past 4 months. When she inquired as to the reasons for the troubles, officials at a Social Security office in your city today explained that shes dead. Four months ago, her check was returned and marked "deceased," so all her benefits were canceled. Because of the error, Mrs. Riggs fears that her check for next month may also be late, and she says she needs the money to buy food and to pay her rent. She lives alone in a one-bedroom apartment and says she has already fallen behind in her rent and is afraid she will be evicted. Social Security officials said that they will correct the problem as soon as possible and that she will receive a check for all the benefits she has missed during the past 4 months, but that it may take several weeks to issue the check. They suggested that she apply for welfare until the check arrives.

SECTION VI: LOCALIZING YOUR LEAD

Write only the lead for each of the following stories.

1. The state Department of Transportation today announced plans for next year. It will spend a total of $418 million to build new roads and to improve old ones. The amount represents a $14.5 million increase over last years total. The money comes from a state gasoline tax amounting to 4 cents per gallon sold. The department allocates the money on the basis of need, with the most congested and dangerous areas receiving the most help. Included in the allocations for next year are $17.8 million, allocated to widen from two to four lanes state highway 17-92, which runs through the southeastern part of your city for a distance of approximately three miles. Construction work on the highway project is expected to begin in four months and to be completed within one and one-half years.

2. Three persons have been killed in the crash of a single-engine plane. Police have identified the victims as Mr. and Mrs. Joel Skurow of Atlanta, Georgia, and Melville Skurow of 4138 Hennessy Court in your community. Joel and Melville are brothers. The plane, flown by Joel, crashed on the outskirts of Atlanta at 7:30 a.m. today. Cause of the crash is unknown. No one on the ground was injured. Friends said Melville Skurow was visiting his brother, an attorney in Atlanta. Skurow is a carpenter and was thirty-seven years of age. The plane, valued at $34,800, was fully insured.

3. The annual Conference of U.S. Mayors is being held in New York City this week. Mayors from throughout the United States hold an annual convention to discuss problems of mutual interest. At the closing session today they elected their officers for the forthcoming year, and they elected your mayor, Sabrina Datolli, first vice president. Approxi-

mately 1,460 mayors were in attendance at the convention, which next year will be held in Las Vegas.

SECTION VII: UPDATING YOUR LEAD

Write only the lead for each of the following stories.

1. William MacDowell, 28, a house painter who lives at 1429 Highland Drive, is being tried for the murder of a cocktail waitress, Ethel Shearer. His trial opened last Thursday, and witnesses last Friday said a ring found in MacDowells home belonged to the murder victim. MacDowell took the stand today and said he knew the victim and had bought the ring from her for $60 for a girlfriend. If convicted, MacDowell could be sentenced to life in prison. He is currently on parole after spending 8 years in prison on an armed robbery charge.

2. There was a grinding head-on collision on Cheney Road yesterday. Two persons were killed: Rosemary Brennan, 27, and her infant daughter, Kelley, age 2, both of 1775 Nairn Dr. The driver of the second car involved in the accident, Anthony Murray, 17, of 1748 North 3 Street, was seriously injured, with multiple fractures. Police today announced that laboratory tests have confirmed the fact that Brennan was legally drunk at the time of the accident.

3. The state Legislature passed a law which prohibits doctors from performing abortions on girls under the age of 16 without the consent of their parents or guardians. The law specifies that doctors found guilty of violating the law can be fined up to $5,000 and can lose their licenses to practice medicine in the state. The law, which was signed by the governor, will go into effect at midnight tonight. The Legislature adopted the law after news media in the state revealed that girls as young as the age of 11 were given abortions without their parents knowledge or consent. The law is intended to prevent that. The parents consent must be in writing. The law stipulates that the girl who is pregnant must also agree to the abortion so her parents cannot force her to have one unwillingly.

EXERCISE 3

LEADS

<u>PRO CHALLENGE</u>

WRITING BASIC NEWS LEADS

INSTRUCTIONS: Write only a lead for each of the following stories. As you write your leads, consult the checklist on Page 127. When you finish, you can compare your work to a professional's. A professional journalist has been asked to write a lead for each of these stories, and these leads appear in a manual available to your instructor. You may find, however, that you like some of your own and your classmates' leads better.

1. There was an accident occurring in your city at 7:10 this morning at the intersection of Post Road and Rollins Avenue. Charles R. Lydon was driving north on Post Road and proceeded to enter the intersection in his van at a speed estimated at 40 mph. His van struck a fire engine responding to an emergency call, with its lights and siren in operation. Two firemen aboard the vehicle were hospitalized; however, their condition is not known at this point in time. Lyden was killed instantly in the serious and tragic accident. Authorities have not yet determined who was at fault. The truck was traveling an estimated 25 mph and responding to a report of a store fire. However, it was a false alarm. Lydens van was totally destroyed. Damage to the truck was estimated at $50,000.

2. There was a report issued in Washington, D.C. today. It came from the Highway Loss Data Institute, an affiliate of the Insurance Institute for Highway Safety. It shows that there are advantages to driving big cars. A study by the institute found that small two-door models and many small or midsize sport or specialty cars have the worst injury and repair records. Many of these small cars show injury claim frequencies and repair losses at least 30 percent higher than average, while many large cars, station wagons and vans show 40 percent to 50 percent better-than-average claim records. According to the analysis, a motorist in a four-door Oldsmobile Delta 88, for example, is 41 percent less likely than average to be hurt in an accident.

3. An article appeared today in the Journal of the American Medical Association. The article concerns the dangers of hot dogs. "If you were trying to design something that would be perfect to block a childs airway, it would be a bite-size piece of hot dog," says a researcher. He concluded that children under 4 should "never be given a whole hot dog to eat," and that hot dogs should never be cut crosswise. The hot dogs are so dangerous that every five days, it is estimated, someone, somewhere in the United States, chokes to death on them. Other risky foods for young kids up to 9 years of age include: candy, nuts, grapes, apples, carrots and popcorn.

4. The family of Kristine Belcuore was grief-stricken. She was 51 years old and died of a heart attack last week. She left a husband and four children. Because her death was so sudden and unexpected, an autopsy had to be performed before the funeral last Saturday. It was a big funeral, costing more than $7,000. More than 100 friends and relatives were in attendance. Today, the family received an apologetic call from the county

medical examiner. Mrs. Belcuors body is still in the morgue. The body they buried was that of a woman whose corpse had been unclaimed for a month. The error was discovered after the medical examiners office realized the month-old corpse had disappeared. Someone probably misread an identifying tag, they said. Also, the family never viewed the remains, they kept the casket closed throughout the proceedings. A relative said, "We went through all the pain and everything, all over the wrong body, and now we have to go through it again."

5. Its another statistical study, one that surprised researchers. For years, researchers thought that advanced education translated into greater marriage stability. Then they discovered that marital disruption is greater among more highly educated women than any other group (except those who haven't graduated from high school). Now a sociologist at The Ohio State University has conducted a new study which explains some of the reasons why women with graduate degrees are more likely to be graduated from their marriages as well. The key fact seems to be timing. Women who married early, before they began graduate school, are more likely to have established traditional family roles which they find difficult to change. When the wife goes back to school and no longer wants to handle most of the housework, it causes resentment on the part of the husband. If the husband refuses to pitch in and do his share, it creates tension. Such unhappiness on both sides often leads to divorce. Indeed, a third of the women who began graduate school after they were married ended up separated or divorced. By comparison, only 15.6 percent of those who married after they had finished an advanced degree ended up divorced or separated. They seem more likely to find husbands supportive of their educational goals.

6. The Department of Justice, as it often does, conducted a crime-related survey. It questioned long-term prisoners. It found that new laws limiting the ownership of guns do not discourage handgun ownership by career criminals. The report concludes, however, that even though curbs on legitimate retail sales of guns have failed to attain the goal of keeping weapons out of the hands of criminals, the laws still may serve other useful functions. The report explains that criminals get their weapons most often by theft or under-the-counter deals. The department surveyed 1,874 men serving time for felonies in 11 state prisons and found that 75 percent said they would expect little or no trouble if they tried to get a handgun after their release from prison. Fifty-seven percent had owned a handgun at the time of their arrest. Thirty-two percent of their guns had been stolen, 26 percent acquired in black market deals, and others received as gifts from family and friends. Only 21 percent had been bought through legitimate retail outlets.

7. Thomas C. Ahl appeared in Circuit Court today. He pleaded guilty last week to robbing and murdering two restaurant employees. In return for pleading guilty prosecutors promised not to seek the death penalty. He was sentenced today. Ahl is 24 years old, and the judge sentenced him to two life terms, plus 300 years. It is the longest sentence ever given anyone in your state. Ahl will be 89 before he can be considered for parole. The judge explained that Ahl had a long history of violence and brutality, and that the public deserved to be protected from him. There had been no reason for him to shotgun the two employees to death. Ahl himself admitted that they had not resisted him in any way.

8. The International Standardization Organization, which is composed of acoustics experts, today opened its annual convention. The convention is meeting in Geneva, Switzerland. Delegates from 51 countries are attending the convention, which will

Harcourt Brace & Company

continue through Sunday. An annual report issued by the organization warned that noise levels in the world are rising by one decibel a year. If the increase continues, the report warned, "everyone living in cities could be stone deaf by the year 2020." The report also said that long-term exposure to a noise level of 100 decibels can cause deafness, yet a riveting gun reaches a level of 130 decibels and a jet aircraft 150.

9. A 19-year-old shoplifting suspect died last Saturday. Police identified him as Timothy Milan. He lived at 1112 Huron Avenue and was employed as a cook at a restaurant in the city. A guard at Panzer's Department Store told police he saw Milan stuff 2 sweaters down his pants legs, then walk past a checkout line and out of the department store. The guard then began to chase Milan, who ran, and 3 bystanders joined in the pursuit. They caught up with Milan, and, when he resisted, one of the bystanders applied a headlock to him. A police officer who arrived at the scene reported that Milan collapsed as he put handcuffs on him. An autopsy conducted to determine the cause of death revealed that Milan died due to a lack of oxygen to the brain. Police today said they do not plan to charge anyone involved in the case with a crime because it "was a case of excusable homicide." The police said the bystanders did not mean to injure Milan or to kill him, but that he was fighting violently—punching and kicking at his captors and even trying to bite them—and that they were simply trying to restrain him and trying to help capture a suspected criminal, "which is just being a good citizen."

10. Several English teachers at your citys junior and senior high schools require their students to read the controversial book, "The Adventures of Huckleberry Finn." The book was written by Mark Twain. Critics, including some parents, said last week that the book should be banned from all schools in the city because it is racist. After considering their complaints and discussing them with his staff, the superintendent of schools, Gary Hubbard, announced today that teachers will be allowed to require reading the book in high school English classes but not in any junior high school classes. Furthermore, the superintendent said that it will be the responsibility of the high school teachers who assign the book to assist students in understanding the historical setting of the book, the characters being depicted and the social context, including the prejudices which existed at the time depicted in the book. Although the book can no longer be used in any junior high school classes, the school superintendent said it will remain available in junior and senior high school libraries for students who want to read it voluntarily. The book describes the adventures of runaway Huck Finn and a fugitive slave named Jim as they float on a raft down the Mississippi River.

E X E R C I S E   4
LEADS

CAMPUS STORIES

INSTRUCTIONS: Write only a lead for each of the following stories. Assume that all the stories occurred on your campus. As you write the leads, consult the checklist on Page 127. A professional has been asked to write a lead for each of these stories, and the leads appear in a manual available to your instructor. However, you may find that you like some of your own and your classmates' leads better.

1. A journalism professor at your school has sparked a heated debate. She teaches a course titled "Communication Law." During her class last week Friday, she took her class outdoors and burned a small American flag. She said the flag was "a teaching tool." The class was discussing Supreme Court cases that defined flag-burning as protected speech. The teacher, assistant professor Denise Beall, said she hoped her action would spark debate in the classroom about free-speech issues. "It was not a personal act," she said. "It was a pedagogical one." This morning, about 250 students, led by veterans groups on your campus, gathered to protest the flag-burning. They marched to the building where Beall was teaching the course. The protesters entered the building, stood outside the room where the class was in session, and sang the national anthem. The students also said the Pledge of Allegiance and chanted "U.S.A." In a statement issued soon thereafter, the president of your school said Beall had used "extraordinarily bad judgment" in burning the flag. But, your president said, it would be inappropriate for the school to do anything further to question or punish her teaching techniques.

2. At first, it seemed like a wonderful idea! Your schools president learned the wife of the President of the United States was going to be in the area. He proceeded to invite her to deliver your schools commencement address for this spring's graduating class—and she accepted. Now, opposition is arising. About a week ago, a half-dozen senior women began circulating a petition opposing her delivering the commencement address and, thus far, more than 300 of their classmates have signed it. "To honor the First Lady as a commencement speaker," says the petition, "is to honor a woman who has gained recognition through the achievements of her husband, which contradicts what we have been taught over our years of study—that women should be honored for their achievements, not their husbands." The president of your institution has scheduled a meeting for late Friday to discuss the issue with members of the graduating class.

3. College students have an unusual problem that has gone largely unnoticed in the past. Some call it "freshman fat." Others call it "the Freshman 5," "the Freshman 10," "the Freshman 15" or even "the Freshman 20." Now, a specialist at your school is studying the issue and finding some truth to the folklore. Freshmen women, she found, are more than twice as likely to gain a significant amount of weight as similar women who don't go to college. Of your schools incoming freshmen last year, 26% gained weight. By comparison, 9% of a group of comparable young women in your community who did not enroll in college gained weight. Freshman Fat isn't considered a serious health

threat. Five or 10 extra pounds don't make a big difference for most people. The best remedy, in fact, may be to ignore the extra weight: sooner or later, your eating habits are bound to settle down. A constellation of factors lies behind Freshman Fat: sudden freedom from parental rules; overabundance of choices; erratic, late hours; a more sedentary life; a social life that revolves around eating and drinking. And stress. Food is the age-old comforter. Linda Kasparov, a licensed dietitian at your school, conducted the study and released all the information about the results of it today.

4. Theres a heated, controversial debate at your school. The school has a foundation that invests its money in various stocks, bonds and properties. A reporter for your student paper last week uncovered the fact that some of the money is invested in tobacco companies. Now some people want the foundation to eliminate those stocks from its investment portfolio. The editor of your student paper advocates the elimination of such stock and, in an interview with you today explained quite persuasively that, "Cigarettes have been responsible for millions of deaths, and owning shares in the companies that produce them sends a conflicting message to both students and the public. Furthermore, the foundation, and thus our school, is benefiting from those deaths: from the sale of a product known to kill its users." The Board of Regents met at 8 a.m. this morning, and the topic was one of several on its agenda. It voted 8–1 that the foundation not be ordered to sell any of its tobacco stocks.

5. Last week a group of medical researchers conducted an unusual survey of the women on your campus. As part of an effort to learn more about students needs and ways of improving student health care, doctors at your student clinic conducted an unusual survey, personally contacting and interviewing a random sample of 1,044 women on campus last week. The women were interviewed in person and were also asked to complete anonymous questionnaires developed by the researchers. The researchers found that almost 1 in 10 had had an abortion at some point in her life. "I was shocked, to be quite frank," said Robert Einhorn, the clinics director. "We have some students who come to us, learn they're pregnant, and ask about their options. Some want a referral to a clinic that performs abortions, and there are a number of names that we give them. But I never thought we were talking about this number of students. Of course, some reported having their abortions years ago—as young as the age of 12." More specifically, 9.41 percent of the women students surveyed said they have had an abortion. 1.7% of the women students have had two abortions.

6. Five students on your campus, all members of a fraternity, Sigma Kappa Chi, have been arrested as the result of a hazing incident. The investigation began after one SKC pledge was hospitalized Saturday with serious internal injuries and another with a sprained back. Each of the five was charged with two counts of battery. The incident occurred during a fraternity meeting Friday at which members "beat pledges with wooden paddles and canes and subjected them to other forms of physical and verbal punishment," according to Detective Sgt. Albert Wei, who headed the investigation. One of the two injured students, sophomore Roland Dessaur, was hospitalized for kidney damage and dehydration. Another sophomore, Eddie Muldaur, was treated for a sprained back and bruised buttocks. State laws require hospital officials to report injuries that appear to be the result of a crime. Thus, hospital officials notified the police and, as the investigation continued, four other pledges were taken to the hospital and also examined, then released. Several suffered contusions, Wei said. A university spokesman said both university and national fraternity officials are investigating to determine what disciplinary action, if any, should be taken against the fraternity.

Harcourt Brace & Company

E X E R C I S E   5

LEADS

<u>PRO CHALLENGE</u>

CITY, STATE AND NATIONAL LEADS

INSTRUCTIONS: Write only a lead for each of the following stories. As you write the leads, consult the checklist on Page 127. The first set of stories involves events in your city; the second set involves events in your state; and the third set involves events in the nation. A professional has been asked to write a lead for each of these stories, and the leads appear in a manual available to your instructor. However, you may find that you like some of your own and your classmates' leads better.

CITY BEAT

1. The restaurant is located at 480 Parkside Dr. and specializes in Chinese cuisine. It is owned by Fred Lee, who also does all the cooking. City health inspectors suspended its license late yesterday. They complained of poor food handling and storage. "The condition of the licensed premises was so serious that it was condemned as posing an immediate threat to public health," the citys emergency license suspension order states. Chester Garland, a city health inspector, said the city suspends licenses only when there are serious violations. "It has to be something that is a major problem," Garland said. "We don't just do it on minor stuff." Garland added that the restaurant has consistently failed to comply with city health codes. Violations cited yesterday by city inspectors include rodent and roach infestations. The inspectors found rodent droppings strewn about storage areas and on canned goods. Garlands report adds: "A mouse was seen running across the dining room. A live mouse was spotted in the pantry. Another mouse jumped on an inspector. Toxic materials were stored in food-preparation and dish-washing areas. Food was found improperly stored in a janitors closet as well as in uncovered containers and in locations less than 6 inches off the floor."

2. Marlene Holland is a junior at Colonial High School. She was enrolled in a biology class there last term and objected when, as part of her class assignments, she was asked to dissect worms, frogs, and a fetal pig. She said the assignments violated her religious beliefs. The teacher then gave her a grade of "F" on the assignments, and she flunked the course as a result. Her parents sued the school district, and the trial was supposed to begin at 8 a.m. next Monday. The lawsuit charged that the Board of Education violated her freedom of religion by giving her failing grades for refusing to participate in dissection experiments. There was a settlement today. "I learned that its worth it, in the end, to act on your convictions," the girl said when interviewed after the settlement. The board's attorney, Karen Bulnes, said the district decided to settle, giving her a passing grade based upon her other work, a grade of "B," because Marlene would have proven in a trial that her refusal to cut up dead animals stemmed from sincere religious beliefs. The district also agreed to pay $12,500 in legal fees, which will go to the American Civil Liberties Union, which represented her. Marlene said her spiritual doctrine bars her from harming animals or cutting them up. They also keep her from wearing leather or wool, eating meat, or drinking milk. She also shuns makeup, which is often tested on animals.

3. Todd Lefforge is an orthodontist who has been working in your community for 11 years. He is 36 years old and lives at 537 Peterson Place. He has a practice of about 750 current patients. He has treated approximately 5,000 more in the past. Today he announced that he has AIDS. He was diagnosed with AIDS three days ago. He immediately closed his practice. He also wrote a letter to all his patients, mostly children, and their parents. His letter, which parents began to receive today, says, "I am very sorry for any anxiety this may cause to anyone." The citys Department of Health has set up an emergency center at its downtown office where, starting today, his patients can be tested for the AIDS virus and counseled about their fears. Leforge, who decided to immediately close his practice, said he tried to be reassuring in his letter. "I have always followed the CDC [Centers for Disease Control] guidelines regarding infection and sterilization procedures," he wrote. "I feel no patients could have been infected by me." Dr. Cathleen Graham, M.D., head of the citys Health Department, agreed that: "The risk is minimal. But the long odds don't lessen the fears of a parent. Since we're dealing primarily with children, its more emotional. Its going to be a traumatic time."

4. Your police department arrested a thief at 11 p.m. last night: Mark Johnsen, 43, of 2463 Pioneer Road. After his arrest, Johnson promptly confessed. Talking to a reporter, he said: "I worked construction, but it was hard and I didn't like it, so I quit. I could make better money stealing, and it only took an hour or two a day." Johnson estimates that he broke into about 300 homes during the last 12 months. "I'd make $2,000, maybe $3,000, a week," he said. He sold his loot, mostly jewelry, to fences, pawnshops, and flea markets. He was arrested shortly after 11 p.m. after leaving a house with a VCR and jewelry, Detective Karen Sweers said. Neighbors called the police after seeing him enter the house. Detectives later found about $10,000 in rings, watches, coins and other jewelry in his car and at his girlfriends apartment. Johnsen was released from prison about two years ago after being convicted of strong-armed rape, robbery and kidnapping. "He's a career criminal," Sweers said. "He has spent 15 of the last 17 years in the prison system." He is being held without bail on charges of burglary and grand theft. Investigators are trying to track down the owners of dozens of stolen coins, rings and necklaces.

5. The accident occurred yesterday at your citys airport. A plane crashed on takeoff. Gusty crosswinds were at least partly to blame, said airport officials. The plane was a single-engine Cessna 172 Skyhawk. It crashed shortly after 4 p.m. yesterday afternoon. The Federal Aviation Administration has been notified and is investigating the crash. The pilot was Joel Fowler, age 23, of 2606 Hillcrest Street. The identity of his 3 passengers was not immediately available. All survived the crash. "It was a miracle we only got scratches," said Fowler, who added that they were "out cruising" in the rented plane, and that he was practicing a few touch-and-go landings. A touch and go is where the plane hits the runway for a split second and then goes airborne again. As the craft touched the runway it was going about 70 mph and being tossed by the wind. Fowler said, "It was real tough." He gave it full throttle to climb back into the air, but in an instant the plane veered right, a wing struck the pavement and it turned upside down, "spewing pieces everywhere." The four, stunned but otherwise not seriously hurt, unbuckled their seat belts and piled out of the plane immediately. The passengers were taken to Regional Medical Center for examination and treatment of cuts, bruises and shock.

STATE BEAT

1. It was an interesting little idea proposed today by a state senator from your city: Neil Iacobi. Today Iacobi made a proposal that would affect most newspapers in your state, or

at least those that publish editorials. Iacobi said he is drafting legislation that would require newspapermen to sign the editorials they write so people know the writers identity. "Its one of the most blatant attempts at press-bashing in recent memory," responded Tony DiLorento, executive director of the State Press Association. Iacobi said he has already found 32 co-sponsors for his bill. Violations would be punishable as second-degree misdemeanors. "It doesn't say you can't write something—only that you have to sign what you write," Iacobi said. "Editorialists should be accountable to their readers. They can attack you and tear you apart and do anything to you, and no one even knows who they are. That's not right or fair. Only cowards would do something like that."

2. State Senator Karen Simmons proposed another new law today. She introduced it in the state senate. To protect the environment she wants to ban disposable diapers but expects strong opposition among working mothers and day-care centers. "We're running out of landfill space," Simmons, a Democrat, said. "But there are young mothers who are going to scream and holler." Many day-care centers will not accept children who wear cloth diapers instead of disposable diapers. "You just cannot handle cloth diapers as sanitarily," said Denise Abdondanzio, a spokesman for the states day care centers. Simmens filed her bill (SB 1244) to ban disposable diapers effective Jan. 1. Without a ban, she said, disposable diapers will fill up landfills, "causing problems long after the babies have babies."

3. Richard Clair, head of your states Department of Corrections, testified before a legislative committee in your state capital today. He reported that, 10 years ago, 4.5% of the people in the states prisons were women. Five years ago it was 6.4%. Today women are 8.7% of the inmates in state prisons "and the percentage seems certain to continue to increase." There are also more older inmates: inmates age 51 and older. The percentage has jumped from 3.8% to 4.6% during the last 10 years, Clair said. Women and the elderly present special problems for a prison system historically geared toward young men. Medical costs for women and older inmates are higher than for young men. And because there are fewer women in the system, there are fewer facilities for them, prompting charges of unequal treatment. Women tend to commit drug-related and economic crimes rather than crimes of violence. Yet in prison they have less access than men to programs that could help them, such as drug treatment, education, and job training programs.

4. Merchants in the state say they are delighted with a new law the governor signed today. It will go into effect on the 1st of next month. Basically, it stiffens check-bouncing penalties. Amy Woods, director of the State Federation of Independent Businesses, said the bill will send a stern message to the writers of bad checks. "We're delighted," Wood said. "SFIB has 15,000 members in the state, and we've lobbied hard for a bill like this." The bill makes check-bouncers liable for paying three times the face value of each bad check if they fail to make good on their bills within 30 days after receiving a written demand for payment. It also requires the writer of a bad check to pay all service charges, court costs and attorney fees incurred in the collection effort. Damage awards are limited to a total of $2,500 per check.

5. Last spring, Rachel Young was named the states "Outstanding Teacher." She is a high school economics teacher. She was invited to give a speech today at the annual convention of the National Education Assn. in the state capital. The main thrust of her speech was to criticize the fact that many high school students hold part-time jobs. She called minimum wage jobs "the silent killers of quality education," and explained that too many teens jeopardize their futures by working part time in high school. She continued in her speech: "Flipping burgers and running a cash register teach youngsters next to nothing and leave them scant time to study, keep up on current events, or participate in

extra curricular activities. If you look at these students, few have to work to help support their families, put food on the table, or save up for college. Instead, most working teens are middle class students who labor to buy themselves flashy cars, pay car insurance premiums or clothe themselves in the latest fashions. They are trapped in seeking material goods, and they come to school truly tired, truly burned out. They're sacrificing their future earnings and career satisfaction because these jobs compromise their ability to make the most of their high school years."

NATIONAL BEAT

1. The Census Bureau issued a report today concerning the problem of illiteracy. The Census Bureau set out to determine how many people currently living in the United States are literate or illiterate in the English language. It administered literacy tests to 3,400 adults in the United States. It found the illiteracy rate for adult Americans whose native language is English is 9%. For adults whose native language is not English, the illiteracy rate climbed to 48%. A large portion of those people are, by their own account, probably literate in their native language, according to the study. Of the native English speakers who failed the test, 70% had not finished high school. The test has a sampling error of 1 to 2 percentage points.

2. The Centers for Disease Control issued a report Friday that, for many, will be pleasing. It concerns Americans consumption of hard liquor. That consumption has fallen to its lowest level since 1959. The average American drank 0.85 gallons of spirits last year, compared with 0.84 gallons in 1959, according to the Alcohol Drug Abuse and Mental Health Administration. Distilled spirits are hard liquors such as whiskey, rum, vodka, or gin. Beer and wine, which are fermented but not distilled, are considered separately. CDC statistics, however, show that consumption of alcoholic beverages as a whole is on the decline. The statistics indicate that some drinkers are switching to lower-alcohol drinks such as wine coolers and light beers as a result of their concern for physical fitness, nutrition and alcohol abuse. Two out of three American adults drink. But just 10 percent of those adults drink half of all the alcohol consumed in the nation.

3. The President lost a battle in Congress today. Congress decided against spending $12 million for a cause the president favored. The project involved huge dish-shaped antennas which listened for radio signals from outer space. It was cut from NASA's budget. The House today approved a $14.29 billion budget for NASA in a 355–48 vote. If the Senate agrees with the House, the space agency budget for next fiscal year will be $2 billion above current spending levels but $800 million below what the president requested. The president wanted included in the budget $12 million for the alien-search project. NASA's search for extraterrestrial intelligence, a project known as SETI, was to cost $100 million over 10 years. Its sophisticated radio antennas have picked up only static since the program began last year. "Our country can't afford this," said Rep. Ronald Machtley, R-R.I., who suggested that the money be spent on education. "I'd rather see a search for terrestrial intelligence in our schools," he said.

4. The Department of Veterans Affairs today admitted that its made a little mistake. The mistake cost an estimated $5.7 million a year. Each year, the Veterans Affairs Department pays more than $14.7 billion in disability compensation and pension benefits to more than 2.8 million veterans and to nearly 1 million surviving spouses and other dependents. An audit of those payments revealed that the Department of Veterans Affairs has been paying benefits to more than 1,200 veterans who are dead. The exact total was 1,212 veterans who were reported dead. About 100 of the veterans have been dead a

Harcourt Brace & Company

decade or more. Auditors said the department could have reduced the erroneous payments by matching VA benefit payment files with death information maintained by the Social Security Administration. In the past, the department relied on voluntary reporting of deaths as a basis for ending benefits.

5. The nations homebuilders are concerned about a problem that affects young adults—but also the entire nation (and its economy as well). The problem is affordable housing. At its annual convention, currently being held in Las Vegas, Nevada, the National Homebuilders Association revealed that a survey it commissioned shows a drop in homeownership rates over the last 10 years among young families—and a rapidly dwindling stock of low-cost rental housing. The associations members expect the problems to continue. The homeownership rate among families in the 25-to-34 age group has fallen to 45%, largely because they don't have the cash for a down payment or the income to qualify for a loan. At the same time, rents are at record high rates in much of the country, making it harder for young families to accumulate the money needed for a down payment. Wayne Doyle, the associations President, offered no concrete solutions to the problem, which has sent the homebuilding industry into the doldrums, with fewer sales and higher unemployment rates. "Young families face a difficult situation," Doyle concluded. "They must accumulate enough savings to make a down payment but they are finding it harder to obtain good jobs, and also find that more and more of their money is going for rent, so its harder to save anything for a house." By comparison, the homeownership rate for 65-to-74 year olds is 78.2%.

CHAPTER 6 ☆☆☆☆☆

ALTERNATIVE LEADS

Everybody hates editors. Writers especially. They give editors stuff they can't possibly print the way it is, and when the editors make it printable, the writers curse them instead of thanking them.

(An editor quoted in "A Corner of Chicago" by Robert Hardy Andrews)

The previous chapter described basic summary leads. That type of lead is more common than any of the alternatives—and probably easier to write. While reading your local newspaper, you may find that 95 percent of its stories begin with a summary lead. Yet increasingly, experienced reporters are using alternative types of leads.

Journalists call the alternatives "soft leads." There are at least a dozen variations, but most soft leads begin with a story's most interesting details—often a question, quotation, anecdote or description. A summary of the story's most important details may appear later, perhaps in the third or fourth paragraph. Or the soft lead may move directly into a story without any attempt to summarize it.

Writing an alternative lead requires thought and imagination: the ability to recognize and convey an interesting idea uniquely. It does not require an unusual story. In the example below, the lead first appears as a routine report about a convention. The alternative lead captures the news of the convention better:

TYPICAL SUMMARY: The annual convention of the Association of Alternative Newsweeklies is being held this week in Nashville.

ALTERNATIVE LEAD: T-shirts and sandals are preferred to pinstripes and wingtips. An air of cynicism and sarcasm supplants a somber civility. Men sport ponytails, not neckties.

At first glance, the annual gathering of the Association of Alternative Newsweeklies looks more like a Woodstock reunion than a newspaper convention.

(Editor & Publisher)

Here is another example in which creativity lends freshness to a story about a has-been fighter:

Middleweight "Sailor" Danny Grogan, who never has been anywhere, is making a comeback.

(The Associated Press)

Good reporters create a variety of leads, choosing the appropriate type of lead for each story. There is a danger, according to Paula LaRocque, assistant managing editor and writing coach at The Dallas Morning News, in getting caught up in one writing trend over another. She urges writers not to follow trends. "Compelling leads are as individual as writing, and writing is as individual as thinking," she comments. In other words, reporters will write better leads if they use their intelligence, inventiveness and imagination—their thinking skills—instead of trying to put their writing into a formula.

When reporters finish a story, their editors expect it to be well written: clear, concise, accurate and interesting. If a story meets these criteria, editors are unlikely to object if its lead uses an alternative form. Similarly, they are unlikely to object to a summary lead that creatively and freshly captures the essence of a story.

Harcourt Brace & Company

CRITICISMS

During the 1940s, the Wall Street Journal became one of the first daily newspapers to use soft leads. Since then, other dailies, including the Los Angeles Times, The Miami Herald and The Boston Globe, have become known as "writers'" newspapers. Dailies are giving their reporters more freedom to experiment with their writing.

Proponents of soft leads say it does not matter whether a lead is hard or soft; what matters is whether it works. They disparage the traditional summaries as "suitcase leads." In the past, they explain, newspapers tried to jam too many details into leads. They suggest that summary leads are unnatural and make it more difficult for reporters to write good stories. They further explain that summary leads eliminate the possibility of surprise and make all stories sound alike.

Reporters using soft leads see their stories as hourglass-shaped, with three parts: (1) an introduction; (2) a turn or transition; and (3) a narrative that tells the story, usually in chronological order. Roy Peter Clark, a proponent of experimentation in writing, insists the hourglass form is a more natural way to tell a story. Like good storytellers, reporters start at the beginning of a tale and go on to the end, thus presenting facts in a normal, logical sequence. Clark adds that the key to a good story is the turn—the transition from the lead to the narrative.

The more literary style of soft leads may also help newspapers compete with television. The style's proponents explain that television can report the news more quickly than newspapers but that, by using soft leads, newspapers can make their stories more interesting.

Critics—primarily other reporters and editors—call the style "Jell-O Journalism." They complain that soft leads are inappropriate for most news stories: too arty, literary, dangerous and unprofessional. Critics add that soft leads are too long and fail to emphasize the news. If a story begins with several paragraphs of description or quotations, for example, the story's most important details may be lost because they are buried in a later paragraph. Critics also complain that some reporters are straining to write fine literature, and many lack the necessary ability.

The following lead is an example of the problem: an alternative lead that is poorly written and is thus likely to make the reader impatient. You have to read more than 145 words before getting to the news—the main point of the story:

> Eleanor Lago considers herself an intelligent, educated woman.
> She's read the information provided her by the Grand Rapids Township Board. She's talked to friends and neighbors. And she intends to vote Tuesday in a special election that could determine the township's future.
> "I just want to do what's best," says Lago.
> Like many residents, though, she's not sure what that is.
> An unusual battle is being fought in this smallest of Kent County townships, a raggedy-shaped 16 square miles set cheek to jowl against the cities of Grand Rapids, East Grand Rapids and Kentwood.
> The battle is not about zoning, the more typical flashpoint of local politics. Nor is it about leaf burning ordinances or other grass-roots laws in this suburb of nearly 11,000 people.
> This battle is about what the community can do to keep from being nibbled to pieces by annexation.

The writer's intention was good: describing an intelligent voter who is confused about an important issue. The introduction would have been more effective, however, if cut in half. The writer could have eliminated some description, cut the clichés and avoided saying what the election was *not* about.

The following sections describe different types of alternative leads and show good examples of each.

Harcourt Brace & Company

Tips from a Pro

WRITING IMAGINATIVE LEADS

Roy Peter Clark, a proponent of experimentation in writing, offers these tips for writing leads:

1. Keep leads short. Even a very long story can flow from one carefully crafted sentence.
2. Never forget the news. If it is not in the first paragraph, put it in a "nut graph" near the top of the story.
3. If a lead is delayed, you have a responsibility to give readers a reason to continue. Include elements that dramatize the news, foreshadow events, create a sense of foreboding or of anticipated surprise.
4. Even if you begin your story with hard news, look for an opportunity later to retell events in a chronological narrative.
5. Keep the lead honest. Don't begin with the most startling or sensational anecdote if it is not organically related to the news.
6. When you find a good lead that violates any or all these rules, use it.

"DELAYED" OR "BURIED" LEADS

A "delayed" lead is the most common type of alternative leads. Some reporters call it a "buried" lead. Typically, a delayed lead begins with an interesting example or anecdote that sets a story's theme. Then a "nut graf"—perhaps the third or fourth paragraph—summarizes the story and provides a transition to the body. The nut graf moves the story from a single example or anecdote to the general issue or problem. Like a traditional lead, it summarizes the topic. In addition, it may explain why the topic is important.

Here are two examples of delayed leads. The first is by Walter R. Mears, a special correspondent for The Associated Press, who takes a different approach to writing about a company filing for bankruptcy. The second is by Sabra Chartland of The New York Times, who wrote about a business side of athletics most people rarely think about:

WASHINGTON (AP)—Time was, writing meant typewriting. Words like these— written on a television screen—were composed on the solid keyboard, banged noisily onto a piece of paper, XXXXd out when they weren't quite right, ripped out and scrapped when the paragraphs just didn't work.

It's easier and faster with the computer, a reality that pushed Smith Corona Corp., the last big-name American typewriter manufacturer, into bankruptcy on Wednesday.

Cal Ripken, Jr., less than two months from breaking Lou Gehrig's streak of 2,130 consecutive games, is famous for his endurance on the baseball field. For a less celebrated example of his stamina, consider the more than 10,000 autographs he will sign this year.

The vast majority will not be the old-fashioned face-to-face kind. Rather, Mr. Ripken signs balls by the boxload, hundreds at a time, in his hotel room or at home, to be sold at a big profit. . . .

After giving some details about how Ripken signs the balls, how much an autographed ball costs and what Ripken makes from the sale of each, Chartland gets to the point of the story in the fourth paragraph:

Ten years ago, mass-autographed merchandise was a rarity. Today, these balls, helmets, jerseys and athletic shoes are a $500 million industry. . . .

You can start a story about a complex or abstract problem by showing how the problem affects a single individual—someone your readers may know or identify with. Or you can use an anecdote that illustrates the problem and is likely to arouse readers' interest in the topic.

Some delayed leads surprise their readers with an unusual twist. If a story is only three or four paragraphs long, journalists may save the twist for the last line. If a story is longer, they use the twist to lure readers to the nut graf, which then provides a transition to the following paragraphs.

MULTIPARAGRAPH LEADS

Other newswriters think of a lead as a unit of thought. Their summary leads consist of two or three paragraphs that flow into each other as if they were one:

SAVONA, N.Y.—Eric Smith has a thatch of coppery hair, freckles and gold wire-rim glasses. The 14-year-old used to ride his bike everywhere, play drums in the school band and crack the other kids up with his cackle of a laugh. On Tuesday, he goes on trial for second-degree murder.

Eric is accused of bludgeoning 4-year-old Derrick Robie, whose body was found Aug. 2 in a vacant lot near his home in this sylvan village of 930 people in western New York.

(The Associated Press)

COLORADO SPRINGS—A mountain was over their shoulders, a deer was in front of the 12th tee and a 16-year-old invaded the leader board. The 50th United States Women's Open met the wilderness today, and the results were minor gusts, a severe rough, sloping greens and, out of the blue, a course record score of 66.

Jill Briles-Hinton, who sneaked her miniature schnauzers into her hotel room, played miniature golf here, too. Her putting on the Broadmoor Resort's East course was deadeye, and her crawling "miracle" uphill birdie putt on the 18th hole landed her a four-under-par 66 and the first-round lead.

(The New York Times)

USING QUOTATIONS

Beginning writers particularly should avoid using quotations in leads. Why? Because a source usually does not provide a quote that meets three criteria for serving as a lead: (1) It summarizes the entire story (not just part of it), (2) it is brief, and (3) it is self-explanatory. Some editors prohibit the use of quotation leads because quotations lack clarity and, when used in leads, are too long and complicated. As with the use of any quote in a story, the source's statement should be so effective the reporter cannot improve it. When used in the first line of a story, a quote must also tell the reader the point of the story:

"I wanted to slam the plane into a mountain so I could die with my husband," said Betty Smith, whose husband died at its controls. But then she thought of her children on the ground.

"Our children can't read, add or find countries on a map," the nation's teacher-of-the-year said at a congressional hearing today.

If a quote is only sensational, then it does not meet the criteria noted above. You can use it in the story, but not in the lead. You can startle readers or grab their attention in other ways with your lead. Remember that the lead provides the organization for the rest of the story. If the quote does not lead readers into and set the stage for the rest of the story, then it will only confuse and discourage them. Even within the body of a story, a quote should be brief. In the lead, brevity is a virtue because a complicated, long quote will raise unnecessary questions.

Be particularly careful to avoid quotations beginning with words needing identification or explanation later: words such as "he," "she," "we," "they," "it," "that" and "this." If such words are first in a story, readers have no way of knowing to whom or what the words refer. When the subject's identity is revealed later in a story, readers may have to reread the quotation to understand its meaning.

Leads using a quotation can often be rewritten with a brief introduction placed *before* the quotation to enhance its clarity:

> "It was saucer-shaped and appeared to have a glass window section running around the center." That's how a woman described the flying object she saw hover above Crystal Lake on Monday and Tuesday nights.
>
> REVISED: A woman who saw a flying object hover above Crystal Lake on two nights said, "It was saucer-shaped and appeared to have a glass window section running around the center."

USING QUESTIONS

Questions can make effective leads. Some editors prohibit question leads because they believe news stories should answer questions, not ask them. Question leads often run the risk of being clichés.

To be effective, question leads must be brief, simple, specific and provocative. The question should contain no more than a dozen words. Moreover, readers should feel absolutely compelled to answer it. Avoid questions if the readers' responses may discourage them from continuing with the story:

> Are you interested in nuclear physics?

The question should concern a controversial issue readers are familiar with: an issue that interests and affects them. Avoid abstract or complicated questions that would require a great deal of explanation.

The following question is ineffective because it is too abstract, long and complicated. Moreover, it fails to ask about issues that everyone is certain to care about:

> If you were on vacation miles from your house, and you thought the mechanics at a service station deliberately damaged your car, then demanded an exorbitant fee to repair it, would you be willing to file criminal charges against the mechanics and return to the area to testify at their trial?

The following questions also fail, but for different reasons. The first question asks about an issue unlikely to concern most readers. The second question is flippant, treating a serious topic as a trivial one, and unanswerable:

> Have you thought about going to prison lately?

> Someone was swindled today. Who'll be swindled tomorrow?

The following are more effective leads. Notice that immediately after asking a question, the reporter answers it:

Are students better off if their principals live in the school district?

They sure are, insist some in Grand Rapids and Spring Lake, where they've been debating whether people who run public schools should be required to live in their district.

(The Grand Rapids [Mich.] Press)

LANSING—Prisons are the fastest-growing consumers of state budget dollars, right? Wrong.

Taxpayer-funded health care for state and public school retirees has grown fourfold in the past eight years.

(The Ann Arbor [Mich.] News)

SUSPENSEFUL LEADS

Some reporters write leads to arouse readers' curiosity, create suspense or raise a question in their minds. By hinting at some mysterious development explained in a later paragraph, this type of lead compels readers to finish a story:

Don't try to tell Kent Owen crime doesn't pay. It could be saving his life.

(The Tampa [Fla.] Tribune)

As a Highland Springs all-state safety, he wore No. 5.
As a Virginia Tech freshman defensive back, he wore No. 22.
Last month, Harold Banks became No. 81.

(Richmond [Va.] Times-Dispatch)

The first story explained that Owen, who was HIV positive, resorted to illegal means to get the drug AZT. The second story reported the shooting death of a troubled star.

DESCRIPTIVE LEADS

Other leads begin with descriptive details and move gradually into the action. The description should be colorful and interesting, so that it arouses readers' interest in the topic. The description can also help summarize a story.

The following examples show the effectiveness of descriptive leads. Notice the use of adjectives in the first lead: "back," "neatly dressed," "earnest," "mimeographed," "sex-education," "rousing" and "weekly." As you read the second lead, notice its effective use of descriptive verbs—"hit," "glided," "skidded" and "sank":

It's Thursday morning, and the back room of the restaurant is filled with neatly dressed men holding earnest conversations over eggs and pancakes.

Mimeographed pamphlets are handed out. A sex-education book is passed around, causing heads to shake negatively. A rousing prayer is delivered.

The Decency in Education Committee of Lee County is holding its weekly meeting.

(The Associated Press)

It hit the bridge with a deafening roar and then, suddenly, there was silence. There was no sound at all, those who watched said later, as the Air Florida 737 jetliner glided into the river, skidded across the gray ice and sank slowly into the icy waters.

(The New York Times)

SHOCKING LEADS—WITH A TWIST

Reporters like "shockers"—startling leads that immediately capture the attention of readers. The following examples have an unusual twist that adds to their effectiveness:

CHARLESTON, W.Va.—Not long after Pat and Fred Grounds moved into their new home, they noticed they weren't getting any mail.

First they thought the mail hadn't been forwarded. Then they were told they had no mail.

Only after more than a week and many phone calls did the post office tell them the truth: Their mail carrier was afraid of catching AIDS from them.

(The Associated Press)

It was one of those split-second things. A family outing, a bump in the road, a freak shot—a toddler is dead.

(The Tampa [Fla.] Tribune)

IRONIC LEADS

Closely related to shockers are leads that present a startling or ironic contrast—again, details likely to arouse readers' curiosity, as in the following examples:

MONTAGUE, Mich.—Amanda Frale and Brianne Roesler went searching for shells and lost treasure at the beach, but found only dead fish and trash. So the 7-year-old cousins wrote a letter to the mayor, their grandfather.

(The Associated Press)

Otters are cute. They're playful. They sustain the Monterey Bay area's ceramic figurine industry.

They're also necrophiliacs and spouse abusers. Teen mothers routinely abandon their babies to die and engage in other practices that might draw serious frowns.

In what could be a blow to their tourist appeal, the first comprehensive study of the endangered California sea otters reveals a dark side we'd probably rather not know.

(San Jose [Calif.] Mercury News)

DIRECT-ADDRESS LEADS

Reporters occasionally use a form of direct address, speaking directly to their readers:

Stop your whining. So what if it got up to 97 degrees on Wednesday, tying the record for a July 12, set in 1954?

(Chicago Tribune)

To the states of matter you learned in school—solid, liquid and gas—add another: a frozen gas that exists nowhere in the universe except a Colorado lab where scientists are making it.

(Chicago Tribune)

UNUSUAL WORDS USED IN UNUSUAL WAYS

If you are clever and have a good imagination (or a good grasp of literature), you can use a common word or phrase in an uncommon way:

> Patrick Buchanan took his presidential campaign to the Alamo Friday, the scrappy underdog at the ultimate shrine to impossible battles.
>
> *(Houston Chronicle)*

> Tommy Hilfiger, the pushy young menswear designer who was supposed to go out of style faster than a Nehru jacket, is hanging on like a navy blazer.
>
> *(Wall Street Journal)*

This style is difficult, because what seems funny or clever to one person may seem corny or silly to another. Also, the subjects may be too serious for such a light touch:

> A man who punched a highway patrol officer in the face will pay through the nose for the blow.

The story explained that a judge ordered a man to pay $40,000 to a state trooper he punched in the face during a routine traffic stop. The trooper suffered a broken nose.

OTHER UNUSUAL LEADS

The following leads are difficult to categorize. All the leads are unusual, yet effective. Notice their simplicity, brevity and clarity. Also, notice the leads' emphasis on the interesting and unusual. The first lead introduces a story about an unusually high number of spring blossoms. The second lead describes the birth of quadruplets. The third lead reports the loss of a school bond issue by 515 votes. The fourth describes an undercover officer trying to catch some thieves.

> Bees are euphoric.
>
> *(Greensboro [N.C.] News & Record)*

> It's a boy!
> It's another boy!
> It's a girl!
> It's another girl!
> "That's enough!" exclaimed Carol Abella of Tempe. "What more does he need for Father's Day?"
> "Diapers," answered David Abella.
>
> *(The [Phoenix] Arizona Republic)*

> Five hundred and fifteen. The number will stick in the minds of parents and teachers here like bubble gum in hair.
>
> *(San Mateo [Calif.] Times)*

> The man who stumbled out of the Miami Beach paddywagon into the county's alcoholic referral center at about 10 p.m. wore filthy, ragged dungarees.
> He smelled of dirt and beer.
> He was loud.
> He was obnoxious.
> He was a cop.
>
> *(The Miami Herald)*

E X E R C I S E   1

ALTERNATIVE LEADS

EVALUATING ALTERNATIVE LEADS

INSTRUCTIONS: Critically evaluate the following leads, each of which uses one of the alternative forms discussed in this chapter. Select the best leads and explain why they succeed. Point out the flaws in the remaining leads. As you evaluate the leads, look for lessons—"do's and don'ts"—that you can apply to your own work.

1. Are you afraid of snakes?
2. Could you swim 40 miles, jog 100 miles or bike 400 miles in one month?
3. Brenda DeVitini got up at dawn to jog. She planned to use a high school track two blocks from her house, a track she had used every morning for the last four years.
   A paper carrier found her body there an hour later.
4. "I didn't come here to make you come to your feet," the Rev. Tyrone Burns told 100 students Tuesday. "I came here to make you come to your senses."
5. "I'll let you guys have it with both barrels," a member of the state Legislature told members of the Association of Secondary Teachers, who held their state convention in the city today.
6. A 16-year-old girl who said she "considers abortion murder" was placed in jail today because she refused to obey her mother and have an abortion.
7. Should America's 1 million excess dairy cows be donated to impoverished nations or destroyed as ordered by the federal government to maintain the price of dairy products?
8. With tears forming in his eyes, Albert Chmielewski whispered goodbye to his mother.
   Moments later, Chmielewski was handcuffed and led from the courtroom on his way to prison. A jury of nine men and three women had just found him guilty of burglary.
9. On July 8, Rhonda Harmon attended a birthday party at a lounge on Princeton Street. She left at about midnight, and friends saw her get into a light-colored van.
   No one has seen or heard from her since.
10. An off-duty police officer thought she would take her family into a KFC restaurant for a bite to eat.
    But what she walked into was the middle of an armed robbery.
11. "You've had enough contact with the legal system." That's the message that Judge Bruce R. Levine today gave a man appearing before him for the third time this year.
12. Stopping for a picnic lunch Friday, Cindy Lowry began walking her horse toward a field off the trail. In seconds, they were covered with hundreds of stinging bees.
    Cindy survived. Her horse, Dan, did not.

Harcourt Brace & Company

E X E R C I S E   2

ALTERNATIVE LEADS

WRITING ALTERNATIVE LEADS

INSTRUCTIONS: Write only the leads for the following stories—but not routine summary leads. Instead, write the types of alternative leads described in this chapter.

1. There was a strange party in Los Angeles yesterday. The honoree wasn't there, however. He is Richard ("Dick") Hoglinn, a former employee of the Hughes Aircraft Co. Friends and former colleagues hold an annual party on behalf of Hoglinn, who worked as an aircraft engineer. He went to lunch one day and never came back. The party yesterday was held at Tequila Willie's Saloon & Grill. People at the party said the disappearance seven years ago of Hoglinn "symbolized rebellion against the corporate world." Some added that they themselves have sometimes thought of disappearing when the pressures of family and job begin to get to them. But Dick really did it. Some party-goers wore "Dick" masks. Hoglinn, still in his early 30s, left behind a wife of 12 years and two young children. Another employee reported spotting him at the Los Angeles International Airport around midnight the day he disappeared. Every year since the disappearance, Hughes employees celebrate the anniversary of his flight. The parties attract people who didn't even know Hoglinn.

2. Jill Laszlo is a psychologist at Michigan State University. She talked to you today about her primary area of research: how people spend their time. People are always talking about how busy they are, says Prof. Laszlo, but that may be bunk—a convenient excuse. For 25 years, she has been studying the way Americans spend their waking moments. She has found a steady increase in the amount of their free time. People feel that the work week has been increasing and leisure time has been decreasing. "In fact, since 1965," Laszlo reports, "men have gained seven hours of free time in a week, to 41 hours from 34 in a week. Women have gained six hours of free time, to 40, from 34." Yet people feel starved for time. Women, Laszlo adds, "have more free time than they did two decades ago, all of which has gone into watching television." TV now consumes 37% of the free time of American women and 39% of the free time of American men. There has always been a large segment of the population that feels rushed, she continued. But only in recent years has lack of time become a valid excuse, "a convenient cover-up." In response to a question you asked, Laszlo further stated, "Many people say they don't have time to read newspapers, but its just another way of saying they'd rather be doing something else."

3. For years, children everywhere have been hearing and reading "Little Red Riding Hood." Now, the story has become involved in a controversy in your city. As a result, it has been pulled from the recommended reading and discussion lists for all elementary school children. The book will remain in school libraries, but teachers will no longer read and discuss the tale with their students nor encourage their students to read it on their own. Why? The heroine has wine in the basket of goodies that she is bringing her ailing grandmother. "It gives the younger ones the wrong impression about alcohol," said Karen Johnsen, your school districts assistant superintendent for elementary instruction. "If they should refrain, why give them a story saying its OK?" School Board member Jane

Tribit agreed, saying, "I don't think the basket of wine is a good concept for kindergarten or first grade." She said she would rather see "a nice thing like cookies and cakes."

4. Two youngsters in your city have a pet rabbit. They are Shannon Simmons, 9, and her brother, Chris, 7. They are the children of Rachel and Wayne Simmons of 708 E. Lisa Lane. The rabbit, which they've named "Jimmy," lives in a cage in their fenced back-yard. Occasionally, they let Jimmy out to play in their house or yard. Most of their neighbors like Jimmy, too. But one of them lodged an anonymous complaint, saying Jimmy should go. Your citys Code Enforcement Board agrees. The Simmons were told today that they have 15 days to get rid of the rabbit. Mr. Simmons then got in touch with their county commissioner, Anne Chen, who says the order "is preposterous." Todd Drolshagen, head of your citys Code Enforcement Board, said: "We received a com-plaint, and we're required to enforce the law. It states that a family can't keep farm ani-mals in a residential neighborhood, and a rabbit is listed in the definition of farm animals. The problem is, where do you draw the line? One rabbit? Two rabbits? Six rab-bits? Two dozen rabbits?" Chen said, "I have a great appreciation for the circumstances, and I'm going back and trying to see what the intent of the Planning and Zoning Com-mission was way back when the ordinance was passed. Another option is getting the zoning regulations changed—modifying the ordinance to allow a family to keep a sin-gle pet rabbit in their home." Chen then added that, "The two children here paid for the rabbit with money their grandma sent them two Easters ago. The fact that they have had the rabbit for over two years makes them responsible owners. My Easter bunnies al-ways ran away in six months."

5. The U.S. governments Census Bureau issued some statistics today. In a report from Washington, it discussed the net worth of the richest Americans. It found that, by last year, 1 out of every 100 American families had a net worth of $1,000,000 dollars or more. That does not mean the families have an income of $1,000,000 dollars or more, but only that if they sold everything they owned and then paid their debts that they would have that amount left over. The report also drew a profile of the average Ameri-can millionaire. The average millionaire, it found, is an entrepreneur: a white male in his early 60s, married to his first wife, with a business "catering to the ordinary needs of his neighbors." Most millionaires are from middle-class or working-class backgrounds and worked hard to get their money: 10 to 12 hours a day, six days a week, for 30 years or more. Washington, D.C. was tops, with 1.7 millionaires for every 100 households. The state of Connecticut was next, with 1.6.

EXERCISE 3
ALTERNATIVE LEADS

PRO CHALLENGE

INSTRUCTIONS: Professionals have written alternative leads for the following stories. Write an alternative lead for each of the stories. When you finish, you can compare your work with the professionals'. Their leads appear in a manual available to your instructor. You may find, however, that you like some of your own and your classmates' leads better.

1. In many ways, it was a rather common robbery. Fortunately, the police succeeded in capturing the apparent perpetrator. This is the story. Employees at the First Union Bank, 3720 Kohlar Boulevard, pushed an alarm button at 2:38 p.m. yesterday after a lone man came into the bank and demanded money. The man said he had a sawed-off shotgun under his raincoat. A teller gave him money in a paper bag he carried. She also slipped in an exploding dye pack. Just as the man left the bank the pack detonated, and the man tossed the bag containing the money into the bushes. Witnesses said he then fled on foot. Officers started combing the area, looking for a man in a yellow shirt, blue jeans, and raincoat. They lifted the lid of a trash bin behind the McDonalds at 3782 Kohlar Blvd. and found him there. He was crouched among the half-eaten burgers and fries. Police identified him as Alan Franklin, age 23, of 820 Apollo Drive, Apartment #223.

2. Judge Samuel McGregor performed the unusual wedding Monday. He married Sunni McGrath and Wallace A. Svec. It wasn't a fancy wedding. There was no cake or dress or hugs, not even a kiss. They weren't allowed. Why? Because McGregor performed the wedding in his courtroom, minutes after sentencing McGrath to a years probation for drunken driving. Immediately after the wedding ceremony, the bride was ordered back to prison. She is serving time there for other crimes. Thus, their honeymoon will be delayed. "It was real different. But I feel really good because I love him to death," McGrath said from her jail cell yesterday afternoon. The two have dated for three years and said they wanted to marry to avoid problems with prison visitation rights and requirements. McGrath is scheduled to be released in three months, and the couple has plans for a traditional wedding—flower girl and all, at that time. At yesterdays ceremony a blue jail uniform served as her wedding gown. For security reasons—so they could not pass anything to one another (notes, drugs, weapons, or anything)—an attorney stood between the couple as they exchanged vows. The couple longed to kiss. The judge suggested that they wave instead. They did. They also blew kisses. McGrath said she planned to spend her wedding night watching television. Svec wasn't certain what he would do. Because McGrath was already on probation for burglary, grand theft and possession of cocaine, the arrest for drunken driving resulted in her being returned to jail. She said she committed the other crimes to support a drug habit which she said she has kicked.

3. It was 12:40 a.m. today and the incident occurred at a home located at 4772 E. Harrison Ave. Two men were involved: Michael Uosis and Edward Beaumont, 40. Uosis lives in the home and, a few weeks ago, was robbed. This morning Uosis heard someone banging at a window of his home. He thought it was the man who had robbed him, coming back to rob him again. So Uosis went to a closet, got out a .38-caliber revolver and fired a single shot at the window. Uosis said he didn't see anyone and didn't mean to shoot

anyone and only fired the gun to scare away whoever was outside. "I didn't mean to shoot him," Uosis said. "He was a good friend, and I didn't know it was him outside. I didn't even see who it was outside." Neither the police nor Uosis know why Beaumont, who used to work with Uosis, both as postal workers, until Uosis retired three years ago, had gone to the house at 12:40 a.m. Beaumont is in serious condition in the intensive care unit at Regional Medical Center. Hospital officials said that Beaumont may be paralyzed as a result of the gunshot wound to his head. Police charged Uosis with aggravated battery, and he was released from the city jail after posting $2,500 bail. If convicted, he could be sentenced to as much as 15 years in prison and fined up to $10,000. Under state law, it is illegal for a resident to use unnecessary force against an intruder unless the resident is defending himself or another occupant of the home against death or great bodily harm.

4. There was another burglary in the city. A pair of burglars struck VFW Post #40 at 640 Sherwood Dr. Both burglars appeared to be teenagers. Janitor Steven Cowles heard them. Cowles, age 70, didn't catch them, however. He said, "I'm getting old, and it would have been a chore catching up with them. They lit out." Cowles went to work at the VFW post at about 5 a.m. today and almost tripped and fell over two knapsacks filled with expensive liquor and cigarettes from the post. "I knew something was funny. Then here's those two kids coming around the corner by the popcorn machine," he said. "I let out a big noise and said a few things. I had two loaves of stale bread for the ducks I feed every morning and an old box of Entenmann's sticky buns. I started hitting them with the bread, and then I threw the buns at them. That's when they dropped everything and ran. I went to a phone and called the cops."

5. The drama started when Lillian Sodergreen parked her car and ran into the supermarket to buy a gallon of milk and other groceries. She told her son in the back seat to sit still and be quiet while she was gone. Her daughter was already sleeping. She said it is the last time she will leave the children alone. The admitted criminal is Troy Dysart, 21. Troy is a car thief and admits it. He insists, however, that he is not a kidnapper. He wanted a car to steal for a joy-ride and, at approximately 8:30 a.m. Tuesday, noticed a car left running, with the keys in the ignition, parked outside a supermarket: Albertsons at 4240 Michigan Street. Normally, he's careful. "There are rules to follow," he explained in an interview with you in his cell in the city jail. "My number one rule is: 'Make sure you don't get more than you bargained for.'" But he was "moving too fast," he said. So he didn't see the children in the back seat: Troy Sodergreen, age 4, and his little sister, Jena, age 8 months. "I saw the keys and got in, but I didn't notice the kids," he continued. He peeled out of the supermarkets parking lot. "When I turn around the corner, I looked to my side and saw the little girl lying on the seat, and then another kid. I saw the kids and say, 'Oh, damn.' I freaked out and parked the car." Dysart is now charged with grand theft and kidnapping. He added, "I didn't want nothing to do with the kids. I didn't touch the kids. My wife has three kids. I don't need no more kids. I'm going to tell the judge the same thing. He can charge me, but I didn't know they were there. Why would I want more kids?" The children were unharmed.

Harcourt Brace & Company

CHAPTER 7

THE BODY OF A NEWS STORY

When you can't find anything wrong with the story you've written, there is something wrong with you. There never has been a story that couldn't be improved upon. When you're having trouble finding fault with your own stuff, reflect how easy it is to criticize anyone else's.

(Morton Sontheimer, "Newspaperman")

The portion of a news story that follows the lead is called the "body." It contains the information a reporter believes readers need to know. The information can be presented in two basic styles: inverted pyramid or narrative. As this chapter will explain, the former packages data in an orderly manner, and the latter tells a story. Neither technique works better with all readers, all stories or all reporters. Both styles require thorough reporting. To be effective, reporters must include a story's facts while also making the story interesting. Both styles of organization require reporters to present the facts and connect the information with effective transitions.

Think of writing a news story as driving a train along a track. The rails give the story direction, while the railroad ties—who, what, when, where, why and how—provide a foundation. The train's engine is the lead; it must be powerful enough to pull the rest of the story. Like the whistle of the engine, a story's lead must capture the reader's attention. Each car that follows the lead represents a paragraph containing information and providing structure. The cars (paragraphs) can be arranged in any sequence—for example, from most important to least or chronologically—that seems most effective. The train is strengthened when research, verification, multiple sources, quotes, anecdotes and descriptions fill the cars. The amount of information needed to complete the story decides the number of cars in the train. Holding the train cars together are couplings, which represent the transitions between paragraphs of information. Without strong transitions (couplings) the paragraphs, and consequently the story (train), disconnect from each other.

This chapter discusses the two styles of writing and the techniques reporters need to write effective bodies for their news stories.

THE INVERTED PYRAMID STYLE

Reporters using the inverted pyramid style of writing normally summarize a story in the lead and present the facts in descending order of importance. Consequently, they place the story's most important details in the second paragraph. They continue to add details in decreasing order of importance. Each paragraph presents additional information: names, descriptions, quotations, conflicting viewpoints, explanations and background data. Beginning reporters must learn this style because it helps them to structure the way they think: to decide what is most important and what is least important. It also helps reporters discover "holes" in their information—details that have not been collected and need to be found.

The primary advantage of the inverted pyramid style is that it allows someone to stop reading a story after only one or two paragraphs. Doing so still allows that person to learn the story's most important details. The inverted pyramid style also ensures that all the facts are immediately understandable. Moreover, if a story is too long, editors can easily shorten it by deleting one or more paragraphs from the end.

The inverted pyramid style has several disadvantages. First, because the lead summarizes facts that later paragraphs discuss in greater detail, some of those facts may be repeated in the body. Second, a story that follows the inverted pyramid style rarely contains any surprises; the lead immediately reveals every major detail. Third, the style makes some stories more complex and more difficult to write. Fourth, readers with less than a high school education cannot easily understand stories written in this style. Fifth, the style locks reporters into a formula and discourages them from trying new styles. "If you go out looking just for an inverted pyramid," says Jane Foy, a writing consultant, "you're just sitting there like a goldfish waiting to be fed the lead."

Many writing coaches discourage the use of the inverted pyramid, saying it is overused, confusing and often irrelevant. Because newsrooms traditionally use the style, however, it is a difficult habit to break. Daily deadline pressures also encourage its use, because coming up with new styles requires additional thinking and, perhaps, more rewriting.

If two cars collide and several people are injured, an inverted pyramid story about the accident might contain the following sequence of paragraphs:

Lead . . . . .Summarizes the story
Paragraph Two . . . . .Identifies the injured
Paragraph Three . . . . .Explains how the accident occurred
Paragraph Four . . . . .Reports charges filed against driver(s)
Paragraphs Five, Six, Seven . . . . .Quotes driver(s), police officer(s) and witness(es)
Paragraph Eight . . . . .Describes unusual damage to the cars
Paragraph Nine . . . . .Describes traffic problems caused by the accident
Paragraph 10 . . . . .Presents minor details

Normally, news media emphasize either the role that people play in a story or the story's impact on the lives of those people. Consequently, paragraph two identifies the injured people. Damage to the cars, a much less important fact, is reported later. Notice that if the damage was not unusual, the story might not mention it. Paragraph three describes the accident itself—the recent action and main point of the story. Quotations, such as those used in paragraphs five, six and seven, add detail and color as well as a pleasing change of pace. Paragraphs eight, nine and 10 are less essential and might be deleted if space is limited.

Not every reporter would present all the facts in the same order; some variation is inevitable. However, most reporters would begin with a summary lead, followed by the most important of the remaining facts. Usually that means the victims' identity, particularly if they were seriously injured, and a description of the accident.

As another example of the inverted pyramid style, imagine that the police in your community arrested three high school students and charged them with auto theft. A newspaper reporter might present the details in the following order:

1. Three students admitted last night that they stole a dozen cars from a faculty parking lot at Wilson High School.
2. Police arrested the youths after noticing a stolen car parked near a theater on Palmer Avenue. The youths were arrested when they returned to the car at 11:15 p.m. after watching a movie.
3. The youths, all sophomores at the school, admitted stealing 12 cars during the past year, according to police.
4. Each youth was charged with 12 counts of auto theft and released to the custody of his or her parents. They are scheduled to appear in Juvenile Court at 11 a.m. Monday.
5. Principal John Blanchard said the school administration was baffled by the thefts, which continued to occur even after security was improved at the parking lot.

6. All the cars were recovered within a week of being stolen. However, one was badly damaged in an accident, and some parts were stripped from the others.
7. Police did not identify the youths because they are juveniles.

Notice how the leads in the following stories summarize their topics, and how the second and third paragraphs present their most important details. Neither story ends with a summary or conclusion; instead, the final paragraphs present the least important details. The stories are cohesive because their leads summarize their main topics and because each of the subsequent paragraphs presents additional information about those topics:

Burglars took an estimated $4,000 worth of appliances and jewelry from a home at 1424 Balchner Drive late Sunday morning.

The owners, Linda and Henry Ruiz, returned home at noon after taking their four children to church. They found a back door pried open and the house ransacked.

"I didn't know what to think," Linda Ruiz said. "The house was a mess, and we were afraid the burglars were still inside. It was really quite scary."

The burglars took a television set, a stereo, two cameras, jewelry and several kitchen appliances.

Neighbors said they saw an unfamiliar van parked in the driveway of the home at 11 a.m.

A new survey found that Americans believe a happy family life is more important than a good income or satisfactory sex life.

Newsweek magazine conducted the survey and found that 48 percent of its respondents said that a happy family is essential to their lives.

By comparison, 29 percent said a good income is essential, and 24 percent said a satisfactory sex life is essential.

Twenty-one percent rated a clean and healthy environment a top priority, 17 percent mentioned their friends, and 15 percent mentioned their home.

"We were surprised at the results," said Jeremiah Voll, one of the pollsters. "They seem to reflect a change from the self-centeredness of the 1980s. Today's adults seem to realize that not everyone can climb to the top of the career ladder. And once you're there, it's not necessarily as satisfying as people expect."

The respondents were asked six questions and given four options for answering each question: "essential," "very important but not essential," "somewhat important" or "not important at all."

The results are based upon a telephone survey of 1,240 adults in all 50 states.

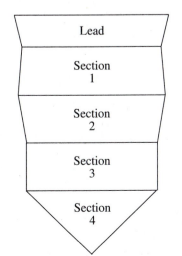

Many of the facts reported in longer news stories are of approximately equal importance. Those stories are more likely to resemble the diagram shown at the left rather than the perfect triangle shown on Page 160. Immediately after the diagram's summary lead, Section 1 presents several paragraphs that contain information of roughly equal importance. Those paragraphs may present some additional information about a single topic, or information about several different but related subtopics. Section 2 presents other details in descending order of importance, and Section 3 presents more facts of about equal importance to one another but of less importance than the facts in Section 2. Section 4 contains the least important details, perhaps routine procedures, background information or a reminder of some related incidents that occurred in the past.

Harcourt Brace & Company

THE NARRATIVE STYLE

A narrative has two components: a story and a storyteller. A storyteller writes much like a playwright or novelist, depicting people interacting with other people and within their surroundings. To write in the narrative style, a reporter must find people who are crucial to the story and record their actions. This technique requires more than just interviewing sources, recording quotes and reporting numbers. It requires observation.

Observation does not mean reporters are free to interject their opinions in a story. It means that, if reporters observe how people important to a story act, and include those details in their stories, the reader can get a better sense of what is occurring. To paint a picture with words, reporters must be specific. That means gathering extra details as part of the recording process. Notice the difference between the following sentences:

> The principal hates what the teacher said about the school.

> While the teacher spoke, the principal left the room shaking his head.

The first sentence presents an opinion. Without using attribution it says the principal hated the teacher's comments. The reader does not know if the writer is reporting fact or the reporter's opinion. The second sentence, however, shows the principal's negative behavior in response to the teacher's comments.

The narrative approach allows reporters to be more creative. Reporters can describe the drama—even if it is not high drama—that took place at a school board meeting, for example. What happened? What did they see? Were people shouting? Were people laughing? Did an exchange take place? Reporters cannot answer these questions and others unless they take extensive notes.

Long-time writing coach Don Fry describes the style this way:

> Narrative writing requires narrative thinking, narrative reporting and narrative forms.

> Narrative thinking means seeing the world in terms of people doing things, not as piles of disparate facts. Actions connect to one another to create meaning, mostly based on human motives. The best journalistic storytellers let their curiosity lead them into stories, because they want to find out why real people do things.

Narrative writing still leads with the news—the most important part of the story—but it gets to the storytelling right away, using conflict, flashbacks, chronology and dialogue. Generally, such stories have a beginning, a middle and an end, each of relatively equal importance. It is more difficult to cut the final paragraphs of narrative stories than of stories written in the inverted pyramid style.

The following story is the example from Page 160 written in a narrative style:

> For three youths, their last joy ride was to see the new James Bond movie. Police charged the Wilson High School students with 12 counts of auto theft. Police accused them of stealing cars from a faculty parking lot at the school.
> "We were just having fun," said one student before he was placed in a police cruiser.
> "Yeah, we just like different cars," said another, as he was led to a second waiting cruiser. "Our parents wouldn't let us use theirs, and the faculty drive some really nice cars."
> The third student refused to comment, but police said all three confessed to the thefts.
> Some moviegoers coming for the second showing of the Bond movie thought the flashing blue police lights were part of the theater's promotion of the movie. "I can't believe the police were actually arresting someone," Sarah Kindstrom said.

Harcourt Brace & Company

Police arrested the three, all sophomores, when they walked out of The Strand Theater on Sunday and entered the stolen car, which was parked on Palmer Avenue. Detective Myron Neely said an officer on routine patrol spotted the white Toyota Camry, which matched the description of one stolen Saturday while its owner was directing a school play.

"At least this car hasn't been damaged," Neely said. All the other cars, although recovered within a week of being stolen, were marred. One was badly damaged in an accident, and parts had been stripped from the others.

"We are happy this rash of thefts has been solved," principal John Blanchard said. "But we're disappointed the thefts were apparently caused by some of our own students."

"One of the students was in my class," said teacher Tina M. Alvarez, who was called to the scene to identify her car, the most recent to be stolen in the year-long crime spree. "She was a good student. I can't believe she would be a part of this."

"It is baffling," Blanchard added, shaking his head.

The thefts continued even after security at the parking lot was improved 10 months ago. The school district added lights, closed one entrance to the lot and asked the police to cruise the area more regularly.

All three students, whose names were not released, are scheduled to appear in Juvenile Court at 11 a.m. Monday.

While narrative style can be a refreshing change from the inverted pyramid style, it is not appropriate for all stories.

WRITING THE SECOND PARAGRAPH

The second paragraph in a news story is almost as important as the lead—and almost as difficult to write. Like the lead, the second paragraph should emphasize the news. In addition, the second paragraph should provide a smooth, logical transition from the lead to the following paragraphs.

While writing their stories' second paragraphs, some reporters fail to emphasize the news. Other reporters fail to provide smooth transitions. As a result, their stories seem dull or disorganized. The following pages discuss both these problems and present some solutions.

Avoid Leapfrogging

Reporters often refer to an individual in their lead and begin their second paragraph with a name. However, many reporters fail to clearly link the two: to say that the individual referred to in their lead is the person named in their second paragraph. Readers are forced to guess, to make that assumption. They will usually guess right—but not always.

This problem is so common that it has a name: "leapfrogging." To avoid it, provide a one- or two-word transition from the lead to a name in the second paragraph:

LEAPFROGGING: A 55-year-old man wept Wednesday after a Circuit Court jury found him innocent of burglary and sexual battery.

Gary Lee Phillips was arrested two months ago.

REVISED: A 55-year-old man wept Wednesday after a Circuit Court jury found him innocent of burglary and sexual battery.

The defendant, Gary Lee Phillips, was arrested two months ago.

Continue with the News

After providing a smooth transition between the lead and the second paragraph, continue with the news: more information about the topic summarized in your lead. Mistakenly, some reporters shift to a different topic, a decision certain to confuse their readers:

> CORVALLIS, Ore.—The police spend more of their time responding to domestic squabbles than to any other type of call.
>
> Merritt Tendall has been the police chief in Corvallis for 15 years. He has seen many wrecks and much crime, but says he never wanted any other job.
>
> REVISED: CORVALLIS, Ore.—The police spend more of their time responding to domestic squabbles than to any other type of call.
>
> "We hate those calls," said Police Chief Merritt Tendall, who has been chief 15 years. "You never know what to expect. It's my biggest problem. We settle most of the disputes in a few minutes. But people get angry and irrational, and some take their anger out on us."

Before revision, the story seems to discuss two different topics. The lead summarizes a problem that confronts police officers everywhere: family disputes. The second paragraph shifts to the police chief's career and goals. It fails even to mention the problem of family disputes.

Names, Names—Dull, Dull

Reporters sometimes place too much emphasis on their sources' identities. As a result, their second paragraphs fail to convey any information of interest to readers. Note how the following example can be revised to emphasize the news—what the source said, saw or did, not who he is:

> A construction worker was killed Monday afternoon when a gust of wind toppled the frame for a new apartment building on Conway Road.
>
> An electrician, Dodge Hewitt of Beatty Electrical Supply, was killed in the mishap.
>
> Julian Prevatte, a carpenter for John McCormack & Sons, was an eyewitness to the accident.
>
> REVISED: The frame for a new apartment building collapsed Monday, killing a construction worker at a Conway Road site.
>
> A gust of wind toppled a wall, which fell on electrician Dodge Hewitt, striking him on the head. He died before emergency crews could reach him.
>
> Julian Prevatte, a carpenter at the site, said he tried to warn the victim when the frame began to collapse. However, the noise made by a saw drowned out his shouts.

Background: Too Much, Too Soon

Avoid devoting your entire second paragraph to background information. The second paragraph in the following story is dull because it emphasizes routine, insignificant details:

> On a typical day, Meals on Wheels delivers 720 meals to the city's shut-ins.
>
> Lucinda Nankin, community relations director for Meals on Wheels, said, "Providing services and identifying resources to enable the homebound and elderly to remain independent has been the role of Meals on Wheels for 30 years."

The story shifts from the news—the number of meals that Meals on Wheels delivers to your city's shut-ins—to the organization's purpose. Yet that purpose has not changed since Meals on Wheels was established 30 years ago. Thus, the second paragraph says nothing new, nothing likely to retain readers' interest in the story. Fortunately, the problem is easy to correct:

On a typical day, Meals on Wheels delivers 720 meals to the city's shut-ins.

But a typical day is hard to describe, said Lucinda Nankin, community relations director for the organization. Making sure the proper food gets to each individual can be a nightmare. Also, the number of meals fluctuates from day to day.

"There always seems to be something that makes it challenging to deliver the meals," she said. "Some days it's as simple as having to deal with bad weather. Other days, people refuse to open the door to a stranger."

In the revision, the second paragraph describes a "typical" day and explains that the number of meals fluctuates—details central to the story, not minor or unnecessary ones.

The second paragraph in the following story is strong. It continues with the news: the main point summarized in the lead (the story's action and other important details). The story's second paragraph contains no minor details, unnecessary names or background information:

Laura Goldfarb wiped the tears from her eyes Wednesday as she told a judge and jury how she was tied up and robbed in her home two years ago.

Goldfarb said she was drinking a cup of tea after lunch when she heard a knock at the back door. As she unlatched the door, a man pushed it open, pointed a gun at her chest and ordered her to remain silent.

IMPROVING YOUR SENTENCES: A BRIEF REVIEW

Write naturally, the way you talk. Be clear and direct. No one would use the following sentences in a casual conversation with friends, yet beginning reporters used them in news stories:

Killed in the accident was a 7-year-old girl.

The vehicle damage is estimated to be $4,000.

Angry words were exchanged between the two drivers.

The sentences are awkward because they fail to use the normal word order: subject, verb and direct object. Moreover, all three use passive verb forms: "was," "is" and "were." Here are two more examples and their revisions:

The team's victory was witnessed by only 17 spectators.
REVISED: Seventeen spectators witnessed the team's victory.

Editors are looking for qualities in reporters that include creativity and aggressiveness.
REVISED: Editors want reporters who are creative and aggressive.

Shorten Your Sentences

Beginners use sentences that are too long and complicated. Yet the longer a sentence, the more difficult it is to understand. Moreover, when too many ideas are crammed into a sentence, no idea receives the clarity and emphasis it deserves.

As you read the following sentences, you are likely to stop and start again, because both sentences contain more ideas than most readers can absorb at a glance. Reread each sentence and count the number of ideas it contains:

UNICEF officials, who have found that 40,000 children die each day, mostly in developing countries, call the death toll "the greatest single stain on our civilization today," and are asking for an unprecedented world summit to save the lives of an estimated 100 million children in the next decade by, during each of the next 10 years, taking the money spent in a single day on the world's military forces and reallocating that money to feed the hungry.

Number of ideas in the sentence: _____

Judge Marilyn Picott today threw out a manslaughter charge halfway through the trial of a teen-age girl accused of killing her stepfather, Fritz Walker, as he beat her mother, ruling that the girl had every right to shoot him after coming home from high school and seeing her parents in a bloody knife fight and her younger brothers and sisters screaming in terror.

Number of ideas in the sentence: _____

Readers may count up to 12 ideas in the first sentence, and 10 in the second. To make your sentences more readable, make them shorter:

Forty thousand children, mostly in developing countries, die each day, according to UNICEF officials. Officials call the death toll "the greatest single stain on our civilization today." UNICEF plans to ask world leaders to reallocate money spent on military forces to feed the hungry. The officials estimate that they could save the lives of 100 million children in the next decade if, each year, they take the money spent in a single day on the world's military forces and use that money to help the hungry.

A teen-age girl accused of killing her stepfather, Fritz Walker, was released today. Judge Marilyn Picott ruled that the girl was justified in shooting Walker.

After coming home from school, the girl saw her parents in a bloody knife fight and heard her younger brothers and sisters screaming in terror. Walker had a history of spouse abuse. Picott's action came halfway through the girl's trial on a manslaughter charge.

A sentence does not have to be long to be overloaded. If the ideas it contains are unrelated, as in the following examples, even a very short sentence may have to be divided:

Born in New Hampshire, he has red hair.

Petrowski, who has a wife and six stepdaughters, was elected mayor by only 27 votes: 382,917 to 382,890.

Avoid Choppy Sentences

A few writers go to the opposite extreme, using a series of very short, simple sentences. Although a typical sentence or paragraph should be short and simple, some variety is necessary to keep paragraphs from becoming too choppy and repetitive, as in the following example:

The youth was sentenced to prison at 9:45 a.m. today. The judge was C.R. Revere. The youth's attorney immediately appealed his conviction. The state Court of Appeals reversed the sentence. The youth was freed at 4:45 p.m.

REVISED: Seven hours after his conviction, a youth walked out of jail. The state Court of Appeals said his trial was filled with errors that infringed on his rights. The youth went to jail at 9:45 a.m. Following an immediate appeal by his attorney, the youth was freed at 4:45 p.m. The appeals court reversed Judge C.R. Revere's decision.

Vary your sentence length. Remember, however, that long sentences should be uncomplicated, and it is better to make sentences too short than too long.

Also vary your wording so that successive sentences and paragraphs do not begin with the same words, or with very similar words. When writing a story about a government report, for example, you may be tempted to begin several paragraphs in a row with words like: "The report said . . ." "The report added . . ." "It said . . ." "The report also said . . ." "It continued . . ." and

Harcourt Brace & Company

"The report concluded . . ." But if every sentence or paragraph begins with the same or very similar words, your story will be dull and repetitious.

USING TRANSITIONS

Transitions help stories move from one fact to the next in a smooth, logical order. Again, think of your story as a train. The engine is your lead, and each car that follows is a paragraph. The couplings that hold the cars together are your transitions. Reporters introduce new ideas by relating them to ideas reported earlier in a story. Often, the natural progression of thought, or sequence of facts and action, is adequate. Or reporters may repeat a key name or pronoun:

> The company's president, Eva *Stoudnaurer*, opposed the plan. *Stoudnaurer* said the company cannot afford to construct a new plant.

> *Lt. Lee Marey* said the Navy is a small, elite force that offers an effective deterrent to nuclear war.
> *She* added that submarines have become more important than battleships and aircraft carriers.

The first example repeats the name of the company president. In the second example, the pronoun "she" refers to the lieutenant mentioned in the preceding paragraph. Reporters can also repeat other key words, ideas or phrases:

> Richard *Nolles*, editor of the Weekly Outlook, said the *newspaper* tries to report the truth even when its *readers* do not want to hear it.
> "*A newspaper* that reports only what its *readers* want to hear is dodging its moral obligations," *Nolles* said.
> In a speech Wednesday, *Nolles* added that many *readers* want to avoid unpleasant news, and threaten to cancel their subscriptions when he reports it.
> "But if a problem exists, *they* need to know about it so *they* can correct it," he said.
> "Ignorant citizens can't make wise decisions."

Transitional Words

You can sometimes use a single word to lead your readers from one idea to the next. Many of the transitional words you use are likely to refer to the time: words such as "earlier" and "later," "before" and "after," "promptly" and "tardy." Other common transitional words are:

Time

delayed	meanwhile	once
eventually	next	seldom
finally	now	sometimes
formerly	occasionally	soon
frequently	often	then

You may also provide a time transition by using the hour, day of the week, month, season, year, decade or century ("an hour later," "the previous Saturday" and so on).

Other types and examples of linkage words include:

Additions

again	beyond	new
also	extra	other
another	furthermore	together
besides	moreover	too

Causations

accordingly	hence	then
because	since	therefore
consequently	so	thus

Comparisons

agreeing	identical	opposite
conflicting	inconsistent	related
contrary	like	separately
different	objecting	similarly

Contrasts

although	however	still
but	if	until
conversely	nevertheless	while
despite	simply	without
exactly	solely	yet

There are also dozens of phrases that you can use as transitions, to move the story along from one idea to another. Examples include:

along with	for instance	in other business
as a result of	for that reason	on the contrary
aside from	in addition	on the other hand
at last	in an earlier	until then
at the same time	in another	years earlier
due to	in contrast	with the exception of
for example	in other action	

Transitional Sentences

Transitional sentences link paragraphs that contain diverse ideas, but the sentences should do more than report that another idea was "introduced" or "discussed." They should present some interesting details about the new topic so readers will be motivated to finish the story. Mistakenly, beginners often use vague generalities. A good transitional sentence often summarizes the topic it introduces, revealing whatever was said or done about it. The following paragraphs then discuss the topic in more detail:

> He also discussed the television coverage of the president's funeral.
> REVISED: He said the television coverage of the president's funeral was misleading.

> He also talked about the city's schools.
> REVISED: He said the city's schools are too old and overcrowded.

Here are two examples of weak transitions, which fail to say anything likely to sustain readers' interest in the topic:

> The board also heard the concerns of a school bus driver.

> She then presented information about the cost of maintaining the museum.

Here are two stronger transitional sentences that are more specific and interesting:

> A school bus driver told the board that bad weather causes most delays.

> The cost of maintaining the museum will increase 7 percent next year.

Harcourt Brace & Company

Questions as Transitions

Like leads, transitional sentences occasionally take the form of questions. The questions should be short and, as in the following examples, should be immediately followed by their answers—the new details or topics that reporters want to introduce:

> Where does she get the ideas for her books?
> "People," she said. "Most people can give you a good story. And I talk to everyone."

> Forty-seven percent of the students enrolled in the university will earn a degree within the next six years, according to Robert McMahon, director of the Office of Institutional Research.
> What about the other 53 percent? They will drop out or transfer to another institution.
> Why? A study just completed by McMahon found that most students who drop out of school accept full-time jobs, get married, have children or say they lack the money needed to continue their education.

AVOIDING CONCLUSIONS

A well-written story includes all the information readers need to understand the subject. That means readers get just the right amount of material—not too much, not too little. When experienced reporters have nothing more to add, they stop.

Avoid Stating Opinions and Mentioning Additional Topics

Resist the temptation to end news stories with a summary, conclusion or opinion of any kind. Again, think of your story as a train. Just as trains no longer end with cabooses, news stories do not need conclusions. The following are inappropriate:

> Is Miss Roth a good teacher? We certainly believe so.

> The remainder of the meeting was concerned primarily with the complaints and comments of those present about conditions at the hospital. Also discussed were some suggestions on ways those conditions could be improved.

The first example contains an opinion rather than a fact. If the story was well written, and if it clearly described Miss Roth, her performance and her students' reaction to her, readers should not have to be told she is a good teacher. Facts reported earlier in the story should have made that obvious. The second example introduces an idea never discussed in the story. It fails to describe specifically the conditions that disturbed people and the suggestions made to improve those conditions. Every topic mentioned in news stories must be fully explained, including topics mentioned in final paragraphs.

The second problem is a common one. As students approach a story's concluding paragraphs, many simply *mention* the story's final topics without reporting what was said or done about them. Here are two examples:

> Zoning was the final topic on the council's agenda.

> After concluding his speech, Nader answered the audience's questions.

Remember, your readers were not there. As a newswriter, you have an obligation to inform, not confuse. If a topic is important enough for you to mention, you should provide enough details to

Harcourt Brace & Company

inform your readers about it. These examples fail to do so. The first example mentions "zoning," but fails to present any specific details about it or to summarize the council's discussion and action. The second example fails to report the specific questions and answers. Thus, it does not present any meaningful information to readers.

Ignore the Routine and Unimportant

Reporters sometimes mistakenly end their stories by telling what did not happen. A list of everything that did not happen today would be endless; by tomorrow, the list would be dull and repetitious. Thus, as you write a story's final paragraphs, avoid the temptation to report that:

No one was killed.

No charges were filed.

No one else was injured.

The burglar has not been caught.

No one saw the car's license number.

No one was able to describe the thief.

Police searched the area but found nothing.

Similarly, an alert reporter or editor would eliminate the following conclusions because they state the obvious:

Police are looking for the thief.

The victim said she hopes to get well soon.

City officials said they are proud of the program's success.

Don't End Your Story Too Soon

Some stories end too quickly. When you write a news story, be thorough. Assume your editor has allowed enough space or time for every important detail to be printed or broadcast. If you are uncertain about whether a fact is important enough to be included in a story, place that fact in the story's final paragraph. If your editor (or instructor) considers the fact unimportant, it can easily be deleted. If you fail to include an important fact, you may have difficulty adding it later.

ALTERNATE STYLES

Although most news stories follow either the inverted pyramid or the narrative style, several alternatives are available.

Chronological Order

Reporters tell some stories in chronological order. This natural sequence of events creates a smooth, logical flow of ideas. This passage appeared in a news story that Newsday, a daily on Long Island, N.Y., published about the Challenger space shuttle disaster:

. . . But then at 11:38 a.m., the gleaming ship rose from a new launch pad, a majestic 700-foot stream of snow-white vapor trailing behind. Onlookers cheered, as is the custom at space shots, and a NASA spokesman described the progress of the flight.

Challenger reached a speed of 1,977 mph—three times that of sound—and was 10.4 miles over the Florida terrain. Mission Control in Houston sent the routine order: "Challenger, go throttle up."

Commander Francis (Dick) Scobee increased power to the main engines as planned and then spoke what proved to be his final words: "Roger, go throttle up."

At that point, officials said, Challenger, one of four U.S. space shuttles, was to enter a period when maximum force would be brought to bear on the vehicle by atmospheric conditions and wind force.

Television viewers then were able to see flames racing toward the space vehicle from an aft section, in the area of the craft's solid-fuel booster rockets. Almost immediately there was a titanic explosion, and Challenger, which had been carrying 526,000 gallons of highly volatile propellant, began rapid disintegration.

A space center employee watching the flight said in horror: "It's too soon. It's too soon. It can't be separation (of the boosters)." Another said simply: "I can't believe it. . . ."

Especially when writing a brief, dramatic story, you can begin with a summary lead, provide a short transition, then report all the remaining details in chronological order. The transition can be brief—often just four or five words, as in these examples:

Witnesses gave this account:

A passenger described the accident:

Here is a complete story that uses this technique. All the students in a reporting class interviewed a young woman who witnessed a shooting, and one student wrote the following account. Notice that she summarizes the story in the lead, provides a brief transition, then tells the remainder of the story in chronological order:

A sheriff's deputy shot and killed a young man outside a Pizza Hut on Thomasville Avenue Monday afternoon.

The shooting occurred in front of dozens of witnesses in the restaurant. One of the witnesses, 28-year-old Lillian Dysart, described the events:

"I was having dinner with my boyfriend in the Pizza Hut when I noticed two men and a woman talking with two sheriff's deputies in the parking lot. The men were being loud and boisterous, and the deputies were trying to get them to leave. My boyfriend, Mike, recognized one of the deputies and went out to see if he could help.

"Suddenly, one of the men pulled a knife and cut a deputy in the face. I went to help and, when I got outside, I could see the other deputy had drawn his gun and was pointing it at the man, saying, 'Stay back and drop the knife.' The man lunged at the deputy, who then shot him in the chest."

The assailant was pronounced dead at Memorial Regional Medical Center. The Sheriff's Department did not immediately identify him.

The injured deputy, Laurie Anne Slater, was released from a hospital Tuesday morning.

The following story is more unusual. It is told entirely in chronological order, without a summary lead:

Michael quickly realized that A Place for Us wasn't the place for him.

Overweight and suffering from stress, the New Yorker had flown to Los Angeles to attend what was advertised as a weight-loss clinic in sunny Southern California.

Harcourt Brace & Company

The air fare was free, and the treatment, he was told, was fully covered by his Blue Cross plan.

But when Michael reached Los Angeles, he was shocked to find himself booked into a psychiatric hospital in a run-down section of suburban Bellflower, where he was diagnosed as suffering from psychotic depression and bulimia—conditions he denies ever having.

Then he was told he could not leave.

(Los Angeles Times)

Tips from a Pro

ALTERNATE STYLES

Professional reporters wrote the following stories. Both stories are effective, yet neither uses newspapers' traditional inverted pyramid style. The first story is presented informally, and as a series of unfortunate coincidences. The second story is reported in chronological order.

HOMESTEAD, Fla. (AP)—"Hey," Luther Germantown said to his family, "why don't we all take a nice drive to Disney World for Christmas?" "Great idea," everybody said. "We'll have a fine time."

It didn't exactly work out that way.

Germantown and eight family members started out Friday in two cars hauling two campers for a Christmas weekend at Disney World.

Then:

- The bolts holding the transmission onto his car fell out.
- He lost some of the replacement bolts.
- The drive gear went, and the car was towed to a Fort Pierce transmission shop.
- The transmission shop, Germantown learned the next day, was closed for the weekend. While trying to recover the keys he had slipped under the door, he set off a burglar alarm.
- After explaining the situation to suspicious police officers, he had the car towed to another transmission shop. But after workers told him it couldn't be fixed for days, he took the limping car back on the highway.
- It caught fire.
- The car was towed again (this is the third time, if you're counting) to another shop, and this time it was fixed, sort of.
- Back on the highway, the muffler fell apart, and the radiator hose, weakened by the small fire, ruptured.
- Giving up, Germantown and family returned home. The car was towed there (fourth time).
- They found that the house had been burglarized of more than $400 worth of tools.

The following story appeared in a special section published by The Milwaukee Journal. "Each year," The Journal explained, "hundreds of thousands of people die of heart disease. Many of those deaths could be prevented by timely treatment using medical techniques not available until recent years."

Joseph Krushas awoke at 4 a.m. on the day that almost became the last day of his life.

"I just didn't feel right," the 55-year-old assistant principal at Forest Home Avenue Elementary School recalled of that morning, Sunday, Feb. 1.

"I just felt uncomfortable. There was no burning in my chest or shortness of breath or sweating. I lay down but I couldn't get comfortable. I woke up my wife and told her to take me to the hospital."

She drove him to Community Memorial Hospital of Menomonee Falls, where initial tests did not disclose any problems. He was admitted to the intensive care unit as a precaution.

About 8 a.m., he began to die. His face suddenly got hot. A severe, crushing chest pain followed. His face turned gray, he began to sweat profusely, and his blood pressure began dropping. His blood pressure dipped to 60; normally it would be twice that high. It was well below the level of shock.

Tests showed he was in the throes of a massive heart attack affecting his heart's left pumping chamber. David E. Engle, a cardiologist who happened to be in the hospital at the time, took over the case. The entire front and side of the chamber showed a serious injury, Engle said.

"I brought his wife into a room and frankly told her he was in the middle of a heart attack, that things were not going well and that he might die," Engle recounted.

At the same time, he ordered that Krushas get intravenous streptokinase, a drug that can dissolve blood clots. The aim was to break up the presumed clot in one of the three coronary arteries feeding his heart.

Exactly 30 minutes later, Engle noticed evidence on the electrocardiogram that Krushas' heart was getting normal blood flow.

"I turned to him and asked him how he felt," Engle said. "He said at that moment the chest pain began to ease. His blood pressure at that point began to rise and came back to normal. We did an EKG a short time later and found it was normal."

Engle had Krushas transferred to St. Joseph's Hospital, which has a complete catheterization laboratory and backup surgery team. Within a few hours after the heart attack began, a thin tube was being threaded into his heart through an artery in his groin.

After injecting dye, Engle confirmed that the streptokinase had dissolved a clot in the left anterior descending coronary artery. That artery is so crucial to the survival of the heart that physicians have macabrely dubbed it the "widow maker" because clots that develop in it often are lethal.

An X-ray examination of the artery showed Engle that at the site of the clot, the artery had been narrowed to only 5 percent of its normal diameter by a buildup of fatty deposits. Without further treatment, Krushas would be at risk of a future heart attack if another clot formed there or if further buildup of plaque completely choked off the flow of blood.

(continued on next page)

So Engle inserted another tube with a small sausage-shaped balloon at the end, guided it into place at the site of the narrowing and inflated it. The rigid, inflated balloon flattened the deposits against the inner walls of the artery, widening the channel and restoring normal blood flow.

Less than five hours had elapsed since that first crushing pain in the hospital.

On Feb. 8, a week after he first woke up feeling uncomfortable, Krushas went home. Less than three weeks later, he was back at work.

Without the treatment with clot-dissolving drugs and balloon angioplasty, Engle said, "I think he would have died."

Did you notice the second story's sentence structure? Almost every sentence, beginning with the lead, uses the normal word order: subject, verb, direct object.

Reread the fifth paragraph. Do you like its opening sentence: "About 8 a.m., he began to die"? What makes that sentence so effective? Notice its simplicity: It contains no unnecessary adverbs or adjectives, only a simple statement of the facts. The sentence also demonstrates the principle that understatement is usually more effective than exaggeration.

Count the number of words in the story's average sentence, then compare the sentence length to that of a recent sample of your work.

Complex Stories

Stories that contain several major subtopics may be too complex to summarize in a brief lead. Each week the U.S. Supreme Court is in session, it announces all its decisions on a single day. Several of those decisions may be important. To save space, most newspapers report all the decisions in a single story. Reporters can mention only one or two of the most important decisions in their leads, so they often summarize the remaining decisions in the second, and sometimes the third, paragraphs of their stories.

After summarizing all the major decisions, reporters discuss each in more detail, starting with the most important. By mentioning all the decisions in the stories' opening paragraphs, reporters alert readers to the stories' entire contents. Readers interested in the second or third decision immediately learn that it will be discussed later in the story. If, in contrast, the lead and following paragraphs mentioned only the most important decision, readers might mistakenly assume that the entire story concerned that one decision. Many might stop reading before reaching the story's account of other decisions that might be of greater interest to them.

The following story begins with the Supreme Court's most important decision and then, in subsequent paragraphs, summarizes other decisions announced the same day:

WASHINGTON—The Supreme Court Monday banned the private possession of machine guns. A National Rifle Association lawyer called it "the first ban on firearms possession by law-abiding citizens in American history."

In a defeat for the NRA, the justices refused to hear a Georgia gun manufacturer's argument that the Second Amendment "right of the people to keep and bear arms" allows him to make or possess a fully automatic weapon.

The Court also decided cases involving: anti-abortion protests, the sanctuary movement, libel and local regulation.

Harcourt Brace & Company

NRA lobbyist Jack Lenzi said his organization was "disappointed but not surprised." He said the federal ban is "an infringement on the rights" of about 100,000 Americans who collect automatic weapons.

Gun control and law enforcement groups told the high court that the NRA's argument would permit private persons to have "bazookas, hand grenades, Stinger missiles and any other weapon of mass destruction. . . . The public safety implications of such a position are truly staggering."

In other matters, the court:

• Refused to lift limits on demonstrations by opponents of abortions at a Dayton, Ohio, abortion clinic and a ban on protests by the opponents at the homes of the clinic's staff and patients.

• Left intact the criminal convictions of eight sanctuary movement members who helped Central American aliens smuggled into this country.

• Heard arguments in a libel case in which a psychologist says a New Yorker magazine staff writer made up quotes attributed to him.

• Agreed to decide whether communities may regulate the use of pesticides or whether such local regulations are preempted by federal law.

Reporters often use lists in news stories that involve several diverse ideas, subtopics or examples. If all the ideas or examples are important, reporters may begin a news story by summarizing one or two main points, adding a brief transition and presenting the other ideas or examples in a simple, orderly list:

Assailants attacked three women in the college's parking lots, and Police Chief Alvin Schwab today warned other students that the attacks may continue.

To protect themselves, Schwab recommended that women:

• Avoid dark areas.

• Park in areas that will be lighted when they return.

• Tell friends where they are going and when they will return.

• Keep their car doors locked and windows rolled up when driving alone.

• Check their car's floor and back seat for intruders before getting into the vehicle.

• Report any suspicious activities to the campus police.

Later in a story, reporters can discuss each point in greater detail. The initial summary may contain all the essential information about a topic; in that case, it need not be mentioned again.

Each item in a list must be in parallel form. If one item begins with a noun and uses an active verb and a complete sentence, then every item in that list must do the same. For example, each item in the story below is an incomplete sentence that begins with a verb:

The governor said he wants to raise the state's sales tax and to increase state spending on education.

He told the National Education Association he would use the money to:

• Raise teachers' salaries.

• Test new teachers to assess their competence.

• Place more emphasis on English, science and math.

• Reduce the number of students in each class.

• Give schools more money to educate gifted students.

Reporters also use lists to summarize less important details placed at the end of news stories. Lists are particularly useful when the details are minor and concern several diverse topics that would be difficult to organize in any other manner:

Donald M. Schoen, a Republican candidate for governor, last night promised to cut the state's budget and taxes by a "minimum of 10 percent."

Schoen, mayor of Madison for the past eight years, also promised to dismiss 10 percent of the state's employees.

Harcourt Brace & Company

"People complain that the government has become too big and that it imposes too many taxes and places too many restrictions on their lives," he said at a fund-raising dinner held last night at Pine Hills Country Club.

On other subjects, Schoen said:

EDUCATION—School budgets should be frozen until educators trim administrative costs and improve students' test scores.

CRIME—Only 19 percent of the serious crimes committed in the state are solved. Fewer than 2 percent of the criminals responsible for those crimes are convicted and sentenced to prison. Penalties should be harsher, and criminals should be kept in jail until they have served their full terms, without parole.

MEDIA COVERAGE—News media devote too much attention to staged campaign activities and "have failed to critically analyze candidates' qualifications and positions on major issues."

Some newspapers number each item in a list. Others mark each item with a dash, bullet, asterisk, check mark or some other typographical symbol.

THE NEED TO BE FAIR

Regardless of how you organize a story, it must be balanced, fair and accurate. Reporters who write about a controversial issue have an obligation to present every significant viewpoint fully and fairly. They must exercise particular care when their stories might harm another person's reputation. A reckless or irresponsible charge may destroy an innocent person's reputation, marriage or career.

If a story contains information critical of an individual, that person should be given an opportunity to respond. It is not enough to get the person's response after a story has been published and report it in a later story, because not everyone who read the original criticism will see the second story. The New York Times has a policy requiring that: ". . . a person mentioned derogatorily or critically in a story should immediately be given a chance to respond. If the person is unreachable, consideration should be given to holding the story over. If holding it over is deemed inadvisable, mention should be made in the story that efforts to reach the person were unavailing, and the efforts should be renewed the next day. . . . This is a cardinal, unbreakable rule."

For example, a story about the Biosphere experiment reported:

The futuristic, privately financed project has been accused of hucksterism, scientific amateurism and deception in the much-publicized test of a prototype space colony.

But backers and some outside scientists say the $150 million experiment succeeded in its main mission: keeping eight people alive for two years as they grew most of their own food and recycled water, waste and most of the air.

(The Associated Press)

If the subject of a negative story is unavailable or refuses to respond, that fact should be mentioned. A brief sentence might explain:

Attempts to reach a company employee were unsuccessful.

OR: A vice president at the company declined to comment about the charges.

OR: Company officials did not return phone calls made by reporters.

THE FINAL STEP: EDIT YOUR STORY

After finishing a story, edit it ruthlessly. Author Kurt Vonnegut recommends, "If a sentence, no matter how excellent, does not illuminate your subject in some new and useful way, scratch it out." Vonnegut also urges writers to have mercy on their readers, explaining: "Our audience requires us to be sympathetic and patient teachers, ever willing to simplify and clarify—whereas we would rather soar high above the crowd singing like nightingales."

Thus, remembering their audience, good reporters will reread and edit their stories. Mistakenly (and lazily), less competent reporters immediately submit their stories to an editor. Those reporters may think their stories are so good that they will not need any editing. Or, those reporters may expect the editor to correct all their errors. That attitude involves some risks. If an editor fails to notice the errors, the reporters will be embarrassed when the errors appear in print. Moreover, the reporters will be held responsible for the errors.

Or, an editor may decide the stories require extensive changes, perhaps even total rewriting. When that happens, reporters often complain about the changes.

If reporters correct their own errors, they will develop reputations as good writers and be rewarded for their efforts: given better assignments, raises and promotions.

CHECKLIST FOR WRITING NEWS STORIES

Use the following checklist to evaluate all your stories.

1. Place the most important details in your lead.
2. Throughout the story emphasize the details most likely to interest and affect your readers.
3. Include details from your observations to create a picture your readers can visualize.
4. In the story's second paragraph, continue to discuss the topic initiated in your lead.
5. Do not leapfrog. If your lead mentions an individual, and your second paragraph begins with a name, provide a transition that makes it clear you mean the same person.
6. Make your sentences clear, concise and to the point. (Avoid passive verbs. Also, use the normal word order of subject, verb, direct object.)
7. Vary your sentence structure.
8. Avoid overloading your sentences.
9. Provide transitions to lead your readers from one sentence or paragraph to another smoothly and logically.
10. Make your transitional sentences specific; say something intriguing to sustain readers' interest in the topic.
11. If you use a question as a transition, make it clear, short and simple.
12. Avoid generalities that have to be explained in a later sentence or paragraph. Be specific.
13. Resist the temptation to end your story with a summary, conclusion or opinion.
14. Report only what happened; omit mentions of what did *not* happen.
15. If you report your story in chronological order, provide a concise transition from the lead to the body.
16. If your story discusses several major subtopics, mention all the major subtopics in your story's opening paragraphs so your readers know what to expect.
17. If you use a list, make sure each item is in parallel form.
18. After finishing your story, critically edit and rewrite it.
19. Count the words in your sentences. How many words are in your average sentence? How many words are in your longest sentence? Critically examine sentences that contain more than 25 words. Consider rewriting your story if your average sentence contains more than 20 words.

SUGGESTED READINGS

Anderson, Douglas A. *Contemporary Sports Reporting*, 2nd ed. Chicago: Nelson-Hall, 1993.
Best Newspaper Writing. St. Petersburg, FL: Poynter Institute for Media Studies. (This book, published every year since 1979, contains prize-winning articles, followed by an editor's comments and question-and-answer sessions with the writers.)

Brooks, Terri. *Words' Worth: A Handbook on Writing & Selling Nonfiction.* New York: St. Martin's Press, 1989.

Cappon, Rene J. *Associated Press Guide to News Writing.* New York: The Associated Press, 1991.

Garrison, Bruce. *Professional News Writing.* Hillsdale, NJ: Erlbaum, 1990.

Hohenberg, John. *The Professional Journalist,* 5th ed. New York: Holt, Rinehart and Winston, 1983.

Izard, Ralph S., Hugh M. Culbertson and Donald A. Lambert. *Fundamentals of News Reporting,* 6th ed. Dubuque, IA: Kendall/Hunt, 1994.

Metz, William. *Newswriting: From Lead to "30,"* 3rd ed. Englewood Cliffs, NJ: Prentice-Hall, 1990.

Scanlan, Christopher, ed. *How I Wrote the Story,* rev. ed. Providence, RI: Providence Journal, 1986.

Sims, Norman, ed. *The Literary Journalists.* New York: Ballantine, 1984.

Sloan, William D., Valarie McCrary and Johanna Cleary. *The Best of Pulitzer Prize News Writing.* Columbus, OH: Publishing Horizons, 1986.

Teel, Leonard R. and Ron Taylor. *Into the Newsroom: An Introduction to Journalism.* Englewood Cliffs, NJ: Prentice-Hall, 1983.

Harcourt Brace & Company

EXERCISE 1

THE BODY OF A NEWS STORY

SECTION I: TRANSITIONS

Critically evaluate the following transitions. Which transitions provide a smooth, specific, informative and interesting introduction to the next idea?

After evaluating the transitions, give each of them a grade from A to F.

1. Why would a former nurse open a hot dog stand? (Grade: _____)
2. He went on to provide guidelines and hints by which journalists might hone their skills. (Grade: _____)
3. The council heard representatives of the Coalition for the Homeless, a nonprofit organization, explain why the city needs a new shelter. (Grade: _____)
4. Asian students said they expected Americans to be friendlier. (Grade: _____)
5. The problem library officials are most concerned about is smoking. (Grade: _____)
6. Only 23 percent of the women said they would like to give up their jobs and stay home full-time to raise their children. (Grade: _____)
7. Frank Yamer, a business major, also encountered a number of problems when he transferred from another school. (Grade: _____)
8. The university's math department awards the lowest percentage of As (14.1 percent) and the highest percentage of Fs (15.6 percent). (Grade: _____)
9. Officials explained how the plan will ease overcrowding at the three schools. (Grade: _____)
10. A man who lives across the road was working outside at the time and saw the accident. (Grade: _____)
11. Forty percent of the teen-agers said they never worry about catching AIDS. (Grade: _____)
12. Dr. Kostyn said there is a shortage of about 2,200 certified math and science teachers in the state. (Grade: _____)

SECTION II: SECOND PARAGRAPHS

Critically evaluate the second paragraph in each of the following stories. Judge which of the second paragraphs are most successful in: (1) providing a smooth transition from the lead, (2) continuing to discuss the topic summarized in the lead and (3) emphasizing the news (details that are new, important and interesting).

After evaluating the second paragraphs, give each of them a grade from A to F.

1. Jewel C. Harris, 42, of 2245 E. Broadway Ave. was arrested and charged with aggravated battery after her car struck a bicyclist, police say.

   Jerry R. Harris, 24, also of 2245 E. Broadway Ave., was transported to Memorial Hospital with cuts, bruises and a broken leg. (Grade: _____)
2. The School Board has expelled eight more students for using drugs, bringing the total this year to 81.

   Only one of the eight students appeared before the board last night to defend herself. She was accused of selling marijuana to a classmate. (Grade: _____)

3. The new Alcohol Information Center on campus acknowledges a slow start with its responsible drinking program. But program coordinators have plans to change that.

   Karen Dees is one of the program's coordinators. She wants to make sure that students understand the philosophy of responsible drinking. "We're not affiliated with any religious sect," she said. "Our main goal is to keep heavy drinkers off the streets and keep them from harming themselves and others." (Grade: _____)

4. County Commissioner Anne Chen wants pornographic movies banned from cable TV.

   In an interview Friday, Chen said that watching pornography can be psychologically damaging to children. "I'm not talking about R-rated movies," she said. "I'm talking about hard-core stuff that shows animals, whips and chains used in sexual acts." (Grade: _____)

5. A man claiming to have a bomb tried to rob the First Federal Savings and Loan Co. at 9:05 a.m. today.

   A man carrying a brown paper bag told a teller that it contained a bomb and that he would kill everyone in the bank unless she gave him $10,000. (Grade: _____)

6. A 22-year-old auto mechanic and his wife delivered their triplets at home Monday because there was no time to drive to a birthing clinic.

   Barbara and Paul Wyman of 2020 Lorry Lane delivered their triplets at 4:30 a.m. The babies and their mother are reported in excellent condition. (Grade: _____)

7. Complaining that college administrators are insensitive to their needs, 50 handicapped students, some in wheelchairs, picketed the Administration Building Friday.

   About 10 percent of the student population is handicapped, but there is no way of determining how many there really are. When the Rehabilitation Act of 1973 was passed, the disclosure of information about handicapped students was prohibited. The law is intended to ensure that a handicapped student is not discriminated against and denied entrance into a college. (Grade: _____)

8. The police in Reno, Nev., feel safer and more confident since the PR-24 Baton replaced their night stick.

   Officer Jim Balliet said the concept of a baton was derived from a martial arts weapon called the tonfa. Lon Anderson, a New Hampshire police officer, developed the baton and brought the idea to a company to manufacture it, Balliet said. (Grade: _____)

9. Two soldiers who were abducted, robbed and tied in a woods said their captors apologized, saying they became robbers in order to feed their children.

   The young couple told the soldiers that they had also abducted several other people but never enjoyed it. (Grade: _____)

10. Peter Laguna, a 24-year-old Alabama man, went on trial Wednesday on charges of armed robbery.

    The first witness was Lynita Sharp, a clerk who was working at the convenience store when it was robbed on July 18. (Grade: _____)

11. The School Board voted Tuesday to construct an elementary school on Grant Avenue.

    Two years ago, the Meadow Woods Subdivision offered to give the board land for the school. (Grade: _____)

12. A 22-year-old man today pleaded innocent to violating his probation, arguing that his poor education made it impossible for him to understand the instructions given by his parole officer.

    The defendant, Henry Forlenza, told the judge that he dropped out of high school and never learned to read. (Grade: _____)

E X E R C I S E 2
THE BODY OF A NEWS STORY

PRO CHALLENGE

WRITING COMPLETE NEWS STORIES

INSTRUCTIONS: Write complete news stories based on the following information. Be thorough; include in your stories most of the information provided. Because much of the material is wordy, awkward and poorly organized, you will have to rewrite it extensively.

    When you finish, you can compare your work to a professional's. Experienced reporters have also been asked to write stories for each set of facts, and their work appears in a manual available to your instructor.

1. Theres a totally new idea starting to be implemented in your city. Some call it "a pilot program." Others call it "a satellite school." Your School Board likes the idea because it saves the board money. Businesses like it because it helps them attract and retain good employees. There was a meeting of your citys School Board last night. Greg Hubbard, superintendent of your citys school system, recommended the idea, and the School Board then proceeded to vote 6–1 in favor of trying the new idea. Whats the idea? Its to mix companies and classrooms. Recently, plans were announced to construct a major new General Electric manufacturing plant in your city. The plant will employ a total of more than 600 employees, many of them women who will work on assembly lines, helping make small appliances for the new General Electric plant. To attract and retain qualified women, many of whom have young children, the plant wants a school to be located on its premises. It offered to provide, free of charge, free space: to construct a separate building on its premises with 3 rooms built according to the School Boards specifications. Its the wave of the future, Hubbard told the School Board last night. Its a win-win situation, he added. He explained that it is a good employee benefit, and it helps ease crowding in the districts schools if some students go elsewhere. The details are being negotiated. To start with at first, the school will have three rooms and serve about 60 kindergarten and first-grade children of employees. The school district will equip the classrooms and pay the salaries of a teacher and a teachers aide for each classroom. At this point in time there are only approximately 20 school districts in the entire country trying the idea. Students will eat in the factorys employee cafeteria and play on a playground also provided by the new factory. Parents will provide transportation to and from the facility. Equipping each classroom will cost in the neighborhood of approximately $10,000. The price is about the same as for a regular classroom. Hubbard said if the program is successful, it will expand to other companies. A company will have to supply a minimum of 20 children to justify the cost of the program which could, if successful, serve young students in 2nd and possibly 3rd grades as well. The program is thought to attract and retain more employees— to reduce the rate of attrition, thus saving companies the cost of training new employees. That is especially important in industries with many low-paying positions in which there is often a high turnover. Its also a solution to working parents who feel there is never enough time to spend with their children. Hubbard said one of the nice things is that many will have the opportunity to ride to and from work and also have lunch with their children.

2. They're all heroes, but no one knows exactly how many of them there are, nor all their identities. They were shopping late yesterday evening at the Colonial Mall in your city. The mall closes at 10 p.m., and it was about 9:50 pm when the incident occurred. There was a serious incident: a robbery. Among the other stores in the mall is a jewelry store: Elaine's Jewelry. An unidentified man walked into the store and, before anyone could respond, pulled out a hammer, smashed two display cases, and then proceeded to scoop up with his hands handfuls of jewelry, mostly watches and rings. Elaine Benchfield is the owner of the store, and also its manager, and she was present at the time and began screaming quite loudly. People heard her screams, saw the man flee, and, according to witnesses, 8 or 10 people began pursuing the man through the mall. As the chase proceeded, the posse grew in number. "Things like that just make me mad," explained Keith Holland, one of the shoppers who witnessed the crime and joined the posse. The chase ended in one of the shopping malls parking lots. Once outside in the parking lot, even more people started joining the posse, yelling at and chasing the man. Asa Smythe, a jogger who says he jogs a distance of 20 miles a week, said he knew the man might out-sprint him for a short distance, but that he also knew he was going to follow the man to hell if he had to. "He couldn't lose me, no way he could lose me," Smythe said. Smythe is a former high school football player and Marine. He succeeded in catching up with and tackling the man. More shoppers, an estimated 15 or 20 by police, then surrounded the man, holding him there in the parking lot until police reached the scene. The people stood in a circle around the man, threatening him, but also applauding and shaking hands among themselves, proud of their accomplishment. The suspect has since then been identified by police officers as Todd Burns, age 23, of 1502 Matador Dr., Apt. 302. He has been charged with grand theft and is being held on $25,000 bond at the county jail. Police officer Barbara Keith-Fowler, the first officer to reach the scene, said she thinks Burnes was happy to see her. Burnes was not armed, and was apparently frightened, police said, by the crowd. At one point in the chase he threw them the bag of loot, apparently hoping they would stop following him. A bystander retrieved the bag and returned it to Blancfield, who said it contained everything stolen from her store. A grateful Blanchfeld then proceeded to tell you, when you called her on the phone, that the people who helped her were a super bunch of people and made her feel wonderful. Blanchfeld added that she thinks people responded as they did because they are sick and tired of people getting ripped off.

3. Its a most unusual controversy. It involves an act at a circus the Shriners in your city put on to raise money for their charitable activities. In addition, the Shriners, who put the circus on every year at this time in your city, invite free of charge hundreds of the citys ill, mentally handicapped and needy children. One of everyones favorite acts involves six cats that look like rather typical household pets. The circus opened last Friday, with shows to continue every nite at 8 p.m. this week through this coming Saturday evening. There will also be a show at 2 pm Saturday afternoon. After seeing the first shows last weekend, some people began to complain about an act put on by Sandra Kidder of Farmers Branch, Texas, a suburb of Dallas. Kidder travels from city to city with the circus and explains that she enjoys traveling and loves her animals, all cats. The cats dive through flaming hoops, and thats what people have complained about. Her cats do it for love, Kidder said when you interviewed her today. They'll do anything for her, she said, because she loves them and they love her. Someone, however, filed a complaint with the citys Humane Society. The complaint charges that Kidder terrifies and starves her cats, endangering their lives to get them to do the trick. Annette Daigle, who filed the complaint, resides in her home at 431 E. Central Blvd. Her complaint states that the cats are forced to perform highly unnatural behaviors for them—that the last thing a cat wants to do is go near fire. Diagle said she is not the only one concerned about the cats

welfare but that other people who also feel the way she does that the cats are being starved, terrorized, endangered, and abused don't want to get involved in the controversy. Kidder responded to you that she feeds her cats one good meal a day at the end of their performance. She couldn't do it sooner, she said, because, if they had just eaten, her cats would fall asleep in the middle of their act. Kidder then went on to add that she would never do anything to hurt or endanger her cats. In addition to jumping through flaming hoops, her cats during each act also leap from stool to stool; jump high in the air; stand on their hind legs; stand on their front legs; sit on their haunches in the begging position like dogs; and walk across a stretched wire, like tight-rope walkers. She calls them her "fabulous flying felines." They're professionals, she concluded. Finally, in addition, Kidder added that its easier for her cats to jump through the flaming rings than to master many of the other, simpler-looking tricks. They're not scared of the flaming hoops, she insists. They're only scared if someone is mean to them. They need to feel that you love them. The hardest thing for them to learn to do is to stand up on their hind legs. Its not natural for them, but they'll do it for her. She also further revealed that they're not special cats. Friends gave her some. She picked up others at a pound. Renee Chung-Peters, head of your citys Humane Society, said she is in the process of investigating the complaint. Chung-Peters said she will watch tonights show and hopes to examine all the cats immediately after the show. When you contacted Kidder, she said that she has no objections to that.

4. An estimated 12,000 people in your city and surrounding area will be affected by the news. A chain of health spas called "Mr. Muscles" is closing. Its the areas largest spa, with 6 clubs located throughout the city. It closed without warning. The company is owned by Mike Cantral of 410 South Street. Normally, the spas open at 6 a.m. and, when people went to them today, they found a simple notice taped to the doors at all 6 saying, "Closed Until Further Notice." Cantral was unavailable. His attorney, Jena Cruz, said the company is bankrupt and she doesn't expect it to reopen. She said she will file a bankruptcy petition for the spas in federal court, probably early next week. Hundreds and hundreds of regular members showed up at the clubs today and found the doors locked, the lights out, and the equipment inside sitting unused. Employees, estimated to total 180 in number, were also surprised. They said they did not know the spas were in trouble and had no inkling they were about to close. Several said they are worried about whether or not they will be paid for their work during the last two weeks. They are paid every two weeks, and their normal payday is tomorrow. Some members paid up to $499 a year for use of the facilities. Some have paid for 3 or 5-year memberships. An undetermined number bought lifetime memberships for $3,999. The clubs have been open for more than 15 years. The state Department of Consumer Affairs is investigating the closing. Kim Eng, director of the department, said she did not know if any members could get refunds on their memberships but said if the company goes bankrupt that seems unlikely. Cruz said the clubs were losing a total of $3,000 a week. She added that there is no money left to return to members. The state attorneys office is also investigating members complaints. The company opened its first spa in 1981, then began an aggressive expansion program. Atty. Cruz said the company borrowed money to buy land for its spas and to build the spas, each of which cost a total of well over a million dollars to build and equip, and that it has not been selling enough new memberships in recent months to make the payments on all its loans.

5. It was a dreadfully tragic incident and involved a 7-year-old girl in your city: Tania Abondanzio, the daughter of Anthony and Deborah Abbondanzia. The girl was admitted to Mercy Hospital last Friday morning. She was driven to the hospital by her parents. She was operated on later that morning for a tonsillectomy. She died Saturday morning.

Harcourt Brace & Company

Hospital officials investigating the death announced, during a press conference this morning, that they have now determined the apparent cause of death: that the girl was given the wrong medication by a pediatric nurse. They did not identify the nurse, saying only that she has been suspended, pending completion of the investigation. The girls parents were unavailable for comment. Tania was a 2nd grade student at Washington Elementary School. Her physician, Dr. Priscilla Eisen, prescribed a half milligram of a pain reliever, morphine sulphate, after surgery. Hospital records show that, somehow, by mistake, the nurse gave the girl a half milligram of hydromorphone, a stronger pain reliever commonly known as Dilaudid. The victim was given the drug at 2:30 p.m. Friday afternoon and developed severe respiratory problems at 2:40 p.m. She also complained of being hot and went into an apparent seizure. An autopsy conducted over the weekend to determine the cause of her problems showed results, also announced during the press conference today, that were consistent with the hospitals report, police said. Police are treating the death as accidental. After developing respiratory problems, the girl was immediately transferred from the medical facilitys pediatrics ward to the intensive care ward and remained in a coma until Saturday morning, when doctors pronounced her brain dead. She was then taken off a respirator and died minutes later at 9:40 a.m. Saturday morning. The nurse involved in the unfortunate incident noticed she had apparently administered the wrong drug during a routine narcotics inventory when the shifts changed at midnight Friday. She immediately and promptly notified her supervisor. The two drugs are kept side by side together in a locked cabinet. Hospital officials said a dosage of a half-milligram of hydromorphone is not normally considered to be lethal, not even for a child. Dr. Irwin Greenhouse, hospital administrator, said in a statement released to the press today that, "Our sympathy goes out to the family, and we will stay close to them to provide support." He declined to comment further. Hydromorphone, a narcotic used to treat pain, is six to seven times more potent than morphine. Children sometimes are given a half milligram of hydromorphone to control coughing, a druggist you consulted said. The druggist added that the dosage did not sound outrageous to her, but rather sounded very reasonable, as a matter of fact. The drug is generally used for pain relief after surgery or as medication before an operation, the druggist also informed you, asking that she not be identified by name, a request that you agreed to honor.

6. A lone man robbed a bank in the city. He entered the Security Federal Bank, 814 North Main Street, at about 2:30 p.m. yesterday. Bank officials said he first went into the bank with the excuse of obtaining information about a loan, talked to a loan officer and then left. When he returned a few minutes later, he was brandishing a pistol and demanded money from the banks tellers. Glady Anne Higginbotham, the banks manager, said he forced two tellers to lie on the floor. He then jumped behind a counter and scooped up the money from five cash drawers. As the gunman scooped up the money, he also scooped up a small exploding device disguised to look like a packet of money and stuffed it into his pockets along with the rest of the cash. The device contains red dye and tear gas and automatically explodes after a specified amount of time. The length of time before the explosion is determined by each individual bank using the device. The device is activated when someone walks out of a bank with it. As the gunman left the bank, he ordered four customers to lie down on the floor. Most of the customers were unaware of the robbery until told to get down on the floor. Witnesses believe the gunman sped away from the scene in a pickup truck parked behind the building. Police say they found a red stain in the rear parking lot and surmise that the device exploded just as the robber was getting into the truck. An eyewitness told police he saw a late-model black pickup truck a few blocks away with a red cloud coming out the window a few moments after the robbery but was unable to get the license number. Detective Myron A. Neeley said, "That guy should be covered with red. The money, too. Just look for a

red man with red money. You can't wash that stuff off. It just has to wear off. It explodes all over the place—in your clothes, in your hair, on your hands, in your car. Its almost like getting in contact with a skunk." An FBI agent on the scene added that many banks now use the protective devices in an effort to foil bank robbers and that the stain will eventually wear off humans but stays on money forever. He estimated that the man will be covered with the red dye for at least the next two or three days. The man was described as a white man. He is between the ages of 25 and 30 years of age. He is about 6 feet tall. He weighs about 180 pounds. He has long blond hair. His attire includes wire-rimmed sunglasses, a gold wedding ring, a blue plaid shirt, blue jeans and brown sandals.

Harcourt Brace & Company

E X E R C I S E 3

THE BODY OF A NEWS STORY

WRITING COMPLETE NEWS STORIES

INSTRUCTIONS: Write complete news stories based on the following information. Be thorough: include in your stories most of the information provided. Because much of the material is wordy, awkward and poorly organized, you will have to rewrite it extensively.

1. It began with a routine inspection. Health inspectors in your city inspect every restaurant and bakery, normally twice a year. The inspections are a surprise. They are not announced in advance. Rather, the inspectors drop in unexpectedly. Last Friday, they dropped in at a bakery on Moore Street: the Kalani Bros. Bakery. It is one of the largest in the city, with 40 employees. It supplies more than 100 grocery stores and restaurants with breads, pies, cakes and other pastries. After the inspection Friday, the Health Department proceeded to suspend the bakers license, effective immediately. The Kalani brothers, Charles and Andrew, say they will appeal to the city council, which meets tonight. During an inspection a year ago, health inspectors found cockroaches, mice droppings, flour beetles and other health problems. There have been two inspections since then, and they found that some problems were corrected, but new problems—such as inadequate refrigeration and garbage thrown on floors—had arisen. The inspectors returned again last Friday—a fourth time—to determine whether all the problems had been corrected. Under emergency provisions of city health laws, a business can be closed immediately—its license temporarily suspended—to protect the public health if a dangerous situation exists. After a hearing, the license can be permanently revoked. City inspectors said, despite their repeated warnings, the problems had not been corrected; some had gotten worse. So Friday, they temporarily suspended the license. Attorney Margie Allen, who represents the brothers, said she does not believe the sanitation problems are as bad as city officials allege and that most have been corrected and that the remainder are in the process of being corrected. She adds that the brothers are losing $13,000 a day in lost business and may permanently lose some customers, who are getting their bakery goods from rivals during the shutdown. "There has been no hearing here," Allen said. "Their business is being destroyed by an edict, without proper legal safeguards. We'll appeal tonight to the city council and, tomorrow, to the courts, if necessary."

2. Its an idea being tried in many places. County commissioners want an impact fee. The county has been growing so rapidly, they point out, that it is impossible, without some additional sources of income, to provide the necessary services. The county needs more fire stations and more firefighters and sheriffs deputies. The county needs a bigger sewer system, a bigger jail, better roads, new schools and more teachers to accommodate all the new residents moving to the county. A task force of 12 county officials has been looking into the matter during the past three months, and they revealed their report at a press conference at 9 a.m. today. The county commissioners will consider the report at their next meeting: next Tuesday night at 8 pm. The task force recommends that new people moving to the county should be required to pay for the expanded services they want and need. Taxes should not be raised. Rather, each time a new house is built, an "impact fee" should be assessed. The money would be used for needed capital improve-

ments. New businesses would also be assessed: 5% of the cost of their construction. The plan is expected to raise about $18 million dollars a year. The impact fee for hooking up to the county sewage system for a single-family home would cost $2,500. The impact fee for a water connection would be $1,000. The fees for apartment units would be $1,800 and $750, respectively. There would be other fees for roads, education and police protection. The county would then issue $260 million dollars worth of bonds during the next five years to build three new sewer plants, a new water treatment plant, a jail, two fire stations, and several new schools, including a brand-new high school. The impact fees would be used to repay the bonds. Developers object to the idea, saying that the proposed fees would raise the price of each new home more than $5,000 and that many people could not afford that kind of money. The countys goal is to get ahead of growth and to maintain a high quality of life for the countys residents. There will be a series of public hearings, the task force said, but no dates or locations have been set. The task force warns that, without new fees, growth will have to stop. The county will be forced to stop granting any new building permits because it will not have the water and sewage capacity to handle future growth. Roads and schools will become overcrowded, forcing double sessions at the schools. Police and fire protection will deteriorate.

3. A new law that goes into effect next fall will affect elementary, junior high and high school students throughout the state. The state Legislature enacted the law, and the governor signed it today. Basically, the law prohibits the sale of so-called junk food at public schools. So, as a result of the laws passage, the content of all school vending machines will undergo a drastic change. The machines no longer will contain any candy bars, gum, soda or other foods with a high sugar content. Instead, they will be replaced by foods which are considered by many to be more healthy, foods such as canned soups and juices, jerky, toasted soy beans, sunflower seeds, yogurt, nuts, cheese, popcorn, pretzels, ice cream and milk. The law was supported by physicians, dentists and educators, who testified in legislative hearings that many students bought snacks and soft drinks from machines instead of eating the more nutritious meals served in school cafeterias. Other persons, primarily food manufacturers and vending-machine operators, opposed the law. Students, too, generally opposed it, claiming that their rights were being violated and that they were old enough to make their own decisions about what they want to eat. Some school principals also opposed the law, pointing out the fact that the law will be costly since they receive a percentage of the receipts of the vending machines located in their buildings. Some big high schools earn up to $20,000 a year from machines and use the money to buy materials that would not otherwise be available, such as supplemental textbooks, library materials, calculators for their mathematics laboratories, television cameras for their communications classes, and athletic equipment. School bands and athletic programs will be hurt most severely by the loss of revenue. The practice of showing free movies at some schools may also come to a quick end, since many were financed by vending machine revenues. Critics said it was inconsistent for schools to teach good nutrition in classes and then make food with a high sugar content easily available. The ban will be in effect only during school hours, so the junk food will still be able to be sold after school hours, such as during school dances and sports events, so schools can continue to earn a limited amount of money from their sale. One proponent added, "There's simply no sense in talking to kids about dental care and good nutrition and selling them junk food at the same time." Opponents responded that students will buy candy anyway, simply going off campus to buy it.

4. Thomas E. Richardson is 28 years old and a city policeman and alive today because while on duty he wears a bullet-proof vest supplied free of charge by the city. He lives

at 5421 Jennings Road with his wife, Inez, and two children: Mary, 8, and Suanne, 5. He has been a policeman since leaving the Army 4 years ago. Without the vest, he might have died last night. Richardson went on duty at 4 p.m. and shortly after 10 p.m. the police received an anonymous phone call about a suspicious person loitering behind a restaurant at 640 Aloma Avenue. Responding to the call, Richardson spotted a man matching the description he was given and, when he pulled his patrol car to the curb and got out, he said without warning the man drew a 38 cal. revolver from a jacket pocket and without saying anything fired four shots at him. Two shots struck Richardson. Two struck his patrol car. The first two shots hit Richardson in the chest, and he was spun around and knocked against the car door by the impact of those two shots. A third bullet shattered a left rear window of the patrol car and the fourth bullet entered the left rear door of the patrol car. After catching his breath, Richardson returned fire, blasting six shots at the suspect who fell to the ground. Richardson was treated at Mercy Hospital for severe bruises on the chest, including one bruise that doctors say is directly above his heart, in a hospital emergency room. The suspect, who was killed in the exchange of gunfire, has not yet been identified. A police spokesman said they do not yet know why he opened fire at Richardson. The police department purchased bullet-proof vests for all its outside policemen last year, but wearing them is voluntary and many officers do not because they are heavy and uncomfortable, particularly during the hot summer months.

5. The police today celebrated the first anniversary of an innovative program. The program is for senior citizens—usually persons 65 and older, although any person who lives alone and is over the age of 55 can participate if that person wants to do so. The program is called "Project Reassurance." Each day, elderly persons who participate in the program call Dorothy Morovchek, a clerk, and two aides at the police department between the hours of 7 and 9 a.m. If they do not call by 9:15 a.m., Miss Morovchek will dispatch a police officer to the persons home to determine whether the person is safe, and the officers have keys to each participants home so they do not have to break their way in. Since the program started a year ago, Miss Morovchek says it has saved three lives, including the life of a woman who police officers found lying on the kitchen floor of her home after having suffered a heart attack before she was able to call the police that morning. Altogether, a total of 318 persons in the city participate in the program at the current time, and police say they will not impose any limitations on the number of participants in the future. Miss Morovchek adds that the elderly like the program for a second reason as well, since many feel alone, and it gives them someone to talk to every morning. One elderly person who uses the service says, "Its a thrill to hear a voice. My wife died four years ago, and I don't have anyone else to talk to. I also feel now like I have some security. I know someone's there to help if I need it."

6. The case involves another unusual lawsuit. As a result of it, if you are blind, or going blind, you may have to wait longer to receive cornea transplants. Your states supreme court ruled on the matter today. It issued a decision saying that medical examiners can no longer remove corneas from the eyes of a deceased without the permission of relatives. A state law, adopted in 1994, gave medical examiners the right to remove corneas without permission of the family of the deceased. The law applied to bodies under the jurisdiction of medical examiners, such as victims of accidents, murders, suicides and other unexplained deaths. Since then, attorneys opposed to the law have argued that it violates a familys right to decide the disposition of a loved ones remains. There was a test case. It involved a woman who died two years ago, at the age of 31. She has not been identified, in part because she committed suicide. During the autopsy of her body, both corneas were removed from her eyes. Later, when her relatives learned of that action, they objected on the grounds of their religious beliefs. Your State Supreme Court,

ruling on the case today, said the state law violates a familys right to decide the disposition of a loved ones remains. The ruling is expected to be appealed to the U.S. Supreme Court. People at an eye bank in your state say the decision could drastically affect cornea procurement. The director of the eye bank said the ruling could extend the waiting period for the sight-restoring surgery from a week or two to a year or longer. "I think this will have a disastrous effect on our ability to obtain an adequate number of corneas to serve our patients," said the medical director of the eye bank. On the other hand, presenting the other point of view, parents have complained that they did not even know about the law until after the corneas of their deceased children were removed. The law permitted the removal of the corneas, the transparent tissue forming the outer coating of the eye and covering the iris and pupil, as long as the family didn't object. The law did not require the medical examiner to notify the family of the procedure. So many families may not have objected because they did not know what was being done. About half of the 50 states have similar laws governing the procurement of corneas. In states where there is no law giving medical examiners the authority to remove corneas, the typical wait for a transplant is from three to six months. "In every state where theres a similar law, the waiting list is very small," a doctor said.

Harcourt Brace & Company

EXERCISE 4

THE BODY OF A NEWS STORY

REPORTING CONTROVERSIAL STORIES (QUOTING OPPOSING VIEWPOINTS)

INSTRUCTIONS: Write complete news stories about the following controversies. As you write the stories, present both sides of each controversy as fully and as fairly as possible. Also, try to integrate those conflicting viewpoints. Instead of reporting all the opinions voiced by the first source, and then all the conflicting opinions voiced by the second source, try—when appropriate—to report both opinions about the story's most important issue, and then both opinions about the second, third and fourth issues.

STORY 1: POLICE RESPONSE TIME

FACTS: Two armed gunmen robbed the Jewelry Shoppe at 1118 Main Street at about noon yesterday. They escaped with about $1,200 in cash and with jewelry valued at about $35,000 to $40,000. The two gunmen, described as being in their mid-20s, wore business suits when they entered the store and said they wanted to look at a watch then drew their handguns and forced the owner, Thomas Hoequist, to empty several cash registers and to open several display cases containing watches, rings, pearl earrings and necklaces, which they scooped up. "They knew what they wanted," Hoequist said. "They took only the best." Two clerks and five customers in the store at the time were made to lie face down on the floor.

ONE SIDE: Hoequist told reporters covering the robbery: "I'm very upset, very upset. The first police car didn't arrive until 10 minutes after I pushed a silent alarm button we have in the store, and its connected directly to the police station. I pushed it as soon as I saw their guns, but the men escaped before the police arrived. We've had some false alarms in the past. I've pushed the button by mistake once or twice myself, and so have the employees. Then two or three police cars would come screeching into our parking lot in a minute or two. The officers would all jump out of their cars holding shotguns and revolvers. Yesterday, the only guns I saw were the ones pointed at me."

THE OTHER SIDE: Police Chief Barry Kopperud, interviewed in his office late yesterday, said: "Our records show that 9 minutes elapsed before the first police car arrived on the scene, but all the units in that district were extremely busy on other calls. We aren't required to respond to calls within a specified length of time, and sometimes we can't. Its not uncommon for us to reach the scene of a complaint within 2 or 3 minutes, and thats what we try to do when its a real emergency. That didn't happen yesterday because there was a four-minute delay before the first patrol car was dispatched to the store because all the cars in the district were extremely busy. It took another 5 minutes for the car to get there because it was miles away in another district at the time. We had a problem because, at the same time the call was received, several patrol cars were chasing a man driving a stolen car. Another car had just arrived at Midtown Park, where a young woman who had been severely beaten had just been found. It was a long dispatch time, but there are times when we are extremely busy. Every day, our heaviest volume of calls comes between 11 a.m. and midafternoon. It really comes down to a problem of money. Without more money, we can't put more cars on the road, but people say their taxes already are too high. It really wasn't a factor here, but you've also got to consider that we've had 10 false alarms from this store in the last year. After a while, its like crying wolf; you just don't believe it anymore. It makes you more reluctant to move an officer from where he's really needed."

STORY 2: HOUSING PROJECT

FACTS: Your City Council voted last night on a proposal to locate a low-income housing project in the 4200 block of Forest Boulevard, which is part of the Creekside Village subdivision. The project would consist of 14 two-story brick buildings. Each building would house 6 to 8 families. The project would cost $6 million and would be federally subsidized. It would serve the elderly, the handicapped and low-income families. After last nights meeting, at which many people loudly and vigorously objected to the plans, the City Council vetoed the proposal by a unanimous vote of 7 to 0. The plans were presented to the City Council by the Tri-County Housing Authority, which is a semi-autonomous public body but which needs the approval of local governing boards to locate its projects within the boundaries of their jurisdictions.

ONE SIDE: The director of the City Housing Authority, Tom Chinn Onn, told the City Council before the vote: "I'm really disappointed in the opposition here tonight. We have a backlog of over 900 applicants waiting to find public housing. This would go a long way toward meeting that need. Low income people are the ones who'll be hurt, badly hurt, if this isn't approved. Everyone seems to be saying they want to help the poor, but no one wants them in their own neighborhoods. Everyone complains when we try to place them in a nice neighborhood. And a lot of what you're hearing tonight about this project is emotional rather than factual. Its all scare tactics. Studies done by Don Brame (the citys traffic operations engineer) show that the project would add only 600 to 800 additional vehicles on the areas roads on a daily basis, and thats a very liberal estimate considering that about a third of the units would be occupied by older people who probably wouldn't drive much. The elderly also wouldn't need other city facilities, like schools. Now, we've already spent more than $160,000 planning this project, and all the money will be wasted, just totally wasted, if you reject this proposal, and we've got nowhere else to go with it. Everyone says they want to help the poor, but they want to help them somewhere else. Thats real hypocrisy. This is a chance for the members of this council to be real statesmen and do some real good for some needy people. This means a lot to them, so I ask you to approve these plans."

THE OTHER SIDE: Residents of the neighborhood voiced the following complaints during the council meeting. Frank D. Shadgett of 8472 Chestnut Drive said, "This thing would cause all sorts of problems: crowded roads, crowded schools, more kids in the streets. We don't have enough parks, and there's only one junior high school and one high school that serve our neighborhood, and both have been filled for years. Now, if you dump this project on us, you'll have to bus some of our children out of their neighborhood schools, or you'll have to bring in some portable classrooms. There are other places that could handle the project better. It just doesn't fit in our neighborhood. You should come out and look at the area before coming up with an idea like this. A lot of our homes cost $100,000 or $150,000 or more. You put this project in the middle of them, and it'll hurt our property values." Another person, James Lasater of 374 Walnut Drive said: "The area is zoned for single-family homes and thats why we invested here. We've got our life savings in our homes, and this will hurt us. We've got no lack of compassion for the cause, but it just doesn't belong here. We want to protect our neighborhood and keep our neighborhood the way it is. We object to this bunch of bureaucrats coming in and changing its character. Its a good area to live in, and we don't want that to change." An attorney representing the neighborhood, Michael Perakis, said: "The area is one of the most stable and beautiful single-family neighborhoods in the city, and these people are only interested in maintaining that status. Right now, you're in danger of violating your own laws if you put this project in Creekside Village. There's been no proper hearings to rezone the land, and this project doesn't fit its current zoning restrictions. The zoning laws are intended to prevent this very kind of thing, this invasion of a residential neighborhood with a nonconforming project of any type."

STORY 3: SCHOOL ATTENDANCE INCENTIVE PROGRAM

FACTS: Greg Hubbard, superintendent of schools in your city, has adopted a unique but controversial pilot program. Last year, the citys school district lost $1,132,000 in state funds because it had an overall 6.4 percent absenteeism rate, compared to a statewide average of 5.3%. To try to solve the problem, Hubbard persuaded the members of the school board to set up a $25,000 fund to pay students at Roosevelt High School the equivalent of 25 cents a day—a maximum of $5 a month. Last fall, students in the school began getting a coupon worth 25 cents for every day of attendance. Students can exchange their tokens in the schools student bookstore for school supplies such as notebooks and pencils. Since then, the absentee rate at the 1,410-student school has averaged about 13.7%, compared to 15.2% for the same period last year, when it had the worst attendance in the city.

ONE SIDE: In an interview in his office today, Supt. Hubbard said: "We're trying this program out in one high school where our worst truancy problems exist. Then if it works, we may expand it to other schools. Under this program, a student can earn the equivalent of $5 a month just for being there—for attending school and compiling a perfect attendance record. They are credited with the equivalent of 25 cents for every day they make it to school and to all their classes on time. They don't actually get any cash. They get coupons they can use in the school store. We mark up the prices of goods sold in the store about 50%, so it really costs us a lot less than the students receive. So far as I know, the idea has been tried in only two or three other school districts, including one in San Diego, and I just thought we might try it here. We've really got nothing to lose. Some students just don't see any other reason to attend school. My responsibility is to give teachers an opportunity to teach the students, and getting them to attend class is a necessary first step. We already can see the results. Attendance is up, and inquiries have been pouring in from other school districts from all over the state and from news organizations as far away as England and Japan. There's a tremendous curiosity about it. It sort of shocks some parents to pay children to go to school, but nothing else has worked. If this works, it could save us thousands of dollars a year in lost state aid, and certainly the students are better off being in school."

THE OTHER SIDE: Stephen I. Wong is chairman of the citys School Advisory Committee, which is composed of one parent representative from each school in the city. Wong is opposed to the program. Today he said: "The program gambles with taxpayers money. The 25 cents they give students comes out of our tax money. If attendance improves by 25 percent or more over a full year, we'll recover the money in increased state aid. But if the attendance figure remains low, we'll lose money. So we're gambling, and that just doesn't seem right. Its also materialistic and amounts to bribery. We shouldn't have to pay our children to do something as basic as going to school because then they expect to get paid for everything. Already, we've got some students in that high school complaining they aren't being paid enough, and students in other schools are demanding that they get paid, too. These kids are winding up with some very unrealistic ideas about how the world works and about what education is all about. Besides, the whole thing is cosmetic. It doesn't solve our real problems. The long-term remedies for truancy lie in more fundamental changes. I'll admit attendance is up so far this year, but not very much, and we don't know the real reason. It could be the money, or it could be something totally different. You also have to recognize that, once these students get to high school, they don't have to do well. They can flunk all their classes and still get paid. Some of these students also could be disruptive, so it may be better for other students if they don't come to school. Its a hell of a mess."

STORY 4: BANNING HANDGUNS

FACTS: In a close vote at a City Council meeting in your community last night, the members voted 4 to 3 to ban the sale and possession of handguns, except by law enforcement officers and by those persons holding a permit issued by the chief of police. The law goes into effect on Jan. 1 of next year, and those persons now possessing handguns will, according to the law, have to dispose of them by that time. First-time violators of the law will face a fine of $50 to $500. A second offense carries maximum penalties of up to six months in jail or a fine of up to $500, or both.

ONE SIDE: Councilman Luis Ramirez, who spoke and voted in favor of the law, said during last nights meeting: "Theres no question, the law is valid and doesn't infringe on an individuals constitutional rights. We recognize the deep-seated convictions of a number of persons that they should be permitted to possess handguns for the purpose of protecting themselves and their families and property. But in this case the public interest outweighs the claim of personal interests. We're adopting this law for the overall good of the entire city, to help protect all its citizens from the careless and lawless use of handguns. I'm sure that hundreds of other cities are going to follow our example and consider similar measures. If they do, a lot of lives could be saved. Theres no sense to the current slaughter. People can't use handguns to hunt with. Their only purpose is to shoot people. They're used mostly by criminals and, in this city alone, we have 8 or 10 people killed by guns every year and many more seriously injured. There also are hundreds and hundreds of robberies committed with handguns. This law will help put a stop to that. If people want to hunt, they can still buy a rifle or shotgun, and they can use a rifle or shotgun to protect themselves in their homes if they want. But its harder for a criminal to conceal a weapon that large when he goes into a grocery store or restaurant with the intention of robbing it."

THE OTHER SIDE: Margaret Ungarient, an attorney representing the citizens opposed to the ban, said at the meeting: "We plan to appeal. The law infringes on citizens constitutional right to keep and bear arms. Its also a matter of self-defense. Criminals do use some handguns in committing crimes. But that doesn't mean the solution is to take away everyones gun. Law-abiding citizens would comply with this law, but criminals never would. So the criminals would be the only ones with guns, and everyone else would be at their mercy. The council has, in effect, ruled in favor of a minority element that has for a long time been trying to deny the rights of other individuals. We won't rest until this gets reversed in a court of law. If we have to, we'll take this all the way to the Supreme Court."

CHAPTER 8

QUOTATIONS AND ATTRIBUTION

The function of the press is very high. It is almost holy. It ought to serve as a forum for the people, through which the people may know freely what is going on. To misstate or suppress the news is a breach of trust.

(Justice Louis D. Brandeis, U.S. Supreme Court)

Reporters obtain much of their information by listening to other people, and they can convey that information to readers in the form of (1) direct, (2) indirect or (3) partial quotations. Direct quotations present a source's exact words and consequently are placed entirely in quotation marks. Indirect quotations are not placed inside quotation marks because reporters use their own words to summarize, or paraphrase, the source's remarks. Partial quotations take key phrases from a source's statement and quote them directly:

INDIRECT QUOTATION: Mrs. Ambrose said journalism students should deal with ideas, not mechanical techniques.

PARTIAL QUOTATION: Mrs. Ambrose criticized the "trade-school atmosphere" in journalism schools and said students should study ideas, not mechanical techniques.

DIRECT QUOTATION: Mrs. Ambrose said: "Journalism students should be dealing with ideas of a social, economic and political nature. There's too much of a trade-school atmosphere in journalism schools today. One spends too much time on minor technical and mechanical things, like learning how to write headlines."

WHEN TO USE DIRECT, INDIRECT AND PARTIAL QUOTATIONS

Reporters use direct quotations when their sources say something important or controversial and state their ideas in an interesting, unusual or colorful manner. Direct quotations are so much a part of news stories that reporters and editors may think a story is incomplete without its quota of quotations. But reporters who merely decorate their stories with quotations are not using them effectively.

Jack Hart, the writing coach and staff development director for The Oregonian in Portland, has identified several instances when direct quotations are appropriate:

- Use quotations to let the sources talk directly to the reader.

- Use quotations when you cannot improve on the speaker's exact words or cannot match the speaker's wit, rhythm, color or emotion.

- Use quotations to tie a controversial opinion to the source.

- Use quotations as evidence for a statement.

- Use quotations to reveal the speaker's character.

One of George Bush's first statements after he became president fit several of these criteria, and many of the nation's news media quoted him. Bush said:

> I do not like broccoli. I haven't liked it since I was a little kid and my mother made me eat it. And I'm president of the United States, and I'm not going to eat any more broccoli.

If you listen carefully, you will hear all kinds of people say things that will fascinate your readers. When you hear one of those quotations, record its exact wording, then use it in your story.

Direct quotations do not have to be long. Four words spoken by President Richard M. Nixon during the Watergate scandals fascinated the American public not only because the president said them but also because he felt the need to say them: "I'm not a crook."

Reporters use indirect quotations when their sources have not stated their ideas effectively. By using indirect quotations, reporters can rephrase their sources' remarks, stating them more clearly and concisely. Reporters can also emphasize the sources' most significant remarks and reword or eliminate remarks that are unclear, irrelevant, libelous, pretentious or otherwise unprintable:

> ORIGINAL STATEMENT: He said, "I fully intend to resign from my position as mayor of this city."
> PARAPHRASED: The mayor said he plans to resign.

> ORIGINAL STATEMENT: Mrs. Czarski said, "Women do not get the same tax and insurance benefits that men receive, and they do not receive maternity benefits that even start to cover what they should."
> PARAPHRASED: Mrs. Czarski said women receive neither the same tax and insurance benefits as men nor adequate maternity benefits.

Reporters avoid partial, or fragmentary, quotations. Most partial quotations are awkward, wordy or unnecessary. Sentences that contain several partial quotations are particularly distracting. The phrases should be paraphrased or used in indirect constructions, with the quotation marks simply eliminated:

> FRAGMENT: He said the press barons "such as William Randolph Hearst" created "an amazingly rich variety" of newspapers.
> REVISED: He said the press barons such as William Randolph Hearst created an amazingly rich variety of newspapers.

Reporters also avoid using "orphan" quotes—that is, they do not place quotation marks around an isolated word or two used in an ordinary way. The addition of quotation marks to emphasize individual words is inappropriate. Similarly, there is no reason to place quotation marks around profanities, slang, clichés or grammatical errors:

> He complained that no one "understands" his problem.
> REVISED: He complained that no one understands his problem.

> She said that having to watch her child die was worse than "hell" could possibly be.
> REVISED: She said that having to watch her child die was worse than hell could possibly be.

At worst, an orphan quotation may be libelous. A New York newspaper included this sentence in a story about a murder case: "As police delved into his tangled business affairs, several women described as 'associated' with Brenhouse (the victim) were questioned at Hastings Police Headquarters." One of those women, who was named in the story, sued for libel. She argued—

Harcourt Brace & Company

and the court agreed—that readers would infer from the quotation marks around "associated" that she had been having a love affair with the victim.

Reporters use partial quotations only for statements that are particularly controversial, important or interesting. The use of partial quotations also helps attribute the statements more clearly to their sources:

Hendricks said he killed the girls "because they laughed at me."

Phil Donahue accused the television critic of "typing with razor blades."

The petition urged the City Council to ban the sale of Penthouse and Playboy magazines "for the sake of our wives and children."

USING DIRECT QUOTATIONS EFFECTIVELY

Direct quotations should illustrate a point, not tell an entire story. Stories composed entirely of quotations seem poorly organized because they lack natural transitions. The following story contains a pleasing combination of quotations and paraphrases:

She started dancing six months ago after a friend told her about the job. Debbie (who does not want her last name used) said: "I knew my friend was dancing topless, but I didn't think I could ever do it. At the time, though, I was desperate to find a job, so I agreed to try it."

Debbie said she felt guilty the first time she appeared topless in front of other people but "after the first time, it seemed there was nothing to hide anymore."

Now, after dancing topless for half a year, Debbie says: "I really enjoy it because there is no actual work involved. I love to dance anyway and I can pick my own hours around my class schedule and, with tips, earn $1,400 a week."

Few of Debbie's classmates know about her job. She explains: "It's not that I'm ashamed of what I do. It just makes it easier for me to know that no one in the audience will be sitting beside me in a class the next morning. I know the general public thinks that what I do is pretty low, and I don't want other students to say, 'There goes that topless dancer.'"

Be careful to use quotations only when they provide some additional information about a topic. Reporters often summarize a major point, then use a direct quotation to explain the idea or provide more specific details about it:

Karcher's girlfriend was instructing a class of lifeguards and asked him to help administer their final test. Karcher said: "My job was to go out in the lake and act like I was drowning. I was to bite, scratch, tear—anything to try to keep them from rescuing me."

A quotation should not repeat facts reported earlier in a story, as in this example:

Company officials said they are not worried about the upcoming audit.
"We're not expecting anything to worry about," treasurer Peter VanNeffe said.

Quotations can also help describe a story's dramatic moments. Because of their importance, those moments should be described in detail and placed near the beginning of a story. The following quotations are so interesting and dramatic that they compel readers to finish the story:

As the grease and flames spread, she panicked and poured water on them. "That just made the flames go higher," she cried. "I knew the whole house was going to burn down, so I picked up my baby and ran outside."

"After the accident I must have passed out for a minute," she said. "Then I woke up and realized the car was on fire. I thought I was going to die. I wasn't badly hurt, but I couldn't get out. I couldn't move."

"I was confused," the girl said. "I woke up at about 2 a.m. and saw this strange man standing near my bed. I didn't know why he was there, and at first I thought my parents had visitors or something. Then I realized he was a prowler."

Quotations help to reveal the personalities of the people in the news, showing them to be unique, interesting individuals. A story about a middle-aged woman who returned to college included this revealing quotation:

"Very practically, I came back to college to get my degree in education because I wanted to be busy and couldn't quite see myself as a 40-year-old checkout clerk in some supermarket. Fifteen years of my life consisted of runny noses and coffee klatches with the neighbors. Now my kids wipe their own noses and the neighbors are still having coffee klatches, and I'm going to be a senior next term."

Using Exact Words and Ellipses

Reporters usually follow one of two approaches—the pragmatic or the purist—on the matter of whether to use a source's exact words in a quotation. The pragmatic approach holds that people rarely speak in clean, complete sentences. Instead, they pause, stutter and repeat themselves. Pragmatists say reporters should use common sense and correct obvious slips of the tongue: errors that would make the source look bad or passages that make the reader's job more difficult. They may go further and correct obvious factual errors. They call it "doctoring," "massaging" or "cleaning up" a quotation. The pragmatists are most likely to clean up the quotations of people unaccustomed to dealing with the media. They are less likely to correct quotations from prominent sources whose language seems careless or inappropriate.

The purist approach says quotation marks are sacrosanct—that every word placed inside quotation marks should be a source's exact words. Purists fear that if they alter a quotation, they may be accused of fictionalizing or lying to their readers. They add that the practice of doctoring quotations destroys their richness and originality and may make sources sound more eloquent than they really are. Moreover, the purists fear that readers do not understand why reporters clean up quotations and that any changes make it easier for sources to claim they were misquoted.

A recent, highly publicized libel case involved the propriety of changing quotations, but the case was resolved in a way that lends support to both schools of thought. Psychoanalyst Jeffrey Masson sued journalist Janet Malcolm and The New Yorker magazine over a profile of him that was published in 1983. The profile was based on extensive interviews of Masson that Malcolm had tape-recorded, but Masson said Malcolm had made up some defamatory quotations and attributed them to him. One of the disputed quotations was on tape, but Masson said it had been taken out of context. The other quotations were not on the tapes, but Malcolm said Masson made some of the controversial statements when the tape recorder was broken or not present. She said she had made handwritten notes of those conversations but lost them after she made a typed version.[1] The case reached the U.S. Supreme Court in 1991 on the question of whether the deliberate alteration of quotations may be evidence that the author knowingly published a falsehood about a libel plaintiff.

The Supreme Court refused to say that all alterations of quotations are evidence of deliberate falsehood. The court recognized that quotations do not always present the exact words of the speaker, and evidence that a reporter simply cleaned up grammar and made other stylistic changes is not going to be enough for a plaintiff to win a libel suit. Only if the reporter has materially changed the meaning of the source's words and the change is defamatory can it be the basis for a libel suit, the court said.

Using the source's exact words eliminates questions about accuracy. It also is the approach most news organizations require. If you are uncertain about the source's exact words (or think a

---

[1]Malcolm announced in 1995, after a second jury trial, that she had found her missing handwritten notes.

statement needs rewriting), use an indirect rather than a direct quotation. If you doctor a quotation or make a mistake, you may seriously injure your source's reputation as well as your own. Whether you use the speaker's exact words or an indirect quotation, you always have an obligation to present that person's views as faithfully as possible.

Everyone, even the purists, recognize a few exceptions to the principle of using a person's exact words in direct quotations. They usually involve the deletion of unnecessary words, grammatical errors and profanities:

> ORIGINAL STATEMENT: He said, "Look, you know I think nuclear power is safe, absolutely safe."
> REVISION: He said, "Nuclear power is safe, absolutely safe."

Reporters may add an ellipsis (three periods) if they delete a number of words, such as an entire phrase or sentence. An ellipsis that appears at the end, rather than the middle, of a statement that is a complete sentence should have four periods. Policies vary from news organization to news organization, and some journalists do not use ellipses in reporting ordinary interviews. Reporters are more likely to use them when quoting formal statements or documents.

Correcting Grammatical Errors

Normally, reporters correct the grammatical errors in direct quotations. An editor at The New York Times has explained: "Cultured people are not expected to maintain in conversation the rigid grammatical standards normally applied to writing, so we delete their false starts and grammatical lapses. Failing to do so would make those we quote seem illiterate by subjecting their spoken language to the standards of writing." Similarly, The Associated Press Stylebook says, "Quotations should be corrected to avoid the errors in grammar and word usage that often occur unnoticed in speech, but are embarrassing in print." For example:

> GRAMMATICAL ERROR: An usher said, "The people started pouring in, and there weren't no way to stop them."
> REVISED: An usher said, "The people started pouring in, and there wasn't any (*or* was no) way to stop them."

Some sources are so well known for the way they misuse words or create confusing sentences that reporters should not clean up their statements. The late Casey Stengel, a baseball manager, was famous for sentences like this one describing an unusually lucky player: "He could fall in a hole and come up with a silver spoon." A more recent example is Alexander Haig, who was President Ronald Reagan's first secretary of state. Haig's use of nouns as verbs and convoluted sentences became known among Washington reporters as "Haigspeak." On one occasion, Haig said, "I'll have to caveat any response, Senator, and I'll caveat that."

Deleting Profanities

Reporters delete most profanities. Editors and news directors explain that their newspapers and programs are seen by entire families. Some children read newspapers and watch news programs, but even some adults are likely to be offended by four-letter words. News organizations are becoming more candid, and many publish mild profanities that are essential to a story. However, most forbid the publication of casual profanities—those used habitually and unnecessarily by many people:

> PROFANITY: "Shit, I wasn't going to try to stop that damned idiot," the witness testified. "He had a knife."
> REVISED: "I wasn't going to try to stop that idiot," the witness testified. "He had a knife."

Harcourt Brace & Company

Stressing Answers, Not Questions

When reporters quote someone, they normally stress the source's answers, not the questions they asked the source. The use of both questions and answers is unnecessary, repetitive and dull. Reporters can either omit the questions or incorporate them into the answers:

> INCORRECT: The president was asked whether he plans to seek a second term, and he responded that he would not announce his decision until next winter.
>
> REVISED: The president said he would not announce his decision regarding a second term until next winter.
>
> OR: In response to a question, the president said he would not announce his decision regarding a second term until next winter.
>
> OR: During a question-and-answer session after his speech, the president said he would not announce his decision regarding a second term until next winter.

Explaining Quotations

Sometimes reporters start a paragraph with a quotation, then they realize readers need background information to understand the quotation. Here's an example:

> "We're mobilizing for an economic war with other cities and states," the mayor said of his plan for attracting new businesses to the city.

The backward construction forces readers to complete the sentence before they can figure out what the topic is. Instead of using this "said of" construction, turn the sentence around and use a partial quotation or an indirect quotation. For example:

> The mayor said his plan for attracting new business amounted to mobilization for an economic war with other cities and states.

Reporters occasionally insert in parentheses the clarifying information a quotation may need. The use of parenthetical matter should be sparing. If reporters pepper their stories with parenthetical explanations, the stories become more difficult to read. Each bit of parenthetical matter forces readers to pause and absorb some additional information before moving on with the rest of the sentence. Here are examples of acceptable and unacceptable uses of parentheses:

> UNACCEPTABLE: "When (head coach Tom) Whitman decides on his starter (at quarterback), the rest of them (the players) will quit squabbling," the athletic director said.
>
> REVISED: The football players will quit squabbling when head coach Tom Whitman selects a starting quarterback, the athletic director said.
>
> ACCEPTABLE: Dr. Harold Termid, who performed the operation, said, "The technique dates back before the 20th century, when it was first used by the French to study ruminants (cud-chewing animals)."

Avoiding Weak Quotations

In an effort to brighten their stories, some reporters use whatever quotations happen to be available. Yet a weak quotation is worse than none. If a quotation bores or confuses people, many will immediately stop reading a story. A story about a stadium sound system contained this quotation:

> "For that type of sound system, that reading isn't particularly loud," Pugsley said.

The quotation is neither interesting nor colorful, and the information could have been conveyed more concisely in a paraphrase. Compare that quotation with this next one, from a story about an

Harcourt Brace & Company

itinerate preacher and his family. The preacher's wife said the family had just returned from a missionary trip across Eastern Europe, and she described the journey this way:

"It's drive and preach, drive and preach," she said. "It's horrible, and it's glorious."

The quotation concisely and forcefully conveys the monotony and exhilaration the preacher's wife experienced on her travels. The reader who encounters this quotation is likely to want to know more about the preacher and his family.

Reporters can never justify a weak quotation by responding, "But that's what my source said." The quotations reporters use reflect their judgment and interviewing techniques. Use only strong quotations—quotations that are clear, concise, dramatic and interesting.

Sometimes a source will give you only routine, boring quotations such as, "I really love to play football." Continue your interview, asking better questions, until you get a better response. Here's the type of quotation you want:

"I really love football," Joe Lozado said. "I've been playing since I was 7 years old, and I would feel worthless if I couldn't play. There's no better feeling than just before a game when you run out on the field with all your buddies and see the crowd. You can feel the excitement."

Asking questions that encourage the source to elaborate on her or his ideas or reactions often will produce good quotations.

Some reporters go farther and dream up what they think sources should say and then try to get them to say it. James Carville, the political consultant who directed Bill Clinton's 1992 presidential campaign, has written: "There's no one who has dealt with the national media who has not gotten any number of phone calls saying, 'I'm writing a story and I want to say this. Can you say it for me?'" This practice is unethical and it distorts the news. Let the source say what is on his or her mind; the good reporter, who should also be a good listener, usually will find plenty of things to quote.

Avoid quotations that state the obvious: something your readers already know. The following quotations are likely to sound familiar, because they appear dozens of times every year. You may see these quotations in newspapers or hear them on radio and television:

"We really want to win this game," coach Riley said. (Readers already know this. Does any coach want to lose?)

"If we can score some points, we can win this game," Tran Ogbondah said. (A team that does not score points obviously cannot win.)

Equally weak are quotations that are vague and self-serving—quotations that enable sources to praise themselves and their programs:

Lyons called her program a success. "We had a terrific crowd and a particularly good turnout," she said.

Reading or listening to someone's self-praise is no more interesting than watching a videotape of someone else's vacation.

Editorializations

Avoid unintentional editorials. If worded carelessly, partial quotations, and even the form of attribution used, can express an opinion:

EDITORIALIZATION: The mayor made it clear that the city cannot afford to give its employees a raise.

REVISED: The mayor said the city cannot afford to give its employees a raise.

EDITORIALIZATION: Each month, Sen. William Proxmire presented the Golden Fleece Award "for the biggest, most ironic or most ridiculous example of wasteful government spending."

REVISED: Each month, Sen. William Proxmire presented the Golden Fleece Award for what he considered "the biggest, most ironic or most ridiculous example of wasteful government spending."

Before revision, the first sentence editorialized by saying the mayor "made it clear"—that she stated a fact in a convincing manner. Others might regard the statement that the city cannot afford pay raises for employees as an opinion or political posturing. The second sentence reported as fact Proxmire's claim that all the recipients of his "award" wasted the government's money; yet many of the recipients disagreed, and some provided convincing evidence that Proxmire was wrong.

THE NEED FOR ATTRIBUTION

The Purpose of Attribution

Reporters are experts in finding things out. They rarely possess expertise in the topics they write about, such as law, medicine, finance or international relations. Instead, reporters must rely on the expertise of their sources. Attribution lets the readers know who the reporter's sources are. Ideally, all direct quotations, opinions, evaluations and second-hand statements of fact should be attributed to specific individuals. This information lets readers draw their own conclusions about the credibility of the story.

Reporters can attribute information to people, documents or publications, but not to places or institutions. For example, reporters can quote a hospital official, but not a hospital:

INCORRECT: The hospital said the epidemic has ended.
REVISED: A hospital spokesperson said the epidemic has ended.

INCORRECT: Atlanta announced that all city offices will be closed next Monday.
REVISED: The mayor of Atlanta announced that all city offices will be closed next Monday.

You should not attribute a direct quotation to more than one person. Instead, eliminate the quotation marks. Two or more people rarely use exactly the same words.

Levels of Attribution

Reporters and sources need to agree at the start of an interview on how the source's statements will be attributed. Ideally, every source should be fully identified, but sometimes a source wants his or her identity withheld. Experienced reporters and sources have worked out a shorthand for describing how much of the source's identity may be revealed and how much of what the source says may be published.

On the record attribution means that everything the source says may be published and quoted directly, and the source may be fully identified by name and title. Reporters should try to keep on the record as much of every interview as possible. This allows readers to see or hear the source's exact words and know who the source is.

When an interview is *on background,* the reporter may quote the source directly but may not attribute the statements to the source by name. The reporter may describe the source by her or his position. When you see stories that attribute information to a "senior State Department

Harcourt Brace & Company

spokesperson," "congressional aides," "reliable sources in the Treasury Department" or "sources close to the president," you are reading stories based on background interviews. If you agree to let the source give you information on background, you should try to describe that person as precisely as possible. To say the information came from "a government employee" is meaningless. If you can say the source is "an aide to the speaker of the House," you will have given your readers more information. The source often will try to keep the identification as vague as possible; you must try to make it as precise as possible.

On deep background is a variation of the backgrounder. This level of attribution is sometimes called the Lindley Rule, named after Ernest K. Lindley, a Newsweek reporter who used it to get U.S. military leaders to talk about their strategy and objectives during World War II. When the source is on deep background, she or he may not be quoted directly and may not be identified in any way. The reporter must publish the information without any attribution or with a phrase like, "It has been learned that. . . ." Unless reporters have a high degree of confidence in the source and the information—and the approval of their supervisors—they should stay away from information given on deep background.

Off the record is the final level of attribution. It generally means that the source's information cannot be used, but that is often misunderstood. Some people will say they are speaking off the record when they really mean they are speaking on background. Also, reporters and sources sometimes disagree as to exactly what "off the record" means. The U.S. State Department's Office of Press Relations says reporters may not use "off the record" information in any way. Reporters, however, sometimes use off-the-record information as leads. Almost every "secret" is known by several people, sometimes hundreds of people. Once reporters know what they are looking for, they usually can locate public records or sources willing to speak publicly, either of which may verify the information.

Some reporters refuse to listen to off-the-record statements. If you cannot publish or broadcast the information, why listen to it? Others see it as an opportunity to gain insight into official thinking. Or it may help them put the information they can publish in a more accurate context.

Anonymous Sources

If reporters should keep sources on the record as much as possible, why do so many stories use anonymous sources?

Sometimes sources want to remain anonymous for legitimate reasons. (See the nearby sidebar for guidelines on when to use anonymous sources.) Corporate or government officials who want to blow the whistle on waste, fraud or other illegal or unethical conduct at their workplace may fear retaliation. Many have lost jobs or been demoted because they disclosed truths that made their supervisors uncomfortable. The Seattle Times made effective use of anonymous sources when it published a story saying U.S. Sen. Brock Adams had sexually harassed several women over a period of 20 years. The investigation began after Kari Tupper, a congressional aide, publicly accused Adams of having drugged and molested her. Although Tupper took her story to prosecutors, no charges were brought because the federal district attorney concluded the case had no merit. The Times, however, started getting phone calls from women who reported similar experiences with Adams but did not want to be publicly identified. Eventually, the Times agreed to publish a story detailing the women's charges so long as the accusers signed affidavits and promised to come forward if Adams sued the Times for libel. Adams abandoned his re-election campaign but denied the sexual harassment charges.

Anonymous sources often pose threats to the independence, accuracy and credibility of journalists. Benjamin Bradlee, the former executive editor of The Washington Post, deplored the continued abuse of unattributed information and said: "Why, then, do we go along so complacently with withholding the identity of public officials? I'm damned if I know. I do know that by doing so, we shamelessly do other people's bidding: We knowingly let ourselves be used. . . . In short, we demean our profession."

Anonymous sources often try to influence the way journalists cover the news. In Washington, high-level government sources often demand that their briefings be "on background" or "on deep background." The officials use these briefings to place administration policy in the best possible light. They think they can do that most effectively when their identities and their political motives are hidden from the general public. Reporters abide by the background rules officials set because of the competitive pressures they face to get the story.

Anonymous sources also may provide inaccurate information. Whether or not they do so intentionally, their anonymity protects them from any consequences of their mistakes. The same is not true of the media that publish the information. Several news organizations that covered the inmate riots at the Southern Ohio Correctional Facility at Lucasville received inaccurate information from anonymous sources. For instance, the Cleveland Plain Dealer said 19 had been killed in the riots, and the Portsmouth (Ohio) Daily Times said between 50 and 150 were dead.

GUIDELINES FOR USING ANONYMOUS SOURCES

Editors are becoming more reluctant to use anonymous sources. Journalism critics say reporters can get more information on the record by threatening to ignore all information from sources who demand anonymity. If some sources insist on remaining anonymous, reporters might seek the same information from other sources who are willing to be identified. On the rare occasions when justification exists for using anonymous sources, news directors and editors tell their reporters to follow guidelines like these:

1. Do not use anonymous sources without the approval of your supervising editor or news director.
2. Be prepared to disclose the identities of anonymous sources to your editors or news directors and, possibly, to your news organization's lawyer.
3. Use anonymous sources only if they provide facts that are essential to the story, not just interesting quotations or opinions. Be sure the source is appropriate for the story and that she or he is in a position to give authoritative information. Even then, information from anonymous sources should be verified.
4. Be sure you understand the motives of the anonymous source, such as whether the source is carrying a grudge or trying to puff a program or an agency. The motives help you evaluate the reliability of the information.
5. Identify sources as specifically as possible without revealing their identities so that readers can judge their importance and reliability. For example, instead of attributing information to "an informed source" or "a key official," you might attribute it to "an elected city official." This tells the reader the level of government in which the official works and alerts the reader to the fact that the official may have political interests. Never include any misleading information about the identity of a source, even if your motive is to protect the source.
6. Explain in the story why the source does not want to be identified.
7. Never allow a source to engage in anonymous attacks on other individuals or groups. Anonymous attacks risk involving you and your employer in a libel suit and are inherently unfair to the person attacked.

Both newspapers relied on unidentified sources, and both were wrong. In fact, nine inmates and one guard died in the riots.

A final problem with anonymous sources is that under some circumstances a promise to keep a source's identity secret can be enforced in court. The U.S. Supreme Court has ruled that a source whose identity is revealed after confidentiality was promised may sue for damages. The court said the law protects people who are injured when they rely on an explicit promise and that promise is broken. That law applies to everybody, the court said, including news organizations.

Statements that Require Attribution

Reporters do not have to attribute statements that report undisputed facts, such as the fact that World War II ended in 1945, that Boston is in Massachusetts or that three people died in an accident. Attribution is also unnecessary in stories that reporters witness. However, reporters must attribute the information given to them by other people, especially: (1) statements about controversial issues, (2) statements of opinion and (3) all direct and indirect quotations. News stories that fail to attribute such statements appear to present the reporter's personal opinions rather than the opinions of the sources. Two or three words of attribution are usually adequate:

> UNATTRIBUTED: The Birthing Center is an alternative for pregnant women who prefer more personalized care.
> ATTRIBUTED: Director Sally Malone said the Birthing Center is an alternative for pregnant women who prefer more personalized care.

You should attribute statements that criticize a person or organization. Again, clearly indicate that you are reporting what someone else said—not expressing your own opinions or those of the news organization you work for:

> UNATTRIBUTED: Congress has failed to deal effectively with the problem of unemployment.
> ATTRIBUTED: The Democrats said Congress has failed to deal effectively with the problem of unemployment.

Also attribute statements that assign blame. For example:

> UNATTRIBUTED: Acting in self-defense, the deputy shot the teen three times in the chest.
> ATTRIBUTED: The deputy said she was acting in self-defense when she shot the teen three times in the chest.

Statements that imply carelessness or recklessness or culpable conduct can become the basis for lawsuits. Careful attribution, particularly if the statements can be attributed to official sources, will reduce the risk of being sued.

WORD CHOICE IN ATTRIBUTING STATEMENTS

The words used to attribute statements must be accurate and impartial. For straight news stories, they also should be in the past tense.

Some form of the verb "to say" best describes how sources communicate information. For variety, reporters sometimes use such verbs as "comment," "reply," "declare," "add," "explain," "state," "continue," "point out," "note," "urge," "suggest" and "warn." Each of these has a more specific meaning than "say" and can be used only when that meaning accurately reflects the source's behavior. "Explain," for instance, means to make something comprehensible or less obscure. Unless the source was discussing a complicated or unclear topic, "explain" would not be an appropriate verb for attribution:

> ACCEPTABLE: She explained that tort law requires that the injurious consequences of a person's actions be foreseeable before that person can be held liable for damages.

> UNACCEPTABLE: The city council meeting will begin at 8 p.m., he explained.

In the first example, the source talks about a point of law that may be confusing or unclear to the average reader. The source's explanation increases understanding of the issue. The statement in the second sentence is obvious and needs no explanation; the most appropriate verb of attribution is "said."

Many editors object to the use of verbs such as "hope," "feel," "believe," "want" and "think." Editors say reporters know only what their sources tell them, not what those sources hope, feel, believe, want or think. Other words are even more inappropriate. People speak words—they do not "grin," "smile," "chuckle," "laugh," "sigh" or "cough" them. Reporters should rephrase such sentences:

> INCORRECT: "It's a wonderful movie," she smiled.
> REVISED: "It's a wonderful movie," she said.
> OR: "It's a wonderful movie," she said with a smile.
> OR: Smiling, she said, "It's a wonderful movie."

The words "claimed" and "admitted" are especially troublesome. The word "claimed" casts doubt on a source's remarks. It suggests that the remarks are controversial and possibly wrong. Similarly, the word "admitted" implies that a source conceded some point or confessed to an error, charge or crime. By comparison, the word "said" is almost always appropriate. It may sound awkward at first, but "said" is a neutral term, and reporters can use it any number of times in a single story.

Attribution should also be concise. Each of the following phrases (which have actually appeared in news stories) can be replaced by either "said" or "added":

made it clear that	said that he feels that
further stated that	brought out the idea that
went on to say that	went on to say that in his opinion
let it be known that	in making the announcement said that
also pointed out that	continued the speech by urging that
emphasized the fact that	responded to the question by saying that
stated in the report that	concluded the speech with the comment that

GUIDELINES FOR THE PLACEMENT AND FREQUENCY OF ATTRIBUTION

Attribution may be placed at the beginning or at the end of a sentence, or at a natural break within it. However, it should never interrupt a thought:

> "I shall," Gen. MacArthur said, "return."
> REVISED: Gen. MacArthur said, "I shall return."

> ACCEPTABLE: "Some men are killed in a war and some men are wounded," President Kennedy said, "and some men never leave the country. Life is unfair."

Readers and listeners should be told who is speaking as soon as conveniently possible; they should never have to guess. If a quotation is long, the writer should place the attribution at the beginning or end of the first sentence or after the first meaningful clause in that sentence. The attribution should not be delayed until the end of the second or third sentence. Similarly, if a quotation contains only one sentence, but that sentence is long, the attribution should come at or near the beginning of that sentence—not at the end:

> "However close we sometimes seem to that dark and final abyss, let no man of peace and freedom despair. For he does not stand alone. If we all can persevere, if we can in every land and office look beyond our shores and ambitions, then surely the age will dawn in which the strong are just and the weak secure and the peace preserved," the president said.
>
> REVISED: "However close we sometimes seem to that dark and final abyss," the president said, "let no man of peace and freedom despair. For he does not stand alone. If we all can persevere, if we can in every land and office look beyond our shores and ambitions, then surely the age will dawn in which the strong are just and the weak secure and the peace preserved."

Attribution should come at the beginning of any quotation where there is a change of speakers. If reporters fail to provide transitions from one speaker to another, particularly when the statements are contradictory, readers may not understand who is speaking:

> The newspaper's editor said he no longer will accept advertisements for X-rated movies. He explained: "These movies are worthless. They contribute nothing to society and offend our readers. They're depressing and pornographic."
>
> "Newspapers have no right to pass judgment on matters of taste. If they do, they should also ban the advertisements for other products considered harmful: cigarettes, liquor and pollutants like automobiles," a theater owner responded.

These two paragraphs are confusing. Readers beginning the second paragraph might mistakenly assume that the editor has begun to contradict himself. The writer can avoid the confusion by placing a brief transition at the beginning of the second paragraph, such as the following: "However, a local theater owner responded, 'Newspapers have no right. . . .'"

Direct Quotations

A direct quotation should be attributed only once, regardless of the number of sentences it contains:

> INCORRECT: "I'm opposed to any laws that prohibit the sale of pornography," the attorney said. "The restriction of pornography infringes on Americans' First Amendment rights," he said. "I like to picture myself as a good guy defending a sleazy thing," he concluded.
>
> REVISED: "I'm opposed to any laws that prohibit the sale of pornography," the attorney said. "The restriction of pornography infringes on Americans' First Amendment rights. I like to picture myself as a good guy defending a sleazy thing."

Even when the direct quotation continues for several paragraphs, it needs attribution only once:

> Capt. Bonventre eliminated the Police Department's motorcycle squad. "The main reason is that there are more injuries to motorcycle officers," he said. "I want to protect my officers. They think there's no danger on a cycle. Well, that's just optimistic thinking; there's a real danger.
>
> "Officers have much more protection in a car. I think that's pretty obvious. If an officer gets in a hot pursuit and crashes, he stands a better chance of escaping injury when he's in a car.
>
> "Also, almost any situation, even traffic, can be handled better in a patrol car than on a motorcycle. There are some places a motorcycle can go more easily, but a car certainly commands more respect."

Harcourt Brace & Company

Reporters also must avoid "floating" quotations: direct quotations that lack clear attribution to a speaker. Direct quotations need attribution only once, but that attribution must be clearly attached to the quotation. Careless writers sometimes name a source in one sentence and then deliver an unattributed quotation in the following sentence or paragraph. The reader then must figure out whether the quotation comes from the person just named or someone who will be identified later. The uncertainty halts the reader. Several such delays can cause the reader to put down the newspaper. Clear attribution makes the reader's work easier:

INCORRECT: The sociologist said there is a trend toward vocationalism on college campuses.

"Many students now demand from college not a chance to think, but a chance to become qualified for some job."

REVISED: The sociologist said there is a trend toward vocationalism on college campuses.

"Many students now demand from college not a chance to think, but a chance to become qualified for some job," she said.

Another practice causes even more confusion. Some reporters use a quotation, then attribute it in the following paragraph:

INCORRECT: "I was scared to death. I knew I was hurt, and I needed help."

These were the words today of an 18-year-old student trapped in her wrecked car.

REVISED: An 18-year-old student who had been trapped in her wrecked car said: "I was scared to death. I knew I was hurt, and I needed help."

Partial Quotations

On the rare occasions when writers quote partial sentences, they take care to separate them from complete sentences that are also being quoted. The separation is necessary to avoid confusing pronoun shifts. You can solve the problem most easily by (1) placing some attribution between the partial quotation and the full-sentence quotation or (2) paraphrasing the partial quotation:

INCORRECT: Ross said he expects to find a job "within a few weeks. And when I do get a job, the first thing I'm going to buy is a new car."

ACCEPTABLE: Ross said he expects to find a job "within a few weeks." He added, "And when I do get a job, the first thing I'm going to buy is a new car."

BETTER: Ross said he expects to find a job within a few weeks. "And when I do get a job, the first thing I'm going to buy is a new car," he added.

The original passage is confusing because of a shift in pronouns. The first sentence uses the third person, referring to Ross as "he." But in the second sentence, which is the full quotation, Ross refers to himself in the first person. Rewriting the partial quotation eliminates the confusion.

Indirect Quotations

Indirect quotations (or paraphrases) need even more attribution than direct quotations. Every idea or opinion in an indirect quotation—sometimes every sentence—must be attributed. Moreover, the location of the attribution should vary because paragraphs become clumsy and repetitive if reporters simply add the words "she said" at the end of each sentence:

The police chief insisted that the death penalty must be retained. The death penalty, harsh as it may seem, is a form of justice designed to protect the lives and rights of law-abiding citizens. Without it, criminals' rights are overly protected. Because of the almost endless mechanisms of the appeal system, it is unlikely that an innocent person would be put to death.

REVISED: The police chief insisted that the death penalty must be retained. He said the death penalty might seem harsh, but it is a form of justice designed to protect the lives and rights of law-abiding citizens. Without it, he said, criminals' rights are overly protected. Because of the almost endless mechanisms of the appeal system, it is unlikely that an innocent person would be put to death, he said.

The journalist could not attribute the police chief's remarks by placing the entire paragraph within quotation marks, because the remarks may be someone else's summary of what the police chief said. Similarly, editors cannot convert an indirect quotation written by a newspaper reporter into a direct quotation. However, editors can take a statement out of quotation marks and reword it provided they do not change its meaning.

While every sentence of indirect quotation should have attribution, writers should avoid inserting phrases that may unnecessarily attribute a quotation twice. For example, the following sentence reports that a fire chief made an announcement, then adds that he "said":

In making the announcement, the fire chief said arsonists caused 20 percent of the blazes reported in the city last year.

REVISED: The fire chief said arsonists caused 20 percent of the blazes reported in the city last year.

GUIDELINES FOR CAPITALIZING AND PUNCTUATING QUOTATIONS

The Use of Quotation Marks

Use double quotation marks to set off quotations. Only the quotation—never the attribution—should appear within the quotation marks:

INCORRECT: "The motorcycle slid sideways and skidded about 100 feet, she said. The driver was killed."

REVISED: "The motorcycle slid sideways and skidded about 100 feet," she said. "The driver was killed."

If a quotation continues for several sentences, all of them should be enclosed within a single set of quotation marks; quotation marks do not have to be placed at the beginning and end of each sentence in the quotation:

INCORRECT: "I did not see the car when I stepped out onto the street." "But when I saw the headlights coming at me, I knew it was going to hit me," she said.

REVISED: "I did not see the car when I stepped out onto the street. But when I saw the headlights coming at me, I knew it was going to hit me," she said.

Like any other part of a news story, a long quotation should be divided into short paragraphs to make it easier to read. New paragraphs should begin at natural breaks in the quotation, usually at changes in topic, however slight. Place quotation marks at the beginning of a long quotation and at the start of each new paragraph. Place closing quotation marks only at the end of the entire quotation, not at the end of every paragraph:

The senator added: "Perhaps the most shocking example of the insensitivity of the Bureau of Indian Affairs' educational system is the manner in which boarding school dormitories have been administered.

"Psychiatrists familiar with the problems of Indian children have told us that a properly run dormitory system is the most crucial aspect of boarding school life, particularly in elementary schools.

Harcourt Brace & Company

"Yet, when a 6-year-old Navajo child enters one of the boarding schools and be-comes lonely or homesick, he must seek comfort from an instructional aide who has no training in child guidance and who is responsible for as many as 100 other unhappy children.

"The aide spends most of his time performing custodial chores. At night, the situa-tion worsens as the ratio of dorm aides to children decreases."

When a quotation appears within another quotation, use double quotation marks to identify the overall quotation and single quotation marks (or an apostrophe on the keyboard) to indicate the quotation within the quotation:

During his 1960 presidential campaign, John F. Kennedy joked, "I got a wire from my father that said: 'Dear Jack, Don't buy one vote more than necessary. I'll be damned if I'll pay for a landslide.'"

If the passage has a quotation within a quotation within a quotation, use double quotation marks to indicate the third level of quotation, as in this example:

The senator said, "I had a voter tell me, 'I'm fed up with tax cheats' getting away with "murder" and I want to see them pay.'"

Other Punctuation

If the attribution comes before a quotation that contains just one full sentence, the attribution should be followed by a comma. If the attribution is placed before a quotation that contains two or more sentences, it should be followed by a colon. The attribution is not followed by a period in either case:

CORRECT: James Thurber said, "It is better to know some of the questions than all of the answers."

CORRECT: Mark Twain said: "I apologize for writing a long letter. If I'd had more time, I'd have written a shorter one."

INCORRECT: The council member said. "We need to raise the speed limit."

REVISED: The council member said, "We need to raise the speed limit."

When reporters place the attribution after a quotation, they use a comma (not a period) at the end of the quotation and place the period after the attribution to punctuate the entire sentence:

INCORRECT: "I'm feeling better." she said.

REVISED: "I'm feeling better," she said.

The comma or period at the end of the quotation should always be placed *inside* the quotation marks. There are no exceptions to this rule. Colons and semicolons should be *outside* the quota-tion marks. Whether a question mark or an exclamation point should appear inside or outside the quotation marks depends on the meaning. If the quotation is a question or exclamation, put the question mark or exclamation point inside the quotation marks. Otherwise, leave it outside the quotation marks:

CORRECT: The senator asked, "How much will the program cost?"

INCORRECT: Why did you say, "It's time to leave?"

REVISED: Why did you say, "It's time to leave"?

Capitalization

The first word in a quotation that is a complete sentence is capitalized, but the first word in a par-tial quotation is not:

INCORRECT: He said, "life is just one damned thing after another."
REVISED: He said, "Life is just one damned thing after another."

INCORRECT: He called journalism "Literature in a hurry."
REVISED: He called journalism "literature in a hurry."

Word Order

Journalists place the words of attribution in their normal order, with the subject appearing before the verb. That is the way people talk, and it is usually the most graceful way to write:

Said Ronald Reagan, "I've noticed that everybody who's for abortion has already been born."
REVISED: Ronald Reagan said, "I've noticed that everybody who's for abortion has already been born."

"Hard work is good for you. Nobody ever drowned in sweat," insisted the executive.
REVISED: "Hard work is good for you. Nobody ever drowned in sweat," the executive insisted.

However, if you place a long phrase between the subject and verb, the normal word order may be awkward. In that case, place the verb first and the subject second:

"It will cost $2 million," Smith, a 29-year-old architect employed by the California firm, said.
REVISED: "It will cost $2 million," said Smith, a 29-year-old architect employed by the California firm.

CHECKLISTS FOR QUOTATIONS AND ATTRIBUTION

Quotations

1. Use quotations sparingly—to emphasize a point or change pace rather than to tell the entire story.
2. Place only the exact words of the source within quotation marks.
3. Each quotation should serve a purpose, such as reveal the source's character, describe or emphasize a point or present additional details.
4. All direct quotations should be clear, concise, relevant and effective.
5. Report only the source's answers, not the questions you asked.

Harcourt Brace & Company

6. For a one-paragraph quotation that includes two or more sentences, place the quotation marks only at the beginning and end of the entire quotation, not at the beginning and end of each sentence.
7. Capitalize the first letter of all quotations that are full sentences but not of partial quotations.
8. Avoid awkward combinations of partial and complete quotations.
9. Divide long quotations into shorter paragraphs; place quotation marks at the beginning of each paragraph, but at the end of only the final paragraph.
10. Use single quotation marks for quotations that appear within other quotations.
11. Eliminate orphan quotations and floating quotations.
12. Make sure the quotations do not repeat facts reported elsewhere in the story.

Attribution

1. Attribute all second-hand information, criticisms, statements about controversial issues, opinions and all direct and indirect quotations. (Do not attribute undisputed facts.)
2. Punctuate the attribution properly. Put a comma after attribution introducing a one-sentence quotation and a colon after attribution introducing two or more sentences of quotation.
3. Put the attribution at or near the beginning of a long quotation.
4. Attribution that appears in the middle of a sentence should come at a natural break rather than interrupt a thought.
5. Vary sentences and paragraphs so that all do not begin with attribution.
6. Place the attribution outside the quotation marks.
7. Attribute each direct quotation only once.
8. Attribute each separate statement of opinion in indirect quotations.
9. Attribute statements only to people, documents or publications, never to places or institutions.
10. Provide transitions between statements from different sources, particularly when a quotation from one source immediately follows a quotation from a different source.
11. Select the verb of attribution that most accurately describes the source's actual meaning and behavior.
12. Do not use such verbs as "hope," "feel," "believe," "think," "laugh," "cough" and "cry" for attribution.
13. Make the attribution as concise as possible.

Harcourt Brace & Company

Name _____ Class _____ Date _____

E X E R C I S E   1

QUOTATIONS AND ATTRIBUTION

IMPROVING QUOTATIONS AND ATTRIBUTION

SECTION I: AVOIDING DOUBLE ATTRIBUTION

Rewrite the following sentences, attributing them only once.

1. A report issued Tuesday by the U.S. Department of Justice said the number of serious

   crimes committed in the United States declined 3% last year.

2. Speaking to more than 3,000 people in the Municipal Auditorium, she continued by

   stating that only the Democratic Party favors universal health care.

3. The Census Bureau issued a report today stating that, according to data it gathered last

   year, 5.2 million people in the U.S. are homeless, including 620,000 children.

SECTION II: CORRECTING PLACEMENT ERRORS

Correct the placement of the attribution in the following sentences.

1. People under 18, she said, should not be allowed to drive.

2. Another important step is to, she said, lower the books prices.

3. "The average shoplifters are teen-age girls who steal for the thrill of it, and housewives

   who steal items they can use. They don't have to steal; most have plenty of money, but

   they don't think it's a crime. They also think they'll get away with it forever," Valder-

   rama said.

SECTION III: CONDENSING WORDY ATTRIBUTION

The attributions in the following sentences are too wordy. They appear in italics and contain a total of 76 words. How many of the words can you eliminate? Rewrite the attribution, if necessary.

1. *She concluded her speech by telling the scouts that* the jamboree will be held August 7–13.

2. *He was quick to point out the fact that, in his opinion,* the president has "failed to act effectively to reduce the federal deficit."

3. *She expressed her feelings by explaining that she believes that* all those convicted of drunk driving should lose their licenses for life.

4. *She also went on to point out the fact that the results of federal studies show that,* by recycling 1 ton of paper, you can save 17 trees.

5. *In a speech to the students Tuesday, he first began by offering them his opinion that* their professors should emphasize teaching, not research.

6. *He continued by urging his listeners to remember the critical point that* the country's energy policy has failed: that the U.S. is not developing alternative fuels, nor conserving existing fuels.

SECTION IV: IMPROVING ATTRIBUTION

Correct all the problems in the following attributions and quotations.

1. He said: "after a certain number of years, our faces become our biographies".

2. Andy Rooney declared "if dogs could talk, it would take a lot of fun out of owning one".

3. "Because that's where the money is" Willie Sutton answered when asked why he robbed banks.

4. He continued by claiming that there are "two" types of people who complain about their taxes: "men" and "women."

5. "Blessed is he" said W. C. Bennett "who expects no gratitude, for he shall not be disappointed". explained Bennett.

6. Mother Teresa then spoke to the youths, telling them that. "The most terrible poverty is loneliness and the feeling of being unwanted."

7. "My views on birth control" said Robert F. Kennedy "Are somewhat distorted by the fact that I was the seventh of nine children".

8. Being a police officer is not always fun and exciting, says Hennigan. "Some things you'd just as soon forget." "Some things you do forget."

9. "The art of taxation." claimed a French statesman long ago "Consists in so plucking the goose as to obtain the most feathers with the least hissing".

10. Dr. Hector Rivera said they test for AIDS at the clinic "but do not treat the disease." "People come in to be tested scared to death." "Some leave the clinic relieved, and some don't." he said.

11. Her friendships, home, and family are the most important things in her life. "My husband is my best friend." "Maybe that's why we've lasted so long." "You really need to be friends before you're lovers".

12. "I cheat because professors give too much work." It's crazy, he said. "They don't take into consideration that some people have jobs, families and other outside interests." continued the history major. He then continued by adding that he's never been caught.

13. "My son thinks I'm old." "But I'm actually in good health for my age." "Of course, I have the usual aches and pains of an 80-year-old." "But I can still take care of my own house, and I still enjoy it." "My son thinks I should move into one of those retirement apartments and watch Wheel of Fortune all day." said he.

14. Jo Ann Nyez, a secretary, grew up in Milwaukee and described a childhood fear: There was this house at the end of my street and none of us would dare go near it on Halloween. It was supposed to be haunted. The story was that the wife had hung herself in the basement and the husband killed and ate rattlesnakes.

Harcourt Brace & Company

E X E R C I S E 2
VERBS OF ATTRIBUTION

Below are several verbs that reporters often use as substitutes for "said" when attributing statements. Define each of these verbs and give an example of how it may be correctly used for attribution.

add	mention
affirm	note
announce	observe
assert	point out
assure	pronounce
aver	propound
claim	recite
comment	respond
conclude	reveal
continue	set forth
declaim	specify
declare	state
discourse	suggest
emphasize	tell
explain	urge
express	utter
inform	warn
maintain	wonder

E X E R C I S E   3

Answer Key Provided: See Appendix D

QUOTATIONS AND ATTRIBUTION

WORDING, PLACEMENT AND PUNCTUATION

Make any changes necessary to improve the attribution in the following sentences and paragraphs. Also correct style, spelling and punctuation errors.

1. "Our goal is peace". claimed the president.

2. Benjamin Franklin said: "death takes no bribes".

3. She said her son refers to her literary endeavors as, "moms writing thing".

4. He is a scuba diver and pilot. He also enjoys skydiving. "I like challenge, something exciting."

5. "The dangers promise to be of indefinite duration." the president said referring to the Mideast crisis.

6. "Freedom of the press is not merely freedom to publish news." "It is also freedom to gather the news. We cannot publish what we cannot gather." said columnist Jack Anderson during a speech last night.

7. Jesse Owens expressed the opinion that "I think that America has become too athletic." "From Little League to the pro leagues, sports are no longer recreation." "They are big business, and they're drudgery." he continued.

8. The man smiled, "It's a great deal for me." "I expect to double my money," he explained.

9. When asked what she likes most about her job as a newspaper reporter, the woman responded by saying—"I'm not paid much, but the work is important. And it's varied and exciting." She grinned: "Also, I like seeing my byline in the paper."

10. The librarian announced to reporters that the new building "will cost somewhere in the neighborhood of about $4.6 million."

Harcourt Brace & Company

11. "Thousands of the poor in the United States," said the professor, "die every year of diseases we can easily cure." "It's a crime," he said, "but no one ever is punished for their deaths."

12. Thomas said students should never be spanked. "A young boy or girl who gets spanked in front of peers becomes embarrassed and the object of ridicule."

13. The lawyer said, "He ripped the life-sustaining respirator tubes from his throat three times in an effort to die. He is simply a man" the lawyer continued "who rejects medical treatment regardless of the consequences. He wants to die and has a constitutional right to do so."

14. Bobby Knight, the basketball coach at Indiana University, said. "Everyone has the will to win." "Few have the will to prepare." Knight added that. "It is the preparation that counts."

15. She said she firmly believes that the federal government "must do more" to help cities "support and retrain" the chronically unemployed.

E X E R C I S E   4

QUOTATIONS AND ATTRIBUTION

USING QUOTES IN NEWS STORIES

INSTRUCTIONS: Write complete news stories based on the following information. Use some quotations in each story to emphasize its highlights, but do not use quotations to tell the entire story. Use the most interesting, important and revealing quotations, not just those that happen to appear first.

1. Carlos Vacante is a police officer who has worked 3 years for your citys police department. Last night he had an unusual experience. This is his story, as he told it to you in an interview today: "I remember his eyes. They were cold, the eyes of a killer. He was pointing a gun at me, and it fired. I smelled the gunpowder and waited for the pain. I thought I was dead. The whole thing had started at about 11 p.m. This man was suspected of stealing from parked cars, and I'd gotten his description by radio. Then I spotted him in a parking lot. This morning we learned he's wanted in the robbery and murder of a service station attendant in Tennessee. There's no doubt in my mind he wanted to kill me last night just because I stopped him. I was an object in his way. I'd gotten out of my car and called to him. He started turning around and I spotted a handgun in his waistband. As he drew the gun and fired, I leaned to the right and dropped to one knee. It was just a reflex that saved my life. When I heard the shot, I thought he hit me. I couldn't believe it was actually happening to me. I thought I was going to cash everything in. Then I was running—zig-zagging—behind some cars. He fired another shot, but my backup arrived, and he fled. Maybe 60 seconds had passed from the time I spotted him. Five minutes later, we found him at the back door to a house, trying to break in and hide. I ordered him to stop, and he put his hands up and said, 'You got me.' I still smell the gunpowder this morning. I thought I was dead."

2. The citys Ministerial Alliance spoke out today against the death penalty. A copy of a resolution it adopted will be sent to the governor and to every member of the state legislature. As its spokesman, the Rev. Stuart Adler declared: "None of us is soft on crime. There must be just punishment for those who commit violent crimes, but what we are saying is we stop short of taking another persons life. We object because several independent studies have concluded that the death penalty is no deterrent to crime, rather the violence of the death penalty only breeds more violence. Also, the method of sentencing people is inconsistent. There is a great disparity between the victim being black or white. Defendants accused of killing black victims often are not sentenced to death, but when the victim is white, the death penalty is often imposed. People are frightened by the amount of violence in our society, and they've been sold a bill of goods. They've been told that the death penalty is a deterrent, and yet every major study disproves that reality. We're not getting at the deeper causes. We're a violent society, and getting more violent. Half the households in this city have guns, and it's inevitable some are going to use them. If we're really serious about stopping crime and violence, we have to recognize and correct its root causes: poverty, racial and sexual discrimination, broken homes and unloved children. Also drugs and alcohol. That's what's responsible for most crimes. And television. Studies show the average child in America witnesses, on television, 200,000 acts of violence by age 16. So we're against the death penalty. It's not going to solve our problems, and it's not fair, not fairly applied. It'll take time, but we

intend to abolish it, and we'll persist. We're already beginning to stimulate discussion, and we expect that discussion to spread."

3. A rise in insurance rates is being blamed for a rise in hit-and-run motor vehicle accidents within the state. Richard Byrum, state insurance commissioner, discussed the problem during a press conference in his office today. He said, "The problem is serious. At first, we thought it was a police problem, but police in the state have asked my office to look into it. There has been a dramatic increase in hit-and-run accidents in the state, particularly in big cities where you find the higher insurance rates. I'm told that last year we had nearly 28,000 motor vehicle accidents in the state, and 4,500 were hit-and-run. People are taking chances driving without proper insurance coverage, or they're afraid of a premium increase if they have insurance and stop and report an accident. They seem to think, 'What the heck, no one saw it, and I won't get caught,' and they just bug out of there. If you look at the insurance rates in the state, it's practically impossible for some people to pay them, and as insurance rates go up, the rate of leaving the scene of an accident increases. Drivers with the worst records—those with several accidents and traffic citations—pay as much as $3,600 a year in insurance premiums, and they may pay even more than that if they are young or have a high-powered car. Even good drivers found at fault in an accident may find their rates going up several hundred dollars for the next three to five years. So leaving the scene of an accident is definitely tied to the economic situation, yet the insurance company people I've talked to say they can't do anything about it. It's just not realistic to expect them to lower their rates; they aren't making that much money. Right now, I'm not sure what we'll do about the situation. In the meantime, we can expect more hit-and-run accidents and more drivers going without any insurance coverage because of its high cost."

Harcourt Brace & Company

E X E R C I S E   5

QUOTATIONS AND ATTRIBUTION

USING QUOTES IN NEWS STORIES

INSTRUCTIONS: Write complete news stories based on the following information. Use some quotations in each story to emphasize its highlights, but do not use quotations to tell the entire story. Use the most interesting, important and revealing quotations, not just those that happen to appear first.

1. Michael Ernest Layoux, 22, is a clerk at a convenience store at 1284 East Forest Boulevard. He was robbed late yesterday. Here is his account of the incident: "First, you have to understand where the store is. It's located in a remote area in the northeast corner of town. There's nothing around that's open at night, so I'm all alone in the store. I started carrying a gun to work last year after I read where two clerks at another convenience store in the city were robbed and killed. Carrying a gun is against company policy, but I figured I had to protect myself. We're open 24 hours, and the store has a history of holdups, particularly at night when there aren't any customers in the store. But it never happened to me personally before. Just after 11, when the store was empty except for me last night, this guy walks in and asks for a pack of Winston cigarettes. I handed him a pack, and then he pulled a gun and says, "You see what I got?" He had a pistol, and he held it low, level with his hip, so no one outside the store could look in and see it. Then he asked me for the money, and I gave it to him. We never have more than $30 in cash in the register. It's company policy. We put all the big bills we get into a floor safe we can't open. So he didn't get much, maybe $20. Then he motioned for me to move toward the cooler. We have a big cooler in the back for beer and soda and other stuff we have to keep cold. When he started shoving me toward the cooler I really got scared. There's no lock on the cooler, so he couldn't lock me in while he was getting away. There's no reason for him to put me in the cooler; I could walk right out. The only thing I could figure was that he wanted to shoot me, and he wanted to do it in some place where no one could see what was happening. That's where the two other clerks were shot last year, in a cooler in their store. Since they were killed, I've kept a .25-caliber pistol under the counter, and when he motioned for me to get into the cooler I shot him. He'd started turning toward the cooler, and then he must have heard me cocking the pistol because he started jerking his head back around toward me. I shot him 3 times in the chest and side, but I didn't know right away that I hit him. He just ran out through the front door. He didn't even open it. He ran right through the glass. I called the police, and they found his body in a field about 200 yards away. He was dead, and now I've lost my job. But I wouldn't do it any different. The police talked to me for almost two hours, and they said it was OK, that I acted in self-defense. Then this morning, just after 8, I got a call at home from my district manager, and he said I'm fired because it's against company policy to have a gun in the store. It's a real shame, because I'm still a college student, and I need the job. I can attend classes during the day and then work at night at the store. I've been doing it for 4 years now, and I want to graduate in a couple more months. But I can understand the companys rules. Most people don't know how to handle guns. I do. I've been around them and using them all my life."
Company officials refused to comment about the robbery or the firing.

2. Lillian Shisenaunt is a pharmacist. She was elected president of your County Pharmacists Association at a meeting held last year. During an interview with you today, she
talked about an issue of concern to pharmacists, one that the pharmacists talked about at
their meeting last night, along with possible solutions. She said: "We find that we've got
an awful lot of older people taking three or four or five different drugs all at once. If
they think that's going to do them any good, they're fooling themselves. We find that, in
many cases, the medicine—the dosage and the way its taken—are all wrong. Patients,
especially the elderly, sometimes get all their different drugs confused, and then they
take two of one and none of the others. Even when the elderly take all the right pills,
sometimes the different drugs nullify each other. Different doctors these people see give
them prescriptions without knowing what else a patient is taking for some other problem. So some of these oldsters become real junkies, and they don't even know it. As
they get older and have more problems, they take more and more medication. After a
few years, their children think their minds are going because they're so heavily sedated
all the time. But if they get a good doctor, or a good druggist, they probably can stop
taking some of the medicines, and then they don't actually have all the problems people
think they have. A lot of these older people aren't senile; they just take too many different drugs, and then it hits them like senility. Drug companies don't help. If you look at
most drug companies, they test their products on healthy young adults, a 25-year-old,
180-pound male. Then the companies set a normal adult dosage based on the clinical
tests with these young adults. But the things that determine how drugs affect you
change with age, so what the drug companies set as a normal daily dosage doesn't always fit an older person with a number of conditions. If you look at studies of hospital
emergency rooms, you'll find that people over 60 are admitted twice as often for adverse drug reactions as the young. Most people don't know that. They think about all
the problems of the young, not the old. But most of the problems can be solved, and
without too much effort. People should talk to a good pharmacist or physician. Unfortunately, we find that most people are scared of their doctors and don't ask them enough
questions and don't understand what their pharmacists have to offer. Patients also
should make a list of all their different medicines and dosages each time they go to a
doctor and tell him what they're taking. Then when they get a new prescription, they
should write down the doctors instructions, and they should get all their prescriptions
from just one pharmacist so the pharmacist knows everything they're taking and can
watch for any problems. If they ask, the pharmacist can color code their pill bottles so
they can't be confused. But patients also have a responsibility for their own health care.
Each morning, they should sort out all that days pills ahead of time, and then they'd be
less likely to make a mistake."

CHAPTER 9

INTERVIEWS AND POLLS

The First Amendment . . . presupposes that right conclusions are more likely to be gathered out of a multitude of tongues than through any kind of authoritative selection. To many this is, and always will be, folly; but we have staked upon it our all.

(Learned Hand, American jurist)

Reporters interview people to gather newsworthy information and opinions. Sometimes interviews provide reporters with facts about events they were unable to witness. Other times, reporters interview sources to obtain opinions or colorful quotations about events in the news.

Unfortunately, interviews are notoriously unreliable. People forget or fail to notice important details, or they misunderstand things that are said or done. Others want to promote a cause or gain recognition for themselves. Thus, they reveal only their side of an issue—and present that side as favorably as possible. For these reasons, interviews produce more useful opinions and analysis than facts.

Reporters themselves may do things that diminish the reliability of interviews. Their own prejudices may cause them to overlook or forget information. Or the source and the reporter may be too uncomfortable with each other to communicate well. Sources may doubt the competence of reporters who are much younger—or older—than they are. Even the way reporters word their questions may influence the answers they receive.

Through months and years of practice, perceptive reporters improve their interviewing skills. By studying the advice of more experienced reporters, beginners can avoid many of the problems likely to arise during interviews. This chapter will discuss those problems and recommend solutions to them.

ARRANGING AN INTERVIEW

When a reporter needs only a few specific pieces of information, the interview may last only a few minutes and often may be conducted over the telephone. Other interviews, when the reporter wants to write about a person in depth, may last hours or days and are always done in person.

Reporters usually do not make advance arrangements for very brief interviews; but for more formal interviews, they call to make appointments. The reporters identify themselves and the news organizations they work for and explain why they want to conduct an interview. Then the sources can gather information to prepare for the interview.

Reporters try to interview top officials, such as mayors of cities and presidents of businesses, rather than secretaries, assistants, public information officers or other subordinates. Reporters want to interview people who have first-hand knowledge of their topics and can immediately answer all their questions. Also, because top officials have more power, their opinions are more important than those of their subordinates.

Sometimes, however, reporters learn more from interviews with subordinates, who may have more detailed knowledge about a particular issue than does the top official. A U.S. senator, for example, may have only superficial knowledge of most of the hundreds of issues and bills be-

Harcourt Brace & Company

fore Congress at any given time, but the senator's aides, who usually concentrate on specific legislative areas, will have more information about particular issues. Whether you can learn more from an interview with the top official or the subordinate will depend on the purpose of your interview.

A thorough interview about a specific topic requires at least one hour, often two or three hours. A wider-ranging interview may require several two- or three-hour interview sessions over a period of several days or weeks. One journalist's interviews with Albert Speer, who had been a high official in Nazi Germany, lasted 10 days and nights.

Reporters usually conduct interviews in their sources' homes or offices because they are likely to be more comfortable in familiar surroundings and to speak more freely. Newsrooms are poor places for interviews because they are noisy and chaotic, especially for strangers. Reporters also avoid luncheon appointments. Luncheon meetings involve too much time, too many distractions and too much expense.

PREPARING FOR AN INTERVIEW

To prepare for an in-depth interview, reporters may spend hours, days or even weeks learning all they can about their sources and about the topics to discuss with them. How much time reporters spend in preparation depends on the purpose of the interview and the type of story they plan to write. Whatever the purpose of the interview, reporters who are prepared have important advantages:

* They will not waste time by asking about issues that have already been widely publicized.

* They will not ask boring questions.

* They will not embarrass themselves by appearing ignorant. On the other hand, reporters sometimes want to feign ignorance about a topic to elicit more in-depth, revealing explanations.

* They are more likely to recognize newsworthy statements and ask intelligent follow-up questions about them.

* They are more likely to notice if their sources are avoiding certain topics or are presenting only one side of a controversial issue.

* They encourage their sources to speak more freely because sources are more likely to trust reporters who seem knowledgeable.

Reporters who fail to prepare for an interview will not know what to ask or how to report the information they get. Some sources will try to manipulate ignorant reporters or avoid difficult topics. Sometimes, sources will immediately end the interview—and scold the unprepared reporters.

The preparation of good questions may be the most important step in the interviewing process. Sources rarely reveal startling new information without some prompting. As you prepare for an interview, ask yourself, "What questions would my audience want to ask?" Also ask yourself, "Which facts are new, important and likely to interest or affect the public?" After deciding exactly what you want to know, ask your source about those specific points. Good interviewers write their questions in advance, then check off each question as they ask it to make sure they do not forget an important one.

The best questions tend to be short, specific and clearly relevant. Vague questions elicit abstract generalities rather than specific details. Long questions are hard to understand and consume too much interview time.

Harcourt Brace & Company

Reporters avoid asking questions that can be answered with a simple yes or no. They want colorful quotations and interesting details, so they ask questions that require sources to give more detailed answers. They may ask the sources to describe or explain an event or tell how or why it occurred.

The questions should be arranged in a logical order, so that a source's answer to one question will lead into the next. Reporters may structure interviews in a variety of ways, depending on the nature of the interview and the reporters' preferences. Some organize their interviews to begin with general questions and gradually focus on more and more specific issues. Others go in the opposite direction, starting with specifics and moving to more general matters. Still others may remain at roughly one level of specificity but organize their questions so as to cover an entire issue systematically. With all these strategies, reporters usually ask their most important questions first so that if they run out of time, they will still be able to produce a good story.

Reporters save their most embarrassing and difficult questions for the end of interviews. By then, their sources should be more comfortable about answering questions. Moreover, if a source refuses to answer the awkward questions and abruptly ends an interview, reporters will have already obtained most of the information needed for their stories.

CONDUCTING AN INTERVIEW

Live interviews with celebrities or important officials appear so often on television that people may think them typical of all journalistic interviews. Live interviews, however, are probably the worst model for journalistic interviewing. Even the few people who do them well—ABC's Ted Koppel is one—recognize their limitations. The live interview usually lasts just a few minutes and allows little chance to ask challenging questions. Taped interviews, such as those on CBS's "60 Minutes" and ABC's "Prime Time Live," are better examples of journalistic interviews. So are the profiles of noted individuals that appear in The New Yorker magazine.

Reporters should arrive promptly for interviews and dress appropriately. Too many college students dress informally, regardless of the circumstances, then wonder why their sources fail to give them much time, information, trust or respect.

Reporters often begin important interviews with a minute or two of small talk. They may mention a subject of mutual interest or ask about something interesting or unusual they notice in the source's home or office. The reporters want to put the source at ease and to establish a friendly relationship so the source will be more willing to answer their questions.

When the serious questioning begins, reporters should take control of the interview—and then remain in control. They should decide which matters are most important and focus the discussion on those matters. If the source lapses into generalities, reporters should ask more specific questions. If the source strays from a topic, reporters should ask questions immediately that refocus the conversation. Reporters cannot let a source waste time or evade important questions.

Thus, good interviewers must be good listeners. They must listen carefully to ensure that a source has answered their questions—and that they understand the answers. Reporters must ask the source to repeat or explain any comment that is unclear. If the source fails to provide some important information, reporters must ask follow-up questions. Or, if the source unexpectedly raises an interesting point, reporters must ask for more details, temporarily setting aside their remaining prepared questions. Print reporters also ask the source to spell names and to repeat important numbers. Later, they verify the accuracy of these spellings and numbers.

Reporters occasionally ask a source to repeat important facts two or three times. Each time a source recalls a fact, he or she may add additional and sometimes important details. However, reporters should not argue or debate with a source. They should encourage the source to express his or her opinions as fully and freely as possible. Few sources will speak freely after reporters disagree with them.

After asking all their prepared questions, reporters should ask the source whether any other information should be included in the story. Although some sources will have nothing to add,

Harcourt Brace & Company

others will provide valuable information. A source may mention related issues, new developments of great importance or facts of personal interest about which the source may begin to speak more candidly and enthusiastically.

Before ending an interview, reporters should be certain that they understand everything that has been said. As a precaution, they should ask how and where they can reach the source if a question arises while they are preparing the story.

Good reporters interview several people before they write about a topic. When they interview one person, reporters typically learn only what that person wants them to know or perceives to be the truth. By interviewing several people, reporters can verify the sources' remarks and obtain a fuller account of the topic. The additional interviews are essential when reporters are writing about controversial issues.

During interviews, print and radio reporters observe their sources so they can describe them if it is appropriate to do so. Thus, reporters may describe a source's height, weight, posture, hair, voice, gestures, facial expressions, clothing, jewelry, car, office or home.

Reporters and sources should set the ground rules for attribution at the beginning of the interview. If a source says the interview is off the record or on background, the reporter should ask what the source means by those terms. ("Off the record" and "on background" are explained in Chapter 8.) Reporters should try to keep all information on the record. If they cannot, they may cancel the interview and seek the information elsewhere. Reporters need not cooperate with a source who grants an interview but only at the end says it was off the record. Most reporters would feel free to report all the information they received under those circumstances.

Some sources will want to review stories before they are published. Most newspapers prohibit this practice. If a story draws on several sources, arranging for each source to review it might take so long that the story would lose its news value before it was published. Also, some sources might try to edit the stories. To avoid the problem, reporters can tell sources that deadline pressures make the practice impossible, or that it violates their newspapers' policies. If a source persists, reporters should give the source the name of an editor to call.

Note Taking

Another major problem, especially for beginners, is note taking. Only a few experienced reporters take no notes during interviews, fearing that the pen and notepad may make sources nervous. Instead they try to remember everything their sources say, and write their notes later. Most interviewers take copious notes, writing down much more information than they can possibly use. During the interview, reporters may not know which facts they will need or want to emphasize in their stories. If they record as much as possible, they are less likely to forget an important point or to make a factual error. Later, they can discard the unimportant and irrelevant items.

Few reporters know shorthand. Few, if any, schools of journalism in the United States teach or require it. However, many reporters develop a shorthand of their own for taking notes. They leave out some words, abbreviate others or jot down only key words, phrases and ideas and fill in the details soon after the interview. Just about every reporter writes down names, numbers and good quotations. Reporters learn to recognize good quotations and key statements as they are spoken and train themselves to remember those quotations long enough to write them down, word for word.

If a source speaks too rapidly, reporters can ask the source to slow down or repeat an important statement. Reporters might say: "Could you wait a minute? That's an important point, and I'd like to write it down." Then, to be certain that they have recorded it accurately, reporters can read the statement back to their source. Reporters also can gain time by asking the source an unimportant "dummy" question, then catch up on their notes while the source answers it.

If their note taking makes a source nervous, reporters can pause to explain that the notes will help them write more accurate and thorough stories. Reporters can also show or read their notes to the source.

After completing an interview, reporters should review their notes immediately, while everything is fresh in their minds. They may want to fill in some gaps or be certain that they understand everything a source said. Reporters should write their stories as soon as possible after their interviews. The longer they wait, the more likely they are to forget some facts and to distort others.

Reporters who tape-record interviews can concentrate on the questions they want to ask and on their sources' responses to those questions. Tapes also provide verbatim and permanent records, so reporters make fewer factual errors and sources are less likely to claim that they were misquoted. And when reporters replay the tapes, they often find important statements they failed to notice during the interviews.

Despite these advantages, few reporters use tape recorders, especially for routine stories, because they require too much time to use. After taping a one-hour interview, reporters would have to replay the entire one-hour tape at least once, and perhaps two or three times, before writing their stories. It also might be difficult to locate a particular fact or quotation on the tape. By comparison, reporters can review their handwritten notes in a few minutes and easily find a particular fact or quotation.

In the past, reporters feared that their sources might freeze at the sight of a tape recorder and that the recorders might break or run out of tape. Modern tape recorders, however, are more reliable, less obtrusive and longer-playing.

Even though tape recorders have become small enough to hide in a pocket, they should be used openly. If reporters intend to record an interview, they have an obligation to inform their source of that fact. In 12 states (California, Delaware, Florida, Illinois, Maryland, Massachusetts, Michigan, Montana, New Hampshire, Oregon, Pennsylvania and Washington), it is illegal to record a conversation without the consent of all parties to the conversation. Twelve states (Alabama, California, Delaware, Georgia, Hawaii, Kansas, Maine, Michigan, Minnesota, New Hampshire, South Dakota and Utah) prohibit the use of hidden cameras in private places.

As a final alternative, reporters may record major interviews but augment the tapes with written notes. The reporters can consult their notes to write the stories, then use the tape recordings to verify the accuracy of important facts and quotations. If the tape recorder has a counter that indicates how much tape has played, the reporter can use that to note the location of important or interesting quotations.

SPECIAL INTERVIEW SITUATIONS

The ideal journalistic interview is a face-to-face conversation between a single reporter and a willing source. This situation gives the reporter the opportunity to watch the source's expressions and ask follow-up questions, both of which increase the likelihood the reporter will get complete and accurate information. Also, the willing source is likely to encourage the reporter's questions and elaborate freely on answers. Some interviews, however, occur in less favorable conditions. The source may be hostile, the interview may be conducted on the telephone or the source may be dealing with several reporters at once.

Dealing with Hostile Sources

Most people cooperate with reporters because interviews are mutually beneficial. Reporters benefit by getting the information they need to prepare their stories. Sources may enjoy seeing their names in print, welcome the opportunity to tell their side of a story, hope to promote some cause or want to inform the public about an issue they consider important. Sources also may cooperate because they are flattered that reporters consider their opinions important or because they are curious about how the media operate.

However, some people are hostile and refuse to talk to reporters. They may fear that a topic is too complex for reporters to understand or that reporters will be inaccurate or sensational. Or they may complain—sometimes justifiably—that reporters have misquoted them or made other errors in previous stories. Some people are too nervous to talk to reporters. Others may consider a topic unimportant, dislike a particular newspaper or fear that a story will harm them.

When reporters encounter a hostile source, they may try to learn why the source is hesitant to speak to them. After learning the reason, they may be able to overcome that specific objection. Reporters also may try to convince sources that they will benefit from a story's publication—for example, that favorable publicity will help them and the organizations they represent. Reporters may argue that the source will appear ashamed or evasive if she or he refuses to comment about an issue, whereas if the source explains his or her side, the story may be less damaging.

In another technique, reporters obtain as much information as possible from other people, including the source's critics. Then they confront the source and ask for a comment on the information. Alternatively, reporters may pretend that they have already obtained all the information they need for a story. If a reporter possesses or appears to possess enough information to prepare a story, then the reluctant source may talk in the hope of portraying that information in as favorable a light as possible.

Reporters should never deal with hostile sources by trying to bully or intimidate them or by trying to deceive them about the purpose of the interview. Information obtained from a source who has been intimidated may be unreliable, and sources who have been led to believe an interview will be about one topic, when in fact the reporters want information about something else, will feel unprepared to respond fully.

Telephone Interviews

Reporters conduct many interviews by telephone, often without having time to prepare their questions. People who have stories they want published in a newspaper often call reporters unexpectedly, and the reporters may want to interview them on the spot. Editors or news directors may tell reporters to call immediately and interview people involved in spot news stories, such as crimes, accidents and fires.

Telephone calls save enormous amounts of time, since reporters do not have to leave their newsrooms, drive to a source's home or office, wait until the source is free, conduct the interview, then walk back to their cars, drive back to their offices and return to their desks.

Experienced reporters will cradle a telephone on one shoulder and type their notes directly onto a computer. Some sources become upset when they hear the clicking of the keyboard and realize that reporters are typing everything they say; they begin to speak more cautiously and try to end the interview as quickly as possible. If a source cannot be soothed, reporters can begin to take their notes more quietly in longhand. Sources used to dealing with reporters become accustomed to the noise.

Despite their advantages, telephone calls are not a satisfactory means of obtaining in-depth interviews about controversial or complex issues and personalities. It is difficult to cultivate sources known only by telephone and never seen face-to-face, and it is, therefore, difficult to persuade those sources to talk for a long time and to answer questions about embarrassing or personal matters. Thus, telephone interviews tend to be brief and superficial. If reporters want to conduct longer, in-depth interviews, they try to visit the source in person.

Press Conferences

A press conference, where a source deals with dozens of reporters at once, is less personal and rewarding for journalists than a one-to-one interview. Most press conferences, including presidential press conferences, are more convenient for sources than for reporters. People who are used to dealing with the media find it easier to manipulate reporters at a press conference for a number of reasons. First, sources often begin with long statements that consume much of the time and present only their side of an issue. Second, they usually choose which reporters will get to ask questions and thus can ignore reporters who ask tough questions. Third, reporters rarely follow up one another's questions, so the source's answer to a given question is seldom challenged. Finally, reporters usually save their best questions for when they have an opportunity to be alone with a source so that if the questions produce a good story, they do not have to share it with anybody. For all these reasons, press conferences tend to deal with a number of topics, none in any depth.

WRITING THE INTERVIEW STORY

Reporters rarely use a question-and-answer format for their stories; this format requires too much space and makes it difficult for news readers and viewers to grasp quickly a story's highlights. Instead, reporters begin most interview stories with a summary lead, then present the story's highlights in the following paragraphs. All the information is presented in the order of its importance, not the order in which it was provided by a source. Reporters must be sure, however, that in rearranging the information they keep every direct and indirect quotation in its proper context. Background information is kept to a minimum and presented in later paragraphs. Also, reporters vary their style of writing so that every sentence and every paragraph does not begin with the source's name.

As they begin to write, reporters study their information, decide which facts are most newsworthy and then emphasize those facts. They discard clichés, platitudes and self-praise, as well as statements that are repetitious, irrelevant or obvious. This task is more difficult than it may seem. A student interested in the U.S. space shuttle program interviewed a representative of the National Aeronautics and Space Administration. The NASA source overwhelmed the student with facts about the technological benefits of the Apollo and Skylab projects. Those were the facts that filled the reporter's story. They were accurate but irrelevant to the student's purpose of writing about the space shuttle program. Had the student kept the interview focused on that program, the story would have kept its focus, too.

Interview stories should use quotations to provide highlights and bring sources to life, not to tell an entire story. A journalism student shadowed police reporter Karen Kaeppler and later wrote a story that included this effective mix of quotations and paraphrases:

Kaeppler has worked the evening police beat at The Daily Telegraph for almost two years. She is scheduled to move to another beat—a daytime beat—next month. She does not know what she will be covering, but is anxious to move on.

"This job is really wearing on me hard," Kaeppler said. "It's ugly. It's all death and destruction. Nobody wants to help you or give you any information. Those in trouble don't want to jeopardize their cases, and most of the police just don't like reporters."

According to Kaeppler, the only thing tougher than being a reporter in the midst of a bunch of cops is being a woman reporter.

"I've devised my own way to deal with it, though," Kaeppler said. "At first I had a really hard time. The police wouldn't take me seriously. They would say condescending and sexist, harassing things to me just because I'm a woman. Some of them even went so far as to come on to me. At first it really bothered me, then I realized the only way I could get them to take me seriously was to prove to them that I am serious about what I do. So, when I ask a question about a case and they reply by telling me how pretty I am, I ignore the remark and repeat my question."

Do not expect your sources to be totally candid—especially not while they are talking about themselves, their work or their programs. Never allow a source to use or manipulate you in order to engage in self-praise. Either ignore the self-praise or, if the topic is important, ask your source for evidence—specific facts—to support the claim. Even better, interview people who have other points of view about the topic.

CONDUCTING AN INFORMAL POLL

Reporters often want to know what people think of issues in the news. Traditionally, reporters have gathered opinions through interviews with local experts or people they happen to encounter on a street. Informal polls of this type are fast and cheap, but they cannot accurately describe public opinion because they do not use truly random samples that represent a cross-section of the general population. If a reporter goes to an area where there are many banks and law offices to get public reaction to some issue, she or he is likely to hear comments different from those that factory workers would express. For this reason, reporters cannot generalize about the results of informal polls. All they can report are the opinions of the people interviewed; they cannot suggest that the opinions reflect the sentiment of the community as a whole.

The unreliability of informal polls has encouraged some news organizations to employ more scientific techniques. To conduct a truly accurate poll, reporters must interview a random sample chosen from all the residents in their community. Because that is difficult, some news organizations hire professionals to conduct their polls, especially during election campaigns. A few organizations employ reporters who have the expertise to conduct scientific polls using random samples—usually samples of several hundred people. Because of their more scientific procedures and carefully worded questions, the reporters can accurately determine public opinion about important issues.

Still, informal polls often are interesting and enable reporters to localize issues in the news. If you are asked to conduct an informal survey—to ask a dozen people whether they favor a new tax, for example—encourage people to respond with more than a simple yes or no. Ask people why they favor or oppose the tax. If they respond with vague generalities, push them to be more specific. If the responses are dull, vague or unclear, your story will be equally uninteresting.

Your lead should describe as specifically as possible your major finding, which usually is the opinion expressed by a majority of the people you interviewed. The lead must do more than report that you conducted a poll or that the people you interviewed were "divided" about the issue. People are divided about every controversial issue, and the fact that you conducted a poll is not newsworthy; only the results are likely to interest your readers. For these reasons, three of the following leads need to be revised. Only the fourth is well written:

NOT NEWS: One hundred college students were polled Tuesday about the nation's pornography laws. (This fails to report the news—the results of that poll.)

OBVIOUS: One hundred college students responded with varied answers Tuesday when they were asked, "Should Congress legalize the sale of pornography?" (This states the obvious—the fact that people disagree about a controversial issue.)

VAGUE: One hundred college students were interviewed Tuesday, and a majority said the sale of pornography should be legalized for adults, but not for children. (This lead is too vague; it fails to reveal the size of that majority.)

BETTER: Sixty-eight out of 100 college students interviewed Tuesday said the federal government should legalize the sale of pornography to adults but not to children. (Note that this lead does not imply that 68 percent of all college students hold this opinion.)

The two or three paragraphs following the lead should summarize other highlights or trends. The fourth paragraph might quote the exact question you asked each respondent. If you shift directly from the lead to a quotation from one of the people interviewed, the transition will be too abrupt and your story will seem disorganized. Also, if the quotation placed in the second paragraph reflects the opinion of just one person, it is probably not important enough to merit that position in the story.

Fully identify every person you quote. Identify most sources by name, age and address (or home town for people from outside your community). Because of fear of crime and concerns about privacy, some news organizations no longer use addresses; instead, they identify sources by occupation, neighborhood or home town. If you are interviewing experts or community leaders, identify them by name, title and organization. Identify students by their major and year in school, faculty by their rank and department, and nonacademic employees by their departments and job titles. Some people may refuse to identify themselves. You have three choices for dealing with them: (1) Ask them why they do not want to be identified and try to overcome their objections; (2) offer to identify them by age or occupation instead of name; or (3) thank them and find others who are willing to be identified. Your editor or news director may tell you which of these options to follow.

You do not have to quote everyone you interview; quote only those who say something colorful, important or unusual. Paraphrase or discard responses that are awkward, wordy, unclear or repetitious. Select only a few of the most interesting statements, then devote several paragraphs to these remarks. If you quote 10 or 20 people and devote one paragraph to each, your story will seem too choppy and superficial.

If two people make similar replies to your poll question, combine their responses in a single sentence or paragraph. Note, however, that because two people are unlikely to use exactly the same words, you cannot attribute a direct quotation to both of them. Instead, paraphrase their responses or indicate that several people expressed the same opinion, then quote one of them to illustrate that point of view. For example:

> Lionel Jackson and Eugene Bushnell, both seniors majoring in political science, said the state's sales tax discriminates against the poor.

> Three students said they had dropped out of college for a year or more. Marsha Dilte, a senior, explained: "I was running out of money, and I really wasn't certain what I wanted to do. After two years of working as a secretary, I had enough money to finish college and knew I wanted to be a nurse."

Arrange quotations in a logical order, grouping similar responses and placing transitions between those groups. Look for trends—perhaps consistent differences between the responses of men and women, young and old, students and nonstudents. (Be careful not to imply that such trends are present in the entire population.)

First quote people who expressed the majority viewpoint, then people who expressed opposing viewpoints. Some opinions may be divided into even smaller groups. For example, if the respondents who favor an issue gave four reasons for their beliefs, you might begin by quoting respondents who mentioned the most popular reason, then quote respondents who cited the second, third and fourth most popular reasons.

Transitions should be interesting. Many summarize the viewpoint of the group of quotations that reporters are about to present. The following transitions appeared in a story about high school students' opinions of the Army. The paragraphs following each of these transitions quoted students who expressed the viewpoint that the transition summarized:

> Fourteen students said they consider service in the Army a patriotic duty.

> Seven students said they plan to join the Army because they want to travel but cannot afford to go overseas by themselves.

> Four women said the Army offers higher salaries than civilian employers and is more willing to promote women.

Harcourt Brace & Company

Do not include simple yes or no responses when reporting the opinions expressed by your respondents. If the fourth paragraph in your story quotes the question that each respondent was asked, and the 10th paragraph reports that one person responded yes, readers may not understand that the person was responding to the question presented six paragraphs earlier:

> Mary Alton responded, "Yes."
> REVISED: Mary Alton agreed that the president's relationship with Congress is deteriorating.

Be specific and clear in characterizing responses, even if it means that you must briefly restate an idea:

> Sandy Roach more or less agreed with Miss Hass.
> REVISED: Sandy Roach agreed that government workers are overpaid but said it is the fault of politicians, not of the unions representing government workers.

Never criticize or attach labels to your respondents' answers. Do not refer to any answers as "interesting," "thoughtful" or "uninformed." Simply report whatever your respondents said, and let your readers judge the remarks for themselves. (Your readers' conclusions may be quite different from your own.) Also avoid making comments about the manner in which people responded to your questions, and be especially careful to avoid trite generalities. For example, do not report that one person seemed "sincere" or that another seemed "apathetic." However, you can report specific details, such as the fact that one person paused for nearly a minute before answering your question and then talked about the question for nearly 30 minutes.

Some of the people you attempt to interview may be undecided about or unfamiliar with your topic. People who are undecided or uninformed usually constitute a small minority and can be mentioned in your story's final paragraphs. In the final paragraphs, you might also describe the methods you used to conduct your poll: the exact number of people interviewed and the way you selected those people. Never summarize or comment on your findings in the final paragraphs; a news story contains only one summary, and it belongs in the lead.

CHECKLISTS FOR INTERVIEWS AND POLLS

Arranging the Interview

1. Call in advance to arrange the interview. Always identify yourself, your news organization and the reason for the interview.
2. Always interview the best available sources, usually top officials or their subordinates most knowledgeable about the issue.
3. Tell the source in advance how long you expect the interview to last. In-depth interviews usually require an hour or more.
4. Plan to conduct the interview in a setting that will be comfortable for your source.

Preparing for the Interview

1. Learn as much as you can about your source and the issues you want your source to discuss.
2. Prepare your questions in advance and phrase them so as to encourage the source to speak at length rather than just replying yes or no.
3. Arrange your questions in a logical order.

Conducting the Interview

1. Arrive for the interview on time and wear appropriate clothing.
2. Reach an agreement on whether the interview is on the record, on background, on deep background or off the record. Try to keep as much of the interview as possible on the record.
3. Put the source at ease with small talk before starting the interview.
4. Take control of the interview, keep it focused on the topic, and encourage the source to provide details rather than generalities.
5. Listen carefully to make sure the source has answered your question and that you understand the answer. If anything is unclear, ask the source to repeat the comment or explain it.
6. Observe the source's appearance, mannerisms and surroundings in order to describe the person when you write the story.
7. After you have asked all of your questions, ask the source whether there is anything else that should be included in your story. Also ask about when and where you can reach the source if you need more information as you write the story.
8. Take thorough notes, being especially careful to include important facts and figures, the spellings of names and interesting quotations.
9. If you want to tape-record the interview, ask the source's permission in advance.

Writing the Story

1. Begin with a summary lead and follow with the highlights of the interview. Arrange the information in the order of its importance, not in the order in which the source gave it to you.
2. Keep the source's comments in context.
3. Use quotations to enliven the story, not to tell it.
4. Ignore the source's statements of self-praise or include competing points of view in the story.

Informal Polls

1. Ask questions that encourage respondents to say more than yes or no. Try to get beyond vague generalities to more specific issues and details.
2. Make the lead as specific as possible in describing the results of the poll.
3. Don't shift abruptly from the lead to quotations from respondents. Use three or four paragraphs after the lead to describe your findings and report the exact wording of the question asked.
4. Look for trends or groups of similar responses.
5. Write strong transitions between sections of the story.
6. Do not criticize or editorialize about the responses; simply report them.
7. Never imply that the results of an informal poll can predict how the community in general thinks about an issue.

SUGGESTED READINGS

Best Newspaper Writing. St. Petersburg, FL: Poynter Institute for Media Studies. (This book, published every year since 1979, contains prize-winning articles, followed by the editors' comments and question-and-answer sessions with the writers. Several of the writers have published exceptional interviews, and some discuss their interviewing techniques.)

Biagi, Shirley. *Interviews That Work: A Practical Guide for Journalists*, 2nd ed. Belmont, CA: Wadsworth, 1992.

Harcourt Brace & Company

Brady, John. *The Craft of Interviewing*. Cincinnati: Writer's Digest, 1977.

Donaghy, William C. *The Interview: Skills and Applications*. Glenview, IL: Scott Foresman, 1984.

Killenberg, George M., and Rob Anderson. *Before the Story—Interviewing and Communication Skills for Journalists*. New York: St. Martin's Press, 1989.

Sincoff, Michael Z., and Robert S. Goyer. *Interviewing*. New York: Macmillan, 1984.

Stewart, Charles J., and William B. Cash Jr. *Interviewing Principles and Practices*, 3rd ed. Dubuque, IA: William C. Brown, 1985.

Yates, Edward D. *The Writing Craft*, 2nd ed. Raleigh, NC: Contemporary, 1985.

Harcourt Brace & Company

E X E R C I S E 1

INTERVIEWS AND POLLS

DISCUSSION QUESTIONS

1. How would you respond to a source who, several days before a scheduled interview, asked for a list of the questions you intended to ask?
2. Do you agree that reporters have an obligation to inform their sources when they plan to record an interview even when it's legal to do so?
3. If a story's publication is likely to embarrass a source, do reporters have a responsibility to warn the source of that possibility? Does it matter whether the source is used to dealing with reporters?
4. Would you be willing to interview a mother whose son just died? Would it matter whether her son drowned in a swimming pool, was murdered or was a convicted killer executed in a state prison?
5. Imagine that you wrote a front-page story about students' use of marijuana on your campus. To obtain the story, you promised several sources that you would never reveal their identities. If, during a subsequent legal proceeding, a judge ordered you to identify your sources, would you do so? Or would you be willing to go to jail to protect your sources?

CLASS PROJECTS

1. List 10 interviewing tips provided by other sources.
2. Interview an expert on body language or nonverbal communication, perhaps someone in your school's psychology or speech department, then report on the information's usefulness to journalists. You might also invite the expert to speak to your class.
3. Interview an expert on interviewing, perhaps a faculty member in your school's psychology department. You might also invite the expert to speak to your class.
4. Interview government officials who frequently deal with reporters. Ask those officials what they like and dislike about the interviews and how they try to handle the interviews and the reporters conducting the interviews.
5. Ask several government officials which local reporters are the best interviewers, then interview those reporters about their interviewing techniques. You might invite one of those reporters to speak to your class.
6. Ask every student in your class to write one paragraph about each of the three most newsworthy experiences in his or her life. Then select the students with the most interesting experiences and have your entire class interview them, one by one, and write news stories about their experiences.

Harcourt Brace & Company

E X E R C I S E   2

INTERVIEWS AND POLLS

INTERVIEW WITH AN INJURED BICYCLIST

INSTRUCTIONS: Write a news story based on the following interview with Marsha L. Taylor. The interview provides a ver-batim account of an interview conducted this morning, two days after she was released from a local hospital after being injured in a bicycling accident. "Q" stands for the questions that Taylor was asked during the interview at her home, and "A" stands for her answers, which may be quoted directly. Taylor manages a McDonald's restaurant and lives at 2012 Lincoln Blvd. in your city.

Q: How long have you been bicycling?

A: I started when I was in college, but I didnt do any serious cycling until after I had gradu-ated. I spent that first summer looking for work and cycling was a way of filling in time and keeping fit while I waited for interviews. Eventually I got involved with some groups of cyclists and participating in weekend rides and even some races. Since then its been a major part of my life. I cant imagine what my life would be like without bicycling.

Q: How active have you been in bicycling recently?

A: I rode a lot this year. Um, I guess I must have ridden at least maybe 3,500 miles be-cause in the spring I rode in the annual Governors Bicycle Tour, which goes across the state. And in the fall I rode in a tour across the United States.

Q: How did your accident happen?

A: Well, a lot of it is hazy too me, but it happened shortly after I finished the U.S. tour. I had been back in town about two weeks and I was just out for a short ride of an hour or so. I was riding down 72nd Street almost to Southland Boulevard when a car hit me from be-hind and sent me flying off my bike. That's all I remember until I was in the hospital.

Q: What were your injuries?

A: Gee, you might as well ask what wasn't injured. I had a mild concussion, a broken neck, six broken ribs, a broken arm, and a broken pelvis.

Q: Were the doctors worried about your condition?

A: Yeah, somewhat. They didnt think there was anything they couldnt control, but there was a lot of stuff broken. They were especially concerned about the broken neck. One doctor said I had what they call a hangmans fracture. She said it was a miracle that I wasnt paralyzed.

Q: Was your recovery pretty smooth?

A: No. In fact I got worse at first. After a couple of weeks, they sent me to a rehabilitation facility, but then I developed complications. The doctors discovered I had some internal injuries. My intestine was perforated and my liver and gall bladder were injured. All that caused my skin to change color, start turning bright orange. When my mother saw me she said I looked like a Halloween pumpkin. I had to go back to the hospital be-cause of those complications. But for that, I probably would have been out in two months instead of four. I still have to go back for rehabilitation three times a week.

Q: Have you changed your attitude about cycling since your accident?

A: No. I still want to ride. If I could, Id be out there right now, but its hard to ride a bike when you have to use crutches. If you, you know, take precautions and are careful, bi-cyclings pretty safe.

Q: What kind of precautions?

A: Well, the main thing, you know, is protective clothing, especially the helmet. I never ride unless I have my helmet. It probably saved my life this time.

Q: How long have you lived here?

A: Let's see, ah 15, years now, ever since I started work for McDonalds.

Q: How long have you been manager there?

A: Four years.

Q: How old are you?

A: Ah, 37. Old enough, yeah.

EXERCISE 3

INTERVIEWS AND POLLS

INTERVIEW WITH A ROBBERY VICTIM

INSTRUCTIONS: Write a news story based on the following interview with Michele Schipper, a sophomore majoring in journalism at your college. The interview provides a verbatim account of a robbery that occurred yesterday. "Q" stands for the questions Ms. Schipper was asked during an interview this morning, and "A" stands for her answers, which may be quoted directly. (This is a true story, told by a college student.)

Q: Could you describe the robbery?

A: I pulled up into the parking lot of a convenience store on Bonneville Drive, but I pulled up on the side and not in front where I should have, and I was getting out of my car, and I was reaching into my car to pull out my purse when this guy, 6 foot tall or whatever, approached me and said, "Give me your purse." I said, "OK." I barely saw him out of the corner of my eye. And then, I, um, so I reached in to get my purse. And I could see him approaching a little closer. Before then, he was 4 or 5 feet away. So I turned around and kicked him in the groin area, and he started going down, but I was afraid he wouldn't stay down, that he would seek some kind of retribution. So when he was down, I gave him a roundhouse to the nose. I just hit him as hard as I could, an undercut as hard as I could. And I could hear some crunching, and some blood spurted, and he went on the ground, and I got in my car, and I went away. I called the cops from a motel down the street. They asked where he was last I seen him, and I said. "On the ground."

Q: Did the police find him?

A: No, he was gone.

Q: Had you taken judo or some type of self-defense course?

A: No, but I used to be a tomboy and I used to wrestle with the guys, my good friends, when I was young. It was a good punch. I don't know, I was just very mad. My dad, he works out with boxing and weightlifting and everything, and I've played with that, so I've got the power.

Q: Could you describe the man?

A: I didn't see him well enough to identify him, really, but I hope he thinks twice next time.

Q: What time did the robbery occur?

A: This was about 4 in the afternoon, broad daylight, but there were no other cars parked around, though.

Q: Did you see the man when you drove up, or was he hiding?

A: There was a dumpster, and I guess he came from behind the dumpster, like he was waiting there, just like he was waiting there. And I guess he was waiting around the dumpster, because no one was standing around when I pulled up, I remember that.

Q: Were there any witnesses who could describe the man?

A: There was no one around, there were no cars parked. The clerks were inside the store. I didn't see any pedestrians around and, after I did it, I didn't wait to find if there were any witnesses because I wanted to leave right away.

Q: Was the man armed?

A: Out of the corner of my eye I realized I didn't see any weapon. And I guess I thought he was alone. You register some things; you just don't consciously realize it.

Q: What was your first reaction, what did you think when he first approached and demanded your purse?

A: I didn't think of anything, really, you know. I just reacted. I was very, really indignant. Why, you know, just because he wanted my purse, why should he have it? There was really only $10 in there, and I probably wouldn't really do it again in the same situation. And my parents don't know about it because they would be very angry that I fought back.

Q: Had you ever thought about being robbed and about what you would do, about how you would respond?

A: It just came instinctively, and after the incident, you know, I was shaking for about an hour afterwards.

Q: About how long did the robbery last?

A: It really only lasted a second, just as long as it would take for you to kick someone and then to hit them and then drive away in the car. It really only lasted a second.

Harcourt Brace & Company

E X E R C I S E 4
INTERVIEWS AND POLLS

INTERVIEW: MURDER TRIAL

INSTRUCTIONS: Write a news story based on the following transcript from a murder trial. "Q" stands for the questions of District Attorney Ramon Hernandez, and "A" stands for the answers of Frank Biegel, one of the defendants. The questions and answers are the men's exact words and may be quoted directly.

BACKGROUND INFORMATION

Biegel, 43, of 782 12th Ave. and Eric A. Knapp, 27, of 2314 N. 11th St. are accused of robbing a service station of $83 last July and of abducting and murdering the attendant, Larry Totmann, age 17. Biegel testified this morning, the second day of the trial.

Q: Well, let me ask you this. Did you commit a robbery at a service station on Baytree Road last July 14?

A: Yes, I did.

Q: And did you help take the attendant, Larry Totmann, out to a campground somewhere away from that station?

A: Yes, sir.

Q: And did you personally see Eric Knapp, your co-defendant, shoot and kill that attendant?

A: Yes, sir.

Q: Describe for us how you and Knapp went about robbing and murdering Totmann.

A: It wasn't me. It was Knapp that shot the kid, not me. We had gone up to the gas station, got my car filled with gas. While I was . . . I went in the bathroom. While I was in the bathroom some other people drove up in a car, young kids it sounded like, and they had an argument with the attendant about using the telephone. When it was all over, I came out, and I got back in the car while Knapp put a gun on him.

Q: All right. Did the young people who had driven up, did they leave before you got back into the car?

A: Yes, sir.

Q: Then what happened?

A: I started the car, and Knapp made the kid take all the money out of the register, and he found a gun hidden under the counter and put it in a box with the money.

Q: Tell us what happened after that.

A: Well, sir, Knapp told the kid to get into the car with us, and, uh, I drove out of town about five miles.

Q: Where was Knapp all that time?

A: He was in the back seat with the kid. He had his gun on him, and the box with the money.

Q: And then what happened?

A: I was driving out toward a campground I use sometimes, and Knapp told me to stop. He told the kid to get out of the car and lay down in some bushes along the road. I didn't know he was going to shoot the kid, I swear. The kid hadn't caused us any trouble, and I thought we'd just dump him there so he couldn't call the cops right away.

Q: But Knapp shot him, didn't he?
A: Yes, sir.

Q: How many times?
A: Four. He fired four shots. I don't know how many times he hit him.

Q: Did Knapp shoot him in the head?
A: Well, sir, I couldn't see that. It was dark, and they were off the side of the road. I just heard the shots and saw like blue flames coming out of his gun.

Q: Uh, how far away from Totmann was Knapp when the shots were fired?
A: Not over three or five feet. He was standing right over him.

Q: Did Totmann say anything or try to run away?
A: No, he just kept lying there. He'd done everything we said, and I don't think he expected it. He just lay there; he never moved.

Q: What . . . well, what did you do after that?
A: I drove Eric home. We had a couple beers at his apartment and divided the money. There wasn't much, not even a hundred dollars.

Q: What did you do with the gun?
A: The next night we went out and threw both guns down a sewer. It was over on the other side of town, near a ballpark.

Q: Do you know why Knapp decided to kill Totmann?
A: He told me the kid recognized him, that the kid had seen him before. And he . . . he was afraid the kid might've seen my license number, the license number on my car.

Q: Why didn't you try to prevent the murder?
A: How could I? I didn't know he was going to shoot anyone, I really didn't. We'd never talked about that. I thought we'd just drop the kid there and leave.

Q: Can you tell us why you've decided to confess?
A: The murder wasn't my idea; I didn't pull the trigger. I didn't know Eric was going to shoot the kid. I don't think I should die, and I thought maybe if I cooperated, I wouldn't get the death penalty.

Q: Have the police or anyone else promised you anything in return for testifying against Knapp?
A: No sir. No one's promised me anything, nothing at all. I wish they would.

E X E R C I S E   5

INTERVIEWS AND POLLS

INTERVIEW WITH A MURDER WITNESS

INSTRUCTIONS: Write a news story based on the following interview with a bookkeeper at the North Point Inn. "Q" stands for the questions she was asked during an interview at her home this morning, and "A" stands for her answers, which may be quoted directly. (The interview is based on an actual case: a robbery and murder at an elegant restaurant.)

Q: Could you start by spelling your name for me?
A: N-i-n-a C-o-r-t-e-z.

Q: You work as a bookkeeper at the North Point Inn?
A: Yes, I've been there seven years.

Q: Would you describe the robbery there yesterday?
A: It was about 9 in the morning, around 7 or 8 minutes before 9.

Q: Is that the time you usually get there?
A: At 9 o'clock, yes.

Q: How did you get in?
A: I've got a key to the employee entrance in the back.

Q: Was anyone else there?
A: Kevin Blohm, one of the cooks. He usually starts at 8. We open for lunch at 11:30, and he's in charge.

Q: Did you talk to him?
A: He came into my office, and we chatted about what happened in the restaurant the night before, and I asked him to make me some coffee. After he brought me a cup, I walked out to the corridor with him. That was the last I saw him.

Q: What did you do next?
A: I was just beginning to go through the receipts and cash from the previous night. I always start by counting the previous days revenue. I took everything out of a safe, the cash and receipts, and began to count them on my desk.

Q: About how much did you have?
A: $6,000 counting everything, the cash and receipts from credit cards.

Q: Is that when you were robbed?
A: A minute or two or less, a man came around the corner, carrying a knife.

Q: What did you do?
A: I started screaming and kicking. My chair was on rollers, and when I started kicking, it fell. I fell on the floor, and he reached across my desk and grabbed $130 in $5 bills.

Harcourt Brace & Company

Q: Did he say anything?

A; No, he just took the money and walked out.

Q: Was he alone?

A: I don't think so. I heard someone—a man—say, "Get that money out of there." Then someone tried to open the door to my office, but I'd locked it. Three or four minutes later, the police were there.

Q: Is that when you found Mr. Blohm?

A: I went into the hallway with the police and saw blood on a door in the reception area. It was awful. There was blood on the walls and floor. Kevin was lying on the floor, dead. He had a large knife wound in his chest and another on one hand.

Q: Can you describe the man who robbed you?

A: He was about 5 feet 10, maybe 6 feet tall, in his early 20s, medium build.

Q: What was he wearing?

A: Blue jeans, a blue plaid button-up shirt and blue tennis shoes.

Q: Did you see his face?

A: He had a scarf, a floral scarf, tied around the lower part of his face, cowboy style. It covered the bottom half of his face.

Q: Did the man look at all familiar, like anyone you may have known or seen in the restaurant?

A: No.

Q: Did you notice anything unusual that day?

A: I saw a car in the parking lot when I came in, one I didn't recognize. It didn't belong to anyone who worked there, but that's all I remember.

Q: Do you have any idea why someone stabbed Blohm?

A: No. Kevin might have gotten in his way or tried to stop him or recognized him or something. I don't know. I didn't see it. I don't know anything else.

E X E R C I S E   6

INTERVIEWS AND POLLS

INTERVIEW WITH A SUSPECT

INSTRUCTIONS: Write a news story based on the following interview with Irene Barber, a woman arrested for stealing her own clothes. Assume that you interviewed Mrs. Barber today and that she lives in your community.

This is a true story, and Mrs. Barber was interviewed especially for this book. Because this is a verbatim account of the interview, you can use direct quotations. Assume that the incident occurred today and that the clerk and the owners of the shop declined to talk to you.

The interview is more complicated than most because Mrs. Barber quotes other sources, and one of those sources is profane. Thus, before beginning to write your story, you may want to discuss the problems with your classmates and instructor. You may also want to discuss the issue of polishing direct quotations—for example, of eliminating words such as "uh" and "you know."

Being new in the area, I needed to find a dry cleaners to take clothing to, and there was one that was convenient in a little shopping center, and uh, so, I went in there, took six pieces of clothing, two shirts of my husbands, two pairs of his pants and two of my blouses. And I went back a couple of days later and found that the pants were OK, but his shirts were not even pressed under the arms or anything, and my blouses, one of them was stained on the front, and the pockets were all wrinkled and, and did not look like what I would want to take home and wear. So she said, well, we can redo them. I said, all right. So, about a week later, I had to go to the pharmacy next door and, while I was waiting for the prescription, I thought, I'll run next door and pick up my clothing. And so I went in, and the two shirts of my husbands were pressed and in better shape, but my blouses were in worse shape than they were the first time they sent them in. The stains were still in front of the white one, and the other one, the pockets were pressed, but nothing else seemed to be pressed. So I told the girl I would just take them home. She said, I can send them back again, and I said, well, obviously you can't get them right, so I'll just take them with me. So she proceeded to ring up the amount and told me it was eight dollars and sixty cents. And I looked at her and I said, you're charging me for those blouses? She said, yes, I have to. And I said, I'm not going to pay you for ruining my blouses. She said, you have to. My boss will fire me if you don't. And I said, well, tell you what, let me talk to him on the phone. So she got him on the phone and, uh, he told me that I had to pay for it, and I said, well, I'm paying you for a service that obviously you did not perform. And he said that if I did not pay for it he would have me arrested and charged with merchandise theft plus assault, which I thought, what in the world is he thinking about? So, uh, he, uh, proceeded to tell me that, uh, he was going to call the police, and I told him, don't bother, I will. And he proceeded to call me an asshole. So I hung up the phone and picked up the phone and called the police and said that I was at the dry cleaners and that I was going to walk out with my clothes. And, uh, the lady said it would be a while, and I said that was OK, I'll wait. So I went back and sat on the bench they had there. But, uh, the phone rang again, and it was the owner, and I heard him talking to the girl. And she said, I'm not going to get myself hit, and I thought, what is he telling her to do? So anyway, I looked, and sitting on the stool behind the counter was my blouses, and she was in the back on the phone, and so I went over and picked up my blouses and walked out the door with them. Not with intending to leave, but just to get out, to get my blouses, I guess. Uh, so I walked down to the corner, and I thought, I have to get my husbands prescription. So I put the, I went into the pharmacy, still shaking, still upset. And, uh, got the prescription and, uh, I went back out, put my clothes, prescription in the car and stood on the corner and waited to see if the police would get there, and I didn't see them, didn't see them, assuming it would be a while like the dispatcher told me. And, uh, so I went back to the phone and I called, and I said, yes, I'm waiting at the dry cleaners. She said, the police officer is there. You'd better go back down there. So I walked back down there, and they had already started to file a report saying that I had stolen my blouses and, uh, so I walked in, and the police officer said, yes, they called the police, and I said, no, I did. And he sort of looked at me funny, and I said, my blouses were not clean. I left with them. And he set me down, and he said, now, when you stepped over the threshold you broke the law because when you turn items over to be repaired or to be worked on, uh, cleaned, they are their possessions. So, he said, do you have any ID, and I said, in the truck, and he said, OK, let's go get it. So we walked out there, and he said, you have to pay them first, then go after them in court. This is the law, you know, and he said, not that I always agree with it, but this is the law. So he said, are you willing to make restitution? Do you have the money to pay for it? I said, of course I have the money to pay for it. You know, I didn't walk out knowingly stealing them. And so he said, OK. So we walked back in there, and he said to the girl, she's willing to make restitution, you know, will you accept that? The girl said, I don't know, I have to talk to the owner. It's a husband and wife combination and, so, they got ahold of the owners, and they said, no, don't accept one penny from her, have her arrested. So the police officer said, I'm sorry, he said, put your purse up on the counter. And I said, you are going to handcuff me, and he said, yeah, I have to. So he handcuffed me, and walked me out to the cruiser. They took me down to jail, and they chained me to the wall. So then, while we were sitting there, the sergeant came walking by and said, what did she steal, and the officer that arrested me said, her own clothes. So they, they found this comical, and yet here I was in the process of being booked on merchandise theft. So the sergeant went over and got a book, and he was trying to figure out how we could lower it, and uh, he went through the book and found out that there is such a law as service theft, which is lower than merchandise theft. So anyway, he decided to write that in there, and the phone rang. They asked for the lieutenant, I believe he was, that arrested me, and he got on the phone, and he put it on hold and said, it's the lady who owns the shop. She wants to talk with you. I said, I'm not going to barter with her, you know, this is, at that point I was angry, and I wasn't sure what to do. I wasn't to a point of being afraid yet. It was the point. It was eight dollars and sixty cents, and it was the point that the man—usually service-oriented companies will do whatever they can to accommodate you—I guess, um, so anyway, the wife got on the phone, and she wanted to talk to me. So here I am, with my arm chained to the wall, talking to this woman, and she said, where do you stand, and which I thought was the funniest line, because I said, what do you mean where do I stand? I stand in jail being booked on merchandise theft, and she said, well, we want to know, you know, what you plan on doing, and I said, at this point I don't know. She said, well, not always can you see stains on clothing when you take them in. If you're not a trained eye, you don't know that it's on there before. And I said, well, I heard the girl on the phone tell you and your husband that the stains were not on those blouses when I brought them in. She said, well, they don't always see everything, they don't find things in pockets, and so I said, you hire incompetent people? She didn't have anything to say to that. And then she said, we're not animals here, we are human beings. And I said, yes, that's why I'm chained to the wall, and she said, how barbaric, and I said, yes ma'am, it is, thanks to you. And she said, well if you promise not to pursue it any further we will come down and drop the charges. And with that I didn't, I couldn't, even answer that. I handed the officer back the phone because I thought, how dare you, you know, I'm not going to barter with you. So anyway, they started to get more things out, and they were preparing to fingerprint me, and to photograph me, and the phone rang again, and it was the husband this time. And he got on the phone, and the officer said, well, you need to get down here shortly, because after I'm

Harcourt Brace & Company

done fingerprinting her and photographing her we will take her in the back, strip search her, and take her down to the county jail. So, uh, at that point, you know, they said, they, they want to talk to you. And I said, I don't want to talk to 'em. Anyway, at that point the officer said, you know, let's make you more comfortable. At that point he took me off of the wall and said, come over here and sit down. He started filling out the paperwork. And, uh, before he was finished the owner came in and, and I told the officer, I don't want to talk to him. I don't want to, you know, he needs to sign that release, and I'll give him his eight dollars and sixty cents. So that was, that was the finale of it. But he just, he is a very cocky man as far as the way he carries himself. I don't understand how he can be in a service-oriented business but, uh, anyway, I paid my eight dollars and sixty cents.

Harcourt Brace & Company

EXERCISE 7

INTERVIEWS AND POLLS

CONDUCTING A POLL

INSTRUCTIONS: Interview a minimum of 10 people, about half men and half women. Ask them a single question concerning a controversial issue; then write a news story about their opinions. The respondents may be students, professors, nonacademic employees, visitors or anyone else you encounter on your campus. Conduct your interviews separately, not simultaneously with other members of your class—if only because it is disconcerting for a respondent to be approached by two or three people, all asking the same controversial question. Identify yourself, explain why you are conducting the poll, then ask the single question selected by your instructor or class. You may want to use one of the following questions:

---

1. Do you believe that newspapers and radio and television stations in the United States report the news fairly and accurately?
2. Should faculty members be allowed to date their students, or should your college or university adopt some rules prohibiting the practice?
3. Should your college or university adopt rules prohibiting faculty and students from saying things that are racist or sexist?
4. Would you want your state legislature to adopt a law making it legal—or illegal—for women to serve as surrogate mothers for childless couples?
5. If you saw another student cheating on a test, would you try to stop the student or report the student to your teacher? Why?
6. If the administrators at your school learned that several students had AIDS, would you want them to allow the students to continue to attend classes with you? Why?
7. Should state prison officials allow journalists to photograph or videotape executions?
8. Should the government prohibit the sale of pornographic magazines or the showing of pornographic movies?
9. Should churches and other religious organizations be required to pay property taxes for the municipal services, such as police and fire protection, that they receive?
10. Should the federal government require television manufacturers to equip all sets with a computer chip that would allow parents to block out violent programs?
11. Do you think the number of terms any one person may serve in Congress should be limited by law?
12. Do you think an unwed mother should be required to identify the father of her child before she can receive welfare benefits so the father can be ordered to help support his child?

Harcourt Brace & Company

CHAPTER 10

IMPROVING NEWSGATHERING AND WRITING SKILLS

Five Rules for Developing Writing Talent

First: Care about it tremendously. Get on fire with the idea that writing is fascinating, thrilling, heartbreaking, better than anything in the world.

Second: Work like the devil. Take hold of this job and sweat at it. Scramble.

Third: Write! Write all the time, any kind of stuff. Prepare for the thousands of words you are going to write by writing hundreds of thousands.

Fourth: Hang around people who know how to write.

Fifth: Read everything that stimulates you, but leave the cheap stuff alone and don't bank too much on the best sellers.

(Henry Justin Smith, managing editor of the *Chicago Daily News*)

When a major event occurs, such as the O.J. Simpson murder trial or the Oklahoma City bombing, dozens and sometimes hundreds of journalists rush to the scene, gather information and then transmit that information to the public. All the journalists write about the same event, but some of their stories are much better than others. Why?

Some reporters are particularly adept at gathering the information needed to write exceptional stories. They go beyond the superficial, critically examine all the information they are given and ask probing questions. They also search for alternative sources of information and are good observers. These reporters notice and record details that help reveal the truth and make their stories more colorful, descriptive and interesting.

Other reporters produce exceptional stories because of their command of the English language. Their language is forceful, and their stories are written so clearly and simply that everyone can understand them. These reporters describe the people, places and events involved in news stories and use quotations that enable those people to speak directly to the public. Their stories are so descriptive and specific—their images so vivid—that the audience is able to imagine the scenes the reporters describe.

Skilled reporters can transform even routine events into front-page stories. A reporter who is unimaginative about or indifferent to a topic may write a three-paragraph story that, because of its mediocre writing, will not be used. Another reporter, excited by the same topic, may go beyond the superficial—may ask more questions, uncover some unusual developments and inject more color into the story. The second reporter may write a 20- or 30-inch story about the topic and, because of its excellence, the story may be published at the top of Page 1.

A reporter named Barry Bradley uncovered and wrote an exceptional front-page story about a mugging. Bradley described his reporting process:

> Sometimes the best news stories are those you might have missed had you not done a little extra snooping or asked that one extra question. The old saying "leave no stone unturned" applies to no business as much as it applies to the news business.

I picked up a press release at the local police station. These releases contain the barest essentials regarding police activities. Many times a set of facts on a press release may seem dull. But a little effort can turn these facts into an interesting story.

The facts said an elderly man was robbed at knife-point. I did some nosing around and found that the man lived in a nursing home. How did the robber get into a nursing home? And, why did the robber choose such an unlikely spot? I also discovered the man was 71 years old and in a wheelchair. Then I found out the man lost $4 and a pocketknife in the robbery. To make matters worse, that was about all he had. That little tidbit was enough to warrant front-page space. The story looked much better now than it did when I first saw the bare facts.

I went to the nursing home, interviewed him and took some pictures. I found out he beat the mugger soundly with his cane before the mugger got away with his cash and belongings. He was a feisty gent who had been in three wars and wounded in two. This made the story good enough for my editors to submit it to an annual writers' contest sponsored by the local press club. Just think. I would have missed the story if I hadn't been nosy enough that day.

The same principle of going beyond the superficial might be applied to any type of story—to stories about the awarding of a scholarship, the celebration of an anniversary or retirement, the construction of a school, the election of a mayor or the damage caused by a storm. A good reporter will always begin by obtaining as much information about a topic as possible. The reporter may interview witnesses, consult experts, visit the scene or examine some documents, always observing and recording details of even minor significance—details that will help readers or viewers understand the topic and that will make the story more interesting.

To help you improve your newsgathering and writing methods, this chapter will discuss pointers on how to be specific and thorough in your writing and how to identify particular people and define unfamiliar terms. This chapter will show you how to use examples, description and humor to improve your stories. You'll also look at newswriting habits to avoid, and review grammar and word usage.

BE SPECIFIC, DETAILED AND THOROUGH

Good writing is specific, and good writers fill their stories with illustrative details. Generalities are less interesting and a sign of hasty writing. To be specific, reporters must take time and be perceptive in gathering information and in presenting that information in their stories.

Here are two good examples of paragraphs filled with specific details. The first paragraph was the lead in a story on a hospital's cost mark-up to patients. The second paragraph appeared in a story about a male athlete's chances of becoming a professional basketball player. Count the number of specific details in each paragraph:

All-Saints Hospital pays $8.35 for a pair of crutches and then bills patients $103.65 for them. Rubber arm pads for crutches, which cost the hospital 90 cents, add another $23.75 to the patient's bill, and the 71-cent rubber tips cost the patient $15.95.

In a typical year, about 500,000 students play for their high school basketball teams, and 12,000 play for their college teams. The National Basketball Association will draft about 160 players, and 50 will be employed in the NBA — for an average of three years.

Good reporters avoid vague sentences and qualifiers, words such as "young" and "old," "big" and "little," "early" and "late," "high" and "low," "fast" and "slow." Other vague qualifiers are: "rather," "very," " much," "quickly" and "a lot." Entire phrases may be too vague, as in the following examples:

Harcourt Brace & Company

at an early age	only recently
traveled extensively	never finished his formal education
for several years	within a short time

What is "an early age," for example? Audience members are forced to guess; one person might guess two months, and another might guess eight years. Similarly, one person might assume "a short time" means five minutes, whereas another might assume it means 10 days. And someone who "never finished his formal education" might have left school after the sixth grade or after his junior year of high school.

When more specific details are added to sentences, their meanings become not only clearer but more interesting:

> They said the land used to be cheap, but now is at a premium.
> REVISED: They said speculators bought the land for $320 an acre and are selling it for an average of $50,000 an acre. A bank paid $100,000 an acre for a corner lot, and developers paid $150,000 an acre to build a shopping center.

Reporters who understand a topic sometimes forget that audiences know less about it than they do. Consequently, they sometimes fail to provide a clear explanation:

> A reporter covering Indiana's U.S. senators devoted all the coverage to the senior senator because the senator had done a favor for the reporter concerning a drunken-driving incident.
> REVISED: Goligoski said the reporter for an Indiana newspaper was charged with drunken driving and put in a Washington, D.C., jail.
> The senior senator from Indiana quietly arranged for the reporter's release, and the reporter began to write favorable stories about the senator.
> "It was obvious that the reporter was paying back the favor," Goligoski said.

Before the paragraph was revised, it failed to explain the incident adequately. The paragraph mentioned "a favor" but did not specifically describe it. It also mentioned "a drunken-driving incident" but failed to provide any meaningful information about that incident.

News stories should be so detailed and thorough that all the questions an audience might logically ask about their topics are answered. Some journalists no longer attempt to answer the six major questions—who, what, where, when, why and how—in their leads. Nevertheless, the answers to all six questions should be presented somewhere in every story. Reporters must also answer all the questions raised by their stories' subtopics. Yet stories containing the following statements failed to answer the questions they obviously raise:

> She said the institution of marriage should be abolished. (Why?)

> He retired from undercover work after he was thrown out a second-story window. (When? Where? Why? By Whom? And with what result?)

Sentences and paragraphs should be so complete, clear and specific that they do not require any later explanation. Notice how easily the following sentences can be rewritten to clarify their meaning:

> Tipton remarked that he has never had a problem like this before.
> REVISED: Tipton said it is the first time he has been accused of shoplifting.

> The girl and her boyfriend tried to obtain a marriage license but were turned down because of the age requirements.
> REVISED: The girl and her boyfriend tried to obtain a marriage license but were turned down because neither is 17, the minimum age for marriage in the state.

Before they were revised, the first example vaguely referred to "a problem like this," and the second example mentioned "the age requirements." Neither example explained what the phrases meant. They raised more questions than they answered.

Harcourt Brace & Company

The same problem arises when stories report a topic was "mentioned" or "discussed." If a topic is important enough to be included in a news story, that topic should be fully explained. Stories should reveal what was said—the substance of the discussion—not just the fact that a discussion took place. This type of error often appears in leads but may arise anywhere in a news story:

She also mentioned that people must not have had some diseases if they want to donate blood.
REVISED: She added that the blood bank rejects potential donors who have had malaria, hepatitis, diabetes or venereal diseases.

She also discussed the federal tax structure.
REVISED: She said the federal tax structure places too heavy a burden on middle-income families.

As an alternative, you may be able to delete the portions of a sentence or quotation that are too vague:

He said the county fair will feature 25 rides and various other activities.
REVISED: He said the county fair will feature 25 rides.

The YWCA counselor said, "We have 800 girls in the program, and it's meeting with a large measure of success."
REVISED: The YWCA counselor said, "We have 800 girls in the program."

Mistakenly, some students begin their paragraphs with a generality, then present more specific details in the sentences that follow. If you begin with the specific details, the generality may become unnecessary and redundant:

Yahari Harris was also active in the community. She served as president of the PTA at Roosevelt High School and as vice chair of the League of Women Voters. She was a member of the Democratic Party and attended St. Paul's Episcopal Church.
REVISED: Yahari Harris served as president of the PTA at Roosevelt High School and as vice chair of the League of Women Voters. She was a member of the Democratic Party and attended St. Paul's Episcopal Church.

He called the conditions in the cafeteria "critical and hazardous." He explained that the cafeteria's french fry bins are fire hazards, its refrigerators often break and its storeroom is infested with roaches and mice.
REVISED: He said the cafeteria's french fry bins are fire hazards, its refrigerators often break and its storeroom is infested with roaches and mice.

Sweeping generalizations, a form of exaggeration, are impossible to verify and often wrong. Consequently, few good journalists will claim everyone in a community considers an issue important, everyone mourns the death of a prominent person or everyone is celebrating a holiday.

Exaggerations in news stories are artificial, wordy and ineffective. They also tend to be trite and to state the obvious. There is no need to report an explosion was "violent," a murder was "brutal" or an ambulance "rushed" someone to a hospital.

IDENTIFY, DEFINE AND EXPLAIN

Journalists should never assume audience members are familiar with a topic. News organizations may have published earlier stories about the topic, but not everyone will have seen those stories. Consequently, reporters must always identify, define and explain unfamiliar topics. The information should be expressed as simply and briefly as possible; often, it can be stated in a short phrase or sentence.

Reporters identify virtually all the people mentioned in news stories, and they usually present the identification the first or second time a person is mentioned. Readers should not be forced to guess a person's identity nor wait until the end of a story to learn who the person is. Journalists identify most people by reporting their ages, occupations and addresses. However, they usually report a street name only for the people who live in their communities. If someone lives outside the area in which a newspaper circulates, the paper reports only the person's hometown.

Journalists use a variety of other descriptive phrases to identify the people mentioned in news stories. Military papers use soldiers' ranks, and college papers list students' years in school, majors and hometowns. Stories that mention a child usually identify the child's parents, because they are more likely to be known to readers. Other stories describe people's achievements and goals.

If a title is short, reporters place it before a name—for example: "Sheriff Keith Kirby" or "Sen. Clair Valle." If journalists refer to the same person later in a story, they use only the person's last name; they do not repeat the title. If a title is long, reporters place it after a name or in the following sentence as a description of the person's position. Usually the title before the name is capitalized, whereas the description given after the name is lowercased:

Associate Superintendent for Planning and Government Relations Jung Sook Li said Friday the school is unsafe.

REVISED: Jung Sook Li, the associate superintendent for planning and government relations, said the school is unsafe.

Assistant Deputy Commander for District II Ralph Phillips said the American Legion's membership is declining.

REVISED: An American Legion official, Ralph Phillips, said the organization's membership is declining. Phillips is the assistant deputy commander for District II, which includes California, Arizona and New Mexico.

If a person has several titles, place no more than one before a name, regardless of how short the titles may be:

Sociologist and Human Resources chair Ruth Heebner said she opposes the fee.

REVISED: Sociologist Ruth Heebner said she opposes the fee. Heebner chairs the Human Resources Committee.

Junior medical technology major and recent Peace Corps volunteer Martina Diaz said she expects to graduate next June.

REVISED: Martina Diaz, a junior majoring in medical technology, said she expects to graduate next June. She served in the Peace Corps in Africa last year.

Journalists have several reasons for identifying so specifically the people mentioned in news stories. Because some sources are more believable than others, a source's identity may affect a news story's credibility. Some people are more interesting than others, and reporters may attract a larger audience if they identify a prominent or popular person involved in a story.

Journalists also identify the people involved in news stories to protect the innocent from adverse publicity. When it failed to adequately identify a man mentioned in several stories, a newspaper in Orlando, Fla., was forced to publish a separate story to exonerate an innocent man. The first stories reported that a man named Kenneth Bray was remodeling a famous hotel in the city, and the hotel would appeal to a homosexual clientele. The hotel was owned by Kenneth Edward Bray, but some citizens began to call Kenneth Lee Bray, a U.S. probation officer living in Orlando. The reporter had failed to fully identify Kenneth Edward Bray—to report his middle name, age or address—in earlier stories.

In extreme cases, proper identification protects news organizations from libel suits. If a journalist reports that a man named Ralph Ussery has been charged with rape, but fails to provide any further identification, the news organization may libel every local resident named Ralph

Ussery. The Ralph Usserys who have not been charged with rape might sue the paper for libel. If the journalist reports Ralph Ussery, 47, of Georgia Avenue has been charged with rape, the journalist identifies the particular individual who is that age and living at that address.

Reporters must also identify or define unfamiliar places and locations. They should try to avoid words that are not used in everyday conversation. When an unfamiliar word is necessary, journalists must immediately define it. Stories that fail to define unfamiliar terms may annoy as well as puzzle readers and listeners. A story about a 19-year-old Olympic skater who collapsed and died before a practice session at the University of Texas reported she died of clinical terminal cardiac arrhythmia. The journalist placed the term in quotation marks but failed to define it. Yet many people would be interested in the death of an Olympic skater and would wonder why an apparently healthy young athlete had died. Because the story failed to define the term, it failed to satisfy their curiosity about the cause of the young woman's death.

Here are three techniques journalists can use to define or explain unfamiliar terms:

1. Place a brief explanation in parentheses:

   The university employs 620 full-time faculty members and 338 adjunct (part-time) instructors.

   The law would ban accessory structures (sheds, pool houses and unattached garages) in new subdivisions.

2. Place the explanation immediately after the unfamiliar name or term, setting it off with a colon, comma or dash:

   While shopping at the mall, they saw some furniture made from polyvinyl chloride: commonly called plastic pipe.

   Amy and Ralph Hargis of Carlton Drive filed for bankruptcy under Chapter 13, which allows them to repay their creditors in monthly installments over a three-year period.

   About 800 foreign students at the university are on F-1 student visas — which means that they are allowed to stay in the United States only until their educations are complete.

3. Place the explanation in the next sentence:

   LeClaire failed the sobriety tests, and a breathalyzer test indicated she had a blood alcohol level of 0.29. The legal limit for blood alcohol levels is 0.10.

   The major banks raised their prime rate to 12.5 percent. The prime rate is the interest rate banks charge their best customers.

Instead of using an unfamiliar term and then defining it, journalists may eliminate the term and use the definition or explanation instead:

   He wants to improve the student-teacher ratio to 1:18.
   REVISED: He wants to provide one teacher for every 18 students.

   She said the school will have K-6 facilities.
   REVISED: She said the school will accept children from kindergarten through the sixth grade.

A journalist reported that a new hospital had "138 private rooms, 72 semi-private rooms and 15 ICU-CCU units distributed over two patient floors." Some people might know the difference between a private and semi-private room; others would not, however, and might also stumble over the terms "ICU-CCU" and "two patient floors." All four terms can easily be avoided:

The hospital has 138 rooms that contain one bed, 72 rooms that contain two beds, and 15 intensive-care and critical-care units. All rooms for patients are located on two floors.

Journalists using these techniques can make even the most complicated stories understandable. For example, an environmental reporter for The Arizona Daily Star in Tucson wrote about several wells contaminated by trichloroethylene. The topic was complex, yet reporter Jane Kay's stories were clear and dramatic. Kay explained that the chemical, also called "TCE," is an industrial degreaser that may cause cancer in humans. The wells contaminated by TCE were closed, and government officials assured people their drinking water was safe. But after hundreds of interviews, Kay discovered, "For 10 to 30 years, many South Side Tucson residents unknowingly got minute quantities of TCE almost every time they turned on the tap water." As many as 20,000 people "drank TCE at home, inhaled it in the shower and absorbed it through their skin when they washed the dishes."

Kay added:

TCE is a tasteless, odorless, colorless—and very toxic—chemical. It is volatile, meaning that it evaporates quickly, much like common household cleaning fluids.

Only a teaspoon of it poured into 250,000 gallons of water—about the amount used by five people in an entire year—would create a taint slightly beyond the 5 parts per billion suggested as a guideline for safety by the state Department of Health Services.

Apparently as a result of the TCE contamination, residents of Tucson's South Side suffered from an unusual number of serious illnesses, including cancer.

Large numbers—millions, billions and trillions— also need explaining. For example, if you saw a story reporting that failing savings and loan companies cost the nation $500 billion, could you really comprehend that number? As a reporter, you can help your audience understand large numbers by converting the numbers into something more familiar, perhaps something related to their own lives:

The county's residents and businesses produce about 2,200 tons of garbage each day, or 6.7 pounds per resident.

Last year in this state, a serious crime was committed every 29 seconds, and a violent crime every three minutes. Every citizen had a 1-in-11 chance of being a victim.

When fallen junk-bond king Michael Milken agreed to a $500 million settlement that would cut his personal net worth to about $225 million, USA Today reporter David Craig wrote: "That's still not bad. Someone earning $50,000 a year would need 4,500 years to make that."

Similarly, The Washington Post reported that an investment bank offered to pay $20.6 billion to take over RJR Nabisco Inc., the conglomerate that makes Oreos, LifeSavers and Camel cigarettes. RJR Nabisco rejected the offer, saying it wasn't big enough. If $20.6 billion cannot buy a cookie company, what is it good for? A writer at The Post calculated that it could:

- Provide shoes for every American for a year.

- House 2 million criminals in prisons for a year.

- Sponsor 80 million destitute children around the world for one year.

- Match the combined fortunes of the six richest people in the United States.

- Cover the cost of every movie ticket bought in the United States in the past 4½ years.

- Buy every advertisement in every magazine published in the United States for the past four years, or every radio ad for the past three years.

Harcourt Brace & Company

If you list several items in a sentence and must explain them, place that explanation before the list, not after it. If the explanation does not appear before the list, people may not immediately understand the relationship between the items or the significance of the list:

> Attempting to elude a police officer, no driver's license, fleeing the scene of an accident and driving while intoxicated were the charges filed against the mayor.
>
> REVISED: The mayor was charged with attempting to elude a police officer, driving without a license, fleeing the scene of an accident and driving while intoxicated.

> To obtain a better salary, better hours and more opportunities for advancement are the reasons the woman gave for changing jobs.
>
> REVISED: The woman said she changed jobs to obtain a better salary, better hours and more opportunities for advancement.

THE IMPORTANCE OF EXAMPLES

Specific examples make stories more interesting, personalize them and help audience members understand them more easily. If you wrote about a teen-ager who became an alcoholic and flunked out of college, you might describe specific examples of the problems she experienced:

> She said school became unimportant, adding: "I can remember staying up all night before my public health final. When I took the test I was smashed. And if that wasn't bad enough, then I ran the entire 10 blocks back to my apartment so I could drink some more. Of course, I flunked public health."

Specific examples are especially important in stories about abstract issues. Sometimes numbers help put those local or national issues into perspective. If you wrote about the lives of people who drop out of college, you would have to report the percentage of students who drop out of college nationally, their reasons for dropping out and what they do afterward: join the military, get married or find a job. In addition to reporting the general trends, a good writer would illustrate the story by describing the lives of two or three dropouts—specific examples of the trend. Similarly, The New York Times began a story about the chemical contamination of fish by describing the story's impact on a single person:

> Sitting in his Fulton Market office one morning, Abe Haymes swallowed his shot of scotch from a paper cup, slapped his chest and declared: "I've been eating fish every day of the week for the past 40 years. Do I look sick?"
>
> Like the rest of the city's fish dealers, Abe Haymes is angry about recent publicity concerning mercury . . . contamination of fish.

The following story, published by The Miami Herald, uses three examples to illustrate the impact of a paralyzing disease. Ironically, the disease was caused by a vaccination program intended to protect Americans from a dreaded strain of influenza:

> WASHINGTON—At first none of them believed anything significant was happening. Their fingers tingled because the weather was bad. They were "coming down with something." That's what caused the tender areas on their heads.
>
> Then the symptoms came with savage swiftness.
>
> • Judy Roberts of Lakeland, Fla., tried to wiggle her toes in a tight-fitting pair of sandals and found she couldn't feel them. She took off her shoes—and found she couldn't feel her feet.
>
> • Maryalice Beauton of Chula Vista, Calif., was eating a hamburger. Astonished, she realized she hadn't tasted anything.

Harcourt Brace & Company

• Herman Bauer of Pittsburgh was shopping with his family when his legs began to buckle. Confused and embarrassed, he grabbed onto a wall and called for help.

They didn't know it yet, but for these people and hundreds of other Americans, the preliminary stages of a paralyzing disease known as Guillaine-Barre syndrome had just begun. . . .

THE USE OF DESCRIPTION

Descriptions, like quotations, make stories more interesting and help people visualize scenes more easily. But many journalists are reluctant to use descriptive phrases; they summarize whatever they hear but are less likely to describe what they see, feel, taste and smell. Typically, a student who attended a speech by an expert in communications technology handed her instructor a story that said:

> The speaker, John Mollwitz, showed some examples of electronic newspapers and talked about how they fit into the newspaper industry.

The student failed to describe what the electronic newspapers looked like and how they "fit into the newspaper industry." She also neglected to mention that the crowd intermittently applauded Mollwitz, who developed some profitable electronic newspapers.

When told to describe something, most students rely too heavily on adverbs and adjectives. Nouns and verbs are more effective. Nouns and verbs are less redundant and less opinionated than adverbs and adjectives.

William L. Laurence won two Pulitzer Prizes for his work at The New York Times. Laurence was aboard the plane that dropped an atomic bomb on Nagasaki during World War II, and he wrote a story that contained this description of the event:

> Captain Bock swung around to get out of range; but even though we were turning away in the opposite direction, and despite the fact that it was broad daylight in our cabin, all of us became aware of a giant flash that broke through the dark barrier of our arc welder's lenses and flooded our cabin with intense light.
>
> We removed our glasses after the first flash, but the light still lingered on, a bluish-green light that illuminated the entire sky all around. A tremendous blast wave struck our ship and made it tremble from nose to tail. This was followed by four more blasts in rapid succession, each resounding like the boom of cannon fire hitting our plane from all directions.
>
> Observers in the tail of our ship saw a giant ball of fire rise as though from the bowels of the earth, belching forth enormous white smoke rings. Next they saw a giant pillar of purple fire, ten thousand feet high, shooting skyward with enormous speed.

Reporters who want to describe an object must learn to use concrete, factual details as opposed to trite phrases and generalities. Readers should be able to visualize the scene in their minds:

> VAGUE: A tall fence surrounds the construction site.
> BETTER: The construction site is surrounded by a 6-foot chain-link fence topped by three strands of barbed wire.

> VAGUE: There were about 50 men and women working in the area.
> BETTER: About 50 men and women were working in the area, and most wore hard hats, some yellow, some white and others red. Four of the workers had tied nail pouches around their waists. Others smoked cigarettes and looked weary in their dirty white T-shirts, jeans and sunglasses.

Harcourt Brace & Company

Tips from a Pro

STORIES NEED A SENSE OF PLACE

By **Lucille S. deView**
Writing Coach
The Orange County Register

Schoenecker was held in a 12-man jail in the center of Mineral County, a remote 600,000 acres of rolling hills, brisk creeks and snow-capped peaks that is home to about 1,500 residents.

About 1,000 of them live in Superior, which along with the 1920 jail has four bars, two markets, a brick courthouse and a Chevrolet dealership with just one car on display.
—*Janine Anderson from Superior, Mont.*

Creating a sense of place is essential to good writing. Some novelists, poets, journalists do this so well that we speak of Isak Dinesen's Africa, Carl Sandburg's Chicago, Bobbie Ann Mason's South, Joan Didion's Los Angeles.

To create a sense of place, imagine yourself as a camera focusing on detailed close-ups or capturing the broader scene with a wide-angle lens.

CLOSE-UPS

Use your senses. What do you see—sky-scrapers, hovels, meadows, cement? What do you hear—birds, sirens, whistles, waves? What do you smell—chemicals, flowers, garbage, perfume? What do you feel—nostalgia, alarm?

Who are the people? What ages? Backgrounds? What do they do with their days? Don't see people as quaint; to do so is to overlook their truth, however much it may differ from yours. What distinguished Anderson's description of Superior, Mont., was her respect for the town and its residents.

Hang out where people hang out. Robert Frank received a good tip for a story about Garden Grove police officers by hanging out at a restaurant they frequent. Charlie Finnic found a mission for the homeless when he methodically combed every street on his beat, looking for stories.

Take along your Polaroid and snap candid shots of streets, parks, cemeteries, industries to augment your notes. Look for contrasts—the ugly and beautiful, the soft and the tough.

What are the architectural styles, the costs of buildings? What does the presence or absence of lawns, trees, flowers say? What is the local history? The prospect for change?

DISTANCE SHOTS

Characterize the entire town, the entire neighborhood within a region. What is typical, what not? Is it like any other place on Earth?

YOU CAN'T TELL ALL

A sense of place need not be lengthy but your research should be thorough, the better to help you select telling details and weave them into exciting prose.

Be the writer. The camera.

Vagueness also becomes a problem when reporters attempt to describe other people. Instead of presenting factual details, some reporters mistakenly present generalities or their personal impressions of those people's appearance and character, as in the following examples:

She spoke with authority.

She seemed to enjoy talking about her work.

Harcourt Brace & Company

Neither of these sentences is an actual description. The first sentence concludes the woman spoke "with authority" but fails to explain why the writer reached that conclusion. The second sentence reports she "seemed to enjoy" talking about her work, but does not specifically describe either the speaker or what she said.

Generalities are often inconsistent among observers. One student reported a woman "seemed relaxed and very sure of herself." Everything about her "conveyed calmness." Yet, another student concluded, "She seemed nervous." The students could have avoided the problem by reporting specific details as opposed to their impressions, opinions and conclusions.

Reporters must learn to observe and describe specific details. If they are important to the story, include descriptions of people's voices, mannerisms, facial expressions, posture, gestures and surroundings. Include details about or descriptions of their height, weight, age, clothing, hair, glasses, jewelry and family, if they help to bring an image alive. Each factor can be described in detail. For example, a journalist describing a woman's hands might mention their size, calluses, nails, smoothness or wrinkles or veins, and jewelry. Thus, when you are asked to describe another person, look at the person carefully, then report specific facts about that person. Avoid generalities and conclusions:

> VAGUE: He is a large man.
> BETTER: He is 6 feet tall and weighs 210 pounds.
>
> VAGUE: Butler looked as though he had dressed in a hurry.
> BETTER: Butler's shirt was buttoned halfway, his socks were mismatched, his shoelaces were untied and his hair was not brushed.

Reporters can include a descriptive word or phrase almost anywhere in a news story, or they can devote an entire sentence or paragraph to description:

> He leaned back in his chair, laced his fingers together across his round belly and clenched the cigar in the corner of his mouth.
>
> She is 70 years old, but her thick brown hair is only slightly graying. As she spoke, she leaned back on a pillow and nervously smoked a long, dark cigarette. She has only a small table and a cot in her living room, and both are covered with knickknacks. She takes her guests into her bedroom to sit and talk.

Descriptions help the audience see the situation or person through the eyes of the reporter. When describing people, however, remember not to write anything about a woman that you wouldn't write about a man in the same situation and vice versa. Don't note, "The woman had long slender legs" if you wouldn't write in the same situation, "The man had long slender legs."

THE USE OF HUMOR

Editors constantly look for humorous stories and often place those stories on Page 1. But for most writers, humorous stories are particularly difficult to write. Journalists should not try to inject humor into stories that are not obviously humorous. If a story is funny, the humor should be apparent from the facts themselves. Journalists should not have to exaggerate or point out the humor by labeling it "funny" or "comical." Author and economist John Kenneth Galbraith has explained: "Humor is an intensely personal, largely internal thing. What pleases some, including the source, does not please others."

When columnist James J. Kilpatrick wrote an article about conservative William F. Buckley Jr., he did more than report Buckley "had a sense of humor." He gave a specific example of Buckley's wit. Kilpatrick reported Buckley had once run for mayor of New York City; when asked what he would do if he won, he replied, "Ask for a recount."

Similarly, a story about the peculiar laws in some cities never called the laws "peculiar" or "funny." Instead it simply listed them so people could judge the humor of the laws for themselves. The laws made it illegal to:

- Take a cow on a school bus

- Take a bath without a bathing suit

- Break more than three dishes in a single day

- Ride a horse not equipped with a horn and taillight

If you were writing about Ann Landers, you might give an example of her famous wit so audience members could judge it for themselves:

> While attending an embassy reception, Landers was approached by a rather pompous senator.
> "So you're Ann Landers," he said. "Say something funny."
> Without hesitation Landers replied: "Well, you're a politician. Tell me a lie."

Try to include some humor in your stories when appropriate, but remember understatement is more effective than exaggeration. Simply report the facts you think are humorous, then hope others will laugh.

NEWSWRITING HABITS TO AVOID

Avoid Stating the Obvious: Platitudes

Dull, trite, obvious remarks are called "platitudes," and journalists must learn to avoid them. News stories should not state obvious facts already known or easily figured out. Platitudes that have appeared in news stories include:

> As it has in most areas of modern life, science has entered the profession of firefighting in recent years.

> Superhighways, high-speed automobiles and jet planes are common objects of the modern era.

The second example appeared in a story about technological changes that had occurred during the life of a 100-year-old woman. The sentence would have been more interesting if it had described the changes in more detail and clearly related them to the woman's life, such as:

> Lila Hansen, who once spent three days on a train to visit relatives in California, now flies to California in three hours every Christmas.

Students have included these platitudes in their stories:

> Counselors help students with their problems.

> The mayor said she was pleased by the warm reception.

> The sponsors hope the art show will attract a large crowd.

The sources in these stories stated the obvious—what they were expected to say. Their statements sound familiar because these platitudes have been used before, perhaps millions of times.

Other platitudes appear in direct quotations. However, that does not justify their use. Such dull quotes should be deleted:

The newly elected mayor said, " I hope to do a good job."

The committee chair said, "Homecoming weekend is going to be big and exciting."

When people stop reading a story, they rarely think about why it bored them. If people re-examined the story, they might find not just one, but a series of platitudes. Platitudes say nothing that hasn't been heard before. Thus, people might quit reading the story because it is no longer interesting or "news" worthy.

To avoid platitudes, reporters must be alert, particularly when conducting interviews. Sources often give obvious, commonplace answers to the questions they are asked. If a bartender is robbed at gunpoint, there is no reason to quote him as saying he "was scared." Most people confronted by guns are scared, and they often say so. If journalists wanted to quote the bartender—or any other source—they would have to ask more penetrating questions and to continue their interview until they received more specific, interesting or unusual details.

Avoid Personification

Avoid treating inanimate objects as if they were human. Objects such as buildings, cars, stores and trees cannot hear, think, feel or talk. Yet some writers treat them as people. The writers see—and repeat—the error so often they no longer recognize it, and continue to personify almost everything, from committees to entire countries. Here is an example that appeared in The New York Times:

China has decided "in principle" to accept Peace Corps volunteers for the first time, Foreign Minister Wu Xueguian told a luncheon meeting at the National Press Club.

An editor at The Times suggested a correction for the sentence: ". . . Foreign Minister Wu Xueguian said at a luncheon meeting at the National Press Club."

Similarly, students have written:

Memorial Hospital treated her for shock and a broken arm.

She was driving west on Hullett Avenue when two cars in front of her slammed on their brakes.

Can a hospital treat patients, or is that the job of a hospital's staff? Similarly, can a car slam on its own brakes? Of course not! Such personifications are easy to correct:

The store said it will not reopen.
REVISED: The owner of the store said it will not reopen.

The intention of the road was to help farmers transport their crops to market.
REVISED: The road was built to help farmers transport their crops to market.

Personification contributes to two other problems. First, it handicaps audiences. People cannot determine a story's credibility if journalists fail to identify their source. Readers can assess the credibility of a statement attributed to their mayor or governor, but not the credibility of a statement attributed to their city or state.

Second, personification allows people to escape responsibility for their actions. Officials cannot be held responsible for their actions if journalists attribute an official's actions to a city or state, for example.

Avoid First-Person References

Except in extraordinary circumstances, journalists should remain neutral bystanders. They should not mention themselves in news stories. Journalists should not have to use the words "I,"

Harcourt Brace & Company

"me," "we" or "us," except in direct quotations—when they are quoting some other person. When they appear outside quotation marks, the words are likely to be confusing. Reporters who use the word "we" rarely explain whom they are referring to, yet their subject is not always clear. Moreover, it is a mistake for reporters to assume all people fit into any category they describe:

> He said we must work harder to improve the city's schools.
> REVISED: He said parents must work harder to improve the city's schools.

> The governor said we are being hurt by inflation.
> REVISED: The governor said residents of the state are being hurt by inflation.

Avoid the Negative

For clarity, avoid negative constructions. Your sentences should be cast in positive, rather than negative, form, as in the following examples:

> The student did not often come to class.
> REVISED: The student rarely came to class.

> The defense attorney tried to disprove her client's sanity.
> REVISED: The defense attorney tried to prove her client was insane.

Sentences containing two or three negatives are wordy and even more difficult to decipher. As you read the following examples, you may have to pause and struggle to determine their meaning:

> The women said they are not against the change.
> REVISED: The women said they favor the change.

> The senator said she will not accept any campaign contributions from people who do not live in her district.
> REVISED: The senator said she will accept campaign contributions only from people who live in her district.

In most cases, you can correct the problem by changing just a word or two:

> Most people are not careful readers.
> REVISED: Few people are careful readers.

> The financial planner said he can help people not go into debt.
> REVISED: The financial planner said he can help people avoid debt.

Avoid an Echo

Avoid an echo—the unnecessary repetition of a word—as in these examples:

> Her annual salary was $29,000 a year.

> In Japan, cancer patients are usually not told they have cancer.

Writers sometimes repeat a key word or phrase for emphasis or to demonstrate an important similarity. If the repetition is needless, however, the result is likely to be awkward, distracting or confusing.

Harcourt Brace & Company

Avoid Gush

Reporters also avoid "gush"—writing with exaggerated enthusiasm. They write news stories to inform members of a community, not to please their sources. News stories should report useful information. They should not praise nor advocate.

Because doing so is fast and easy, too many journalists obtain all their information from a single source, often an official responsible for the issue being discussed. Officials try to impress or manipulate journalists in an attempt to obtain more favorable publicity, and often they succeed. They reveal only the information that makes them, their policies and their institutions look good.

To avoid this problem, journalists must talk to several sources to obtain a variety of viewpoints and verify statements made by officials. Journalists must also prepare for each interview so they can ask knowledgeable questions and recognize evasive responses. Perhaps even more important, journalists must learn to ask for more specific details supporting officials' claims. The following statements lack those details, so they enable the officials to engage in self-praise:

> "We feel we are providing quality recreational programs for both adults and children," Holden said.

> Police Chief Barry Kopperud said the city's mounted horse patrol, which began one year ago, has become a great success.

When a journalist finishes an article, it should sound like a news story, not a press release. Yet, one travel story gushed Mexico is "a land of lush valleys and marvelous people." Other examples of gush include:

> The fair will offer bigger and better attractions than ever before.

> The event will provide fun and surprises for everyone who attends.

This gush cannot be rewritten, because there is nothing of substance to rewrite. It should simply be deleted.

There is a second type of gush: an escalation in modifiers. Columnist Donna Neely explains that what used to be called "funny" is now called "hilarious" and what used to be "great" is now called "fantastic" or "incredible."

These exaggerations appear everywhere: in news stories, press releases, advertisements and everyday speech. Sports writers call athletes not just "stars," but "superstars." Advertisers call their inventories "fabulous" and their sales "gigantic."

Avoid Contrived Titles and Labels

Some students come up with their own labels to attach to subjects. Most of those labels are unnecessary, opinionated and awkward. Many are also ridiculous. One writer referred to a young girl with an unusual illness as "the diseased student." Other students have referred to "a two-car, three-person accident" and "the county's school bond-financed building program." If a label is so artificial that you have never heard or used it before, and would not use it in a conversation with friends, do not use it in a news story.

Here are other examples of awkward, contrived labels:

> a yellow-clad man

> the well-patrolled parking lot

Such labels—also called "false titles"—often appear as a jumble of modifiers piled before a name:

Harcourt Brace & Company

Twenty-two-year-old Seminole Community College business major Nina Thomas won the $5,000 prize.

REVISED: Nina Thomas, a 22-year-old business major at Seminole Community College, won the $5,000 prize.

Contrived labels also arise when journalists try to make something more important than it is, as in these examples:

This is the third worst storm in five weeks.

Except for Sunday, this is the coldest day we've had in a month.

Inexperienced reporters use the time as a label, treating it as if it were a significant factor that could be used to distinguish one event from another. Thus, they may describe "a 10:05 a.m. fire," "an 11:20 a.m. drowning" or "a 2:15 p.m. storm."

Avoid Vague Time References

Unless your instructor suggests otherwise, do not use the words "yesterday," "today" and "tomorrow" in print news stories; you are too likely to mislead your readers. Instead, use the specific days of the week: "Sunday," "Monday," "Tuesday" and so forth. Many of the stories that appear in daily newspapers are written the day before their publication or even earlier. Certainly, most stories in weekly newspapers are written more than a day in advance. For people to read the event happened "today"—the day the story was written—would be misleading.

For example, if a fire destroyed a home at 5 p.m. Tuesday, journalists would write about the story later that Tuesday night, after the fire. Reporters could not say the fire occurred "today" because readers who received the paper Wednesday morning would assume that "today" meant the day they were reading the story—Wednesday. To avoid confusion and errors, always use the name of the day of the week.

Journalists also avoid the word "recently" because it is too vague. They use more precise terminology.

Avoid the Present Tense

Print journalists avoid the present tense and terms such as "at the present time" because many of the events journalists report end before readers receive the newspaper. Even though it is true, a reporter working on deadline should not say, "A fire at the Grand Hotel threatens to destroy the entire block." Firefighters would almost certainly extinguish the blaze before readers received the paper hours later. For the same reason, a reporter covering a fatal accident should not say, "The victim's identity is not known." Police might learn the victim's identity in a few hours, and local radio and television stations might broadcast the person's name before subscribers received their papers. Consequently, reporters must use the past tense, clearly indicating that the situations they are describing existed at some time in the past:

A fire at the Grand Hotel threatens to destroy the entire block.
REVISED: A fire at the Grand Hotel was still threatening to destroy the entire block at 11:30 p.m.

The victim's identity is not known.
REVISED: Police were unable to learn the victim's identity immediately.

Avoid Excessive Punctuation

Journalists avoid excessive punctuation, particularly exclamation points, dashes and parentheses. Exclamation points are rarely necessary and should never be used after every sentence in a story, regardless of that story's importance.

Reporters avoid excessive parenthetical matter because it creates an obstacle that makes reading and listening more difficult. Parentheses interrupt the flow of ideas and force people to pause and assimilate some additional, often jarring, bits of information:

> She (the governor) said the elderly population (people 65 and older) has grown twice as fast as any other segment of the state's population during the last 20 years.
>
> REVISED: The governor said the percentage of people 65 and older has grown twice as fast as any other segment of the state's population during the last 20 years.

Sources use a lot of pronouns and vague references. Students often quote these sources, adding explanations within parentheses. If an explanation is necessary, then a direct quote is not a good idea. Instead, reporters use partial quotes or paraphrase what a source has said:

> "I wish they (school administrators) would quit fooling around," she said. "They say they don't have enough money (to hire more teachers), but I don't believe that. I know they have it (the money); it's just a matter of priorities—of using their money more wisely."
>
> REVISED: She said the school administrators should "quit fooling around." They say they do not have enough money to hire more teachers, but she does not believe that. "It's just a matter of priorities—of using their money more wisely," she said.

Avoid "It," "This," "These," "Those" and "That"

Reporters use words such as "it," "this," "these," "those" and "that" with caution because their meanings are often unclear. Reporters must be particularly careful to avoid starting a sentence or paragraph with one of these words unless its antecedent is obvious. To avoid confusion, reporters can repeat a key word or rewrite a foggy sentence to clarify its meaning:

> Commissioner Terry Benham, who represents Scott County on the Transit Authority, said the bus system is no longer losing money. He attributed this to the elimination of routes that had consistently shown losses.
>
> REVISED: Commissioner Terry Benham, who represents Scott County on the Transit Authority, said the bus system is no longer losing money because routes that had consistently lost money have been eliminated.

Avoid Cluttered and Convoluted Sentences

For clarity, news stories should be emphatic. Facts that are important should never be slipped into stories as minor clauses or phrases that receive little emphasis within long, cluttered sentences:

> James Loach admitted that he robbed Anders of $170 and said he tied the Vanguard Theater employee's hands with a rope, but he denied that he killed the son of Central High School Principal Robert Anders.
>
> REVISED: James Loach admitted he robbed Anders of $170 and said he tied Anders' hands with a rope, but he denied he killed the youth.
>
> Anders, the son of Central High School Principal Robert Anders, worked at the Vanguard Theater.

The first sentence began by mentioning Anders, but later referred to "the Vanguard Theater employee" and to "the son of Central High School Principal Robert Anders." The sentence failed to make it clear Anders himself was the theater employee and the son of the high school principal. At best, the inclusion of these facts was confusing. At worst, it was misleading, because readers might assume the story was describing three different people.

As your sentences become more complicated, they are also likely to contain more errors. The following sentences, written by students, illustrate the problem:

> She said advice for a swimming pool with the algae would be not to swim in the pool.

> Primarily a rental area, the commission wants to rezone the neighborhood and encourage single-family ownership over rental properties.

The first sentence, in effect, warns swimming pools not to swim in the pool. The second sentence calls the commission a rental area.

MORE ON GRAMMAR AND WORD USAGE

To become an effective writer, you will have to understand more than the basics of grammar and word usage. You will have to become an expert. Understanding the following suggestions will help.

Use Parallel Form

Every item listed in a series must be in parallel form. If the first verb in a series uses the past tense, every verb in the series must use the past tense. Or, if the first verb ends in "ing," all must end in "ing":

> The man was running from the dog, crying and bled.
> PARALLEL FORM: The man was running from the dog, crying and bleeding.

> Police said the plastic handcuffs are less bulky, not as expensive and no key is needed to remove them from a suspect's wrists.
> PARALLEL FORM: Police said plastic handcuffs are less bulky, less expensive and less difficult to remove from a suspect's wrists.

Use Articles Correctly

Use the articles "a," "an" and "the" correctly. The words "a" and "an" are indefinite articles, used to refer to one member of a broad category or class of objects (for example, "they want to buy a table"). The word "the" is a definite article, used to refer to a specific person or object (for example, "that is the table they want to buy").

As a general rule, use an indefinite article ("a," "an") when referring to a person or object that has not been mentioned earlier in a story. Use the definite article ("the") when referring to a person or object mentioned earlier in a story.

If it is misused, the definite article may mislead people because it often suggests that the object being referred to is the only such object in existence. If, for example, a story reports three people were taken to "the hospital," yet the story's earlier paragraphs never mentioned the hospital, the sentence implies the area has only one hospital, the hospital at which those people are being treated. Similarly, if you reported someone ate lunch at "the McDonald's in Chicago," your sentence would imply, wrongly, that there is only one McDonald's in the entire city.

Check for Subject-Verb and Noun-Pronoun Agreement

If the subject is singular, use a singular verb, and if the subject is plural, use a plural verb. Similarly, if a noun is singular, use a singular pronoun, and if a noun is plural, use a plural pronoun:

> A team of researchers have been gathering the information.
> REVISED: A team of researchers has been gathering the information.

> The groups failed in its attempts to obtain more money.
> REVISED: The groups failed in their attempts to obtain more money.

Nouns such as "committee," "family," "group," "jury" and "team" are confusing. The Associated Press Stylebook explains that all those nouns take singular verbs and pronouns because they denote a single unit:

> The team won their third victory in a row.
> REVISED: The team won its third victory in a row.

> The jury reached their verdict at 11:10 p.m.
> REVISED: The jury reached its verdict at 11:10 p.m.

Collective nouns refer to a group or quantity regarded as a single unit and also take singular verbs and pronouns. For example: "A thousand bushels is a good yield."

SOME FINAL GUIDELINES

1. Begin by obtaining a good, solid foundation for the story: all the information audiences might want to know about the topic. To add to the story's credibility and depth, consult several credible sources, not just one, and report every viewpoint.
2. If the story is complicated, decide which facts are most important and decide how to organize them. Plan the transitions between different ideas and the point at which to end the story.
3. Emphasize the human element in every story: the people involved in the story, or the people affected by it. People are interested in other people: their interests, values, habits, jobs, eccentricities, families, problems, triumphs and tragedies.
4. Ken Fuson, an award-winning reporter for The Des Moines (Iowa) Register, suggests reporters look for unexpected or unusual ways to present the facts in their stories. For example, while writing about a town's isolation, Fuson began: "State Center is 45 miles from Des Moines, 15 miles from Ames and 13 miles from the nearest McDonald's."
5. Place the information to emphasize at the beginning or end of a sentence. Avoid burying it in the middle of a sentence, since it receives less emphasis there. Because people are most likely to remember whatever they saw last, many experts believe information placed at the end of a sentence is likely to have the greatest impact.
6. When mentioning several objects or numbers in a story, always check their arithmetical consistency. If, for example, seven people received awards, list their names, and count to be certain it is a listing of seven, not six or eight, recipients.
7. Be consistent in the description of, or reference to, topics. If writing about a hospital, for example, use the hospital's full name the first time it is mentioned. Later in the story, refer

Harcourt Brace & Company

to it as "the hospital." The hospital's full name does not have to be repeated. Because different labels might confuse an audience, do not call the building a "hospital" the first time it is mentioned and later refer to it as a "structure," "building," "medical facility" and "health center."

8. If using a specific figure, such as 41 or 471, do not use approximations such as "about." Use approximations only when rounding off a figure, such as, "About 700 people attended the concert." Similarly, when indicating the time, do not write "the fire started at about 8:03 a.m." Write either "at 8:03 a.m." or "at about 8 a.m." Whereas "8:03 a.m." is a specific time, "about 8 a.m." is an approximation of time.

9. Avoid loaded words that might prejudice audience members for or against a subject. When they attribute statements, journalists avoid the word "claim" because it implies doubt, suggesting the statements may be false. The word "only" is even more troublesome. If a journalist comments, "Only three people were killed," the use of "only" suggests those deaths were unimportant.

10. Avoid contractions: "doesn't," "hadn't" and so on. Many papers prohibit their use except in direct quotations.

11. Avoid overusing the words "that" and "then"; both words can usually be deleted. "Then" is especially troublesome because some writers habitually—and monotonously—add it to most of their sentences.

12. Avoid using too many pronouns in a sentence. They become confusing and repetitive, as in these examples: "She said she would be happy to help her if they could finish the work after the test." Or: "He said he had a bomb in the bag he was carrying, and he threatened to blow up the bank if he did not get their money."

13. Tell audience members how or where the information presented in each story was obtained: from a press conference, speech, interview or telephone conversation. The source does not have to be emphasized or placed in a story's lead, but it should be included somewhere, perhaps in a brief phrase or sentence (for example, "during a press conference in her office, the governor said she opposes legalized gambling in the state").

14. If you are unable to obtain an important fact or some information audience members might expect or need, explain why the information could not be included in the story: "University officials said it will take several days to calculate the average faculty member's salary." Or: "Rescue workers said they will not know how many people were killed until all the water is pumped out and they are able to search the entire mine."

15. Never create or manufacture any information; report only the facts obtained from reliable sources. If additional information is needed, research the topic more thoroughly; never make up any information. News stories are based on fact, not fiction.

16. Be original. Go out and personally gather the information needed for a story. Do not rewrite information already reported by other media. By the time it is copied, the information is likely to be old, and many audience members may have seen or heard it before. Moreover, you may be accused of plagiarism.

CHECKLIST FOR IMPROVING NEWSGATHERING AND WRITING SKILLS

1. Use words in your story properly. Try to include descriptive, specific and interesting words.
2. Do not start sentences with the words "it," "this," "these," "those" and "that," unless their antecedents are clear.
3. Eliminate generalities and vague qualifiers: words such as "young," "big," "late," "fast," "very" and "a lot."
4. Use the articles "a," "an" and "the" correctly.
5. Use strong verbs—colorful, descriptive verbs.
6. Refer to topics consistently, and avoid loaded words and opinionated or artificial labels.

Harcourt Brace & Company

7. Avoid mentioning yourself in the story and using the words "I," "me," "we," "us" and "our," except in direct quotations from a source.

8. Use singular verbs with singular subjects, and plural verbs with plural subjects.

9. Place the explanation before rather than after items in lists.

10. List items in a series in parallel form.

11. Write your story with detail and explanation, so it answers all the questions one might logically ask about the topic.

12. Identify everyone mentioned in your story, define unfamiliar words and explain unfamiliar concepts. Also, identify people only once—normally, the first time you mention them in your story.

13. Define a large number—millions, billions or trillions—by converting the number into something more familiar, perhaps something related to your reader's lives.

14. Emphasize the human element: the people involved in, or affected by, your story. Use examples to personalize topics and explain abstract concepts.

15. Provide specific, factual details, as opposed to generalities and personal impressions, to describe the objects or people mentioned in your story.

16. Present humor in a clear, straightforward manner, without labels or exaggeration.

17. Avoid misleading statements about the time of the story. Use the specific day of the week—not "yesterday," "today" or "tomorrow"—and avoid suggesting your story will continue indefinitely.

18. Avoid gush, exaggeration, contrived labels and excessive punctuation.

19. Avoid personification: do not suggest that inanimate objects can talk, think or feel.

20. Avoid an echo: do not unnecessarily repeat the same word in a sentence.

21. Avoid platitudes: do not state the obvious, such as the fact that a government official was happy to be elected.

22. Do not bury important facts in a convoluted sentence or paragraph.

23. Cast your sentences in positive rather than negative form.

24. Explain how or where you obtained your information. If you were unable to include some important information, explain the reason for its omission.

25. Make certain your story is original and based entirely on facts that you were able to verify—not on "facts" you have made up or assumed.

Tips from a Pro

LOOK FOR DETAILS THAT TELL ALL

By **Lucille S. deView**
Writing Coach
The Orange County Register

Writers, please note:

The time to search for telling details is when you're on the scene, not when you sit down to write the story with less than total recall.

Journalism guru Elliott Osborn, in his book, "The World of Oz," cites this how-to example:

An editor phoned a reporter in New Orleans. The religion section of the paper, it

(continued on next page)

seems, was doing a story on a confrontation in that city between an archbishop and an excommunicated parishioner, Una Gaillot. The confrontation, about desegregation, had taken place on the archbishop's lawn.

The editor asked the reporter to answer just two questions.

"No. 1, what does the archbishop's house look like? Is it wood or stone or brick? Is it Victorian with ivy on the walls? What kind of day was it? Was it balmy and overcast or hot and muggy? What does the archbishop look like? Is he old and bespectacled or what? How did he walk when he came out of the house? Did he stride angrily? Or did he walk haltingly, leaning on a cane? How was he dressed? What is the walkway like? Is it concrete, brick or gravel? What do the grounds look like? Are there oak trees and rose bushes, magnolias and poppies? Were birds singing in the bushes? What was going on in the street outside the house? Was an angry crowd assembled? Or was there the normal business traffic, passing by oblivious to the drama? What were Mrs. Gaillot and her friends wearing? Did they have on Sunday best or just casual clothes? What happened when the archbishop confronted Mrs. Gaillot? Was he stern and silent? Or did he rebuke her? What was the exact language she used?

"Now," the editor said, "question No. 2."

No, the writer did not include the answers to every question, but might have found an interesting contrast between the serenity of the surroundings (if, indeed, they were serene) and the chaos on the lawn.

Were the tempers in tune with the temperature that day? And why were the speakers mere voices instead of being flesh and bone? The possibilities were infinite.

WHAT A DIFFERENCE A DETAIL MAKES

Compare the writing in the following.

Traditional: "Jim Valvano, a former basketball coach who is fighting cancer, attended the game last night at the arena."

From Sports Illustrated by Gary Smith: "He entered the arena with his wife on his arm and a container of holy water from Lourdes in his black leather bag. His back and hips and knees ached. That was the disease, they told him. His ears rang and his stomach turned and his hands and feet were dead. That, they said, was the cure. Each step he took brought a rattle from his bag. Twenty-four tablets of Advil were usually enough to get him through the day."

Traditional: Krystal Wilhelm sits on the steps of the Merlin Apartments waiting for a date.

From the Spokane Chronicle by Julie Sullivan: "Krystal Wilhelm crouches on the seventh stair of the Merlin Apartments, thin knees pulled against her 16-year-old stomach, insides cramping. She's dope sick. Living in the Merlin, one cracked cement step from the street, the Coeur d'Alene girl knows impure drugs are an occupational hazard. She rocks with cramps. But she needs $2 for a pack of cigarettes and that means going upstairs, finding her shoes and heading out into the cold for a 'date.'"

Traditional: The annual skipday at the stadium was canceled this year. It's a day when men become truants from their jobs to watch the first weekday game of spring training.

From the Miami Herald by Geoffrey Tomb: (Lead) "Trash swirled on the street outside the stadium. Inside, the place was empty. Still. Under the stands the lifeless air had no aroma of red hots, no splash of bright yellow mustard, no underfoot crunch of peanut shells. . . . (Ending) Miami Stadium is dark and silent. They skipped skipday."

WRITE WITH THE SENSES

Look and really see. Listen and really hear. Sniff the air. Feel the textures underfoot, the gravel or melting tar. Taste the salt spray, bite into the apple you've plucked from the tree.

Test yourself. The next time you return from an interview, before you begin writing, list every detail of the person (height, weight, color eyes, style of hair, posture, voice, gestures). Describe the setting, a la Elliott Osborn.

Harcourt Brace & Company

SUGGESTED READINGS

Cappon, Rene J. *Associated Press Guide to News Writing: A Handbook for Writers from America's Leading News Service.* New York: The Associated Press, 1991.

Kennedy, George, Daryl R. Moen, and Don Ranly. *Beyond the Inverted Pyramid: Effective Writing for Newspapers, Magazines and Specialized Publications.* New York: St. Martin's Press, 1993.

Ricchiardi, Sherry, and Virginia Young. *Women on Deadline: A Collection of America's Best.* Ames, IA: Iowa State University Press, 1991.

Rothmyer, Karen. *Winning Pulitzers: The Stories Behind Some of the Best News Coverage of Our Times.* New York: Columbia University Press, 1991.

Sloan, Wm. David, Julie K. Hedgepeth, Patricia C. Place, and Kevin Stoker. *The Great Reporters: An Anthology of News Writing at Its Best.* Northport, AL: Vision Press, 1992.

Zinsser, William. *On Writing Well: An Informal Guide to Writing Nonfiction,* 4th ed. New York: Harper-Perennial, 1990.

EXERCISE 1

IMPROVING NEWSGATHERING AND WRITING SKILLS

RECOGNIZING AND CORRECTING NEWSWRITING ERRORS

SECTION I: DESCRIBING PEOPLE

Which of the following descriptions are most effective? Rank them from best (No. 1) to worst (No. 5), then discuss them with your instructor and classmates.

1. He is an attractive blond: young, slender, articulate and intelligent. (Rank: _____)
2. She walked into the courtroom wearing a blue suit, dark glasses, a gold bracelet and five gold rings. (Rank: _____)
3. It was a dreary scene: ugly and unpleasant, and that may have contributed to their illness. (Rank: _____)
4. Jorge cried when a bailiff snapped handcuffs on his wrists after the jury foreman read the verdict of guilty. (Rank: _____)
5. Linn is an 18-year veteran of the Police Department. His tall, heavy-set appearance and no-nonsense attitude befit a man in his position. (Rank: _____)

SECTION II: DEFINING AND EXPLAINING

Define or explain each of the large numbers or unfamiliar terms in the following sentences.

1. Their son has meningitis.
2. A single B-2 Stealth bomber costs $800 million.
3. Pioneer 10, a satellite launched on March 2, 1972, is 4.2 billion miles from the sun.

SECTION III: AVOIDING UNNECESSARY PARENTHESES

Eliminate the parentheses, and other errors, from the following sentences.

1. She (the mayor) said (in response to a question about property taxes) that she opposes any such proposal (to increase them).
2. Despite the loss (now estimated at $4.2 million) she said the company should be able to pay all their debts before the deadline (Dec. 30).
3. The governor predicted that, "They (members of the Legislature) will approve the proposal (to increase the sales tax) within 60 days."

SECTION IV: AVOIDING PERSONIFICATION

Rewrite the following sentences, eliminating all their examples of personification and other errors.

1. Slamming on its brakes, the car turned to the left, then skidded off the road and collided with a tree.
2. The corporation, which denied any responsibility for the deaths, will appear in court next month.

Harcourt Brace & Company

3. The committee issued their report Monday, saying they will discuss the problem in a press conference at 11 a.m. Monday.

SECTION V: AVOIDING FALSE TITLES

Rewrite these sentences, eliminating their false and contrived titles.

1. Assistant solid waste disposal director Carlos Alicea said he opposes the fee.
2. President of the Michigan Avenue boat shop Robert Ellerbee discovered the 7:05 a.m. fire.
3. The door of the 1213 Ashland Avenue home of the two female senior college students was pried open.
4. The typical 1990s American family spends 37 percent of its weekly food-budgeted dollars in restaurants.
5. The Seventh Avenue lawn furniture manufacturing company damaged by the 7:10 a.m. Tuesday fire hopes to reopen next week.

SECTION VI: AVOIDING THE NEGATIVE

Rewrite the following sentences in positive form.

1. She cast a no vote for the proposal to raise property taxes.
2. Not until late August did she finally receive the check for $820.
3. The mayor said she would not be disinclined to vote against the bill.
4. The students do not have any limitations on which songs they can choose.
5. The restaurant is not far away.

SECTION VII: USING PARALLEL FORM

Rewrite these sentences in parallel form.

1. He was charged with drunken driving and an expired drivers license.
2. Her injuries include a broken left arm, permanent blindness in her left eye, an 84-day hospital stay and bills exceeding $240,000.
3. To join the club, one must be a sophomore, junior or senior; studying journalism; be in good academic standing; and have demonstrated professional journalistic ability.
4. She said the other advantages of owning her own business include being independent, not having a boss, flexible hours and less stress.
5. Under the conditions of her probation, the teen-ager must obey her parents, complete her high school education, not possess drugs or associate with people who do, and she is restricted from drinking alcohol.

SECTION VIII: IMPROVING SENTENCES

Rewrite the following sentences, correcting all their errors. Some sentences contain more than one error.

1. He said the book were a good read.
2. The article went on to add that most of todays most popular comedians are women.

3. She said that before marijuana is legalized, there has to be more extensive research pointing in the direction of its being a harmless drug.
4. She wants to establish a program where convicted juveniles would be required to perform some sort of community service and not go to jail.
5. The latest fire occurred Sunday night in a basement room used by the school band, causing an estimated $30,000 damage and destroyed 80 of their uniforms.

Harcourt Brace & Company

EXERCISE 2
IMPROVING NEWSGATHERING AND WRITING SKILLS

WRITING NEWS STORIES

INSTRUCTIONS: Write complete news stories based on the following information. Critically examine the information's language and organization, improving it whenever possible. To provide a pleasing change of pace, also use some quotations in your stories. Go beyond the superficial; unless your instructor tells you otherwise, assume that you have enough space to report every important and interesting detail.

1. It was almost like a popular movie titled "Home Alone" that you may have happened to see in a theater or on a tape at home on your VCR. It involved an 11-year-old girl in your city, Andrea Jones of 4851 Edmee Cir. When you interviewed her today, Andrea said she doesn't feel much like a hero. "I was scared," she said. "I thought he was going to see me and beat me up or something if he got in, so I tried to hide at first." In fact, Andrea used her imagination—and a baseball bat—to thwart a would-be burglar who tried to break into her familys home when she was home alone. The incident began when Andrea was home alone, watching television at approximately 6 p.m. last night. Her parents and 3 sisters had left the house to go pick up a pizza for dinner. They had been gone for only a few minutes and were due back very shortly. Andrea told you that she was watching television and heard a noise. "I saw a man at the window and ran to my bedroom to hide in the closet," she said. "Then I remembered the bat there. I went back into the dining room and saw this guy opening the window. He put his hand in first. He was coming in the window, and had his left hand on a table there. I took the bat and hit it as hard as I could. I, uh, really smashed it hard. He screamed like real loud, man, and ran away. Then, uh, I called 911." Police Detective Jack Noonan was at the scene and, when questioned by you, commented on the case, stating that: "Preferably, we would like to see someone in an incident like this call 911 first. It's safer that way. Someone could get really hurt in a situation like this. In this case, the girl was lucky. She kept her head, and she was really brave about it. She was home alone and decided she should protect herself and her house. She must have really walloped the guy. There's a lot of blood on the window and table, so now we're looking for someone who's injured." Police found the bad guy later last night. After the break-in, they notified hospital emergency wards to be on the look-out for a man suffering from trauma to his left hand and, shortly after 1 a.m., received a call from the Regional Medical Center, where a man matching a description Andrea gave the police came in for treatment of a very badly cut, broken, swollen, and painful left hand. He has been arrested and charged with attempted burglary. Police identified the man as Steven Jabil, 23, of 800 Crestbrook Loop, Apt. 314.

2. It was a fatal accident and involved two small planes. They collided at an estimated height of 800 feet above your city shortly after 8:30 a.m. today. Three people were aboard the planes. No one on the ground was seriously hurt, although the wreckage fell on and near several homes. "It could have been a lot worse," Police Chief Barry Koperud said. "People living in the area were very fortunate." The dead include the pilot of one plane, identified as Sharon Noruse of 4740 Valley View Lane. She was flying a single-engine Piper Cub. It collided in the air with a single-engine Cessna 172. The Piper, which was towing a banner, belonged to Aerial Promotions, Inc., said police. The pilot, Nouse, had worked for Aerial Promotions, Inc. for three months. The Cessna, carrying a

flight instructor and his student, belonged to the Pratt Air Academy. The names of the two deceased individuals in the Cessna were withheld pending notification of their next of kin. Both businesses are located at the Municipal Airport. The Cessna crashed into the roof of the house owned by Bobby and Dawn Correia of 9542 Holbrook Dr. Some members of the family—Mrs. Correia and their youngest child, a boy named Sean, age four—were home at the time and ran out when the Cessna slammed into their home. They were not injured at all. The Correias retired to the home of a neighbor who said they were too distraught to be interviewed. Other family members later joined them there. A block away, Mr. and Mrs. Elton Amanpour and their two children, Casey and Carmen, were eating dinner when the Piper fell in front of their house at 823 E. Pierce Av. A fuel tank from the Cessna smashed into the ground in front of Trina Greenhouse, who was smoking a cigarette on her front porch at 9557 Holbrook Dr. She was taken to Regional Medical Center after she complained that fuel got into her eyes and was burning them. According to other eyewitnesses, the two planes were very close to each other. People at the airport said the planes apparently tried to land at the same time. They are in the process of reviewing air traffic control tapes to determine which plane had been given clearance to land. Some witnesses said they heard a dull thud moments before the planes plummeted to the ground. Ronald Lin said he was standing in his back yard at 6287 Airport Boulevard when the collision occurred. "It was a loud, dull impact," he said. "There was no explosion. It was more like a blunt impact. I looked up and couldn't believe what I was seeing. There was a moment when both planes just seemed to stop in midair for a second, and then they both fell to the ground." Lori Kaeppler of 9540 Holbrook Dr., a neighbor of the Correias, said, "When it first hit, it sounded like a car hit our house or something. I ran to the front door and yelled to my husband, 'Call 911, we have a plane in the Correias house.' There wasn't any fire or anything, and I went in the house to see if I could help. I spotted this one guy in the wreckage in the kitchen, almost cut in half. Before our children were born, I worked as a nurse, and I reached in to feel his pulse but couldn't find it. Later, I saw the other guy sprawled on our roof. He must have been thrown there and, obviously, he was dead." Witnesses said it appeared the Cessna clipped the wing of the banner plane, then got caught up in the banner, sending both to the ground.

3. Some said she shouldn't be charged with murder. She wasn't. She's a doctor. She had a patient with leukemia. She admitted helping her patient commit suicide. Today she was cleared by a state board of charges of misconduct. The 7-member board—your states Board for Professional Medical Conduct—could have revoked her license to practice medicine. Instead it concluded that the actions of Dr. Catrina Lowrie were "legal and ethically appropriate." Lowrie is an internist at the Regional Medical Center in your city. No one might have known what she did, but she described it in a public speech sponsored by your citys chapter of the Hemlock Society, and an anonymous caller called the police about what she said. In the speech she described how she prescribed barbiturates for a patient and made sure the patient knew how many to take to kill herself. The patient, who has since been identified as Irma Cain of 427 Hidden Lane, was 37 years old and, her husband and parents said, in terrible, hopeless pain. They supported the doctor in the matter, their attorney said, but they refused to talk to you about it. Cain decided to commit suicide rather than undergo chemotherapy for cancer which would have given her only a 25% chance of survival. Her death occurred six months ago. Last month, a grand jury investigated the matter and then cleared the doctor of criminal responsibility for the womans death. Now the board, which issued its ruling late yesterday, said that the doctor did nothing medically improper in prescribing the barbiturates because "she could not have known with certainty what use a patient might make of the drug she prescribed, and which was totally appropriate and needed by her

patient." Lowrie said in a statement that the ruling "seemed like a very thoughtful decision." The members of the board stated that they were not condoning "so-called assisted suicide." They added that this case differed from other recently publicized cases in that Lowrie had a longstanding relationship with her patient. In addition, she did not directly take part in ending her patients life. Rather, she prescribed pills needed to alleviate the patients pain, and the patient, by herself, took them all at once in a successful attempt to terminate her own life and very painful suffering from the deadly disease.

4. Janet C. Herholtz is a professor of sociology at the University of Wyoming. She was in town today to give a speech at the annual convention of the American Association of Sociologists. During her speech, she discussed the topic of murder, about which she wrote her Ph.D. dissertation. She is also in the process of writing a book about murder and, at the University of Wyoming, teaches an unusual course titled, "The Epidemic of Murder." She explains that each year one out of every 10,000 Americans is murdered, and that in five years more Americans are murdered than were killed during the entire war in Vietnam. Yet, she said, many popular stereotypes about murder are false, totally without foundation. "The most likely murderer is a victim's relative," she explained. "Almost a third of all victims are related to their killers. The murderers are husbands, wives, lovers, neighbors, friends and acquaintances—people who can no longer endure chronic frustrations. Most murders are committed by men in their 20s—often because they blame other people rather than themselves for their problems. In two-thirds of the murders, they use guns. I should mention the fact that the probability of being murdered varies from one area of the country to another and from one race to another. People in the South are three times more likely to be murdered than people living in New England, and people who live in a large city are twice as likely to be murdered as people living in a suburb or rural area. Also, black men are 10 times more likely to be murdered than white men, and black women five times more than white women. In 90 percent of the cases, blacks are murdered by blacks, and whites by whites." Dr. Herholtz blames the use of alcohol for many murders, along with drugs, rising frustrations, permissive parents, joblessness and marital instability.

5. What can you do to maximize the span of your life? Raymond W. Herron, author of a book titled, "Centenarians," autographed copies of his book at area bookstores today and, during a press conference at 9:30 a.m. this morning, answered the questions of local reporters from newspapers and radio and television stations in the area. In response to their questions, he said a major factor is work. "Old age is not a time to be sedentary, but to be active. Work is an invaluable remedy against premature old age—hard work. If you study the background of people who live to be 100, you'll find few of them are lazy. Most worked hard all their lives, and many are still working." Herron noted that Russia claims to have almost 20,000 centenarians, many more than any other country in the world, and that the highest age claimed by Russia is 167, attained by Shirali Mislimov, who passed away in the year 1982. Herron noted that Russia reports that healthy old people seem to have several characteristics in common. Most live in rural areas. More than 99 percent are married. Most have large families. All are moderate eaters and drinkers and stick to a regular diet of plain foods. Much of their work is physical. Other studies, Herron continued, have found that people seem to live longer if they live in high places, drink well water and talk a lot. In the United States, he continued, researchers often note the effects of "pension illness"—the fact that people who retire deteriorate quickly in health and mind and often die within a few years after reaching their 65th birthdays, whereas people who continue to work maintain a better health and enjoy considerably longer lives. What are the average American's chances of living to be 100? Less than 1 out of 50,000, responded Herron.

Harcourt Brace & Company

CHAPTER 11

SPECIALIZED TYPES OF STORIES

Always, when time permits, read your story before submitting it. If you can't cut out at least a couple of words, you're not doing a sufficiently critical job of reading. One of the toughest things in the writing trade, and one of the best for a writer, is to cut your own copy.

(Morton Sontheimer, "Newspaperman")

In addition to the news stories discussed in previous chapters, reporters write more specialized types of stories, including brights, followups, roundups and sidebars.

BRIGHTS

Brights are short, humorous stories that often have surprise endings. Some brights are written in the inverted pyramid style: They begin with a summary lead, then report the remaining details in descending order of importance. Other brights have unexpected or bizarre twists, and reporters may try to surprise their readers by withholding those twists until the stories' final paragraphs. Brights that have surprise endings are called "suspended-interest stories" and, to keep their endings a surprise, usually begin with intriguing or suspenseful facts—some details likely to interest readers. A suspended-interest story cannot begin with a summary lead, because it would reveal the surprise ending.

Editors and news directors search for humorous stories and display the best ones prominently in their newspapers and news broadcasts. Brights entertain viewers and readers, arouse their emotions and provide relief from the seriousness of the world's problems. Here are examples of summary leads for brights:

> What's the worst gift you ever received for Christmas? Does the word "fruitcake" strike fear in your heart?

> DAVENPORT, Iowa (AP)—Two Davenport men were arrested Wednesday on charges of riding a horse on a sidewalk, riding a horse without lights and failure to pick up manure.

The suspended-interest story that follows begins so routinely that at first it may mislead the audience; its bizarre twist is not revealed until the final paragraphs:

> Police killed an intruder after he set off a burglar alarm in a clothing store on Main Street shortly after 1 a.m. today.
> Police entered the store after customers in a nearby tavern heard the alarm and surrounded the building until the officers arrived.
> Police found the intruder perched on a counter and killed it with a fly swatter.
> "It was my third bat this year," declared a police officer triumphantly.

Harcourt Brace & Company

Here are two more brights. The one on the left begins with a summary lead. The one on the right does not, and its ending may surprise you:

College students often complain about sloppy roommates, and Oscar—the first pig to be evicted from an apartment in the city—may be the sloppiest of all.

Oscar is a 6-week-old, 20-pound Hampshire pig. His owners claim that Oscar is only slightly different from other pets that live in the Colonial Apartments on University Boulevard. But the complex's owners say Oscar has to go.

"He's dug up the entire back yard," co-owner Sean Fairbairn said. "Besides that, he's noisy, and he stinks. We've gotten all sorts of complaints."

Oscar has lived in an old hay-filled refrigerator in Todd Gill's patio for a week. The patio is fenced in, but neighbors complained to the owners. The owners then told Gill and his roommate, Wayne Brayton, that Oscar has to go by noon Saturday.

"I don't think it's fair," Gill said. "People love Oscar. He runs around and grunts and squeals, but nothing too obnoxious. We've only let him out a couple times, and he's dug a hole under the fence once or twice, but no one's complained to me."

Gill and Brayton bought Oscar last week at a livestock auction.

The briefcase was on the floor near the Police Department's information desk for about 45 minutes. A clerk got suspicious. Maybe it contained explosives, she thought.

She called the department's bomb squad, and it evacuated the building. Members of the bomb squad then carried the briefcase outside and blew it up in a vacant lot.

That's when they learned that the briefcase belonged to their boss, Police Chief Barry Kopperud. He left it at the information desk while visiting the mayor.

"It's my fault," Kopperud said. "I should have mentioned it to someone. My officers did a good job, and I'm proud of them. They did what they were trained to do: to be alert and cautious."

Kopperud added that his son is likely to be upset, however. Today is the boy's seventh birthday, and Kopperud had his present in the briefcase.

FOLLOWUPS

"Followups," which are also called "second-day" and "developing" stories, report subsequent developments in stories that were reported earlier. Major stories rarely begin and end in a single day, and news organizations prepare a fresh article or package each time a new development arises. So stories about a trial, a legislative session, political campaign or flight to the moon may appear in the media every day for weeks. Reporters for The Daily Oklahoman said several months after a bomb destroyed the federal building in Oklahoma City that their paper still was running daily followup stories. They expected the story to remain in the news for years because of trials and appeals.

Although the followup story is tied to a past event, its lead always emphasizes the latest developments. Followups may summarize previous developments, but that information is presented as concisely as possible and placed later in the story.

Followup stories about disasters are especially common. On Monday, news organizations may report that an explosion trapped 47 miners in a West Virginia coal field. They will report later developments on Tuesday, perhaps that rescuers have found 21 bodies. On Wednesday, the news media may report that seven miners have been found alive. Followup stories published on Friday may describe the funerals held for the known dead. Rescue workers may find all the remaining bodies on Saturday, and work in the mine may resume the following Tuesday. Weeks later, another followup story may report that state and federal investigators have determined the cause of the explosion. Months later, the final followup may report that lawsuits filed against the mine's owners have been dropped in return for payments of $260,000 to each victim's family.

The following leads from The New York Times trace new developments over five months after President Bill Clinton nominated Dr. Henry W. Foster Jr. to be the U.S. surgeon general:

WASHINGTON, Feb. 7—President Clinton's nominee for Surgeon General was dealt another blow today as anti-abortion forces stepped up their assault on his record, saying he had participated in a study designed to help women induce their own abortions.

WASHINGTON, Feb. 15—With a majority of the Senate still undecided on the fate of his nomination to be Surgeon General, Dr. Henry W. Foster Jr. went to Capitol Hill today to begin lobbying for support.

RUSSELL, Kan., April 15—The Senate majority leader, Bob Dole, said today that he would oppose President Clinton's choice for Surgeon General and might block the nomination from coming to a vote.

WASHINGTON, May 26—Benefiting from the swing vote of a freshman Republican, President Clinton's beleaguered choice for Surgeon General, Dr. Henry W. Foster Jr., cleared his first political hurdle today when the Senate Labor and Human Resources Committee sent his nomination to the full Senate.

WASHINGTON, June 22—The nomination of Dr. Henry W. Foster Jr. to be Surgeon General died in the Senate today when Democrats failed for a second and final time to end a Republican filibuster.

Because each new development in a newsworthy situation prompts a followup story and each followup story recapitulates earlier stories, some viewers and readers grow weary of the repetition and believe the news media do it only to sensationalize stories. People who were unhappy with the amount of coverage given to the murder trial of O.J. Simpson often expressed such views. And yet news organizations cover such events intensely because large numbers of readers and viewers are interested. Americans were so enthralled with the Simpson trial that the audiences for the nightly network news broadcasts were down as much as 10 percent because people were watching live coverage of the trial on cable channels CNN and Court TV.

Sometimes a followup story does not report new events but adds information unavailable earlier. The Federal Bureau of Investigation's arrest of a notorious computer thief who had stolen thousands of data files, including more than 20,000 credit card numbers, received front-page coverage in The New York Times. The next day, The Times followed up the initial story with another that described how the computer thief's work exposed the vulnerabilities of the Internet.

Followup stories are becoming more common as news organizations devote more resources to making sure important stories are followed to their conclusions. Some organizations have established regular columns or segments for followups. In the past, critics complained that journalists, like firefighters, raced from one major story to the next, devoting most of their attention to momentary crises. Critics added that when one crisis began to subside, reporters moved on to the next, so older stories disappeared from the news before they had been fully resolved. To address this problem, news organizations now regularly return to important topics and tell readers what has happened since the topics dropped out of the headlines. Followups may relate that an area devastated by a hurricane has been rebuilt or that victims of an accident are still suffering from its consequences.

Harcourt Brace & Company

ROUNDUPS

To save space or time, news organizations run roundup stories that summarize several different but related events. Traffic roundups are most common; instead of publishing separate stories about each traffic death that occurs in a single weekend, newspapers and broadcast stations summarize a dozen or more fatal accidents in a single story. Or news organizations may report all the weekend crimes, fires, drownings, graduation ceremonies or football games in roundup stories.

Another type of roundup story deals with a single event but incorporates facts from several sources. Reporters may interview half a dozen people to obtain more information about a single topic, to verify the accuracy of facts they have obtained elsewhere or to obtain new perspectives. For example, if your mayor resigned unexpectedly, you might interview her and ask why she resigned, what she plans to do after leaving office, what she considers her major accomplishments and what problems will confront her successor. You might then (1) ask other city officials to comment on the mayor's performance and resignation, (2) ask the city clerk how the next mayor will be selected and (3) interview leading contenders for the job. All this information would be included in a single roundup story.

The lead in a roundup story emphasizes the most important or unique developments and ties all the facts together by stressing their common denominator, as in the following examples of roundup leads:

> Eleven people, including three teen-agers who were driving to the state fair, were killed in traffic accidents reported in the region last weekend.

> Gunmen who robbed four service stations during the weekend escaped with a total of $3,600. All four stations are located along Highway 141 on the west side of the city.

After the lead, roundup stories usually organize facts and quotations by topic, starting with the most newsworthy accident, crime, fire or drowning and moving on to the second, third and fourth most important. Some beginning reporters make the mistake of organizing their material by source. For example, they might write a crime roundup by reporting first all the information they got from the police chief and then all the information they got from the county prosecutor. Stories organized by source are disjointed and repetitious. Each source is likely to mention the same topics, and if the story is organized by sources, the comments about a particular topic will be scattered throughout the story.

SIDEBARS

Sidebars are related to major news stories but are separate from them. Sometimes, news organizations use them to break long, complicated stories into shorter, more easily understood ones. Other times, sidebars report information of secondary importance. Sidebars may give readers additional information about the main topic, usually from a different source or perspective. They may provide background information, explain a topic's importance or describe the scene, emphasizing its color and mood. If fire destroys a nightclub, news organizations may publish or broadcast a sidebar in which survivors describe how they escaped. If a prominent person receives an award (or is arrested or injured), the main story will describe that award, arrest or injury, and a sidebar may describe the person's character or accomplishments. Similarly, when a new pope is selected, sidebars may describe his personality, past assignments, philosophy and previous trips to the United States. Other sidebars may describe his new home in the Vatican and problems confronting Catholic churches throughout the world.

Sidebars are usually briefer than the main news stories and are placed next to them in a newspaper or just after them in a newscast. If, for some reason, the sidebars must be placed on a different page of a newspaper or later in a newscast, editors or producers will tell the audience where or when the related stories will appear. Because some people read or view only the sidebars, most briefly summarize the main stories even when the two stories are close together.

CHECKLISTS FOR WRITING SPECIALIZED STORIES

Brights

1. Choose either an inverted-pyramid style or a suspended-interest style for the story.
2. If you use a suspended-interest approach, write a lead that will intrigue readers without revealing the bizarre or amusing twist the story takes at the end.

Followups

1. Write a followup each time there is a newsworthy development in a continuing story.
2. Stress the new developments in the lead and body of the story.
3. Summarize the important background and earlier developments.

Roundups

1. Emphasize the most important or unique incident or development in the lead.
2. Explain in the lead what is common to all the incidents reported in the roundup.
3. Organize subsequent facts by topic, not by source.

Sidebars

1. Focus the lead on background, color, mood or some other aspect of the story different from that emphasized in the lead to the main story.
2. Summarize the news event described in the main story.

EXERCISE 1

SPECIALIZED TYPES OF STORIES

BRIGHTS

INSTRUCTIONS: Use the following information to write "brights," a series of short, humorous stories. Write some brights that have a summary lead and others that have a surprise ending.

1. SQUIRRELS

University officials are blaming squirrels for a rash of problems students, teachers and staff members have been experiencing with their cars. One person whose car has been damaged by squirrels is Oliver Brooks, an associate professor of English, 5402 Andover Dr. One of the headlights in his van went out a few weeks ago. He replaced it, but it still didn't work. When he opened the hood, however, he was surprised to find a squirrels nest. "There was a big squirrels nest in the corner where the light wires were," he said. Brookes spent $184 to get the wiring replaced. Linda Kasparov, university dietitian, 9301 Lake St., had a similar experience. She was driving home one night when the headlights, speedometer and oil-pressure gauge on her new sedan all quit working. She pulled into a service station and asked the attendant what was wrong. She said, "The attendant put up the hood and then jumped back exclaiming, 'My God, what have you got in there!'" She said there was a nest made of sticks, string and plastic bags. One of the bags started moving, and when the attendant pulled it out, he discovered three baby squirrels. The squirrels had chewed through every wire in the engine compartment except two. The repair bill for Kasparov was $425. Laura Ruffenboch, a wildlife professor at the university, said the insulation on many electrical wires is made from a soybean derivative, and the squirrels may find that attractive. She also said it was unusual for squirrels to make nests in cars that are used regularly.

2. MISDIRECTED LOVE

Joseph R. DeLoy told the judge today that he's in love. DeLoy, 26, said he loves a 29-year-old woman, Patty McFerren. DeLoy met McFerren while they were both shopping at a su-permarket in the city. DeLoy asked McFerren for a date. McFerren refused. "But she was wonderful, and I could tell she really liked me, so I called her," DeLoy said. In fact, DeLoy tried to call McFerren more than 200 times, sometimes in the middle of the night. However, it wasn't really her number that he called. By mistake, he got the wrong number and called Patrick McFerren instead. The two McFerrens are unrelated and do not know each other. Their listings in the phone book are very similar. Patty is listed as "P. McFerren." Patrick is listed as "P.J. McFerren." Patrick informed DeLoy that he was dialing the wrong number. DeLoy said he didn't believe him and continued to call. "I was hoping that she'd answer," DeLoy said in court today. Patrick installed an answering machine so he could screen the calls, and the machine got a heavy workout. Finally, Patrick called the police, and they told DeLoy to stop making the calls, but no charges were filed against him. The calls continued, so Patrick sued, accusing DeLoy of intentional infliction of emotional distress and invasion of privacy. The calls were a costly mistake for DeLoy. In court today, DeLoys attorney explained that his client was acting "on his heart and hormones, not his head." A jury of 5 men and 7 women decided that his calls were worth $25 each—for a total of $5,000. The jury ordered DeLoy to pay that sum—$5,000—to Patrick. "I'm satisfied," Patrick said.

3. UNDERAGE DRIVER

Charles Todd Snyder was charged with drunk driving following a traffic accident in your city one week ago. He was also charged with driving without a drivers license in his possession. He was scheduled to appear in court at 9 a.m. this morning. He failed to appear in court. As a consequence, Judge Edward Kocembra ordered police to go to Snyders home and to haul Snyder into court. Police went to the address Snyder had given officers at the time of the accident: 711 Broadway Avenue. The police returned to the court at approximately 10:15 a.m. and appeared before Judge Kosembra with Snyder. Snyder was in his mothers arms. He is a 13-month-old child, and his mother insisted that he drinks only milk and that the only vehicle he ever drives is a stroller. So the judge apologized for the inconvenience and told the officers to give Snyder and his mother a ride back to their home. Snyder, apparently frightened by the unfamiliar surroundings and people, cried. Police said that whoever was stopped had falsely given the arresting officers Snyders name and address when he signed the drunken driving ticket and the ticket for driving without a drivers license in his possession. They told the judge that they have no idea who that person might be.

4. TRUCK THEFT

There was a motor vehicle theft which occurred in the city at some time in the middle of last night. The vehicle was taken from a building located at 7720 Avonwood Dr. The building was unlocked at the time, and 12 occupants sleeping in an upstairs room said they heard nothing unusual. They were all in bed by midnight and the first got up at 6 a.m., discovering the theft at that time. Police describe the missing vehicle as a bright canary-yellow fire truck, marked with the name of the city fire department. The custom-made truck cost a total of $192,000 and was delivered to the city just three months ago. Firemen said it had a full tank of gas, about 50 gallons. However, it gets only 1½ miles to the gallon. It contained enough clothing and equipment for six firefighters, a dozen oxygen tanks, 1,000 feet of hose, four ladders (each up to 60 feet tall), plus miscellaneous other equipment. The people sleeping upstairs were all firefighters and the building was a fire station. The firefighters suspect that someone opened the stations main door, then either pushed or towed the truck silently outside and started its engine some distance away from the building. It is the first time in its history that the city fire department has reported that one of its trucks has been stolen. It was not insured. The keys are always left in the truck to reduce the response time when firefighters receive a call for help.

5. INHERITANCE

The will of a local man, Benjamin Satterwaite, 74, of 307 E. King Boulevard was filed in Probate Court today. Satterwaite died on the twentieth of last month of cancer. He had lived alone in his home, neighbors said, for at least the past 20 years. He was a retired postal clerk. According to the will, Satterwaite left a total estate of $1,471,400.38. Much of the money was earned in the stock market. Neighbors said they were surprised by the amount. Satterwaite was not a miser but lived frugally, and neighbors said they did not suspect that the deceased was a millionaire. Satterwaite left the entire estate to the U.S. government, explaining that, "Everybody seems to be living off the government, so maybe someone ought to help it out." He had no known relatives.

6. BANK REGULATIONS

Abraham Burmeister is president of the First National Bank, the largest bank in your community. Each year, in accordance with new federal laws, the bank is required to send all its customers copies of some complex new federal rules concerning the regulation of

Harcourt Brace & Company

banks and the procedures followed for money transfers by means of electronic banking. Consequently, the First National Bank prepared a 4,500-word pamphlet describing and summarizing those new federal rules and then sent copies of the rules to all its 40,000 regular depositors and customers. Like many other bankers, Burmeister objected to the federal law, saying it imposed a needless burden and needless expense on bankers since the federal laws that banks are being forced to explain are too complicated for the average person to understand and too dull and uninteresting for people to spend time trying to read. To prove his point, on the last page of 100 of the 40,000 copies of the rules he took a gamble and inserted a special extra sentence. The sentence said, "If you return this pamphlet to any of the banks tellers within the next 30 days, they will give you $50." The 30 days passed yesterday and not one person turned in a single copy of the 100 special pamphlets and requested the $50 due on demand, apparently because no one read the pamphlets. Bank officials calculated that it cost somewhere in the neighborhood of $25,000 to prepare, print, address and mail the pamphlets to the 40,000 bank customers, and they said that is a waste of money, yet they must do it every year, even though obviously no one reads the things, as they have just proven with their interesting little experiment.

7. DRUNKEN RIDER

Lynita L. Sharp admits she was intoxicated last night but says she should not be charged with drunk driving. Sharp, 5836 Bolling Dr., was riding her 2-year-old filly horse along a state highway when Scott Forsyth, a corporal in the sheriffs department, came along. Forsyth said he saw Sharp sitting on her horse in the middle of the road. He said the rider looked to be sick or asleep. He turned on the blue lights on his cruiser, and the horse bolted off. Sharp said she was spending the weekend with her friends who own the farm where her horse is stabled. She had spent part of the evening at the local tavern and was riding home. Sharp said the cruisers light spooked the horse and caused her to lose control of it. Forsythe issued Sharp a ticket for operating a vehicle while under the influence of an intoxicating substance. Sharp said her horse, Frosty, is not a vehicle. "Vehicles can't think, but Frosty can think for herself," Sharp said. "I've fallen asleep in the saddle before, but it doesn't matter because Frosty knows the way home." Donald Hendricks, the assistant county attorney, said the state law does not require that a person be operating a motorized vehicle in order to be cited for drunk driving. The law was changed in 1991, he said, and since then 23 people who were not operating motorized vehicles, including a bicyclist and a man in a wheelchair, have been arrested for driving while intoxicated.

EXERCISE 2

SPECIALIZED TYPES OF STORIES

FOLLOWUP STORIES

INSTRUCTIONS: Write a story summarizing the initial set of facts and then just the lead for a followup story about the later developments. Or your instructor may ask you to write a complete news story about each day's developments.

YESTERDAY

Two boys were playing in Nichols Lake in Lakeside Park in your town. They were wading along the shore of the lake at about 12 noon at a point where the bottom drops off steeply. The two boys were Randy Stockdale, age 9, son of George and Lillian Stockdale, 472 Bolling Dr., and Edward McGorwan, age 10, son of Karen McGorwann, 4320 Elsie Drive, Apt. Six. Edward waded too far from shore, lost his footing and was unable to get back to shore. He and Randy started to yell for help. A man whose name has not been released by police heard their screams and ran to the lake to help. James Kirkman, a cab driver who was taking his lunch break in the park, heard the screams, too. He radioed his dispatcher who called 911. Kirkman said later that the unidentified man waded out as far as he could and tried to reach out to Edward, but the boy had drifted too far from shore. "When the boy went under and didn't come back up for air, this guy dove under to find him. But he didn't come back up, either," Kirkman said. Police Officers Kevin Barlow and Eddie Linn arrived on the scene at 12:18. Barlow immediately stripped to his shorts and started diving into the lake to find the victims. After several dives, he came back up with Edward McGorwan, who was unconscious. Linn tried to resuscitate the boy, but he was still unconscious when he was taken by ambulance to the Regional Medical Center. Barlow continued to search for the unidentified man for another 20 minutes until Dorothy Heslin, a scuba diver who assists the police on a volunteer basis, arrived. She pulled him from the water about 1:15 p.m. Wayne Svendson, a paramedic, tried to resuscitate the man. Svendson said the water was unusually cold and hypothermia had set it, which was indicated by the fact the mans skin had started to turn blue. The man was taken to the Regional Medical Center. Dr. Catrina Lowrie, a physician at the Medical Center, said the man was pronounced dead when he arrived. She also said that Edward McGorwan was in critical condition. Officer Barlow also was treated at Regional Medical Center for minor shock caused by the long period of time he spent in the water looking for the victims. He was released that afternoon.

TODAY

This morning, the police department released the name of the man who died trying to save Edward McGorwann from Nichols Lake. His name is William McDowell and he is an unemployed housepainter. He was 30 years old and he had lived at 1429 Highland Dr. Police Chief Barry Koperud said, "McDowell risked his life without hesitation to try to save someone in trouble. He was a real hero." Also this morning, Dr. Lowrie at the Regional Medical Center announced that Edward McGorwann had died. "He spent the night on a respirator, but his condition did not improve. This morning, at his mothers request, we took Edward off the respirator. He died less than half an hour later." McDowells sister lives in your town. Her name is Janice Carson and she lives at 2197 Marcel Av. She said her brother had dropped out of Colonial High School one year before graduating and joined the navy. He spent six years in the navy, and after he left he held a succession of jobs, including electronics technician, cook, construction worker and painter. She said he always enjoyed his jobs but was too restless to stay at one for more than a couple of years. "I guess some people would call him a drifter, but to me he was a free spirit. He loved people but he didn't want to be tied down with a house and a mortgage and all of that. There were only two things he never learned how to do. He couldn't hold a job for more than two years and he could never say no to anyone who needed help," she said with tears in her eyes.

E X E R C I S E 3

SPECIALIZED TYPES OF STORIES

FOLLOWUP STORIES

INSTRUCTIONS: Write a story summarizing the initial set of facts and then just the lead for a followup story about each of the later developments. Or your instructor may ask you to write a complete news story about each day's developments.

BACKGROUND

Years ago, tuberculosis ranked among the worlds most lethal diseases, and it remains a serious health problem in developing countries. The number of Americans with tuberculosis has declined dramatically over the last half century. Only approximately 23,000 new cases were reported in the U.S. last year, about 1,000 of them in your state. Basically, TB is a bacterial infection. It usually affects the respiratory system. It is spread through coughing, sneezing, singing or talking. Because of advances in the field of medicine, it is rare for a death to occur because of TB. Modern treatment succeeds virtually 100 percent of the time. Doctors can prescribe medications to stop the disease if the infection is detected early enough. However, TB can be fatal if undetected. Symptoms include a prolonged and unexplained cough, night sweats, and sudden weight loss. To test for TB, a small amount of dead bacteria is injected into the skin of the upper arm of a person. Health workers know there is an infection when natural anti-bodies, formed to fight the illness, respond to the dead bacteria, and harden the skin around the test area.

ORIGINAL STORY

Maureen Verdugo, principal of Kennedy High School, called a special assembly at the beginning of classes at the school today and made a startling announcement. Verdugo revealed to the students that a 16 year old student enrolled at the school, whose exact identity she in no way revealed, other than as a tenth grader, has been diagnosed as suffering from the disease tuberculosis. Verdugo continued on by announcing that city health officials were notified by the students doctor and will be available at the school all five days of classes next week to give free TB tests to every student enrolled in one of the 16 yr. olds classes, as well as to students known to be the victims friends. "Anyone else—students, faculty members, and school personnel—who fears they may have been infected will also be tested free of charge. The tests will be administered in the school clinic, and students will be excused from their study halls and other free periods to take the tests," Verdugo said. The clinic will be open from 7 am to 5 pm and people can also visit it before or after their classes. "I've been working in high schools for 30 years," Verdugo went on to say, "and this is the first time I've had a problem like this. But I want to reassure you that there's no reason for panic. We're taking all the necessary precautions and have the situation well under control."

WEDNESDAY OF THE NEXT WEEK

On Monday and Tuesday of this week the citys Public Health Dept. had its personnel at the school, busily testing for tuberculosis students that may have come in contact with the infected 16 yr. old student enrolled in Kennedy High School. Initial tests were given free of charge at the school clinic. About 250 of the schools students were singled out by school authorities as having regular contact with the infected teen, either by being enrolled in the kids classes or by having some other close contact with the guy. Other students and teachers went in on their own. The testing is continuing and the final results will be announced sometime during the course of next week.

Of approximately three hundred students tested Monday and Tuesday, six showed signs of infection and were advised to have more testing done on them. "Infected students are being advised to undergo chest X rays and possibly sputum tests to determine whether they have developed TB," said Cathleen Graham, head of the citys Public Health Dept. "Those who are merely infected with the bacteria will be prescribed an antibiotic to prevent the onset of the disease. If the disease has progressed further, students will have to undergo more extensive drug therapy."

Some parents were frightened and dissatisfied. Tanaka Holland, mother of Sophomore Andrea Holland, said during an interview today: "When I called the school with some questions they were totally uncaring, and their procedures stink. Every student in the whole school should be tested. Just because a child wasn't in a class with the carrier doesn't mean they didn't come in contact with the disease," Mrs. Holland said. A second parent, James R. Waundry, agreed, adding, "This isn't anything to mess with. I've heard that people can die of tuberculosis, and how do we know that, uh, it's not going to come back? We've told our son, Paul, to stay home this week, and we're thinking of putting him in a private school."

FRIDAY OF THE FOLLOWING WEEK

In all, 581 Kennedy High School students were tested after learning that a 10th grade schoolmate had TB, Kennedy High School Principal Maureen Verdugo announced today. A total of 23 of the 581 students have tested positive for exposure to tuberculosis but none of the 23 have developed the disease. "The students are not contagious but must take antibiotics for six months to prevent the disease," said Joseph Perez, a health official employed by the city.

Greg Hubbard is the citys superintendent of schools. Hubbard said during a press conference today that he believes that this TB outbreak was the worst in the citys entire history. Hubbard said there is nothing the district can do to prevent occasional health problems like this one. "You're always subject to this kind of thing with the number of kids we have," he said. Health officials added that no one will ever know exactly how the outbreak started.

E X E R C I S E   4

SPECIALIZED TYPES OF STORIES

FOLLOWUP STORIES

INSTRUCTIONS: Write a story summarizing the initial set of facts and then just the lead for a followup story about each of the later developments. Or your instructor may ask you to write a complete news story about each day's developments.

DAY 1

Twelve people have been selected to hear the murder trial of Sara Kindstrom, 27, of 4828 North Vine Street. She is charged with the first-degree murder of her live-in boyfriend, Frederick C. Taylor, 25. If convicted of the charge, she could be sentenced to life in prison and would have to serve at least 25 years before becoming eligible for parole. Taylors death occurred last summer, on August 4 at about 7 p.m. Taylor was killed by shots from a .22 caliber pistol. This morning, assistant county attorney Donald Hedricks and Kindstroms attorney, assistant public defender Marilyn Cheeseboro, spent several hours questioning 42 potential jurors before selecting an 8-man, 4-woman panel to hear the case. The trial will begin at 9:00 a.m. tomorrow before Circuit Court Judge Randall Pfaff.

DAY 2

A neighbor, Martha Rudnick, testified: "My husband and I heard her screaming, but that wasn't unusual. They were always fighting over there. The police had been there a dozen times, but it never seemed to do any good. This time I heard the gun. Right away, I knew they were shots, but I thought he was shooting her. He was always threatening to kill her. I ran next door to see if I could help Sara. But when I got outside, Freddy was crawling out their front door, and she was coming after him with the gun, still shooting him. She was shooting him in the back, and he was just lying there, bleeding on the sidewalk. She kept pulling the trigger, but the gun must have been out of bullets and was clicking every time she pulled the trigger. I could see her face was all red and swollen and bleeding where he'd hit her, and it wasn't the first time I'd seen her like that."

DAY 3

Police Sergeant Michael Barsch said: "I interrogated her as soon as we got her to the police station. She told me she'd shot him and that she hoped she'd killed him. It was his gun, but we checked and found that she'd used it before. He'd taught her how to shoot it. He'd taken her target shooting and hunting with him. We also found a box of shells in her purse, with 9 shells missing, and found that she'd bought the box herself at a sporting goods store near her home about a week earlier."

DAY 4

Jurors seemed to be spellbound as they listened to the fascinating testimony of Sara Kindstrom today. She told a tearful story of bloody beatings and verbal, physical and sexual abuse at the hands of her live-in boyfriend, whom she is accused of killing. During her 5½ hours of testimony today, Kindstrom said: "He was going to kill me. It wasn't a matter of whether he'd kill me, but when he was going to do it. I met him a year ago, and he moved right in with me, and at first it was really nice. Then he lost his job and got sicker and

Harcourt Brace & Company

sicker. We could sleep together for a month and not have sex. Then we'd fight and he'd force himself on me. I work as a waitress, and when I got home Aug. 4 he was waiting for me. He started calling me names and hitting me and accused me of running around with other men, and that's not true. I'd never do that, but he was always jealous. I tried to keep quiet and make supper, but he started drinking. Later, we started arguing again. He was telling me that if I left, he'd move someone nice in. I said it was my house, and he said I'd be dead and then it would be his house. He was hitting me really hard, and I was bleeding. Then we were in the bedroom, and I just couldn't take it anymore. He kept a pistol in a bedroom closet, and I had it in my hand. I don't remember getting it out, but I must have, and it started going off. I don't remember pulling the trigger. He looked surprised and then he just fell to the floor without saying anything. I knew I'd hurt him, but I didn't think he was dead. I didn't mean to kill him."

DAY 5

In his closing arguments, the prosecuting attorney said: "The defendant did not have to murder Fredrick Taylor. She could have called the police for protection. She could have charged Taylor with assault, and she could have forced him to leave her house. But she never sought help and consistently returned to the man who beat her. She may regret it now, but she killed him. If she only wanted to protect herself, she could have shot him once, possibly twice, and escaped. But she fired 9 bullets, and all nine hit him—mostly in the back. She continued firing those bullets even after Taylor was down on the ground, trying to crawl to safety. That's murder in the first degree."

In her closing arguments, the public defender said: "This woman acted in self-defense. She was repeatedly and brutally beaten by Fredrick Taylor during their 12-month relationship. We also know Sarah Kindstrom believed that Taylor eventually would have killed her. She killed him to protect herself from rape and murder. Imagine yourself in that situation. You're being beaten, badly beaten. Dazed, confused, in need of protecting yourself, you pick up a gun and begin to shoot. You're acting in self-defense, to protect your own life, and you may not be entirely rational at a moment like that."

DAY 7

After two days of deliberation, the jury announced that it found the defendant guilty of murder in the second degree rather than of murder in the first degree. The maximum penalty for a conviction of that type is from 5 to 18 years in prison.

DAY 10

The judge today sentenced the defendant, Sara Kindstrom, to a term in a state prison of the minimum sentence of 5 years. In sentencing Kindstrom to the minimum prison term the judge noted the extenuating circumstances in the case, including her brutal treatment at the hands of her victim and her apparent effort to defend herself. However, the judge complained that she used excessive force in that defense. She will be eligible for parole in as short a time as a period of 18 months, with time off for good behavior.

EXERCISE 5

SPECIALIZED TYPES OF STORIES

ROUNDUPS—MULTIPLE SOURCES

INSTRUCTIONS: Write a single news story that summarizes the following information. Organize the information in a clear, logical, cohesive manner. As you write the story, correct the spelling, style, grammatical and vocabulary errors. Also be thorough; report every issue in depth. Notice that the sources' comments appear in quotation marks, so you can quote them directly.

BACKGROUND

The Sunnyview Retirement Home is an 8-story brick building located at 410 Hillcrest Street in your community. The building is a former hotel. Ten years ago it was renovated and turned into apartments for retirees. It is privately operated, for profit, with 110 apartments, including 30 for a single resident and 80 for two residents, often couples, sharing an apartment. About 175 people were living there when a fire broke out at approximately 7:10 a.m. this morning. As many as 150 firefighters from throughout your region, including nearby communities, were called in for assistance in battling the blaze and assisting in rescuing all the victims from their peril.

FIRE CHIEF TONY SULLIVAN

"Its the worst damn fire I've ever seen. We've got seven dead we know of and maybe 20 more that've been taken to hospitals with various injuries, some pretty serious. We just can't tell for sure. There could be lots more in the building, people who couldn't get out. I can't send my men in yet to look for them, not at this point, because its not safe. We've got the fire out, but it was a fierce one, and some floors and walls were weakened and are liable to collapse at any time. We may have to pull them down or they could fall on my men. It may be another day before we're able to make a thorough search and recover all the bodies."

RESCUE WORKER JOHN CHARLTON

"People I've talked to say the fire started on the first or second floor. The fire itself wasn't so bad, except on the first couple of floors. Everything on those floors is gone. The fire didn't spread to the upper floors, but most of the deaths occurred up there. It was the smoke that did it. People said they couldn't breath, and then a lot of them were old and in bad shape to begin with. We've taken the survivors that weren't hurt none to a church just across the street, and they're mostly resting there now. I don't know where they'll go tonight, where they'll sleep. The Red Cross is setting up an information center for relatives at the church. We've, uh, got all sorts of relatives that've been in and out all morning, looking for their people and apparently bringing them home with them, so we don't know who's missing or dead or home safe with their families."

RETIREMENT HOME DIRECTOR MILDRED ANCHALL

"We don't know how the fire started, just that it started somewhere on the second floor, and our alarms sounded at 7. It happened so fast, it spread so fast, that all we could do was try and get everyone out. No one had time to stop and get a list of all our residents, and

Harcourt Brace & Company

now they've been taken a half-dozen different places. We don't have any way of knowing who's safe and who's missing. Besides our residents, I've got my staff to worry about, and some visitors who were in the building. It's a tragedy, a real tragedy, something like this. You hear about things like this happening but never think it could happen at your home."

BUILDING INSPECTOR RALPH SCHWEITZER

"We inspected the building just a couple weeks ago, and it satisfies all our codes. When it was remodeled 10 years ago we didn't require sprinklers, and they would have saved everyone, would have put the fire out in a minute or two, so they would have really prevented a tragedy like this. Anyone building a nursing home today is required to put in sprinklers, and this is what we have in mind to prevent, a real serious tragedy like this one."

SURVIVOR STEVEN MINH

"I'm 82, and I've been living here since it opened 10 years ago. Nothing like this ever happened here before. Its like I was back in World War II or something. I lived on the eighth floor, and people up there were screaming for help. The smoke was real bad, and some of us don't move so quick anymore. The firemen got up there real fast and led us down the stairs. There were some real heroes up there. I saw firemen carrying a half-dozen people down 6 or 8 flights of stairs when they could hardly breath themselves, and a lot of us would be dead without them. We couldn't have lasted much longer with the smoke and all. I'd just like to know what started the fire because it spread so fast. One minute everything was OK, then we were all choking on the smoke."

SURVIVOR BETSY AARON

"It was terrible in there. We began hearing fire alarms, but they weren't loud enough. By the time we realized what it was and went out into the hall it was full of smoke. I had a third-floor apartment, so I was able to get right out. I just took an elevator downstairs. Other people said they weren't working, but that must have been later, after I was out, that the elevators stopped working. When I got out on the street and looked up I saw people I knew leaning out their windows and shouting 'Help me! Help me!' I couldn't do anything for them, not anything at all."

FIRE MARSHAL R.J. HILTON

"We haven't pinpointed the cause of the fire yet. It's too early, but my personal feelings are, strictly on a preliminary basis, it seems to have been an accidental fire that started in one of the apartments. It'll be at least a day or two before we have anything official on that."

EXERCISE 6

SPECIALIZED TYPES OF STORIES

ROUNDUPS—MULTIPLE EVENTS

INSTRUCTIONS: Write a single roundup story that summarizes all three of the fires described below.

FIRE 1

Two police officers patrolling Main St. reported a fire at Frishe's Bowling Alley, 4113 Main St., at 3:32 a.m. today. They smelled smoke, got out of their squad car and traced the smoke to the bowling alley. Firefighters said the fire was confined to an office, where it caused an estimated $10,000 damage. Firefighters found evidence of arson and notified police that the office apparently had been set on fire after it was burglarized. Two cigarette machines, a soft-drink machine and a door leading to the office had been pried open. Police said the thieves probably set the fire to hide the robbery. Art Mahew, manager of the bowling alley, estimated that $20 was missing from the three machines and $50 was taken from a cash box in the office. He added: "That's all the money we keep in the building at night. Except for some change for the next day's business, we just don't keep any money in the building at night. It's too risky. This is the third robbery we've had since I started working here four years ago."

FIRE 2

Firefighters were called to 1314 Griese Drive at 8:23 a.m. today. They found a fire in progress on the second floor of the two-story home. The home is owned by Mr. and Mrs. Timothy Keele. Mr. and Mrs. Keel and their four children escaped from the home before firemen arrived. Firefighters extinguished the blaze within 20 minutes. The fire was confined to two upstairs bedrooms and the attic. Smoke and water damage were reported throughout the house. No one was injured. Damage was estimated at $20,000. Mrs. Keel told firemen she had punished one of her children for playing with matches in an upstairs closet earlier in the morning. Fire marshals said the blaze started in that closet and attributed the fire to the child playing with matches. Mrs. Keel added that she was not aware of the fire until a telephone repairman working across the street noticed smoke, came over and rang her doorbell. When she answered, he asked, "Do you know your house is on fire?"

FIRE 3

Firefighters responded to a call at the Quality Trailer Court at 10:31 a.m. today after neighbors were alerted by screams from a trailer occupied by Mrs. Susan Kopp, age 71. Flames had spread throughout the trailer by the time firefighters arrived at the scene. The firefighters had to extinguish the blaze, then wait for the embers to cool before they were able to enter the trailer. They found Mrs. Kopp's body in her bedroom in the trailer. A spokesman for the Fire Department said she had apparently been smoking in bed, then awoke when her bedding caught fire. She died of suffocation before she could get out. Neighbors who heard her screams were unable to enter the trailer because of the flames, smoke and heat.

Harcourt Brace & Company

E X E R C I S E   7

SPECIALIZED TYPES OF STORIES

ROUNDUPS—MULTIPLE EVENTS

INSTRUCTIONS: Write a single story that summarizes all three of the following committee actions in your state's legislature.

ANTI-CRIME LEGISLATION

The Judiciary Committee of the state Senate held hearings today on S.B. 167, which is aimed at reducing crime. The bill would impose mandatory minimum sentences for persons convicted of felonies where that person had already served at least one year in the state prison; increase penalties for possession or distribution of drugs in "drug free zones," which are areas around schools and other places where juveniles congregate; reduce a prisoners "good time" credit from six months to three months per year but add an additional three months credit per year for inmates who participate in treatment or educational programs; and create "boot camps" for nonviolent offenders who have no prior convictions. The sponsor of the bill is Sen. Neil Iacobi, a democrat from your town. Iacobi said, "This bill will guarantee citizens that repeat violent offenders will spend at least 25 years in prison." He also said the bill creates "positive time" as an alternative to "good time." "Under my plan, inmates will earn additional time off their sentences only if they participate in substance abuse programs or job-training programs that will help re-integrate them into society once they are released," Iacobi said. Guillermo Vasquez, the director of the state Department of Corrections, said, "Boot camps are a viable intermediate sanction for nonviolent offenders. They will free up space in the prisons for the violent offenders. My only recommendation would be to allow judges to sentence second-time nonviolent offenders to boot camps and not just first-time offenders." Circuit Court Judge JoAnn Kaeppler, from your town, said she thought the mandatory minimum sentence provision was unwise. "Most judges are doing a good job of matching the severity of the sentence to the crime. If you take away the discretion judges now have, you will be filling the states prisons with people who could be better dealt with in other ways." The Committee took no action on the bill yesterday.

DRUNKEN DRIVING

A bill that would increase penalties for persons arrested for drunken driving and that would lower the legal level of a drivers blood-alcohol content was the subject of testimony before the House Transportation Committee today. A fourth conviction for drunken driving would be increased from a misdemeanor to a Class D felony, punishable by up to five years in prison and a fine of up to $10,000. Subsequent convictions, now treated as Class D felonies, would be treated as Class C felonies, which carry maximum penalties of 20 years in prison and fines of $25,000. The bill, H.B. 355, would also change the legal standard for intoxication from a blood alcohol content of .10 percent to .08 percent. The bill is sponsored by Rep. Mary Hayes, a Republican from Ellerton. Rep. Hayes said, "I'm not trying to stop anyone from drinking who wants to. I just want to stop those people from driving." Marlene Stoudnaur, M.D., your citys medical examiner, testified that the lower standard for intoxication was justified. "Impairment of a drivers ability begins before that person reaches the .08 level. Even a blood alcohol content of .08 represents a serious hazard. To reach that level a 170-pound man would have to have four drinks in one hour. That's not social drinking." Beverly Cheng, executive director of the State Restaurant Association, testified against the bill. "Lowering the blood alcohol content level will not stop heavy drinkers. The heavy drinker doesn't care what the B.A.C. level is and changing it will not deter that person. You should be focusing on treatment for those who are caught rather than punishment," Cheng said. The committee took no action on the bill.

MINIMUM WAGE

The state Senate Business and Labor Committee heard testimony on S.B. 223, a proposal to raise the states minimum wage from $6.25 an hour to $7.25 an hour over a two-year period. The bill is sponsored by Sen. Micus Circenis, a Democrat from Willow Creek. Circenis said raising the minimum wage would assist the state in attracting business because it would help get people off welfare and lower the states tax burden for welfare programs. "The fact is the minimum wage is probably the best vehicle for economic development as well as the best tool for fighting poverty." Raymond Herrin, a professor in the School of Social Work at your university, testified that poverty is spreading most rapidly among families with children. Raising the minimum wage would help, Herrin said, but it will not solve the problem. "A recent study of welfare reform in this state concluded that it takes a $9 an hour job to support a mother and child. So raising the minimum wage to $7.25 will not even approximate a living wage." Amy Woods, director of the State Federation of Independent Businesses, said, "S.B. 223 will inhibit the creation of new jobs, especially by small businesses, which tend to be labor intensive. In a lot of these businesses, labor is the major cost. The only way they can deal with a higher minimum wage is to reduce employment." After the hearing, Sen. Margaret Van Den Shuck, a Democrat from your town, moved that S.B. 223 be advanced to the full Senate. The motion was defeated on a 3-4 vote, which kills the bill for this legislative session.

Harcourt Brace & Company

EXERCISE 8

SPECIALIZED TYPES OF STORIES

SIDEBARS

INSTRUCTIONS: Use the following information to write two separate stories: first a news story reporting the fire, then a sidebar based on the interviews with Mrs. Noffsinger.

MAIN STORY

The Grande Hotel is located downtown at the corner of Wisconsin and Barber Avenues. It is a seven-story structure with a total of 114 rooms. It was constructed and opened for business in the year 1924. In recent years the hotel has been in an obvious state of decline, unable to compete with new facilities in the city and with the convenience of motels located along highways which now bypass the city. Many of the hotel rooms have been rented on long-term leases, often to elderly persons who like its downtown location, which is more convenient for them, since many facilities they use are in walking distance and buses are easily available for other trips they want to make. Three persons died in a fire at the hotel last night. The cause of the fire is undetermined. It started in a third-floor room. It spread and also destroyed the fourth, fifth, sixth and seventh floors before it was brought under control at 4:30 a.m. today. At about 11 p.m. a guest called the lobby to report the odor of smoke. A hotel employee used a passkey to enter the third-floor room where the fire originated and found it totally engulfed in flames. The room is believed to have been vacant at the time. The employee sounded a fire alarm in the hotel and called firefighters. It was the first five-alarm blaze in the city in more than 10 years. Every piece of fire equipment in the city was rushed to the scene, and off-duty firefighters were called in to assist. Fortunately, said Fire Chief Tony Sullivan, no other fires were reported in the city at the same time or he would have had to send a truck and men from the scene of the hotel blaze. Hotel records indicate that 62 persons were registered in the hotel at the time the blaze initiated; 49 had long-term leases and 13 were transients. All the transients were located on the second floor and escaped safely. The dead, all of whom had long-term leases, have been identified as Mildred Haserot, age 58; Willie Hattaway, age 67; and Pearl Petchsky, age 47. The bodies of all three victims were found on the fourth floor, where they lived. Fire Chief Tony Sullivan said this morning the hotel is a total loss and that some walls are in danger of collapse. He said: "The fire was already out of hand when our first units reached the scene. I was called from home, and by then the flames were breaking out through the third- and fourth-floor windows. We were really lucky there weren't more people killed, but the hotel people knocked on the door of every room that was occupied to get everybody out. Most guests used a back stairway, and we were lucky the elevators kept working for awhile even after my men got into the building, otherwise the loss would have been worse. I'm also told that the top two floors were empty, and that helped keep down the loss of lives."

The Red Cross is caring for survivors, finding them new rooms and providing clothes and emergency allocations of cash, a total of $250 per person. Five people were injured, including one fireman who suffered from smoke inhalation. The others suffered from burns, some serious, and also from smoke inhalation. Three are being treated at Mercy Hospital. Two have been released, including the fireman. Their names and conditions are unknown at this time.

SIDEBAR

Nora Noffsinger, 74, has been a resident of the Grande Hotel for the past nine years. She paid $880 a month rent for one room on the fifth floor. A retired bookkeeper, she said afterward: "It was dreadfully expensive, but it was a charming old building and I had lots of good friends living there. I was asleep last night when I heard someone pounding on my door. I don't know who it was, but he told me to get out fast, and I did. All I had on were my pajamas and a robe, but I could see the smoke, even up there on the fifth floor, and I was scared; I knew right away that it was bad. Everyone else was scared too, but we all knew what to do. We'd talked lots about what we'd do if there was ever a fire because you hear so often about fires in old hotels, and we wanted to be prepared. We all kept flashlights in our rooms and planned to go down the back stairway unless the fire was there, and it wasn't. The lights were still on, so we didn't even need our flashlights. Now the Red Cross put me in a motel room a few blocks away, and I guess I should be happy I'm safe, but I lost everything—my clothes, a little money I'd kept hidden in a secret place, all my photographs. My husband's dead, you know, and I lost all my pictures of him. I don't know what I'll do now; I don't have any children. I'm all by myself, except for my friends, and they all lived at the hotel with me."

Harcourt Brace & Company

EXERCISE 9

SPECIALIZED TYPES OF STORIES

SIDEBARS

INSTRUCTIONS: Use the following information to write two separate stories, first a news story reporting the Senate's action and then a sidebar based on the interview with the sheriff.

MAIN STORY

The state Senate today approved a bill overwhelmingly. The bill has already been approved by the house and now goes to the Governor, who has indicated that she will sign it. The bill was passed almost unanimously by angry lawmakers who want inmates housed in jails throughout the state to help pay the costs of their room and board. There were only 2 votes against the measure in the senate and none against it in the house. The bill will go into effect next January 1st. It will require persons housed in a jail within the state to reveal their incomes and, if they can afford it, to pay the entire cost of their room and board behind bars, or whatever share of the cost they can reasonably afford. The bill requires the State Department of Offender Rehabilitation to draw up guidelines on how prisoners will disclose their finances and how much they will be required to pay. The department will consider a number of relevant variables, such as whether a prisoner must support a family and devote all his or her income to that family. The idea for the bill arose a number of months ago when lawmakers touring a state prison were told that some inmates received Government benefits (mostly Social Security and veterans' benefits). The lawmakers were told that some of the prisoners opened bank accounts in the prisons and that the money they received piled up so they had thousands of dollars accumulated in the accounts when they were released. A subsequent survey requested by legislative leaders found 19,000 inmates in the state and that, of that total, 356 received government payments of some type. The same survey found that the inmates had a total of $8.1 million in inmate accounts at state prisons. Prison officials cautioned that the prisoners may have more money deposited in banks outside the prison system and that it would be difficult to locate those accounts. To enforce the new bill, lawmakers stipulated that prisoners who refuse to disclose their finances cannot be released early on parole. Officials have not yet determined how much each prisoner will be charged. Lawmakers also noted that some inmates may have other assets, such as farms, homes, automobiles, and stocks and bonds, and that those prisoners can also be expected to help defray their prison expenses.

SIDEBAR

Gus DiCesare is the county sheriff. He has held that position for 11 years. To retain the position, he must run for re-election every four years. As sheriff, DiCesare is in charge of the county jail, which has a capacity of 120 inmates, mostly men but also a few women. Criminals sentenced to terms of less than one year in prison usually are sentenced to the county facility rather than to a state prison. Despite its capacity of 120 persons, the county jail usually holds 140 to 150 persons—20 or 30 more than its rated capacity. When interviewed today about the legislatures approval of the bill in question, DiCesare said: "Hey, I think its a great idea. Some of these prisoners got more money than I'll ever have. When we pick them up, they're driving fancy cars, living in big homes and carrying a thick wad of money. Not most of them, but there're always a few in here, mostly drug dealers. We sentence them to jail as punishment, but it punishes honest taxpayers who pay to keep them in here—pay for this building, their food, clothes, jailers and all the rest. A couple of years ago, we calculated that it cost about $55 to keep one prisoner here one day. Hell, if they can afford it, prisoners should help pay for it all; that could be part of their punishment. I'll bet our costs are up to nearly $90 a day apiece now, and they're still rising. It'd help me too. I've got a damned hard problem trying to run this place on the budget the county gives me. With a little more money, I could improve the food, come up with more recreational facilities and maybe even try to rehabilitate a few prisoners—bring in some teachers and counselors and that type of thing. Now, all I really do is keep them locked behind bars all day, and that's not going to rehabilitate anyone."

Harcourt Brace & Company

CHAPTER 12

WRITING OBITUARIES

Death can make even triviality momentous.
(Edward Le Compte, "And Obituaries Are the Last Writes")

Although most journalists do not get a lot of outside recognition for it, their work on the obituary page—the description of someone's life and notice of death—produces one of the most popular sections of the newspaper. Obituaries are closely scrutinized by loved ones, generally inspected by local townspeople and perused by others who have moved away but still subscribe to their hometown newspaper.

It is hard for some people to believe that obituaries are as popular as the comics section or "Dear Abby"; however, readership studies have found that 40 to 50 percent of a newspaper's readers look at obituaries daily. And the percentage increases with age. For example, while about 45 percent of 18- to 24-year-old readers express "at least some interest" in obituaries, more than 60 percent of readers over 60 are "definitely interested" in them. By comparison, about 87 percent of readers look at a newspaper's front page; 66 percent at its local news; 47 percent at the weather; 44 percent at the comics, sports and food pages; 41 percent at the editorial page; and 37 percent at the business page.

Obituaries are popular because of their importance to the people involved. Few other stories are as likely to be clipped, pasted in scrapbooks or mailed to friends. Also, obituaries are well read because only newspapers report them. Radio and television stations may mention the deaths of celebrities, but only newspapers have the time, space and staff necessary to report, write and publish obituaries for everyone in their communities.

Obituaries are reports that people have died. For most journalists, writing an obituary is the art of saying something positive and accurate about the dead person. Typically, an obituary announces a person's death, briefly describes the person's life and family, then summarizes the funeral arrangements.

Unfortunately, most obituaries seem cold and impersonal. Few convey the feeling that the people they describe possessed unique personalities and sets of experiences. When obituaries are not written well, one reason is likely to be that few newspapers devote enough resources to obituaries. Often, a single reporter is assigned to write all of a newspaper's obituaries. That may mean hurriedly writing 10 or 15 obituaries before every deadline.

A second reason few obits seem warm or lively is that newspapers often assign obituaries to their newest and least experienced reporters. Some newspapers even hire people without any journalistic training to write obituaries, thus freeing experienced reporters for assignments believed to be more important. Or, editors assign beginning reporters the task of writing obituaries because the basic organization of the story stays the same from one obituary to another. The inexperienced writer can thus mechanically group similar attributes such as clubs or professional experiences together within the same paragraphs in an obituary, feeling assured that "the formula" has been followed.

A third reason obituaries seem detached or unfeeling is that journalists often do not take time to go into depth. They put facts together into a report without leaving their desks. They rarely call friends or family to capture the personality of the person who died—which is curiously contrary to the way journalists cover the people involved in other types of stories.

Many journalists consider the task of obituary writing unpleasant, so they lack enthusiasm and forgo effort. Like most other Americans, journalists are uncomfortable with death, and are reluctant to question the friends and relatives of people who just died. Too many journalists consider an obituary as a reflection of death only, not an opportunity to capture another's unique life and personality.

A final reason few obituaries are given the proper time and attention is reporters realize they are unlikely to receive many rewards for writing good obituaries. Today that may be changing. A few newspapers have begun to devote more attention to obituaries, and some reporters have begun to win prizes for their work—even to become nationally famous for it.

Newspapers try to publish an obituary for everyone who lived in their geographical region and for well-known community members who may have moved away from the area. Newspapers in smaller communities usually publish longer obituaries. Everyone in a small community knows almost everyone else, including the deceased. In large cities, a smaller percentage of readers will know each person who died. Thus, the amount of space devoted to obituaries varies depending on the type of newspaper. Other problems arise because all of a newspaper's obituaries have to fit into a limited space. The addition of headlines and perhaps photographs consumes more space, leaving even less room for each obituary. A few newspapers in very large cities no longer print everyone's obituary because they simply do not have enough space. Adopting the practice of radio and television stations, they report only the deaths of the most prominent members of their communities.

OBITUARIES ARE NOT NEWS STORIES

Some people confuse obituaries with news stories. If a newsworthy individual dies, or if someone's death is unusual, newspapers will publish a news story about events surrounding the person's death. That news story will include standard news elements, such as quotes from a variety of people. Usually a newspaper will also publish an obituary in the following day or two, once funeral arrangements have been determined. The main difference between the news story and the obituary is that the obituary emphasizes the person's life, not death.

OBITUARIES ARE NOT FUNERAL NOTICES

Obituaries should not be confused with paid funeral notices. Funeral directors write and place funeral notices, and the fee for publishing them is added to the cost of funerals. Newspapers publish funeral notices in alphabetical order usually near the obituaries or among a newspaper's classified advertisements. All are one paragraph long. Some indicate the person's name and funeral arrangements only, while others include relatives' names. A paid funeral notice ensures publication of someone's death. Thus, everyone with some type of memorial observation will usually have a funeral notice, and some will have both an obituary and funeral notice (and perhaps a news story, as well). The difference between a funeral notice and obituary is that the paid funeral notice written by the funeral home emphasizes funeral arrangements. The free obituary written by a reporter describes the person's life.

SOURCES OF INFORMATION FOR OBITUARIES

Funeral homes give newspapers all the information they need to write most obituaries. Funeral homes, eager to have their names appear in newspapers as often as possible, obtain the information when families come in to arrange services. Some funeral homes have the families fill out special forms provided by their local newspapers, and immediately deliver the completed forms to the papers. Just before their daily deadlines, reporters may call the funeral homes to be certain they have not missed any obituaries.

If the person who died was prominent, reporters may learn more about the person by going to their newspaper's library and reading previous stories published about him or her. Journalists may also call the person's family, friends and business associates to obtain additional information and a recent photograph. Most people cooperate with reporters; they seem to accept such requests as part of the routine that occurs at the time of death. Also, people want their friends' and relatives' obituaries to be accurate, thorough and well written.

THE CONTENT OF OBITUARIES

Lead

An obituary begins by identifying the person who died. The typical lead reveals the person's name and identification and at least one unique or outstanding fact about that person's life, usually the person's major accomplishment. The inclusion of some unique or outstanding fact is essential; it makes obituaries more interesting and keeps them from looking alike. For example:

> Dr. Anna J. Simmons of North Blossom Drive died of a heart attack at St. Agnes Hospital Monday. She was 85.
> REVISED: Anna J. Simmons, who delivered more than 10,000 babies during the 40 years she worked as an obstetrician at St. Agnes Hospital, died at the hospital Monday.

> Thomas R. Jackson, 79, of Jefferson Street, a retired executive, died Monday at his home after a lingering illness.
> REVISED: Thomas R. Jackson, who began work as a mailroom clerk for the nation's largest insurance company and 30 years later became the company's president, died Monday at the age of 79.

The original leads contained dull, routine facts: the people's ages, addresses and causes of death. Dull, routine facts make dull leads. The revisions contain more specific and interesting facts about their lives and accomplishments. Other good leads might describe a person's interests, goals, hobbies, philosophy or personality.

Body

After the lead, an obituary should summarize the individual's life. Information commonly presented, and its approximate order, in an obituary includes:

1. Identification (full name, age, address)
2. Unique or major attribute
3. Time and place of death
4. Cause or circumstance of death
5. Major accomplishments
6. Chronology of early life (place of birth, moves, education)
7. Place and date of marriage
8. Occupation and employment history
9. Honors, awards and offices held
10. Additional interests and accomplishments

11. Membership in churches, clubs and other civic groups
12. Military service
13. Surviving relatives (spouse, children, grandchildren, etc.)
14. Religious services (location, officiating clergy, pallbearers)
15. Other burial and funeral arrangements

After gathering the specific details needed for a good obituary, begin by summarizing the most important, interesting or unique aspect of the person's life. An obituary's second and third paragraphs should immediately develop the primary idea summarized in the lead. If, for example, your lead reports that the deceased was a plumber who played the violin, immediately begin to describe that person's work and hobby. Mistakenly, beginners quickly shift to chronological order and, in their second paragraph, report the obituary's earliest—and usually least interesting—details: the dates the person was born, graduated from high school, married or retired.

If time and space are available, reporters should include some anecdotes about the person's life, and recollections of friends and relatives, as well as other biographical highlights. Direct and indirect quotes help make obituaries more interesting, as in the following example:

> Madeline K. Royal, a pioneer in the field of journalism, is fondly remembered for her joyous spirit.
>
> "Maddy was always looking forward to traveling, family reunions, meeting friends and doing more free-lance writing," said Jeanette Howard, a longtime friend. "She gave others hope for the future."
>
> A faculty member in the journalism department at the University of Iowa, Miss Royal died of a heart attack Saturday in her home. She was 62.
>
> Miss Royal, who lived in Iowa City, Iowa, was born in Correctionville, Iowa, and began her journalism career at the age of 15 by writing stories for the Correctionville News. She received her bachelor's and master's degrees in journalism from the University of Iowa.
>
> A longtime resident of Des Moines, Miss Royal was publicity director for the National Arts Museum; public affairs officer for Drake University; and a gardening columnist for The Des Moines Register.
>
> Miss Royal was the first female sports editor of the University of Iowa yearbook and the first female member of the Football Writers Association of America.
>
> Surviving is one brother, Geoffrey of Houston.
>
> Visitation will be from 2 to 4 p.m. Tuesday in Skyline Funeral Home, 4538 Roanoke Blvd., Iowa City, Iowa.
>
> The funeral is scheduled for 11 a.m. Wednesday in the funeral home, with the Rev. Adaline Reeser officiating. Burial will immediately follow in Gentle Rest Cemetery, Iowa City.
>
> Memorials may be sent to the journalism department at the University of Iowa for a scholarship in Miss Royal's name.

Policies vary on how newspapers refer to the deceased. Some use only the last name ("Smith"), while others add a courtesy title ("Mrs. Smith" or "Mr. Smith") to sound more respectful of the deceased.

Most newspapers no longer print the specific street address of the deceased. One reason for the omission is to preserve the privacy of survivors. Another reason is that burglars assume the house will be empty during funeral services. Furthermore, swindlers often prey upon a person's survivors.

The list of survivors normally includes only an individual's immediate family. It begins with the name of the person's spouse and continues with the names of parents, brothers and sisters, and children. Some newspapers list the number but not the names of grandchildren and great-grandchildren, while others do list the names. Few newspapers list more distant relatives, such as nieces, nephews and cousins, unless they are the only survivors or are themselves people of note.

Harcourt Brace & Company

Recently, some newspapers have begun to list the names of other survivors—nonrelatives, such as live-in friends who played an important role in the person's life. Newspapers usually report the town where survivors live, but not their specific street addresses.

Normally, information about the religious services, burial and surviving relatives appears at the end of an obituary. The information should be as specific as possible so that mourners will know when they can call on the person's family, and when and where they can attend the funeral and burial.

The following obituary illustrates newspapers' typical format:

Margaret Treeford Holleanna, 69, a teacher at Hawthorne Elementary School for 37 years, died Wednesday at Mt. Hope Hospital.

Although she was offered several jobs as an elementary school principal, she never accepted them. She once explained: "I always loved the children in my classroom. Too often, being an administrator means pushing papers, not teaching children."

She was born in Holland, Mich., to John and Margaret Windsor Treeford. She was graduated cum laude with a bachelor's degree in education at Michigan State University. She obtained her master's in education at Ohio University. It was in Athens, Ohio, that she met and married her husband, Charles Holleanna.

Mrs. Holleanna was a member and a past president of the City Women's Club and a past president of the State Federation of Women's Clubs.

She was also a member of St. Andrew's Presbyterian Church, the Sunshine Society, Chaminade Club, Eastern Star and Daughters of the American Revolution.

Survivors include her husband, Charles, and a daughter, Marlene Sanders of Kalamazoo, Mich.

The funeral will be held at 1:30 p.m. Saturday at the Pine Garden Chapel, with the Rev. Robert Kurber of St. Andrew's Presbyterian Church officiating. Interment will follow in Greenwood Cemetery.

Friends may call from 2 to 4 and from 7 to 9 p.m. Friday at the Pine Garden Chapel, 430 N. Kirkman Road.

The family requests that memorial contributions be made to the American Cancer Society.

Some newspapers try to report the cause of every death. However, others do not, often because that information is difficult to obtain. Many people are reluctant to reveal the cause of their relatives' deaths, particularly if they died of diseases with social stigmas, such as AIDS or cirrhosis. For years, people were also reluctant to mention cancer, so obituaries used the euphemism that people "died after a long illness." A similar euphemism—"died after a lingering illness"—continues to appear in many papers.

Newspapers are most likely to report the cause of a celebrity's death. And, because it is unexpected, they are also more likely to report the cause of a young person's death.

Some newspapers consider suicide a private matter, never to be reported in any manner. Yet, other newspapers report suicides in separate news stories, while still other newspapers always note the cause of death, even when it is suicide, in obituaries. When newspapers do report suicides, they carefully attribute the determination of the cause of death to some authority, usually the coroner. Whatever the cause, obituaries rarely include details of death because the obituary reviews a person's life. If you work for a newspaper, you will be expected to follow the policies set by its executives; in other cases, use your own judgment.

ADDITIONAL GUIDELINES FOR WRITING OBITUARIES

Obituaries become more interesting when reporters go beyond the routine and do more than list the events in a person's life—that is, when they take the time to include additional details and to explain their significance. For example, instead of reporting that a woman served in the Army and graduated from college, an obituary might tell what the woman did in the Army, where she attended college and what she studied. Similarly, instead of simply reporting that a man retired 10 years earlier, the obituary might reveal what he has done since his retirement. The reporter might describe the person's character and physical appearance. If the person who died was young, his or her goals might be reported. An obituary might describe the person's hobbies.

Reporters avoid eulogies, euphemisms and sentimentality. They report that people have died, not that they have passed away, departed, expired or succumbed. Obituary writers must also avoid the flowery language used by funeral directors and by grieving friends and relatives—terms such as "the loved one."

Other problems encountered by obituary writers are unique. Many people are reluctant to reveal their relatives' ages, particularly if they had falsified or kept them a secret during their lifetimes. Also, obituary writers may prefer to report that someone died in a hospital, but not identify the hospital because the information may unfairly harm its reputation. Reporters would identify the hospital if there were any suspicions that it might be responsible for the death, but not if the person obviously died after a serious accident or illness.

Journalists need to be careful when strangers call with obituaries for other people. The callers are often able to provide all the necessary information. They may explain that they will not be using a funeral home because a friend's or relative's body will be cremated by a private burial society or donated to medical research. Often people call because the deceased was a member of the community, but moved to another town. People described in these obituaries occasionally call newspapers the next day, insisting that they are not dead. Because pranksters sometimes call newspapers and give them obituaries for living people, editors often require their reporters to call a second source and confirm the details in every obituary before it is published. Author Mark Twain experienced the problem while traveling in Europe. After learning that newspapers in the United States had reported he was dead, Twain sent a cable saying, "Reports of my death have been greatly exaggerated."

Even the information provided by funeral directors should be checked for errors. Survivors are likely to be upset and flustered about the death of their friend or relative. Thus, when they make funeral arrangements, they may be mistaken about some of the information they give to funeral directors. They may not know or remember some facts and may guess at others. Furthermore, funeral directors may make some mistakes while recording information and may misspell names, especially names of unfamiliar individuals and cities.

Obituary writers must be especially careful and accurate. Obituaries are usually the last stories written about a person. If a reporter makes an error, it is likely to infuriate the person's friends and relatives. The error may also be difficult to correct.

OBITUARIES FOR CELEBRITIES

Newspapers publish longer, more colorful obituaries for well-known people such as politicians, athletes and entertainers. The Associated Press and other news services prepare some celebrities' obituaries in advance and update them periodically. When that person dies, a reporter adds a lead, and the news service disseminates the obituary across the country.

Obituaries for national celebrities emphasize different types of information. Because few readers are likely to know a national celebrity personally and attend the funeral and burial, the obituary may not mention those services. Instead, it will emphasize the celebrity's personality and accomplishments.

Typical leads for obituaries of famous people include the following:

BEVERLY HILLS, Calif.—Dinah Shore, the honey-haired, down-to-earth entertainer who won hearts over half a century in radio, television, records and movies, died of cancer Thursday. She was 76.

Harcourt Brace & Company

Her smooth contralto voice earned her 10 Emmy Awards—more than any other per-former—nine gold records and the USO Medallion Award as the first entertainer to visit GIs in the front lines in World War II.

(The Associated Press)

NEW YORK—Tennis great Arthur Ashe, the first black to win the prestigious Wim-bledon tournament, died Saturday of pneumonia resulting from AIDS, a hospital spokeswoman said. He was 49.

During his tennis career he won 33 titles, earned more than $1.58 million and ranked No. 1 or 2 in the world off and on during the late 1960s and 1970s.

(Reuters)

To reveal a celebrity's character or philosophy, an obituary may reprint the person's most in-teresting or controversial statements. Obituaries for Jacqueline Bouvier Kennedy Onassis quoted a response about the tabloid stories written about her: "The river of sludge will go on and on," she said. "It isn't about me." An obituary for former president Richard Milhous Nixon reported he had described himself as "an introvert in an extrovert's business."

Other obituaries quote people who knew the celebrities. The following quotation appeared in an obituary for Louis Armstrong, jazz trumpet player, singer, composer and orchestra leader:

Armstrong's wife, Lucille, once said of him: "Life with Louis is a laugh a day. Why, that man even wakes up happy. I tell him sometimes, 'Louis, it's against the law of av-erages for you to be so happy all the time.' But he always finds something to laugh about just the same."

(The Associated Press)

Obituaries describe the hurdles that celebrities overcame. Actor Richard Burton was a coal miner's son, born in South Wales. Sammy Davis Jr. was born in Harlem, joined his father's vaudeville act when he was 3 and never attended school. Davis lost an eye in a car wreck, and worked in clubs and hotels that refused to serve him or to let him stay overnight because he was black. Actress Lucille Ball was the daughter of an electrician and left home at the age of 15 to study acting. A drama teacher in New York City told Ball that she had no talent and advised her to return home. Ball was so poor that to get by she stole the tips left on coffee-shop counters.

Even on the day a celebrity dies, reporters may recall anecdotes: tales that will make readers laugh (or simply reveal more about the person's life and character). Actress Bette Davis died of cancer at the age of 81 and had once said that she did not care about aging. Obituaries, however, reported that she had celebrated her 70th birthday "by hanging a black wreath on her door and needlepointing a pillow that read, 'Old age ain't no place for sissies.'"

Similarly, when Newsweek magazine published an obituary for Eddie Rickenbacker, a World War I ace who became head of Eastern Airlines, the magazine reported that Rickenbacker had been badly injured years earlier when a DC-3 crashed as it approached Atlanta:

In the hospital, he heard the radio voice of Walter Winchell announce that he was dying. "I began to fight," Rickenbacker recalled later. "They had me under an oxygen tent. I tore it apart and picked up a pitcher. I heaved it at the radio and scored a direct hit. The radio fell apart and Winchell's voice stopped. Then I got well."

Obituaries also explain how celebrities died. Sammy Davis Jr. died of throat cancer at the age of 64. Supreme Court Justice William O. Douglas entered a hospital on Christmas Eve, "suf-fering from pneumonia, and was treated for progressive respiratory and kidney failure."

REPORTING THE GOOD—AND THE BAD

Most journalists insist that obituaries should not simply praise individuals, but should report their lives: both the good and the bad. After Harry Reasoner's death, Andy Rooney (a colleague at CBS) reminisced:

In pure intellect, Harry was the smartest of all the TV correspondents—but he did more dumb things than any of them. He would not have died at the age of 68 if this were not true. He smoked three packs of cigarettes a day. He drank martinis, a lot of them. Four years ago, he had his cancerous left lung removed and continued to smoke heavily.

"I can stop drinking if I have to," he said to me one day two years ago, "but I can't stop smoking." That was the last time I ever said anything to him about smoking.

He died of almost everything. His other lung, his liver and his kidneys had deteriorated, and in early June he had brain surgery. . . .

Another example of reporting the bad happened years ago in Europe—with good results. Alfred Nobel was born in Stockholm in 1833 and became a chemist and engineer. Nobel invented dynamite and other explosives, became an armaments manufacturer and accumulated an immense fortune. In 1888, Nobel's brother died, and a newspaper in Paris published an obituary for Alfred by mistake. The newspaper's obituary called Alfred "a merchant of death." Nobel was so shocked by the obituary's description of him that, when he died in 1896, he left the bulk of his estate in trust to establish the Nobel Prizes for peace, literature, physics, chemistry and physiology or medicine. Thus, Nobel used his wealth to honor people who have done the most to advance humanity "rather than simply kill them off, as his products had done."

Newspapers that publish negative information in obituaries do not have to fear lawsuits. A person who has died cannot sue the newspapers for libel; nor, in most cases, can the person's relatives. Thus, the decision to publish or to suppress critical information is influenced by the information's newsworthiness, good taste or impact on the community, not by any legal considerations.

Newspapers are more likely to publish negative information about public figures than about private citizens. Also, large dailies are more likely than smaller daily and weekly newspapers to mention a person's indiscretions. Smaller newspapers tend to be more protective of their communities and of the people living in them. Journalists in smaller cities may know the people who died and fear that the critical information would anger the people's friends and relatives and be disturbing for the entire community.

JIM NICHOLSON: NO. 1 IN OBITUARIES

Jim Nicholson started an obituary page for the Philadelphia Daily News in 1983. Earlier, Nicholson worked as an investigative reporter and was nominated for a Pulitzer Prize. While working for the Daily News, Nicholson has become famous and has repeatedly been honored as the nation's best obituary writer.

While most newspapers publish long obituaries only for celebrities, Nicholson writes colorful obituaries of ordinary Philadelphians. Nicholson writes about bus drivers, school crossing guards, sanitation workers and retirees. He calls these people the real heroes in our society and explains that:

Most people never make the paper because they never murdered anybody, dealt in narcotics, got locked up or elected to public office. But what I write about are the most important people in the world—[those] who make your water run, your street cars and buses operate, deliver the vegetables. Who would you miss more when he goes on vacation, the secretary of state or your garbage man?

A colleague at the Philadelphia Daily News adds:

On Jim's obit page, you read about laborers, plumbers, pastors, housewives; you read about their pride and their small kindnesses. You read about the security guard who died with no survivors and few possessions who was a World War II hero. You read about the elderly storekeeper who gave away as much as she sold, and listened to her customers' troubles.

Nicholson calls his job "the most rewarding I've ever had." Nicholson explains that, as an obituary writer, he has "touched more lives positively than I have with anything else I've done." In addition, an obit "is the last—and sometimes only—time we can say someone lived a life and their being here mattered." He adds:

> Any one of my obits will outlive any investigative thing I've ever done. People save these forever. Some people will Xerox 200 to 300 copies and take them to the funerals. They'll put them next to the register and people will sign in and take a copy. People laminate my obits and give them to friends.

CHECKLISTS FOR WRITING OBITUARIES

Nicholson recommends the following guidelines for writing obituaries:

I. What Does a Good Obituary Contain?

1. *Basic facts:* Name, age, occupation, area of residence, organizational memberships, awards, survivors, services, memorials.
2. *Character portrait:* Drawing on quotes from friends and family, the reader should be able to see the outlines of a personality. The reader may be able to relate the person to someone the reader knows or even to the reader himself or herself. The ultimate acclaim may be when a reader thinks: "I wish I had known this person."
3. *Quotes:* Quote people the way they talk—fragmented sentences, dangling prepositions. Anyone who has read grand jury or court testimony or tape transcripts knows this is how most of us talk.
4. *Warts and wrinkles:* Cleaning up someone's act after they have died really does not serve the cause of the deceased or loved ones. A sanitized portrait is indistinguishable from any other. It is the irregularities of personality and human shadings of temperament which give us all identity. A person described as being a strict parent, impatient with unprofessional conduct, and openly hostile toward insurance representatives becomes real to the reader. The person is no longer an oil portrait of George Washington hanging on the wall. The subject is in a Polaroid snapshot, caught in the act of living.
5. *Historical notes:* Sometimes, in a few sentences or paragraphs, you can put people in their youth or childhood, and thus place the reader in another era of the city's or town's history. For example:

> Bob Smith was raised in the east end of town in the early 1920s, when Zeke Clayton's blacksmith barn was still standing only a few hundred yards from the Smith family's clapboard house. Years later, Bob would tell his grandchildren how he would wake up most mornings to the hard ping of a hammer bouncing against an anvil.

II. The Interview

1. The funeral director, who has had time to deal with the family and evaluate the members, can usually point the reporter to the most articulate or composed family member or friend. He or she will gladly furnish the home phone number.

2. Sometimes it is best to open the interview with known facts that the interviewee can recall and recite easily. Some facts, such as services or burial, may already be known to the reporter, but the objective is to get the individual talking. As the interview progresses, more pertinent questions can be asked. For example: "Why did your father choose to become a tree surgeon?" The response may be: "Well, after his father was gunned down by the Capone mob for holding back numbers receipts, my dad had to quit school in the ninth grade to help his mother support the family."

3. Remember, you are not writing about death, you are writing about life. The interview can go as any feature-style interview would progress. The fact that the subject is dead is almost incidental, although how some people face death can be an important part of an obituary because it may reveal how they handled the previous 70 or 80 years of their life.

SOME FINAL SUGGESTIONS

1. A woman is said to be survived by her husband, not her widower. Similarly, a man is survived by his wife, not by his widow.
2. A Catholic funeral Mass is celebrated, said or sung, and the word "Mass" is capitalized.
3. Many editors object to reporting that a death was "sudden," explaining that most deaths are sudden.
4. Because burglars sometimes break into surviving relatives' homes while they are attending a funeral, most newspapers no longer print survivors' addresses in obituaries.
5. Medical experts often conduct autopsies to determine the cause of death. When that happens, simply report that, "An autopsy will be conducted." If you report, "An autopsy will be conducted to determine the cause of death," you will be stating the obvious—and thus wasting your readers' time and your newspaper's space.
6. Avoid suggesting that one relationship is inferior to another. Unless the family requests that you do so, do not create separate lists of natural children and adopted children, or of sisters and half-sisters, for example.

SUGGESTED READINGS

Caughey, Bernard. "The Popularity of Obituaries." *Editor & Publisher*, April 23, 1988, pp. 46 and 146–147.

Duffy, Glen. "Death Takes a Job: How Reporter Jim Nicholson Learned to Relax and Love Writing Obits." *Philadelphia*, December 1988, pp. 131–132.

Lippman, Thomas W., ed. *The Washington Post Deskbook On Style*, 2nd ed. New York: McGraw-Hill, 1989. (See Chapter 4: "The Craft of the Obituary.")

Nicholson, Jim. "Obituary Writing," in Don Fry, ed., *Best Newspaper Writing 1987*. St. Petersburg, FL: Poynter Institute for Media Studies, 1987, pp. 227–263.

Rambo, C. David. "Obits Provide Lifelong Reading Appeal: Subtle Changes Are Afoot, Although Getting It Right Remains Rule No. 1." *Presstime*, June 1990, pp. 46–48.

Storm, Bill. "A Different Type of Obit Page: Jim Nicholson of the Philadelphia Daily News Writes Obituaries Not Only about the Upper Class, but also about the 'Common' Man and Woman." *Editor & Publisher*, June 6, 1987, pp. 100 and 149.

Tips from a Pro

GRIEF AND ANGUISH: HOW TO INTERVIEW DURING A CRISIS

By **Lucille S. deView**
Writing Coach
The Orange County (Calif.) Register

People are generally at a loss for words in a crisis.

I know. When my mother died and my newspaper phoned for an obituary, relatives handed the phone to me. My life-work is words, but in my grief, I couldn't find any.

"Look around the room," my colleague said on the phone. "Something there must remind you of your mother's life."

I saw mother's framed drawing of praying hands. I started talking and could hardly stop.

Compassion and empathy may guide us when we interview people enduring a tragedy but we need to maintain our professionalism for our sake and theirs; to remain calm.

It sometimes helps to explain that the information we request will enable us to tell the story of the deceased as a person, not as a statistic.

At the scene of a fire or accident, try to draw concerned friends or relatives aside, away from the sight of the body or the devastation.

Don't be afraid to express your concern. Edna Buchanan, a Pulitzer Prize-winning police reporter for the Miami Herald and now a novelist, saw more than her share of grisly crimes. But in a talk to student journalists, she said she never failed to express her sympathy to the bereaved before asking tough questions.

Offer to help. It is not amiss to say, "Here's a Kleenex," or "Can I get you a glass of water." This encourages the person under stress to see you as a human being, not a reporter.

Be careful, however, not to touch someone unless you are sure your sympathetic gesture is welcome. Sometimes what is meant to be kind is resented as an invasion of that person's space.

E X E R C I S E   1
WRITING OBITUARIES

INSTRUCTIONS: Write obituaries based on the information given below. Use your own judgment, based on what you have read in this chapter, in deciding whether to use the most controversial details.

OBITUARY 1: VERONICA BLACKFOOT

Identification: Veronica Dawn Blackfoot. Born in 1927. Address: 2045 Wentover Ave.

Circumstances of death: Died at 2:30 a.m. today in General Hospital. Blackfoot was admitted to the hospital almost five weeks ago and was being treated for breast cancer.

Funeral services: A memorial service at St. Agnes Non-Denominational Church will be held at 8 p.m. Friday. Graveside services scheduled for 1 p.m. Saturday at Wildwood Cemetery. There will be no viewing of the body. The family requests no flowers and that expressions of sympathy be in the form of contributions to St. Agnes Non-Denominational Church.

Survivors: Widower, Johnny. One daughter: Pamela of Oklahoma City, Okla. One adopted son: Robert of New York City. Three grandchildren.

Accomplishments: Born and attended elementary and high schools in Chicago. Graduated from the University of Illinois in 1949. Graduated from Marquette University law school in Milwaukee in 1952. At Marquette, she was editor of the law review journal. Opened an office in this city in August of that year. Elected city council member in 1958 and retained that post until 1964. Was head of the Chamber of Commerce from about 1975 to 1980. At the time of her death, was senior partner in the law firm of Blackfoot, Perez and Tinsel. She was a member of the County Bar Association (of which she was president in 1971), the American Bar Association, Overeaters Anonymous and the Defense Law Institute. She was director of a local bank and also on the board of directors of the hospital in which she was a patient when she died.

OBITUARY 2: LYNN SHEPARD

Identification: Lynn Marie Shepard. Age 20. Address: 854 Maury Road, Apt. 107B.

Circumstances of death: Taken to the emergency room at Mercy Hospital at 1 a.m. yesterday, where she died shortly thereafter. An autopsy conducted later in the day revealed that she died "of symptoms brought about by the ingestion of a large quantity of cocaine."

Funeral services: 5 p.m. tomorrow at Hines Brothers Funeral Home. Burial immediately following at Memorial Park Cemetery.

Survivors: Her parents, Frank and Helen Shepard of 107 Eastbrook Avenue. Three sisters, Patricia, Virginia and Carol, all at home. A brother, William, a soldier stationed in Germany. Also, her college roommate of the last two years: Timothy Bolankner, also of 854 Maury Road, Apt. 107B.

Accomplishments: Salutatorian of her senior class at Central High School, where she was a member of the girls' volleyball team, a member of the homecoming court during her senior year and also school treasurer during her senior year. Now, a sophomore studying business administration at your school. She compiled a 3.8 gpa during her first full year of college and was on the Dean's List. A member of Delta Delta Delta Sorority and the Business Honor Council. Worked part-time as a waitress at the Steak & Ale Restaurant. Hoped to someday own her own business.

E X E R C I S E   2
WRITING OBITUARIES

INSTRUCTIONS: Many newspapers give blank obituary notice forms to local funeral homes and ask the people working there to fill out the forms when friends and relatives come in to arrange a funeral. The system makes it easy for newspapers to obtain all the information needed to write most obituaries. Use the information in these forms to write obituaries for the individuals they describe.

OBITUARY NOTICE

Please supply the information asked for below and send to the newspaper office as quickly as possible after death. Relatives, friends and neighbors of the deceased will appreciate prompt reporting of this news so that they may attend funeral services or send messages of condolence.

Full Name of Deceased _Col. Thomas M. Martin_

Address _1637 Leet St._

Age _About 61_

Date of Death _Late afternoon yesterday_

Place of Death _In back yard—he was working in his rose garden_

Cause of Death _Stroke, we think_

Time and Date of Funeral _Monday at 2 p.m._

Place of Funeral _St. Timothy's Episcopal Church_

Place of Burial _Sunset Gardens behind Sunset Funeral Home on 55th St._

Officiating Cleric _May Alvarado_

Place of Birth _Pearl City, Hawaii_

Places and Length of Residences _Col. Martin moved around a lot as a child—his father was in the military. After graduating from West Point, he was in Okinawa, Japan, for 2 years, embassy duty in Germany for 4 years, stationed at Pearl Harbor for 6 years, then state-side at various military installations._

Occupation   Retired, after being twice passed over for promotion to general

Did Deceased Ever Hold Public Office (When and What)?   No—was often asked

to do so, but Col. Martin always declined the public spotlight.

Name, Address of Surviving Husband or Wife   Pre-deceased by second wife,

Rebecca Stewart Martin. His first wife divorced him and also pre-deceased him.

Maiden Name (if Married Woman)

Marriage, When and to Whom   Rebecca Stewart Martin in 1979 in San Antonio,

Texas

Names, Addresses of Surviving Children   Daughters Anna Linn Martin of Albu-

querque, N.M., and Rebecca Martin Bell of Marengo, Iowa; son David of this town

Names, Addresses of Surviving Brothers and Sisters   None

Number of Grandchildren (Great, etc.)   Annie Martin Bell

Names, Addresses of Parents (if Living)   No

Additional Information   Col. Martin went to high school in France while his father

was stationed there for 4 years. He graduated from West Point 108th in a class of 482.

He was a deacon in St. Timothy's Episcopal Church, where he was a member for many

years. He also taught Sunday School there. He was a member of the American Rose

Growers Society. Growing roses was always an active hobby of his. He once said that

their beauty reminded him of his wife, who loved flowers. He did a lot to progress the

research and development of hybrid tea roses. He won many awards for his roses. The

well-known "Rebecca" tea rose was a hybrid developed by Col. Martin.

Harcourt Brace & Company

OBITUARY NOTICE

Please supply the information asked for below and send to the newspaper office as quickly as possible after death. Relatives, friends and neighbors of the deceased will appreciate prompt reporting of this news so that they may attend funeral services or send messages of condolence.

Full Name of Deceased Iris Norcross

Address 112 52nd St.

Age She always gave her age as 38, but relatives said she was 43.

Date of Death This morning

Place of Death Knowles AIDS Research Center in New York City

Cause of Death Infected with the AIDS virus

Time and Date of Funeral Wednesday at 11 a.m.

Place of Funeral Thompson and Thompson Funeral Home on 4220 Agee Avenue,

and then another ceremony in Cleveland, Ohio, next Thursday

Place of Burial Greenlawn Cemetery in Cleveland, Ohio, next Thursday

Officiating Cleric Maynard Brown

Place of Birth Cleveland, Ohio

Places and Length of Residences Ms. Norcross lived in Cleveland, Ohio, until she

was 20. She graduated from Cleveland's Eastern High School, and then went to Cleve-

land Community College where she received an associate's degree in accounting. Then

she went to Bowling Green University in Ohio and received a B.S. in business

management. She moved here right afterward when she was offered a job with the

Restaurant Ritz chain. After about four years, she started her own accounting business.

She also did some consulting.

Occupation Owner of Norcross Accounting Services

Did Deceased Ever Hold Public Office (When and What)? No

Harcourt Brace & Company

Name, Address of Surviving Husband or Wife _Ex-husband Gerald Willis_

Maiden Name (if Married Woman) _Never changed name_

Marriage, When and to Whom _Gerald Willis from 1976 to 1978_

Names, Addresses of Surviving Children _None_

Names, Addresses of Surviving Brothers and Sisters _Sisters Jamella Norcross and_

Zena Johnson, both of Cleveland, Ohio

Number of Grandchildren (Great, etc.) _None_

Names, Addresses of Parents (if Living) _Rita Norcross and stepfather Jim Trevors, of_

Cleveland, Ohio

Additional Information _Ms. Norcross was a volunteer at the Rape Crisis Center for_

about 7 years, where she has been publicly recognized for her dedication to the Center.

She began to work at the Rape Crisis Center after she herself was counseled there

following a brutal rape in her home and a trial in which her rapist—a jealous ex-

boyfriend—was convicted by the jury. She was very active in the First Presbyterian

Church for 10 years where she was an Elder. True to her adventuresome personality to

be unafraid of new experiences, when Ms. Norcross became ill with the AIDS virus a

few years ago, she volunteered to be used as a research subject for new treatments.

She said that if her one life could save many others, then she will have died for a good

cause.

EXERCISE 3
WRITING OBITUARIES

A. Write an obituary for another student in your class. Assume the student died of unknown causes early today, and that the student's funeral arrangements have not yet been made. Do not write a news story about the person's death, but an obituary about his or her life. Include the student's philosophy and goals and interesting experiences or major accomplishments. You might also describe the student's physical traits. Avoid generalities and clichés.

B. During a two-hour class period, go out onto your campus and look for two people together, both strangers to you. With their consent, interview one of those persons about the "deceased" other person. Continue the interview until you obtain some good (specific) quotations about the "deceased." Then return to your classroom and write an obituary before the end of the period. Assume the person died of unknown causes early today and the funeral arrangements have not yet been made.

C. Write an in-depth obituary for one of the celebrities listed below. Briefly report the person died of unknown causes at home last night and the funeral has not yet been scheduled. Do not make up any other facts, or report only what you remember about the person. Instead, use your campus library to thoroughly research the person's character and accomplishments. (Consult and, on a separate page, list a minimum of 10 sources you used while writing the obituary.)

After your lead, immediately report additional highlights—interesting and important details—that help describe the person's life, character and accomplishments. Avoid dull lists, and avoid reporting the information in chronological order. More routine details (such as the person's place of birth, education and survivors) should be placed near the end of the obituary, not near the lead.

People about whom you might write an obituary include:

Athletes
Peggy Fleming
George Foreman
Florence Griffith Joyner
Monica Seles
Lee Trevino

Authors and Journalists
Helen Gurly Brown
Walter Cronkite
Katharine Graham
Charles Kuralt
Andy Rooney

Entertainers
Johnny Carson
Glenn Close
Leonard Nimoy
Brooke Shields
Barbra Streisand

Political Figures
Fidel Castro
Hillary Rodham Clinton
Mikhail Gorbachev
H. Ross Perot
Margaret Thatcher

Your mayor, governor, senator or representative

Others
Marcia Clark
Billy Graham
Ralph Nader
Colin Powell
Gloria Steinem

Harcourt Brace & Company

CHAPTER 13

PUBLIC AFFAIRS REPORTING

Knowledge will forever govern ignorance, and a people who mean to be their own government must arm themselves with the power that knowledge brings.

(President James Madison)

Sometimes you hear people refer to the news media as "the Fourth Estate." Some people attribute that phrase to a British politician and political thinker, Edmund Burke, who supposedly once said the three traditional classes, or estates, of society—the king, the clergy and the commoners—were represented in Parliament but in the reporters' gallery sat a fourth estate more powerful than the other three. Whatever its origin, the term recognized the power of the British and American press around 1800 to inform and shape popular opinion on public affairs.

News organizations continue to devote substantial time and money to reporting on public affairs. The term "public affairs reporting" encompasses more than reporting on government, but the latter remains one of journalism's most important tasks. For the reporter on the local newspaper's police beat as well as those covering the White House for the television networks, recording the actions and policies of government consumes much of the working day. This chapter introduces public affairs reporting at the local level, focusing on the coverage of crimes and accidents, local government officials and agencies, and criminal and civil court cases.

The public affairs reporter, to be successful at any level, must cultivate certain habits. Among them are the following:

- **Diligence:** The public affairs reporter, whether assigned to the county courthouse or the Pentagon, must follow a regular pattern of checking sources. Reporters have discovered important stories simply by regularly inspecting documents filed with the register of deeds or contracts awarded by government agencies.

- **Knowledge of sources:** The sources for public affairs stories may be the people who work in government or who are affected by its decisions. Or the sources may be the records governmental agencies keep. The public affairs reporter must know how to use both people and documents to find information quickly.

- **Accuracy:** Government agencies deal with complicated matters. The reporters who cover public affairs must report the details of these issues correctly, whether they are the name and address of a person arrested for a crime or a contractor's winning bid on a street improvement project.

- **Ability to write clear explanations:** The reporter not only must understand what government agencies are doing but must be able to explain issues and decisions clearly to readers, listeners or viewers. Unless the reporter explains governmental actions clearly, citizens will not understand how their lives and interests may be affected.

Reporters who can develop these traits may find public affairs reporting to be the most rewarding and satisfying aspect of their work, for nothing else a journalist does can affect so many people.

Harcourt Brace & Company

CRIME AND ACCIDENTS

The first assignment many newspaper reporters have is the police beat. Beginning television or radio reporters may have more varied assignments, but covering crimes and accidents will be a major part of their jobs.

Not all police reporters are beginners; some have covered that beat for many years. Nevertheless, the police beat is an excellent training ground, for several reasons:

- It forces young reporters to learn the community, both physically and sociologically.

- It trains reporters in news values and in the need for accuracy.

- It gives reporters an opportunity to develop sources who will serve them for many years.

The police beat imposes a great deal of stress on reporters. Police reporters mostly cover breaking news, so the deadline pressures are constant. More important, their jobs expose them to the harshest aspects of urban life, such as murders, fatal accidents and suicides. And being on the streets places police reporters in more danger than most other reporters. Some reporters burn out because of the stress of police reporting, while others thrive on it. Many news organizations rotate police reporters to other beats after a few years, partly to prevent burnout but also to prevent reporters from becoming too friendly with the police officers they cover.

The police reporter's work will vary with the size and type of community she or he is covering. In a small community, almost any crime, even a minor theft, may be newsworthy. In big cities, where two or three homicides a day are common, only the most bloody, most unusual crimes will receive detailed coverage. Police reporters also cover the activities of the department, including community service projects, promotions, retirements and internal investigations. They may cover traffic accidents, but usually only the most noteworthy ones.

A lot of the information for these stories is available at police headquarters or the precinct stations. Reporters may be able to write their stories without ever leaving headquarters or the newsroom. But experienced reporters know that they must go to the scenes of crimes and accidents to be able to report on them vividly. The reporter needs to be on the street, talking to the victims, witnesses, suspects and investigating officers.

Police Sources

The suspicion that exists between reporters and law enforcement officers sometimes prevents thorough reporting. Police forces are organized along military lines, and many members follow the military ideals of duty, discipline and deference to superior officers. Reporters tend to be more individualistic and less deferential to authority than police officers are. A more important obstacle is that police officers are wary of news coverage. They fear that stories will sensationalize their work, portray them in a bad light or get them in trouble with their superiors. They usually see few if any benefits from news coverage, except under circumstances they can control. For their part, reporters tend to see police officers as tight-lipped and secretive, using claims of privacy or investigative necessity to keep interesting and important information from the public.

Police reporters need to set aside their prejudices and work to overcome this mutual suspicion and distrust, because they need information from police sources to write their stories. The first step toward gaining the confidence of police officers is to spend as many hours as possible at police headquarters and precinct stations. Reporters should chat with officers about their work and their professional concerns. Reporters also should try to get permission to ride with officers in patrol cars. Those who do will see how officers spend their time and will learn what their lives

Harcourt Brace & Company

are like. The best way reporters build trust with police officers is to prove their professionalism by reporting on police matters accurately and thoroughly and by treating sources fairly.

Different police departments handle relations with news organizations in different ways. In some cases reporters may be able to speak with the officers and investigators who are working on a particular crime or accident. Other departments may channel all information through an officer at police headquarters, a practice most journalists dislike.

Edna Buchanan, a former police reporter for The Miami Herald, says journalists, especially print reporters, need details to make their stories complete. A police department's public information officer, who may never visit a crime scene, cannot furnish those details. Only the officers who were present know what a reporter needs. Buchanan learned the importance of asking for details when she neglected to do so while covering a homicide. The case at first appeared to be routine: A man had been shot and his body dumped in the street. Only later did Buchanan learn that the victim had been wearing a black taffeta cocktail dress and red high-heeled shoes.

Some police departments forbid reporters from talking with the officers who worked a crime or accident. Such policies provide all the more reason to go to crime and accident scenes. Being there lets reporters gain some sense of the incident, locate witnesses and victims and write a more thorough story, but even then reporters may encounter obstacles. Police officers control crime and accident scenes to protect lives and property and preserve evidence. News reporters would agree with those goals. Some officers, however, become overly protective and impose unreasonable limits on reporters. This and other issues relating to news gathering are discussed in Chapter 20, Communications Law.

Documentary Sources

Police keep records of most of their activities. The records help police plan their investigations, keep track of suspects, prepare to testify in court and justify their budget requests, among other things. Police officers do not prepare their records for the convenience of news reporters, but many police records are open to the public, including journalists. The reporter who wants to cover police matters thoroughly must learn what records are available and how to read them.

Record-keeping policies vary from state to state. The police reporter needs to know what records describing local police activities are open to the public under state open-records laws. What follows is a brief description of some of the more common types of records of crimes and accidents available from police departments and other agencies:

- **Police blotter:** This document goes by different names, but it usually is a record of all calls for assistance received by the police. The log provides such basic facts as the location of an event, the time and a brief description. It may also show who has been arrested, the charge and the time of the arrest. Blotter information is sketchy and best serves as a lead to other sources.

- **Incident reports:** The incident report gives a more complete description of a crime. It will tell you the nature of the crime, the location, the name of the victim, when the crime occurred, what property was stolen or damaged (if relevant) and the name of the investigating officer. Other information may or may not be available, depending on the law of the state. For example, Alaska law prohibits the disclosure of the addresses and phone numbers of all witnesses and victims; it also keeps confidential the names of victims of kidnappings, sex crimes and certain crimes involving minors. Some states make available sections of the incident reports that provide a narrative of the crime; other states consider that information part of the investigative record and close it to the public. Police everywhere treat as confidential any portion of the record that identifies suspects who have not been arrested.

Harcourt Brace & Company

- **Search warrants and affidavits:** Police officers usually have to get a warrant from a magistrate before they can legally search private property. Police investigators get warrants by filing affidavits with the court identifying the place they want to search and telling why they want to search there and what they expect to find. The warrants and the affidavits usually become public records once the search is complete. The affidavits help reporters understand what police are doing and why. Sometimes courts will seal the warrants and the affidavits if the search is part of a larger investigation and police do not want to alert other possible suspects.

- **Autopsy reports:** In cases involving violent or unexplained deaths, coroners perform autopsies to determine the cause and manner of death. The cause of death is the medical reason the person died, such as gunshot wound to the heart or poisoning. The manner of death refers to the circumstances—namely, whether the death was an accident, a suicide or a homicide. Autopsy reports are not public records in all states. In Massachusetts, for example, they are considered medical records that are closed to the public. In Kansas, Wyoming and Maryland, however, autopsy reports are explicitly identified as public records.

- **Arrest reports:** The arrest report describes the person who has been arrested and the offense, names the officers involved, lists the witnesses and, eventually, gives the outcome of the case.

- **Criminal history information:** Information that a suspect has prior arrests and convictions is likely to turn public opinion against that person and make it harder for him or her to receive a fair trial. To protect the suspect's right to a fair trial, law enforcement authorities are reluctant to disclose such information. Some states severely limit access to it; others erase or expunge it after a certain period. Nevertheless, criminal history information is a public record in most states, and reporters have a right to ask for it. Some states have computerized their criminal history files, but usually, for a fee, a person's criminal record is accessible to journalists.

- **Accident reports:** These records describe motor vehicle accidents and identify the time and place of the accident, drivers involved, passengers, injuries and property damages. The reports usually describe how the accident occurred as reconstructed by the investigating officer.

Although a number of records are available to reporters, most states allow police to withhold investigative records. Some states allow the withholding of almost any kind of investigative record, even if it is not part of a criminal investigation. Other states say police can withhold only the records of active criminal investigations; once the investigation is complete, the records become public. The names of confidential sources and undercover police officers, along with information about confidential investigative techniques, usually can be withheld indefinitely. Privacy laws may also allow police to keep some records confidential, such as the name of a rape victim or the identity of a juvenile suspect. Police sometimes use laws protecting personnel records as an excuse to withhold information about investigations of police misconduct. These secrecy provisions mean the police reporter must combine human and documentary sources to prepare complete news reports.

The Problem of Libel

A story saying that a person has been arrested in connection with an infamous crime is likely to harm that person's reputation. Therefore, reporters covering the police and courts must be careful to avoid libel lawsuits. Reporters can state that a person has been *charged* with a crime. However, reporters cannot say that the person is *guilty*—that the person actually committed the crime—until after that person has been convicted by a judge or jury. Criminal defendants in the United States are presumed innocent and have a right to be tried in a court of law, not by a mob on a street corner or by their local daily.

The following story does not libel the defendant because it never reports or implies that the defendant committed the crime. Rather, the story seems to be describing two different people: (1) the defendant and (2) the criminal. The reporter is careful not to say that the defendant actually committed the crime:

> A 27-year-old woman is suing a downtown hotel because she was raped in the hotel's parking garage on her wedding night.
>
> On Tuesday, the woman filed a suit in Circuit Court, charging that the Grand Hotel failed to adequately protect its guests.
>
> The hotel's general manager, Lillian DeLoy, responded that the hotel's security is adequate.
>
> According to the woman's attorney, James R. Lopez, the rape took place in front of an empty security office—a glassed-in booth with a view of the entire garage.
>
> The attack occurred when the bride returned to her parked car for a suitcase at about 11 p.m. Police arrested a suspect a short time later.
>
> The suspect, Myron Jaco, 18, of 141 Pine St., has been charged with sexual battery and is scheduled to stand trial next month.

Elements of Crime and Accident Stories

Most crime stories have summary leads. For unusual crime stories, reporters sometimes use delayed leads, which place an anecdote or a quotation ahead of the most newsworthy facts. Nevertheless, all crime stories contain basically the same information:

- Any deaths or injuries, when they occur. These are often the most important facts and should appear early in the story.

- The nature and value of any property stolen or damaged.

- As complete an identification of the suspect as possible: the suspect's full name, including middle initial, as well as his or her age, address and occupation. Complete identification of the suspect guards against the possibility that readers or viewers will confuse the suspect with someone else who has a similar name; that kind of confusion leads to libel suits.

- Identification of victims and witnesses. To protect them, some news organizations will not publish their addresses. News organizations also routinely withhold the names of victims of sex crimes.

- Whether any weapons were used in the commission of the crime and, if so, what types.

- The exact charges filed against the suspect.

- A narrative of the crime.

News stories should describe the specific crimes involved, not just the legal charges. The legal charges often fail to reveal exactly what happened. Moreover, because they are expressed in general terms, the same legal charges could be repeated in thousands of stories:

VAGUE: Three people arrested in a church parking lot Sunday morning were charged with petty larceny.

REVISED: Three people arrested in a church parking lot Sunday morning were charged with siphoning gasoline from a car.

Never report a suspect's race or religion unless it is clearly relevant to your story. In the past (and sometimes even today) reporters mentioned the race only of suspects and criminals who were minorities. Race is relevant, however, in the description of a specific individual, such as:

Witnesses described the thief as a white male, about 25 years old and 6 feet tall. The thief has a mustache, a scar on his left cheek and is missing several front teeth.

While describing a crime, do not mention the fact that it was committed by an "unidentified" man or woman. Criminals rarely announce their identities, and most crimes are never solved. Thus, most criminals are never "identified." Similarly, if police do not know a criminal's identity, you cannot report that the police are looking for "a suspect." If the police do not know who committed a crime, they have no suspect.

Accident stories are similar to crime stories in many of their elements. Here are some of the major points to include in accident stories:

• Any deaths or injuries. Again, this is usually the most important information.

• Property damage.

• The identities of the people involved in the accident.

• The types of vehicles involved, such as cars, trucks or buses.

• Any citations given to any of the drivers.

• Any unusual conditions at the time of the accident, such as fog, rain or snow.

• A narrative of the accident.

Do not say that a person "received" injuries. People "receive" gifts, but they normally "suffer" or "sustain" injuries.

For both crime and accident stories, report only what occurred, not what has not occurred. Avoid statements like the following:

No one was hurt.

There are no suspects.

Officers searched the neighborhood but were unable to find the vandals.

LOCAL GOVERNMENT

Americans have always been suspicious of government. That suspicion is embodied in the federal Constitution, which provides for a limited government, separation of powers, and checks and balances—all intended to prevent government from becoming too powerful. Similar restraints operate on state and local governments. Recently, that suspicion of government has deepened to disgust and loathing, mostly directed at the federal government but also at all other levels of government.

Journalism is built on coverage of government. The idea of newspapers and broadcast news programs as watchdogs of the public interest has motivated generations of reporters, editors and producers. Given the close connection between journalism and government, perhaps it is no surprise that public respect for the press also has declined.

A recent survey found that 71 percent of Americans believed that the press did more to hinder than to help the search for solutions to public problems. Some critics suspect reporters and politicians collaborate in creating phony crises so that the politicians have something to do and journalists have something to cover. Others complain that news organizations ignore complicated stories about issues that affect the lives of millions, such as the economic impact of international trade agreements, in favor of more sensational stories, like the murder trial of O.J. Simpson. And still others complain that news organizations, driven by stockholders' demands for ever-greater profits, are cutting investigative reporting and other costly hard-news projects and filling their columns and broadcasts with fluff.

Scholars and journalists have put forward various proposals to reinvigorate public affairs journalism. One of the more ambitious and hotly debated proposals is an approach called "public journalism" discussed in the chapter on news. Proponents of this approach contend news organizations should do more than report what public officials say; they should try to find out what issues interest citizens and then help them discuss and resolve those issues. To some extent, this requires journalists to abandon the ideal of objectivity and become involved in public affairs. Public journalism advocates warn that news organizations should limit their involvement to encouraging public participation and should avoid becoming advocates for any particular party, candidate or set of policies. Critics of public journalism say this approach risks excessive entanglements between journalists and public officials and undermines the traditional obligation of journalists to identify problems for readers and viewers.

The debate over public journalism may be confusing, but it indicates the importance that journalists and citizens place on public affairs reporting. Styles in public affairs reporting may change, but reporters who are skilled and interested in writing about city hall, the county courthouse or the local school district always will be valuable. These local governments are closest to the people. They are also the ones that local news organizations must cover for their readers, viewers and listeners; no one else can do it.

Obstacles to Thorough Coverage

Although citizens and journalists agree that coverage of local government is important, that coverage is often incomplete. Some numbers help explain why. There are 86,692 local units of government in the United States, including cities, counties, school districts and a variety of special districts that oversee such things as housing, water and power. By comparison, there are only 1,532 English-language daily newspapers and 1,481 television stations. True, there are also 9,746 radio stations and 8,293 weekly newspapers; but many stations broadcast little or no news, and weeklies often cover only the immediate community.

The picture appears more dismal when you compare employment figures. The total full- and part-time employment for all local governmental units is 11,103,000. Federal estimates put total newspaper employment at 452,000 and total radio and television employment at 225,000. Not all of those 11 million government workers make news, but only about 110,000 of the newspaper, radio and television workers actually cover the news. And many of those 110,000 are covering sports, business or lifestyles, not local government.

Small numbers of reporters in newsrooms across the country have the difficult task of watching many governmental units and their departments and subdivisions. Even a small daily paper may have to cover a dozen city and county governments. In urban areas, a daily newspaper's coverage area may include hundreds of governmental units. Television journalists often must cover more governmental units than print reporters because their signals reach larger areas. Given these realities, it is no wonder many people complain about the superficiality of much local news coverage.

The murder trial of O.J. Simpson received intense coverage. When Simpson was acquitted, two fiercely competitive newspapers—the New York Post and the New York Daily News—published the same headline and Associated Press photo on their front pages. The two lower photographs show reporters covering Simpson's trial. Some were working in a courthouse pressroom while others, especially photographers, were outside a courthouse entrance.

Harcourt Brace & Company

City and County Governments

City governments provide a wide range of services for their residents: police and fire protection, sewage treatment, water, street construction and maintenance, and parks and recreation services. Some cities also provide trash pickup and disposal, public transportation and electricity or natural gas. Others may operate hospitals or have some control over the local school system. They also adopt ordinances regulating such things as local speed limits, zoning and the use of outdoor signs by businesses.

County governments usually have more limited powers. They collect taxes levied by all the governments in the county. They may assess the value of all real and personal property, and they may hear appeals from citizens who believe those assessments are too high. County governments are repositories for records of births, deaths, marriages, real estate transactions and motor vehicle registrations. County governments also supervise elections and handle voter registration in many states.

Although it is difficult to generalize, city governments tend to have more professional managers than county governments, and cities tend to be less open than counties to the press and public. Usually, only the mayor and city council or city commission members are elected. In many cities, the mayor has little real power; much of the responsibility for administering the city rests with a city manager who is hired by the council. Cities often hire other top officials, such as the police chief, fire chief, finance director and public works director. Some city commissioners have both executive and legislative functions. Under this system, each commissioner directs some aspect of the city's operations, such as finance, public works or police, and collectively the commissioners vote on policies and ordinances. Communities within the same state or even the same county may have very different forms of government, so reporters must make sure they know how each city is organized.

The list of elected officials is longer in counties than in cities, sometimes including the county commissioners or supervisors, the clerk, register of deeds, assessor, sheriff and treasurer. These elected officials may feel more need to respond to the public, so they may be more accessible to reporters and citizens. Counties also may conduct their business in less formal ways than cities. The "good ol' boy" atmosphere of the 1940s and 1950s lingers in many county courthouses.

Local Budgets and Taxes

Reporters covering city or county government may report on a wide variety of issues, including the awarding of contracts for construction or major equipment purchases, creation of fire protection districts, zoning disputes and the regulation of adult movie theaters. The most important story, however, is the budget. The budget determines how much money a local government will have to collect from taxpayers and how it will spend that money for the coming year. It is the blueprint by which local governments work.

City budgets are set by the council or commission, county budgets by the commissioners. Usually department heads or officeholders submit their budget requests for the coming year. The council or the commission reviews the requests and makes the changes it considers prudent. Some states have statutory limits on the amounts by which local governments may increase their spending. If so, the council or commission may have to make difficult choices to keep the budgets within the limits.

Local governments get some money from federal and state governments, sales taxes, local income taxes, user fees and other miscellaneous sources, but property taxes provide the bulk of local revenue. Personal property includes such things as automobiles, boats, stocks and bonds. Real property is land and buildings. The county or city assessor determines the value of property for tax purposes. The assessor tries to determine the market value of the property—how much it

Harcourt Brace & Company

would sell for. Some states tax property on its full market value. Others apply the tax only to a portion of the market value. Still other states assess different classes of property differently, applying the tax to, say, 100 percent of the market value of residences but to only 80 percent of the market value of farmland.

The local government determines how much money it must raise from property taxes by determining how much it needs to spend in the coming year and then subtracting all revenue from sales taxes, federal or state grants, user fees, income taxes and so forth. The remainder is divided by the total assessed valuation of the community to produce the tax levy.

Here's an example: Say a city council has decided to set next year's budget at $15 million. The council expects to take in $5 million from sales taxes, state and federal grants and various fees. The remaining $10 million will have to come from property taxes. Assume the total assessed value of all real and personal property in this city is $700 million. Dividing $10 million by $700 million produces a tax rate of .01429 cents per dollar.

Most readers and viewers will see the tax rate as just another number. The news reporter must explain it in terms that will have meaning to them. One way is to say how much people will have to pay in taxes for every $100 in the assessed valuation of their property. Multiplying the tax rate of .01429 by 100 yields 1.43. That means people will pay about $1.43 in taxes for every $100 of taxable property they own.

Another way to explain property taxes to readers is to show what the tax bill would be for a typical home or car. Say the average price of a home is $75,000 and personal homes are assessed at 100 percent of their market value. Multiply $75,000 by the tax rate, .01429. The result, $1,071.75, is the amount the owner of that average home would have to pay in real property taxes next year.

Any individual in a community may pay taxes to several different governments: the city, county, school district, fire protection district, sewer district, natural resources district and others. The combination of taxes any individual pays will vary from city to city or even within cities.

City and County Sources

Covering city hall or the county courthouse requires establishing a routine for visiting the various offices and departments in each and taking the time to get to know each officeholder or department chief. Reporters also should cultivate contacts among the assistants, staff members and secretaries who work in the various offices. Such workers can be very helpful in steering reporters toward information for a story.

Some local officials fear press coverage or want to control information released to the press. Instances where local governments have tried to control information abound. The Aberdeen, S.D., City Commission ordered all city employees to get approval from their department heads before they made any statements to reporters about city rules, regulations or internal decisions. The commission believed that city employees were spending too much time in media contacts, even though it was not part of their official duties, and that news organizations were getting incomplete information from lower-level officials. In a similar incident in Memphis, Tenn., a new mayor ordered department heads to refer all questions from news reporters to him. Neither of these policies endured. The Memphis mayor quickly rescinded his order because of press criticism, and a federal judge ruled the Aberdeen policy interfered with the free speech rights of city employees.

When they do talk, government officials often speak in jargon and technical terms: "ad valorem taxes," "capital outlays," "declaratory judgments," "percolation ponds," "promissory notes," "rapid infiltration basins," "secured and unsecured debts" and "tangible personal property." If a legal or technical term is essential to a story, the reporter should define it. Otherwise, those terms should be replaced with something simpler and more familiar. For example, while writing about plans to fix a sewer system, one reporter explained that the repairs were necessary

Harcourt Brace & Company

"because of groundwater infiltration." Another reporter explained more clearly that the sewer pipes were so old and cracked that water was leaking into them.

City hall and county courthouse reporters also need to be familiar with public records. Every state provides for some degree of public access to local government records. Not every document held by government is a public record, not every entity connected with the government is a public agency, and some public records are exempt from disclosure. The definitions of "public record" and "public agency" vary from state to state, and so do the kinds of records that are exempt from disclosure. Nevertheless, here are some local government records usually available to the public:

City or County

- **Purchase orders (paid and not paid):** These show what products or services were obtained from what vendors at what prices.

- **Payroll:** This record tells not only how much each employee was paid but also deductions, time records, sick leave, vacations and other absences. Although payroll information is usually obtainable, governments can and do withhold the Social Security numbers of employees. Other personnel information often is exempt from disclosure.

- **Bids and bid specifications:** When a governmental unit plans a major construction project or a major equipment purchase, it usually asks for bids. State laws may require local governments to seek bids for all purchases above a certain amount. The bid specifications are the government agency's description of what it wants to buy or build and are sent to all contractors or vendors that might want to submit bids. The businesses submit sealed bids, which are opened at a public meeting. The specifications are public records as soon as the local government has distributed them. The bids become public records when they are opened.

- **Licenses:** Cities issue licenses for various kinds of businesses (liquor stores and food markets), occupations (private detectives and security guards), pets and a variety of other things.

- **Inspection reports:** Fire department officers inspect certain public buildings regularly for fire hazards, and the reports they prepare usually are public records. So are reports prepared by building inspectors who examine new buildings.

- **Zoning records:** Maps, reports, petitions and case files pertaining to planning and zoning actions are usually public.

County

- **Real estate assessment records:** These records reveal the owner, legal description and assessed value of the land and buildings for each piece of property in a community. The records usually are cross-indexed so they can be accessed in a number of different ways.

- **Motor vehicle registration records:** These records show who owns what vehicles, their value and the taxes paid on them.

- **Deeds:** The register of deeds office keeps track of all transfers of real property in a county. The records reveal who owns what property, when it was purchased and from whom. In some states, the actual sales price of a piece of real estate is confidential.

For generations, local governments have kept these records and many others on paper. Now, computers are changing the way governments do business. The electronic transformation of public records has created both problems and opportunities for reporters. Most states consider records public whether they are in electronic or paper form. However, states differ on whether reporters and citizens should be able to get the records in electronic form. The difference is important because reporters can analyze data that are available in electronic form in ways that would be impossible with paper documents.

Erik Kriss and Jon Craig of the Syracuse (N.Y.) Herald-Journal, matched data from two computer databases to show that the New York Legislature had padded its payroll with more than 800 political appointees, given jobs to many relatives of legislators, kept retired legislators on the payroll, and operated three duplicate radio and television stations, among other things. Boston Globe reporters David Armstrong, Shelley Murphy and Stephen Kurkjian used a computer database with information on 30,000 elevators and escalators in Massachusetts to prepare a story documenting the decline in elevator safety. These stories were possible because reporters could use computers to examine the electronic versions of thousands of public records quickly. To sift through so many paper records would have taken more manpower than most news organizations could afford to devote to a single project. Of course, the reporter must understand database and spreadsheet programs to be able to use electronic records effectively.

School Districts

Public education absorbs more local tax money than any other area of government. That fact should encourage local news organizations to provide thorough and continuing coverage of schools. Most journalists, however, say education is poorly covered.

The responsibility for the poor news coverage of education rests partly with journalists and partly with educators themselves. Understanding what teachers and administrators are doing requires that reporters learn something about curriculum, educational methodology and child psychology, among other things. These are difficult subjects to master, so many news organizations simply focus on what school boards decide or top administrators say. Yet such coverage reveals little of what happens to children in the classroom. Educators have compounded the problem with their fondness for opaque jargon, calling libraries "learning resource centers" and schools "attendance centers." Many of them also tend to fear news coverage, sometimes out of a desire to protect students and teachers, but other times to protect themselves from criticism.

There are important stories about education that will interest readers, but they require patience and time. The Reno (Nev.) Gazette-Journal, for instance, found that rich schools were getting richer and poor schools were falling behind in spite of efforts to equalize the distribution of money for schools. A Chicago Sun-Times investigation discovered that 20 years of inadequate maintenance had left many schools in poor condition. And KIRK-TV in Houston reported that many "bilingual" teachers recruited from Central and South America spoke no English, forged college transcripts and were unprepared to teach. Other issues reporters on the education beat can and should examine include programs for bringing disabled students into mainstream classrooms, methods of teaching reading, policies for dealing with weapons in schools, and teacher pay and benefits.

Education reporters need to realize there is a hierarchy of sources in school districts and those who are highest and most often quoted may have the least knowledge of what is happening in classrooms. Boards of education usually concentrate on financial and administrative matters; rarely do they get involved in curriculum issues. The superintendent of schools has day-to-day authority to direct the district and carry out policies set by the board. Superintendents generally deal willingly with reporters, but their knowledge of the classroom is limited. In larger districts, a number of assistant superintendents and program administrators may report to the superintendent. They may have information about specific areas, such as elementary education, art education, nutrition and foreign language instruction. Principals and teachers know the most about what is happening in classrooms, but they may be among the least accessible sources.

Harcourt Brace & Company

Schools are semipublic places. Officials try to control access to school buildings to protect students and prevent disruptions of the educational atmosphere, but sometimes officials use the restrictions to harass reporters. When a lesbian group started handing out fliers at a local school, the Springfield (Mass.) Union-News sent a reporter to cover the event. The reporter was questioning demonstrators and taking photographs when the superintendent arrived and asked the demonstrators and the reporter to leave. They did, but later the superintendent sent the newspaper a letter saying that the reporter was barred from all public schools in the district and if she entered any school it would be considered trespassing. The Union-News sued to prevent the district from enforcing that decree, but the suit was withdrawn after a settlement allowed the reporter to enter schools but only to attend public meetings. In another incident, a Hackensack, N.J., reporter was arrested for trespassing when she entered a school without permission to meet a sexual assault victim who had agreed to be interviewed. The reporter was convicted in municipal court, but that decision was later reversed. Such cases are rare, but reporters who want to cover stories about classroom activities should arrange their visits in advance with the teacher and the building principal and possibly with the superintendent as well.

Some school records are closed to the public. Educational records on specific students are closed by state and federal laws. Directory information on specific students, such as name, age, address, major areas of study, and height and weight (for athletes), is usually available unless a student objects to its release. Personnel records for district employees and supervisors usually are confidential, too.

Although student and personnel records are closed, state laws open other records that can assist reporters. All records on school district revenues and expenditures are open to the public. In spite of the confidentiality of personnel records, some salary information is likely to be public. Sometimes only salary ranges or salary scales are available. Other states make public the salaries of employees in specific positions. In addition, districts and individual schools usually prepare a variety of reports for state education officials. School districts may submit several reports describing curriculum, personnel, students and district finances. Reporters probably can find records about the school lunch program, including analyses of menus and receipts and expenditures. If a district operates school buses, it probably keeps inspection and servicing records on those buses. State officials also may inspect individual districts on a regular basis for accreditation or approval. The reports of these inspections, which may include recommendations for upgrading school facilities, curriculum or personnel, can give reporters criteria for evaluating school performance and progress over time. The range of records may be great. Officials in a state's department of education can give reporters information about what records are kept by schools in the state.

COURTS

Much of what Americans know about the judicial system comes from the trial of O.J. Simpson on charges that he murdered his ex-wife, Nicole Brown Simpson, and Ronald Goldman. That trial was televised in its entirety, and although many Americans saw little or nothing of the proceedings, many others followed them closely. The public certainly learned a lot from that trial—about police procedures, about DNA evidence and about how trials are conducted—but in fact the Simpson case was not typical. For one thing, most crimes never result in trials. They go unreported or unprosecuted, or the defendant negotiates a plea bargain. For another, the criminal cases that do go to trial are seldom as long or theatrical as Simpson's. One rarely sees attorneys attacking each other in court or in news interviews, jurors accusing one another of bias or racism, or analysts providing instant criticism of a judge's rulings.

Even if most trials lack the ballyhoo of O.J. Simpson's, they still can form the stuff of interesting and important news stories. Crimes disrupt the community and challenge its moral order. People want to know that the moral order will be maintained. They also want to know that law enforcement officers, prosecutors, defense attorneys and judges are doing their jobs. As the Simpson trial entered its final weeks, the people of Philadelphia were confronting evidence that a band of rogue police officers had lied, destroyed some evidence, planted other evidence and used beatings to extract confessions. These revelations cast doubt on hundreds of criminal prosecutions and led to the freeing of many people who had been wrongly imprisoned. The Philadelphia case was less sensational than the Simpson trial, but it demonstrates how the public can benefit from news coverage of the criminal justice system.

General Information about the Court System

Criminal cases begin when the state charges someone with violating a criminal statute. Courts also hear cases in which one individual sues another. These are called civil cases and they involve such matters as divorce, contracts, personal injury, antitrust issues and more. Civil cases rarely attract the same degree of press attention as criminal cases, but they may change more lives. The outcome of the O.J. Simpson trial affected few people other than Simpson and the relatives of the victims. While Simpson was being tried, a New Mexico woman won $2.9 million in damages (later reduced to $640,000) in a civil suit against the McDonald's restaurant chain. She said she was severely burned when she took the lid off a cup of coffee to add cream and sugar and spilled it on her groin. The coffee was served at 180 to 190 degrees. As a result of that suit and the publicity it received, McDonald's and other fast food restaurants started placing warnings on coffee cups that the beverages are served very hot. News stories and editorials—some of which were inaccurate—inspired outrage over this case and made reform of the legal system a major political issue.

Knowledge of the court system is important for all reporters, not just those who make the courts their beat. Courts are important sources for all kinds of information. Business reporters, education reporters, even sports reporters may follow paper trails to state and federal courts. A business reporter may want to find information about a corporation that plans to locate a new factory in the community. The corporation's public relations office may provide a lot of facts, but only what the corporation is willing to release. To go beyond that, other sources are needed, and one possibility is court records. If the corporation has sued or been sued, it will have disclosed a lot of information to the other party as part of a pretrial process called discovery. Some of that information may become part of the court record available to the public. The records are likely to reveal the corporation's finances, structure and operating style.

Court systems vary from state to state, but the general outlines are similar, and all resemble the federal court system. The federal system has three tiers. The lowest level is the district court, where a case is first heard before a judge and jury. The intermediate level is the U.S. Court of Appeals, which has 13 circuits and hears appeals from losing parties in both criminal and civil cases. The highest level is the U.S. Supreme Court, which also hears appeals but only when the justices think a given case involves an important legal issue, when lower courts have reached conflicting results or when a decision seems contrary to established law. In addition, the federal system has specialized courts, such as bankruptcy, tax and claims courts, which hear only cases of a particular nature.

State court systems usually have three tiers corresponding to those in the federal system, but the names of the courts may differ. In California, the trial courts are called superior courts; in New York, supreme courts. Elsewhere they may be called circuit courts or district courts. The intermediate courts may be known as courts of appeal or appellate divisions; like the federal appeals courts, they hear cases where the losing party in the trial court believes the law was not properly applied. Each state also has a final appellate court, but again the names vary. In New York, the Court of Appeals is that state's highest appellate court. In Massachusetts, it is called the Supreme Judicial Court. Most states call it the supreme court. States, too, may have specialized lower courts, such as small claims courts, municipal courts, juvenile courts and others.

The steps in a court case are similar for criminal and civil cases, but there are differences that may affect news coverage. Also, court procedures may differ from one state to another or between federal and state courts. Reporters who are going to cover courts regularly should spend some time with local judges, prosecutors and defense attorneys to learn the procedures in the state. Bar and press associations have collaborated in many states to produce handbooks for reporters. These handbooks can be valuable resources as reporters follow court cases, both criminal and civil. What follows is a summary of some of the major phases in criminal and civil cases and issues they present for news coverage.

Criminal Cases

Pretrial Stages

Court action in a criminal case usually begins when a complaint is filed against the defendant. This happens at the initial appearance, when the defendant is brought before a judge and informed of the charges. Misdemeanors can be settled at this level. If the case is a felony, the judge sets bail and a date for a preliminary hearing.

The purpose of the preliminary hearing is to persuade a judge that the state has probable cause to believe that a crime has been committed and that the defendant committed it. Preliminary hearings are open to the press and public, but judges and attorneys may worry that the press and public will hear facts that are prejudicial to the defendant but that will never be introduced at the trial. Judges may try to avoid this problem by sealing statements and evidence and by closing portions of the preliminary hearing. At the end of the preliminary hearing, the judge may either free the defendant or have the defendant bound over for trial.

Most states use preliminary hearings in place of grand jury action. Only about half the states use grand juries, and their use is often limited to investigating public corruption or some similar task. In the federal system, however, no person can be tried for a felony unless that person has been indicted by a grand jury. Grand jury proceedings are closed to the press and public, but reporters can sit outside grand jury rooms and observe the people who are brought in to testify. Members of a grand jury and attorneys are sworn to secrecy. Anyone who violates that oath risks being charged with contempt of court. Reporters who publish stories based on grand jury leaks may be subpoenaed to testify about their sources; if they refuse to identify the sources, they may be held in contempt. Federal grand jury witnesses usually are free to talk to reporters and to describe their testimony after they have been examined, but witnesses in some states are sworn to secrecy. The U.S. Supreme Court has limited the ability of states to impose secrecy requirements on witnesses. The court, in declaring a Florida statute unconstitutional, said the state's interest in secrecy does not outweigh the free speech rights of the witness once the grand jury's investigation is complete. When the grand jury finds probable cause to believe the defendant committed a crime, then it will vote a bill of indictment, or a "true bill." Grand juries also may issue presentments, which give the results of their investigations.

Once defendants have been charged either by a grand jury indictment or by an information filed by a prosecutor, they are arraigned in the trial court. The defendants enter their pleas, and trial dates are set. Because defendants have a constitutional right to a speedy trial, trials usually begin within two or three months of arrest, unless the defense requests delays. Before the trial begins, both sides must disclose all their witnesses and exhibits to each other. Also, the defense and the prosecution at any time may reach a plea agreement, which usually requires the defendant to plead guilty to a lesser charge or to some of the charges if others are dropped.

Trial

The trial begins with the selection of 12 jurors (unless the judge alone hears the case in what is called a bench trial). Prospective jurors are asked whether they have a connection to the case or

Harcourt Brace & Company

any of the people involved. If they do, they can be dismissed. Attorneys for each side also have a limited number of opportunities to dismiss prospective jurors without giving a reason. These are called peremptory challenges, and lawyers use them to exclude jurors who they believe will view their clients unfavorably.

Jury selection, like the rest of the trial, is almost always open to the public and the press, although in highly publicized cases, the court may protect the jurors' identities. The prospective jurors may be referred to by number rather than by name. In this way overly eager reporters and people with opinions about the case cannot reach a juror by telephone or in person.

The presentation of testimony is always open to the public, unless some overriding interest justifies closing the courtroom. Such an interest might be the protection of a child from the emotional trauma of testifying in public about a sexual assault. Documents introduced as evidence become court records and also are open to the public. Here, too, the court may limit access in certain cases. For example, the court may prohibit public access to or copying of photographs, audiotapes or videotapes containing salacious or gory material.

Stories about court proceedings should provide specific summaries of each day's proceedings. Mistakenly, beginners often emphasize a witness' identity or topic instead of summarizing what the witness specifically said about the topic. Leads usually do not have to reveal whether a witness testified for the state or defense; that can be reported later. The news—a summary of the witness' most telling remarks—is more important:

> VAGUE: The trial of William Allen Lee, who is accused of shooting his girlfriend, began Tuesday with the testimony of a prosecution witness who described what he saw on the day of the murder.
> REVISED: A neighbor testified Tuesday that he saw William Allen Lee shoot his girlfriend, then carry her body into a house the couple shared at 914 W. 22nd St.

The trial ends when the jury delivers its verdict. Jury deliberations are closed to the public, but reporters try to talk to jurors after the trial to find out what evidence and arguments were most persuasive and how the jurors evaluated the witnesses, the attorneys and the defendant. Occasionally judges try to protect jurors from news reporters even after the trial is over. After a notorious securities fraud case, the judge advised jurors not to speak to the press and prohibited journalists from repeatedly asking jurors for interviews. A federal appeals court ruled that this order violated the First Amendment rights of news organizations. The appeals court left intact that part of the trial court's order prohibiting journalists from asking jurors about comments by or opinions of other jurors.

Post-Trial

If the trial ends in acquittal of the defendant, the reporter will want to interview the defendant, the defense attorney, the prosecutor, the jurors and the witnesses for a post-trial wrap-up. If the defendant is convicted, the next major step is sentencing. Congress and state legislatures in recent years have taken away some of the discretion judges traditionally have had in imposing sentences. Nevertheless, judges still can impose sentences within fairly broad ranges, depending on the crime. Convicts usually undergo a series of examinations by psychologists and penologists to determine the appropriate sentence. These officials' recommendations are contained in presentence evaluations. The severity of the sentence depends partly on these evaluations and partly on other factors, such as any mitigating or aggravating circumstances associated with the crime. Presentence evaluations are closed to the public, although some of the information in them may come out at the sentencing hearing, which is open to the public.

A convicted defendant always may appeal, but to succeed, he or she must show that the trial court made some error of law that was so grave as to warrant reversing the conviction and ordering a new trial. Appeals courts are reluctant to do so. Nevertheless, the appeals process may go on for years, particularly in cases where the death penalty has been imposed. Appeals may be heard in a number of state and federal courts.

Harcourt Brace & Company

Civil Cases

Pre-Trial

A civil case begins when one party files a complaint in court against another party. The person filing the complaint is the plaintiff and the other party is the defendant. The complaint states the factual and legal basis for the lawsuit and tells the court what kind of relief the plaintiff wants. In many cases, the plaintiff wants money to compensate for injuries, lost wages, lost property or misfortunes arising from the defendant's conduct. Other times, the plaintiff may ask for a court order prohibiting the defendant from doing something or requiring the defendant to do something. This is called equitable relief. Plaintiffs may ask for both kinds of relief in some cases.

Reporters should be skeptical of the amounts of money demanded in lawsuits. Plaintiffs can demand any amount they want, even though it is obviously exorbitant. To attract news coverage, some lawyers encourage their clients to demand huge amounts, often hundreds of thousands of dollars, as compensation for minor injuries. The plaintiffs normally settle for much less, often a small fraction of what they demanded. Consequently, news story leads generally should not emphasize the amount demanded.

The complaint presents only the plaintiffs' charges; defendants are likely to deny those charges, and a judge or jury may decide (months or even years later) that the charges are unfounded. Thus, a news story should indicate clearly that the charges are the plaintiffs' allegations, not accepted facts. For example:

> Because of the accident, Samuelson will require medical care for the rest of his life.
> REVISED: Samuelson's lawsuit says he will require medical care for the rest of his life.

Whenever possible, the story should include the defendant's response to the charges. If legal documents do not include the defendant's response, reporters often can obtain it by calling the defendant or his or her attorney. The following example and revision illustrate the inclusion of a defendant's response. They also illustrate the need to condense, to simplify and to attribute the claims in a plaintiff's lawsuit:

> He was caused to slip, trip and fall as a direct result of the negligence and carelessness of the store because of a liquid on the ground. This fall injured his neck, head, body, limbs and nervous system and caused him to be unable to lead a normal life and to lose his normal wages for a prolonged period of time.
> REVISED: The suit charges that he slipped and fell on a wet sidewalk outside the store, dislocating his arm and shoulder and tearing several ligaments.
> The store's manager responded, "He was running to get out of the rain and slipped and fell on the wet pavement."

If the defendant cannot persuade the court to dismiss the complaint, he or she must file an answer, which sets forth his or her version of the facts and interpretation of the law. Both the complaint and the answer are public records.

As the case goes forward, both sides engage in the discovery process, during which each side takes sworn statements from witnesses and from the opposing parties. They seek documents and other evidence from each other. The discovery process happens outside of court, and the press and public have no right of access to it. Information exchanged between the lawyers for the two sides remains confidential unless it is filed with the court. Even then, the side producing the information may ask that the court impose a seal or restrictive order on information that is highly personal or that might disclose trade or business secrets.

In some jurisdictions, the practice of sealing the records in court cases has become almost routine. Reporters have even found cases with names like *Sealed* v. *Sealed*. Sealing court records offers something for everyone involved in the case: Defendants want records sealed to avoid bad publicity; plaintiffs sometimes can get larger payments from defendants in return for

Harcourt Brace & Company

agreeing to seal records; and judges like anything that encourages pretrial settlements and reduces caseloads. But the practice deprives the public and even government agencies of information about problems and about how the courts function. The U.S. Food and Drug Administration, for instance, was ignorant of the problems women were experiencing with silicone breast implants because of secrecy provisions imposed in the many lawsuits filed against the implant makers. Some states have tried to limit the sealing of court records in recent years, either through legislation or through changes in court rules.

Trial

The civil trial proceeds much as a criminal one, and it is usually just as open to the press and public. The trial may be heard by a judge, who decides the case alone, or by a jury. Some states use juries that have fewer than 12 members to hear civil cases.

A civil trial, like a criminal one, ends with the jury presenting its verdict. However, a civil trial is more likely to be halted by a settlement between the parties. At any time in a lawsuit, the two sides may reach an agreement to end it. Judges usually encourage such settlements, preferably before trial but even after the trial has started. The parties to the case usually keep secret the terms of any agreement. Sometimes, however, a settlement must have court approval and so may become public record.

Post-Trial

The losing party in a civil case may ask the judge to set aside the jury's verdict and render a verdict in his or her favor; this is called a judgment notwithstanding the verdict. The loser also may ask for a new trial. Neither request is granted frequently. More commonly, the losing party appeals the verdict to a higher court. Again, the loser must argue that the trial court committed a legal error so serious as to warrant a reversal of the verdict or a new trial. Appeals are usually unsuccessful.

A NOTE ABOUT THIS CHAPTER'S EXERCISES

Many of the documents available to a public affairs reporter—lawsuits and police reports, for example—provide all the information needed for minor stories. Examples of such documents are reprinted in the following exercises. Write a news story about each document. Unless the instructions say otherwise, assume that the police reports have been prepared by officers who investigated incidents in your community, and that all the other legal documents have been filed in your city hall, county courthouse or federal building.

Most of the exercises use genuine copies of actual government documents. Even the most unusual police reports are based on actual cases.

CHECKLISTS FOR PUBLIC AFFAIRS REPORTING

Crimes and Accidents

1. Spend time at the police station and talk to officers; try to learn their concerns.
2. Get as much information as possible from the investigating officers, witnesses, victims and suspects.
3. Learn what records are available at the police station and what information they contain and do not contain.
4. When writing crime stories, avoid implying that a suspect is guilty.
5. Avoid referring to a suspect's race or religion unless it is clearly relevant to the story.

Local Government

1. Learn how your local governments are organized, what their powers and limitations are and how the various governmental units interact.
2. Study the budgets of units of local government and learn how they raise their money.
3. Develop a routine for visiting the local government offices on your beat, and become familiar with the people who work in those offices.
4. Learn what public records are kept in each office and how to use them.
5. Go beyond covering school board meetings; visit schools and talk to principals, teachers, parents and students.

Courts

1. Remember that the state files criminal charges against people suspected of violating criminal laws, whereas civil cases are usually between private parties.
2. Learn how courts are organized in your state, the names of the various courts and what kinds of cases they hear.
3. Learn how court records are kept and how to find the records on any particular case.
4. Do not imply that a defendant in a criminal case is guilty; only the jury can decide that.
5. Be skeptical of allegations and damage claims that appear in civil complaints; they present only one side of the story.
6. Be alert to the possibility that a plea bargain or a settlement will end a case before or during a trial.

SUGGESTED READINGS

Blau, Robert. *The Cop Shop: True Crime on the Streets of Chicago*. Reading, MA: Addison-Wesley, 1993.

Buchanan, Edna. *The Corpse Had a Familiar Face*. New York: Random House, 1987. (Reprinted in paperback by Charter Books.)

Campbell, Don. *Inside the Beltway: A Guide to Washington Reporting*. Ames, IA: Iowa State University Press, 1991.

Gelman, Mitch. *Crime Scene: On the Streets with a Rookie Police Reporter*. New York: Times Books, 1992.

Griffin, Robert J., Dayle H. Molen, Clay Schoenfeld and James F. Scotton, with others. *Interpreting Public Issues*. Ames, IA: Iowa State University Press, 1991.

Kelly, Patricia A. *Police and the Media: Bridging Troubled Waters*. Springfield, IL: Charles C. Thomas, 1987.

Killenberg, George M. *Public Affairs Reporting: Covering the News in the Information Age*. New York: St. Martin's Press, 1992.

McIntyre, Bryce T. *Advanced Newsgathering*. New York: Praeger, 1991.

Press, Charles, and Kenneth Verburg. *American Politicians and Journalists*. Glenview, IL: Scott, Foresman/Little, Brown, 1988.

Strentz, Herbert. *News Reporters and News Sources: Accomplices in Shaping and Misshaping the News*, 2nd ed. Ames, IA: Iowa State University Press, 1989.

Ward, Hiley H. *Reporting in Depth*. Mountain View, CA: Mayfield, 1991.

Weaver, Paul H. *News and the Culture of Lying*. New York: Free Press, 1994.

Weinberg, Steve. *The Reporter's Handbook: An Investigator's Guide to Documents and Techniques*, 3rd ed. New York: St. Martin's Press, 1995.

Harcourt Brace & Company

E X E R C I S E 1

PUBLIC AFFAIRS REPORTING

911 EMERGENCY: A CHILD'S HEROISM

A 6-year-old girl placed the following call to a 911 dispatcher. Assume that the girl placed the call in your city today. She is Laura Burke, the daughter of Lynn and Randy Burke of 412 Wilson Avenue.

Police arrested a neighbor, Andrew Caspinwall of 416 Wilson Avenue, and charged him with raping Mrs. Burke. Bail has been set at $250,000, and Caspinwall, 24, is being held in the county jail.

DISPATCHER:	"911 emergency. Hello?"
GIRL:	"My mommy needs help."
DISPATCHER:	"What's wrong?"
GIRL:	"Somebody's hurting my mommy."
DISPATCHER:	"Where do you live?"
GIRL:	"At home with my mommy and daddy."
DISPATCHER:	"No, uh, that's not what I mean. Can you tell me where your house is, your address?"
GIRL:	"Wilson Avenue."
DISPATCHER:	"Do you know the address, the number?"
GIRL:	"Hurry. My mommy's crying."
DISPATCHER:	"No, honey, do you know your address?"
GIRL, CRYING:	"I gotta think. It's, uh, it's, uh, 4 something, I'm not sure. 412. 412."
DISPATCHER:	"OK. I'll send help."
GIRL, CRYING:	"Hurry."
DISPATCHER:	"What's your name?"
GIRL:	"Laura. Laura Anne Burke."
DISPATCHER:	"Can you tell me what's wrong, who's hurting your mother?"
GIRL:	"A man. He came in the back door and hit my mommy."
DISPATCHER:	"Where are you now?"
GIRL:	"Upstairs."
DISPATCHER:	"Does the man know you're there?"
GIRL:	"No. I'm hiding."
DISPATCHER:	"Where are you hiding?"
GIRL:	"In my mommy and daddy's room. Under the bed."
DISPATCHER:	"Can you lock the door?"
GIRL:	"I don't know. Maybe."
DISPATCHER:	"Don't hang up. Just put the phone down and go lock the door. Then come back, talk to me some more."
GIRL:	"My mommy. What'll happen to my mommy?"
DISPATCHER:	"We've got three police cars coming. They'll be there in a minute. Now go lock the door, and don't let anyone in until I tell you. OK?"
GIRL:	"I guess so."
DISPATCHER:	"Hello? Hello? Laura, are you there?"
GIRL:	"I locked the door."

DISPATCHER:	"How old are you, Laura?"
GIRL:	"Six."
DISPATCHER:	"You're doing a good job, Laura. You have to be brave now to help your mommy. Tell me, is the man armed?"
GIRL:	"What's that mean?"
DISPATCHER:	"Does he have a gun?"
GIRL:	"No. A knife."
DISPATCHER:	"OK, a knife. Is the man still there, Laura?"
GIRL, SOBBING:	"I don't know. I'm afraid. Will he hurt me too?"
DISPATCHER:	"No one will hurt you, Laura. Be brave. The police are outside now. They'll be coming into your house. You may hear some noise, but that's OK. Stay in the bedroom, and don't let anyone in, OK?"
GIRL:	"OK."
DISPATCHER:	"Your daddy's coming too. We've found your daddy."
GIRL:	"Soon?"
DISPATCHER:	"The police say they're in your house. They're helping your mommy now. They've found your mommy, and they're going to take her to a doctor, a hospital."
GIRL:	"The man?"
DISPATCHER:	"He's been caught, arrested. It's OK. It's safe to go downstairs now. There are people there to help you. They want to talk to you, Laura. Can you unlock your door and go downstairs? Laura? Hello? Are you there? Laura? Hello? Laura?"

E X E R C I S E   2

PUBLIC AFFAIRS REPORTING

911 EMERGENCY: THE DAHMER TAPES

Police officers in Milwaukee, Wis., found 11 mutilated bodies in an apartment rented by Jeffrey L. Dahmer. Dahmer, 31, confessed to killing a total of 17 people, and pleaded that he was insane. One of Dahmer's victims was a 14-year-old Laotian boy, Konerak Sintha-somphone, whom the police might have saved. When he was finally arrested, Dahmer told police that two officers had been at his apartment two months earlier to investigate a 911 call involving the 14-year-old. The officers left the boy at the apartment, and Dahmer then killed him.

The police later released this transcript of the 911 call. It reveals that a Milwaukee resident named Glenda Cleveland called the police at 2 a.m. the previous May 27. Mrs. Cleveland told a 911 dispatcher that her daughter and a niece had seen the boy on a street corner, and that the boy needed help. In a follow-up call, Mrs. Cleveland, 37, asked the officers if they were certain that the boy was an adult.

A week before the tape's release, the two officers were suspended with pay, but not identified. A lawyer representing the officers said they had seen no evidence at Dahmer's apartment to suggest that anything was wrong. Also, they believed that the naked male was a man living with Dahmer. The officers' lawyer added that they tried to interview the boy, but that he seemed to be seriously intoxicated.

Assume that the Milwaukee police (1) have already found the bodies and interviewed Dahmer, (2) suspended the officers one week ago and (3) released the transcript today. Write a news story that summarizes the transcript's content. Since this is a verbatim copy of the transcript, you can quote it directly. Include whatever background information seems necessary.

DISPATCHER: "Milwaukee emergency. Operator 71."

WOMAN: "OK. Hi. I am on 25th and State. And there's this young man. He's butt-naked and he has been beaten up. He is very bruised up. He can't stand. He is . . . butt-naked. He has no clothes on. He is really hurt. And I, you know, ain't got no coat on. But I just seen him. He needs some help."

DISPATCHER: "Where is he at?"

WOMAN: "25th and State. The corner of 25th and State."

DISPATCHER: "He's just on the corner of the street?"

WOMAN: "He's in the middle of the street. He (unintelligible). We tried to help him. Some people trying to help him."

DISPATCHER: "OK. And he's unconscious right now?"

WOMAN: "He is getting him up. 'Cause he is bruised up. Somebody must have jumped on him and stripped him or whatever."

DISPATCHER: "OK. Let me put the fire department on the line. They will send an ambulance. Just stay on the phone. OK?"

WOMAN: "OK."

[The dispatcher transferred the call to the fire department and the woman asked for an ambulance, saying a "butt-naked young boy or man or whatever" needed help.]

WOMAN: "He's been beaten up real bad. . . . He can't stand up. . . . He has no clothes on. He is very hurt."

FIRE
DEPARTMENT
DISPATCHER: "Is he awake?"

WOMAN: "He ain't awake. They are trying to get him to walk, but he can't walk straight. He can't even see straight. Any time he stand up he just falls down."

DISPATCHER: "25th and State? All right. OK."

[The woman hung up. The next part of the tape is a police radio transmission of a dispatcher reporting the woman's call to a street officer.]

DISPATCHER: "36. I got a man down. Caller states there is a man badly beaten and is wearing no clothes, lying in the street, 2-5 and State. Anonymous female caller. Ambulance sent."

OFFICER: "10-4."

[A Milwaukee emergency operator received information from the sheriff's department, checking on another call that reported a male dragging a naked male who looked injured.]

EMERGENCY
OPERATOR: "OK. We will get someone out."

[The next conversation involved an officer reporting back to the dispatcher over the police radio.]

OFFICER: "36. . . . Intoxicated Asian, naked male. (Laughter.) Was returned to his sober boyfriend. (More laughter.)"

[An officer advised (C-10) that the assignment was completed (C-18) and the squad was ready for new duties (10-8). There was a 40-second gap in the tape, then:]

OFFICER: "Squad 65."

DISPATCHER: "65."

OFFICER: "Ah, give myself and 64 C-10 and put us 10-8."

DISPATCHER: "10-4 64 and 65."

OFFICER: "10-4. It will be a minute. My partner is going to get deloused at the station." (Laughter.)

DISPATCHER: "10-4."

[A woman later called Milwaukee Emergency and told the dispatcher that 10 minutes ago her daughter and niece "flagged down" a policeman after they "walked up on a young child being molested by a male guy." She said the officers took no information from the girls, and the boy was naked and bleeding. The woman said further information "must be needed." The dispatcher asked the location of the incident, and the woman repeated that her daughter's and niece's names were not taken.]

WOMAN: "The fact is a crime was being committed. I am sure you must need, you know, some kind of information based on that."

[The call was transferred, and the woman repeated the squad number and the address of the incident. The woman asked if squad car 68 "brought someone in, a child being molested by an adult that was witnessed by my daughter and niece."]

WOMAN: "Their names or nothing was taken down and I wonder if this situation was being handled. . . . What it indicated was that this was a male child being raped and molested by an adult."

[The police agent referred the call to another district after getting the address of the incident. The woman repeated her story again to another official. Eventually, she reached an officer who was at the scene.]

OFFICER: "Hello. This is . . . of the Milwaukee Police."

WOMAN: "Yes. There was a squad car number 68 that was flagged down earlier this evening. About 15 minutes ago."

OFFICER: "That was me."

Harcourt Brace & Company

WOMAN: "Ya, ah, what happened? I mean my daughter and my niece witnessed what was going on. Was anything done about the situation? Do you need their names or information or anything from them?"

OFFICER: "No, not at all."

WOMAN: "You don't?"

OFFICER: "Nope. It's an intoxicated boyfriend of another boyfriend."

WOMAN: "Well, how old was this child?"

OFFICER: "It wasn't a child, it was an adult."

WOMAN: "Are you sure?"

OFFICER: "Yup."

WOMAN: "Are you positive? Because this child doesn't even speak English. My daughter had, you know, dealt with him before, seeing him on the street."

OFFICER: "Hmmm. Yea. No. He's, he's, oh, it's all taken care of, ma'am."

WOMAN: "Are you sure?"

OFFICER: "Ma'am. I can't make it any more clear. It's all taken care of. That's, you know, he's with his boyfriend and, ah, his boyfriend's apartment, where he's got his belongings also. And that is where it is released."

WOMAN: "Isn't this, I mean, what if he's a child and not an adult. I mean are you positive this is an adult?"

OFFICER: "Ma'am. Ma'am. Like I explained to you. It is all taken care of. It's as positive as I can be. OK. I can't do anything about somebody's sexual preferences in life."

WOMAN: "Well, no, I am not saying anything about that, but it appeared to have been a child. This is my concern."

OFFICER: "No. No. He's not."

WOMAN: "He's not a child?"

OFFICER: "No, he's not. OK? And it's a boyfriend-boyfriend thing. And he's got belongings at the house where he came from."

WOMAN: "Hmmmm. Hmmm."

OFFICER: "He has got very . . . pictures of himself and his boyfriend and so forth. So . . . ."

WOMAN: "Oh, I see."

OFFICER: "OK."

WOMAN: "OK. I am just, you know, it appeared to have been a child. That was my concern."

OFFICER: "I understand. No, he is not. Nope."

WOMAN: "Oh. OK. Thank you. 'Bye."

Harcourt Brace & Company

EXERCISE 3

PUBLIC AFFAIRS REPORTING

Submitting Agency __Fire Department__					Name of Deceased (last, first, & middle) Lora Anne and Karen Lynn Dolmovich		Comp. No. 82471
Description Of Deceased	Sex	Descent	Hair	Eyes	Location of Occurrence 714 N. 23rd Street	Dist. 7	Type (Trf, Nat) Accident
Height	Weight	Age	Build	Complexion	Location of Original Illness or Injury 714 N. 23rd Street	Dist. 7	Type Orig. Rpt.

Identifying Marks & Characteristics	Date/Time Original Ill/Inj. 8 p.m. yesterday	Occupation of Deceased None	Date & time Rptd to P.D. 8:05 p.m.
See below	Date/Time Deceased Discovered 8:05 p.m. yesterday	Date/Time Death Occurred 8 p.m. yesterday	Relatives Notified By Were on scene
Clothing and Jewelry Worn None	Removed To (Address) Mercy Hospital		Removed By Paramedics
	Probable Cause of Death Electrocution	Reason (quarrel - illness - revenge - etc.) Accidental	
Deceased's Residence Address 714 N. 23rd Street	Investigation Division or Unit Notified & Persons Contacted Coroner's Office		
Deceased's Business Address None	**DEATH REPORT**		UCR 48-B-8216

CODE: R- Person Reporting Death   D- Person Discovering Death   I- Person Identifying Deceased   W- Witness   Day Phone ——— X

CODE	Nearest Relative	Relationship	Notified	Address	City	I	Phone	X
RDI	Sandra M. Dolmovich		☐YES ☐NO	Res. 714 N. 23rd St. Bus. 2318 N. Main Street	Yours Yours		824-2791 365-7884	
	Name			Res. Bus.				
				Res. Bus.				

Doctor in Attendance None	Business Address	Phone

Source of Call (How notified & By Whom)
Call came from girls' mother. Rescue Squad paramedics dispatched at 8:06 p.m.

Medical Examiner's Name Marlene Stoudnour	Medical Examiner Case No. SD-24-8928

DISPOSITION OF PROPERTY   [X] RELEASED TO M.E.   RECEIPT [X] YES ☐ NO   ADDRESS _____

☐ RELEASED TO RELATIVES   NAME _____

(1) Reconstruct the circumstances surrounding the death. (2) Describe physical evidence, location found & give disposition.

Sandra M. Dolmovich, natural mother of Lora Anne Dolmovich, age 3, and Karen Lynn Dolmovich, age 5, reports that shortly after dinner last night she left her two girls playing in a bathtub as she straightened up the kitchen. After a few minutes, when the mother could not hear the girls splashing around, she went into the bathroom to check. She found both the girls lying face down in the water. A hair dryer, which was plugged in, was also in the water. The victims' mother says she normally kept the hair dryer on a radiator next to the bathtub. She says she immediately pulled the cord and then pulled both girls from the water and called the Fire Department Rescue Squad. The dispatcher received the call at 8:05 p.m. and paramedics Svendsen and Povacz reached the scene at 8:11 p.m. They report finding no heartbeat and immediately administered CPR and oxygen at the scene. Not getting any response, they took the victims to Mercy Hospital, where they were both pronounced dead on arrival at the emergency room. The victims' mother says she used the hair dryer in the bathroom each morning and that her girls sometimes played with it. It has a warning against immersion imprinted in the plastic body of the dryer. Autopsies are scheduled for tomorrow.

If additional space required, use reverse side.

Supervisor Approving Haskell	Emp. No. 1481	Interviewing Officer(s) Svendsen and Povacz	Emp. No.	Person Reporting Death (signature) X
				Indexed Yes	Checked Yes

602-07-21A   **DEATH REPORT**

Harcourt Brace & Company

EXERCISE 4

PUBLIC AFFAIRS REPORTING

POLICE DEPARTMENT

STOLEN PROPERTY

OFFENSE (GRAND OR PETIT) Grand	U.C.R. CLASSIFICATION FR-721-83-4498	CR NO. 14	SHIFT NO. 1	CASE NO. 83-4751

NAME AND ADDRESS OF OCCURRENCE Bert's Shell Station, 4800 Conway Road	AREA 7	OCCURRED (DATE & TIME) 11 a.m. yesterday	DAY OF OFF. Yesterday	DISP. 9:07a	ARR. 9:15	IN SER. 9:40	DATE OF REP. Today

OWNER OF PROPERTY Rene J. Firment	AGE - SEX - RACE 19 M W	RESIDENT ADDRESS 2474 Colyer Road	RES. PHONE 350-6974	BUSINESS ADDRESS 4800 Conway Road	BUSINESS PHONE 644-0292

REPORTED BY Same as above

DISCOVERED BY Same as above

WITNESSED BY None

OWNERS OCCUPATION Service station attend.	TYPE OF PREMISES (RES. OR BUS.) Service Station		LOCATION OF PROPERTY STOLEN

MODEL NO. - SERIAL NO. - CALIBER	METHOD USED TO COMMIT CRIME Swindle	GENERAL TYPE OF PROPERTY TAKEN Cash	INSURANCE COMPANY

COST OF PROPERTY (NEW AND AT TIME OF THEFT) $100		MODUS OPERENDI		NO. PRIOR THEFTS REPORTED

VEHICLE USED BY OFFENDERS	MAKE	MODEL	YEAR	BODY STYLE	COLOR	LICENSE	STATE	YEAR
None seen								

☐ SUBJECT ☐ SUSPECT ☐ JUVENILE	AGE - SEX - RACE	RESIDENCE ADDRESS Unknown	INCARCERATED YES ☐ NO ☒ No	WHERE	OCCUPATION

KIND OF PROPERTY RECOVERED None	VALUE	PROPERTY RECEIPT	DETECTIVE NOTIFIED -- DATE AND TIME

REMARKS (INCLUDED DETAILED DESCRIPTION OF PROPERTY TAKEN) Firment said a very well dressed young couple, both about 30, walked into the service station at about 11 a.m. yesterday, and the woman asked to use the restroom. While she was in the restroom, the phone rang, and Firment said he answered it in the station office from a man who told him his wife had left her wedding ring on a bathroom sink at the station. The caller said the ring was a genuine diamond worth $2,000 and offered a $200 reward if the ring was found. As Firment was still on the telephone, the woman then walked out of the restroom with a ring, and Firment told her of the offer. The couple said they were on their way to a friend's wedding and couldn't wait for the reward. The caller, who was still on the phone at that point, told Firment to give the couple $100 and said Firment would receive the $200 when he came down to pick up the ring later in the afternoon, so the couple and Firment would split the reward 50-50. Firment said he then proceeded to give the couple the suggested amount, and they left, walking south on Conway Road. The caller never came to the station yesterday, and Firment said he went to a jeweler early today and determined that the ring was a fake and worth only about $6. He called the department at about 9 a.m. today. He was unable to provide clear descriptions of either perpetrator and said he didn't see them get into a vehicle of any kind. Detectives will interview him later today and try to get some kind of description.

REPORTING OFFICER'S SIGNATURE Cullinan	BADGE NO. 4287.3	AREA	APPROVED BY Forsythe	PERSON REPORTING CRIME Rene Firment

(A)

(B)

				STATE TWX MSG. NO.
				LOCAL TWX MSG. NO.

REFERRED TO: Detective Bureau

SUPERVISOR: E. G.

DISPOSITION	☐ CLEARED BY ARREST	☐ EXCEPTIONALLY CLEARED	☐ UNFOUNDED	☐ PENDING

CT 284

E X E R C I S E   5

PUBLIC AFFAIRS REPORTING

POLICE DEPARTMENT

STOLEN PROPERTY

U.C.R. CLASSIFICATION 84762.41	CR NO. 11	SHIFT NO. 2	CASE NO. 89306411

OFFENSE (GRAND OR PETIT)
Grand

NAME AND ADDRESS OF OCCURRENCE
3405 Virginia Ave.

AREA 7

OCCURRED (DATE & TIME) Sometime in the past week

DAY OF OFF Unknown

DISP. 8:20a

ARR. 8:32

IN SER. 10:12a

DATE OF REP. Today

OWNER OF PROPERTY
Dr. William J. Gulas

AGE 46 SEX M RACE B

RESIDENT ADDRESS 3405 Virginia Ave.

RES. PHONE 273-1364

BUSINESS ADDRESS 851 Morse Boulevard

BUSINESS PHONE 442-8090

REPORTED BY
Mrs. Gulas

AGE 29 SEX F RACE B

" "

DISCOVERED BY
Mrs. Gulas and family

WITNESSED BY
No known witnesses

OWNERS OCCUPATION
Medical doctor

TYPE OF PREMISES (RES. OR BUS.)
Residence

LOCATION OF PROPERTY STOLEN

MODEL NO. - SERIAL NO. - CALIBER
Checking serial numbers presently

METHOD USED TO COMMIT CRIME
Front door pried open, pry marks found

GENERAL TYPE OF PROPERTY TAKEN
Household furnishings

COST OF PROPERTY (NEW AND AT TIME OF THEFT)
$20,000

MODUS OPERENDI
Used truck to move everything out of home

INSURANCE COMPANY
Prudential

NO. PRIOR THEFTS REPORTED
Two

VEHICLE USED BY OFFENDERS
Exact vehicle unknown, but probably a large truck

MAKE MODEL YEAR BODY STYLE COLOR LICENSE STATE YEAR

☐ SUBJECT ☐ JUVENILE
☐ SUSPECT

AGE - SEX - RACE

RESIDENCE ADDRESS

WHERE

OCCUPATION

INCARCERATED ☐ YES ☐ NO
DATE AND TIME

KIND OF PROPERTY RECOVERED
None

VALUE
None

PROPERTY RECEIPT

DETECTIVE NOTIFIED

REMARKS (INCLUDE DETAILED DESCRIPTION OF PROPERTY TAKEN) The family, including four children, had been vacationing in New Orleans for a week and got home at about 8:20 this morning and found the house totally looted. Almost everything is gone. All their furniture, clothes, appliances, yard tools, dishes, etc. Even the rugs were pulled up. About the only thing left were the drapes, so everything looks normal from the outside. Whoever was responsible must have had plenty of time, since they even took food from the kitchen shelves, plus the kitchen stove, refrigerator, a washer and a dryer, and a freezer the family says was half full of meat. Neighbors don't report hearing anything unusual, but the house is isolated on a 1½ acre lot. The house has been robbed twice before, and the family installed a burglar alarm system they say they paid $840 for just before leaving on vacation. It's been tampered with and silenced. Even some interior doors are missing from the home. Because of the previous robberies, much of the property was new, bought as replacements for property stolen earlier. Tire marks are apparent on the front lawn but are too old to make a good impression. We're continuing to interview people in the neighborhood. Because of the previous break-ins, the family hadn't told anyone that they wouldn't be home, and no one was checking the house while they were out of town. The break-in is similar to one of the previous entries, and the same thieves may have returned with a truck. Little was taken in that previous entry.

REPORTING OFFICER'S SIGNATURE
(A) George Oldaker

BADGE NO. 310

AREA 2

APPROVED BY
D.N.

PERSON REPORTING CRIME
Mrs. Gulas

STATE TWX MSG. NO.

LOCAL TWX MSG. NO.

REFERRED TO: Detective Bureau

SUPERVISOR: Griffin

DISPOSITION ☐ CLEARED BY ARREST ☐ EXCEPTIONALLY CLEARED ☐ UNFOUNDED ☒ PENDING

(B)

CT 284

Harcourt Brace & Company

SHERIFF'S DEPT.

MISCELLANEOUS INCIDENT

2. CASE NO.
84761004

11. RADIO NO	12. ZONE	5. DATE	6. DISP.	7. ARR.	8. IN SERV.	64. WEATHER	14. VICTIM'S NAME	DOB 7/11/34	RES. PH. 641-7838
42	15	Yesterday	4:25 p.	4:31 p.	5:15 p.	Clear, sunny	Gregory L. Herwarth	A S R	BUS. PH. 644-2360

73. FURTHER POLICE ACTION REQUIRED	48. PROPERTY RECEIPT	150. MIRANDA WARNING READ	ADDRESS	CITY	STATE	ZIP
☒ YES ☐ NO	☐ YES ☐ NO	☒ YES ☐ NO	4401 Baltimore Avenue (Yours)			

41. PERSON OR UNIT NOTIFIED	TIME	15. REPORTED BY		
		Unknown caller		RES. PH.
		ADDRESS	CITY	STATE ZIP

50. VEHICLE USED	MODEL	MAKE	YEAR	BODY STYLE
18 foot motor boat, 45 horsepower motor				

53. COLOR	52. LICENSE TAG NO.	STATE	YEAR EXPIRES	4A. NATURE OF INCIDENT	74. DATE
White	SB45-721-63	(Yours)		Victim struck by motorboat	

55. IDENT. MARKS (ACCESSORIES,DAMAGE,ETC.)	47. STORAGE RECEIPT	10. ADDRESS OF OCCURRENCE	9. OCCURRED
	☐ YES ☐ NO	South end of Crystal Lake	Yesterday

4. U C R CLASSIFICATION (WHERE APPLICABLE)

31. ☐ SUBJECT ☐ JUV. ☒ SUSPECT ☐ UNK.	NAME	DOB 3/28/60	ADDRESS	CITY AND STATE
	Vernon Sindelar	A S R	4164 Mandar Drive	(Yours)

RES. PH. 293-5495	OCCUPATION	INCARCERATED	
BUS. PH. 644-6648		☒ YES ☐ NO	WHERE County jail, freed on $1,000 bail at 10 p.m. yesterday

DISTURBANCES NO ASSAULT	☐ NEIGHBOR DISPUTE ☐ LOUD PARTY ☐ LOUD NOISE (VEH.)	☐ TENANT-LANDLORD ☐ LOITERING ☐ DOMESTIC	☐ JUVENILE ☐ PROWLER ☐ LOUD RADIO, STEREO, ETC.	☐ BARKING DOG ☐ OTHER	☐ SHOOTING IN AREA ☐ STRAY ANIMAL ☐ FIREWORKS	☐ HEALTH LAW VIOLATION ☐ DISORDERLY CONDUCT
POLICE SERVICE	☐ OBSCENE OR THREATENING CALLS ☐ MENTAL ILLNESS ☐ INDECENT EXPOSURE	☐ FOUND PROPERTY (DRUGS,ETC.) ☐ VANDALISM ☐ LOSS PROPERTY	☐ DAMAGE TO PROPERTY ☐ ACCIDENTAL NON-TRAFFIC	☐ DANGEROUS OR HAZARDOUS SITUATION	☐ LOST TAG	☐ HUMANE SOCIETY
POLICE SERVICE	☐ SUSPICIOUS PERSON ☐ SOLICITORS ☐ SUSPICIOUS VEHICLE	☐ SUSPICIOUS INCIDENT ☐ DOG BITE ☐ OTHER	☐ TRAFFIC HAZARD ☐ IMPROPER PARKING ☐ RECKLESS DRIVING	☐ DRUNK DRIVER ☒ DRUNK PEDSTN. ☐ BOATING TROUBLE	☐ INFORMATION ☐ MAKE INVESTIGATION ☐ ASSIST OTHER AGENCY	WHAT AGENCY ☒ ACCIDENT ☐ CAPIAS ☐ OTHER
PUBLIC SERVICE	☐ OPEN DOOR/WINDOW (NO ILLEGAL ENTRY) ☐ BUILDING CHECK	☐ CONTACT MSG ☐ VERBAL ☐ NOTE	☐ UNABLE ☐ ESCORT ☐ SP. DETAIL	☐ OTHER	FAULTY, ACCIDENTAL/UNINTENDED ALARMS ☐ ROBBERY ☐ BURGLAR	☐ SILENT ☐ FIRE ☐ AUDIBLE
ACTION TAKEN	☐ SCENE SECURED ☐ NO ADDRESS / COMPLAINANT	☐ ALL PARTIES G O A ☐ CIVIL MATTER-ADVISED	☐ UNFOUNDED	GENERAL INFO. ☒ SEE NARRATIVE		70. WILL VICTIM PREFER CHARGES ☒ YES ☐ NO

1. ODCN	60. CONTACT INFORMATION
	Other witnesses: Darla and Savilla Gould, 4178 N. 11th Ave.

33. NARRATIVE   Herwarth was riding on an innertube being towed by a boat operated by his wife, Ruth. Another couple, Mr. and Mrs. Wayne Morrill of 382 Arlington Circle was in the boat with her. They say the boat operated by Sindelar approached from the west at high speed, suddenly veered straight at Herwarth, its propeller striking him and amputating his right arm at the shoulder. Herwarth was unconscious when we arrived at the scene, and an ambulance took him to St. Nicholas Hospital. His wife and the two Morrills pulled him from the water. They and witnesses allege that Sindelar stopped after the accident but did nothing to help. He appeared to be drunk, and we administered a Breath Analyzer test. He flunked, the alcohol in his blood being .14%, and we charged him with operating a power boat while under the influence of alcohol. Doctors at the hospital say Herwarth also suffered a broken collar bone and several broken ribs but is expected to survive.

20. REPORTING OFFICER'S SIGNATURE	ID NO.	13. DISTRICT	19. APPROVED BY	21. PERSON REPORTING CRIME
(A) Charles Cullinan	42813	7	Forsythe	Unknown caller
(B)	ID NO.	36. GRID	24. STATISTICS	22. FOREIGN AGCY.
				23. LOCAL MSG NO.

30. DISPOSITION (WRITE IN)	28. REFERRED TO	SIGNATURE	27. RECORDED BY	25. INDEXED BY	29. RELEASE REPORT
	County attorney		C.R.	M.A.	☒ YES ☐ NO

RECORDS

E X E R C I S E   7

PUBLIC AFFAIRS REPORTING

SHERIFF'S OFFICE

ZONE __1__ UNIT __#17__	**COMPLAINT REPORT**	CASE NO. __131-8864__
GRID __14__	PAGE __One__ OF __One__	OTHER AGCY CASE NO. _____
MESSAGE NUMBER __131-148__		DATE __Today__ MONTH DAY YR

TIME RECEIVED __11:35 p.m.__   TIME DISPATCHED __11:37 p.m.__   TIME ARRIVED __11:42 p.m.__   TIME IN-SERVICE __1:20 a.m.__   WEATHER __OK__

NATURE OF CASE __Armed Robbery__   CHANGED TO _____   F.S.S.__ FEL. __XX__ MISD.__

LOCATION OF OCCURRENCE (INCL. NAME OF BUSINESS/SCHOOL) __McDonald's Restaurant   3220 McCoy Road__

VICTIM: __Taylor__ (LAST)   __Marsha__ (FIRST)   __Lynn__ (MIDDLE)   AGE __29__ R/S__ DOB MO. DAY YR.

HOME ADDRESS __2012 Lincoln Avenue__   PHONE __420-9780__

CITY __(Yours)__   STATE _____   ZIP _____

BUSINESS ADDRESS __3220 McCoy Road__   PHONE __420-6064__

CITY __About 1 mile south of the city on McCoy Road__   STATE _____   ZIP _____

REPORTER ☐
WITNESS ☐ __Six other employees, all available at the restaurant__   PHONE __420-6064__

CITY __(Yours)__   STATE _____   ZIP _____

PROPERTY MISSING/STOLEN

QUAN.	ITEM	DESCRIPTION - SERIAL NO. - MFG NO. - ETC	EST. VALUE $ STOLEN	RECOVERED
		Approximately $3,700 in cash	$3,700	None

☐ MISSING ☐ SUSPECT ☐ ARRESTED ☐ WITNESS ☐ OTHER

NAME __Unknown__ (LAST) (FIRST) (MIDDLE)   AGE __ R/S__ DOB MO. DAY YR.

ADDRESS _____   PHONE _____

CITY _____   STATE _____   ZIP _____

BUSINESS OR SCHOOL ADDRESS _____

HEIGHT __ WEIGHT __ HAIR __ EYES __ COMPLEXION __ OCCUPATION _____

CLOTHING, ETC., _____

VEHICLE INVOLVED

☐ USED   ☐ STOLEN   ☐ TOWED   ☐ DAMAGED   ☐ BURGLARIZED   ☐ WRECKER   ☐ OTHER _____

YEAR __ MAKE __ MODEL __ BODY STYLE __ COLOR __ DECAL _____

LICENSE TAG NO. _____   STATE __ YEAR EXPIRES __ I.D. OR VIN NO. _____

REMARKS: _____

ENTERED FCIC/NCIC ☐ YES ☐ NO   BOLO ☐ YES ☐ NO   MESSAGE NO. _____

NARRATIVE: Taylor, manager of the restaurant, was taking inventory with two assistant managers in a back room. Four other employees were cleaning the restaurant which had closed at 11 p.m. The front doors were locked, but when an employee opened a back door to take out some trash, three robbers wearing Halloween masks forced their way in. One gunman put a revolver to Taylor's head. Another of the managers was told to round up the other employees in the building. Taylor was forced to open a safe at gunpoint while the other six employees were taken to a small lounge used by employees. The two assistant managers were made to lie face down on the floor, and the other employees were seated at a table and told to put their heads down. Taylor was brought into the room after five cash register drawers in the safe had been emptied of about $3,700. The gunmen then ordered the employees to place their pocketbooks and jewelry on the table and took them as well. The employees then were warned they would be shot if they moved as the men left. The victims waited about five minutes before leaving the room and calling for help.

DISPOSITION: __Referred to Detective Bureau__

FURTHER POLICE ACTION TAKEN   YES ☐   NO ☐   REFERRED TO __Detective Bureau__

__Deputy Cullinan__   __Forsythe__
REPORTING OFFICER'S NAME (PRINT)   I.D. NO. (INITIAL)   APPROVED BY

RECORDS

Harcourt Brace & Company

EXERCISE 8

PUBLIC AFFAIRS REPORTING

TRAFFIC ACCIDENT REPORT

MAIL TO: ACCIDENT RECORDS BUREAU, DEPT. OF HIGHWAY SAFETY & MOTOR VEHICLES

TIME & LOCATION

DATE OF ACCIDENT: Month Day Year	DAY OF WEEK Yesterday	TIME OF DAY 11:40 p. M
COUNTY (Yours)	CITY, TOWN OR COMMUNITY	LOCAL ACCIDENT REPORT NUMBER 34178004

IF ACCIDENT WAS OUTSIDE CITY LIMITS, INDICATE DISTANCE FROM NEAREST TOWN 1½ ☐ Feet ☒ Miles ☐ N ☒ S ☐ E ☐ W Of (Your City) City, Village or Township

ROAD ON WHICH ACCIDENT OCCURRED S. R. 17 Use State or County Road Number or Name ☐ Exit Ramp ☐ Entrance R. ☐ At its intersection with ☐ Influenced by intersection Highway Number or Name of Intersecting Street and Node

IF NOT AT INTERSECTION 400 ☒ Feet ☐ Miles ☐ N ☐ S ☐ E ☐ W Of County Road 41 Show nearest intersecting street or highway, bridge, RR crossing, underpass or curve

☐ Feet ☐ Miles ☐ N ☐ S ☐ E ☐ W of Node

IS ENGINEERING STUDY NEEDED (if so explain) No DO NOT WRITE IN SPACE ABOVE

TYPE MOTOR VEHICLE ACCIDENT	OVERTURNING	OTHER NONCOLLISION	PEDESTRIAN	MV IN TRANSPORT	MV ON OTHER ROADWAY	HIT AND RUN
	PARKED MV	RAILWAY TRAIN	PEDALCYCLIST	ANIMAL	FIXED OBJECT XXX	OTHER OBJECT	NON-CONTACT

VEHICLE 1

TOTAL NO. MOTOR Vehicles Involved	YEAR	MAKE Ford	TYPE (Sedan, Truck, Bus, etc.) Sedan	VEHICLE LICENSE PLATE NO. B678-510	STATE Yes	YEAR Cur.	VEHICLE IDENTIFICATION NO. 811-423084

Area of Vehicle Damage 1 2 4 | Damage Scale 1 | Damage Severity 1 | AMOUNT (Approximate) | Safety Equipment | VEHICLE REMOVED BY Bob's Shell

NAME OF INSURANCE (Liability or PIP) Allstate POLICY NO. 963-818-59 Owner ☐ Driver ☒ ☐ Owner's Request ☐ Other (Explain) ☒ Rotation List

OWNER (Print or type FULL name) Alton J. Reimer ADDRESS (Number and street) 2529 Barbados Avenue CITY and STATE/Zip Code (Yours)

DRIVER (Exactly as on driver's license) Same as above ADDRESS (Number and street) CITY and STATE/Zip Code

OCCUPATION Student	Driver's License Type A	DRIVER'S LICENSE NUMBER 471380059	STATE Yes	DATE (Month, Day, Year) OF BIRTH Age 17	RACE W	SEX M	Safety E.	Eject. X	Injury X

OCCUPANTS

	Name	ADDRESS – Number and Street	City and State/Zip Code	AGE	RACE	SEX	Safety E.	Eject.	Injury
Front center	Marlene Anne Guyer	4043 S. 28th Street		17	W	F			X
Front right									
Rear left									
Rear center									
Rear right									

VEHICLE 2 or PEDESTRIAN

YEAR	MAKE	TYPE (Sedan, Truck, Bus, etc.)	VEHICLE LICENSE PLATE NO.	STATE	YEAR	VEHICLE IDENTIFICATION NO.

Area of Vehicle Damage | Damage Scale | Damage Severity | AMOUNT (Approximate) | Safety Equipment | VEHICLE REMOVED BY

NAME OF INSURANCE (Liability or PIP) POLICY NO. Owner ☐ Driver ☐ ☐ Owner's Request ☐ Other (Explain) ☐ Rotation List

OWNER (Print or type FULL name) ADDRESS (Number and street) CITY and STATE/Zip Code

DRIVER (Exactly as on driver's license) ADDRESS (Number and street) CITY and STATE/Zip Code

OCCUPATION	Driver's License Type	DRIVER'S LICENSE NUMBER	STATE	DATE (Month, Day, Year) OF BIRTH	RACE	SEX	Safety E.	Eject.	Injury

OCCUPANTS

	Name	ADDRESS – (Number and Street)	City and State Zip Code	AGE	RACE	SEX	Safety E.	Eject.	Injury
Front center									
Front right									
Rear left									
Rear center									
Rear right									

PROPERTY DAMAGED-Other than vehicles Utility pole	AMOUNT $500	OWNER – Name State Power & Light,	ADDRESS – Number and Street 2480 S. Main Street	CITY and STATE/Zip Code

INVESTIGATOR – Name and rank (Signature) Cpl. Alvarez	BADGE NO. 3814	I.D. NO. 684172	DEPARTMENT Highway Patrol ☐ F.H.P. ☒ C.P.D. ☐ S.O. ☐ Other	DATE OF REPORT

SHEET One OF Two SHEETS

Harcourt Brace & Company

DIAGRAM WHAT HAPPENED – (Number each vehicle and show direction of travel by arrow)

INDICATE NORTH WITH ARROW

POINT OF IMPACT

Vehicle	1	2	
	☒	☐	Front
	☐	☐	Right front
	☐	☐	Left front
	☐	☐	Right side
	☐	☐	Left side
	☐	☐	Rear
	☐	☐	Right rear
	☐	☐	Left rear

DESCRIBE WHAT HAPPENED – (Refer to vehicles by number)

Reimer was trying to pass a truck driven by J. Vernon Flavell, 827 N. Pigeon Road. Flavell estimates he was traveling about 50 mph and the car was going 60 to 70 mph at the time. Skid marks confirm the car was going 59 mph. Reimer apparently lost control of the car as he pulled alongside Flavell's vehicle and his car ran off the left side of the road, struck a utility pole and stopped, rightside up, in a field 87 feet from the edge of the pavement. Neither occupant was wearing a seat belt, and Reimer was ejected through the windshield, apparently on impact with the utility pole. Guyer remained in the vehicle. Hospital officials say Reimer died of massive head injuries. The girl has been admitted to the hospital's intensive care unit with multiple internal injuries and is listed in serious condition. We were unable to interview either victim at the scene of the accident, Reimer being dead when we arrived at the scene.

WHAT VEHICLES WERE DOING BEFORE ACCIDENT

VEHICLE No. 1 was traveling ☒☒☐☐ On S.R. 17 at 59 M.P.H. Approximately

VEHICLE No. 2 was traveling ☐☐☐☐ On _____ at _____ M.P.H.

Vehicle 1 2		Vehicle 1 2		Vehicle 1 2		Vehicle 1 2	
☐ ☐	Going straight ahead	☐ ☐	Making right turn	☐ ☐	Slowing or Stopping	☐ ☐	Starting from parked position
☒ ☒	Overtaking	☐ ☐	Making left turn	☐ ☐	Changing lanes	☐ ☐	Stopped or parked
						☐ ☐	Other (explain above)

WHAT PEDESTRIAN WAS DOING

PEDESTRIAN was going ☐☐☐☐ (check one) ☐ Along ☐ Across or into _____ from _____ to _____ Color of Clothing ☐ Dark ☐ Light

☐ Crossing at Intersection	☐ Stepped into path of Vehicle	☐ Getting on or off Vehicle ☐ Playing in roadway
☐ Crossing not at Intersection	☐ Standing in roadway	☐ Hitching on Vehicle ☐ Other roadway
☐ Walking in roadway - with traffic	☐ Standing in safety zone	☐ Pushing or working on Vehicle ☐ Not in roadway
☐ Walking in roadway - against traffic	☐ Lying or Sitting on roadway	☐ Other working on roadway ☐ Other (explain above)

DRIVERS AND VEHICLES	VEHICLE 1	VEHICLE 2
PHYSICAL DEFECTS (Driver)		
VEHICLE DEFECTS		
CONTRIBUTING CIRCUMSTANCES		

ACCIDENT Characteristics						
LIGHTING CONDITION	Dark	ROAD DEFECTS	None	TRAFFICWAY CHARACTER	Light	CLASS OF TRAFFICWAYS 7
WEATHER	Overc	TRAFFIC CONTROL	None	TRAFFICWAY LANES	Two	TYPE TRAFFICWAY 3
ROAD SURFACE	Dry	TYPE LOCATION	Str.	VISION OBSCURED	No	

WITNESSES other than occupants

NAME	ADDRESS – Number and street	City and State / Zip Code
J. Vernon Flavell, 827 N. Pigeon Rd.		(Yours)

FIRST AID GIVEN BY
J. Vernon Flavell

☐ Doctor or Nurse ☐ Cert. First Aider (Police) ☐ Cert. First Aider ☐ Other (Explain)

CHEMICAL TEST: YES NO TEST RESULTS:

INJURED TAKEN TO Memorial Hospital BY: Cleary Ambulance

☒ Priv. Ambulance ☐ Other (Explain) ☐ Gov't. Ambulance

Driver No. 1 ☒ ☐ Not yet in
Driver No. 2 ☐ ☐

ARREST

NAME	CHARGE	Citation No.
NAME	CHARGE	Citation No.

PHOTOGRAPHS TAKEN
☒ Yes ☐ No
☐ Invest. Agency
☐ Other (Explain)

TIME NOTIFIED OF ACCIDENT	TIME ARRIVED AT SCENE	WAS INVESTIGATION MADE AT SCENE (If not where)	IS INVESTIGATION COMPLETE (If not why)
11:44 19 P. M	12:03 A. M	Yes	Need to interview surviving passenger

E X E R C I S E　9

PUBLIC AFFAIRS REPORTING

TRAFFIC ACCIDENT REPORT

MAIL TO: ACCIDENT RECORDS BUREAU, DEPT. OF HIGHWAY SAFETY & MOTOR VEHICLES,

TIME & LOCATION

DATE OF ACCIDENT	Month	Day	Year	DAY OF WEEK Yesterday	TIME OF DAY 11:35　p.　M

COUNTY (Yours)	CITY, TOWN OR COMMUNITY	LOCAL ACCIDENT REPORT NUMBER 34178005

IF ACCIDENT WAS OUTSIDE CITY LIMITS, INDICATE DISTANCE FROM NEAREST TOWN　4　☐ Feet　☒ Miles　N S [E] W　or　(Your city).　City, Village or Township

ROAD ON WHICH ACCIDENT OCCURRED　U.S. 141　Use State or County Road Number or Name　☐ Exit Ramp　☐ Entrance R.　☐ At its intersection with　☐ Influenced by intersection　Highway Number or Name of Intersecting Street and Node

IF NOT AT INTER-SECTION　2　☐ Feet　☒ Miles　N S [E] W　or　State Route 19　Show nearest intersecting street or highway, bridge, RR crossing, underpass or curve

☐ Feet　☐ Miles　N S E W　of Node

IS ENGINEERING STUDY NEEDED (if so explain)　None

DO NOT WRITE IN SPACE ABOVE

TYPE MOTOR VEHICLE ACCIDENT

OVERTURNING	OTHER NONCOLLISION	PEDESTRIAN	MV IN TRANSPORT	MV ON OTHER ROADWAY	HIT AND RUN
PARKED MV　xxx	RAILWAY TRAIN	PEDALCYCLIST	ANIMAL	FIXED OBJECT	OTHER OBJECT	NON-CONTACT

VEHICLE 1

TOTAL NO. MOTOR Vehicles Involved	YEAR	MAKE Buick	TYPE (Sedan, Truck, Bus, etc.) Sedan	VEHICLE LICENSE PLATE NO. 7D-8434	STATE Yes	YEAR Cur.	VEHICLE IDENTIFICATION NO. 817-93200745

| Area of Vehicle Damage | | | 4 | 5 | 6 | Damage Scale 1 | Damage Severity 1 | AMOUNT (Approximate) | Safety Equip-ment | VEHICLE REMOVED BY Halston Towing |

NAME OF INSURANCE (Liability or PIP)　Liberty Mutual　POLICY NO.　84-992-8341　Owner ☒☒　Driver ☐　☐ Owner's Request　☐ Other (Explain)　☒☒ Rotation List

OWNER (Print or type FULL name)　Mr. and Mrs. Harry Ralph Novogroski　ADDRESS (Number and street)　2891 Norris Avenue　CITY and STATE/Zip Code (Yours)

DRIVER (Exactly as on driver's license)　Harry R. Novogroski　ADDRESS (Number and street)　2891 Norris Avenue　CITY and STATE/Zip Code (Yours)

OCCUPATION Machinist	Driver's License Type A	DRIVER'S LICENSE NUMBER 74-892-4837		STATE Yes	DATE (Month, Day, Year) OF BIRTH 3/23/27	RACE B	SEX M	Safety E.	Eject.	Injury X

OCCUPANTS	Name	ADDRESS – Number and Street	City and State/Zip Code	AGE	RACE	SEX	Safety E.	Eject.	Injury
Front center									
Front right									
Rear left	Mary Ruth Novogroski	2891 Norris Ave.		15	B	F			X
Rear center	Margaret Sue Novogroski	2891 Norris Ave.		11	B	F			X
Rear right	Matthew Harold Novogroski	2891 Norris Ave.		9	B	M			X

VEHICLE 2 or PEDESTRIAN

YEAR	MAKE Chevy	TYPE (Sedan, Truck, Bus, etc.) Pickup truck	VEHICLE LICENSE PLATE NO. 7d-3680	STATE Yes	YEAR Cur.	VEHICLE IDENTIFICATION NO. 935-8780341

| Area of Vehicle Damage | 1 | 2 | 3 | | | Damage Scale 1 | Damage Severity 1 | AMOUNT (Approximate) | Safety Equip-ment | VEHICLE REMOVED BY Halston Towing |

NAME OF INSURANCE (Liability or PIP)　Not yet determined　POLICY NO.　Owner ☐　Driver ☐　☐ Owner's Request　☐ Other (Explain)　☒☒ Rotation List

OWNER (Print or type FULL name)　Donald Edward Guerin　ADDRESS (Number and street)　1045 Eastview Road　CITY and STATE/Zip Code (Yours).

DRIVER (Exactly as on driver's license)　Same as above　ADDRESS (Number and street)　CITY and STATE/Zip Code

OCCUPATION City fireman	Driver's License Type A	DRIVER'S LICENSE NUMBER 62-311-3828		STATE Yes	DATE (Month, Day, Year) OF BIRTH 11/3/56	RACE W	SEX M	Safety E.	Eject.	Injury

OCCUPANTS	Name	ADDRESS – (Number and Street)	City and State/Zip Code	AGE	RACE	SEX	Safety E.	Eject.	Injury
Front center									
Front right									
Rear left	None								
Rear center									
Rear right									

PROPERTY DAMAGED–Other than vehicles　None　AMOUNT　OWNER – Name　ADDRESS – Number and Street　CITY and STATE/Zip Code

INVESTIGATOR – Name and rank (Signature) Cpl. Alvarez	BADGE NO. 3814	I.D. NO. 684172	DEPARTMENT Highway Patrol	☐ F.N.P.　☒ C.P.D.　☐ S.O.　☐ Other	DATE OF REPORT

SHEET　One　OF　Two　SHEETS

DIAGRAM WHAT HAPPENED – (Number each vehicle and show direction of travel by arrow)

INDICATE NORTH WITH ARROW

POINT OF IMPACT

Vehicle 1	Vehicle 2	
☐	☒	Front
☐	☐	Right front
☐	☐	Left front
☐	☐	Right side
☐	☐	Left side
☒	☐	Rear
☐	☐	Right rear
☐	☐	Left rear

DESCRIBE WHAT HAPPENED – (Refer to vehicles by number)

Novogroski had experienced a flat tire and drove onto the shoulder, completely leaving the roadway with his vehicle, to change it. His wife was outside with him, apparently holding a light of some type, when vehicle #2 struck the rear of their car, crushing the couple between the two vehicles, apparently killing them outright. Guerin was not injured and was wearing a seatbelt at the time. Three children in vehicle #1 were injured and taken to Eastbrook Hospital, although the extent of their injuries was not immediately determined. Gasoline ignited, setting both vehicles totally ablaze, burning one of the children who had not yet gotten out of the car. Bystanders helped pull the child out, as did Guerin.

*WHAT VEHICLES WERE DOING BEFORE ACCIDENT

VEHICLE No. 1 was traveling ☐☐☒☐ On U.S. 141 at 0 M.P.H.

VEHICLE No. 2 was traveling ☐☐☒☐ On U.S. 141 at 50 M.P.H.

Vehicle 1	Vehicle 2		Vehicle 1	Vehicle 2		Vehicle 1	Vehicle 2		Vehicle 1	Vehicle 2	
☒	☐	Going straight ahead	☐	☐	Making right turn	☐	☐	Slowing or Stopping	☐	☐	Starting from parked position
☐	☐	Overtaking	☐	☐	Making left turn	☐	☐	Changing lanes	☒	☐	Stopped or parked
									☐	☐	Other (explain above)

*WHAT PEDESTRIAN WAS DOING

PEDESTRIAN was going (check one) ☐☐☐☐ N S E W   ☐ Along   ☐ Across or into .... from .... to ....

Color of Clothing ☐ Dark ☐ Light

☐ Crossing at intersection	☐ Stepped into path of Vehicle	☐ Getting on or off Vehicle	☐ Playing in roadway
☐ Crossing not at intersection	☐ Standing in roadway	☐ Hitching on Vehicle	☐ Other roadway
☐ Walking in roadway – with traffic	☐ Standing in safety zone	☐ Pushing or working on Vehicle	☐ Not in roadway
☐ Walking in roadway – against traffic	☐ Lying or Sitting on roadway	☐ Other working in roadway	☐ Other (explain above)

DRIVERS AND VEHICLES

	VEHICLE 1	VEHICLE 2
PHYSICAL DEFECTS (Driver)		
VEHICLE DEFECTS		
CONTRIBUTING CIRCUMSTANCES		

ACCIDENT Characteristics						
LIGHTING CONDITION	Dark	ROAD DEFECTS	None	TRAFFICWAY CHARACTER	Quiet	CLASS OF TRAFFICWAYS 4
WEATHER	Normal	TRAFFIC CONTROL	None	TRAFFICWAY LANES	2 lane	TYPE TRAFFICWAY 2
ROAD SURFACE	Dry	TYPE LOCATION	Hwy.	VISION OBSCURED	No	

WITNESSES other than occupants	NAME	ADDRESS – Number and street	City and State Zip Code
	None		

FIRST AID GIVER BY Donald Guerin

☐ Doctor or Nurse   ☒ Cert. First Aider   ☐ Cert. First Aider (Police)   ☐ Other (Explain)

INJURED TAKEN TO Eastbrook Hospital   BY Cleary Ambulance

☒ Priv. Ambulance   ☐ Gov't. Ambulance   ☐ Other (Explain)

CHEMICAL TEST: YES NO   TEST RESULTS:

Driver No. 1 ☐ ☐ ....

Driver No. 2 ☒ ☐ Negative

ARREST NAME Donald Edward Guerin   CHARGE Manslaughter   Citation No. 8320816

NAME   CHARGE   Citation No.

PHOTOGRAPHS TAKEN ☒ Yes ☐ No

☐ Invest. Agency   ☐ Other (Explain)

TIME NOTIFIED OF ACCIDENT	TIME ARRIVED AT SCENE	WAS INVESTIGATION MADE AT SCENE (If not why)	IS INVESTIGATION COMPLETE (If not why)
11:47 19 P.M	11:54 M	Yes	Yes

Harcourt Brace & Company

EXERCISE 10
PUBLIC AFFAIRS REPORTING

In the Circuit Court of
The 9th Judicial Circuit
in and for (your) County

Division: Probate

Case No.: PR 67-1381

IN RE: GUARDIANSHIP
OF PATRICIA JEAN
WILLIAMS, an Incompetent

JOHN RUSSELL
WILLIAMS, as Guardian
of the Person of
PATRICIA JEAN
WILLIAMS,   *Plaintiff,*

vs.

MERCY HOSPITAL;
ROSS R. GRAHAM,
M.D.; RICHARD M.
CESSARINI, M.D.;
RAMON HERNANDEZ,
DISTRICT ATTORNEY,   *Defendants.*

FINAL DECLARATORY JUDGMENT

THIS CAUSE came for hearing upon the Complaint for Declaratory Relief because of the uncertainty of the law by JOHN RUSSELL WILLIAMS as Guardian of the Person of PATRICIA JEAN WILLIAMS, an Incompetent, against MERCY HOSPITAL; ROSS R. GRAHAM, M.D.; RICHARD M. CESSARINI, M.D.; and RAMON HERNANDEZ, DISTRICT ATTORNEY for the city, the Defendants, wherein Plaintiff seeks a Declaratory Judgment as to the following:

Authorization for JOHN RUSSELL WILLIAMS, as Guardian of the Person of PATRICIA JEAN WILLIAMS, an Incompetent, to direct MERCY HOSPITAL; ROSS R. GRAHAM, M.D.; RICHARD M. CESSARINI, M.D.; and all other attending physicians and health care providers to discontinue and to withhold all extraordinary measures such as mechanical ventilators, respirators, antibiotics, cardiovascular or similar type drugs; that these extraordinary measures should not be utilized, but be discontinued or withheld, in that the doctors agree there is no reasonable possibility of the Ward ever recovering from her present, persistent, "vegetative" (coma-like) state, which is irreversible;

That your Petitioner, JOHN RUSSELL WILLIAMS, surviving son; MERCY HOSPITAL; ROSS R. GRAHAM, M.D.; RICHARD M. CESSARINI, M.D.; and all other treating and consulting physicians and health care providers shall not be held civilly or criminally liable for taking the above action; and

That an appropriate restraining order be issued restraining the Defendant, RAMON HERNANDEZ, DISTRICT ATTORNEY, from prosecuting any of the above named individuals and organizations for withdrawing or withholding all extraordinary measures such as mechanical ventilators, respirators, antibiotics, cardiovascular or similar type drugs.

The Court makes the following findings of fact:

1. That this action is properly brought as a suit for declaratory judgment and relief, and that Plaintiff is the proper party to bring this action.

2. That at all times material hereto, the Plaintiff is a resident of the county in which this action is brought, and PATRICIA JEAN WILLIAMS, the Ward, has been maintained at MERCY HOSPITAL since she was involved in a serious motor vehicle accident 73 days prior to the issuance of this order.

3. That the following findings are based upon reasonable medical certainty and derived from the testimony of ROSS R. GRAHAM, M.D.; RICHARD M. CESSARINI, M.D.; and the records of MERCY HOSPITAL:

   (a) That four electroencephalograms, commonly referred to as EEGs, were performed on PATRICIA JEAN WILLIAMS, the Ward. None of the electroencephalograms indicated any cortical response. The only indication was a flat line.

   (b) That the Ward has suffered severe brain damage, which brain damage is totally irreversible and untreatable with no hope of recovery; and that the Ward is in a chronic and persistent "vegetative" (coma-like) state.

   (c) That the testimony of the doctors revealed that it was their respective medical opinion that all measures which are considered extraordinary lifesaving measures should not be utilized with respect to the Ward, but be discontinued or withheld; however, the decision to withdraw or withhold extraordinary lifesaving measures should be made by the Plaintiff and the family of the Ward.

   (d) That PATRICIA JEAN WILLIAMS, the Ward, requires constant care, and will so require IN THE FUTURE.

4. That PATRICIA JEAN WILLIAMS, the Ward, requires constant care, which care invades the Ward's body and violates the Ward's right to privacy as guaranteed by the Constitution of the United States of America and of this State; and that the State does not have an overriding interest it needs to protect, nor are there overriding medical interests that need to be protected.

5. That the son, JOHN RUSSELL WILLIAMS, has determined, subject to the approval of this Court, that all extraordinary lifesaving measures should not be utilized with respect to the Ward, but be discontinued or withheld from the Ward, PATRICIA JEAN WILLIAMS, and that MERCY HOSPITAL has no objection.

It is, therefore, ORDERED AND ADJUDGED:

1. That JOHN RUSSELL WILLIAMS, as the Guardian of the Person of PATRICIA JEAN WILLIAMS, an Incompetent, has full power to make decisions with regard to the identity of the Ward's treating physicians.

2. That MERCY HOSPITAL; ROSS R. GRAHAM, M.D.; AND RICHARD M. CESSARINI, M.D., are authorized to discontinue or to withdraw all extraordinary measures and life-support systems upon written direction of JOHN RUSSELL WILLIAMS, as Guardian of the Person of PATRICIA JEAN WILLIAMS, an Incompetent.

3. That no one shall be held civilly or criminally liable for taking action authorized by this Order.
4. That the Defendant, RAMON HERNANDEZ, as District Attorney for the city, shall be bound by this decision.

DONE AND ORDERED in Chambers.

BY: _____
RANDALL PFAFF, Circuit Judge

E X E R C I S E   1 1

PUBLIC AFFAIRS REPORTING

In the Circuit Court of
The 9th Judicial Circuit
in and for (your) County

Division: Civil

Case No.: 1-78-1440

THADDEUS DOWDELL
and LAURA DOWDELL,
individually and as next friends
and parents of JAMES
DOWDELL, a minor,   *Plaintiffs,*

vs.

MARVIN FERRELL,
GREG HUBBARD
and (YOUR CITY'S)
SCHOOL DISTRICT,   *Defendants.*

C O M P L A I N T

COME NOW the Plaintiffs, THADDEUS DOWDELL and LAURA DOWDELL, individually and as next friends and parents of JAMES DOWDELL, a minor, by and through their undersigned counsel, and sue the Defendants, MARVIN FERRELL, GREG HUBBARD, AND (YOUR CITY'S) SCHOOL DISTRICT, jointly and severally, for damages and allege:

1. That this is an action for damages of $500,000, exclusive of interest, costs and further demands.
2. That at all times material to this cause, JAMES DOWDELL was and is the minor son of THADDEUS DOWDELL and LAURA DOWDELL, residing together with them in a family relationship as residents of this county.
3. That at all times material to this cause, the Defendant MARVIN FERRELL held and now holds the position of Principal of Kennedy High School, and that the Defendant GREG HUBBARD held and now holds the position of School Superintendent.
4. That the minor JAMES DOWDELL is and has been a student in Kennedy High School for the past three years and has been told that he will graduate from that school on or about the First Day of next June.
5. That the minor, JAMES DOWDELL, of this date, can barely read or do simple arithmetic and obviously has not learned enough to be graduated from high school or to function successfully in a society as complex as ours.

6. That the problem is not the fault of the minor JAMES DOWDELL, who, according to tests administered by guidance counselors at the high school, enjoys a normal IQ of 94.

7. That the failure of the minor JAMES DOWDELL to master the skills expected of high school students is the fault of the Defendants, MARVIN FERRELL, GREG HUB-BARD, and (YOUR CITY'S) SCHOOL DISTRICT, that said defendants failed to employ competent teachers, to maintain discipline, to provide remedial help, and to provide an atmosphere in which learning might take place.

WHEREFORE, the Plaintiffs, THADDEUS DOWDELL and LAURA DOWDELL, individually and as next friends and parents of JAMES DOWDELL, a minor, sue the Defendants MARVIN FERRELL, GREG HUBBARD and (YOUR CITY'S) SCHOOL DISTRICT, jointly and severally, for compensatory damages in the amount of $500,000, exclusive of interest and costs.

FURTHER, the Plaintiffs demand that the minor JAMES DOWDELL be retained in Kennedy High School until he masters the skills expected of a high school graduate.

FURTHER, the Plaintiffs demand trial by jury of all issues triable as of right by a jury.

PILOTO and HERNDON, Attorneys
1048 Westmore Drive
Attorneys for Plaintiffs

BY: _Kenneth J. Piloto_
    KENNETH T. PILOTO

E X E R C I S E 1 2

PUBLIC AFFAIRS REPORTING

WALKER LAWSUIT

INSTRUCTIONS: Write a story based on the following civil complaint filed in federal district court. This is a real case. Assume you are a reporter covering federal courts in Nebraska and this complaint was filed today. Be sure to include the response from the defendant, which follows the complaint.

IN THE UNITED STATES DISTRICT COURT
FOR THE DISTRICT OF NEBRASKA

Case No.: CV95-3189

KENNY W. WALKER, *Plaintiff*

vs.

PDB SPORTS, LTD., d/b/a
DENVER BRONCOS FOOTBALL
CLUB, INC., *Defendant.*

C O M P L A I N T

COMES NOW Plaintiff Kenny W. Walker ("Walker"), pursuant to Rule 3 of the Federal Rules of Civil Procedure, and hereby files his complaint against PDB Sports, Ltd. f/k/a PDB Enterprises, Inc. d/b/a Denver Broncos Football Club, Inc. ("Broncos"), stating and alleging as follows:

PARTIES

1. Walker is an individual and citizen of the State of Nebraska.
2. Broncos is a limited partnership organized and existing under the laws of the State of Colorado with its principal office located in Englewood, Colorado.

INTRODUCTION

3. Walker is a 28-year-old former AP All-American First Team collegiate football player from the University of Nebraska–Lincoln ("Nebraska") who was recruited and later "drafted" by Broncos for employment as a professional football player in the National Football League ("NFL"). Walker is also deaf. Walker lost his hearing at age two after a high fever associated with spinal meningitis. Despite his hearing loss, Walker proved that he could successfully play professional football in the NFL, playing in 16 games in his rookie season (1991–1992), making 16 tackles, 15 assists and three sacks as a defensive lineman and being voted by his teammates as the Most Inspirational Player for the year. Walker's second year with Broncos (1992–1993) was an even greater success, with Walker starting 15 of Broncos' 16 football games and making 20 tackles, 29 assists, 1.5 sacks and 2 fumble recoveries for the year.

Harcourt Brace & Company

4. Despite proving beyond question that a deaf person could play professional football in the NFL (Walker was the second deaf athlete to do so), upon information and belief, Broncos falsely represented to other NFL teams ("Other NFL Teams") that Walker's handicap required an unreasonable accommodation by the Other NFL Teams and otherwise created an undue hardship. Broncos also unlawfully terminated Walker's employment with Broncos due (in part) to Walker's handicap.

STATEMENT OF FACTS

5. On or about April 22, 1991, while Walker was still a resident of the State of Nebraska, Broncos selected Walker in the Eighth Round of the NFL draft.

6. On or about July 12, 1991, Walker reported to football training camp ("Camp") of Broncos. About three weeks later (while still in Camp), Broncos determined that Walker had extraordinary potential and could be a "starter." Broncos originally recruited Walker as a pass-rushing specialist because it believed there would be difficulty giving him signals, but Walker was soon considered by Broncos to be an "every-down" lineman.

7. After a very successful rookie year (1991–1992), Walker became a regular starter for Broncos (1992–1993), starting and playing as a defensive lineman in 15 games played throughout the United States.

8. On or about July 28, 1993, after Walker and Broncos had executed Contracts, Walker's Nebraska Agent executed and thereafter forwarded to Broncos from his office in Omaha, Nebraska, the original "fully executed" Contracts for the 1993–1994 and 1994–1995 seasons. Under the Contracts, Walker was entitled to receive $230,000 for 1993–1994 season and $300,000 for 1994–1995 season, $75,000 if he participated in 50% or more of the defensive plays, excluding special teams, during the regular season and other potential bonuses.

BRONCOS INTERFERENCE

9. On or about August 30, 1993, approximately six weeks after Walker's Nebraska Agent had executed and forwarded the fully executed Contracts to Broncos, Broncos terminated Walker. A few days later (in early September 1993), Walker listed for sale his home in the State of Colorado and began the process of returning to the State of Nebraska.

10. From August 31, 1993, until approximately March 1994, Walker's Nebraska Agent solicited each of the Other NFL Teams in an attempt to secure Walker a position for the 1993–1994 football season. Upon information and belief, Other NFL Teams which had a particular need for a defensive lineman received false and misleading information about Walker from Broncos, which resulted in those Other NFL Teams refusing to consider Walker for employment.

11. Upon information and belief, due to the interference by Broncos, Walker was unable to play professional football in the NFL during the 1993–1994 season and thereafter. While working from and maintaining his permanent residence in Lincoln, Nebraska, however, Walker joined the Hamilton Tigercats and soon thereafter was traded to the Calgary Stampeders ("Stampeders") of the Canadian Football League ("CFL"), for whom he has since played professional football (without the aid of an interpreter). Walker started in 18 regular season and two playoff games for the Stampeders, had 28 tackles, nine sacks and three fumble recoveries and earned CFL lineman of the week honors during the 1994–1995 season.

Harcourt Brace & Company

BRONCOS' TERMINATION OF WALKER

12. Under the Contracts, while Broncos were permitted to terminate the Contracts "at any time if in the[ir] sole judgment . . . , [Walker's] *skill or performance* ha[d] been unsatisfactory as compared with that of other players competing for positions on [Broncos'] roster . . . ," Broncos were not permitted to terminate Walker on account of his handicap. Despite his success, Broncos became increasingly annoyed with having to reasonably accommodate Walker and engaged in inappropriate conduct toward him on account of his disability. Broncos ultimately terminated Walker on or about August 30, 1993, in part due to his handicap.

13. On or about September 19, 1993, Walker's father-in-law, Dan Offenburger ("Offenburger"), a former Athletic Director at Creighton University ("Creighton") (who after resigning from Creighton began working with six national organizations for the physically disabled in sports), without Walker's knowledge or any input from Walker's Nebraska Agent or any other person, corresponded in a letter to Pat Bowlen ("Bowlen"), President and Chief Executive Officer of Broncos, requesting, among other things, that Broncos consider "bring[ing] Kenny back."

14. On September 21, 1993, Bowlen responded to Offenburger's letter, grimly advising that football is a "business," not a "game," and that Broncos' coaches had determined that Walker's "handicap made it impossible for Kenny to continue as a player":

> Thank you for your kind letter concerning Kenny Walker. . . . Unfortunately, football is a high-paying entertainment business, and we are left very little room to treat it only as a game. Our coaching staff felt that Kenny's ability *coupled with his handicap* made it impossible for him to continue as a player. (Emphasis added)

FIRST CLAIM FOR RELIEF

(Tortious Interference with Business Expectancy)

15. Upon information and belief, Broncos committed unjustified intentional acts of interference with respect to Walker's business expectancies, in that, it made statements to Other NFL Teams to the effect that Walker's hearing disability would require an unreasonable accommodation by Other NFL Teams.

16. Upon information and belief, such interference with Walker's potential employment with Other NFL Teams was made by Broncos with malice, that is, with spite or ill will toward Walker or, alternatively, with reckless disregard of the truth or falsity of the statements made to Other NFL Teams.

SECOND CLAIM FOR RELIEF

(Trade Libel)

17. Upon information and belief, Broncos made false and derogatory statements to Other NFL Teams concerning Walker's ability to play professional football in the NFL.

18. Broncos understood the statements made to Other NFL Teams were both derogatory and about Walker's ability to play professional football in the NFL.

19. Broncos' statements to Other NFL Teams were made with malice, that is, in this context, Broncos should have reasonably foreseen that the statements would convey a disparaging meaning.

THIRD CLAIM FOR RELIEF

(Negligent Misrepresentation)

20. Broncos, by and through its agents or employees, was acting in the course of its business when, upon information and belief, it supplied information regarding Walker to Other NFL Teams.
21. Upon information and belief, the information concerning Walker supplied by Broncos to Other NFL Teams was false.
22. Walker is a person for whose benefit the duty to give accurate information to Other NFL Teams was created.
23. Walker's attempt to become employed by one of the Other NFL Teams is a transaction in which the duty by Broncos to provide accurate information regarding Walker was intended to protect Walker.
24. Upon information and belief, Walker has been damaged by Broncos' failure to provide accurate information to Other NFL Teams.

FOURTH CLAIM FOR RELIEF

(Americans with Disabilities Act, 42 U.S.C. sec. 12101 *et seq.*)

25. Walker is an individual with a disability who satisfied the requisite skill, experience, education and other job-related requirements of a professional football player and thus was a "qualified individual with a disability" pursuant to 42 U.S.C. sec. 12111(8).
26. As a qualified individual with a disability, Walker had rights protected by the ADA for equal employment opportunities.
27. Broncos interfered with Walker's enjoyment of his right to equal employment opportunities with Other NFL Teams and discriminated against him in a hostile work environment and in regard to his discharge from Broncos.

WHEREFORE, Walker prays for the following relief against Broncos:

A. Under the First Claim for Relief, for lost profits and other consequential damages;
B. Under the Second Claim for Relief, for pecuniary loss resulting from the false and derogatory statements, including impairment of vendibility;
C. Under the Third Claim for Relief, for pecuniary loss suffered due to disparaging statements;
D. Under the Fourth Claim for Relief, for back pay, front pay, statutory, compensatory and punitive damages, damages for humiliation and emotional suffering, prejudgment interest, reasonable attorney's fees and costs (including expert fees); and
E. For any other or further relief allowed by the pleadings at law or in equity.

BY: _____
Bartholomew L. McLeay
Robert M. Slovek
KUTAK ROCK
1650 Farnam Street
Omaha, NE 68102

RESPONSE FROM BRONCOS

In a brief telephone conversation, the Broncos' general manager, John Beake, denies all the allegations made against the team in Walker's complaint. "We're prepared to vigorously address that in court," he tells you.

EXERCISE 13

PUBLIC AFFAIRS REPORTING

HOUSE BILL 371

INSTRUCTIONS: Write a news story about the bill reprinted here and about your state Senate's debate on the bill, which follows. You may quote the senators' remarks directly. Assume that the Senate debate and vote on the bill happened today. Assume also that your state's House of Representatives has already passed the bill by a vote of 101–23. In the text of the bill, the passages that have lines through them will be deleted from the current law, and passages that are underlined will be added to the law.

H.B. 371

An Act relating to crimes and offenses.

Section 1. Section 28-105, Revised Statutes, is amended to read:

28-105. (1) For purposes of the Criminal Code and any statute passed by the Legislature after the date of passage of the code, felonies are divided into eight classes which are distinguished from one another by the following penalties which are authorized upon conviction:

Class I felony .... Death
Class IA felony.................. Life imprisonment
Class IB felony.................. Maximum—life imprisonment
~~Minimum ten years imprisonment~~
<u>Minimum—twenty years imprisonment</u>
Class IC felony.................. Maximum—fifty years imprisonment
Mandatory minimum—five years imprisonment
Class ID felony.................. Maximum—fifty years imprisonment
Mandatory minimum—three years imprisonment
Class II felony .... Maximum—fifty years imprisonment
Minimum—one year imprisonment
Class III felony.................. Maximum—twenty years imprisonment
Minimum—one year imprisonment
Class IV felony.................. Maximum—five years imprisonment
Minimum—none

(2) <u>A person convicted of a felony for which a mandatory minimum sentence is prescribed shall not be eligible for probation.</u>
Section 2. Section 28-1205, Revised Statutes, is amended to read:

28-1205 (1) Any person who uses a firearm, <u>a</u> knife, brass or iron knuckles, or any other deadly weapon to commit any felony which may be prosecuted in a court of this state~~, or any person~~ who unlawfully possesses a firearm, a knife, brass or iron knuckles, or any other deadly weapon during the commission of any felony which may be prosecuted in a court of this state commits the offense of using ~~firearms~~ <u>a deadly weapon</u> to commit a felony.

(2) <u>(a)</u> Use of ~~firearms~~ <u>a deadly weapon other than a firearm</u> to commit a felony is a Class III felony<u>.</u>

<u>(b) Use of a deadly weapon which is a firearm to commit a felony is a Class II felony.</u>

Harcourt Brace & Company

Section 3. Section 28-1206, Revised Statutes, is amended to read:

28-1206. (1) Any person who possesses any firearm ~~with a barrel less than eighteen inches in length~~ or brass or iron knuckles who has previously been convicted of a felony or who is a fugitive from justice commits the offense of possession of ~~firearms~~ a deadly weapon by a felon or a fugitive from justice.

(2) (a) Possession of ~~firearms~~ a deadly weapon other than a firearm by a felon or a fugitive from justice ~~or a felon~~ is a Class IV felony.

(b) Possession of a deadly weapon which is a firearm by a felon or a fugitive from justice is a Class III felony.

Section 4. Section 29-2221, Revised Statutes, is amended to read:

29-2221. (1) Whoever has been twice convicted of a crime, sentenced, and committed to prison, in this or any other state or by the United States or once in this state and once at least in any other state or by the United States, for terms of not less than one year each shall, upon conviction of a felony committed in this state, be deemed a habitual criminal and shall be punished by imprisonment in a Department of Correctional Services adult correctional facility for a ~~term of not less than ten nor~~ mandatory minimum term of ten years and a maximum term of not more than sixty years, except that:

(2) If the felony committed is manslaughter, armed robbery, rape, arson or kidnapping, as those terms are defined in the Criminal Code, or vehicular homicide while under the influence of alcohol, and at least one of the habitual criminal's prior felony convictions was for such a violation or a violation of a similar statute in another state or in the United States, the mandatory minimum term shall be twenty-five years and the maximum term not more than sixty years.

Section 5. Section 29-2262, Revised Statutes, is amended to read:

29-2262. (1) When a court sentences an offender to probation, it shall attach such reasonable conditions as it deems necessary or likely to insure that the offender will lead a law-abiding life. No offender shall be sentenced to probation if he or she is deemed to be a habitual criminal pursuant to section 29-2221.

Section 6. Section 29-2525, Revised Statutes, is amended to read:

29-2525. (1) In cases where the punishment is capital, no notice of appeal shall be required and within the time prescribed by section 25-1931 for the commencement of appeals, the clerk of the district court in which the conviction was had shall notify the court reporter who shall prepare a bill of exceptions as in other cases. The Clerk of the Supreme Court shall, upon receipt of the transcript, docket the case. The Supreme Court shall expedite the rendering of its opinion on any appeal, giving the matter priority over civil and noncapital matters.

Section 7. The following shall be added to the Criminal Code of the Revised Statutes:

(1) A person commits the offense of assault on an officer using a motor vehicle if he or she intentionally and knowingly causes bodily injury to a peace officer or employee of the Department of Correctional Services (a) by using a motor vehicle to run over or to strike such officer or employee or (b) by using a motor vehicle to collide with such officer's or employee's motor vehicle, while such officer or employee is engaged in the performance of his or her duties.

(2) Assault on an officer using a motor vehicle shall be a Class IV felony.

EXCERPTS OF FINAL DEBATE IN THE SENATE

Sen. Dan Twoshoes, D-Henderson: "If a farmer finds a weasel in his henhouse, he shoots it. I wish we could do the same with some of the two-legged weasels. But at least we can lock them up and keep them away from decent people. That's what this bill will do. It increases the prison sentence for criminals who use deadly weapons—especially guns—in the commission of crimes and it increases the penalties on felons and fugitives who possess deadly weapons. This bill will keep criminals off our streets by preventing judges from placing criminals on probation when this legislature has imposed a mandatory minimum sentence. And most importantly, this bill sets a mandatory minimum sentence for habitual criminals who commit serious crimes."

Sen. Sally Ong, R-Wakarusa: "I agree with Sen. Twoshoes that we need to keep habitual criminals off our streets, and if it were not for one provision, I could support this bill. I speak of the inclusion of vehicular homicide while under the influence of alcohol as one of those offenses requiring a 25-year mandatory minimum sentence. I understand the pain felt by those who lose a loved one in an accident caused by a drunken driver. That's how my brother died five years ago. But the people who drive while drunk need help, not a 25-year prison sentence."

Sen. John Percy, D-(Your city), and chairman of the Judiciary Committee: "I want to address Sen. Ong's concerns about the vehicular homicide provision. The Judiciary Committee debated this provision extensively, and we heard testimony from many people in law enforcement and social work. It was clear to us that a person who abuses alcohol and then drives an automobile is aware that she or he is behaving recklessly. If a habitual criminal engages in such reckless behavior and causes a fatal injury, then that should be treated as an extremely serious crime."

Sen. William Antonucci, R-(Your city): "We're fooling ourselves if we think that this bill will have any impact on crime in this state. Criminals don't think they'll be caught when they rob or kill, so increasing the penalties means nothing to them. What we'll be doing is wasting money warehousing criminals for years and years. The more people we jam into our prisons, the more we are going to have to pay to operate the prisons—even if we let the prisons become pigsties. We would do better to hire more police, prosecutors and judges. We will deter more crime by increasing the chances that crooks will be caught and prosecuted than by increasing the sentences for the few who now are prosecuted."

After debate, the Senate voted 40–12 in favor of the bill. The bill now goes to the governor, Laura Riley, who must sign it before it can become law. Her press secretary says the governor supports the bill and intends to sign it.

E X E R C I S E   1 4

PUBLIC AFFAIRS REPORTING

ORDINANCE NO. 20732

An Ordinance of the City Enacting Chapter 2A, "Alarm Devices," Relating to Privately Owned General Alarm Devices: Defining Terms; Imposing upon the Owner or Manager of the Premises the Responsibility of Deactivating Alarms upon Notification to Do So; Requiring Corrective Action and the Filing of Reports; Prescribing Fees; Providing for Disconnection of Faulty Alarm Devices; Prohibiting the Installation of Telephone Alarm Devices Connected to the Police Department; and Providing for an Effective Date.

WHEREAS, malfunctions of privately owned alarm devices are causing substantial misuse of the manpower and resources of the Police Department of the City by provoking responses to numerous false alarms; and

WHEREAS, telephone alarm devices regulated or programmed to make connection with the Police Department could seize and hold Police Department telephone lines to the exclusion of other calls; and

WHEREAS, false alarms and use of telephone alarm devices create a threat or potential threat to the health, safety and welfare of the people of the City,

NOW, THEREFORE, BE IT ENACTED BY THE CITY COUNCIL THAT:

SECTION 1. Chapter 2A, "Alarm Devices," of the Code of Ordinances of the City is hereby enacted to read as follows:

Sec. 2A-1. *Definitions.* For purposes of this ordinance, the following terms shall have the following meanings:

(a) *False alarm*—the activation of a telephone alarm device or general alarm device by other than a forced entry or attempted forced entry to the premises and at a time when no burglary or hold-up is being committed or attempted on the premises, except acts of God.

(b) *First response*—a response to a false alarm to premises at which no other false alarm has occurred within the preceding six (6) month period.

(c) *Telephone alarm device*—any device which, when activated, automatically transmits by telephone lines a recorded alarm message or electronic or mechanical alarm signal to any telephone instrument installed in any facility of the Police Department.

(d) *General alarm device*—any alarm bell, light or other signaling device which, when activated, is designed to indicate a burglary or hold-up.

Sec. 2A-2. *Duty of owner or manager of premises.* Prior to the installation or use of any type of telephone device or general alarm device, the owner or manager of the premises shall furnish to the Police Department information regarding the full names, addresses and telephone numbers of at least two (2) persons who can be reached at all times and who are authorized to enter the premises and deactivate the alarm device. Owners or managers of premises with telephone alarm devices or general alarm devices already installed shall have thirty (30) days from the effective date of this ordinance to comply with the above notice requirement. If any such person shall fail to appear and reset any such alarm within one (1) hour after being notified by the Police Department to do so, then the owner or manager of the premises shall be charged a fee of forty dollars ($40.00) for the first such occurrence, and a fee of seventy-five dollars ($75.00) for each succeeding occurrence within six (6) months of the last failure to appear.

Sec. 2A-3. *Responses to false alarms; corrective action and reports required; fees charged.*

(a) *Corrective action and report required.* For each response by the Police Department to a false alarm, the owner or manager of the premises involved shall, within three (3) working days after notice to do so, make a written report to the Chief of Police, on forms provided by him, setting forth the cause of the false alarm, the corrective action taken, the name, address and telephone number of the service man, if any, by whom the device has been inspected or repaired, and such other information as the department may reasonably require to determine the cause of the false alarm and what corrective action has been taken or may be necessary.

(b) *Fees charged.* There shall be no fee charged for a first response to premises or for a second or third response within six (6) months after a first response. For a fourth response to premises within six (6) months after a third response, there shall be a fee of forty dollars ($40.00), and for all succeeding responses within six (6) months of the last response, a fee of seventy-five dollars ($75.00) for each such response shall be charged. Upon a failure to pay any such fee within ten (10) days after the occurrence for which it is charged, the Chief of Police shall be authorized to disconnect or deactivate the alarm device involved.

(c) *Authority to disconnect.* Upon failure of an owner or manager of premises to pay any fee specified above within ten (10) days after the occurrence for which the fee is charged, or upon a determination by the Chief of Police that any false alarm, other than a false alarm caused by an act of God, to which a first response is made has resulted from a failure on the part of the owner or manager of the premises to take necessary corrective action, the Chief of Police shall be authorized to disconnect the telephone alarm device or general alarm device, and it shall be unlawful to reconnect such telephone alarm device or general alarm device unless and until appropriate corrective action has been taken and such reconnection is authorized by the Chief of Police; provided, however, that no disconnection or deactivation shall be ordered or made as to any premises required by law to have an alarm device in operation.

Sec. 2A-4. *Telephone alarm devices prohibited.* It shall be unlawful for any person, firm, corporation or association to install any telephone alarm device after the effective date of this ordinance.

SECTION 2. All ordinances or parts of ordinances in conflict herewith are hereby repealed.

EXERCISE 15

PUBLIC AFFAIRS REPORTING

SCHOOL DISTRICT BUDGET

INSTRUCTIONS: Write a news story summarizing the statement from the superintendent of schools and the proposed school district budget which follow. The statement appears verbatim and may be quoted directly. Accompanying the budget are figures showing enrollment by grade and the number of people the district employs. As you write your story, you may want to use a calculator (or a computer spreadsheet program) to find some numbers the budget does not provide, such as the percentage by which spending will increase or the average annual salary for teachers.

STATEMENT ON THE PROPOSED BUDGET

By Gary Hubbard
Superintendent of Schools

The development of this budget for the coming year was a challenging process. The district staff had only one overriding premise: What educational programs will provide every student with the opportunity to reach his or her fullest potential and provide the community with contributing citizens? This is an important goal because if this community is to continue to grow, prosper and maintain its quality of life, we must have educated citizens. This community historically has committed itself to maintaining the quality of the school system, and we are sure it will continue to do so.

This budget proposal shows what the district staff thinks is necessary to maintain the quality of schools and is based on certain assumptions which should be made public:

1. We expect growth in the district's assessed valuation of 28% next year. The county assessor will not certify the final assessed valuation for the district until after the deadline for adopting this budget.
2. The Legislature changed the formula by which state aid is distributed. The impact of that change is not clear, but we expect that state aid will increase only slightly for the next year, but more substantial increases of $700,000 to $1 million may be coming in the two or three years after next.
3. Student spending will remain at about $3,000 per pupil, and the district's enrollment will grow modestly.
4. The ratio of teachers to students will remain constant.
5. No new programs will be started.
6. No programs will be restarted.
7. Salaries and fringe benefits will not increase, but spending on nonsalary items will increase 2.5% in accordance with the consumer price index.

The General Fund Budget shows the staff's proposals for expenditures for most of the district's day-to-day operations, including all instructional programs. All expenses for operating the district's three high schools, nine middle schools and thirty-three elementary schools are in the general fund. It also includes all salaries for administrators, certified teachers and classified non-teaching employees.

The Building and Construction Budget shows spending on the construction of three new elementary schools and the work being done to renovate and remodel two middle schools. The district is nearing completion of the building program voters approved five years ago when they passed a $54-million bond issue. Some of the construction and renovation work

Harcourt Brace & Company

that had been budgeted for this year was delayed because of bad weather. Therefore, money the district had expected to spend last year has been included in this year's budget.

The Interscholastic Athletics Fund Budget covers expenditures on interscholastic sports, such as football, girls' volleyball, girls' and boys' basketball, boys' baseball and girls' softball. Salaries for full-time coaches come from the General Fund. The salaries paid from the Interscholastic Athletics Fund go to referees, parking attendants, concessions workers and security personnel.

The Debt Service Fund shows district payments on the principal and interest for the various bond issues outstanding.

Definitions of Budget Categories:

* Salaries—Funds paid to employees under regular employment contracts with the district.
* Benefits—Funds for the district's share of Social Security, retirement, unemployment benefits, health insurance and death benefits.
* Contracted Services—Funds to pay for services provided by individuals or firms outside the district. Examples are attorneys' fees, consultant fees and maintenance agreements on equipment.
* Supplies—Funds for consumable materials used in providing district services, such as textbooks, pencils, chalk, paper, floor wax, gasoline, etc.
* Instructional Development—Funds allocated to improve instructional programs and for professional growth activities by employees.
* In-District Travel—Funds paid to reimburse district employees who are required by their job assignments to travel within the district.
* Repair Equipment—Funds allocated to repair equipment such as typewriters, film projectors, lighting fixtures and musical instruments.
* Replace/New Equipment—Funds for the purchase of equipment to provide new services or enhance current programs. Examples are microcomputers, copying machines, vehicles, tools and furniture.
* Fixed Charges—Funds allocated to purchase various kinds of insurance for the district.
* Transfer—Funds transferred from the General Fund to support athletics, debate, journalism and other student activities.
* Contingency—Funds budgeted for unexpected personnel and non-personnel items and which can be expended only with board approval.

SCHOOL DISTRICT BUDGET

Description	Last Year Actual	This Year Budget	Next Year Proposed
GENERAL FUND			
Beg. Balance 9/1	14,727,807.00	17,552,056.00	14,174,366.00
Receipts			
Property Taxes	91,798,484.00	91,485,010.00	102,793,572.00
State Aid	29,236,428.00	31,373,050.00	31,427,590.00
Other Local	5,785,741.00	5,847,000.00	5,971,000.00
County	857,522.00	1,000,000.00	841,000.00
State	18,744,139.00	21,566,000.00	21,451,000.00
Federal	2,950,850.00	3,457,000.00	3,625,000.00
Total Receipts	149,373,164.00	154,728,060.00	166,109,162.00
Total Revenue Available	164,101,335.00	172,298,116.00	180,283,528.00
Property Tax Rate	1.5571	1.6453	1.4126
Valuation	5,572,804,000.00	5,702,528,000.00	7,301,758,000.00

(continued)

Harcourt Brace & Company

Description	Last Year Actual	This Year Budget	Next Year Proposed
Expenditures			
Personnel Expenses			
Salaries			
Administration	7,924,457.00	8,320,440.00	8,447,610.00
Certificated	76,144,423.00	80,556,450.00	87,034,960.00
Classified	19,413,780.00	21,297,550.00	21,982,000.00
Total Salaries	103,482,660.00	110,174,440.00	117,464,570.00
Benefits	26,117,570.00	29,405,560.00	30,723,020.00
Total Personnel Expenses	129,600,230.00	139,580,000.00	148,187,590.00
Non-Personnel Expenses			
Contract Services	1,716,125.00	2,588,010.00	2,570,590.00
Supplies	6,685,297.00	7,586,510.00	7,650,980.00
Utilities	3,081,556.00	3,036,980.00	3,566,700.00
Professional Development	386,739.00	384,430.00	391,930.00
In-District Travel	171,513.00	163,900.00	163,750.00
Repair Equipment	265,977.00	317,430.00	317,930.00
Replace/New Equipment	2,738,604.00	3,093,640.00	3,147,250.00
Fixed Charges	1,507,858.00	1,409,200.00	1,447,400.00
Transfers	395,380.00	363,650.00	348,150.00
Total Non-Personnel Expenses	16,949,049.00	18,943,750.00	19,604,680.00
Total Expenses	146,549,279.00	158,523,750.00	167,792,270.00
Contingency	0.00	100,000.00	0.00
Grand Total Expenses	146,549,279.00	158,623,750.00	167,792,270.00
Ending Fund Balance	17,552,056.00	13,674,366.00	12,491,258.00
BUILDING AND CONSTRUCTION FUND			
Beginning Balance 9/1	3,383,807.00	54,536,777.00	46,633,343.00
Receipts			
Property Taxes	8,206,489.00	7,895,636.00	6,419,926.00
In Lieu of Taxes	241,790.00	260,000.00	260,000.00
Interest on Investments	97,280.00	1,550,000.00	1,730,000.00
Land Leases	5,024.00	10,000.00	5,000.00
City Reimbursements	510,898.00	580,000.00	75,000.00
Miscellaneous	42,394.00	50,000.00	50,000.00
Roof Replacement Fund	0.00	1,000,000.00	900,000.00
Motor Vehicle Taxes	28,578.00	20,000.00	20,000.00
Bond Proceeds	53,705,054.00	0.00	0.00
Tax Anticipation	0.00	5,828,700.00	3,198,344.00
Total Receipts	62,837,507.00	17,194,336.00	12,658,270.00
Total Available	66,221,314.00	71,731,113.00	59,291,613.00
Expenditures			
Construction	8,535,662.00	29,923,852.00	55,390,460.00
Renovation	2,933,242.00	1,150,000.00	1,000,000.00
Connectivity	0.00	0.00	1,225,000.00
Roof Replacement	0.00	1,000,000.00	959,153.00
Purchase of Sites	7,883.00	0.00	0.00
Tax Collection Fee	75,892.00	80,000.00	82,000.00
Rating and Management Fees	131,858.00	0.00	0.00
Contingency	0.00	500,000.00	0.00
Not Completed Projects	0.00	3,545,348.00	1,000,000.00
Principal/Interest Accrual	0.00	0.00	335,000.00
Total Expenditures	11,684,537.00	36,199,200.00	59,991,613.00
Ending Balance	54,536,777.00	35,531,913.00	0.00

(continued)

Description	Last Year Actual	This Year Budget	Next Year Proposed
DEBT SERVICES FUND BUDGET			
Beginning Balance 9/1	799,305.00	8,689,915.00	1,342,124.00
Receipts			
Property Tax	2,305,785.00	7,075,000.00	7,442,500.00
In Lieu of Tax	61,198.00	100,000.00	100,000.00
Motor Vehicle Taxes	7,578.00	10,000.00	10,000.00
Interest	159,196.00	218,660.00	100,000.00
Refunding	7,945,815.00	0.00	0.00
Total Receipts	10,479,572.00	7,403,660.00	7,652,500.00
Total Available	11,278,877.00	16,093,575.00	8,994,624.00
Expenditures			
Bond Principal			
4,280,000 Issued six years ago	325,000.00	3,225,000.00	0.00
5,000,000 Issued five years ago	345,000.00	4,005,000.00	0.00
3,500,000 Issued four years ago	240,000.00	380,000.00	415,000.00
4,220,000 Issued three years ago	110,000.00	180,000.00	190,000.00
8,020,000 Refunding two years ago	430,000.00	1,255,000.00	1,285,000.00
54,480,000 Issued last year	0.00	475,000.00	1,475,000.00
Total Principal	1,450,000.00	9,520,000.00	3,365,000.00
Bond Interest	1,091,477.00	6,096,168.00	5,529,489.00
Tax Collection Fee	21,455.00	70,000.00	70,000.00
Management Fees	26,030.00	33,241.00	30,135.00
Total Expenditures	2,588,962.00	15,719,409.00	8,994,624.00
Ending Balance	8,689,915.00	374,166.00	0.00
INTERSCHOLASTIC ATHLETICS FUND BUDGET			
Beginning Balance 9/1	71,272.00	72,303.00	72,229.00
Receipts			
Football	125,036.00	75,000.00	75,000.00
Basketball (Boys')	48,922.00	40,000.00	50,000.00
Basketball (Girls')	24,794.00	25,000.00	25,000.00
Other	104,148.00	100,000.00	100,160.00
Transferred from General Fund	294,120.00	238,390.00	228,230.00
Total Receipts	597,020.00	478,390.00	478,390.00
Total Available	668,292.00	550,693.00	550,619.00
Expenditures			
Salaries, supplies, equipment	595,989.00	505,964.00	505,964.00
Total Expenditures	595,989.00	505,964.00	505,964.00
Ending Balance	72,303.00	44,729.00	44,655.00
SUMMARY OF ALL FUNDS			
Total Available Revenues	242,269,818.00	260,673,497.00	249,120,384.00
Total Expenditures	161,418,767.00	211,048,323.00	237,284,471.00
Ending Balance	80,851,051.00	49,625,174.00	11,835,913.00

Harcourt Brace & Company

DISTRICT ENROLLMENT

Grade	Last Year	This Year	Next Year
Kindergarten	2,348	2,193	2,349
1st	2,367	2,347	2,225
2nd	2,378	2,377	2,347
3rd	2,415	2,371	2,373
4th	2,421	2,406	2,386
5th	2,326	2,424	2,398
6th	2,322	2,319	2,435
7th	2,292	2,367	2,302
8th	2,071	2,289	2,335
9th	2,118	2,082	2,265
10th	2,078	2,141	2,112
11th	1,969	2,015	2,089
12th	2,070	2,057	2,006
Special Education	296	367	367
Head Start	267	265	265
Total	29,738	30,020	30,254

DISTRICT EMPLOYMENT (FULL-TIME EQUIVALENCY)

Category	Last Year	This Year	Next Year
Administration	127.95	131.30	132.30
Certificated	2,225.63	2,313.38	2,369.26
Technician	62.00	65.70	136.14
Office Personnel	270.60	274.55	263.05
Paraeducators	574.74	599.97	549.54
Tradespersons	435.13	467.50	467.55
Total	3,696.05	3,852.40	3,917.84

CHAPTER 14 ☆☆☆☆☆

SPEECHES AND MEETINGS

A free press is not a privilege but an organic necessity in a great society. Without criticism and reliable and intelligent reporting, the government cannot govern. For there is no adequate way in which it can keep itself informed about what the people of the country are thinking and doing and wanting.

(Columnist Walter Lippmann)

Many news stories report what important or interesting people say in speeches or the actions people take at public meetings. Even in small towns, dozens of speeches and meetings happen every week. In large cities, there may be thousands. Some speeches and meetings involve government agencies. Others are sponsored by clubs, schools, churches or business and professional organizations. Journalists cover only the most newsworthy speeches and meetings: the ones that are likely to affect or involve large numbers of people.

News organizations often produce two stories about major speeches and meetings: an "advance" story before the speech or meeting and a "follow" story afterward.

ADVANCE STORIES

Advance stories alert readers, listeners and viewers to coming events they may want to attend, support or oppose. Most advance stories are published the same day a speech or meeting is announced, or shortly thereafter. As a reminder to their audiences, news organizations may publish a second advance story a day or two before the speech or meeting occurs.

News organizations publish several advance stories about events of unusual importance. If, for example, the president of the United States announced plans to visit your city, local newspapers and radio and television stations would immediately report those plans. As more information became available, news organizations would publish additional advance stories about the president's schedule, companions and goals—and about opportunities the public would have to see the president.

All advance stories emphasize the same basic facts:

- what will happen

- when and where it will happen

- who will be involved

The advance stories for speeches identify the speakers, report the times and places they will appear and describe their topics. The advance stories for meetings identify the groups scheduled to meet, report the times and places of the meetings and summarize the agendas. Advance stories also may mention the event's purpose or sponsor, whether the public is invited, whether those who attend will have an opportunity to participate and whether there will be a charge for admission. Some news organizations publish advance stories only for those events open to the general public.

Harcourt Brace & Company

The leads for advance stories should emphasize what is important and unusual, not just the fact that someone has scheduled a speech or meeting. Often, leads mention celebrities who will be involved in the events or the topics that will be discussed. For example:

Singer and actress Barbra Streisand has agreed to perform in Washington, D.C., at a dinner expected to raise more than $5 million for the Cancer Society.

Members of the American Civil Liberties Union will meet at 8 p.m. Friday at the YMCA to discuss charges that the Police Department refused to hire an applicant because he is a homosexual.

Advance stories are short and specific. They often contain only three or four paragraphs:

The last time the City Commission discussed Memorial Hospital there was standing room only.

The city planner's advice for Tuesday's meeting? Come early if you want a seat.

The commission will meet at 4:30 p.m. to discuss a 10-year master development plan that would change the hospital from a community to a regional facility.

The commission will also discuss spending $10,810 for signs, installing speed bumps in hospital parking lots and driveways and the proposed closing of Eddy Drive.

Because of time limitations, broadcasters usually carry advance stories for only the most important speeches and meetings. Newspapers run more advance stories, but to save space, they may publish them in roundups or digests (often called "Community Calendars") that list all the newsworthy events for the coming week.

COVERING THE SPEECH OR MEETING

Speeches and meetings quickly become routine assignments for most reporters, but covering them effectively requires the development of some basic reporting skills: advance preparation, sound news judgment, accuracy, an ear for interesting quotations and an eye for compelling details.

Reporters may cover speeches about topics with which they are unfamiliar or meetings about complicated issues. Meetings of some public agencies can be particularly confusing. In larger communities, a city council might vote on issues without discussing them at its regular meeting because all the discussion will have occurred in committee meetings days or weeks earlier. Unless the reporter is familiar with the committee action, she or he might misunderstand the full council's action or fail to recognize newsworthy details about an issue.

Planning and preparation help reporters cover speeches and meetings. Reporters usually try to learn as much as possible about the participants and issues before a speech or meeting. As a first step, reporters may go to their news organization's library and research the topic for the speech or meeting, the speaker or the group.

Reporters who cover meetings should learn all the participants' names beforehand in order to identify the people who are speaking or making decisions. So they understand everything that is said, reporters should also learn as much as possible about every item on the agenda. Reporters can get agendas before many meetings. The agendas identify what topics the group will consider, and reporters can research those issues. In case any unexpected or confusing issues arise, reporters may arrange to see the leading participants to ask followup questions after a meeting adjourns.

Reporters who cover speeches often try to talk to the speaker so that they can clarify issues or get additional information. The groups that sponsor speeches will sometimes accommodate reporters by scheduling press conferences with the speakers before or after the speech. If no formal press conference is arranged, reporters may ask to see speakers for a few minutes immediately

Harcourt Brace & Company

after their appearances. Reporters also like to get advance copies of speeches, when the speakers make them available. Then, instead of having to take notes, reporters can follow the printed text, simply checking to be certain that the speaker does not depart from the prepared remarks.

Some steps reporters take are common to covering both speeches and meetings:

- Arrive early and find a seat that will allow you to hear and see as much as possible. Some public bodies that the media regularly cover set aside special seating for reporters.

- Introduce yourself to the speaker, if possible, or the participants in the meeting, if this is a group you have never covered before. You may also have an opportunity to ask a few quick questions or arrange for an opportunity to talk with the speaker or the participants later.

- Take detailed notes. The more thorough your notes, the easier it will be for you to recall and understand what was said or done and to reconstruct it for your audience.

- As you listen to the speech or the meeting, try to think of groups or individuals who might have different points of view or who might be affected by any actions taken. You should try to reach these individuals or groups later so that you can provide your audience with as complete a news story as possible.

FOLLOW STORIES

Follow stories are published after speeches or meetings and report on those events in detail. Therefore, they are much longer than advance stories. They are also more difficult to write because they involve a multitude of issues and participants. Seven members may attend a council meeting, hear a dozen witnesses, then vote on four issues. Many of the issues may be complex. Yet, to save space or time, reporters may have to summarize all the proceedings in a single story.

Writing Effective Leads

A mistake inexperienced reporters commonly make is to begin their follow stories for speeches and meetings with leads so broad they contain no news. The overly broad lead may say, for example, that a speaker "discussed" a topic or "voiced an opinion" or that a group "considered" or "dealt with" an issue. Here are examples of overly broad leads:

FOLLOW STORY LEAD (SPEECH): The president of the Chamber of Commerce discussed the dangers of higher taxes in a speech Tuesday night.

FOLLOW STORY LEAD (MEETING): The Government Affairs Committee of the state Senate held a public hearing Wednesday on a bill that would restrict campaign contributions to lawmakers.

Neither lead contains any news. The advance stories for these events would already have informed readers and viewers that the Chamber of Commerce president was going to talk about high taxes and that the Senate committee was going to hold a hearing on a bill to limit campaign contributions. The news is what was said or done about these issues. The leads might be revised as follows to emphasize the news:

REVISED LEAD (SPEECH): If the city continues to raise its property taxes, major businesses will begin moving elsewhere, throwing thousands of people out of work, the president of the Chamber of Commerce warned Tuesday night.

Harcourt Brace & Company

REVISED LEAD (MEETING): By a vote of 5–2, the Senate Government Affairs Committee approved Wednesday a proposal to prohibit campaign contributions to lawmakers while the state Legislature is in session.

Usually leads for follow stories will stress the main point of a speech or the most important action taken or the main point of discussion in a meeting:

FOLLOW STORY LEAD (EMPHASIS ON MAIN POINT): Every American has a right to a decent home, and the federal government should do more to help people obtain one, former President Jimmy Carter said here Friday night.

Although former presidents are newsworthy people, the most newsworthy point here is the call for federal assistance for housing for the poor, not the fact that the recommendation came from Jimmy Carter. At other times, who said something is more important than what was said:

FOLLOW STORY LEAD (EMPHASIS ON SPEAKER): Attorney General Janet Reno said on a television program yesterday that she would not have approved the raid on the Branch Davidian cult near Waco, Texas, if she had known it would end with more than 80 deaths.

(The Washington Post)

Many people criticized the government's decision to use force to end the standoff at the Branch Davidian complex, but the fact that the person who ordered the attack now has second thoughts makes this story newsworthy. Sometimes, the most important news is not made in the speech or the meeting but in reaction to it:

FOLLOW STORY LEAD (EMPHASIS ON REACTION): Two dozen hecklers forced Sen. Jim Davis to cut short his campaign speech in Hallsville Tuesday.

Campaign speeches are usually routine, with candidates delivering the same speech over and over. The fact that hecklers disrupted the candidate's speech in this case is more newsworthy than the speech itself.

Experienced writers disagree over the use of direct quotations as leads. Some say that quotations should never be used in the lead. The reporter is better able to write a summary lead than a speaker is, and quotations, no matter how interesting, may be more effective in the body of the story than in the lead. As a rule, a writer should use a quotation in the lead only if it accurately and succinctly states the most newsworthy point of the meeting or speech. In practice, few quotations will satisfy that standard.

Organizing the Story

If a speech or meeting involves several important topics, briefly summarize all of them in the story's opening paragraphs. Then, report each topic in detail, starting with the most important. If the opening paragraphs mention only one topic, readers or listeners will think the story discusses only that topic. If that topic fails to interest them, they may stop paying attention.

Here are three solutions to the problem of organizing a story about a speech or meeting:

Solution 1

If a speech or meeting involves several major topics, select the one or two most important topics and summarize them in the lead. Summarize the remaining topics (rarely more than two or three) in the second paragraph. Then discuss the topics in the order of their importance. For example:

The School Board has adopted a $14 million program designed to reduce the high school dropout rate from 24 to 10 percent.

In other action Thursday night, the board voted to build an elementary school on Hartz Drive and to require every new teacher to pass a series of competency tests.

Solution 2

If a speech or meeting involves several major topics, select the most important and summarize it in the lead. Provide a brief transition, and then give summaries of the meeting's other major topics, using numbers, bullets or some other typographical device to introduce each item. Remember that such lists must be parallel in form: if the first element in a list is a complete sentence, the following elements must also be complete sentences.

Normally, reporters will return later in the story to each topic, discussing it in more detail. Here is an example:

> Carlos Diaz, a Democratic candidate for governor, promised last night "to cut the state's taxes by at least 20 percent."
> Diaz said the state can save billions of dollars a year by:
> • Eliminating at least 10 percent of the state's employees.
> • Hiring private companies to build and operate the state's prisons.
> • Establishing a "workfare" system that will require every able-bodied adult on the state's welfare rolls to either work or go to school.
> • Reforming the state's school system by abolishing tenure and reducing the number of administrators.

Solution 3

If a speech or meeting involves one major topic and several minor topics, begin with the major topic and, after thoroughly discussing it, use bullets or numbers to introduce summaries of the minor topics in the story's final paragraphs:

> In response to questions asked after her speech, LeClarren said:
> • Most colleges are still dominated by men. Their presidents, deans, department chairs—and most of their faculty members, too—are men.
> • A subtle, often unintentional, discrimination steers women away from fields traditionally dominated by men—from mathematics, business and engineering, for example.
> • When two college students marry, the husband rarely drops out to support his wife. Rather, the wife drops out to support her husband.
> • Some parents discriminate against their college-age children by giving more help and encouragement to their sons than to their daughters.

Never, in a story's final paragraph, simply report that a speaker or group "discussed" or "considered" another topic. If a topic is important enough to mention, give readers meaningful information about it. As specifically as possible, summarize the discussion or action:

> VAGUE: Finally, Commissioner Cycler expressed concern about the Senior Citizens Center on Eisenhower Drive.
> REVISED: Finally, Commissioner Cycler said several people have called her to complain that the staff at the Senior Citizens Center on Eisenhower Drive is arrogant and unhelpful.

Solving Problems of Sequence and Attribution

Two common weaknesses in speech and meeting stories are the reporting of events in chronological order and the failure to vary the location of the attribution.

Some beginners report events in the order in which they occurred, as if the events' sequence was somehow important to readers. The agendas for meetings rarely reflect the importance of the topics discussed. Major issues may be taken up early or late, but there is no reason to make a reader or a viewer endure descriptions of minor actions before learning about important ones.

Harcourt Brace & Company

While speeches usually have a more logical order, speakers rarely put their most important points at the beginning. Rather, they save them for the middle or end of the speech.

Experienced reporters write most follow stories in the inverted-pyramid style, presenting information in the order of its importance—not in the order in which it arose during a speech or meeting. Reporters can move statements around and may begin their stories with a statement made at the end of a one-hour speech or meeting, then shift to a topic discussed midway through the event. If topics brought up early are unimportant, reporters may never mention them at all.

The second problem beginners have with speech and meeting stories occurs when they start every paragraph with the speaker's name and attribution. As a result, their stories become dull and repetitious.

When you finish a story, look at your paragraphs. If you see this pattern or something like it, your paragraphs need rewriting:

> City Manager Faith An-Pong began by discussing the problems that recycling is creating for the city.
> Next, An-Pong said . . . .
> Turning to a third topic, An-Pong said . . . .
> She then went on to add that . . . .
> Continuing, An-Pong said . . . .
> In conclusion, she added . . . .

Writing Transitions

Transitions shift a story from one idea to another. A good transition will show readers how two ideas connect and arouse their interest in the topic being introduced.

Transitions should be brief. The repetition of a key word, phrase or idea can serve as a transition to a related topic or shift to a new time or place. If the change in topic is more abrupt, a transitional sentence or question may be necessary. The transition should not, however, simply report that a speaker or group "turned to another topic." Instead, the transition should function as a secondary lead, summarizing the new topic by giving its most interesting and important details:

> WEAK TRANSITION: The board also considered two other topics.
> REVISED: The board also considered—and rejected—proposals to increase students' health and athletic fees.

> WEAK TRANSITION: Hunt then discussed the problem of auto insurance.
> REVISED: Hunt then warned that the cost of auto insurance rose 9.6 percent last year and is expected to rise 12 percent this year.

REMEMBER YOUR READERS

Reporters should write with their readers in mind, clarifying every issue so that readers can understand it, and making the story interesting so that they will want to read every word. More important, reporters should focus on issues that are of interest and concern to readers, showing how events will affect readers and their neighborhood, city or state. Sometimes reporters forget this rule and try to please the people they are writing *about* instead of the people they are writing *for*.

One news report of a city council meeting began by saying three employees received awards for working for the city for 25 years. That type of award is common and, although important to the recipients, is unimportant to almost everyone else. The story later discussed a topic more likely to interest readers: plans for the city government to help people with low incomes buy their own homes.

Harcourt Brace & Company

Here is an example of a lead that fails to emphasize the information most likely to interest or affect readers. Mistakenly, the lead emphasizes a routine, bureaucratic procedure:

The City Council has approved issuing $12 million in bonds for improvements at the Regional Airport.

REVISED: The City Council will spend $12 million to expand the Regional Airport's parking lots and to construct an observation tower and restaurant for visitors.

Provide Clarity and Detail

News stories about speeches and meetings help readers understand the ideas and issues of the day. To accomplish this, the stories must be as specific as possible. The following sentence appeared in a story about a meeting and, until it was revised, failed to convey any meaningful information to readers:

VAGUE: Mary Scott Butler, a city council member from Waynesville, also spoke out against the property tax lid.

MORE SPECIFIC: A state law intended to slow the growth of local property taxes will cripple the ability of governments to deal with emergencies and local problems, said Mary Scott Butler, a city council member from Waynesville.

Jargon, especially the bureaucratic language used at government meetings, is another obstacle to understanding. A story reported that a county commission had imposed "stricter signage requirements" for adult bookstores, theaters and clubs. Instead of repeating such jargon, reporters should give specific details. In this case, the commissioners limited the size and location of outdoor signs advertising adult entertainment businesses.

Check Facts

The reporter has an obligation to go beyond what is said or done at the speech or meeting to check facts, find opposing points of view and get additional information and comments.

People say things in speeches that may not be true or may be largely opinion. And because the speech represents the views of only the speaker, there may be no one present who can challenge or correct the speaker's statements. In the 1950s, Sen. Joseph McCarthy built his political career by making unsubstantiated allegations that individuals or organizations were sympathetic to the Communist movement. Reporters at that time rarely tried to check statements made by speakers, especially U.S. senators. But as journalists came to understand McCarthy's tactics, many realized they had an obligation to check his statements and to point out his falsehoods.

Now, news organizations are more likely to expect reporters to check controversial statements of fact or opinion made in speeches. The degree of checking a reporter may do for any particular story will depend on how much time the reporter has before the deadline and how controversial the speech is. Certainly, reporters should check personal attacks and give the target of the attack an opportunity to respond, preferably in the same story in which they report the attack.

Participants in public meetings may make controversial statements, and reporters should check them. Reporters who cover meetings also have an obligation to get reactions to or different perspectives on actions taken in public meetings. If the city council votes to rezone a particular area, the reporters should get comments from property owners, developers and others involved in the issue, even if they are not present at the meeting.

Double-checking personal attacks and getting responses from the targets may help avoid libel suits in some cases. If a defamatory personal attack is made at a speech or meeting that is

Harcourt Brace & Company

not an official government proceeding, the person who is attacked may be able to sue for libel both the speaker and any news organizations that report the statement. The fact that news organizations accurately quoted the speaker is not a defense. Even when there is no danger of a libel suit, either because the statement was not defamatory or because it was made in an official proceeding, the journalist still has an ethical obligation to check facts, get opposing points of view and give people who have been attacked an opportunity to respond.

ADDING COLOR

Report What You Hear

Quotations, direct and indirect, help the writer describe any debate that takes place in a public meeting. The people who read and view the news need to know why certain actions were taken or why their elected representatives voted a certain way. Simply recording votes and actions will not give readers and viewers the information they need to make informed judgments. They also need to know the competing points of view.

Before the fall of the Soviet Union, a school board considered an exchange program that would allow 32 American high school students to spend a semester there studying and traveling. Two men objected to the program, complaining that it would expose students to Soviet propaganda. The following story uses quotations to describe the participants and illuminate the issues:

> "This is a sneak attempt at changing the students' values," said LeRoy DeBecker of the John Birch Society. "The students will never be shown any of the negative aspects of communism, only propaganda promoting the system."
>
> Erik Lieber, chair of the Pro-Family Forum, agreed that the program should be rejected. "Russia wants only one form of peace," Lieber said. "It wants to completely dominate the world, and this trip will help it."
>
> Catrina Weinstein, a teacher at Colonial High School, disagreed. Weinstein said that she has led students from other high schools on similar trips, and that the trips made the students more patriotic, not pawns of the Communists.
>
> "When the students got home they realized how fortunate they were, so they were more motivated to study our political system," Weinstein said. "All these other comments you've heard are nonsense. These trips introduce students to the Soviet people, not Soviet ideology. The closest we ever came to propaganda was a guide's speaking with pride of his country's accomplishments."
>
> The board voted 6–1 to establish the program, and board member Anna Nemechek explained, "If we're going to be afraid every time our children cross a border, then perhaps we should lock them up in cages and make sure they're well fed."

Describe What You See

Vivid descriptions of participants, audiences and settings add drama to speech and meeting stories. The description can appear anywhere. Here are some examples of descriptive passages:

> Nearly 100 irate parents stormed into Tuesday's School Board meeting, demanding that the Board abandon its plans to stop teaching art and music.
>
> A public hearing on an ordinance that would limit the number of animals allowed in homes drew a standing-room-only crowd to a County Commission meeting Thursday.
> Some of the spectators wore T-shirts inscribed with pictures of their pets, primarily cats and dogs.

Harcourt Brace & Company

About a dozen people stood in the back of the room, holding signs that said, "I'm be-hind our mayor" and "We support the mayor."

A combination of quotations and descriptions can make stories even more interesting:

The spectators cheered and waved cardboard axes in boisterous support.
"Ax the tax," they chanted. "Ax the tax."

Baker loudly objected to each vote in favor of the project.
"We're citizens," she yelled. "You should consider us."
After all the votes were cast, she threw her petition to the floor and stormed out of the room, shouting: "This is not a dictatorship! You should listen to us."

CHECKLISTS FOR REPORTING SPEECHES AND MEETINGS

Advance Stories

1. Report what speech or meeting will happen, when and where it will happen, and who will be involved.
2. Keep advance stories short—normally no more than three or four paragraphs.

Covering the Speech or Meeting

1. Get background information on the group or speaker, including a copy of the agenda or the speech, if available.
2. Learn the names of all participants.
3. Find out if there will be an opportunity to interview the speaker or the participants before or after the event.
4. Arrive early and find a seat where you can see and hear as much as possible.
5. Introduce yourself to the speaker or the participants in the meeting if they do not know you already.
6. Take detailed notes, making sure you record colorful quotations, information about the set-ting of the event and the responses of the participants and observers.
7. Identify and seek responses from people who may be affected by what happens at a speech or meeting or who may have other points of view.

Follow Stories

1. Focus the lead on specific actions or statements to keep it from being overly broad.
2. Organize the story in inverted-pyramid fashion, not according to the order in which state-ments were made or topics considered.
3. Identify all major topics early in the story and develop them in the body of the story in the order of their importance.
4. Vary the location of the attribution in direct and indirect quotations so that the story does not become monotonous.

Harcourt Brace & Company

5. Provide transitions from one topic to another.
6. Avoid vague generalities, and eliminate or explain jargon or technical terms.
7. Check controversial facts and give any person or group who has been attacked in the speech or meeting an opportunity to respond.
8. Include color in speech and meeting stories by providing direct quotations and descriptions of speakers, participants, settings and audience responses.

E X E R C I S E 1

SPEECHES AND MEETINGS

EVALUATING SPEECH AND MEETING LEADS

INSTRUCTIONS: Critically evaluate the following speech and meeting story leads, giving each of them a grade from A to F. Then discuss the leads with your teacher and classmates.

1. The County Commission voted unanimously Tuesday against raising the county tourism tax by one cent to pay for a new baseball stadium. (Grade: _____)

2. A spokesperson for Citizens Against Crime warned parents Wednesday night about violent crime and its impact on families in the city. (Grade: _____)

3. By a vote of 5–4, the City Council rejected Monday night a proposal to build an apartment complex near Reed Road and State Road 419. (Grade: _____)

4. A heated debate took place at the City Council meeting Thursday night over the need for police dogs. (Grade: _____)

5. Fifty percent of the drug abusers entering treatment centers go back to using drugs within a year, Mimi Sota told an audience here Monday. (Grade: _____)

6. The Student Health Fee Committee voted unanimously Friday to increase fees by $6 in the fall and spring semesters and $4 in the summer. (Grade: _____)

7. During a speech to the American Legion last night, former Marine Lt. Col. Oliver North discussed his work in the Reagan White House. (Grade: _____)

8. County commissioners heard testimony from more than 20 people Tuesday morning on plans to license and regulate snowmobiles. (Grade: _____)

9. The County Commission reviewed a resolution Wednesday to create a committee that will identify conservation and recreation lands within the county. (Grade: _____)

10. Blasting opponents of the plan, Mayor Sabrina Datoli last night defended a proposal to establish a police review board. (Grade: _____)

11. Traveling by airplane has never been more dangerous, Ramon Madea charged in a fiery speech Sunday night. (Grade: _____)

12. The City Council voted unanimously Monday to change the zoning along three streets from residential to commercial. (Grade: _____)

13. The business before the School Board flowed smoothly Tuesday night as the board proceeded through the agenda. (Grade: _____)

14. The County Commission continued to struggle with the issue of protecting the water quality in Butler Lake at their meeting Monday. They eventually denied a petition to build a new boat ramp on the lake. (Grade: _____)

15. The County Commission unanimously passed an ordinance that makes it illegal for anyone to possess an open container of alcohol in a vehicle. A previous law made it illegal to drive while drunk, but legal to drink while driving. (Grade: _____)

Harcourt Brace & Company

EXERCISE 2
SPEECHES AND MEETINGS

SPEECHES

INSTRUCTIONS: Write separate advance and follow stories about each of the following speeches. Because the speeches are reprinted verbatim, you can use direct quotations.

1. FIREFIGHTER CONCERNS

Information for advance story:

Tony Sullivan is scheduled to speak to the Downtown Rotary Club Monday of next week. The club meets every Monday noon at the Blackhawk Hotel. Lunch is served and costs $8.50 per person. The public is invited to the lunch, which begins promptly at noon, or the public may come for just the speech, which will begin promptly at 1 p.m. Tony Sullivan is your city's fire chief, and he will speak to the club members about the major concerns of today's firefighters.

Speech for follow story:

Some of you don't know me. My name is Tony Sullivan. When I was 22 years old and had just been discharged from the Army, I didn't know what I wanted to do with the rest of my life. Two of my best friends wanted to join the Fire Department, and they talked me into taking all the physical and written tests along with them. I passed, but they didn't, and I've been associated with the Fire Department for the past 28 years. For the past 6 years, I've been chief.

The Fire Department is much different today than it was when I joined 28 years ago, and we've got much different problems today. I've been asked to talk to you about those problems. Our biggest problems, as you might expect, are low pay and long hours. But we're also concerned about the problems of arson and outdated gear. Now I'd like to talk to you about each of those problems, and in much more detail. As local business people, all of you are affected by the problems, and I hope that you'll be able to help us solve them.

First, the problem of arson. It's gotten completely out of hand. Property owners in this state alone lost at least $1 billion in damaged and destroyed property due to arson last year. We'd estimate, conservatively, that right here in this city 10 to 20 percent of our fires are arson. It's hard to control because the conviction rate for arson is low. And that's because fires oftentimes destroy the evidence. You, as business people, lose money because arson causes higher insurance premiums for everyone. It also causes lower profits, lost wages to workers and lost tax revenue to the city.

Another big problem we face involves the gear we use in fighting fires. A good truck these days costs $300,000. If we want a good ladder truck, one that can reach some of the taller downtown buildings, it may cost twice that much. The city can't afford many, but if we don't have the trucks, then we can't rescue people trapped on the upper floors of those buildings.

Even the protective gear worn by our firefighters is getting terribly expensive. Until recently, all our protective clothing has been made of a highly flammable cotton coated with neoprene, usually black. Black is bad because it absorbs heat and because firefighters can't be seen if they fall and get into trouble inside a dark building or a building filled with

Harcourt Brace & Company

smoke. Then take a look at our helmets; they're far from being the state of the art. They melt in temperatures above 700. In your average fire, the floor temperature is 200 and the ceiling is 1,800. The state-of-the-art helmets can resist heat up to 2,000 degrees, but they cost three times what we're paying now.

One reason why the injury and death rate among firefighters is so high—more firefighters die annually than police—is because our gear is so expensive, and cities won't buy it. They seem to think it's easier to replace firefighters than to outlay the money for better gear.

The heavy physical labor and working conditions also contribute to the high injury rate. When you send people into a fire, and you've got intense heat, broken glass, the danger of whole walls and floors collapsing, and the danger of explosions from unknown chemicals stored in these buildings, it's almost inevitable that you're going to have some injuries and possibly even some deaths. With the proper equipment, we could reduce the number and severity of injuries, but there's no way to completely eliminate them. Danger's a part of our job. We accept that.

Despite the fact that we have a higher death rate than the police, firefighters start out earning $2,000 to $3,000 a year less than they do, and we object to that. It's not fair. When we ask the City Council why, they say because it's always been that way and it would cost too much to pay firefighters as much as the police. We don't think that's right, especially when you consider that the police work only 40 hours a week. Firefighters work 24-hour shifts and an average of 56 hours a week. So they work longer hours for less money.

The next time you hear anyone talking about these problems, and the next time you see us going to the City Council, requesting a larger budget, we'd appreciate your support. With your support, we'll be able to offer you, and everyone else in the city, better fire protection. It's already good, but with your help we can make it even better, and that benefits everyone.

2. ABORTION CRITIC

Information for advance story:

John F. Palladino is an outspoken critic of abortion. He is scheduled to speak at a prayer breakfast next Sunday at the First Baptist Church, 412 North Eastland Ave., in your city. His topic will be, "Abortion: Our Greatest Sin." The public is invited free of charge for both the breakfast and speech. The prayer breakfast will be held in the church's social hall, starting at 7:30 a.m. Palladino is a Republican and unsuccessful candidate for governor in the last election in your state. He was defeated in the Republican primary. Previously, he served three terms in your State Senate. Currently, he lives in the state capital and operates his own real estate firm there. He is chairman of your state's Right to Life Committee, which opposes abortion.

Speech for follow story:

I appreciate your invitation to speak to you today. I also appreciate the help that many of you have given our Right to Life Committee. I recognize that some of you have given us very generous financial donations, and that others of you have helped man our telephone lines and distribute our literature.

I'd like to begin this morning by telling you something of my personal views. Personally, I cannot understand how a woman can achieve sexual liberation by taking the life of her unborn child. I believe that abortion basically is a very selfish, self-centered remedy to those that think the birth of a child is an inconvenience. I think it is an inconvenience for only nine months. After that, there are 3- or 4-year waits to adopt children. I know of many families who go down to El Salvador to adopt children. I have other friends who adopted

Harcourt Brace & Company

little babies from Korea and from many other countries of the world. So no child is unwanted; there's a loving home in this country for every child.

Now some people ask, "What about cases where the mother's life is threatened, or where the mother is impregnated through rape or incest?" My main concern is with the 99 percent of the abortions that do not deal with that, but merely with inconvenience. When the mother's life is in question, and it's a true case of the life of a mother vs. the life of an unborn child, certainly the life of the mother should take precedence—the reason being that there is a good possibility that the mother is already a mother of other children. To say that we're going to deprive these already-born children of their mother to protect the life of an unborn child is improper.

But I find it difficult from a personal standpoint to say that I would agree to abortion in the case of rape or incest because, again, it's an innocent child no matter whether it's the product of a legitimate or illegitimate sexual union. So if I had the authority to stop all abortions, except those that involve the endangerment of the mother's life, then certainly I would agree to that.

Now, in talking about this issue, you have to remember one critical point. Life begins upon fertilization of the egg. If you don't agree with that, certainly at least you have the potential for life at that point, and therefore it should be as jealously guarded as life itself.

The federal and state laws that permit abortion are wrong, absolutely and totally wrong. Abortions are a crime and a sin. When governments adopt these laws, they're saying that life doesn't exist, or that some forms of life aren't as important as others and don't deserve the same protection as others. So even from a political view, abortion is wrong because it allows governments to judge the value of life—to say that there's a point or condition under which some lives can be ended. I think that's a very dangerous position for government to be in. And you have to ask where it'll stop. What other lives will governments decide we can end? Next it could be the sick, the elderly, the insane or the criminals from all our jails. That's not the kind of decision government should be making. All life is precious. All life should be protected by the government—and by us, as individuals.

Thank you.

Harcourt Brace & Company

E X E R C I S E   3

SPEECHES AND MEETINGS

SPEECH: SELF-DEFENSE AGAINST RAPE

INSTRUCTIONS: Write separate advance and follow stories about the following speech. Because the speech is reprinted verbatim, you can use direct quotations while reporting the follow story.

INFORMATION FOR ADVANCE STORY

Albert Innis is a lieutenant in the Detective Bureau of the city's police department. He will speak at the YWCA Friday about the topic of rape. The speech will be open to the public free of charge. Women, particularly, are urged to attend the meeting by the sponsor, the YWCA Young Adults Section. The speech will begin at 8 p.m. in Room 12. Innis has agreed to answer questions from the audience at the conclusion of his speech. Members of the Young Adults Section will hold their monthly business meeting after the conclusion of the speech, and the public is also welcome to attend the meeting. To be eligible for membership in the section, women must be between the ages of 18 and 35. The Young Adults Section is sponsoring the presentation because of public interest in the topic of rape and its importance to women, a club representative said. According to some estimates, there are 10 rapes for every one reported to the police.

SPEECH FOR FOLLOW STORY

I've been asked to come here tonight to talk to you about rape. I'd like to begin by discussing three myths about rape. Two concern the victim, another the rapist. According to one myth, the victim is always young and attractive; movies and television programs perpetuate this myth. The truth is that every woman is a potential victim. Last year, the victims in this city ranged in age from 2 to 91 years. A second myth is that the woman provokes the attack. But sexual assault isn't provoked by a womans behavior or by the way she dresses. The truth is that the rapist selects his victim on the basis of opportunity. Most rapists select as their victims women who appear vulnerable and alone. Third, it's also a myth to think that rape is committed for sexual gratification. Sex is not the motivating factor. Rapists have feelings of hostility, aggression and inferiority, and they enjoy overpowering and degrading their victims; it raises their self-esteem.

Rape can occur virtually anywhere, but it is most likely to occur in the victims home or in the home of the assailant. Often, the assailant is someone the victim knows either closely or by sight.

Most rapists are emotionally unstable, and all rapists have the potential to be violent. Outwardly, they appear to be normal, but most have difficulty relating to other people and establishing lasting relationships.

No one can predict how a woman will react when actually confronted with the threat of sexual assault. Panic and fear are perfectly normal responses. The first few moments you may be too terrified to utter a sound. That's perfectly normal. But if you have thought in advance about the possibility of sexual assault, the shock won't be as great. And if you mentally prepare yourself in advance and think about what you might do, you may be able to react more quickly and effectively.

One tactic available to women is making noise. Sometimes screaming "Fire!" or "Call the police!" or blowing a whistle if you have one with you may frighten away your as-

Harcourt Brace & Company

sailant or bring help. But it may antagonize him. All the alternatives involve some dangers, and screaming can make an assailant angrier, and he may beat you or try to strangle you to keep you quiet. You have to weigh the odds, depending on the situation, of this tactic being successful.

A second tactic is trying to run to safety. But unless you are reasonably certain you can get a good lead and reach safety before he overtakes you, this may be too risky. Make sure you have a place to run where someone will help. If you try running away and your assailant overtakes you, it may make him even more violent.

A third tactic is trying to gain a psychological advantage. Try to defuse your assailants anger and give yourself time to think. If you do something the rapist doesn't expect, it may stop or delay him because rapists want to be in control, and many can't cope with actions they don't expect. This tactic can take many forms—going limp, sinking to the ground and eating grass, hiding your face to stick your fingers down your throat and cause yourself to vomit, making yourself belch, even urinating on your attacker. Crying might be effective in some instances.

You should understand that rapists don't understand or recognize the rights of women as individuals. So it's important to teach them in a way that breaks their fantasies and allows them to see you as an individual with honest feelings and concerns—not as an object. Many of these men put women on a pedestal and, through sexual assault, feel they're cutting women down to size.

You might try to speak calmly and sincerely as one human being trying to reach out to another. Don't beg, plead, cower or make small talk. That's what these assailants expect to hear, and it may antagonize them even more. Talk about something that interests you—anything you can talk about comfortably—a pet, a recent movie you've seen, a book you're reading, a recent death in the family. The important thing is to convince your assailant you're concerned about him as a person.

The last tactic available to you is fighting, but you should keep in mind the fact that all rapists have the potential for inflicting serious harm; they are all potentially violent, so fighting is the last tactic to try if all the others have failed. And if you use this tactic, you have to be willing and able to inflict serious injury. If you try fighting and fail to completely incapacitate your assailant, your risk of receiving serious injury is greatly increased. Most studies show that about half of all rapists carry some weapon, and you have to always assume they're willing to use the weapons. If you are going to fight, use surprise and speed to your advantage. For instance, gently put your hands on the assailant's face and get your thumbs near his eyes, then press his eyeballs suddenly with your thumbs as hard as you can. This will put the assailant into shock and could blind him. Or grab his testicles, squeeze as hard as you can and jerk or pull to inflict immobilizing pain.

There is no universal prescription for foiling sexual assaults. No one can tell you what specific tactics to use. What worked for one woman may not work for you. It all depends upon the circumstances, your basic personality and your perceptions of the rapist. The way you react may depend upon your physical condition. The very thought of sexual assault makes some women so angry that they would rather face the risk of serious injury. Other women may want to escape with the least possible injury or may be more concerned about the safety of other members of their families than with rape or other injury to themselves.

Thank you.

Harcourt Brace & Company

EXERCISE 4

SPEECHES AND MEETINGS

SURGEON GENERAL'S SPEECH

INSTRUCTIONS: Write a news story that summarizes the following speech given by the surgeon general of the U.S. Public Health Service. Assume that the surgeon general spoke at a state PTA convention in your city at 8 p.m. yesterday. This is a verbatim copy of a speech actually given by the surgeon general and can be quoted directly. As you write the story, assume that it is just a few days before Halloween.

I am pleased to be here today with representatives of several organizations who recognize that alcohol is the nations number one drug problem among youth and who share my concern that the alcohol industry has targeted Halloween, a traditional holiday for children, as their latest marketing opportunity.

Just as Saman, the ancient Keltic Lord of the Dead, summoned the evil spirits to walk the earth on October 31, America's modern day distilleries, breweries and vineyards are working their own brand of sorcery on us this year. On radio and television and even at supermarket check-out counters we are being bombarded with exhortations to purchase orange and black 12-packs and even "cocktails from the Crypt."

Well, as your surgeon general I'm here today with my own exhortation: Halloween and hops do not mix.

Alcohol is the number one substance abuse problem among America's youth. In fact, it is the only drug whose use has not been declining, according to our most recent National High School Senior Survey. The National Institute on Alcohol Abuse and Alcoholism reports that, currently, 4.6 million teen-agers have a drinking problem.

Why do so many of our young people drink? There are no easy answers to this question, but clearly the availability of alcohol and its acceptance, even glamorization, in our society are factors. The National Coalition on Television Violence reports that before turning 18, the average American child will see 75,000 drinking scenes on television programs alone.

In just two days many of our young people will be celebrating Halloween. Many children look forward to this day as much as they do Christmas and Hanukkah. Who among us can forget the excitement of dressing up as ghosts and goblins and going from door to door shouting "trick or treat," and coming away with a fistful of candy?

Trick or treat.

This year the alcohol industry has given new meaning to those innocent words of childhood. They are serving up new treats—and new tricks.

They are saying: "It's Halloween, it's time to celebrate, it's time for a drink!" Beer companies offer free Halloween T-shirts, bat sunglasses, and glowing cups. Halloween parties sponsored by a major brewer are being held in nearly 40 cities.

What I say is scary is the possibility of increased carnage on our highways, the real specter of more binge drinking by our young people, and the absolute reality of those smaller, less dramatic cases of health and emotional problems caused by alcohol consumption.

Last year alone, we lost 3,158 young people in alcohol-related crashes, over 60 in every state in the union. Fully 40 percent of all deaths in young people are due to crashes—6,649 last year, and, as you can see, about half are related to alcohol.

What is also scary to me is the encouragement of "binge drinking" by our young people. Some of these Halloween ads encourage the purchase of 12 or 24 packs of beer, and who

Harcourt Brace & Company

will drink all that beer? 43 percent of college students, 35 percent of our high school seniors and 26 percent of 8th grade students have had five or more drinks in a row during the past two weeks. And beer and wine coolers are their favorite alcoholic beverages.

I also find it scary that we continue to think of beer and wine as "soft liquor." There's nothing "soft" about ethyl alcohol. And there's just as much ethyl alcohol in one can of beer or one glass of wine as there is in a mixed drink. That is the hard fact.

Finally, as the nations doctor and as a pediatrician, what I find scariest of all is that alcohol affects virtually every organ in the body. Alcohol consumption is associated with medical consequences ranging from slight functional impairment to life-threatening disease states—among them, liver disease, cancer of the esophagus, and hypertension. Where the organs of the body are concerned, alcohol is an equal opportunity destroyer.

The alcohol industry and its hired guns, the advertising agencies, know these facts. I hope that parents and other concerned adults do too. For if the alcohol industry has chosen to be part of the problem, it is up to you to be part of the solution.

In closing I would like to speak on behalf of those who have no voice in this debate—Americas children and adolescents. Let us not make this year, the year they robbed the kids of Halloween. For their sake and our own, let us keep Halloween sane, safe—and sober.

EXERCISE 5

SPEECHES AND MEETINGS

PRESIDENT GEORGE BUSH'S IRAQI WAR SPEECH

INSTRUCTIONS: This is a transcript of President George Bush's address to the nation on the night in January that allied planes began to bomb Iraq. Assume that the president presented his speech last night. Write a news story that summarizes its content. Because this is a verbatim copy of the president's speech, you can quote it directly.

Five months ago, Saddam Hussein started this cruel war against Kuwait; tonight the battle has been joined. This military action, taken in accord with United Nations resolutions and with the consent of the United States Congress, follows months of constant and virtually endless diplomatic activity on the part of the United Nations, the United States and many, many other countries.

Arab leaders sought what became known as an Arab solution, only to conclude that Saddam Hussein was unwilling to leave Kuwait. Others traveled to Baghdad in a variety of efforts to restore peace and justice. Our Secretary of State James Baker held a historic meeting in Geneva only to be totally rebuffed.

This past weekend, in a last ditch effort, the secretary-general of the United Nations went to the Middle East with peace in his heart, his second such mission, and he came back from Baghdad with no progress at all in getting Saddam Hussein to withdraw from Kuwait.

Now, the 28 countries with forces in the gulf area have exhausted all reasonable efforts to reach a peaceful resolution, have no choice but to drive Saddam from Kuwait by force. We will not fail.

As I report to you, air attacks are under way against military targets in Iraq. We are determined to knock out Saddam Husseins nuclear bomb potential. We will also destroy his chemical weapons facilities. Much of Saddams artillery and tanks will be destroyed.

Our operations are designed to best protect the lives of all the coalition forces by targeting Saddams vast military arsenal.

Initial reports from General Schwarzkopf are that our operations are proceeding according to plan.

Our objectives are clear. Saddam Husseins forces will leave Kuwait. The legitimate government of Kuwait will be restored to its rightful place and Kuwait will once again be free.

Iraq will eventually comply with all relevant United Nations resolutions and then when peace is restored, it is our hope that Iraq will live as a peaceful and cooperative member of the family of nations, thus enhancing the security and stability of the gulf.

Some may ask, "Why act now? Why not wait?" The answer is clear. The world could wait no longer.

Sanctions, though having some effect, showed no signs of accomplishing their objective. Sanctions were tried for well over five months and we and our allies concluded that sanctions alone would not force Saddam from Kuwait.

While the world waited, Saddam Hussein systematically raped, pillaged and plundered a tiny nation—no threat to his own. He subjected the people of Kuwait to unspeakable atrocities, and among those maimed and murdered—innocent children. While the world waited, Saddam sought to add to the chemical weapons arsenal he now possesses an infinitely more dangerous weapon of mass destruction, a nuclear weapon.

And while the world waited, while the world talked peace and withdrawal, Saddam Hussein dug in and moved massive forces into Kuwait. While the world waited, while Saddam

Harcourt Brace & Company

stalled, more damage was being done to the fragile economies of the Third World, the emerging democracies of Eastern Europe, to the entire world, including to our own economy.

The United States, together with the United Nations, exhausted every means at our disposal to bring this crisis to a peaceful end.

However, Saddam clearly felt that by stalling and threatening and defying the United Nations he could weaken the forces arrayed against him.

While the world waited, Saddam Hussein met every overture of peace with open contempt. While the world prayed for peace, Saddam prepared for war.

I had hoped that when the United States Congress, in historic debate, took its resolute action Saddam would realize he could not prevail and would move out of Kuwait in accord with the United Nations resolutions. He did not do that. Instead, he remained intransigent, certain that time was on his side. Saddam was warned over and over again to comply with the will of the United Nations—leave Kuwait or be driven out. Saddam has arrogantly rejected all warnings. Instead, he tried to make this a dispute between Iraq and the United States of America.

Well, he failed. Tonight, 28 nations, countries from five continents—Europe and Asia, Africa and the Arab League—have forces in the gulf area standing shoulder to shoulder against Saddam Hussein. These countries had hoped the use of force could be avoided. Regrettably, we now believe that only force will make him leave.

Prior to ordering our forces into battle, I instructed our military commanders to take every necessary step to prevail as quickly as possible and with the greatest degree of protection possible for American and allied servicemen and women. I've told the American people before that this will not be another Vietnam.

And I repeat this here tonight. Our troops will have the best possible support in the entire world. And they will not be asked to fight with one hand tied behind their back.

I'm hopeful that this fighting will not go on for long and that casualties will be held to an absolute minimum. This is an historic moment. We have in the past year made great progress in ending the long era of conflict and Cold War. We have before us the opportunity to forge for ourselves and for future generations a new world order, a world where the rule of law, not the law of the jungle, governs the conduct of nations. When we are successful, and we will be, we have a real chance at this new world order, an order in which a credible United Nations can use its peacekeeping role to fulfill the promise and vision of the U.N.'s founders.

We have no argument with the people of Iraq. Indeed, for the innocents caught in this conflict, I pray for their safety. Our goal is not the conquest of Iraq. It is the liberation of Kuwait.

It is my hope that somehow the Iraqi people can even now convince their dictator that he must lay down his arms, leave Kuwait and let Iraq itself rejoin the family of peace-loving nations. . . .

And let me say to everyone listening or watching tonight: When the troops we've sent in finish their work, I'm determined to bring them home as soon as possible. Tonight, as our forces fight, they and their families are in our prayers.

May God bless each and every one of them and the coalition forces at our side in the gulf, and may he continue to bless our nation, the United States of America.

E X E R C I S E   6

SPEECHES AND MEETINGS

PRESIDENT BILL CLINTON'S MEMORIAL ADDRESS FOR OKLAHOMA CITY BOMBING VICTIMS

INSTRUCTIONS: This is a transcript of President Bill Clinton's address at the memorial service held on April 23, 1995, for the people who died in the explosion that destroyed the Alfred P. Murrah Federal Building in Oklahoma City. The service was held at the State Fairgrounds Arena in Oklahoma City and was attended by more than 10,000 people. Oklahoma Gov. Frank Keating and the Rev. Billy Graham also spoke at the service. Because the speech is reprinted verbatim, you may quote it directly.

BACKGROUND

The federal building was destroyed by a bomb, made from fertilizer and fuel oil, that exploded the morning of April 19. The number of people known at this time to have died in the blast is 78. In addition, 432 people have been injured, and 150 are still missing. Soon after the explosion, FBI agents announced they were seeking two white males whom they were calling John Doe No. 1 and John Doe No. 2. The agents now suspect Timothy James McVeigh of Kingman, Ariz., is John Doe No. 1 and have charged him with destruction of federal property. Just hours after the bombing, McVeigh was arrested by an Oklahoma trooper for driving without a license plate and carrying a concealed knife. The search for John Doe No. 2 is continuing. FBI agents have been questioning Terry Nichols of Herington, Kan., and his brother James of Decker, Mich. Neither Terry nor James Nichols is suspected of being John Doe No. 2. But federal agents say in affidavits filed in court that the Nichols brothers and McVeigh are involved in right-wing militia organizations and know one another. Other court papers described McVeigh as angry with the federal government because of the assault by federal agents on the Branch Davidian complex in Waco, Texas, on April 19, 1993.

THE PRESIDENT'S SPEECH

Today our nation joins with you in grief. We mourn with you. We share your hope against hope that some may still survive. We thank all those who have worked so heroically to save lives and to solve this crime, those here in Oklahoma and those who are across this great land, and many who left their own lives to come here to work, hand-in-hand, with you.

We pledge to do all we can to help you heal the injured, to rebuild this city and to bring to justice those who did this evil.

This terrible sin took the lives of our American family, innocent children in that building only because their parents were trying to be good parents as well as good workers; citizens in the building going about their daily business; and many there who served the rest of us, who worked to help the elderly and the disabled, who worked to support our farmers and our veterans, who worked to enforce our laws and to protect us.

Let us say clearly they served us well and we are grateful.

But for so many of you, they were also neighbors and friends. You saw them at church, or the P.T.A. meetings, at the civic clubs or the ball park. You know them in ways that all the rest of America could not. And to all the members of the families here present who

Harcourt Brace & Company

have suffered loss, though we share your grief, your pain is unimaginable and we know that. We cannot undo it. That is God's work.

Our words seem small beside the loss you have endured, but I found a few I wanted to share today. I have received a lot of letters in these last terrible days. One stood out because it came from a young widow and a mother of three whose own husband was murdered with over 200 other Americans when Pan Am 103 was shot down. Here is what that woman said I should say to you today.

"The anger you feel is valid but you must not allow yourselves to be consumed by it. The hurt you feel must not be allowed to turn into hate, but instead into the search for justice. The loss you feel must not paralyze your own lives. Instead, you must try to pay tribute to your loved ones by continuing to do all the things they left undone, thus ensuring they did not die in vain."

Wise words from one who also knows.

You have lost too much but you have not lost everything, and you have certainly not lost America, for we will stand with you for as many tomorrows as it takes.

If ever we needed evidence of that, I could only recall the words of Governor (Frank) and Mrs. (Cathy) Keating, "If anybody thinks that Americans are mostly mean and selfish, they ought to come to Oklahoma."

If anybody thinks Americans have lost the capacity for love, and caring, and courage, they ought to come to Oklahoma.

To all my fellow Americans beyond this hall I say, one thing we owe those who have sacrificed is the duty to purge ourselves of the dark forces which gave rise to this evil.

There are forces that threaten our common peace, our freedom, our way of life. Let us teach our children that the God of comfort is also the God of righteousness. Those who trouble their own house will inherit the wind. Justice will prevail.

Let us let our own children know that we will stand against the forces of fear. When there is talk of hatred, let us stand up and talk against it. When there is talk of violence, let us stand up and talk against it. In the face of death let us honor life.

As St. Paul admonished us, "Let us not be overcome by evil, but overcome evil with good."

Yesterday Hillary and I had the privilege of speaking with some children of other federal employees, children like those who were lost here. And one little girl said something we will never forget. She said, "We should all plant a tree in memory of the children." So this morning before we got on the plane to come here, at the White House, we planted that tree in honor of the children of Oklahoma.

It was a dogwood with its wonderful spring flower and its deep enduring roots. It embodies the lesson of the Psalms that the life of a good person is like a tree whose leaf does not wither.

My fellow Americans, a tree takes a long time to grow, and wounds take a long time to heal, but we must begin. Those who are lost now belong to God. Some say we will be with them, but until that happens, their legacy must be our lives.

Thank you all and God bless you.

Harcourt Brace & Company

EXERCISE 7
SPEECHES AND MEETINGS

COUNTY COMMISSION MEETING

INSTRUCTIONS: Assume that your county commission held a meeting at 2 p.m. yesterday. Write a news story that summarizes the comments and decisions made at this meeting.

The members of your county commission began their meeting by listening to plans for a luxury condominium development on Elkhart Lake. The new development will be called "SunCrest." The property is owned by The Roswell Development Corporation, headquartered in Pittsburgh. Carlos Rey, a spokesman for the company, said: "We are planning a series of 10-story buildings overlooking the lake. None will exceed 100 feet in height. They will contain a total of 715 units. Estimated selling price of a unit will be $250,000 and upwards, perhaps to a top of $750,000 for the larger penthouse units. The development is about 5 miles from the nearest town, and we intend to promote it as a vacation and recreation center. We'll have our own well and our own sewer system, with an extensive recreation system centered around the lake. We know that fire protection is a concern. The township fire department serving the area doesn't have a ladder truck capable of reaching the top of a 10-story building. We'll donate $600,000 for the purchase of one." The commission voted 5–2 to approve the plans and to rezone the land from agricultural to PUD: Planned Unit Development.

Next, at 3 p.m., the commission honored and presented plaques to two 15-year-old girls. The girls, Doreen Nicholls and Pamela DeZinno, were walking along a river in a county park last week and saw a young child fall from a boat. Both girls dove into the river and pulled her out. While Doreen then proceeded to administer CPR, Pamela called for help, thus saving a life.

Appearing next before the commission, Sheriff Gus DiCesare asked it to require a three-day wait before a pistol could be bought from any gun dealer in the county. "I do not think that 72 hours is too long for someone to wait to buy a handgun," Sheriff DiCesare said. "There are a lot of cases where people went out and bought a gun with criminal intent and used it right away to shoot or rob someone. We want a cooling off period." Under the proposed ordinance, a customer would have to provide the dealer with his name, address, date of birth and other information, then wait 72 hours before picking up the pistol. The dealer would mail the information to the sheriffs department, where it would be kept on a computerized file. Sheriff DiCesare said it would speed the identification of the owner of a pistol found at a crime scene. A majority of the commissioners said they favor such a proposal but want to get more information and possibly hold a public hearing to give every citizen an opportunity to speak his mind. They promised to seriously consider it at their next meeting.

The commissioners then decided not to give themselves a raise, rejecting a proposed pay raise on a 4–3 vote. It has been five years since the last pay raise for them. Then their salary went from $47,500 to $51,000 a year. Yesterday, the majority, led by Commissioners Roland Graumann and Anita Shenuski, argued that a raise was "inappropriate." Faith Ellis argued a proposed increase to $56,500 was not out of line because commissioners in other counties earn more. "This is not asking too much," she said. "The county is getting a good deal for the time we put in." Anne Chen responded, "Our work should be done for community service, not just for how much we make."

E X E R C I S E 8

SPEECHES AND MEETINGS

SCHOOL BOARD MEETING

INSTRUCTIONS: Assume that your school board held its monthly meeting at 7:30 p.m. yesterday. Write a news story that summarizes the comments and decisions made at this meeting.

The school board opened its meeting by honoring seven retiring teachers: Shirley Dawsun, Carmen Foucault, Nina Paynich, Kenneth Satava, Nancy Lee Scott, Lonnie McEwen, and Harley Sawyer. Paynich worked as a teacher 44 years, longer than any of the others. Each teacher was given a framed "Certificate of Appreciation" and a good round of applause.

The school board then turned to the major item on its agenda: the budget for next year. The budget totals $418.7 million, up 5% from this year. It includes $6.3 million for a new elementary school to be built on West Madison Ave. It will be completed and opened in two years. The budget also includes a 4.5% raise for teachers and a 6% raise for administrators. Also, the salary of the superintendent of schools was raised by $10,000, to $117,000 a year. The vote was unanimous: 9–0.

The school board then discussed the topic of remedial summer classes. Board member Umberto Vacante proposed eliminating them to save an estimated $1.1 million. "They're just too expensive, especially when you consider we serve only about 900 students each summer. A lot of them are students who flunked their regular classes. Often, if they attend the summer classes, they don't have to repeat a grade. If we're going to spend that kind of money, I think we should use it to help and reward our most talented students. They're the ones we ignore. We could offer special programs for them." Supt. Greg Hubbard responded, "Some of these summer students have learning disabilities and emotional problems, and they really need the help. This would hurt them terribly. Without it, they might never graduate." The board then voted 7–2 to keep the classes one more year, but to ask its staff for a study of the matter.

During a one-hour hearing that followed, about 100 people, many loud and angry, debated the issue of creationism vs. evolution. "We've seen your biology books," said parent Claire Sawyer. "I don't want my children using them. They never mention the theory of creationism." Another parent, Harley Euon of 410 East Third Street, responded: "Evolution isn't a theory. It's proven fact. Creationism is a religious idea, not even a scientific theory. People here are trying to force schools to teach our children their religion." A third parent, Roy E. Cross of 101 Charow Lane, agreed, adding: "People can teach creationism in their homes and churches. It's not the schools job." After listening to the debate, the board voted 6–3 to continue using the present textbooks, but to encourage parents to discuss the matter with their children and to provide in their individual homes the religious training they deem most appropriate for their families.

Finally, last on its agenda, the board unanimously adopted a resolution praising the school systems ADDITIONS: adult volunteers who contribute their spare time to help and assist their neighborhood schools. Last year, Supt. Greg Hubbard reported, there was a total of 897 ADDITIONS, and they put in a total of 38,288 hours of volunteer time.

Harcourt Brace & Company

E X E R C I S E   9

SPEECHES AND MEETINGS

CITY COUNCIL MEETING

INSTRUCTIONS: Assume that your City Council held a meeting at 8 p.m. yesterday. Write a news story that summarizes the comments and decisions made at this meeting.

BACKGROUND

For 10 years, a downtown church in your city (the First United Methodist Church at 680 Garland Avenue) has provided a shelter for the homeless, allowing them to sleep in the basement of its fellowship hall every night and feeding them both breakfast and dinner. The church can house 180 people each night and relies on a staff of more than 200 volunteers. In recent years, they've been overwhelmed, and the church, by itself, is unable to continue to afford to shoulder the entire burden. It has asked for help: for donations and for more room, especially in winter, for the homeless to sleep. Civic leaders have formed the Coalition for the Homeless, Inc., a nonprofit organization, and hope to build a new shelter. The coalition has asked the city to donate a site, valued at $500,000. Coalition leaders said they will then raise the $1.5 million needed to construct the shelter. The coalition leaders say they will also operate the shelter, relying on volunteers; a small, full-time professional staff; and donations from concerned citizens.

FIRST SPEAKER

Ida Levine, president of the Coalition for the Homeless, Inc.:

"As you, uh, know, what we're trying to do here is raise $1.5 million to build the shelter. We're approaching everyone that might be able to help and, so far, have collected about $200,000 and have pledges of another $318,000, and thats just the beginning, in two months. So we're certain that if you provide the land, we'll be able to, uh, come up with all the money for this thing. The site we have in mind is the old fire station on Garland Avenue. The building is so old that its worthless, and we'd tear it down, but its an ideal location for our purposes."

SECOND SPEAKER

Lt. Luis Rafelson:

"I'm here officially, representing the police department, to say that we're all for this. It costs the taxpayers about $350,000 a year to arrest homeless people for violating city ordinances like trespassing on private property and sleeping at night in parks and such. During the average month last year we arrested 300 homeless people, sometimes more. It takes about 2 hours to arrest a person and do all the booking and paperwork, while taking five minutes to transport them to a shelter. So you're wasting police time, time we could be spending on more important things. So if the city spends $500,000 on this deal, it'll save that much in a year, maybe more."

Harcourt Brace & Company

THIRD SPEAKER

Banker Irvin Porej:

"The people who stay in shelters are just like you and me. The difference is that we have a place to go. They're good people for the most part, just down on their luck. This would provide a temporary shelter for them, help them get back on their feet. Until now, we've had churches doing this, and the Salvation Army has a shelter, too, but we should put an end to the church shelters. Its not fair to them because the churches are burdened by a problem that everyone should be helping with, and the problem is getting too big for them to handle."

FOURTH SPEAKER

Council member Sandra Bandolf:

"We have to address this problem. It's not going to go away. And with this solution, it really won't cost the city anything. No one's asking us for money or anything, only for a piece of land that's been lying unused for years."

FIFTH SPEAKER

Council member William Belmonte:

"I suppose I'm going to be the only one who votes against this. Why should taxpayers suddenly start paying for this, people who work hard for their money and are struggling these days to support their families? And what happens if the coalition doesn't raise all the money it needs for the shelter, what happens then? What happens if they breach the agreement? Then we'll be left holding the bag, expected to pay for this damn thing and to support it for years. That'll add a whole new bureaucracy to the city, and where'll the money come from then?"

SIXTH SPEAKER

Trina Guzman, president of the Downtown Merchants' Assn.:

"The members of my association are strongly opposed to this. We agree that the city needs a shelter, that we have an obligation to help the people who are really homeless and needy, but not on Garland Avenue. That's just a block from downtown, and we've been having trouble with these people for years. Some of them need help, have all sorts of problems like alcoholism and mental illness that no one here's talking about. Remember too that these people aren't allowed to stay in the shelters during the day. Theoretically, they're supposed to go out and work, or at least look for work. What some of them do is hang around Main Street, panhandling and annoying people and using our parking lots and alleys for toilets. We've got customers who tell us they won't come downtown any more because they're afraid of being approached and asked for money and being mugged or something. Let's feed these people and help them, but put them out somewhere where they can't hurt anyone."

OUTCOME

The council voted 6–1 to donate the land. Belmont cast the single vote against the proposal.

Harcourt Brace & Company

CHAPTER 15

PUBLIC RELATIONS: WORKING WITH THE NEWS MEDIA

*The press is the best instrument for enlightening the mind of man,
and improving him as a rational, moral and social being.*

(Thomas Jefferson)

WHAT IS PUBLIC RELATIONS?

Public relations is communication meant to project a positive image about an organization or product and to produce a positive reaction from the public about that organization or product.

To achieve that objective, public relations departments are made up of practitioners with a combination of skills. Almost every public relations practitioner is a writer and editor. Practitioners are also researchers, photographers, videographers, layout and design experts, publishers, media specialists, interpersonal communicators, promoters, image-makers, market analysts and financial experts.

The goal for most practitioners is to get their client's name in the news without having to pay for the publicity. Practitioners want the public to respond favorably whenever they hear or see the client's name.

Whereas a journalist's objective is to serve the public, a practitioner's allegiance is to the client. To succeed in getting the client's name in the news, the practitioner must serve the needs of the public and the client. Practitioners cannot plaster their client's name all over the news release or it will look like an advertisement. Instead, they use the client's name within the context of news.

To get their news releases accepted, practitioners think and write like journalists. Practitioners writing news releases about a seminar or speech use the same techniques as reporters do. Thus, the best news releases sound and look as though they were written by journalists.

PUBLIC RELATIONS AGENCIES

Some practitioners work in a public relations agency, representing companies or other organizations either throughout the year or just for special events, such as a 20th anniversary. Public relations practitioners in agencies handle several "accounts" simultaneously. Agencies can be as small as a one-person consultant contracted to write and edit a company's communications, develop brochures or shoot video training tapes. Or an agency can be a large, international network of offices. International conglomerates usually hire worldwide agencies to handle their public relations needs in different cultures.

CORPORATE PUBLIC RELATIONS

Many public relations practitioners work in a public relations department within a company. Some of these corporate practitioners handle internal communications, while others deal with external communications.

Internal Communications

Internal communicators keep in touch with company employees. They ensure that a company's employees, whether in the same building or in a branch office several states away, feel like part of the company.

For example, a machinist in a General Motors plant in Texas may not feel administrators in the Detroit headquarters care much about her. The public relations practitioner makes the machinist aware of her role in the whole company's operations. Via the company newsletter, the practitioner communicates to the machinist and other employees about activities at headquarters as well as in branch facilities. Similarly, a practitioner helps employees understand the reasons a plant in another part of the country is shutting down or how a change in policy will affect them.

Some internal communicators send birthday cards to all company employees to show their company cares about them. Others publish photographs and brief biographies of all new employees in a newsletter or news video. Still others hold companywide competitions or host awards banquets for all personnel. Usually the public relations practitioner stays in the background, facilitating goodwill from company executives: a department head signs the birthday cards the practitioner sends, a CEO announces the competition the practitioner orchestrates and the CEO shakes hands with the winners, and a president reads the practitioner's prepared speech at the awards banquet. Thus, in many ways, the practitioner is similar to a theater director, who never appears onstage but coordinates the performances of others.

External Communications

External communicators promote a positive image of their company to people outside the company. They research and identify different external groups and determine the best way to reach them. To influence or project a positive image, most practitioners write and send news releases and features to the media. Other tools and skills include developing press kits that contain information about the company; setting up speakers' bureaus; staging events; filming news clips; writing public service announcements; holding meetings; and designing posters, brochures and pamphlets. All these activities help disseminate information about the company or its products to the public. Many companies' public relations departments manage all their standard external communication needs, while some companies also hire public relations agencies to handle special needs.

BECOMING A PUBLIC RELATIONS PRACTITIONER

Usually, schools require students majoring in public relations to enroll in a reporting class. The class teaches public relations majors about the media's definitions of news, style of writing, deadlines and other characteristics and policies.

Professionals agree on the class's importance. A survey of 200 members of the Public Relations Society of America found that professionals consider a news reporting course more important for public relations majors than any course in public relations. The professionals were given a list of 38 possible courses and asked to select 13 courses for public relations majors. Ninety percent chose "Basic News Reporting"—their first choice. Eighty-five percent listed "Introduction to Public Relations."

Many journalists who decide to leave the traditional news business—perhaps as many as 45 percent—accept jobs in public relations. Companies hire reporters and editors as public relations practitioners because they have writing skills, which are essential to the job.

WORKING WITH NEWS MEDIA

Many news stories have public relations origins. Practitioners bring information about a company to journalists' attention, often through a news release. If the news release is well written, it has a better chance of being repeated in the media, thus accomplishing the practitioner's goal of transmitting positive news about the company to the public. If a news release is poorly written, it usually is given only a glance before landing in a trash basket. Journalists might also follow up on the idea presented in a news release, but interview their own sources, write their own stories and present their own angles.

Public relations practitioners use media to get information about their client to the public. Therefore, practitioners find out which media outlets will best serve their purposes—newspapers, trade publications, radio or television.

Practitioners check to determine who is in charge of different news departments. They regularly update their files so their releases are not addressed to editors who moved (or died). By sending their news releases to the right editor, practitioners increase the likelihood that the releases will be used. At the same time, practitioners decrease the likelihood they will waste other editors' time—and harm their own reputations in the process. For example, most editors will discard a news release about a company employee's promotion, but a business editor might report the promotion in a weekly column devoted to local promotions. Similarly, most editors would discard a news release about a Christmas program at a church, but a religion editor might mention the program in a roundup about Christmas activities.

News releases sent to radio stations are written in broadcast style and format. Thus, radio announcers do not have to rewrite the releases; they can read them verbatim over the air. News releases sent to newspapers are written in Associated Press style. Public relations practitioners write news releases the same way journalists write newsworthy stories. The more a news release looks like a news story, the more likely it will appear in the news.

In many respects, it may seem as though practitioners are using journalists to achieve their own goals. Yet news releases help journalists stay informed about what is happening in their community. Journalists can still choose whether to use the news releases.

ELEMENTS OF A NEWS RELEASE

Journalists have long complained about news releases. Several studies found that journalists' complaints have remained consistent since the 1960s. Journalists reject news releases for many reasons: They are too long; they lack news elements; they are poorly written; they fail to include important information; they have not been localized; they contain puffery; they arrive too late; they are mailed to the wrong person; they are written more for clients than for journalists and the public.

The following suggestions for writing a successful news release are directed toward print media, but are also helpful for attaining success with broadcast news journalists.

List a Reliable Contact Person and Phone Number

Most journalists follow up on news releases. They need to know whom they can call to obtain more information. Thus, an effective news release lists a contact person, usually a public relations practitioner familiar with the subject of the release. The release also lists a phone number for that contact.

A recent survey found that editors commonly complain that the listed contact person is unavailable when they call for information.[1] As Eloise De Haan of the York (Pa.) Daily Record puts it: "What I hate is you call the person listed as contact and he or she is out of town, can't be reached, and no one else is cleared for comment."

Similarly, a California editor who struggles with a three-hour time difference to the East Coast admonishes: "Don't send us a news release with a contact name and then allow the contact to leave immediately for a long weekend or vacation, or even the afternoon. It is extremely frustrating to get a news release, to have a question, and then learn that the contact listed is unavailable for comment."

Send the Release on Time

Public relations consultant Dick Elfenbein found in a national survey of editors that they prefer to receive news releases in the morning the day prior to their likely publication. Furthermore, many editors prefer to receive news releases by fax. Many editors joke about the "4:45 fax." They feel it is timed purposefully so practitioners can dodge journalists' callbacks. Practitioners' lack of consideration for a newsroom's deadlines and the way journalists work promotes ill-will between practitioners and journalists.

Depend on the Five W's

Journalists respect public relations practitioners who understand the media's definitions of news. Journalists want to be informed about major stories. They do not want to be bothered with stories that are obviously not newsworthy. Journalists discard news releases about such topics.

Linda Morton, a public relations practitioner and professor, found that only 39 of 129 news releases from the PR News Wire contained news elements. In addition, only 25 of 103 university news releases contained news elements.[2]

The best news releases are so good that it is difficult to distinguish between them and the stories written by a news organization's own staff. Here are three examples:

Tina Delgado, assistant professor of music at Rollins College, will present a piano recital at 4 p.m. Sunday in the Annie Russell Theatre.

Women Alone, a group for women who are divorced, widowed or separated, will meet at noon on Friday at the Center for Women's Medicine in the Medical Plaza at 2501 N. Orange Ave.

Philomene Gates, the author of "Suddenly Alone: A Woman's Guide to Widowhood," will speak about widowhood at the Public Library at 10:30 a.m. Saturday.

---

[1] Dick Elfenbein. "Fax Survey." *Editor & Publisher*, June 26, 1993, pp. 18, 19, 37.
[2] Linda Morton. "Researcher Finds Complaints Against Press Releases Are Justified." *Editor & Publisher*, May 8, 1993, pp. 42, 52.

Analyze those leads. Notice that, like good news story leads, all three emphasize the news—and are clear, concise and factual.

Write Well

Another national survey found that editors say many of the news releases they receive are poorly written. The study showed that the average reader must be a third- or fourth-year college student to understand the average press release. In contrast, news organizations strive to write at the 11th-grade level. Journalists are likely to throw away hard-to-read releases and accept those that are easy to understand. Many news organizations rejected this news release:

> Mortalene has begun a multi-center Phase II clinical trial of its Interleukin-2 (IL-2) receptor-targeted Fusion Toxin in patients with moderate to severe plaque-type psoriasis. The randomized, double-blind, placebo-controlled study will evaluate the clinical effects and safety of IL-2 Fusion Toxin at three dose levels compared with placebo in a group of sixty patients.

When writing news releases, practitioners should write as journalists. Words should be simple, and average sentence length should be about 20 words. They should avoid the passive voice as much as possible.

Practitioners should keep their copy clear, eliminate unnecessary words, write short paragraphs and get to the point immediately. They should also limit a news release to one or two pages.

Proofreading is essential. Editors often find important information missing, buried or mistaken—reasons for callbacks, which annoy editors and may give them second thoughts about using the story.

Practitioners should think of news releases as a community service (for newspaper readers and broadcast listeners) and not a client service. Their writing should be lively and to-the-point, not boring and literary.

Localize Information

News releases often present generalized information, failing to indicate how that information affects people in a community. Too often practitioners confuse "localization" and "proximity." In fact, localizing can mean reflecting a psychological as well as geographical closeness. A university's health science center submitted the following three news releases, which illustrate that principle:

> While many Americans may be eating less red meat to lower cholesterol and fat levels, researchers at the University of Florida are investigating the possibility that older Americans should, in fact, be eating more.

> Doctors have some unseasonable advice for pregnant women heading outdoors to enjoy this summer's warm weather: Bundle up.
> Although the risk is small, they could get bitten by ticks carrying Lyme disease, a rare but disabling illness that University of Florida physicians say can be transmitted by infected mothers-to-be to the unborn babies.

> Schoolteacher Dawn Flanegan doesn't have to whisper to her class any more, thanks to a new surgical procedure performed on her vocal cords by a University of Florida surgeon.
> Just a few months ago, the 40-year-old kindergarten teacher could speak only in a hoarse, breathy whisper. She now speaks in tones clearly audible over the telephone,

Harcourt Brace & Company

and she no longer struggles to communicate, although her vocal volume remains slightly weaker than it was previously.

The loss of Flanegan's voice was caused by a paralysis of her right vocal cord, which occurred last November when surgeons found it necessary to sever a nerve during the removal of a noncancerous tumor. The tumor was wrapped around the nerve.

Raising her voice to be heard above a room full of noisy 5-year-olds became so physically exhausting that Flanegan had to quit teaching. The vocal cord paralysis also made it difficult for her to cough, and when she attempted to swallow, food would frequently enter her windpipe instead of the esophagus.

"My voice is very important in managing 24 children from 8 a.m. to 2 p.m. every day," said Flanegan, who has three children of her own. "I couldn't read stories to them; I couldn't help teach them sounds because I couldn't even make some sounds myself after the tumor surgery."

Flanegan's voice loss was evaluated last December at the University of Florida's Voice Disorder Clinic. . . .

The first of the three news releases discusses a topic that concerns many adults—their cholesterol level—but it also points out an unusual or unexpected twist: that older Americans may need more red meat. The second news release concerns another unusual topic: the fact that pregnant women need to bundle up, even in summer, to protect their unborn babies from Lyme disease (a disease often in the news). Notice that the third news release emphasizes the human element: a woman's struggle to overcome an unusual medical problem. These news releases mention their source, but are not blatant advertisements for it.

Additional Considerations

Thousands of news releases are written every day. Journalists receive them in the mail, on fax machines and from a public relations news wire. To make their releases more likely to be read by journalists, practitioners should include:

- The contact's name and telephone number, and the address of the public relations agency or department.

- A short headline summarizing the contents of the release.

- The release date, indicating an appropriate publication date. Normally, news releases are written in advance of an event.

- A journalistic format. Begin one-third of the way down the page and use "more" or "#" on the appropriate pages.

- Creative visuals or photos to attract readers' attention. Visuals, such as graphs, charts and photographs, help illustrate a point. They also catch the eye, drawing readers into the story. Good visuals are creative and to-the-point.

- A letter to the editor indicating more about the sponsoring company or ideas for using the attached news release.

TYPES OF NEWS RELEASES

News releases can achieve a variety of objectives, such as publicizing a new company or pointing out the effects a company has on a community. The most common types of news releases are advance stories, event stories, features and discoveries.

Advance Stories

Practitioners write announcements whenever their company or client will sponsor an activity such as a speech or seminar:

> Reed Hospital will offer "Matters of the Heart—Your Aging Parent and You" from 7 to 9 p.m. Oct. 17 at Reed's Administration Building, 3601 W. Thirteen Mile Road.
>
> The class is free, but participants must register in advance by calling 1-800-000-0000.

Event Stories

Even though practitioners write a story prior to an event, they write it as though the event has already happened and the news organization is reporting on it. The story serves two main purposes: First, it lets journalists know what will occur at the event, in case they want to cover it; second, it frees journalists from writing the story.

Journalists rarely publish such a story verbatim. They attend the event, perhaps simply to verify the story's accuracy. Reporters also rewrite the stories so they do not use the same word-for-word accounts that appear in other publications.

Practitioners also give members of the press copies of speeches before they are delivered. This practice enables journalists to quote the speakers accurately. However, journalists must attend the speeches, because some newsmakers change parts of their speeches at the last moment.

The following story was written about an upcoming presentation at a chemical society's convention. The headline, "Leaves Found to Be Rich Source of Protein for Humans," indicates that the story concerns a topic that interests many readers: health trends. However, this advance could be improved:

> Tobacco and soybean leaves are a better source of protein for human consumption than egg white, cheese and milk, scientists said today. Tobacco protein, particularly, has a more complete complement of essential amino acids, they said.
>
> The researchers have been experimenting with tobacco protein for several years, and have demonstrated that it can be whipped into meringue toppings or added to any foods that are whipped or jellied.
>
> Now they say edible proteins can be extracted as well from the leaves of alfalfa, soybean and sugar beets. Unlike traditional protein sources like meats, eggs and milk, the plant leaves contain no fat or cholesterol, said Austin Black of the University of Iowa today. He spoke here at the 99th national meeting of the Midwestern Chemical Society.
>
> With world population increasing and a shortage of protein for human nutrition imminent, Dr. Black said that leaf protein, being the most abundant protein on earth, can alleviate the supply and demand problem. He also said that after extracting the protein and removing undesirable leaf constituents, the fiber and juice from the leaf could be processed into smoking materials that are less harmful than those on the market now.
>
> "This is especially important for developing countries where the smoking population is increasing and human malnutrition is overwhelming," Dr. Black said.
>
> He described two forms of leaf protein, fraction-1-protein (F-1-p) and fraction-2-protein (F-2-p). F-1-p accumulates inside chloroplasts—where the green pigment chlorophyll occurs—and is the enzyme responsible for fixation of carbon dioxide in photosynthesis. F-2-p represents the remaining protein that surrounds the nuclei of the leaf cells.
>
> The tobacco F-1-p has a protein content of 99.5%; F-1-p's from soybean, sugar beet and alfalfa range between 97.3–98.4% in protein. All F-1-p's are odorless and tasteless, as are all F-2-p's, but they are beige to yellow in color.

Harcourt Brace & Company

In food applications, plant leaf protein can be added to any food that will be whipped or jellied. Dr. Black said that these proteins could serve the same function as egg white and the protein casein in the new commercial fat substitutes. The result would be an even lower fat content and nearly equal or better protein level, he said.

Dr. Black noted that tobacco F-1-p may have pharmaceutical uses, particularly for renal and post-surgical patients. For patients undergoing dialysis, tobacco F-1-p provides a near ideal combination of protein and amino acids and it would be nutritious for post-surgical patients also, he said.

This story has several problems. Although the first paragraph notes "scientists," only one is named and quoted throughout the news release. Dr. Black or the event—the chemical society's meeting—need to be mentioned higher in the story, as in a speech story. In addition, the news release should be simplified by eliminating much of the information in the last four paragraphs.

Features

Practitioners often write feature stories as press releases. Many features can interest a national audience without targeting a specific community. The public enjoys well-written features, and often does not recognize them as publicity. Sometimes features mention the client as the sponsor of an event. At other times, features quote the client as an authority or source.

The following feature describes homebuilders using the Internet for information. The feature mentions a specific distributor, Stevens Construction Inc., in St. Louis. It also quotes the manufacturer, Jackson Windows, headquartered in Jackson, Mich.:

Nearly 80 percent of homeowners now consider themselves buy-it-yourselfers. Yet, only one in five say they rely on the advice of professionals to assist in their product buying decisions, according to a survey by *Better Homes and Gardens Special Interest Publications.*

Instead, that advice could be coming from one of the fastest-growing sources of information for homeowners—the Internet's World Wide Web—say building product manufacturers. The Web grew by 360 percent in just the last quarter, according to *Open Markets Inc.*

"Buy-it-yourselfers demand information about home products where they can reach it, when they want it, " said Daniel Hobbs of Stevens Construction Inc., the local distributor of Jackson Windows and Doors. He said area homeowners are seeking product information once requested only by builders and contractors. "They demand competitive comparisons, details of product features and examples of what the product will look like installed."

Right now, more homeowners are looking for this kind of information on the Internet. "If it's not there, that product may not be considered when it's time to buy," said Marvin Espinoza, vice president of marketing for Jackson Windows, which recently established a site on the Web to provide on-demand information about windows and doors.

With a home computer, modem and browser software, homeowners have everything from product photography to technical information at their fingertips. And, while only two percent of building materials manufacturers have World Wide Web sites now, according to *WebTrack's InterAd Database*, Espinoza expects that number to rise quickly.

Like Jackson Windows, Frigidaire, Electrolux, Master Lock and Grohe Faucets have anticipated this demand and established sites on the Web.

Upon accessing Jackson's home page (http://www.jack.com) through an online service, users may choose informational paths including "Windowscaping," which provides photography and descriptions of design ideas; "Crash Course," including a glossary of window and door terms and energy efficiency ratings terminology; "Jamb Session," which highlights product line options and benefits; and "Windows of Opportunity," where users can request free information about making window decisions by entering their name and mailing address.

"We expect the Web to support our sales personnel," said Hobbs. "Buy-it-yourselfers now have the window and door information they demand—at their fingertips—when and where they demand it."

For free literature about making window decisions, call 1-800-000-0000, or visit Jackson Windows on the World Wide Web at http://www.jack.com

Most news organizations would eliminate the feature's last sentence and both mentions of the company's online home page to keep it from sounding too much like an advertisement.

Discoveries and Results

Universities, hospitals, corporations and research institutes want the public to know about their discoveries and the results of their work. A news release from a university medical center began with the following paragraphs. The rest of the news release explained scientific terms and the researcher's discovery:

Our skin wrinkles. Our hair thins and grays. Our shoulders stoop. But this slide toward senescence may not be inevitable, according to biochemistry Professor Vini Glicco, Ph.D., who has discovered a way to reverse aging in a test tube.

By "refolding" long ribbons of amino acids in muscles, eye-lens and liver proteins, Glicco says he has successfully reversed aging on the molecular level.

Proteins are made up of amino acids, like beads on a necklace, and folded into a three-dimensional structure that determines their function. For years scientists have known that a damaged or missing amino acid results in the production of abnormal proteins that can cause such molecular diseases as Alzheimer's, cystic fibrosis and sickle-cell anemia. But what has confounded scientists is the fact that a protein may have all of its amino acids intact yet *still* be abnormal in shape. Glicco speculated it had to do with the folding, and he was right. . . .

PUBLIC RELATIONS PRACTITIONERS AND JOURNALISTS WORKING TOGETHER

Public relations practitioners provide a valuable service for both their clients and the public. Yet journalists and public relations practitioners often have a difficult relationship. Practitioners complain that journalists generalize from a few bad experiences with practitioners who are ineffective or unprofessional: practitioners who do not understand how the media operate and are indifferent to the media's need for information that is clear, concise, accurate and objective.

Journalists need and respect public relations practitioners with good writing skills: practitioners able to translate complicated information into clear, readable stories. Journalists also appreciate practitioners who understand the media's definitions of news. Journalists want to be informed about major stories. They do not want stories that are not newsworthy.

Good public relations people are available and cooperative. To help journalists meet their deadlines, they respond quickly, no matter what the question, and do their best to provide accurate and complete information at all times.

The best practitioners are also well informed about their own companies and industries. They can find information quickly and will arrange interviews with experts and top executives.

When an important issue arises, some anticipate journalists' questions and make sure that the right corporate officials are available to answer them.

Some people believe the tension between journalists and public relations practitioners is slowly dissipating. However, some tension seems inevitable—and perhaps is healthy: It may keep people in both professions on their toes.

Opinion

PRESS RELEASES NOT KNOWN TO BE NEWSY

By **Mark Nixon**
Lansing (Mich.) State Journal

The Big Orange Stink on my desk is begging me to write about it.

Every time a paper gets shuffled on my desktop, another cloud of the NI-712 odorizer by Neutron Industries grasps me by the throat. It's like being smothered in orange Jell-O.

"What's that *smell*?" asks a passing colleague.

It's a perfumed press release with a half-life of 13,000 years. There's a little printed warning on the orange card which says: "Card may adversely affect some materials."

Yeah, like brain cells.

If you want to know what's wrong with the media today, look no further than the press release. Reporters and editors are being buried alive in news—I use that word loosely—about everything from improved bonding agents in plywood manufacturing to fashion statements out of Buffalo.

The rest of the world worries about nuclear waste and the trade deficit. Journalists want something done about press releases.

Let's stop right here so you can ask yourself, "Why should I care?"

Because somewhere in the daily mailbag is a press release with actual news value, and it might be yours. It might be something newspapers actually want to do a story about. It might—if the editor

hasn't already thrown himself out the window in despair.

Newsworthy press releases do exist. I have personally seen three. When a newsworthy release lands on an editor's desk, it is cause for minor celebration. Editors huddle around it, admiringly. One editor has a few framed on her wall.

Most releases, though, are mass-mailed by corporate boneheads who make more money than newspaper editors—a sore point in itself. Here are some genuine releases that have landed on my desk recently:

- From Aberdeen, S.D.: "Skip Clay, president of Super 8 Management Inc., a subsidiary of Super 8 Motels Inc., has been awarded the Certified Hotel Administrator designation by the Educational Institute of the American Hotel & Motel Association." Way to go, Skip.

- From the Hyatt Regency in Maui, Hawaii: "We recently sent out our astronomy program news mailing and inadvertently left out the actual release. We are now enclosing that release." Nobody in the newsroom remembers the first letter or the actual release. We hope the stars shine brightly in Maui.

- "We are pleased to announce our move to new headquarters effective January 2." That's from the Dynaric

(continued on next page)

company in Fort Lee, N.J. Any day now we expect a letter from Dynaric, telling who they are and what they do.

The biggest perpetrators of the press release glut are governments (surprise, surprise!) and brokerage firms. Cryptic releases like this, flagged "For Immediate Release," come from the agriculture department:

"The psychotropic pesticide Tulephecyamixemol-23 is being considered for waiver from the conditional H-Zeta list." Are we to be alarmed, or relieved?

In this newsroom, the worst offender is the stock brokerage firm, Shearson Lehman Hutton. If I could take their junk mail budget and divvy it up among its clients, I'd be voted CEO of Shearson Lehman overnight.

Shearson Lehman sends us up to 5 letters a day (often duplicates or triplicates). These are often accompanied by fat packets containing meaningless rows of numbers. Fortunately, there's a cover letter that spells it out: "Low-yield pork belly mutuals were transferred to a junk equity fund on the Tokyo Exchange in December."

Read that aloud three times a day, and you understand why our business editor's eyes begin glazing over by 10 a.m.

Some journalists may call this column a heresy. They insist that press releases are the lifeblood of the industry, that we have a duty to welcome the daily flood of dull, useless press releases in order not to interrupt the vital flow of public input.

If they think that, have them send me a press release. I know just the place for it.

SUGGESTED READINGS

Bivins, Thomas. *Handbook for Public Relations Writing*, 2nd ed. Lincolnwood, IL: NTC Business Books, 1991.

Brody, E. W., and Dan L. Lattimore. *Public Relations Writing*. Westport, CT: Praeger, 1990.

Doty, Dorothy I. *Publicity and Public Relations*. New York: Barron's, 1990.

Fisher, Lionel L. *The Craft of Corporate Journalism: Writing and Editing*. Chicago: Nelson-Hall, 1992.

Grunig, James E., ed. *Excellence in Public Relations and Communication Management*. Hillsdale, NJ: Erlbaum, 1992.

Saffir, Leonard, with John Tarrant. *Power Public Relations: How to Get PR to Work for You*. Lincolnwood, IL: NTC Publishing Group, 1993.

Seib, Philip, and Kathy Fitzpatrick. *Public Relations Ethics*. Fort Worth, TX: Harcourt Brace, 1995.

Seitel, Fraser P. *The Practice of Public Relations*, 4th ed. Columbus, OH: Merrill, 1989.

Wilcox, Dennis L., and Lawrence W. Nolte. *Public Relations Writing and Media Techniques*. New York: Harper & Row, 1990.

EXERCISE 1

PUBLIC RELATIONS: WORKING WITH NEWS MEDIA

DISCUSSING NEWS RELEASES

1. Newspapers are full of stories that originated from news releases. Look especially in the business, "Today" or "Leisure" sections of a local paper to identify stories that probably came from news releases. Clip the articles and discuss with your class why you think they originated as news releases.

2. Ask your college newspaper or broadcast station to save news releases for you. Ask the editors which ones they used. Compare the original news releases to the newspaper's or station's story. Discuss with your class how the news releases were changed and possible reasons why.

EXERCISE 2

PUBLIC RELATIONS: WORKING WITH NEWS MEDIA

WRITING NEWS RELEASES

1. Pretend you are a public relations practitioner working in an agency with several clients. These clients want to announce their new products, which are scheduled to appear in stores at Christmas. Write news releases for the following fictitious clients and products (add whatever information you feel is necessary):

   A. Lady GymCo's new exercycle
   B. Laudon Inc.'s new perfume, "Betty Jean"
   C. Mr. Fred's "Crystal" clothes detergent

2. Have some fun with this exercise: Select a common household appliance, such as the clothes washer, dryer, vacuum cleaner or microwave. Write a news release for its introduction to the public.

You might send copies of the following news releases to your student or local paper or broadcast station:

3. Call or visit your college's public relations department and ask for a list of scientists' and professors' recent research results. Use your reporting skills to find information the public would like to know. Write news releases for several of the research results.

4. Ask your college's public relations department for a list of new teachers or administrative promotions. Use your reporting skills before writing a news release for one of each.

5. Write a news release announcing a student organization's next meeting or its next speaker.

6. Has your department invited a speaker for a special occasion? If so, find out if the occasion is for the department only or open to the public. After you have identified your audience, write a news release about the speaker, the special occasion or both.

EXERCISE 3

PUBLIC RELATIONS: WORKING WITH NEWS MEDIA

WRITING NEWS RELEASES

INSTRUCTIONS: The following information is from actual news releases. Write a news release from each set of details. Remember to correct the spelling and use Associated Press style. Use as much information as you feel is necessary. Add phrases and transitions to make the news releases acceptable to editors. List yourself as the contact person for each sponsor, decide on the release date, and write a headline.

1. The following program is sponsored by Memorial Hospital's departments of Social Work, Cardiac Rehabilitation and Marketing Services.
   - Three Memorial experts are to discuss how changes in your outlook and your habits can prevent stress. Our experts are:
     A. Memorial social worker Anna George, who will discuss changes in your routine, how to plan your time carefully, and how to take better care of yourselve.
     B. Exercise specialist Dean Randall from Memorials Department of Cardiac Rehabilitation, who is supposed to discuss how increasing a persons level of physical activity can prevent stress.
     C. Memorial dietician Jamaila Kendall will provide nutritional advise to help you "charge" up your body for a busy day.
   - The fee for the program is $20.
   - 1-800-000-0000 is the toll-free number to call to register.
   - Are you "stressed out"? Do you sometimes feel like your just "spinning your wheels" in your daily routine? With simple changes in your habits, a person can take positive steps toward preventing or reducing stress in their lives. This upcoming program should help you.
   - "Stress Relievers and Life Enhancers" is the title of the seminar.
   - When: October 18, from 7–10 p.m.
   - Where: Memorial Hospital, Rehab. center, classrooms C & D, 746 Purdy St., your city.

2. The following class is sponsored by your state's department of health.
   - Premarital AIDS Education
   - A 1-hr. class for all people applying for a marriage license.
   - The fee for the class is $20 a person or $30 per couple.
   - You must preregister by calling the toll free number of 1-800-000-8799.
   - Your state law requires couples applying for a marriage lisense to be councilled about sexually-transmitted diseases and AIDS. This class meets the state public health department requirements for those applying for a marriage lisense.
   - The one-hour class is held the 1st Tues. & 3rd Thurs. of every month from 5:30–6:30. The next class begins this next Tuesday.
   - The class will be held at Rivera's Family Practice Center, Florence Nightengale seminar room, 114 San Felipe St., your city.

- Participants must bring a photo id to the class.
- Upon completion of the class, you'll recieve a cerificate signed by a Rivera physician that is valid for 60 days.

3. The following information is from Healthy Planning Inc.:

- Healthy Planning, your states first Medicaid clinic plan, is a managed care outpatient program delivered through primary care clinics. Healthy Planning, which provides quality healthcare for the nearby Medicaid community, is an alternative to other healthcare programs (HMO's, PHP's). Instead of administrators making healthcare decisions, in the Healthy Planning plan the patient has control over chosing a primary care physician, and the doctor has control over the delivery of healthcare services.

- Your states first Medicaid clinic plan, Healthy Planning, is offering a free immuniza-tion fare for all ages every Wed. of this month at their Center on Harding St.

- Just in case those shots provoke tears, Healthy Planning will also provide clowns, bal-loons and a shiny red hook-and-ladder fire engine, to help dry those eyes.

- Healthy Plannings director of operations, Tia Pang, said: "We want to provide immu-nizations to anyone who can't afford to go to a physician and recieve shots. We chose this location to reach as many people as possible."

- The immunization fair is from 10 a.m. in the morning to 2 o'clock in the afternoon. The immunizations will be good for rubella, diphtheria, tetnus, polio and hepititis. Verification of all shots will be provided.

- Immunizations are important. For school-age children, back-to-school shopping often means getting the right tools—folders, books, and pencils—to make good grades. However, often parents forget to equip their children with the one tool that will ensure their child can stay in school—immunization shots.

CHAPTER 16

NEWS RELEASES: WORKING WITH PR PRACTITIONERS

Never write to please the writer. Write to please the reader.

(An editor quoted in "King News" by Moses Koenigsberg)

Many of the nation's journalism students are preparing for careers in public relations, and the previous chapter discusses their work. Almost everyone entering other fields of journalism—but especially people entering the fields of print and broadcast news—will work with public relations practitioners.

The relationship between journalists and public relations practitioners is difficult. The two groups depend on one another, but often do not understand or respect one another. This chapter discusses journalists' use of news releases—and the misunderstandings that often arise.

Newspapers are besieged by individuals and organizations seeking publicity. John Mollwitz of the Milwaukee Journal Sentinel says that large newspapers receive thousands of requests for publicity. His newspaper takes in at least eight 15-inch-high boxes of news releases a day. Newspapers published in small towns are likely to receive hundreds of news releases in their mail or on their fax machines daily. In addition, dozens of people may call each of the media or stop at their news desks. Individuals and groups seeking publicity also besiege campus papers.

Most news releases announce an event, promote a cause or enhance an image. Business firms use news releases to describe their growth, to report their latest dividends, to introduce their latest product, to announce employee promotions and to solicit more customers—all in an effort to benefit the business. Charities use news releases to plead for donations and volunteers; politicians to win votes; colleges to attract more students; and parents to obtain recognition for their children—and often for themselves as well.

For most news organizations, news releases are an important and convenient source of information. No news organization can afford to employ enough reporters to uncover every story occurring in its community. Instead, news media depend on the people involved in some stories to notify editors about them: about church and school activities; business and medical news; art, music and theater schedules; speakers; and festivals.

Yet journalists are critical of many news releases they receive. They complain that most news releases are self-serving: written for the benefit of the public relations practitioners' clients rather than for the media or the public.

Reporters assert that many news releases promote or praise rather than report. Journalists discard those news releases and explain that it is not their job to promote or praise even the most outstanding individuals and organizations in their communities. Other news releases concern subjects obviously not newsworthy—subjects likely to interest only the people paying to have them written. In addition, many news releases are poorly written and even incomprehensible to the average person:

ALPHARETTA, Ga.—Electronics Communications Inc. (ECI) today announced a new version of its Remote2 asynchronous remote control communications software that now includes Lotus-Intel-Microsoft (LIM) extended memory support (EMS) and background file transfer.

However, many public relations practitioners write good news releases, containing news elements that journalists require. These practitioners have been trained as journalists and understand how to write stories that journalists will use.

HANDLING NEWS RELEASES

Reporters handle news releases like any other type of story. They critically examine whatever information the news releases provide, then summarize that information as clearly, concisely and objectively as possible. Their task is often difficult because some news releases fail to emphasize any news. Others contain clichés, jargon, puffery and platitudes. Moreover, most fail to use the proper style for capitalization, punctuation and abbreviations.

Typically, editors will discard 100 news releases for every three or four they accept. Even those they accept usually have to be rewritten. Some editors do not even open all the news releases they receive in the mail. Rather, they glance at the return addresses on envelopes and immediately throw away those coming from sources that regularly submit trivia. For example, the major automakers often send out news releases announcing the promotions of executives in Detroit, yet few news organizations run stories about those promotions because they are of little interest to people in other cities and states. Editors reject other news releases because they are unimportant, poorly written and obvious advertisements.

The worst news releases, usually those submitted by local groups unfamiliar with the media, fail to provide all the information that reporters need to write complete stories. They also fail to provide the names and telephone numbers of people whom reporters might call to obtain more information, or explanations of unclear facts. Some news releases provide telephone numbers that journalists can call only during the day, not during the evening, when the reporters employed by morning dailies or the broadcast media often work. Still other news releases are handwritten and submitted after the events they describe have ended and are no longer considered news.

Some editors refuse to use news releases. These editors may be reluctant to use anything submitted by publicists because they distrust the veracity of the information. Or they may decide to use some news releases but, as a matter of principle, instruct their reporters to rewrite them, to confirm them or to add to their information. These editors may explain that they want their stories to be distinctive. In addition, many editors believe that every news release can be improved.

Other editors use news releases primarily as a source of ideas. If editors like an idea provided by a news release, they will assign a reporter to gather more information about the topic, then to write a story about it. Sometimes the published story is much different from the picture presented in the news release.

Many of the people who send news releases to the media know that journalists are likely to rewrite their stories for broadcast or print style, or to change their content. Thus, those people do the best they can to provide all the facts that journalists will need, but do not try to present the facts in perfectly written stories.

This chapter will show how journalists can improve some news releases and rewrite others for local angles, style and newsworthiness.

THE NO. 1 PROBLEM: LACK OF NEWSWORTHINESS

Journalists obviously prefer news releases about topics that satisfy their definitions of news. They look for topics that are new, local, interesting, unusual, relevant and important. Journalists also look for information likely to affect hundreds or even thousands of people. Action is more newsworthy than opinions, and a genuine or spontaneous event is more newsworthy than a contrived one. Unless they serve a very small community, news organizations increasingly refuse to publish news releases about ribbon-cutting and groundbreaking ceremonies. Newspapers also refuse to publish photographs showing people passing a check or gavel.

Too-Small Audience

News organizations would not be likely to use news releases like the following because their topics would not interest many people—except, of course, members of the organizations they mention. Those organizations can use other means, such as newsletters, to communicate with their members. That is not the job of a news organization:

> The American Medical Press held its annual Top Management Meeting this week in Chicago, its largest ever.

> Jim Abboud, Chair of Decisionmakers Corp., has been elected to a second one-year term as Chair of the Management Institute. The Institute is the national association of the management company industry, which includes mutual funds, closed-end funds and unit investment trusts.

Contrived Events

Reporters are likely to discard the following news releases because they announce contrived events:

> The President has joined with the blood bank community proclaiming January as National Volunteer Blood Donor Month and is urging everyone who is healthy to donate blood to help others.

> The governor has proclaimed Nov. 14–20 American Education Week in the State. The theme of this year's event, observed since 1921, is "A Strong Nation Needs Strong Schools."

Every week and every month of the year is dedicated to some cause, and often to dozens of causes. For example, May is Arthritis Month, National High Blood Pressure Month, National Foot Health Month, Better Speech and Hearing Month, National Tavern Month and American Bike Month. Furthermore, the two news releases above tend to state the obvious. Most responsible adults would urge "everyone who is healthy to donate blood to help others." Most adults also recognize the importance of good schools. Thus, stories about such proclamations are trite, dull, repetitive and of little news value.

Rewriting for Newsworthiness

News releases issued by former Sen. William Proxmire, D-Wis., usually started in the same way—with his name. Proxmire was unusually adept at attracting favorable publicity. Every month until his retirement, Proxmire issued a Golden Fleece Award for what he considered "the biggest, most ironic or most ridiculous example of wasteful spending." It was a clever gimmick that attracted publicity for Proxmire because it appealed to an almost universal value: Americans' opposition to government waste. Moreover, many of the examples that Proxmire cited seemed to be truly wasteful.

A student assigned to write a story about one of Proxmire's monthly awards began with this lead:

> Sen. William Proxmire, D-Wis., has given his Golden Fleece of the Month Award for wasteful government spending to the National Aeronautics and Space Administration.

The lead is dull because it emphasizes the routine: the fact that Proxmire gave another of his awards for wasteful government spending, something he did 12 times every year. Moreover, the lead contains three names: Proxmire's, NASA's and the award's.

The lead should have emphasized the news—a specific description of the latest recipient:

> REVISED: The Golden Fleece Award for February has been given for a $14 million to $15 million project designed to find intelligent life in outer space.
>
> Sen. William Proxmire, D-Wis., has complained that the project "is a low priority program that at this time constitutes a luxury that the country can ill afford."
>
> Proxmire presents the Golden Fleece Award each month to what he considers "the biggest, most ironic or most ridiculous example of wasteful spending." The project to find intelligent life in outer space was proposed by the National Aeronautics and Space Administration.

Notice that the revision mentions Proxmire in the second paragraph rather than in the lead, and that NASA is not mentioned until the third paragraph. Also, the introductory paragraphs do not present Proxmire's claims as fact; rather, they are carefully attributed. However, the most important point is that the lead did not have to begin with Proxmire's name, since it is not the newest, most interesting or most newsworthy aspect of the story.

The problem is a common one. Many of the people writing news releases seem to be more interested in pleasing their bosses than in satisfying the media and informing the public. To please their bosses, they begin news releases with their bosses' names.

Other news releases are editorials that philosophize or praise rather than report. Typically, a news release submitted by a state's beef producers declared, "Red meat makes a contribution to America's health and vitality and should be saluted." The news release continued:

> We often overlook the fact that American meat products are known throughout the world for their quality, wholesomeness and delicious flavor. This week is National Meat Week, and it is an excellent opportunity to recognize the important contribution red meat makes to the diets of more than 250 million Americans who have made meat one of the country's favorite foods. Meat is more than a satisfying meal—it's part of a healthy, well-balanced diet.

Most journalists would respond that the media do not have a responsibility to salute the importance of red meat—nor of anything else. That is not their job. Moreover, it is not the type of story the public seems anxious to receive.

News organizations might use the following news releases because they describe topics likely to interest some readers. However, all three news releases would require some rewriting to emphasize the news and conform to the style—especially the type of lead—suitable to newspapers:

A national organization is again sponsoring an important forum that any student interested in the field of journalism should want to attend. Last year's event, held at this same convenient location, was a major success, attracting more than 2,000 journalism students over the two-day period. The group is charging $5 for this year's event.

REVISED: The Society of Professional Journalists is again sponsoring the SPJ Forum, which will give students an opportunity to speak with representatives from 90 college journalism programs.

The forum will be held from 2 to 6 p.m. Saturday and Sunday in the Municipal Auditorium. Admission will be $5.

Programs making war violence exciting and fun entertainment are said to lead the new Fall programs, according to the National Coalition on Television Violence (NCTV). NCTV has just released its most recent monitoring results of prime-time network programs. Violence is portrayed at the rate of about seven violent acts per hour, with new programs taking three of the top four violent spots. ABC continued to be the most violent network for the fourth quarter in a row.

REVISED: Prime-time network programs contain about seven acts of violence every hour, and this fall's new programs are among the most violent, according to the National Coalition on Television Violence.

THE NO. 2 PROBLEM: A LACK OF OBJECTIVITY

A second major problem with news releases is their lack of objectivity. Too many news releases promote rather than report. They contain laudatory adverbs and adjectives, not facts.

Advertisements

The worst news releases are blatant advertisements, obviously intended to help sell commercial products. Most journalists would reject the following news releases for that reason:

Fashion designer Beth Engalls and Ribbon Inc. will launch the first line of Beth Engalls Fashion Glass next spring, according to a licensing agreement signed on Friday. The new line will be available to the trade in March and will appear on retail shelves by late spring.

Ribbon will distribute the line through department stores, sunglass specialty shops, retail chains and optical stores nationwide, as well as in Engalls' U.S. boutiques. The line will debut in Engalls' runway presentation for spring at Abby Park in the Mayes Pavilion.

The collection, consisting of eight ophthalmic and eight sunglass styles, exudes all the charm, whimsical creativity and wit that characterizes the work of Beth Engalls. The styles are designed to enhance one's look with sophisticated coloration and subtle detailing, and will feature Engalls' trademark crown logo on the temple. They will be manufactured to Ribbon's renowned high-performance eyewear standards.

"I am looking forward, no pun intended, to working in a new format like eyewear," said Engalls. "The subtleties in eyewear design are exciting and challenging."

Pierce Electronics, a leading supplier of high technology cellular accessories and enhancement products, introduces Easy Phone, the unique hands-free speakerphone for portable cellular telephones that can travel with the user—from vehicle-to-vehicle.

This product is the complete hands-free solution. Easily transferred from one vehicle to another, Easy Phone is actually two products in one. . . .

Compact and portable, Easy Phone is small enough to fit into a briefcase, purse, or even the vehicle's glove compartment. Easy Phone requires no installation. One end plugs into virtually any vehicle's cigarette lighter receptacle and the other into the user's phone. It's that simple!

Another news release promoted a state lottery, claiming: "This game offers players lots and lots of cash prizes that can be claimed at any lottery retailer, with excellent overall odds."

This type of news release offends journalists. No journalist is going to report anyone's claim that a lottery offers "lots and lots of cash prizes . . . with excellent overall odds." Journalists are also going to throw away any news release from a company claiming "this extraordinary line has the exciting fashion sensibility that only Engalls can bring." Those are advertisements, not news stories.

Laudatory Adjectives and Puffery

Journalists eliminate laudatory adjectives in rewriting news releases. Every speaker does not have to be called a "guest speaker," and none should be labeled "famous," "prominent," "well known" or "distinguished." If a speaker is truly famous, then the public will already know the person—and will not have to be told of his or her fame.

No news story—or news release—should call a program "wonderful," "successful," "timely" or "informative." Similarly, nothing should be called "interesting" or "important." Reporters also avoid phrases such as "bigger and better," "the best ever" and "back by popular demand." Puffery often appears in leads:

Rebecca R. Zaslow, a nationally recognized and respected forecaster in the field of economics and financial investments, will speak in the city November 15.
REVISED: Rebecca R. Zaslow will speak about financial investments—gold, stocks and real estate—at 8 p.m. Nov. 15 in the Municipal Auditorium.

The Creative Art Gallery, devoted exclusively to fine art photography, proudly announces an event of international significance in the photographic community: an exhibition of the works of Jerry N. Uelsmann and Diane Farris.
REVISED: The Creative Art Gallery, 324 N. Park Ave., will exhibit the photographs of Jerry N. Uelsmann and Diane Farris from Jan. 4 to Jan. 29.

Telling the Public What to Do

Instead of reporting any news, other news releases urge the public to act: to donate their time and money, to buy new products, to attend events, to join organizations. For example:

You must see the exciting displays!

You'll miss out if you don't join the festivities!

Make a difference. Send your contributions of $25, $50, $100 or more to help the needy. You'll be glad you did.

Journalists delete such editorial comments or rewrite them in a more factual manner. Reporters may summarize a story and then, in the final paragraph, tell readers how they *can* respond. Reporters will not tell readers that they *should* respond, only how those who want to do so can:

Tickets for the program are available to the public at the Performing Arts Center and by calling 422-4896, for $5 each. Seating will not be reserved, so the public is urged to arrive early and to hear this most important message on the subject of women's rights.

REVISED: Tickets cost $5 and can be obtained at the Performing Arts Center or by calling 422-4896.

OTHER PROBLEMS WITH NEWS RELEASES

Stating the Obvious

Many public relations writers have no journalism training and do not know what makes a successful news story. Some of their news releases have to be rewritten because they state the obvious:

Parents are worried more than ever about the amount of violence in our society.

A representative of the police department today emphasized the importance of wearing seatbelts.

Violence has always been a problem, and generations of parents have worried about its prevalence; thus, it is not news. Similarly, people expect a police officer to encourage seatbelt safety. That is a routine part of any officer's job, and is not news.

The real news, however, is often buried in a news release's second—or even 22nd—paragraph. Here are two examples:

Most people don't like getting "needled" at work, but employees at McQuitty Food Store are signing up for the privilege—and hoping to avoid a bout with the flu this winter.

Wednesday, Oct. 11, the company's annual flu immunization program will open to the public. In a tradition established over the past few years, several employees will don costumes from 7 a.m. to 5 p.m. on Oct. 11. . . .

REVISED: McQuitty Food Store at 1342 Gordon St. will hold its annual free flu shot clinic from 7 a.m. to 5 p.m. Wednesday.

"It's not easy to raise kids in today's fast-paced society, but that's all right," according to the Program Director of the Regional Medical Center's Child Protection Team. Doreen Mayer asserts that levels of stress inherent in child rearing are normal.

Mayer is among several child abuse counselors who will address a community service program titled "Help! My Kids Are Driving Me Crazy," which will be conducted next Wednesday from 7 to 9 p.m. in the RMC Auditorium.

REVISED: The Regional Medical Center will offer a program to help parents who are having difficulty raising their children. The program, titled "Help! My Kids Are Driving Me Crazy," will begin at 7 p.m. Wednesday.

Absence of Solid Facts

Other sentences contain generalities, platitudes, self-praise and gush, but no facts. While rewriting news releases, journalists eliminate every one of those sentences. Here are three examples:

It will be an exciting musical celebration.

An impressive lineup of speakers will share their expertise.

The library has a reputation as a friendly, pleasant place to visit.

Harcourt Brace & Company

Such gush often appears in direct quotations, but that never justifies its use. If a quotation lacks substance, reporters will discard it, too:

City Council member Jaitt stated, "The fair is the best ever, with a dazzling lineup of new entertainment."

"We're very excited about the opening of the new store," said Mark Hughey, president. "The store represents a new direction for us and extends our commitment to provide customers with the highest-quality products at the lowest possible prices."

The platitudes and generalities sound familiar because they are used so often. For example, the following platitudes are similar but appeared in news releases that two different companies used to describe new employees:

We are fortunate to have a woman with Russell's reputation and background as a member of the team. Her knowledge and experience will be invaluable as we broaden our sales and marketing base.

We were impressed with Belmonte's accomplishments and his professionalism. We're extremely pleased with our good fortune in having him join us.

One-Sided Stories

People and organizations submit news releases to the media because they hope to benefit from the stories' publication. Almost all their news releases are one-sided. They present only their sources' opinions, and often present those opinions as fact. The news releases that do mention an opposing view usually try to show that it is mistaken.

Because doing so is fast and easy, reporters may be tempted to accept the information provided by a news release. Reporters who fail to check the facts, however, are likely to make a serious error. For example, a college newspaper missed a major story because it received and immediately published a news release announcing that eight faculty members had been granted tenure or promotions. The news release failed to reveal the real story: the fact that a dozen other faculty members, including some of the college's most popular teachers, had been denied tenure or promotions because they were not considered good researchers. Moreover, the faculty members who were denied tenure were, in essence, fired. A single telephone call to a faculty representative would have uncovered the real news story.

Using the Media

Other news releases encourage controversy. Here, too, news media that publish such news releases allow themselves to be used. For example, Paul N. Strassels, a former tax law specialist for the Internal Revenue Service, has charged that the IRS uses the media to scare taxpayers. Each year, stories about tax evaders who have been sentenced to prison begin to appear in the media shortly before the April deadline for filing income tax returns. Strassels explains: "It's the policy of the IRS public affairs office to issue such stories at the time when you are figuring your taxes. The service knows that prison stories make good copy. It's simple manipulation." A member of Congress accused the IRS of waging "a campaign of terror among the American people." He explained the IRS uses tactics "carefully designed to threaten the American taxpayer" to keep people in a constant state of fear so that fewer will cheat on their taxes.

In dealing with these and all the other problems that reporters encounter while handling news releases, they regularly condense four- and five-page handouts into three- and four-paragraph stories. The news release reprinted here has been reduced by half:

REWRITTEN NEWS RELEASE

NEWS RELEASE

Joyce Jones, organ virtuoso and concert artist, returns to perform her second concert on the Trexler Memorial Organ of St. Paul Lutheran Church at 8:00 P.M., Friday, November 19.

Her dazzling technique left the audience calling for more at her first performance in the Trexler Memorial Concert Series in 1990. Long before that appearance and certainly many times since, she has thrilled audiences all over the United States and Europe.

"Utterly charming . . . dazzling bravura mingled with intelligence," said the Los Angeles Times. The Stuttgarter Nachrichten hailed her performances in Germany as displays of "phenomenal technique . . . played magnificently."

Studying piano at age 4 and composing by age six, her seemingly boundless energy and talent have earned her a wall full of accolades of international recognition. When she is not touring, she is the organist in residence at Baylor University, Texas.

Her program will include: Toccata on "Loge den Herren," Fantasia and Fugue in G minor, Twilight at Fiesole, Sonata: The Ninety-fourth Psalm, In Paradisium and Pageant.

Like all Trexler Memorial Concerts, her performance will begin promptly at 8:00 P.M. Tickets are $10.00 each and are available at the Concert Series Office, 300 E. Church St. Telephone number is 425-6060. Ext. 7117, between the hours of 1:00 and 5:00 P.M. weekdays.

NEWS STORY

Organist Joyce Jones will perform at St. Paul Lutheran Church at 8 p.m. Nov. 19 as part of the Trexler Memorial Concert Series.

Tickets cost $10 and are available at the Concert Series Office, 300 E. Church St. or by calling 425-6060, extension 7117, from 1 to 5 p.m. on weekdays.

Her program will include: Toccata on "Loge den Herren," Fantasia and Fugue in G minor, Twilight at Fiesole, Sonata: The Ninety-fourth Psalm, In Paradisium and Pageant.

Jones is the organist in residence at Baylor University in Waco, Texas. She also performed here during the 1990 concert series.

SOME FINAL GUIDELINES

First, whenever possible, localize the news releases you handle. A news release distributed by the American Journalism Foundation began:

> ARLINGTON, Va.—Sixty-seven students, representing the best of the country's future journalists, will receive more than $186,000 as winners of American Journalism Foundation Scholarships.

The American Journalism Foundation Scholarship Program provides scholarships of $2,500 a year to undergraduates and $4,000 a year to graduate students pursuing full-time journalism or mass communications degrees at four-year U.S. colleges and universities.

The news release ended with a list of the winning students and their universities. Perceptive reporters would localize their stories' leads, focusing on the winning students from their area.

Second, a surprising number of news releases mention raffles and lotteries, and reporters must delete every reference to them. Most newspapers distribute some subscriptions by mail, and postal regulations prohibit using the mail to promote lotteries. Also, many references to lotteries are linked to promotional gimmicks:

Brinks Home Security will be passing out cold drinks to the walkers, and people can sign up for the raffle of a Brinks Home Security system valued at $530.

Americans who recycle aluminum play a large role in the protection of their environment. Now those recyclers can be rewarded with as much as $100,000 for their efforts in Reynolds Aluminum Recycling Company's "Great American Outdoors Game."

"Every time consumers recycle at a Reynolds center between May 1 and October 31, they could possibly win instant prizes from $1 to $1,000," said Deborah Brinkley, Regional Manager of Reynolds Aluminum Recycling Company (RARCO). "In addition, they can also become eligible for the grand prize of $100,000."

Third, avoid unnecessary background information, especially statements about a group's philosophy, goals or organization. The information is rarely necessary. Moreover, it would become too repetitious and waste too much space if reporters included it in every story about a group:

MDCA is a private, nonprofit arts organization dedicated to the presentation and advancement of the fine arts in our area.

Throughout the year volunteers give unselfishly of their time as Big Brothers and Big Sisters. "The lives of boys and girls in this community are enriched by their caring," said Joe Midura, Executive Director, in announcing the Volunteer Appreciation Week event.

CHECKLISTS FOR HANDLING NEWS RELEASES

When evaluating a news release, ask yourself the following questions:

Is the News Release Newsworthy?

1. Is it newsworthy?
2. Does it involve an issue likely to interest or affect many members of your community—or only a few, such as the members of the organization sponsoring the news release?
3. Does it involve a genuine rather than a contrived event, such as a proclamation, groundbreaking or ribbon cutting?

Does the News Release Need Rewriting?

1. Does every paragraph—especially the lead—emphasize the news, or is the news buried in a later paragraph?
2. Does the lead begin by stating the obvious?
3. Does the lead begin with an unnecessary name?
4. Does the lead need to be localized?

Harcourt Brace & Company

5. Is the story clear and concise?
6. Does the story contain every necessary detail?
7. Does the story contain any clichés, jargon, gush, platitudes, generalities or self-praise? Even if they appear in direct quotations, eliminate them.
8. Who does the news release benefit, the public or its source?
9. Is the story objective?
    —Does it contain any puffery: words such as "best," "exciting," "famous," "interesting," "important," "successful" or "thrilling"?
    —Does it promote a private company or commercial product?
    —Does it make any unsubstantiated claims about being the "cheapest," "biggest" or "best"?
    —Does it urge the public to act?
10. Does the news release contain any unnecessary background information?
11. Does the news release present every side of a controversial issue? If it does, are its presentations adequate—that is, fair and thorough?
12. Does the news release contain any references to a raffle or lottery?

SUGGESTED READINGS

Fedler, Fred, Tom Buhr and Diane Taylor. "Journalists Who Leave the News Media Seem Happier, Find Better Jobs." *Newspaper Research Journal*, Winter 1988, pp. 15–23.

Kopenhaver, Lillian Lodge, David L. Martinson and Michael Ryan. "How Public Relations Practitioners and Editors in Florida View Each Other." *Journalism Quarterly*, Winter 1984, pp. 860–865.

Rees, Clair. "Avoiding the Hot-Air Syndrome: Writing for Publication: News Releases and Newsletters." *WordPerfect Magazine*, May 1989, pp. 25–27.

Ryan, Michael, and David L. Martinson. "Journalists and Public Relations Practitioners: Why the Antagonism?" *Journalism Quarterly*, Spring 1988, pp. 131–140.

Sanoff, Alvin P. "Image Makers Worry About Their Own Image." *U.S. News & World Report*, Aug. 13, 1979, pp. 57–59.

Smith, Ron F. "A Comparison of Career Attitudes of News/Editorial and Ad/PR Students." *Journalism Quarterly*, Summer/Autumn 1987, pp. 555–559.

Stegall, Sandra Kruger, and Keith P. Sanders. "Coorientation of PR Practitioners and News Personnel in Educational News." *Journalism Quarterly*, Summer 1986, pp. 341–347.

Guest Column

A PRACTITIONER'S VIEW

By **Frank R. Stansberry, APR**

Research has shown that journalists have a low regard for public relations people in general, yet have a high regard for PR practitioners they know well or with whom they have a good working relationship. This might indicate that journalists have a healthy skepticism of PR people until a PR person's usefulness (or lack thereof) is established.

Ethical PR people see part of their mission as being a news source to journalists. Content analyses of major newspapers show that as much as 50 percent of the news in their business sections, for example, originates with PR people.

PR people do seek publicity for their clients or employers, but ethical practitioners define publicity as "information from an outside source used by journalists because of its news value." An honest, ethical PR person knows that news value is the linchpin of successful publicity.

There may have been a time, decades ago, when unethical PR people were able to influence equally unethical journalists with gifts and favors. If those days ever existed, they are over now. Today ethical journalists and PR people know that their relationship can be, and must be, one of pure professionalism. For both, this means being honest, available and informed.

An ethical PR person will be honest with a reporter, providing the journalist with information, access or interviews in a truthful and timely manner. One of the canons of the Code of Ethics of the Public Relations Society of America holds that members will not obstruct channels of communications in any way, and honest, ethical PR practitioners will honor that commitment.

The ethical journalist has a similar responsibility. Reporters should be up-front about their mission and not mislead news sources about the direction or tone of the reporting. The ethical PR person will honor that honesty by being as cooperative as possible.

"Availability" means that both the PR professional and the reporter should be available to each other whenever possible. Being available can be as simple as accepting or returning a call or as complex as gathering information as deadlines approach. The PR professional should respond as quickly when the news is not favorable as when the news is good. Reporters, likewise, need to listen to a news idea from the PR professional, even if the idea later proves to lack news value. Neither person benefits from a one-way relationship.

Finally, both the journalist and the PR practitioner need to be informed about the other's profession. For PR people, this means understanding not only their employers' business, but also the news business.

A knowledge of the news process begins with an understanding of what the media consider news—and with an understanding of the media's deadlines and special requirements. It also includes an ability to produce tight, concise writing in a style suited to the medium. A public relations person who understands the news process can do a better job of serving both an employer and a journalist.

Journalists, too, need to understand the companies or agencies they cover. What does the company produce? Is it successful? Why? How? A journalist who understands how a news source does business will conduct a better interview and write a better story.

EXERCISE 1
NEWS RELEASES

EVALUATING NEWS RELEASES

INSTRUCTIONS: Critically evaluate the newsworthiness of the following leads. Each lead appeared in a news release mailed to news organizations. Determine if each news release is usable as written, and why. Then discuss your decision with your classmates.

1. Regina M. Heatern, Vice-President of Marketing & Pricing for Old Ironhorse Freight Line, Inc., announced three (3) new simplified pricing programs designed to meet the shipping public's need for cost-effective simplified pricing.

   EVALUATION: _____

2. During October, millions of high school seniors and their families will attend college fairs and tour campuses nationwide as they select a college for next fall. Planning experts at Morris College say that families should not automatically eliminate a college because of its sticker price.

   EVALUATION: _____

3. Parents who refuse to let children believe in Santa Claus may be doing them harm, today asserted a Mt. Sinai School of Medicine psychologist.

   Mr. David M. Kelley stated in the current issue of Parent's magazine, "Being the only one in the classroom who knows for sure that there's no such guy could make a child feel very different, very strange." He said it "would be unusual" if the denial led to a sense of strength.

   EVALUATION: _____

4. Nail polish remover is still being dropped into the eyes of conscious rabbits to meet insurance regulations, infant primates are punished by electric shocks in pain endurance tests and dogs are reduced to a condition called "learned helplessness" to earn someone a Ph.D.

   With the theme "Alternatives Now," People for the Ethical Treatment of Animals (PETA) is sponsoring a community rally on Friday—World Day for Laboratory Animals—at 1 p.m.

   EVALUATION: _____

5. Until recently, a missing lockbox key could be a major security problem for homeowners selling a house. But today, a missing electronic key can be turned off, protecting clients and their homes. More and more homesellers are using an electronic lockbox, the Superior KeyBox from Williams, on their properties to provide added safety, security and convenience for their homes.

   EVALUATION: _____

6. *Natural Gardening*, the world's largest-circulation gardening magazine, has announced that it has retained Balenti Associates to represent its advertising sales in the Midwest and Western United States. The 27-year-old company is one of the largest

advertising sales firms in the United States, with sales offices in the top five U.S. markets as well as major European cities.

EVALUATION: _____

7. "The Changing Face of Men's Fashion" will be illustrated in a fashion presentation in Robinson's Mens Shops at 5:30 on Thursday. A special feature of the event will be commentary on the distinctive directions in men's designs by fashion designer Anna Zella.

EVALUATION: _____

8. In cooperation with the U.S. Consumer Product Safety Commission (CPSC), the Moro Division of the Petrillo Group of Italy is announcing the recall of 31,000 London branch LP Gas Monitor Gauges. Some of these gauges may leak highly flammable propane gas that could ignite or explode. CPSC is aware of 5 incidents of gas leaks catching fire. Two of these fires resulted in burn injuries.

EVALUATION: _____

9. Dr. Zena Treemont, who recently retired after 35 years with the U.S. Department of Agriculture, has assumed her new duties as Chief of the Bureau of Brucellosis and Tuberculosis with the State Department of Agriculture and Consumer Services, Commissioner Doyle Conner announced today.

EVALUATION: _____

10. Women have made much progress against discrimination through social and legal reforms, but they are still the victims of a very disabling form of discrimination that largely goes unnoticed: arthritis.

Of the more than 31 million Americans who suffer from arthritis, two-thirds are women, according to the Arthritis Foundation.

EVALUATION: _____

EXERCISE 2

NEWS RELEASES

EVALUATING NEWS RELEASES

INSTRUCTIONS: Critically evaluate the newsworthiness of the following leads. Each lead appeared in a news release mailed to news organizations. Determine if each news release is usable as written. Then discuss your decision with your classmates.

1. Demand for gas energy in the United States could, under the right conditions, increase as much as 50 percent to approximately 30 trillion cubic feet (Tcf) by the year 2010, according to a study by the American Gas Association (AGA).

   EVALUATION: _____

2. In cooperation with the U.S. Consumer Product Safety Commission (CPSC), Safety Baby Products Company of Denver, Colo., is warning consumers that certain models of its Safety Baby cribs can collapse if not properly assembled.

   EVALUATION: _____

3. Fire safety education in the state's public schools should be stepped up, according to the State Fire Marshal.

   EVALUATION: _____

4. A coalition of farmers, consumers, students and environmentalists has announced a global boycott of all products of the Maynard Corporation. The boycotted items range from ag chemicals and lawn/garden products to sweeteners.

   EVALUATION: _____

5. High interest rates, coupled with low prices for most agricultural commodities, are causing serious "cash flow" problems for farmers, pushing some toward bankruptcy, according to a study by the Institute of Food and Agricultural Sciences (IFAS) at your state university.

   EVALUATION: _____

6. Pregnant women throughout the state are finding it more difficult to locate an obstetrician willing to deliver their babies because of the number of obstetricians—80 last year alone—who are discontinuing this practice because of the high cost of malpractice insurance, according to a survey by the State Obstetric and Gynecologic Society.

   EVALUATION: _____

7. America's largest chain of luggage and gift stores, Chicago-based MERCEDES LUGGAGE & GIFTS, has recently opened its three newest retail stores in Circle Centre (Indianapolis, IN), Regency Square (Richmond, VA) and Seminole Towne Center (Sanford, FL).

   EVALUATION: _____

8. The Crime Prevention Commission has produced a brochure of crime prevention and safety tips that every child should know. This free brochure contains a handy list of home and bicycle safety guidelines as well as rules regarding "dangerous strangers" that should be taught to all youngsters. The cheerful yellow leaflet also includes a panel of emergency numbers for posting near the telephone.

EVALUATION: _____

9. General Electric Company will establish the worldwide headquarters for its new Automation Systems Department near your city, James A. Meehan, General Manager of the Automation Systems Department, announced today.

Automation Systems markets industrial robots designed for parts assembly, arc and spot welding, spraying, material handling, and process applications such as grinding, polishing, and deburring.

EVALUATION: _____

10. The State Supreme Court has suspended a local attorney from the practice of law for three months and one day, effective immediately. The discipline resulted from action brought by the State Bar.

EVALUATION: _____

E X E R C I S E 3

NEWS RELEASES

ELIMINATING PUFFERY

INSTRUCTIONS: Rewrite the following sentences and paragraphs to make them more objective. Many contain puffery.

1. The entry deadline is Friday, March 16th, so hurry and sign up!

2. As a proponent of innovative hiring practices, the companys president has worked diligently to hire older workers, disabled workers and the homeless.

3. The outrageously funny British farce, RUN FOR YOUR WIFE!, will romp across the Lake Street Players stage May 25–27 and May 31–June 2. It will be a fun-filled evening for the entire family, with each hilarious performance starting promptly at 8 p.m.

4. The governor has not wasted any time. Today the governor announced the selection of a special blue-ribbon search committee for the states university system. This important group is composed of 12 distinguished members with a broad range of interests and will immediately begin its vital task of seeking a new chancellor to head the system.

5. If you're looking for something out of the ordinary for an evenings entertainment, the Center for Arts is the place to be at 7 p.m. Friday and Saturday and at 2 p.m. Sunday. Director Chris Allen will introduce "Love, Love, Love," an exciting new muscial comedy certain to please the entire family—and at the low price of only $9.50 a ticket.

6. Johnson is committed to his work and, while serving as head of the Chamber of Commerce in Houston, succeeded in increasing its membership by 41 percent. His goal when he assumes the presidency of the chamber here next week is to achieve the same type of rapid growth. Johnson has already prepared a detailed plan of action outlining the tasks to be accomplished in the months ahead.

7. The stellar cast includes such renowned performers as Hans Gregory Ashbaker as Rodolfo and Elizabeth Holleque as Mimi. Holleque has become one of America's most sought-after sopranos since winning the 1993 Metropolitan Opera National Council Auditions. She thrilled audiences here with her portrayals of Marguerite in Faust last season and is sure to do the same with her rendition of Mimi.

8. Torey Pines is home to a new community of luxury custom homes with lot sizes starting at 1/2 acre and prices from $300,000. In stark contrast to the surrounding properties, which are built on former farmland, Torey Pines stands out as a forest of extremely tall pines and offers a distinctly different skyline. Built by twelve of the areas most renowned custom builders, Torey Pines homes feature floor plans and elevations that are strikingly individual. Eighteen of the finest luxury models will open for the publics inspection and appreciation at noon this Sunday.

Harcourt Brace & Company

E X E R C I S E   4

NEWS RELEASES

INSTRUCTIONS: These are actual news releases mailed to daily or weekly newspapers. Only the locations and the names of some individuals have been changed. Your instructor may ask you to write only the lead for each news release or to write the entire story.

1. RECOVERED ANOREXIC TO SPEAK

"Understanding the Anorexic/Bulimic Family Member" will be the subject of a meeting sponsored by Memorial Hospitals Eating Disorders Unit Monday, Nov. 3, at 6:00 p.m. in the hospital auditorium.

Karen Balliet, a recovered anorexic and the president and director of the state chapter of the American Anorexia/Bulimia Assn., Inc., will be the speaker.

Anorexia nervosa, which is characterized by an intense fear of becoming obese, affects over 100,000 people in the U.S. alone. Bulimia, characterized by recurrent episodes of binge eating often followed by attempts to purge food by vomiting or laxative abuse, is especially prevalent in female high school and college students.

The Memorial Hospital Eating Disorders Unit has been open for two years. It is unique to this area in that it offers both in-patient and out-patient programs. Its staff is available to answer questions concerning these life threatening disorders and to assist patients and family members in coping.

For information about Balliets talk or the Eating Disorders Unit, call the hospital at 767-2267.

2. "INVENTING YOUR LIFE" SEMINAR

On Friday evening of next week, the countys Mental Health Association and the Center for Women's Medicine will present a two-hour seminar designed to provide simple, practical techniques to help women achieve greater success and happiness in every area of their life. Through a combination of lecture and audience participation, participants will be given the tools to "Invent Your Life" the way they want it to be. The featured seminar leader will be Joyce Reynolds from the Swan Center for Intuitive Living in Atlanta, Georgia. Ms. Reynolds states, "When you know how to create what you want, you can be more productive and motivated, and have an excitement for life. You can make your life what you want it to be." The seminar will also include a discussion of how physical health is directly affected by the level of stress in life. Scheduled to begin at 7 PM, the workshop will be held in the Great Hall of the Cathedral of St. Luke's, 130 Dakota Avenue. Pre-registration is encouraged. "Early Bird" registration fees for the seminar are $10 per person for M.H.A. members and $12 for non-members. Registration at the door will be $15 for everyone. Refreshments will be provided. For more information or to register by telephone, please call the Mental Health Association at 843-1563.

3. ANNUAL "STOP, DROP & SHOP" PROGRAM

The city Parks & Recreation Dept. and the Public Library invite you to spend an afternoon of Christmas Fun, Sunday, December 14, 1 p.m.–5 p.m.

Parents can begin by *Stopping* off at the Public Library, *Dropping* off their school age children and *Shopping* for the holidays with their free time, knowing that their children are being well cared for and having fun.

The Public Librarys annual *Stop, Drop & Shop* program will be held at the library from 1 to 5 p.m. Sunday, December 14. Games, films, stories and other activities for school age children will be featured to add to their holiday fun. Its all completely free of charge.

4. FIRST COMMUNITY RESPITE CARE WEEKEND

Alzheimer's, the fourth leading cause of death among adults in the U.S., has a profound impact on the entire family, thus leaving the primary care giver in a "high risk" category for stress related illnesses. Any time off, regardless of how little, is essential in helping reduce that stress.

Next week, on Saturday and Sunday, Sand Lake Hospital will offer the areas first "Community Respite Care Weekend," a new concept. Volunteers will offer time and loving care the entire weekend.

The Community Respite Care Project offers rest or relief to those families who are continually caring for an Alzheimer's loved one. This weekend will give those family members the opportunity to have a weekend off to do just as they please while their loved one is safe and in the caring hands of trained volunteers and nursing professionals.

After this weekends respite, similar respite care will be offered on the first weekend of each month at the Sand Lake Hospital facility. The new program also offers in-home volunteer help and subsidized adult day care.

"Anyone who has an interest in volunteering their time is greatly needed," says Charlotte McFarland. "Our program relies solely on volunteer power to staff both the in-home and hospital respite. We realize many people may find this type of volunteerism difficult, however, the devoted people we do have find much personal satisfaction and reward once they see how much they help and the difference they make to these families."

For more information, call Charlotte McFarland, Respite Project Director, at 425-2489.

5. BLOOD DONORS NEEDED DURING SUMMER MONTHS

Come roll up your sleeve and give a lifesaving gift to a patient who needs you.

The summer is a time for enjoyment and relaxation, but for many local hospital patients who are ill or injured, the summer won't be so much fun. The Blood Bank asks that you help these patients return to good health by donating blood.

"The community blood supply traditionally decreases during this time of the year because many regular donors are on vacation or busy with other activities," said Linda Wallenhorst-Zito, director of communications and marketing at the Blood Bank. "However, accidents and emergencies increase during the summer, and many patients wanting elective surgery are forced to postpone it until more blood becomes available."

Any healthy person at least 17 years old may donate and there is no upper age limit. Donors complete a brief medical questionnaire and health screening that many find a good way to regularly monitor such factors as their heart rate and blood pressure.

For additional information, call your local Blood Bank branch. Come help save a life. Someday, someone may save yours.

EXERCISE 5

NEWS RELEASES

WRITING NEWS BRIEFS

INSTRUCTIONS: Assume that you have been asked to write a column of news briefs that will be published tomorrow in your local daily. Summarize each of the following news releases in a separate story or brief. The news releases are genuine; only a few names and dates have been changed.

1. HELP SUNBANK ALLEVIATE THE YEAR-ROUND PROBLEM OF HUNGER

Nearly one-fourth of the children in this state must go to bed hungry every night. That's no way to let our future generations grow and take shape.

In order to help alleviate the growing concern of hunger in our local state, SunBank has announced that it will begin their seventh annual SunSanta food drive next June 14. Residents of the state are encouraged to bring any canned or nonperishable food items to their nearest SunBank office for distribution to the needy. When the food drive ends on Friday, July 6, the Christian Service Center will pick-up and distribute all donated items to local, needy families and individuals.

For the first time, SunBank is hosting their statewide food drive in the summer months. "When we first began the program seven years ago, there were few food drives during the winter holidays," explained Sara Curtis, Senior Vice President of Marketing. "However, as more and more organizations sponsored year-end food campaigns, we have rescheduled our program for the summer months to help replenish depleted food banks."

Last year, residents of the state donated over 78,000 items to 55 different charities. Clearly, you "can" make a difference. So when composing your vacation packing list, don't forget to drop off your canned goods at your local SunBank office.

2. BUGGY EXHIBIT

The Dodd Science Center is preparing for an invasion of insects. Beginning with a Members Preview Party at 2 p.m. Sunday, DSC hosts the highly successful "Insect Zoo, Arachnids Too" developed and circulated by Great Explorations, Inc. of Boston, Massachusetts. The exhibit celebrates the diversity and splendor of the world of insects. Over 20 species of live arthropods including tarantulas, a bird-eating spider, walking sticks, praying mantises, grasshoppers and native and exotic cockroaches, including the giant hissing cockroaches from Madagascar, will be in residence at DSC during this exhibit, which opens to the public on Tuesday and will continue for 6 weeks. The staff will conduct daily feedings and demonstrations at 10:00 a.m. and 1:00 p.m.

DSC's hours are:

Tuesday–Saturday	9 a.m. to 5 p.m.
Sunday	12 p.m. to 5 p.m.
Monday	Closed

Admission is $3.00 for adults and $2.00 for children ages 3–17. Children under 3 and members of DSC are admitted free. Group rates and programs are available. Call DSC at 259-5572 for further information.

The Centers unique gift shop has a wide variety of books, posters, games, and much more. Don't forget to stop in and buy your favorite glow-in-the-dark critters and insect t-shirts.

3. METRO LIFE CHURCH

Metro Life Church welcomes internationally known Christian leader, author, and speaker Terry Virgo. Terry will be our special guest in our weekly Worship Celebration both this Sunday and the following Sunday.

Terry leads the unusually large Clarendon Church in Brighton, England. In addition, he leads an apostolic team in close relationship with more than 70 churches in the United Kingdom and throughout the world in five other countries.

An acclaimed Bible teacher, Terry has ministered at major national and international conferences. He and his wife Wendy have also authored a number of books, including the popular *Restoration in the Church*.

Senior Pastor Danny Jones invites you to join us for the ministry of Terry Virgo. Childrens ministry will be available for the ages 1–9. Services are at 9 and 11 a.m. each Sunday with Bible Study at 7 p.m. The Virgos will appear at all 3 services both Sundays.

4. CALLING ALL WINNERS!

Its time to gear up for the competition, fun, and prizes at the 87th edition of the State Fair. Although the State Fair is not until June, now is the time to prepare for the states most competitive event.

The theme of next Junes Fair is "Carry on the Tradition" and there are plenty of contests to enter. Whether your interest is sewing, baking, tropical fish, photography, horticulture, fine arts, wood-carving, fashions, cheerleading, wine, or championship livestock, theres a place for you at the Fair. This is your opportunity to showcase your talents to nearly one million people. All entries will be judged by professionals in their field.

To enter most Family Living Events, you must be a resident of the state and entries must be received by the State Fair Authority by Friday, April 1. Wine entries must be submitted by April 15. Livestock deadlines are May 5.

5. WOMEN AND DEPRESSION

MERCY HOSPITAL is sponsoring a free presentation on Women and Depression. Participants will be taught to:

- identify the symptoms of depression
- explore the dynamics of depression
- learn treatment alternatives, including individual and group therapy
- define issues unique to women which impact on identification and treatment of depression

The seminar will be held in the hospital auditorium next Wednesday with registration beginning at 6:30 p.m. The presentation will be from 7–9 p.m. To make a reservation call **MERCY HOSPITAL** at 767-0152 or 1-800-221-0000.

Speakers: Marie Lozando, M.D.—Dr. Lozando is Clinical Director of **MERCY HOSPITAL's** Women's Issues Program.
Deborah L. Carter, Ph.D.—Associate of the Lovell Psychiatric Association.
Phyllis Williams, A.R.N.P., M.S.W.—Associate of Lovell Psychiatric Association.

Harcourt Brace & Company

E X E R C I S E   6

NEWS RELEASES

REWRITING NEWS RELEASES

INSTRUCTIONS: These are actual news releases sent to news organizations. Only the locations and the names of some individuals have been changed. Your instructor may ask you to write only the lead for each news release or to write the entire story. These exercises contain numerous errors in style, spelling and punctuation.

NEWS

FINANCE COMPANY INSTITUTE

For Immediate Release

Customer Value is Focus of Institutes Operations Conference; Theme is "Gateway To The Future"

With competition in the marketplace turning increasingly fierce, how can a company make its mark? One way, to be explored at the Economics Company Institutes 9th annual Management Conference and Vendor Exhibition, is through increased customer value.

This years conference, "Gateway to the Future: Bridging the Milenia" will be held Nov. 28–Dec. 1. in Houston. The Institute expects a record number of attendees and exhibitors.

The keynote address by Dr. Jung Soon Park is expected to be one of the highlights of the conference. Dr. Jung is coauthor of the best selling book, *The Operations of Management Leaders.* She will examine the concept of customer value and share her insights into what it will take for a company to be a true "Management Leader" in the 21st Century.

The Conference will also include enlightening panel discussions on industry consolidation, human resource issues and operations risk management. Representatives from the IRS, the SEC and the mutual fund industry will be on hand to talk about current regulatory concerns. Participants are also encouraged to attend the public information crisis communications mini seminar to learn about developing strategies and plans to help prepare for emergency situations.

In addition, an extensive vendor exhibition will feature the latest products and services which companys will need to give them a competitive edge in the future. Attendees will have the opportunity to test drive cutting edge computer hardware and software, sample high-tech printing techniques and mull over innovative marketing strategies.

Registration for the Conference is $575 for Economics Company Institute members and $750 for nonmembers. Discounted registration fees are available for companies sending more than 3 attendees.

Reduced hotel reservations should be made directly though the Houston Mariott. For additional conference and registration information, please contact the ECIs Conference Division at 212-000-CONF.

CHEESE & SPECIALTY
FOOD MERCHANTS ASSOCIATION

For Immediate Release

Hundreds of new specialty foods and gifts, plus seminars on gift merchandising and customer relations, will be featured at the next Gourmet Food and Gift Show being held on March 6 in your city. Everyone is invited!

The Gourmet Food and Gift Show, sponsored by the Gourmet Food Merchants Association, is the largest show of its kind with over 150 exhibitors from throughout the country showing the latest products to the public, as well as to the retail, gourmet, mail order and gift businesses.

This one day show is designed to include all the products and information necessary to run a specialty food and gifting business. In the exhibit area, there will be experts ready to answer questions about the specialty food and gifting businesses.

Come sample the delights! Products featured are the latest gourmet and specialty foods including cheese, candy and nuts, cookies and pastries, pastas and rice, meats, sausages and poultry, sauces and condiments and many items packaged specifically for the mail order and gift basket businesses.

In addition, accessories as well as gift baskets, gift boxes, packaging and other services will be displayed. Prizes will be awarded for outstanding new food and gift items as well as "Best of Show."

Several prizes will be awarded to lucky attendees. Attendees may register at the show for these prizes.

The show runs from 9:00 to 4:30 on Wed. at the citys Exposition and Convention Center and Arena. Admission is free for all those smart people wanting to come by. If you'd like to be an exhibitor, call the Gourmet Food Merchants Association at 1-800-000-FOOD.

CRIMELINE PROGRAM INC.

<u>For Immediate Release</u>

This weeks CRIMELINE case comes from the files of the County Sheriffs Office.

It was a relatively quiet night last October 18, while Sgt. David Aneja was riding in patrol. He normally worked in the Internal Affairs Section of the County Sheriffs Office, but he liked riding on the street periodically; so when he had the chance to fill in for a friend and fellow sergeant who was on medical leave, he readily volunteered.

Just a few minutes after midnight, Sgt. Aneji spotted a black Chevrolet Nova parked on a dead-end street north of Beville Road directly across from the Forest Lake subdivision.

The vehicle was jacked up in the rear, had wide tires and a Duval County tag. Both the lights and the engine were turned off.

Sgt. Aneji pulled his unmarked police car behind the Nova and got out. At the same time, a male in his mid 20's, 6' tall, 180 pds. got out of the other car. Even though Sgt. Aneja was in uniform, he wanted to make sure that there was no doubt that the man knew he was a police officer, so he reached back in his car to turn on the blue lights. When he stood back up, he heard a shot and felt a sharp pain in his left chest. The bullet struck the deputy's badge and, thankfully, his bulletproof vest. Sgt. Aneja fell to the ground behind his car door. The suspect fired five more rounds through the door, narrowly missing the deputy.

The gunman then jumped into his car and sped off, heading west on Beville Road, with Sgt. Aneja returning fire. Through the whole gun battle, not one word was spoken!

Who was this man, and why was he so bent on killing Sgt. Aneji? If you know, you could earn a reward of up to $1,000 by calling CRIMELINE at 423-TIPS. And, of course, you don't have to give your name. When only <u>you</u> know, we keep it that way.

Facts for Consumers
from the Federal Trade Commission
BUREAU OF CONSUMER PROTECTION   •   OFFICE OF CONSUMER EDUCATION   •   WASHINGTON, D.C. 20580

Vacation Certificates

Immediate
Release

"Gift vacation for two. Have an exciting fun-filled holiday. Deluxe room accommodations for two days and three nights." Sometimes its in Las Vagas. Or Reno. Or Miami. Or it might be in some other vacation spot.

It sounds too good to be true. And it sometimes is. Las Vegas law enforcement officials are warning consumers about vacation certificate promoters who make these claims.

Phone and
Mail Sales

According to these officials, about 100 firms make these offers either directly to consumers—through telephone or mail solicitations—or to businesses who use these vacation certificates as part of their own sales promotions. Consumers don't always get what they expected.

However, the files of Nevada Consumer Affairs Commissioner David Cook are filled with complaints from unhappy people who took the certificate promoter up on the "free vacation" offer. Cook tells of people who traveled to Las Vegas only to find out that—even though they had "confirmed" reservations—the hotel staff had never heard of them.

Deposits
Made in
Advance

Vacation certificates usually cost from $15 to $25. If you buy one—or a local merchant gives you one it bought—you would typically be entitled to a three-day, two-night vacation to Las Vegas or Reno or Miami. According to the conditions on the certificate, you would have to contact the promoter—not the hotel—to make your reservation and would probably have to make a deposit to "hold" it. You might even have to make another deposit when you confirm the reservation.

In some cases, the promoter has a good relationship with the hotel, and the hotel agrees to set aside a block of rooms so the certificates can be redeemed.

However, in some cases vacation certificate promoters get rooms from the hotel **only if the hotel is not already booked up**. If it is already booked up, consumers who want to redeem their certificates may not get their first choice of hotel. They may find promised "first class accommodations" aren't all that classy or that their "vacation site" may be some distance from the main attractions of the resort community.

Harcourt Brace & Company

In fact, as Commissioner Cook indicates, some promoters sell vacation certificates without reserving **any** rooms. They issue counterfeit certificates that are not honored by the hotel, restaurant, or casino indicated. These promoters rake in the money, go out of business overnight, and leave you holding the casino chips.

Some companies, more sophisticated in their sales techniques, simply make it virtually impossible for you to **use** your certificates. They do this by repeatedly refusing your requests for a specific vacation date. You may never get a confirmed reservation. They figure that after a while you'll just give up.

If you do get a date and take the vacation (one promoter said they figure fewer than 2% of the recipients actually do), you might have some unpleasant surprises. You will usually have to pay travel costs and the cost of your meals. Also, your "bonus coupons" for free meals, drinks, discount gambling, show tickets, or golf may not be a bargain at all. For example, an offer of free meals may be limited to the hours of 2 a.m.–5 a.m., and the free tickets for gambling might be available only from certain casinos at odd hours. Very often you'll have to spend your own money first; then the promoter will match it with an equal sum.

The Better Business Bureau of Southern Nevada released a typical standard vacation certificate coupon package showing that you would have to spend as much as $50 of your own money to get a $13.50 value in coupons.

Some vacation certificate offers are completely above board and plainly disclose any limitations they may have. But before you fly off to your free vacation, invest some time checking the reputation of the company. If you can't get straight answers to the questions you ask, don't go.

FROM: Madison Pancake Festival   News Release
      P.O. Box 5029
      Madison

MADISON PANCAKE FESTIVAL

MADISONS Seventeenth Annual Pancake Festival takes place this Saturday and Sunday.

The Festival has always been non-profit, sponsored by the Betterment Association of the Madison Area, Inc. and for the past three years, has been co-sponsored with the Madison Area Jaycees.

Civic organizations, churches, school children, City Hall employees, inmates from the Copeland Road Prison, local businesses and residents from surrounding areas all work together to stage a smooth-running two-day event that over the past 16 years has drawn almost a million people to this small town of 3,200.

From last years proceeds, money was donated to the city of Madison to be used for park improvements. Monies also were donated to the Madison Volunteer Fire Department and the Gateway Ambulance Service. Also a portion of the proceeds were set aside for scholarships for local high school students.

The volunteers successful efforts to stage the Festival show what communities can do on their own—with ingenuity, determination, and effort. *Nobody gets paid. All work is volunteer.* Chief lure of the Festival is the picturesque and historic town itself.

The menu consists of pancakes with your choice of delectable toppings such as nuts, berries (blueberries, raspberries or strawberries), jams, syrups, bananas, and much, much more. These Pancake Plates will be served both days, from 7 AM to 9 PM on Saturday and Sunday. A Pancake Plate will cost $12 for adults and $6 for children 12 and under. That one low price includes the cost of admission to the festival and free refills for an entire day.

Visitors will also be able to purchase tickets for a drawing on a 16-foot boat, a trailer, and a 45 HP outboard motor sponsored by the Madison Volunteer Fire Dept.

There will be over 100 booths to display a large selection of the finest arts and crafts. Booths manned by local clubs and residents will also offer other special foods.

Country music is played continuously both days. The Festival will feature Country and Western artist "Lionel Cartwright" on Sunday at 1:00 and 3:00 PM. Also featured will be clogging, kiddie and carnival rides, hot dogs, ice cream, popcorn, pies, soft drinks, coffee, iced tea and cold beer served in Festival mugs that the purchaser gets to keep as souvenirs of his visit to our event.

Madison has campgrounds and motels for guests who would like to spend the weekend. There are many other attractions in Madison and the surrounding areas: swimming, fishing, camping, hiking, horseback rides, boat tours, glider and plane rides, an observation tower to climb and shopping at the town's many

Harcourt Brace & Company

fine antique stores. In addition, there will also be a gigantic flea market with bargains galore. Visitors are welcome to
set up a table of their own. The registration fee for the flea
market is $10 per table.

   For those planning to come by plane, the City has an airport
with a 2400-foot runway. There is no charge for landing your
plane. Volunteers handle plane parking. There is also an area
close to the Festival at which arrivals in RVs may park for
overnight stays for a modest fee.

CHAPTER 17

FEATURE STORIES

I think the whole glory of writing lies in the fact that it forces us out of ourselves and into the lives of others.

(Sherwood Anderson)

Most news stories describe a recent event—a meeting, crime, fire or accident, for example. Earlier chapters have shown that news stories also inform the public about topics that are important, local or unusual.

Feature stories, by contrast, read more like nonfiction short stories. Many have a beginning, a middle and an end. They focus on facts likely to amuse, entertain, inspire or stimulate. They also inform. Because of these emphases, they are also called "human interest" and "color" stories.

Features may describe a person, place or idea rather than an event. So long as the stories appeal to readers, their topics may be less timely, less local and less earthshaking than those of news stories.

There is no single writing formula, such as the inverted-pyramid form, that reporters must use for every feature story. In general, however, features explore their topics in greater depth than news stories.

To do this, feature writers may borrow techniques from fiction, often using description, sensory details, quotations and anecdotes. They may use characterization, setting, plot structure and other novelistic elements to dramatize a story's theme and to add more details.

Feature stories, however, are journalistic, not fiction or "creative writing." Nothing is made up. Like news stories, features are factual and original. They are fair and balanced, based on verifiable information. They must also be objective—they are not essays or editorials.

SELECTING A TOPIC

The most crucial step in writing a good feature story is the selection of a topic. Ideally, every topic should be fresh, dramatic, colorful and exciting.

The concept of "universal needs" is useful in choosing a topic. Everyone is interested in ideas relating to the needs all human beings have in common and in ways of satisfying those needs. Food, clothing, shelter, sex, health, approval, belonging, self-esteem, productive work, money, leisure and similar needs are subjects no reader can resist.

Feature writers find appropriate topics by being curious and observant. The following exercise is useful to journalists finding a topic: Write the universal needs down one side of a piece of paper. Write some current topics from the news, such as AIDS and unemployment, across the top. Then, where each line intersects, write in a "hybrid" topic combining the two, such as AIDS patients' need for emotional contact or loss of self-esteem among the jobless.

News stories may provide spinoff topics for features. An earthquake, plane crash, international incident or other news event can spark human-interest stories about the reactions of victims, heroism in crises and other "people" angles that bring the event into sharper focus. Features

Harcourt Brace & Company

about major events or social problems can be localized through personal interviews with people who had a relative serving in a war or a friend in a plane crash.

For instance, a college student read several news stories about the street people in her community and noticed that none of the stories quoted the homeless. Instead, reporters relied on the authorities in their community. Police blamed the homeless for a series of minor crimes. Welfare agencies wanted more money to care for the homeless. Church leaders wondered about their responsibilities to the homeless.

The student drove to the area where homeless people congregated, sat on a curb and began to interview one of the homeless people. Others gathered around her, so that in a few hours she was able to complete a dozen interviews. Her feature story revealed that the homeless were not primarily adult males—or bums and criminals. Rather, families with small children had become homeless. For years, many of the families had lived in their own homes. Then a husband or wife became ill or lost a job, often because a factory closed or moved. The couples came to the city looking for work, but were unable to find new jobs or low-cost housing and ended up living on the streets.

Some feature stories are inspired by journalists' personal experiences—and those of friends. If, after little or no training, a reporter's friend is given a gun and hired as a guard, the reporter might ask about the training and qualifications of other "rent-a-cops" who, in many cities, outnumber the police. Students have also written about unwed fathers, student suicides, unusual classes and unusual teachers.

After selecting a general topic of interest to a large audience, reporters must limit it to a manageable size, perhaps by emphasizing a single person, theme or episode. For example, a profile cannot summarize a person's entire life, so journalists might discuss just one aspect: a single experience, trait or achievement that sums up the person's character. If journalists fail to limit their topics, their stories are likely to become too long, disorganized and superficial. They may ramble or skip from one idea to another without adequate transitions and without explaining any of the ideas in detail.

While gathering the information for feature stories, reporters normally consult several sources, perhaps a half-dozen or more, to obtain a well-rounded account. Good reporters gather two or three times more information than they can possibly use, then discard all but the most powerful, telling details.

TYPES OF FEATURE STORIES

Profiles or Personality Features

Profiles describe interesting people. The people may have overcome a handicap, pursued an unusual career, achieved success or become famous because of their colorful personalities. To be effective, profiles must do more than list an individual's achievements or important dates in the individual's life. They must reveal the person's character. To gather the necessary information, feature writers often watch their subjects at work; visit them at home; and interview their friends, relatives and business associates. Completed profiles then quote and describe their subjects. The best profiles are so revealing that readers and viewers feel as though they have actually met and talked to the people.

Some profile subjects may surprise reporters by revealing their most personal and embarrassing secrets. A few sources may ask to have their identities kept secret. Their stories are compelling, and reporters need them, so reporters may have to respect their wishes. Journalists can use their imaginations when interviewing. For example, they can go straight to those involved in a situation. Instead of interviewing the police about a drug problem, or faculty members about students who cheat, reporters may interview the drug users and cheaters themselves—specific individuals who seem to be representative of a larger issue.

Harcourt Brace & Company

The following profile uses a single individual to reveal the problems of the elderly. Notice how the use of quotations enables the woman to tell much of the story in her own words:

She is old—91—but doesn't like to admit it. "It's like admitting defeat," Rilla says. "Why does old age have to be such a hardship? It's supposed to give you time to enjoy things."

Rilla was the oldest of 10 children but is the only one still alive. The youngest died three months ago at the age of 72.

"One of the hardest things I've had to face is watching my family and friends die," she says. "Even my own children are middle-aged and in ill health."

Rilla seems reluctant to discuss old age, but considers herself an authority on the subject. "I've been old for a long time now," she explains. "I just see myself get a little older every day. I guess I'm what's kindly referred to as 'fragile.'" She lives with a daughter and her husband. "I used to have a lot of friends in the neighborhood," she adds, "but they're all dead."

"There's nothing for me to do any more. I can't see to read. I have such bad arthritis that I can't hardly walk from the living room to the kitchen. My garden has all gone to weeds because I can't bend over far enough to work in it."

Rilla says there are a few benefits to old age: "I don't worry about my figure any more. I eat as much as I want as often as I want.

"Of course, I've been able to watch my children and grandchildren grow and develop and become good people. And too, there have been times when I've wanted to die."

Historical Features

Historical features commemorate the dates of important events, such as the attack on Pearl Harbor, the bombing of Hiroshima or the assassination of Dr. Martin Luther King Jr. News organizations also publicize historical features on 100th birthdays and on the anniversaries of the births and deaths of famous people. The following story, distributed by the North American Newspaper Alliance, typifies this kind of historical feature:

MATEWAN, W.Va.—The most infamous episode in the annals of Appalachia erupted on Blackberry Creek 100 years ago.

The feud between the Hatfields and McCoys, two powerful mountain clans, lasted for about 15 years. When the fighting finally subsided, more than 100 men, women and children had been killed or wounded, and the region's residents generally were viewed by the rest of the country as a bunch of murderous moonshine-swilling hillbillies who liked nothing better than to loll about the front porch, picking their toes and taking potshots at each other.

Other historical features are tied to current events that generate interest in their topics. If a tornado, flood or earthquake strikes your city, news organizations are likely to present stories about earlier tornadoes, floods or earthquakes. When President John F. Kennedy was assassinated, news organizations prepared historical stories about the assassinations of Presidents Lincoln, Garfield and McKinley. When the space shuttle exploded, killing seven astronauts, newspapers published features about the astronauts killed in previous accidents.

Historical features may also describe famous landmarks, pioneers and philosophies; improvements in educational, entertainment, medical and transportation facilities; and changes in an area's racial composition, housing patterns, food, industries, growth, religions and wealth.

Every region, city and school is likely to have experienced some interesting events at some time in its history. A good feature writer will learn more about those events, perhaps by consulting historical documents or by interviewing people who witnessed or participated in them.

Adventure Features

Adventure features describe unusual and exciting experiences—perhaps the story of someone who survived an airplane crash, climbed a mountain, sailed around the world, served in the Peace Corps or fought in a war. In this type of feature story, quotations and descriptions are especially important. After a catastrophe, for example, feature writers often use the survivors' accounts to recreate the scene. Many writers begin with the action—their stories' most interesting and dramatic moments:

> "It was the 10th of July, 1969, approximately 5 p.m.," said Steve Jefferson, one of the Vietnam veterans attending classes here. "Myself and two sergeants were driving down the road in a Jeep. Theoretically, we shouldn't have been in this situation. We should have been accompanied by more men in another Jeep, but I always thought that when my time was up, it was up. It was going to happen no matter what.
>
> "There was a white flash and a pop, and the next thing I knew I was lying in the middle of the road.
>
> "I thought we had hit a hole, and that I had flipped out of the Jeep. I always rode kind of haphazardly in the Jeep, with one leg hanging out one side of it. I really thought I had fallen out, and they had kept going without me; you know, as a joke.
>
> "Then I turned and saw the Jeep overturned and on fire by the side of the road. I touched my arm with my good hand, and it was all bloody. It finally dawned on me that it was an ambush. I heard some rifle fire but, at the time, didn't realize they were shooting at me.
>
> "I crawled over to the side of the road, away from the Jeep, and hollered for the other guys. There was no answer. . . ."

Seasonal Features

Reporters are often assigned feature stories about seasons and holidays: about Christmas, Easter, St. Patrick's Day, Friday the 13th and the first day of spring. Such stories are difficult to write because, to make them interesting, reporters must find a new angle. Yet it can be done:

> Thanksgiving, 1989. At the age of 6, Ana had only a vague idea of what Thanksgiving involved. Her knowledge was limited to a family get-together, good food and pictures of Pilgrims and Indians. But a surprise visit from a police officer named Tony changed all that.

Explanatory Features

Explanatory features are also called "local situation" or "interpretive" features or "sidebars." In these features, reporters provide a more detailed description or explanation of topics in the news. Explanatory features may examine a specific organization, activity, trend or idea. After news stories describe an act of terrorism, an explanatory feature may examine the terrorists' identity, tactics and goals. After a bank robbery, an explanatory feature may describe the training banks give their employees to prepare them for robberies or may reveal more about a typical bank robber, including the robber's chances of getting caught and probable punishment.

One followup won a Pulitzer Prize. In 1947, an explosion killed 111 men in an Illinois mine, and Joseph Pulitzer II, publisher of the St. Louis Post-Dispatch, asked his staff to thoroughly review the tragedy. Pulitzer wanted to know what would be done to improve mine safety. What would be done to help the miners' families? Also, who was responsible for the tragedy, and were

Harcourt Brace & Company

they likely to be punished for it? Notice that the story starts with the action. Also notice the reporter's use of specific detail:

> The clock in the office of the Centralia Coal Company's Mine No. 5 ticked toward quitting time on the afternoon of March 25. As the hands registered 3:27 and the 142 men working 540 feet underground prepared to leave the pit at the end of their shift, an explosion occurred.

> The blast originated in one of the work rooms in the northwestern section of the workings. Fed by coal dust, it whooshed through the labyrinth of tunnels underlying the town of Wamac, Ill., on the southern outskirts of Centralia.

> Thirty-one men, most of whom happened to be near the shaft at the time, made their way to the cage and were brought out alive, but the remaining 111 were trapped. Fellow-workmen who tried to reach them shortly after the explosion were driven back by poisonous fumes.

How-to-Do-It Features

How-to-do-it features tell readers how to perform some task. They may describe a tangible project like building a house, planting a garden or training a puppy. They may focus on psychological issues, such as strengthening a marriage or overcoming shyness. Or they may show how newcomers to a city can find a physician or how anyone can organize receipts for tax time.

Inexperienced reporters tend to preach or dictate to readers, presenting their own opinions. Professionals gather facts from several sources, including book and magazine articles. They also interview experts in the field and get tips from people who have completed the task or experienced the changes.

Reporters divide the task into simple, clear, easy-to-follow steps. They tell readers what materials are needed and the cost in money and time. Often they conclude such stories with a list or summary of the process, such as "eight ways to build self-confidence in children."

Unusual Occupation or Hobby Features

Reporters may write about an occupation because it is dangerous, highly specialized (cleaning up oil spills) or exciting (personal fitness trainer to movie stars). They may pick a boring or exacting job (sorting clothes at Goodwill) that is fulfilling to a handicapped worker because it allows him or her to earn money and live independently.

Strange hobbies make good topics, too, because they tend to involve colorful characters. Reporters find collectors and crafts enthusiasts to be passionately involved and often eccentric, quotable and entertaining.

For ideas, journalists scan their papers' meeting notices for hobby club meetings, senior citizens' activities, church and school events and speeches on unusual topics. They ask other people what they do to relax. They read classified ads and seek out magicians, storytellers, psychic readers, basement cleaners and unicycle instructors.

Personal Experience Features

News stories are usually written in the third person, with the reporter a neutral observer or outsider. Feature stories can be written in the first person, with the journalist appearing in the story. Feature stories can also be written in the second person, with the journalist addressing audience members directly. At times, these styles can be extremely effective.

It is tempting for beginning reporters to write about their own experiences because it seems easy; they do not have to interview anyone, spend any time digging for information or conduct any other research. But journalists should use the first person cautiously, especially in their first feature stories. While describing their own experiences, they run a greater risk of selecting poor topics and dwelling on insignificant details and dull generalities:

> During the summer, 20 ardent cyclists (I among them) biked through 300 miles of the Canadian Rockies. In the course of our journey, we encountered many exciting experiences.

The following story is also written in the first person, but is more interesting because it describes a truly unusual experience. The story also emphasizes specific details, descriptions and anecdotes. It was written by M. Timothy O'Keefe, a successful free-lancer and one of the first Americans to visit modern China:

> Any time any of us walked down a street alone, we drew tremendous interest. If we stopped to talk or eat an ice cream bar, we drew a crowd. If we did something interesting, like change the film in a camera, we drew a horde.
>
> The Chinese paid especially close attention to our feet. Leather shoes are a sign of great wealth among the Chinese, and one of the things the crowds discussed about us was how wealthy we might be. The quality of our shoes was a clue.
>
> If we wanted to talk seriously with the Chinese in a particular city, all we had to do was stand on a street corner near our hotel at dusk when the work day was done. In a short time some young man—never a woman—would stop to talk. Often his English was broken and halting simply because he hadn't had sufficient opportunity to practice. Other times the English was amazingly fluent.
>
> Their questions were blunt. They wanted to know how much money we made, what our sex practices were and, in general, what interested young people in the United States. They were especially interested in our music.
>
> Sometimes the Chinese would make strange requests of us. Several wanted to rub our arms to see if our freckles were permanent or would come off. They also were intrigued about the amount of hair on our arms (the guys', of course). And they were always impressed at our larger size, which they ascribed to our different diet.

Behind-the-Scenes Features

Behind-the-scenes stories take readers backstage for an inside view of some event. Reporters often find such ventures fascinating and are able to convey the excitement. Behind-the-scenes stories are based on personal interviews with stage managers, rock group "roadies," library catalogers, night street cleaning crews, caterers, convention decorators and the like.

Journalists look for people who perform jobs out of the public eye but essential to some operation. They interview the source, visit him or her on location and use his or her own words to tell the story. They also include details they observe at the scene, such as atmosphere, working conditions, physical appearance of the person and his or her workspace, specialized terms and conversations between workers.

Behind-the-scenes features convey a sense of immediacy, allowing readers to see, feel, taste, touch, smell and understand the "backstage" work that goes into a public event.

Participatory Features

Participatory features give another kind of inside view, this time through the senses of a reporter who is actually experiencing an event or situation. John Howard Griffin, author of "Black Like Me," was a superb participatory reporter. Griffin turned his skin dark with melanin injections and

Harcourt Brace & Company

entered a black community to find out about life in the South during the late 1950s and early 1960s.

If lack of time and money prohibits total immersion in the world of the subject, you might shadow an attorney, a retail clerk, a parent of preschoolers or an elderly person for an afternoon.

Journalists usually arrange such experiences with the boss, director or person in charge of an agency, making it clear that they are journalists and will write or broadcast a story about the experience. Undercover, cloak-and-dagger approaches, like getting arrested in order to expose jail conditions, are risky and ethically questionable.

Medical Features

Some news organizations have medical reporters. However, general-assignment reporters can find good medical features in any community. Illness and health are vitally interesting to the public, and subjects abound.

Topics with endless variations include: the cost of devastating illnesses, new and radical treatments for common ailments, ethical issues surrounding medical advances, pregnancy, child rearing, mental illness, death and the grief process, new equipment and what it does, support groups, workshops for patients with a chronic disease and volunteer programs.

Journalists gather facts from medical experts, people with a particular condition, relatives and friends. They use quotes, allowing subjects to tell about their experiences and feelings. When interviewing people dissatisfied with their medical treatment, reporters must be careful to avoid quoting libelous statements. "She's obviously a money-grubbing quack" can provoke a lawsuit for the news organization, even if the subject did say it. It's helpful to balance complaints with experts' points of view.

Business Features

Many business features highlight one person or aspect of local commerce. Journalists find ideas by looking for the human interest in stories of promotions, new businesses, the local economy and even the election of club officers.

A wealth of business stories exists in any town. Fad businesses like message balloons and flavored popcorn rise and fall. Dating bureaus, computer software merchants and shopping services for working parents respond to new needs in society. Stories on old, established firms, perhaps focusing on the personality of a founder or dynamic leader, are also of perennial interest.

TYPES OF FEATURE LEADS

Many features begin with summary leads. However, features may also begin with quotations, anecdotes, questions, action, descriptions, shocking facts or a combination of these techniques. The only requirement is that the leads interest people, luring them into the stories.

As the following examples demonstrate, a feature lead can be a unit of thought that contains two, three or even four paragraphs:

> SUMMARY: They come seeking excitement: the thrill of toting a gun and flashing a badge. They leave disappointed to find that the job of an auxiliary Highway Patrol officer includes even mundane tasks.

> QUOTATION: "What grade are you in, Aunt Andrea?" asked her 7-year-old niece. "Let's see, I'm a college senior, so I guess that makes it 16th grade," Andrea said. "I'm in first grade," said Sally. "If you're in 16th grade, you must be old." Old has different meanings for different people. . . .

Harcourt Brace & Company

ANECDOTES AND EXAMPLES: Martha, a 28-year-old, began to suffer from ulcers, headaches and high blood pressure. A doctor advised her to change jobs and, three days later, she became a travel consultant.

Kim, 32, was divorced with four children to support. To increase her income, she began to sell real estate. She earned $49,000 last year—and expects to earn $80,000 this year.

Allison, 25, disliked taking orders from doctors. Moreover, she thought some doctors were lazy and uncaring. So she returned to college and is studying to become an English professor.

Until last year, all three women were nurses. Like thousands of others, they became frustrated by the job's stress, hard work and irregular hours.

QUESTION: Just about all plants and animals live by the clock. But how do they know what time it is?

(The Washington Post)

ACTION OR NARRATIVE: Pepper O'Neill can't keep her hands off people. Walking down the streets of Muncie, she sees men and women with bad posture and knotted muscles, the unmistakable signs of stress—and she wants to help them. She needs to knead them. Pepper is a masseuse with a mission.

SHOCKER: Thousands of the world's children under the age of 5 die each day of illnesses that most Americans shrug off.

DESCRIPTION: On Thursday, Jim Donaldson woke up and prepared for work. He took a shower, brushed his teeth and shaved. Jim then put on his makeup: a little blush here and a little eyeliner there. Afterward, he looked to his wife, Lara, for her approval.

Lara inspected her husband. "You need a little more lipstick, honey."

Jim put on some more lipstick while his daughter, Judy, added a bright red bow to her father's hair. That was the perfect touch. His family all agreed that he looked "absolutely marvelous."

Jim kissed his family good-bye, grabbed his bow and arrow and headed off to another day at the office.

As a member of the Activities Committee at Roubidoux Regional Medical Center in Baltimore, Jim has many annual rituals. On Christmas, he's Santa and on Halloween, he's Dracula. On Valentine's Day, he's a tall, dark and handsome Cupid.

THE BODY OF A FEATURE STORY

Like the lead, the body of a feature story can take a number of forms. The inverted-pyramid style may be appropriate for some features, and chronological order for others. Regardless of the form or style chosen, every feature must be coherent. All the facts must fit together smoothly and logically. Transitions must guide the audience from one segment of the story to the next and clearly reveal the relationship between those segments. Transitions should be brief. They may ask a question; shift to a new time or place; or repeat a key word, phrase or idea.

Reporters should be concise, never wasting their audience's time. Features should emphasize lively details—the action. And they should provide an occasional change of pace. A good reporter rarely composes a story consisting of all quotations or all summaries. Instead, the reporter might use several paragraphs of summary, then some quotations to explain an idea, then some description and then more quotations or summary.

Features should be specific. Instead of saying that a person is generous or humorous, reporters should give specific examples of the subject's generosity and humor. Instead of simply stating that "President Calvin Coolidge was a taciturn man," it would be better to illustrate his reluctance to speak by quoting Coolidge himself:

> A woman meeting President Coolidge for the first time said to him, "My friends bet that I couldn't get you to say three words." The president replied, "You lose."

Successful feature writers also use elements such as characterization, setting, plot and subplot, conflict, time, dialogue and narrative.

Journalists reveal character by using quotations and describing speech patterns, mannerisms, body language, appearance, dress, age, preferences, prejudices, use of personal space and a host of other traits. Reporters can sprinkle touches of these descriptions throughout a story to show what the subject of an interview is like.

The setting reveals character and puts the audience member in a context. Geography shapes physical and mental traits, determines lifespan, influences ways of earning a living. Reporters should tell where a subject grew up, what the person's surroundings are now and how these factors reflect what he or she is.

The plot of a feature story may be thought of as a description of the obstacles that lie between a person and his or her goal. The solution of conflict (frustration induced by the obstacles) presents the theme of every human-interest story. The main plots are human vs. nature, human vs. human, and human vs. the inner self. As reporters interview people and ask them about events in their lives, plots naturally emerge. Often there is a subplot, a secondary line of action that runs in counterpoint to the main action, sometimes helping and sometimes hindering the progress. If journalists listen and identify plot and subplot elements as the subject tells the story, a natural order emerges.

Time can be handled in a variety of ways. To organize some types of features, reporters can use a dramatic episode in the present as an opener, then flash back to the beginning of the story and bring it forward in chronological order. Journalists can foreshadow the future or build in a series of flashbacks, arranged in the order in which they happened. Whatever form reporters choose, they should be sure to use transitional words—"now," "then," "in 1995"—to let the audience know when events are taking place.

Feature stories need dialogue. Reporters may use dialogue to show temperament, plot, events, time, customs, color or continuity. They must be careful to choose only the best, most revealing quotes.

Journalists use narrative to weave a story together. It summarizes, arranges, creates flow and transitions, and links one idea to the next. Narrative should be unobtrusive and subtle.

THE ENDING OF A FEATURE STORY

Features should end with a satisfying conclusion, perhaps an anecdote, quote, key word or phrase repeated in some surprising or meaningful way. Journalists should avoid ending feature stories with a summary. Summary endings are too likely to state the obvious, to be repetitious, to be flat and boring.

After finishing a feature, a professional is likely to edit and rewrite it many times. A professional will also slant the feature for a particular audience, publication or news program, emphasizing the story's relevance and importance to it.

SUGGESTED READINGS

Allen, Linda Buchanan. *Write and Sell Your Free-lance Article.* Boston: The Writer, 1991.

Brooks, Terri. *Word's Worth: A Handbook on Writing and Selling Nonfiction.* New York: St. Martin's Press, 1989.

Garrison, Bruce. *Professional Feature Writing,* 2nd ed. Hillsdale, NJ: Erlbaum, 1994.

Harcourt Brace & Company

Garvey, Mark, ed. *Writer's Market: Where & How to Sell What You Write.* Cincinnati: Writer's Digest Books. (An annual guide.)

Hay, Vicky. *The Essential Feature: Writing for Magazines and Newspapers.* New York: Columbia University Press, 1990.

Jacobi, Peter P. *The Magazine Article: How to Think It, Plan It, Write It.* Cincinnati: Writer's Digest Books, 1991.

Lovell, Ronald P. *Free-Lancing: A Guide to Writing for Magazines and Other Markets.* Prospect Heights, IL: Waveland Press, 1994.

Wilber, Rick. *Magazine Feature Writing.* New York: St. Martin's Press, 1995.

Witt, Leonard, ed. *The Complete Book of Feature Writing.* Cincinnati: Writer's Digest Books, 1991.

EXERCISE 1
FEATURE STORIES

1. GENERATING IDEAS AND SELECTING A TOPIC

A. List some universal needs (such as food, clothing, shelter, sex, love, belonging, self-expression) across the top of a piece of paper. Down the left side, list some pressing social issues (concerns of the elderly, health care, AIDS, unemployment, teen suicide). Draw lines to form a grid. Fill in the spaces in the grid with story ideas created by combining the two topics.

B. Listen and observe to find a feature topic. Ride a city bus to the end of the line, sit in the student union or in a cafeteria. Watch what people do, and listen to what people are talking about. Make a list of potential feature topics.

C. Pair up with another student. Set a timer and write for 10 minutes, completely free and uncensored, about one or more of the following topics: pet peeves; things I avoid writing about; things I am curious about; favorite places in my hometown; a specific holiday, such as Christmas or Thanksgiving; my biggest problem as a child (or teen-ager). Take turns reading your papers aloud to your partner. Discuss how you could conduct research and interviews to make a story from one of the ideas you generated.

2. STORY TYPES

A. Find and clip an example of each story type described in this chapter. As you read and discuss the various types in class, analyze your examples for strong and weak points.

B. List five story ideas of your own for each type.

3. FEATURE LEADS

A. Critically evaluate the following leads. Decide which topics would interest people and which leads pull them into the story:

1. It may be one of the smallest pieces of real estate that you will ever buy, but chances are that your cemetery plot will also be the most expensive. The price of cemetery property goes up at least 10 percent a year, said Roberta Neel, president of Wood-lawn Memorial Park. The current starting price for a 5-by-10-foot plot is between $1,800 and $2,400 at most cemeteries.

2. There was no hesitation. The bowler picked up her ball and smoothly let it roll down the alley. Nine pins fell, leaving just one standing. Anna Hershey took careful aim and knocked that one down too. Perfectly ordinary. Except that Hershey is blind.

3. "How about if I just sit on the floor with you?" asked Judge Clarinda Dubreff after a child complained that she "always sits higher than anybody else." The juvenile court judge took off her jacket, rolled up her sleeves and sat on the classroom floor.

4. Twenty teen-agers plan their own curriculum and live and work at Freedom House School. All 20 are from welfare families, and most have police records.

Harcourt Brace & Company

    5. Pancho is a short, dark-skinned, curly-haired 20-year-old with flashing black eyes, a bouncing step and a Spanish accent.

B. Find and clip a newspaper or magazine feature lead to illustrate each type of lead discussed in this chapter. Identify what kind each is. Then rewrite it as a different type. Also, evaluate the leads: Which leads are most likely to interest readers?

C. Exchange the feature stories you have written for class with another student. Rewrite each other's leads as different types. Decide which type is better for each lead.

4. MISCELLANEOUS EXERCISES

A. Clip five feature stories from a newspaper or magazine and analyze the stories' topics, leads and styles of writing, particularly their organization and development of details.

B. Rewrite the introductory paragraphs of five news stories as feature leads.

C. Take a feature story you have written and read it to class members or a tape recorder. Note the places where you stumble, run out of breath or become confused about a passage's meaning. Reword these spots, shortening sentences and smoothing awkward passages.

Harcourt Brace & Company

CHAPTER 18

WRITING FOR BROADCAST

The function of the press is very high. It is almost holy. It ought to serve as a forum for the people, through which the people may know freely what is going on. To misstate or suppress the news is a breach of trust.

(Justice Louis D. Brandeis, U.S. Supreme Court)

Whereas print news is written for readers scanning the news page with their eyes, broadcast news is written for listeners tuning in with their ears. Another difference between print and broadcast is that the printed word is permanent and can be reread. Broadcast words, once spoken, are gone forever; listeners cannot hear them again if their attention wanders or if they need to clarify a fact or issue. Furthermore, most people like the newspaper for its detailed information, but enjoy broadcast news for quick, up-to-date information. Thus, the story organization and writing style of broadcast news are different from those of print because of the nature of the medium and how people interact with it.

Although the writing style for each medium is different, the types of stories chosen are not. The best stories in broadcast are similar to the best stories in print. They involve the listener. Listeners are drawn into a story either because it is compelling or because it involves them in some way.

In addition to emphasizing similar news elements, print and broadcast journalists must do the same type of background work. They must research their topic to find the best angle, conduct background research on their interview subjects to ask the best questions, and employ good interviewing skills to obtain interesting quotes. Furthermore, they must be good writers and spellers so their copy flows easily for both the announcer reading the story and the listener hearing it.

WRITING FOR YOUR LISTENER

A broadcast journalist must think in terms of listener time, whereas a print reporter thinks in terms of newspaper space. People often listen to broadcast news while doing something else. These competing activities, a listener's short attention span and writing for the ear make a broadcast journalist's job challenging.

Broadcast is written in a conversational, informal and relaxed style. It is written in the way that one friend would talk to another. Sometimes this style includes using contractions, incomplete sentences and first and second person (*I*, *me*, *us*, *we*, *you*) to establish a rapport with listeners.

Also, sentences need to be short and to the point. People cannot listen to a long sentence and always remember to associate its end with what was said at the beginning. Broadcast sentences are declarative, and frequently fewer than 15 words, certainly no more than 20. They should be simple sentences in the active voice, keeping the subject, verb and object together. And they need to be cleared of parenthetical information; instead, use a separate sentence:

Harcourt Brace & Company

WRONG: Taxes, said Texas Republican Bill Archer, who is chair of the national House Ways and Means Committee and who may become a presidential candidate—a race in which there are three presidential hopefuls so far—should be abolished in their present form.

REVISED: The chair of the House Ways and Means Committee says he wants to abolish our current tax structure.

Texas Republican Bill Archer set that as his goal today as he opened hearings on our tax system. . . .

Because broadcast news is aired several times a day, information needs to be presented in an up-to-date format. News is happening NOW. Use "today," "this morning" and "earlier today" to indicate immediacy. And use "yesterday" and "tomorrow" instead of days of the week. Most Associated Press wire stories written for broadcast leave out the time altogether because a listener assumes the stories will concern a recent event or a current issue.

Verbs should be in the present tense to show recency: "says," not "said"; "is presenting," not "presented." If the present tense does not work, then try the present perfect tense:

A heat wave that has baked the Plains for four straight days has caused at least six deaths.

If past tense is used, try to include the time element to reflect immediacy:

Deadheads everywhere are reeling in shock that the music group's lead singer died of a heart attack this morning.

Grateful Dead lead singer Jerry Garcia . . .

Here are a few more hints on writing for a listening audience:

- Round numbers: It is difficult for someone to remember the exact figure of 3, 984. It is easier to remember "almost 4-thousand."

- Give numbers meaning: What does it mean to the listener that people in Greenetown will be taxed an extra $100,000 for an improved fire department? Saying the tax is only "an additional 5 cents per person" gives listeners a different tone and clearer understanding.

- Shorten long titles: Titles do not always describe the position nor job that people occupy. Also, long titles make people forget what else the story has to say. For example, Andrea Maye is the supervisor of the Pharmacy Program of the Health Regulation Division in the Office of Health Services of the Bureau of Occupational and Professional Regulation in the Michigan Department of Commerce. This long title would use most of the time allotted to the story. Shorten the title to a word or two, such as "a supervisor," or to a brief description of the person's job, such as "a state health official."

- Never put an unfamiliar name first in a story because a listener might miss it. Delay it until you have your audience's attention:

    The president of the American Medical Association says it's compiled overwhelming evidence showing tobacco company scientists knew the dangers of their product.

    President Tyler Reeves says that . . . .

- Contrary to newspaper style, omit a person's middle initial, unless it is commonly recognized as part of that person's name. Remember that broadcast is a conversational style, and people are not usually referred to by their initials in conversation.

Harcourt Brace & Company

- Place the description, age or identification before a person's name. Newspaper style, with description often placed after the name, is not conversational. Instead, describe the person beforehand to keep the subject-verb-object phrase together:

  WRONG: Gordon Elliott, 16, a Friendswood high school student, was given the state's Good Citizenship Award earlier today.

  REVISED: A Friendswood teen-ager is the center of attention today at the governor's mansion.

  Sixteen-year-old Gordon Elliott has been given the state's Good Citizenship Award for saving two children from drowning in Grand River last fall. . . .

- Place the attribution before what is said. The broadcast formula "Who Said What" is the opposite of newspaper style ("What, Said Who"). In broadcast news, reporters need to prepare listeners for the quote or paraphrase coming next, to allow them to concentrate on what is being said:

  Judge Lance Ito says the defense suggestion that the killing of Nicole Brown Simpson was a drug hit is highly unlikely.

- Avoid direct quotes: Listeners cannot see a quotation mark, so a journalist needs to paraphrase what someone said. Or a journalist can use indirect quotes. If a direct quote is necessary, then special language is sometimes inserted:

  And quoting directly here, ". . .

  Her exact words were, ". . .

  In her own words, ". . .

- Avoid homonyms: These can be confusing to your listener, who must spend time wrestling with the confusing sentence and may miss the rest of the story.

- Try to avoid pronouns. With four dogs in a story, it is often difficult to figure out which "it" ran away with the prize.

- Use descriptive language, but sparingly. Some descriptive words help a listener to better visualize an event (e.g., "slammed into" instead of "hit"). However, too much description can take away from the rest of the story by confusing the listener or using precious seconds needed elsewhere.

WRITING FOR YOUR ANNOUNCER

Broadcast journalists must understand listeners' ability to hear and remember all the information in a story. Thus, stories are kept short and the style is conversational.

Broadcast copy must also be "announcer-friendly." At some stations, the writer is the announcer, but in many others, they are different people. The copy is often finished only minutes before a newscast is aired, thus allowing an announcer only a single quick practice read before going on-air. Therefore, a writer needs to make a story as readable as possible so it can be interpreted aloud by someone else.

Here are some common tips for writing broadcast copy for an announcer:

- Add phonetic spelling: To mispronounce a name on the air is a sin. However, not everyone knows how to pronounce everything correctly. Announcers often need the name of a place or person spelled out phonetically, either directly after or in the space above the word:

  Juanita Diaz [Wha-NEE-ta DEE-ahz] has placed first in the Rifle Association's annual sharpshooters' contest.

Sometimes, the same spelling is pronounced differently in different regions of the United States. Thus, "Charlotte" can be [SHAR-lot], as in North Carolina, or [shar-LOT], as in Michigan.

- Hyphenate words that go together in a group. Announcers will then avoid taking a breath between these words, saying them as a group:

    The four-month-old baby was unharmed.

    About 12-point-three-million people avoid paying taxes.

- Spell out numbers up to and including eleven so that announcers can easily read them at a glance. Use numerals for 12 to 999, unless they begin a sentence or indicate an age, address or date. Use a combination of numerals and words for large numbers (e.g., 40-thousand). Announcers may pause at the phrase "$10,110,011," but can glide more easily along when reading (and rounding) "about 10-million-110-thousand-dollars":

    Maggie Williams' legal bills from Whitewater have topped 100-thousand dollars.

    Spell out eleven because it may look like two ll's (letter l's) instead of two 11's (numeral ones). For example, an announcer may pause when hit with "11 llamas" instead of "eleven llamas."

- Use words instead of abbreviations or symbols: Spell out titles, symbols and states' names so an announcer can more easily recognize and pronounce them:

    Lieutenant General Smith—not Lt. Gen. Smith

    Texas—not Tex., nor TX

    fifty-percent—not 50%

    two-hundred-dollars—not $200

- Hyphenate some numbers and some abbreviations on second reference. Hyphens let an announcer know that the letters are to be read not as a word, but individually:

    I-B-M

    N-C-A-A, but also N-C-double-A

    Acronyms, such as NATO and NASA, are written without hyphens because they are pronounced the way they are spelled.

    In addition, numbers to be read individually need hyphens:

    That telephone number is 6-7-6-3-4-2-2.

- Avoid alliterations or tongue twisters that might trip up an announcer. Also avoid words in a series that have several snaking "S" sounds or popping "P's." They don't translate well into a microphone.

TYPES OF LEADS FOR BROADCAST STORIES

The traditional summary lead sometimes used for print news is too long for broadcast news because it is difficult to follow when read aloud. Too much information (who, what, where, when,

Harcourt Brace & Company

why and how) frustrates listeners. People cannot digest all that information at once; it should be given to them in separate sentences.

Broadcast news stories follow a "pyramid" formula: The single most important element of a story comes first, followed by the rest of the information. The lead does not have to tell the whole story. And, because newscasts are timed before they are aired, journalists can write a complete story without fearing that the ending sentence or paragraph will be edited out at the last moment.

A broadcast lead should capture listeners' attention immediately or they will be lost to the story forever. The lead must tell listeners one or two important facts and ease them into the details.

The best leads capture listeners' attention by involving them in some way. Many people are going to care about a story regarding a new corn hybrid. Even if they are not farmers, they will be affected by the impact the hybrid corn has on the price of corn in the supermarket. In a college town, most students will be interested in new bicycle laws that will affect the way in which they get to their classes. For others, the story will explain the new paths they see criss-crossing campus.

Yet the lead must not give away too much important information. Listeners usually don't hear the first two or three words of a lead, but "tune in" when they hear something that interests them.

Leads are constantly being rewritten for ongoing stories in each newscast. Whereas newspapers are published once a day and give yesterday's news, broadcast news can be aired any time of the day, as often as necessary. With hourly updates, broadcast stories can tell the news as it happens throughout the day. Thus, broadcast news needs to be rewritten each time to freshen the information, update the story or localize the news.

Four common types of leads are the soft lead, hard lead, throwaway lead and umbrella lead. Each is written to intrigue and interest the listener, and provide a transition into important facts of the story.

The Soft Lead

The soft lead tells listeners that something important is coming up and invites them to continue listening to hear the story. Soft leads, similar to soft news stories, "featurize" information before getting to the hard news. A soft lead usually tells listeners why the information is important or how it affects them:

> LEAD: The space shuttle "Discovery" is up and running.
> REST OF THE STORY: The main reason for this mission is to replace a communications satellite lost when "Challenger" exploded in 1986.
> "Discovery's" liftoff from the Kennedy Space Center in Florida came just six days after "Atlantis" returned from Russia's space station. That's the shortest time ever between U-S missions.
> The launch was scheduled for last month, but was put off for repairs. Woodpeckers had drilled holes into the insulation of the shuttle's fuel tanks.
> The astronauts are expected to be in space for eight days.

Here is another example of a soft lead:

> LEAD: Smoke still fills the air over western Colorado.
> REST OF THE STORY: A wild fire that injured 30 firefighters and threatened homes has already burned 12-thousand acres. High temperatures and strong winds make the job harder for the 15-hundred firefighters who continue working around the clock.

The Hard Lead

Hard leads give important information immediately. Some broadcasters believe that, as a result, the important facts that listeners need to know are gone before listeners realize they need to "tune in" to what is being said. Not everyone agrees:

> LEAD: The man who raped three St. Louis men, killing one of them, was sent to prison for life today.
>
> REST OF THE STORY: Ervine McMitchelle drew a life term for the first-degree murder of Henry LaDouche last year. County Circuit Judge Ashley Monahan also gave McMitchelle 50-to-75-years for each of three counts of rape. The rapes occurred between 1994 and last year.

Here is another example of a hard lead:

> LEAD: More than 165 passengers are safe, after a seven-47 plane made an emergency landing at the Minneapolis Metro Airport today.
>
> REST OF THE STORY: Airport director Jean Richards says shortly after takeoff, a door opened in the luggage compartment. The plane dumped its fuel and returned to the airport. Richards says only one piece of luggage was dropped—and it was recovered intact. She says it appears a hinge came loose from the door. The plane refueled and took off again, after a two-hour delay.

The Throwaway Lead

The throwaway lead intrigues listeners. After they have "tuned in" to the story, the next sentence begins the real lead. A story would make sense without the throwaway lead—but without it, the story might not have attracted listeners:

> LEAD: If you think your pampered pooch or cuddly kitty deserves the national spotlight, here's your chance.
>
> REST OF THE STORY: The International Pet Cemeteries Foundation in Austin, Texas, plans to build a National Pet Hall of Fame by the year two-thousand.
>
> The president of the foundation, Heidi Hills, hopes to provide education about pets and also memorialize famous and not-so-famous pets.

Here is another example of a throwaway lead:

> LEAD: Businesses that work with the government will have to heed a federal pollution-reporting law.
>
> REST OF THE STORY: The president today in Chicago signed an executive order making companies with government contracts report their chemical emissions.
>
> This order is in response to what the president says are Republican efforts to weaken environmental laws. Republicans say that many of the laws are unnecessary and overly bureaucratic.

The Umbrella Lead

The umbrella lead summarizes or ties together two or more related news stories before delving into each story separately. The lead tells listeners the relationship between the separate stories that are subsequently described:

LEAD: Police are looking into the possibility of a connection among 20 recent dog-nappings in the area.

REST OF THE STORY: Mason Animal Shelter Director John Ertos says he has received 12 inquiries about lost dogs since yesterday. Most of these dogs were in fenced-in back yards or on leashes.

In nearby Dansville, police officer Annie Bearclaw says the station has logged eight calls reporting missing dogs within two days.

This is a high number of calls about missing pets—dogs specifically—within a two-day period.

THE BODY OF A BROADCAST NEWS STORY

The traditional inverted-pyramid news story is written with its facts presented in descending order of importance. After each sentence or paragraph, the reader can leave the story, having gleaned an increasingly detailed sense of what happened. Also, print editors can cut the story almost anywhere, knowing that the most important information has already been presented.

In broadcast news, every sentence of a story is important because when listeners leave the story, they are usually leaving the newscast. In addition, listeners generally cannot digest a lot of information all at once, so broadcast stories are short. Every sentence needs to be heard. Stories need to be tight, with no extraneous information or loose ends. Thus, the most important information is given first, followed by other important information. Sometimes facts are presented in descending order of importance, sometimes in chronological order with a narrative format. Overall, sentences are shorter and contain fewer facts than in print style.

Descending Order of Importance

The journalist must first figure out the single most significant piece of information to tell listeners. It goes in a story's lead. Then the journalist must anticipate what else listeners want to know. This information makes up the body of the story.

Although a story may contain several pieces of information, their order is usually dictated by the facts given in the lead. If the lead indicates that a minister was killed late last night, listeners will want to know the victim's name. They will also want to know where, how or why the victim was killed. And they will want to know what police are doing about the case:

A Presbyterian minister has been found dead this morning in her church office.

First Presbyterian Church secretary Robert Abrahm found the door unlocked and the Reverend Sarah Chen dead when he came in to work on the church newsletter.

Police Chief Chris Stagers says Chen died a little before midnight, but they are not yet sure how she died.

Chen had been minister of the First Presbyterian Church for more than eight years.

Chronological Order

In the chronological type of broadcast news story, the climax—the most significant part—makes up the lead. Then, as in chronological print stories, the details are related to listeners in the order of their occurrence. Journalists relate the story in the order of when events happened, not the order in which they found out about each fact:

Police have found a Presbyterian minister dead this morning in her church office.

Police Chief Chris Stagers says the Rev. Sarah Chen died a little before midnight.

First Presbyterian Church secretary Robert Abrahm found the door unlocked and Chen dead when he came in to work on the church newsletter.

Authorities are trying to learn how she died.

Chen had been minister of the First Presbyterian Church for more than eight years.

UPDATING BROADCAST NEWS STORIES

Many radio stations have several newscasts throughout the day. Although some topics may be substituted for others, stations must keep listeners up to date on important, ongoing events. Thus, the same story may be repeated throughout the day, but freshened with new angles or additional interviews or more recent information. The lead sentence and story wording should never stay exactly the same in successive newscasts. Here are two updated leads:

Police are investigating the death of a Presbyterian minister found dead in her office this morning.

Religious fundamentalists could have something to do with a minister's death late last night.

GUIDELINES FOR COPY PREPARATION

The format and aesthetics of broadcast news copy are important because too many extraneous marks can distract an announcer and, consequently, detract from the news story. If an announcer gets confused, then listeners surely will, and will be likely to turn the dial.

Most of the information in this chapter applies to both radio and television broadcast. However, these copy guidelines and some of the following sections are written mostly with the radio journalist in mind, because many students learn about radio before advancing to television:

- Use standard-sized 8½- by 11-inch paper so that all stories fit neatly together and smaller ones don't slip out.

- Type on only one side of the paper so an announcer knows immediately where the next story is, to prevent on-air paper shuffling.

- Set margins for 65 characters a line as a universal line measurement for announcer timing. (About 15 lines, of 65 characters each, make up one minute of air time; the exact timing depends on the individual announcer's pace.)

- Triple-space to visually separate lines for announcing and to give more room for editing.

- Standardize copy with either all uppercase or upper and lowercase letters.

- Place only one story on each page. If more stories are written than can be used during a newscast, the announcer may become confused about which of two stories on a page should be omitted.

- Put a slug in the top left corner of the page. The slug contains the story identification in one or two words, the reporter's name, date and the time of the newscast. If the story is more than one page long, the slug on subsequent pages should include the page number, repeated several times for clarity (e.g., 2-2-2). Rarely is a story more than one page long.

Harcourt Brace & Company

- Begin each story about six lines below the slug. The space between the slug and the story can be used for editing or adding transitions between stories.

- Omit datelines because most broadcasts reach only local listeners. (National wires do use datelines because they are syndicated across the country.)

- Indent the first line of each paragraph of a story five spaces to indicate the beginning of a new paragraph.

- Never split words or related phrases between lines of copy (e.g., "She has been in the news/room . . ."). End lines at natural breaks between words or phrases, to avoid leaving an announcer unprepared and listeners wondering.

- Never split a sentence or paragraph between pages of copy. Again, an announcer needs to read smoothly and should not have to look for extended endings on other pages. Furthermore, the story will sound less confusing if a thought (paragraph) is completed, but the rest of the story (on the next page) happens to be missing.

- Use an end mark at the end of the story to indicate there is no more. Some journalists prefer a traditional end mark (### or -30-), while others use their initials.

- Add "more" or a long arrow pointing to the bottom of the page to indicate that the story continues onto the next page.

EDITING COPY

- Never use newspaper copy editing symbols. They are too difficult for an announcer to interpret while reading on-air:

  WRONG: Police are ~~are~~ ^looking^ for a Kalamazoo woman who ~~feld~~ the Jackson County court house momments after being convicted today.

- To edit a word, black it out completely and rewrite it in the space above it:

  RIGHT: Police are ~~are~~ looking for a Kalamazoo woman who ~~feld~~ fled the Jackson County ~~court house~~ ~~momments~~ Courthouse moments after being convicted today.

- Limit the number of words inserted into copy.

- If the copy requires a lot of editing, type a clean copy. The fewer editing marks, the fewer times an announcer hesitates or stumbles while reading.

- Write the timing of the story (for example, ":20") and number of lines in the top right-hand corner of the copy page. Remember that for most announcers, 15 lines of copy equal one minute of reading time. Some journalists prefer to denote the number of lines. (Count two half lines as one complete line.)

- Circle all information that is not to be read on-air, such as the slug, end mark and timing.

PUTTING TOGETHER A NEWSCAST

Tight, efficient—but thorough—story writing is imperative in broadcast news. CBS news announcer Walter Cronkite was "the most trusted man in America" for many years because of his concise informational, but complete 30-minute newscasts.

BROADCAST COPY EXAMPLE

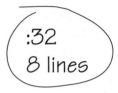

Police are looking for a Lansing woman who fled the Jackson

County Courthouse moments after being convicted today.

Assistant prosecutor Reggie Maxim says the trial had just

ended when Lucretia Morris hit a guard and ran to freedom, at

about three o'clock.

The 28-year-old Morris had just been convicted of assault and

robbery charges from last May.

Sheriff Bobbi McNeil says the woman was wearing jeans, and a

white short-sleeved shirt and tennis shoes.

Police say Morris is dangerous.

# # #

Local and national television newscasts are about 30 minutes long. Some public radio newscasts span a half-hour or more, but many commercial radio newscasts are only five minutes long, made up of mostly 15- to 30-second news stories.

Newscasts become even shorter once the time used for the opening and closing, a commercial break, teasers and promos, transitions between stories, weather and sports is deducted.

Reviewing Copy

A journalist or announcer should read all copy to become familiar with what has been prepared for the newscast. While reading each story, the announcer should confirm that his or her reading

Harcourt Brace & Company

time is in sync with the average number of lines per minute. The announcer should also mark—or personalize—the copy for word emphases or difficult pronunciations.

Timing the Newscast

Let's say that five minutes are allotted every hour on the hour for a radio newscast. To figure out how much copy you need, begin by subtracting one minute for a commercial break and 15 seconds each for the intro and "outro" (ending) to your newscast. That leaves three and a half minutes, which is about 52 lines of copy. Weather and sports updates consume 20 seconds each, taking a total of 10 lines (five lines each). That leaves 42 lines for news copy. With this number in mind, review each story, find the important ones, and add the total lines of copy (by adding the number of lines in all the stories, which should be noted in the top right-hand corner of each copy page). Remember to add a few seconds for transitions between stories. In addition, always keep an extra story available in case you need it to fill time.

A newscast's length is called its "running time." Some announcers combine running time with "back timing" the last two or three stories. For example, the announcer does a practice reading of the last few stories, in this case sports and weather, and notes the exact time it takes. Then the announcer subtracts that time from the end of five minutes—what the clock should say at this exact point. Thus the announcer will know where in the newscast he or she should be at this exact time while on-air. When the announcer reaches these stories on air, he or she compares the time with the run-through. If the announcer is under the allotted time, then the last stories should be read more slowly or another short story should be added. If the announcer is over, he or she should speed up the last few stories to end exactly on time.

Organizing Stories

The order in which stories appear in a newscast often depends on a news organization's policy. Some begin with local news, progress to state news and end with national or international news. Others use just the opposite order. Within each news category, begin with the best stories to gain the listener's attention at the beginning. If the first story—whether in the local or international category—is an attention-grabber, then a listener is unlikely to change stations. Look for a "kicker" to run at the end of the newscast: a lighthearted story that leaves listeners feeling good. Some are humorous, others emphasize human interest.

Adding Transitions

Transitions make newscasts more conversational. As you review each story before a newscast, think about the transitions needed to move from story to story, and pencil them in on the copy. Transitions smooth out the potentially abrupt movement from one subject to another by tying different subjects together. In addition, transitions signal the end of one story and the beginning of another. Some transitions include the following phrases:

> Meanwhile . . .

> Closer to home . . .

To make a transition from one story to another, try to find a commonality in both. Commonalities might include geographic proximity, time sequence or action:

> You might think it's hot today, but forecasters are predicting even hotter temperatures tomorrow in southern Iowa. . . .

Or, transitions can point out differences:

While southern Texas is experiencing heat waves, fierce thunderstorms are ravaging the northern part of the state. . . .

SOURCES FOR BROADCAST NEWS

Broadcast journalists get their news from the same sources as print journalists. However, instead of writing down what a source has said, broadcast reporters tape a source's comments to be played on the air. This change in voice gives variety to newscasts and lends authority to the news. In addition, broadcasters often use the telephone rather than a personal interview. Because newscasts are so frequent, little time is available to work on stories. Common sources for broadcast news include news services and wire feeds, people, newspapers and news releases from public relations agencies.

News Services

In days gone by, wire machines would continuously print out all news, weather and sports stories that correspondents wrote from different parts of the country and beyond. Typically, a subscribing station's morning reporter would open the office door to find yards of paper filled with stories from a wire machine, which typed throughout the night. This Teletype machine would continue to print news and information throughout the day, occasionally ringing a bell for a particularly important story, and stopping only for a change in ribbon or paper.

The old term "rip and read" came from reporters ripping stories off the Teletype and immediately reading them over the air. Often nothing was changed because wire copy coming into broadcast stations was already written in the accepted broadcast style.

Today, the wire services are termed "news services" and Teletype machines have been replaced by computers. The steady clacking of Teletype keys and ringing of the bell have been replaced by the quiet hum of a printer. A continuous stream of stories is no longer printed. Reporters look at national or regional headings and read every story on a screen. They then print only the stories they want to use.

News feeds are another news source. These also are from news services, but instead of being written, they are audio stories that journalists can tape and integrate into their newscasts. At designated times of the day, upcoming story topics and lengths are listed on a computer, and the news feeds sent to subscribing stations. A journalist can tape whichever story is desired. Once the story is taped, the journalist simply adds an intro and outro.

Newspapers

Newspapers are an important source of information. Frequently, commercial broadcast stations have only one or two news reporters, who do not have time to cover all stories in person. Thus, they learn about many important events from a local newspaper. Broadcast journalists rewrite the story in broadcast style for newscasts, giving credit to the newspaper.

Public Relations News Releases

The government and businesses hire public relations practitioners to promote their image or product. News organizations are flooded with news releases announcing events or happenings,

Harcourt Brace & Company

from the promotion of an executive officer to a new product line. Rarely are news releases objective; never are they negative.

However, news releases can be quite helpful on slow news days. Journalists can look to them for additional information about changes within the community or updates on local companies. Ideally, the release should be regarded as a news tip, to be followed up with background research and interviews with competing organizations or people with opposite viewpoints. Unfortunately, too many journalists simply take a news release, shorten it for broadcast and read it on the air.

People

Many good news tips come from people who call stations to give information about an event that has just happened or is about to happen. Following up on these tips with good reporting techniques, such as in-depth questions and research, can lead to more sources and interesting stories. In addition, interviewing people about one subject can lead to tips and ideas on additional subjects.

THE NEWSROOM ENVIRONMENT

Commercial television and public radio stations typically schedule longer and more frequent news and information programs than do commercial radio stations. Thus, they need more journalists, more space for newsrooms and a larger news budget. Commercial radio stations often regard news as a brief update for their listeners. They have small news budgets and sometimes only one journalist. That one journalist, titled "news director," is the entire news staff.

This journalist is responsible for obtaining the news from news releases or a local newspaper, calling sources to verify information or to ask for interviews, writing the news and reading it over the air. This person does not have a lot of time to spend researching stories in depth, and going out to cover events in person is out of the question.

Journalists who prefer talking to a lot of people and covering stories in depth would probably like working at a television station or public radio station better than at most commercial radio stations. Those who can become proficient at conveying the heart of a story in a few words should do well in broadcast news.

CHECKLISTS FOR BROADCAST WRITING

Writing Style

1. Write in a conversational style for the listener.
2. Make your copy "announcer-friendly" for quick, easy reading.
3. Use sentences of about 15 words or fewer.
4. Write in the present tense.
5. Write simple sentences in subject-verb-object order, and eliminate parenthetical phrases.
6. Find the one important news element and highlight it in the lead. The rest of the information should follow in small doses.
7. Do not start a story with a person's name or important information; save it for a bit later, when the listener has "tuned in."
8. Use few numbers, round them and give them meaning.
9. Write out titles, large numbers and symbols.
10. Use descriptive language, but sparingly.

Copy Format

1. Use only one side of the paper.
2. Triple space.
3. Set margins for 65-character lines.
4. Do not split phrases or words between lines. Do not split a sentence or paragraph between pages.
5. Put the slug in the top left-hand corner, then skip about six lines to begin the story.
6. Black out words to be edited. Write in the corrected word above the line.
7. Circle all parts of the text that are not to be read by the announcer.

SUGGESTED READINGS

Bliss, Edward, Jr. *Now the News: The Story of Broadcast Journalism.* New York: Columbia University Press, 1991.

Block, Mervin. *Broadcast Newswriting: The RTNDA Reference Guide.* Chicago: Bonus Books, 1994.

Blumenthal, Howard J., and Oliver R. Goodenough. *The Business of Television.* New York: Billboard Books, 1991.

Campbell, Richard. *60 Minutes and the News: A Mythology for Middle Americans.* Urbana, IL: University of Illinois Press, 1991.

Filoreto, Carl, with Lynn Setzer. *Working in T.V. News: The Insider's Guide.* Memphis, TN: Mustang, 1993.

Gibson, Roy. *Radio and Television Reporting.* Boston: Allyn & Bacon, 1991.

Matelski, Marilyn J. *TV News Ethics.* Stoneham, MA: Focal Press, 1991.

Mayeux, Peter E. *Broadcast News Writing and Reporting.* Dubuque, IA: William C. Brown, 1991.

Papper, Robert A. *Broadcast News Writing Stylebook.* Boston: Allyn & Bacon, 1995.

White, Ted. *Broadcast News Writing and Reporting.* New York: St. Martin's Press, 1993.

E X E R C I S E 1

WRITING FOR BROADCAST

IDENTIFYING BROADCAST STYLE

INSTRUCTIONS: The following are correctly written broadcast leads from The Associated Press. Explain what makes their broadcast style different from the stories written for newspapers. Think about time, verb tense, titles, personal identification, amount of information and a conversational mode.

1. A government official says she found uncontrolled bank fraud at an Arkansas company with ties to the Clintons' Whitewater real estate venture.

2. The jury for the O. J. Simpson case faces another long day of genetic evidence testimony.

3. The director of the Senate Whitewater hearings says the panel might revisit testimony from Maggie Williams—the first lady's top aide.

4. The F-B-I agent in charge of the Oklahoma City bombing investigation has been promoted.

5. The U-S has begun extradition procedures against the political leader of an Islamic militant group.

6. Prosecutors want more time to build a case against a city official accused of illegal trading.

7. Parts of south Louisiana remain under a flash-flood watch as what's left of Hurricane Harriet moves across the state.

8. President Clinton is angrily denouncing the most recent military base closing list as absurd, especially when it comes to California and Texas.

9. A U-N representative calls the overflow of refugees from Serb-toppled Srebrenica [sreh-breh-NIT-sah] an example of human misery.

10. A restaurant in Arkansas has offered free meals to nine Asians who were denied service earlier this week.

EXERCISE 2

WRITING FOR BROADCAST

IDENTIFYING DIFFERENT BROADCAST LEADS

INSTRUCTIONS: The following broadcast leads and the second paragraphs from The Associated Press are written correctly. Identify the style of each lead: hard news, soft news, throwaway or umbrella.

1. The judge in the O. J. Simpson trial is refusing to admit testimony about drug use by a good friend of Nicole Brown Simpson.

   The defense attorneys want to show evidence of drug use by Faye Resnick. They want to support their claim that Nicole Brown Simpson and Ronald Goldman might have been killed by drug dealers looking for their friend Resnick.

2. There is confirmation that inflation is not a problem.

   A representative of the Labor Department says that the June Producer Price index dropped one-tenth of one percent. Not counting food and energy, the index was ahead a modest two-tenths of one percent. The index shows a big decline in energy costs and the largest drop in fruit prices in nearly 20 years.

3. A New York man who tried to exterminate his girlfriend's family will spend the rest of his life in prison.

   A federal judge in Rochester, New York, today gave Hiram Evans five consecutive life terms and four additional life sentences to be served concurrently.

4. Defense attorneys in the O.J. Simpson trial have requested a special prosecutor in the case.

   In court papers released today, Simpson attorneys say there should be an outside investigation of whether police officers lied on the witness stand.

5. Shakespeare's ghost may live again.

   After about 400 years, actors are again on the stage of the Globe Theatre in London. It's a copy of the old building where the playwright's first productions were performed.

6. About a dozen people were killed this morning when a charter flight out of Chicago hit thunderstorms.

   The Sunshine Company plane was rising above lightning and torrential rain on its way to Reno when its engines apparently failed.

7. Several U-S industries are experiencing the effects of NAFTA.

   Asparagus growers are finding that more fresh asparagus is being imported from Mexico because of cheaper prices.

8. Even the North is no escape for hot weather this week.

   According to the National Weather Service, temperatures in northern Michigan will remain in the scorching three digits.

9. Some disgusted citizens are doing something about the new Calvin Klein ads.

    A group in New Hampshire is demonstrating against the company's ads focusing on open crotches. The new ads show young men sitting with open legs and wearing underwear not covered by high-cut jeans shorts.

10. A police officer in New York has quit his job in deference to his principles.

    At a press conference in Manlius today, Jesse Morales called the judicial process a revolving-door penal system.

Harcourt Brace & Company

E X E R C I S E   3

WRITING FOR BROADCAST

WRITING BROADCAST STORIES

INSTRUCTIONS: Write broadcast stories about the following events. Write at least one soft news, one hard news and one throwaway lead. Your stories should not run over 30 seconds. Remember to consult the checklists on pages 461-462.

1. Previously, anyone who parked in a spot reserved for the handicapped in your city would be fined $20. However, your city council met last night and heard complaints that other motorists often use the spaces, making it harder for handicapped people to shop or eat out or go to movies. As a result, the council voted 5-2 to raise the fine to $250—the highest in the state—to discourage able-bodied drivers from using the parking spots reserved for the handicapped. Those spaces normally are close to store entrances. Two members of the Paralyzed Veterans Association were at the meeting to lobby for the stiffer fine, saying it might be the only way to stop offenders. The new law will go into effect in 30 days. State law allows half of the money collected through such fines to go toward enforcing and administering the parking regulations. The rest may be used to build wheelchair ramps and other improvements to enhance access to public buildings.

2. J. T. Pinero is a developer in your community. He is planning to build 350 houses in a 120-acre subdivision which he has named "Deer Run." This morning he was cited by the city. The city also stopped all work on the development. The land had been wooded, and Pinero was charged with clearing the first 30 acres without obtaining city permits. Mayor Paula Novaro said it was the most flagrant violation of the citys tree protection code since her election five years ago. Pinero was cited for cutting down more than 500 pines, oaks, maple, birch and other trees. Under city codes, unauthorized destruction of each tree is punishable by a fine of up to $500. Novaro added that she and other city officials are negotiating with Pinero and his attorney for landscaping and replacement of all the trees. Pinero must also post a $100,000 bond or letter of credit to ensure restoration. If the work is done, Nova said, Pinero might not be fined for this, his first offense. Pinaro said he did not know of the land-clearing and tree-removal permits required by the city.

3. Liz Holton operates a doughnut shop at 2240 Broadway Avenue. Today she was ordered to appear in court at 10 a.m. tomorrow morning. One of her employees is Mildred McCartey. Ms. McCartey was called for jury duty on Monday of last week and served the entire week. When she returned to work at 7 a.m. Monday of this week she found that she had been replaced: fired because of her absence last week. State law prohibits an employer from firing or threatening to fire an employee called for jury duty, and Judge George C. LeClair has ordered Holten to appear in his courtroom to determine whether she should be held in contempt of court. Interviewed today, Holton said she did not know of the law. She said she works 12 to 16 hours a day in the doughnut shop, which she owns. McCartney is her only full-time employee, and she said she cannot afford to have her away for several days at a time—she is unable to run the business by herself with only her part-time help. If held in contempt, she could be fined up to $10,000 and sentenced to six months in jail.

Harcourt Brace & Company

4. Wesley Barlow is an inmate in a Nebraska state prison. He has been charged with swindling dozens of widows out of thousands of dollars. Barlew, 32, is serving an 8-year sentence for burglary. Today he pleaded guilty to new charges against him and was sentenced to an additional 10 years. Barlow had mailed letters to men who recently died. The letters were then received by the mens widows. They sought payment—usually less than $100—"for maintenance and repairs." Some women paid because they assumed their dead husbands had some work done before their deaths, a detective thought. Barlow said he got their names from the obituaries in an Omaha newspaper. The scam was discovered when the mother of an Omaha detective received one of the letters.

5. Researchers at your college issued a report today. After three years of study, they confirmed the widely assumed link between drinking and birth defects. They warned that pregnant women who drink risk injury to their children. Because the scientists don't know how much alcohol may be safely consumed by pregnant women, they recommend absolute and total abstention from all alcoholic beverages during a womans 9-month term of pregnancy. What the doctors found during their three years of study is that children born to pregnant women who drink have higher rates of mental and physical abnormalities. The most common problems among such infants are mental retardation and delays in their physical development. Pregnant women who drink also experience more miscarriages and premature births. The reason for the problems is that alcohol from a mothers system passes directly into the bloodstream of her developing child, and that the alcohol remains in the fetal system longer because it is not metabolized and excreted as fast as it is in the adult woman. Scientists call the problem the fetal alcohol syndrome.

E X E R C I S E 4

WRITING FOR BROADCAST

WRITING SHORTER BROADCAST STORIES

INSTRUCTIONS: Write broadcast stories about the following events. Write at least one soft news, one hard news and one throwaway lead. Although you will find it difficult at first, limit your stories to 20 seconds or less. Remember to consult the checklists on pages 461-462.

1. A teen-ager is paralyzed. The teen-ager, Amy Claunch, 17, was struck by a bullet when a pistol fired accidentally. This morning, a jury awarded her $2 million in damages. Clounch, who is not married, sued both David Gianangeli—also not married—who fired the pistol, and the pistols manufacturer. Clauchs attorney said she probably won't be able to collect even a penny of the award because Gianangeli does not have any money. He dropped out of the school, without graduating, and now works as a gardener, paid little more than the minimum wage. The jury deliberated almost 10 hours before reaching its decision. Clounch had attempted to prove that small handguns are so inherently dangerous that their makers and sellers should be held jointly responsible for harm caused by them, even when they are misused.

2. Its a smart idea, some people say, a way to solve a problem. Other people say its a waste of taxpayers money. The city council in Roseville, a small town near your community, adopted the idea last night. In the last municipal election there, only 23% of the citys registered voters cast a ballot in the race for mayor, a dismal record. It was the lowest percentage in your state. The Roseville city council wants to do something about it, so last night they decided to have a lottery. During the next municipal election, scheduled for the fall of next year, the city will give away $5,000 in cash prizes. The winners names will be drawn from a list of all persons who cast a ballot in the election.

3. A childs life was saved yesterday. Max Rivera and Charles Fusner, employees of the local power company, are the heroes. Cheryl Nichols, 1287 Belgarde Avenue, told police she found her 3-year-old son, Richard, face down and motionless in the familys swimming pool at 4:42 p.m. yesterday afternoon. She screamed and pulled him from the water. The boy had been riding his tricycle around the pool, and it apparently slipped over the edge, dumping him into the cold water. Riviera and Fusner, who were working on nearby electrical lines, heard the screams and rushed to help. Riviera breathed into the childs mouth and Fuzner applied heart massage. A neighbor called the police and fire departments. Fuzner said the child came to after 3 or 4 breaths. Paramedics responding to the call said the boy was in good shape when their rescue unit arrived at the scene a few minutes later. They rushed the boy to St. Nicholas Hospital, where he was examined, then released in good condition. A spokesperson for the power company said company employees are required to take training in cardiopulmonary resuscitation (CPR) because of the dangers they face while working around high-voltage lines.

4. There was a fatal traffic accident on State Road 419 at about 7:00 a.m. this morning. Five persons were killed in the fiery crash. The state highway patrol said a truck was attempting to pass a car about 2 miles west of your city. The truck clipped the back of the

car, sending it into a complete spin. The spinning car came to rest in a ditch, and its driver was not injured. The truck then proceeded to skid out of control and crashed head-on into an oncoming car. The truck and the on-coming car that it hit burst into flames. All four persons in the car died. The truck driver, who was alone in the vehicle at the time, also died. A highway patrol officer said the truck and second car "hit pretty hard, and their occupants probably died before the flames reached them." The patrol officer added that all four persons in the car were tourists from Canada. The truck driver was a resident of your city. Police are withholding all their names pending notification of next of kin.

5. There was a robbery which occurred at approximately 10:30 p.m. last night. A masked gunman entered a pizza parlor at 411 Michigan Avenue. There were three patrons and four employees in the establishment at the time. The gunman quickly emptied a cash register of about $450 in cash, and then he told everyone to empty their pockets. A youth about to enter the pizza parlor noticed the robbery in progress. She immediately called the police. Just as the police arrived, the gunman ran from the pizza parlor and fled into a housing development behind it. The youth followed the gunman. The police released a police dog from their car and ordered it to attack the gunman. The dog caught and bit the youth in her right leg. The youth required 12 stitches in her leg. The gunman escaped. Police are still looking for a suspect.

CHAPTER 19

ADVANCED REPORTING

Nothing less than the highest ideals, the most scrupulous anxiety to do right, the most accurate knowledge of the problems it has to meet, and a sincere sense of moral responsibility will save journalism from a subservience to business interests, seeking selfish ends, antagonistic to public welfare.

(Joseph Pulitzer)

The bulk of this chapter contains advanced reporting exercises. To do well on these exercises, you must apply all the skills you developed in the earlier chapters of this book. Some are longer and more complex than the exercises in previous chapters. However, all the exercises involve the types of stories editors assign reporters during the first years of their careers. The exercises are divided into three types:

- Statistical (Exercises 1–4). These exercises range from the simple to the complex. The challenge is to make the numbers interesting to the reader;

- In-depth (Exercises 5–8). These four exercises are genuine; they involve actual letters, statements and other documents. Only a few names and dates have been changed. Unless the exercises mention another time and location, assume each story occurred in your community today;

- Computer-assisted reporting (Exercise 9). This exercise involves a set of questions to get you thinking like a journalist about where to get information and how to use it to support a story.

USING STATISTICS

Much of the information given to newspaper reporters comes in the form of statistics. Statistics appear almost daily in news stories concerning budgets, taxes, census data, profits, dividends and annual reports. Other news stories concerning rates of crime, productivity, energy consumption, unemployment and inflation are based largely on statistics. Reporters must learn how to present statistics to the public in a form that is both interesting and intelligible.

When given a collection of numbers and asked to write a news story about them, critically analyze the data. Translate as many numbers as possible into words because readers can understand words more easily than statistics. Thus, instead of simply reporting the statistics, you should explain their significance. Look for and emphasize major trends, record highs and record lows, the unusual and the unexpected.

Even better, emphasize your story's human interest. Until it was revised, the example below only gave numbers in a routine and dull series. The revision includes a human element. The reporter found someone who received first aid from the fire department. Another version could have examined the false alarms in greater detail. Did they come from a certain area of the city?

Harcourt Brace & Company

Was anyone caught and prosecuted for making those false alarms? Where were the bomb threats? Was anyone injured?

    The Fire Department's annual report states that last year it responded to the following numbers and types of calls: bomb threats, 60; electrical fires, 201; false alarms, 459; first aid, 1,783; mattress fires, 59; burned pots left on stove, 78; rescues, 18; washdowns, usually of leaking gasoline at the scene of automobile accidents, 227; and water salvage, 46.

    REVISED: When Sarah Kindstrom needed help, the fire department responded. Kindstrom's heart attack last week was one of 5,024 calls the department answered last year. First aid requests were the most common, according to the department's annual report, which was released today.

    The five leading types of calls included, in the order of their frequency: first aid, 1,783; false alarms, 459; washdowns, usually of leaking gasoline at the scene of automobile accidents, 227; electrical fires, 201; and burned pots left on stoves, 78.

    Other common types of calls included: bomb threats, 60; mattress fires, 59; water salvage, 46; and rescues, 18.

Stories that rely too heavily on numbers can be deadly for the reader. The reporter's job is to make the numbers interesting so the reader stays with the story from beginning to end.

If you are writing about a city election, do more than tell your readers who won and the number of votes that each candidate received. Search for additional highlights: For example, did incumbents (or women, blacks, conservatives) win or lose? Were there significant differences in precinct results from previous elections? Did any candidates win by unusually large or small margins? When Paul Gillmore, R-Port Clinton (Ohio), won in a hotly contested Republican Party primary, he did so by 27 votes among the approximately 63,000 cast. Because he ran in a strong GOP district, his victory in the primary essentially meant he was going to Congress. That information makes a story more interesting than merely reporting that Gilmore won, 31,513 to 31,486.

When you must include some statistics in your news stories, present those statistics as simply as possible. Avoid a series of paragraphs that contain nothing but statistics. Use transitions, explanations and commentary to break up long strings of numbers and to make the information clearer and more interesting for your readers.

USING COMPUTERS TO GET ANSWERS

Recently, journalists began viewing numbers in a different way. At many news organizations today, computers rather than pocket calculators help reporters analyze budgets, reports, surveys and polls.

A decade ago, only national or large regional newspapers were using computers to help spot trends and patterns in the information that crossed their desks. A recent compilation of 100 computer-assisted reporting (CAR) stories shows that small news outlets have jumped on the technology bandwagon. A recent survey of editors reported that 66.3 percent of their newspapers use computers as reporting tools in some manner.

Computers have been used in newsrooms for a long time, but primarily as word processors. Newspapers use them for design purposes (pagination), and recently more papers have begun to use them for photographic purposes, eliminating the need for a darkroom.

CAR is really just another method of gathering and analyzing information. Computers provide access to the Internet, where reporters use E-mail to communicate with other reporters and with sources. Journalists also can enter the World Wide Web to gather information about people, places and things. Computers have the power, capacity and speed to enable reporters to analyze data.

But CAR is more than figuring out averages, means and mediums. Journalists use computers to spot trends, patterns, names that may have been hidden. The once formidable and time-consuming task of analyzing reams of material is more easily managed with computers.

Databases are nothing new. A common example is a city's telephone directory. A CAR project compares two or more databases to see what they have in common. For example, The Ann Arbor (Mich.) News got a tip that a local judge running for the state supreme court was strong-arming attorneys for campaign contributions. A reporter approached the story with three databases: a list of all the campaign donations for the judge, a list of attorneys practicing in the county and the results of cases these attorneys argued before that judge.

Other news organizations have used CAR to obtain stories about agriculture, business, child welfare, crime, discrimination, education, the environment, health care, highway safety and the justice system, to name just a few general areas. The opportunities are endless.

It would be impossible to provide here all the information needed to become adept at CAR, but this chapter introduces this growing and important type of reporting. Students are encouraged to pursue these kinds of projects, because news editors and station managers are requiring more CAR skills of new hires. The student who graduates with some basic computer skills in using spreadsheet software (such as QuatroPro, Lotus 1-2-3 and Excel) and relational databases (such as FoxPro, Paradox, dBase and Access) will move to the front of the line in the job market. It will also be important for students to prove that they can apply that knowledge to real stories. You must see the possibilities, develop story ideas and write stories that use these skills.

CAR does not replace good, old-fashioned reporting skills, addressed in earlier chapters of this book. Computers do not provide all the answers; they do not interview sources; and they are only as good as the information that goes into them.

SUGGESTED READINGS

Barnett, Tracy L., ed. *IRE 100 Selected Computer-Assisted Investigations*, Book II. Columbia, MO: Investigative Reporters and Editors and the National Institute for Computer-Assisted Reporting, 1995.

Garrison, Bruce. *Computer-Assisted Reporting*. Hillsdale, NJ: Erlbaum, 1995.

Reddick, Randy, and Elliot King. *The Online Journalist*. Fort Worth, TX: Harcourt Brace, 1995.

Virtual Reality: Newspapers and the Information Superhighway. Reston, VA: American Press Institute, 1994.

Harcourt Brace & Company

St. Louis Post-Dispatch

WRITE & WRONG

By **Harry Levins**
Post-Dispatch Writing Coach

Reporters who write about government budgets find themselves working with numbers that stretch way past the experience of most people. In one year, for example, Missouri's state government spent $4.5 billion. Putting that sort of total in perspective is tough; after all, it comes to $1 for every human being on Earth.

Terry Ganey faced the problem recently when he wrote that the state's budget left precious little in reserve. First, he explained the situation in the state's terms:

> *The budget . . . includes a $67.6 million operating reserve to maintain cash flow and handle emergencies.*

But raw numbers mean little to the average reader. So Ganey decided to refine the numbers further:

> *While that sounds like a lot, it is less than 1.5 percent of the state's total spending and 2.8 percent of general tax revenue expenditures.*

That helps considerably. Most readers grasp percentages more easily than whole numbers. Even so, Ganey decided to take one more step and put the numbers in terms that almost anybody could see clearly:

> *A comparison of the state's situation would be that of a family with a combined annual income of $30,000 setting a budget for a year that leaves $450 in the bank after all its anticipated bills are paid.*

What a nice touch. Ganey had said in his lede the state would have "a very thin bank account." And in his comparison with a middle-class family, Ganey drove home just how thin that bank account would be.

Some years back, Eliot Porter turned the same smooth trick in a story on the water supply in the St. Louis area. He mentioned how much water rolled by each day in the Mississippi River and then noted how much water St. Louis needed each day. The numbers were so big that they were, in effect, meaningless. The next paragraph put the whole thing in focus. Porter wrote words to this effect:

> *In other words, a sightseer, standing by the Arch to watch the river roll past, needs to stand there only four minutes and 42 seconds to see all the water St. Louis needs that day.*

What the paragraph accomplished is clear:

1. It reduced big numbers to a total anybody could fit into perspective. Few people can picture millions of gallons of water, but most of us have a close idea of what four minutes and 42 seconds equals.

(continued on next page)

Harcourt Brace & Company

2. It gave the reader a specific frame for the numbers. Almost all of us have stood at the Arch and watched the river roll by. Porter's use of that image gave us something specific, something concrete to use as an aid to grasp the abstract ideas that we choose to call "numbers."

So good is Porter at this sort of thing that The New York Times lifted his explanation of how to visualize five parts of dioxin for each billion parts of soil:

> *That's the equivalent of five jiggers of vermouth in a thousand railroad tank cars of gin.*

To help people grasp numbers, the people at Dow Chemical put out a small pamphlet titled "How Big Is 'Small'?" It says:

> *We often find reference to "parts per billion" or "parts per trillion" in our reading or conversations about trace impurities in chemicals.*
>
> *What is a part per billion? How big is a part per trillion? And what about a part per quadrillion? Can we get a fix on these infinitesimally small quantities?*
>
> *Well, if you're a 26-year-old male, for example, your heart beats about 72 times a minute . . . a part per billion is equal to one heartbeat out of all your heartbeats since birth (plus half of your prenatal experience)!*
>
> *Let's start with a part per million, . . . that's the equivalent to . . . one drop of gasoline in a tankful of gas for a full-sized car . . . or one facial tissue in a stack of facial tissues higher than the Empire State Building.*

> *Other comparisons . . . part per billion.*
> —*One kernel of corn in enough corn to fill a 45-foot silo, 16 feet in diameter . . .*
> —*One sheet in a roll of toilet paper stretching from New York to London . . .*
> —*One second of time in 32 years.*

> *More comparisons . . . part per trillion:*
> —*One square foot of floor tile on a kitchen floor the size of Indiana . . .*
> —*One drop of detergent in enough dish water to fill a string of railroad tank cars over 10 miles long . . .*

> *How about something really small? Part per quadrillion:*
> —*The palm of one's hand compared to the total land area of the United States . . .*
> —*One human hair out of all the hair on the heads of all the people in the world . . .*

To be sure, Dow has a self-interest in making big numbers look small. We have our own interest—clarity. In making things clear, we can go beyond Dow's comparisons and come up with our own.

We can use the volume of local landmarks like Busch Stadium: one billion equals a stadium sellout of every home game for almost 247 baseball seasons. For area, we can use the figures for St. Louis (61 square miles or 39,040 acres), St. Louis County (500 square miles or 320,000 acres) and Missouri (68,945 square miles or 44,124,800 acres).

Coming up with your own comparisons involves nothing more than a base figure and a calculator—or, as in Ganey's case, a pencil, a piece of paper and a touch of imagination.

Harcourt Brace & Company

EXERCISE 1
ADVANCED REPORTING

INSTRUCTIONS: Write a news story about the results of the following national opinion poll about recent American presidents, based on a random sample of 2,400 people aged 18 and older. Assume the interviews were conducted by telephone last week by members of the National Association of Political Scientists, and the results were announced today. All the figures are percentages. Also, develop a list of sources you would interview to make the story better, along with questions that you would ask each of them.

	Most Loved	Most Powerful	Highest Moral Standards	Did Most to Improve U.S.	Best in Domestic Affairs	Best in Foreign Affairs
Franklin D. Roosevelt	22	23	18	36	29	28
Harry S. Truman	8	9	16	7	7	10
Dwight D. Eisenhower	10	12	13	12	15	15
John F. Kennedy	23	10	5	10	11	13
Lyndon B. Johnson	3	15	2	7	7	4
Richard M. Nixon	3	7	0	2	4	9
Gerald R. Ford	2	3	3	3	5	2
Jimmy Carter	8	3	24	4	5	3
Ronald Reagan	6	4	4	5	4	3
George Bush	5	7	7	5	6	7
Bill Clinton	5	3	5	7	5	3
Undecided or no answer	5	4	3	2	2	3

E X E R C I S E   2

ADVANCED REPORTING

INSTRUCTIONS: Write a news story about the rates of crime in 40 of the nation's largest cities, which are listed below in the order of their overall rate of crime. This list includes U.S. cities with 300,000 or more residents last year. The crime rate in each city is based on the number of serious crimes reported per 1,000 residents.

The FBI conducts its Uniform Crime Reporting Study each year. It collects the statistics from local police departments. The results, released today, cover seven types of crime: (1) murder, (2) rape, (3) robbery, (4) aggravated assault, (5) burglary, (6) larceny and theft and (7) motor vehicle theft.

Also, develop a list of sources you would interview to improve the story, along with questions that you would ask each of them.

Rank and City	Crime Rate Last Year (per 1,000 Residents)	Rank and Crime Rate Two Years Ago
1. Atlanta	192.4	2. 183.8
2. Miami	190.2	1. 206.9
3. Dallas	155.2	3. 167.3
4. Fort Worth, Texas	149.8	4. 156.9
5. St. Louis	146.7	5. 153.3
6. Kansas City, Mo.	129.5	9. 127.2
7. Seattle	126.0	7. 129.1
8. Charlotte, N.C.	125.9	6. 132.4
9. San Antonio, Texas	124.8	10. 127.2
10. New Orleans	124.4	17. 112.6
11. Detroit	121.9	14. 120.9
12. Tucson, Ariz.	118.8	11. 125.5
13. Boston	118.5	15. 120.7
14. Austin, Texas	117.1	21. 106.7
15. Minneapolis	114.4	13. 121.0
16. Houston	113.4	20. 108.2
17. El Paso, Texas	112.4	22. 106.2
18. Portland, Ore.	111.0	8. 127.5
19. Chicago	110.6	28. 99.6
20. Oakland, Calif.	109.1	12. 125.3
21. Washington, D.C.	107.7	26. 102.8
22. Phoenix, Ariz.	107.6	19. 108.7
23. Oklahoma City	106.1	18. 111.9
24. Baltimore	106.0	33. 93.5
25. Fresno, Calif.	105.3	16. 116.9
26. Jacksonville, Fla.	104.6	24. 103.3
27. Memphis, Tenn.	102.0	37. 88.8
28. Albuquerque, N.M.	100.6	27. 99.7
29. Columbus, Ohio	99.1	23. 103.9
30. New York	97.0	29. 96.7
31. San Francisco	96.6	36. 90.2
32. Toledo, Ohio	96.1	30. 95.4
33. Long Beach, Calif.	95.7	31. 94.1

Harcourt Brace & Company

Rank and City	Crime Rate Last Year (per 1,000 Residents)	Rank and Crime Rate Two Years Ago	
34. Tulsa, Okla.	95.3	35.	91.8
35. Milwaukee	93.0	39.	87.6
36. Los Angeles	92.3	34.	92.7
37. San Diego	91.5	32.	93.7
38. Sacramento, Calif.	91.3	25.	103.2
39. Cleveland	91.1	42.	83.5
40. Wichita, Kan.	89.3	40.	87.4

EXERCISE 3

STATISTICAL MATERIAL

UNITED STATES DEPARTMENT OF EDUCATION
WASHINGTON, D.C. 20202

UPDATE ON ADULT ILLITERACY

THE SOURCE

The English Language Proficiency Survey was commissioned by the U.S. Department of Education and conducted by the Bureau of the Census during the last summer. At that time, simple written tests of English comprehension were administered in the home to a national sample of 3,400 adults, ages 20 and over.

MAJOR FINDINGS

Between 17 and 21 million U.S. adults are illiterate, for an overall rate of nearly 13 percent. In contrast to traditional estimates of illiteracy based on completion of fewer than six years of school, this new study shows that illiterate adults are now much more likely to be located in our major cities, and most are under the age of 50. Immigration and reliance on a non-English language are also major factors; nearly half of all adults using a non-English language at home failed the test of English proficiency. More specifically,

- **OF ALL ADULTS CLASSIFIED AS ILLITERATE:**

—41 percent live in central cities of metropolitan areas, compared to just 8 percent in rural areas;
—56 percent are under the age of 50; and
—37 percent speak a non-English language at home.

- **AMONG NATIVE ENGLISH-SPEAKERS CLASSIFIED AS ILLITERATE:**

—70 percent did not finish high school;
—42 percent had no earnings in the previous year; and
—35 percent are in their twenties and thirties.

- **AMONG ILLITERATE ADULTS WHO USE A NON-ENGLISH LANGUAGE:**

—82 percent were born outside the United States;
—42 percent live in neighborhoods where exclusive reliance on English is the exception rather than the rule;
—21 percent had entered the U.S. within the previous six years; and
—About 14 percent are probably literate in their non-English language (judging from their reported education).

THE TEST AND THE DEFINITION OF ILLITERACY

The test employed is called the Measure of Adult English Proficiency (MAEP). The written portion of MAEP consists of 26 questions which test the individual's ability to identify key words and phrases and match these with one of four fixed-choice alternatives. Based on an analysis of the number of questions answered correctly out of 26, a literacy cutoff of 20 was selected as providing the best discrimination between high and low risk groups. Specifically, among native English speakers, less than 1 percent of those completing some college scored below 20, in contrast to a failure rate of more than 50 percent for those with fewer than 6 years of school.

ACCURACY OF THESE ESTIMATES

The standard error of our point estimate (18.7 million) is about 1 million. Thus, we can be quite confident (95 chances out of 100) that the true figure is in the range of 17 to 21 million.

IDENTIFICATION OF HIGH-RISK GROUPS

Six factors were found to be strongly correlated with performance on the written test: age, nativity, recency of immigration for non-natives, race, poverty status, amount of schooling and reported English speaking ability (of persons who use a non-English language at home).

ILLITERACY RATE ESTIMATES*

	Rate	Inverse Rank		Rate	Inverse Rank
UNITED STATES	13				
			MASSACHUSETTS	11	17
ALABAMA	13	31	MICHIGAN	11	17
ALASKA	7	2	MINNESOTA	9	9
ARIZONA	12	25	MISSISSIPPI	16	47
ARKANSAS	15	40	MISSOURI	12	25
CALIFORNIA	14	33	MONTANA	8	4
COLORADO	8	4	NEBRASKA	9	9
CONNECTICUT	12	25	NEVADA	9	9
DELAWARE	11	17	NEW HAMPSHIRE	9	9
DIST. OF COLUMBIA	16	47	NEW JERSEY	14	33
FLORIDA	15	40	NEW MEXICO	14	33
GEORGIA	14	33	NEW YORK	16	47
HAWAII	15	40	NORTH CAROLINA	14	33
IDAHO	8	4	NORTH DAKOTA	12	25
ILLINOIS	14	33	OHIO	11	17
INDIANA	11	17	OKLAHOMA	11	17
IOWA	10	14	OREGON	8	4
KANSAS	9	9	PENNSYLVANIA	12	25
KENTUCKY	15	40	RHODE ISLAND	15	40
LOUISIANA	16	47	SOUTH CAROLINA	15	40
MAINE	11	17	SOUTH DAKOTA	11	17
MARYLAND	12	25	TENNESSEE	15	40

Harcourt Brace & Company

	Rate	Inverse Rank		Rate	Inverse Rank
TEXAS	16	47	WASHINGTON	8	4
UTAH	6	1	WEST VIRGINIA	14	33
VERMONT	10	14	WISCONSIN	10	14
VIRGINIA	13	31	WYOMING	7	2

Rates apply to the adult population age 20 and over. All rates have been rounded to the nearest whole percent.

EXERCISE 4

STATISTICAL MATERIAL

FROM THE OFFICE OF THE GOVERNOR

The annual survey of legislative appropriations for the arts, conducted by the National Assembly of State Arts Agencies, is being released nationwide today. The results show how our state compares to others in the nation.

The complete results of the survey follow:

NATIONAL ASSEMBLY OF STATE ARTS AGENCIES

	Per Capita (¢)		Appropriations ($)		% Change	% of State General Fund	Rank
	This Year	Last Year	This Year	Last Year			
Alabama	24.1	26.2	969,020	1,045,000	−7.2	.0374	42
Alaska	420.3	800.2	2,189,800	4,000,000	−45.2	Not available	
Arizona	35.9	33.1	1,144,800	1,010,200	13.3	.0452	37
Arkansas	42.7	35.6	1,006,754	836,226	20.3	.0588	27
California	47.7	46.0	12,589,000	11,793,000	6.7	.0411	40
Colorado	50.8	30.6	1,640,647	971,459	68.8	.0820	17
Connecticut	52.5	46.0	1,666,166	1,479,000	12.6	.0388	41
Delaware	97.1	80.9	603,900	496,000	21.7	.0647	24
Dist. of Columbia	378.3	283.3	2,368,000	1,765,000	34.1	.1032	13
Florida	111.8	88.9	12,710,386	9,761,077	30.2	.1639	5
Georgia	45.0	37.7	2,687,779	2,200,588	22.1	.0506	32
Hawaii	216.5	208.9	2,282,092	2,170,485	5.1	.1230	8
Idaho	13.5	13.3	134,000	131,400	1.9	.0223	49
Illinois	75.9	57.0	8,758,300	6,559,400	33.5	.0857	15
Indiana	33.4	33.3	1,836,923	1,830,576	0.3	.0551	28
Iowa	34.0	18.0	981,590	522,593	87.8	.0452	38
Kansas	24.6	24.5	602,707	596,288	1.0	.0335	45
Kentucky	53.2	42.0	1,983,300	1,564,400	26.7	.0659	23
Louisiana	20.1	27.0	900,000	1,205,431	−25.3	.0212	50
Maine	40.7	36.4	473,503	420,292	12.6	.0456	36
Maryland	108.7	43.9	4,776,096	1,909,382	150.1	.1079	11
Massachusetts	313.7	282.5	18,265,924	16,379,066	11.5	.2738	1
Michigan	125.5	113.4	11,404,000	10,291,500	10.8	.1863	4
Minnesota	65.7	60.1	2,755,083	2,502,961	10.0	.0539	31
Mississippi	15.8	17.9	411,986	465,827	−11.5	.0277	47
Missouri	87.6	137.9	4,403,292	6,904,051	−36.2	.1316	9
Montana	109.2	78.8	901,745	649,068	38.9	.2457	2
Nebraska	36.5	36.3	585,891	582,749	0.5	.0676	22
Nevada	19.1	19.1	178,642	174,270	2.5	.0338	44
New Hampshire	32.6	33.1	325,500	323,000	0.7	.0712	21
New Jersey	177.9	138.3	13,453,000	10,391,000	29.4	.1488	6*
New Mexico	48.2	50.1	698,800	713,500	−2.0	.0481	33
New York	273.2	249.3	48,590,702	44,218,900	9.8	.2081	3
North Carolina	64.8	63.8	4,050,637	3,936,067	2.9	.0734	20
North Dakota	34.8	34.7	238,268	238,268	0.0	.0421	39

	Per Capita (¢)		Appropriations ($)			% of State	
	This Year	Last Year	This Year	Last Year	% Change	General Fund	Rank
Ohio	84.2	69.7	9,050,963	7,493,265	20.7	.0855	16
Oklahoma	46.5	55.2	1,535,253	1,821,462	−15.7	.0900	14
Oregon	18.4	18.2	494,421	487,048	1.5	.0286	46
Pennsylvania	65.6	56.3	7,780,000	6,724,000	15.7	.0805	18
Rhode Island	62.0	46.2	599,854	444,357	34.9	.0539	30
South Carolina	85.7	77.4	2,869,596	2,555,563	12.2	.1039	12
South Dakota	40.5	40.2	286,873	283,912	1.0	.0775	19
Tennessee	29.0	76.7	1,382,500	3,615,800	−61.7	.0476	35
Texas	18.2	30.3	2,983,955	4,846,064	−38.4	.0546	29
Utah	100.1	94.9	1,646,000	1,568,200	4.9	.1242	10
Vermont	49.5	45.8	264,900	242,902	9.0	.0622	26
Virginia	52.2	34.6	2,979,540	1,947,865	52.9	.0637	25
Washington	38.5	43.2	1,697,395	1,879,419	−9.6	.0360	43
West Virginia	115.8	106.5	2,241,793	2,117,238	5.8	.1488	6*
Wisconsin	24.1	24.2	1,148,600	1,151,500	−0.2	.0226	48
Wyoming	33.2	28.3	169,275	144,605	17.0	.0447	34

*New Jersey and West Virginia are tied for sixth.

Harcourt Brace & Company

E X E R C I S E   5

ADVANCED REPORTING

TELEVISION'S EFFECTS ON CHILDREN

INSTRUCTIONS: This is a verbatim account of a policy statement issued by the American Academy of Pediatrics, warning the public about television's effects on children. Assume the statement was issued today. Write a news story summarizing its content. At the end of your story, list the sources you would interview to write a more thorough story, along with the questions you would ask each source.

POLICY STATEMENT

In 1984 the American Academy of Pediatrics' Task Force on Children and Television issued a statement cautioning pediatricians and parents about the potential for television to promote violent and/or aggressive behavior and obesity. The influence of television on early sexual activity, drug and alcohol abuse, school performance and perpetuation of ethnic stereotypes also was stressed. Advances in our understanding of the effects of television on children have prompted this update of the Academy's policy.

[Last year] the average child in the United States still spent more time watching television than in any other activity except sleeping. According to recent Neilsen data, children aged 2 to 5 years view approximately 25 hours per week, children aged 6 to 11 watch more than 22 hours weekly, and adolescents 12 to 17 years watch 23 hours of television per week. Although the amount of commercial television viewed by children has declined since 1980, the most recent estimates of television viewing do not include VCR use. Therefore, the amount of time that children in our country spend in front of the television set has probably not decreased significantly since 1984.

Television influence on children is a function of the length of time they spend watching and the cumulative effect of what they see. By the time today's child reaches age 70, he or she will have spent approximately seven years watching television. Therefore, television may displace more active experience of the world. For some children, the world shown on television becomes the real world.

In the years since the original statement was released, sufficient data have accumulated to warrant the conclusion that protracted television viewing is one cause of violent or aggressive behavior. Television viewing also contributes substantially to obesity.

Although there is no clear documentation that the relationship between television viewing and sexual activity or the use of alcohol is causal, the frequency of adolescent pregnancy and sexually transmitted diseases, and the prevalence of alcohol-related deaths among adolescents and young adults, represent major sources of illness, injury and death. American teenagers see an estimated 14,000 sexual references and innuendoes per year on television, yet only 150 of these references deal with sexual responsibility, abstinence or contraception. Therefore, the many implicit and explicit messages on television that promote alcohol consumption and promiscuous or unprotected sexual activity are a cause for concern.

The Committee on Communications therefore makes the following recommendations:

1. Efforts should be developed and intensified to teach pediatricians and parents about the influence of television and, furthermore, new initiatives should be developed to promote involvement by parents as well as critical television viewing skills among children.

Harcourt Brace & Company

2. Pediatricians should advise parents to limit their children's television viewing to one to two hours per day. In addition, pediatricians should include advice regarding the effects of television on children and the importance of limiting television time as part of anticipatory guidance during health maintenance visits. Parents should be encouraged to develop television substitutes such as reading, athletics and physical conditioning as well as instructive hobbies.

3. Families should participate in the selection of the programs their children watch. Parents should watch television with their children in order to help interpret what they see. Parents should take advantage of the acceptable programs offered on video cassettes for their children's viewing, if affordable.

4. Pediatricians should continue to support legislation making broadcast of high quality children's programming a condition of license renewal and seek a revival of legislation mandating at least one hour per day of programs of educational and instructional benefit to children.

5. Pediatricians should continue their efforts to ban toy-based programs, because such programs are designed to sell toys to children and constitute program-length commercials.

6. Pediatricians should continue to urge that sexuality be portrayed responsibly by the media.

7. Pediatricians should support efforts to eliminate alcohol advertising on television and also encourage extensive counter-advertising.

8. The Academy should support further research into the effects of television on children, and continue to build coalitions with other groups to monitor and improve television for children.

E X E R C I S E 6

ADVANCED REPORTING

CLUB'S CONTROVERSIAL SCHOLARSHIPS

INSTRUCTIONS: Assume the president of your college has decided to accept $150,000 from a club that discriminates against women, blacks and Jews. He released the memorandum that follows today. Write a news story summarizing its content. At the end of your story, list the sources you would interview to write a more thorough story, along with the questions you would ask each source.

BACKGROUND

Several hundred prominent businessmen belong to the University Club in your city. The club does not admit women, blacks or Jews. One month ago, the club offered to donate $150,000 ($30,000 a year for five years) to your school for scholarships. During a meeting last Thursday, your school's Faculty Senate adopted the following resolutions:

Resolution 13. It is inappropriate for the University to encourage or support faculty involvement or the involvement of other members of the university community with clubs or other institutions that knowingly engage in discriminatory practices on the basis of race, gender, ethnicity or religious preference.

Resolution 14. It is not appropriate for the university to engage in any activity that may lend support or give credence to any club or private institution that knowingly engages in discriminatory practices on the basis of race, gender, ethnicity or religious preference.

MEMORANDUM

TO: The Faculty

FROM: The College President

SUBJECT: University Club

Today I have asked the Faculty Senate to reconsider Resolutions 13 & 14. As written, both are difficult or impractical to implement, yet the principle of nondiscrimination is important to affirm. I intend to meet with the Faculty Senate's leaders to develop new language.

While the Resolutions were general, clearly their purpose was specifically directed to the prospect of the University receiving funds from the University Club for student scholarships. The funds, if accepted, would amount to approximately $150,000 over five years, and are unrestricted in their use at the University. But, well beyond the issue of money is the broader policy question of the University's posture toward donors, and more specifically toward the University Club.

Because of the policy question, and the interest the issue has stirred, I have engaged in broad consultation, on campus and off, to solicit input and to assess the impact of an action either way. I have been impressed with the depth and quality of the discussion this matter has sparked in the community, and by the thoughtful debate that has occurred on campus. John Milton said, "Where there is desire to learn, there of necessity will be much arguing, much writing, many opinions; for opinion in good men is but knowledge in the making."

His words ring true. Knowledge is in the making, and the Faculty Senate's action has shown leadership in bringing an important issue to the public's attention. But, now it is time to decide—based on what is in the best interests of the University.

My decision is to accept the gift for unrestricted scholarship use. The funds will be used consistent with University priorities to recruit and provide assistance to high ability students, minority students and other special talent students. A talented and diverse student body is fundamental to our development. As graduates, they will provide future leadership to the community.

The reasons for my decision are many, but before detailing several of them I must say that this has been a very difficult decision. Discriminatory practices are abhorrent, and this University must be committed in its education and research programs to actions that promote equal opportunity. As we assemble the tools to be able to do so more fully, I am confident that even more progress soon will be evident. My decision now is rooted in my commitment to build the very best university we can. It did not result from votes, loud voices or pressure.

The decision is also difficult because of my belief in the development of a strong Faculty Senate at the University. My preference is to support its work on behalf of the entire faculty, and to affirm the principle of responsible faculty governance. At the same time, we can all recognize the tensions that arise between the expression of transcendent values and life in a vastly imperfect world. Both positions require respect.

It is my judgment that the message conveyed by the Senate's action has been heard clearly throughout the community and in the University Club. I have reason to believe that progress is underway to open up current membership practices, and the Club should be encouraged to move forward with the change process for the good of the community. My hope is that in so doing, its leadership may set an example for all organizations with restrictive practices. This is important to the future of the region. Yet, I also have reason to believe that continued contentiousness from the University at this point will actually impede the progress we all hope will occur.

There may always be differences among reasonable people about the best means to create change, but in this case I believe it will now have to come from within the organization. In the meantime, no moral cause will be advanced by discouraging people with whom we may disagree from doing a good thing.

By accepting funds from the University Club, the University is not lending its support to them. The funds are absolutely unrestricted for scholarship use, and are totally subject to the University's control. The very nature of the gift means that the University is not obligated to do anything except use the funds responsibly. If this were not the case, my decision would be different.

There are other examples in academe where universities separate their actions from those of their donors. They, and we, accept funds from the Ford Foundation even though Henry Ford expressed anti-Semitic views. They, and we, encourage our students to pursue Rhodes Scholarships without fear that we endorse the racial and colonial views of Cecil Rhodes. Members of our faculties do not condone the earlier votes of J. William Fulbright in support of racial segregation by accepting Fulbright Scholarships. While these are not current practices of these organizations, the point is that people and institutions do change over time. The University should be able to exert leadership to help bring it about, but the means to do so will differ in each situation.

The bigger question is the University's relationship to donors generally. The institution is placed in an untenable position if it must begin probing the intentions and character of each donor to assure itself that certain standards of conduct are observed. We do not have standing nor the authority to make such judgments, and in fact, we would expose ourselves to legal liability if we were to do so in a manner that would be construed to be defamatory. If this practice were to start, its logical and simple extensions would confound our better judgment about where to draw the line before we accept a gift.

Harcourt Brace & Company

The above does not suggest, however, that no standard at all should be applied. The University will not accept funds acquired through illegal activity, nor from organizations and individuals whose purposes undermine social order or human dignity. The University will not accept funds from benefactors who seek to endanger our most basic academic values. In Justice Frankfurter's words, these include "determining" for ourselves "on academic grounds who may teach, what may be taught, how it shall be taught, and who may be admitted to study." It is not difficult to draw these distinctions and to apply them rigorously.

Our community is on its way to becoming a major U.S. city, and its aspirations for further development are high. A great future is possible here, and part of that depends on the ability of business people to show the leadership necessary to avail themselves of all the talent that is available. Our setting is so competitive that any exclusionary practices undermine the unity that makes good things possible. The University's increasing stature aids this process: our efforts to advance cultural diversity in the faculty, staff and student body will lead by example. Our own diversity agenda is one of our biggest challenges now, and many people rightfully are monitoring our progress closely. We need to get on with that task as we work with the business community to build a better university.

Despite the many other issues involved, and the negative financial impact this situation has already had, we have to finally remember why we are here. Simply put, we are here to educate students. They are the ones who are either helped or hurt by whatever decision we make. My commitment is to aggressively seek support for them, just as it is to bolster support for the faculty. These funds will help a significant number of students get an education who otherwise would not be likely to do so, or at least not here. We owe them that opportunity, secure in the knowledge that education is the best weapon against racism, sexism and other social ills.

I ask for your support as we move forward. The debate is healthy, and reflective of a university that is maturing rapidly. The mere fact that we can deal openly with it affirms the values for which the institution stands. The subject will stay with us as we get on with our other work.

E X E R C I S E   7
ADVANCED REPORTING

EDUCATIONAL EQUITY

INSTRUCTIONS: The following complaint filed by the National Association for the Advancement of Colored People (NAACP) is genuine. It charges that a public school system discriminated against black students and teachers. Assume your county branch of the NAACP filed the complaint today with the superintendent of your local school system. Write a news story that summarizes the complaint. At the end of your story, list the sources you would interview to write a more thorough story, along with the questions you would ask each source.

NAACP COMPLAINT

The County Branch NAACP contends the School District has ignored educational quality and equity for the black students and black professionals. It appears the School District is in continuous violation of the Fourteenth Amendment—that is, students are not fully de-segregated in the system. Specifically, the NAACP, black parents and concerned citizens have found that:

I. STUDENT CONCERNS

A. Black students are suspended and expelled at a disproportionately higher rate than white students.

B. Black students receive corporal punishment at a far higher rate than white students.

C. Black students are channeled into special education and remedial classes at a far higher rate than white students and are generally kept there.

D. Black students are generally excluded from the gifted classes.

E. Black students are channeled into dead-end programs by counselors in the high schools and are not challenged to enter the discipline courses (biology, chemistry, physics, geometry, trigonometry and calculus).

F. Black students have fewer role models in school-based and central office administration.

G. High potential and gifted black students are recruited by the white schools while the low performing black students are coerced to attend the predominately black schools, and

H. The majority of our black students are not being educated in the School District.

II. PROFESSIONAL CONCERNS

A. Black teachers are denied professional contracts (tenure) at a far higher rate and percentage than white teachers.

B. Black teachers eligible for retirement are constantly harassed and pushed to leave the profession.

Harcourt Brace & Company

C. After gaining experience in predominately black schools, white teachers are recruited from these schools two or three days prior to the opening of schools—thereby reducing the effectiveness of black school faculties.

D. Black teachers that are strong and effective are passed over for promotion to administrative positions.

E. Black principals and black parents are denied participation in the decision-making process as related to school operation, programming and personnel selection.

F. Black principals are denied the right to attain deputy or superintendent status regardless of preparation or experience.

G. Black teachers are not retained in the system but shuttled out after two years of performance, and

H. Black teachers are not treated the same as white teachers in the School District.

III. PHYSICAL FACILITIES

A. The buildings at the predominately black schools are not maintained as well as those at predominately white schools.

B. The furnishings in the predominately black schools are not of the same quality as those in predominately white schools.

C. The buildings at the predominately black schools are in dire need of repair while the predominately white schools are highly maintained.

D. Quality materials in predominately black schools are less than those in predominately white schools.

E. The equipment in predominately white schools is greater in number and quality than that in predominately black schools.

F. The landscaping at predominately white schools is far more attractive than that at black schools.

G. The overall facilities at black schools are inferior to those at white schools.

IV. RECOMMENDATIONS

The County Branch NAACP, parents and concerned citizens recommend that:

A. The predominately black schools be brought up to par via construction, materials, equipment and personnel.

B. Teachers' quotas for schools that are predominately black or white be at least fifty percent of the dominant race in the school.

C. The administration respect the predominately black communities by meeting with the parents and teachers, permitting them to select principals and teachers and to have a say in the operation of the schools.

D. The NAACP Education Committee work with district personnel and parents to study, adjust and/or correct situations that affect the education of black boys and girls in the county, and

E. Further recommendations for effective schooling: The School Board organize each school in the following manner:

Harcourt Brace & Company

1. *Elementary Schools*

    a. Select one teacher from each grade level to serve on a school-based council for a total six persons for curriculum reasons.

    b. Select six (6) parents that are interested, have some knowledge of education, and are strong supporters of the school. Total six (6) for community services.

    c. Elect six (6) citizens to serve on the Council, four of whom should be business leaders.

    d. Assign an Area Superintendent to work with these councils for communication purposes only.

2. *Secondary Schools*

    a. Select one teacher from each department to serve on a school council.

    b. Select interested and knowledgeable parents equal to the number of departments in the school to serve on a school council.

    c. Select six citizens with a minimum of four business persons to serve on a school council.

    d. Assign one Associate Superintendent to work with this council for communication purposes, and

    e. Give them the power to employ the school-based management system: the power to set policies and select all their schools' personnel—their teachers and principals.

3. *Administration*

    a. Select and employ more black administrators at all levels—administrators that project positive images in black communities.

    b. Require all administrative personnel to acquaint themselves with the citizens of black communities.

    c. Have the district board members work closer with the schools and their personnel so as to improve relations with black communities.

    d. Communicate with the school boards of Chicago, Milwaukee, Los Angeles and Colorado regarding their approach to school-based management.

    e. Build more schools in the inner city, where the majority of blacks are concentrated.

    f. Evaluate and react to the above concerns of black parents, citizens and the County Branch NAACP relative to equality in education for blacks.

The County Branch NAACP, black parents and concerned citizens of the county request that the District School Board respond to the aforementioned concerns regarding assurance of quality and equity in education for blacks via a special work session with the above groups.

Harcourt Brace & Company

EXERCISE 8

ADVANCED REPORTING

JUVENILE SHOPLIFTING

INSTRUCTIONS: Write a news story that summarizes this report about juvenile shoplifters. At the end of your story, list the sources you would interview to write a more thorough story, along with the questions you would ask each source.

THE JUVENILE SHOPLIFTER

Shoplifting is the largest monetary crime in the nation. Annual retail losses have been recently estimated at $16 billion nationally and as high as 7.5% of dollar sales. Shoplifting-related costs have been cited as a prime cause in one-third of all bankruptcies in small businesses. Shoplifting losses are on the rise, with a 300 percent increase in the incidence of this crime during the 1980s alone.

Juveniles make up the largest percentage of shoplifters. Several studies have revealed that juvenile shoplifters account for approximately fifty percent of all shoplifting.

To gain further insight into the shoplifting problem, George P. Moschis, Professor of Marketing at Georgia State University, and Professor Judith Powell of the University of Richmond, surveyed 7,379 students ages 7 to 19 in urban, suburban and rural areas using methods that insured anonymity of responses.

Some key findings:

- Approximately one out of three juveniles said they had shoplifted.
- Among teenagers ages 15 to 19, about 43% had shoplifted.
- Male youths shoplift more than females; approximately 41% of the males and 26% of the females reported having shoplifted at some time.
- A large amount of shoplifting is done by relatively few juveniles. Approximately 14 percent of those who admitted to shoplifting indicated repeat shoplifting behavior.
- In comparison with non-shoplifters, youths who shoplift are more likely to believe that shoplifting is not a crime.
- Motives for shoplifting are primarily social rather than economic, especially among girls.
- A great deal of shoplifting is done because of peer pressure, especially among girls.
- About half of the time shoplifting takes place in the presence of peers.
- Shoplifting with peers is more common among girls than among boys (61% vs. 47%).
- Females show greater tendency to shoplift with others with age than males.
- Females tend to shoplift more frequently in the presence of others with age.
- Boys tend to shoplift more frequently alone (less frequently with others) with age.
- Shoplifting done by juveniles is primarily impulsive; four times out of five it is done on impulse.
- Female juveniles who shoplift are more likely to shoplift on impulse. Approximately 87% of females and 76% of males who admitted they had shoplifted decided to shoplift after they entered the store.
- Older teen-age girls are more likely to shoplift on impulse than older teen-age boys.
- Older boys tend to plan out shoplifting more than girls.
- There is a decline in impulse shoplifting with age and an increase in planned shoplifting among boys. No decline in impulsive shoplifting behavior is shown for girls.

- Impulsive (unplanned) shoplifting in the presence of others is not only more common among girls but it also becomes more frequent with age. Impulsive shoplifting among boys in the presence of others does not increase with age.

The findings regarding differences in shoplifting behavior due to age and sex characteristics are expected to apply to other parts of the country, and they are consistent with the results of previous studies.

The authors recommend two broad strategies for reducing shoplifting losses: shoplifting prevention and shoplifting detection. Among shoplifting prevention methods, the authors suggest promotional campaigns that would increase awareness of the seriousness of the crime, and methods that would increase the difficulty of shoplifting. Proposed shoplifting detection strategies focus on educating security-detection personnel to be alert to the shoplifter's early warning signals, including knowledge of characteristics of youths most likely to shoplift.

E X E R C I S E   9

ADVANCED REPORTING

COMPUTER-ASSISTED REPORTING

1. Get an E-mail address for yourself through the proper agency on your campus and sub-scribe to a journalism discussion list. Prepare a weekly report about the mail on the list summarizing what journalists talk about. Discuss the mail in class. What does it tell you about journalists and the journalism profession?

2. Read this chapter's Exercise 5 about television's effect on children. What databases could be checked or developed that would help you find out whether there is any justifi-cation for the policy statement issued by the American Academy of Pediatrics? Discuss your ideas with other members of your class and your instructor.

3. Read this chapter's Exercise 6 about your school's acceptance of a donation from an or-ganization that discriminates against women, blacks and Jews. Develop a list of data-bases—either ones that already exist or ones that you could make—that could add to the impact of the story. Discuss your ideas with other members of your class and your instructor.

4. Read this chapter's Exercise 7 about the NAACP complaint regarding your local school district. What databases could be checked or developed that would help you determine whether the complaint is justified? Discuss your ideas with other members of your class and your instructor.

5. Read this chapter's Exercise 8 about juvenile shoplifters. Develop a list of databases—either ones that already exist or ones that you could make—that could test the findings of the report. Discuss your ideas with other members of your class and your instructor.

6. Develop a computer-assisted reporting project from the information given below. What databases could be generated? What kind of information would be important for your story? What comparisons need to be made? Who needs to be interviewed? What ques-tions need to be asked?

   County commissioners for the past 10 years issued licenses for duck hunting on three small, unoccupied islands in Ford Lake. Each year there are nearly 100 applica-tions for the five licenses the commissioners award. Over the past several years, de-velopers have built a number of homes along the waterfront around the lake. Visitors and residents use the lake for recreational activities—boating, swimming, fishing and picnicking. This year, homeowners want the duck hunting to stop. They claim devel-opment around the lake has made hunting dangerous. They say pellets from the hunters' guns could hit houses and people along the shoreline. Hunters say the pellets never reach shore.

7. How could computer-assisted reporting help you with a story based on the information given below? What other databases would be helpful? Can the health report listed below be divided into sub-databases? What kind of information would be important for

your story? What comparisons need to be made? Who needs to be interviewed for the story? What questions need to be asked?

Every year, the county health department releases a report that lists the leading causes of death. This report provides the address, age, gender and race of each decedent, as well as the cause of death and the date of death. There were 3,245 deaths in the county last year, including 1,201 from all types of cancer. Other leading causes of death were: automobile accidents (525), heart attacks/strokes (432) and gunshot wounds (57).

8. Your editor hands you a computer printout of a database containing information about the 4,000 parking tickets your local police department wrote over the past year. For each ticket, the printout contains this information: license plate number, state where license was issued, year license was issued, the ticket number, where the ticket was issued (including street and block), time of day the ticket was issued, day of the week the ticket was issued, date the ticket was issued, type of parking violation (expired meter, no parking zone, double parked, etc.), make of the vehicle, amount of the fine, date the fine was paid and name of the officer issuing the ticket.

Before your editor will allow you to use a computer to manipulate the data, she wants you to develop three ideas for stories that could result from this single database. She also wants you to list the sources you will need to talk to about each story once the data have been analyzed. Prepare a report for your editor addressing these requirements.

CHAPTER 20

COMMUNICATIONS LAW

Congress shall make no law respecting an establishment of religion, or prohibiting the free exercise thereof; or abridging the freedom of speech, or of the press; or the right of the people peaceably to assemble, and to petition the Government for a redress of grievances.

(The First Amendment to the U.S. Constitution)

The First Amendment's guarantee of "freedom of the press" has never afforded complete freedom to express anything at any time. From the very beginning of the republic, courts have held that the First Amendment does not restrict the ability of the state to prohibit expression that is obscene. In the 20th century, the courts, particularly the U.S. Supreme Court, have elaborated on the meaning of the First Amendment. They have found that it does not apply to advertising, movies and broadcasting in the same way that it applies to newspapers and books. They also have found that the right to gather information is not as broad as the right to publish it. And they have said that the First Amendment does not insulate media businesses from the taxes and regulations to which all other businesses are subject.

Communications law is a broad area involving many aspects of the mass media and a variety of legal principles. You will probably study this subject in more detail in a specialized media law course, if you have not already done so. This chapter will introduce you to three areas of communications law that you will need to know as a professional-in-training. Libel and privacy are covered extensively because the danger of a lawsuit is high and the cost of defending or losing one can be great. News gathering is also covered, though in less detail.

LIBEL

Libel is defamation by written words or by communication in some other tangible form, whereas slander is defamation by spoken words or gestures. Traditionally, the law has treated libel more harshly because the written word carries more weight and is more permanent than the spoken word. Courts said the greater power of written words to injure reputation justified harsher penalties and legal rules more favorable to the plaintiff in libel cases than in slander ones. You might think that broadcast defamation should be treated as slander since it is spoken, and some states do so, either by statute or by judicial interpretation. More commonly, however, courts treat broadcast defamation as libel, since it can be as harmful and as durable as printed or written defamation.

Libel is a major concern for reporters. People who feel injured by something in a broadcast, a newspaper story or an advertisement may be quick to sue. The costs of a lawsuit can be great. Juries may award millions of dollars to a successful libel plaintiff. The largest libel judgment upheld on appeal so far is $3.05 million against CBS for defamatory statements aired by one of its stations about the Brown & Williamson Tobacco Co. Even when media organizations win libel suits, they still may have to spend millions on court costs and attorneys' fees. William Westmoreland, a retired general who commanded U.S. forces in Vietnam, sued CBS for libel in the

Harcourt Brace & Company

1980s. The trial ended in an agreement that involved no monetary settlement, but the two sides spent an estimated $8 million on legal fees; more than half of that expense was borne by CBS.

Libel suits place not only the news organization's pocketbook at risk but also its reputation. News organizations build their reputations on fairness and accuracy. A libel judgment blemishes that reputation, sometimes irreparably. Individual reporters, producers and editors also depend on their reputations for accuracy, thoroughness and responsibility. If they lose a libel suit, they may lose that reputation. They may even lose their jobs. For these reasons and others, journalists must know what constitutes libel and what defenses can protect them in a libel suit.

The Elements of a Libel Suit

A plaintiff in a libel suit involving a statement published in the mass media usually must prove six things: (1) defamation, (2) identification, (3) publication, (4) falsity, (5) injury and (6) fault.

Defamation

The essence of a libel suit is vindication of one's reputation. The plaintiff, therefore, must prove defamation, meaning injury to reputation. A statement is defamatory if it injures a person's reputation so as to lower that person in the estimation of the community or deter third persons from associating or dealing with that person. Judging whether a statement is defamatory involves two steps. The first step requires a determination by the judge that the statement is capable of a defamatory meaning; in the second step, the jury decides whether a substantial and respectable segment of the public actually understood the statement as defaming the plaintiff.

Some statements obviously have the power to injure reputations—for example, statements that a person has committed a crime, has a loathsome disease, is incompetent in her or his business or has engaged in serious sexual misconduct. In other cases, the statement conveys no obviously defamatory meaning. Rather, a reader or listener must put the statement together with previously known facts to come up with a defamatory conclusion. In 1939, for example, the owner of a kosher market sued the meatpacking firm of Armour & Co. for libel because it had published an advertisement listing his store as one that sold Armour bacon. Saying that a person sells bacon is not defamatory by itself, but it becomes defamatory when it is combined with the extrinsic fact that the store is kosher (Braun v. Armour & Co., 173 N.E. 845 [1939]). In cases like this one, the plaintiff must prove that people were aware of the additional facts and that he or she suffered actual monetary loss as a result.

A statement may embarrass or annoy a person but fail to be defamatory. The mayor of a Utah town sued a local newspaper over a number of stories and editorials it had published about him. One of the mayor's complaints involved an editorial that accused him of "repeated and not-too-subtle" attempts to manipulate the press. The Utah Supreme Court said the manipulation charge at worst accused the mayor of trying to use his political position to influence what information was disseminated to the public. "Absent assertions of illegal or at least ethically improper conduct, it is not defamatory to criticize a politician for using his or her office for personal gain," the Utah high court said (West v. Thomson Newspapers, 872 P.2d 999 [Utah 1994]).

An Illinois case illustrates how far one can go in attacking a person. The Belleview News-Democrat had endorsed Jerry Costello's candidacy for chairman of the county board because Costello had said he opposed any new taxes without a referendum. At the first meeting of the county board following Costello's election, the board voted to create a metropolitan transportation system, which entailed new taxes. Two days later, the News-Democrat ran an editorial that said: "Jerry Costello lied to us. . . . The County Board had an opportunity to conduct a binding referendum. . . . That's the very thing Costello had pledged to do. . . . But when the time came to make a decision, he was up there sitting on his gavel." Costello sued, and the Illinois Supreme Court agreed the editorial was defamatory. Saying an official lacks integrity in discharging his or her duties is libelous on its face in Illinois, and the court said the editorial's description of

Costello as a liar implied a lack of integrity on his part (Costello v. Capital Cities Communications, 532 N.E.2d 790 [1988]). The newspaper won the case on other grounds.

Identification

The libel plaintiff must also prove that he or she was identified with the defamatory statement. This requires proving that reasonable readers, listeners or viewers would have understood that the statement was "of and concerning" the plaintiff. It does not matter whether the publisher of the statement intended to refer to the plaintiff, only whether the reader, listener or viewer could reasonably draw that conclusion.

Usually, libel plaintiffs have no trouble establishing identification in cases involving the news media. The sources for or subjects of news stories are usually clearly identified by name. In fact, detailed identification protects reporters against libel suits. Many suits arise from situations in which similar names create confusion. If a Sam Johnson is arrested for dealing cocaine, the commonness of the name creates the possibility of confusion. By making it clear that the person arrested was Samuel H. Johnson Jr. of 3517 N. Forest St., Apt. 303, you have eliminated the possibility that you will inadvertently defame any other Sam Johnsons in town.

The publication of a name is not necessary for identification. A California jury awarded damages to a psychologist, Paul Bindrim, who said he had been libeled by a novel. Bindrim conducted nude encounter-group workshops, one of which was attended by Gwen Mitchell, a novelist. Mitchell later wrote a novel about a psychiatrist who conducted similar nude workshops. The fictional psychiatrist had a different name and different physical characteristics from Bindrim, but the real-life psychologist persuaded the jury there were enough similarities that readers could infer that the novel was about him (Bindrim v. Mitchell, 155 Cal. Rptr. 29 [Cal. Ct. App. 1979]).

Publication

Obviously, when a statement has appeared in a newspaper or on a television broadcast, it has been published. But a statement does not have to be so widely disseminated for a person to sue for libel. All the law requires is that the defendant made the defamatory statement to someone other than the person defamed. In one case a man dictated a letter to his secretary, accusing the addressee of larceny. The secretary then typed the letter. The New York Court of Appeals held that publication took place when the secretary read and transcribed the stenographic notes (Ostrowe v. Lee, 175 N.E. 505 [N.Y. 1931]). If the man had written his own letter and sent it to the addressee in a sealed envelope, there would have been no publication.

Once a libel is published, the plaintiff must sue within the time specified by the state's statute of limitations. In most states, the statute of limitations is one or two years. A few allow as many as three years. Some states have other time provisions that may favor plaintiffs. Texas, for example, says the statute of limitations begins running not from the date of publication but from the time the plaintiff learned of the libel or should have learned of it. In all states, the statute of limitations runs from the most recent publication, so republishing a defamatory statement extends the time during which the plaintiff may sue.

Falsity

For generations, courts presumed defamatory statements were false. A series of Supreme Court decisions beginning in 1964 has changed that. Now many libel plaintiffs must prove falsity when the allegedly defamatory statements involve matters of public concern. The Supreme Court has said that in many libel cases, the parties argue over whether a defamatory statement is true. In those cases, the party that must prove truth or falsity is more likely to lose. Making plaintiffs prove falsity means some defamed persons may not be able to recover damages, but making defendants prove truth means some truthful publications will be punished. When the mass media publish statements about matters of public concern, the Supreme Court said, the First Amendment requires tipping the balance in favor of freedom of the press (Philadelphia Newspapers v. Hepps, 475 U.S. 767 [1986]).

Although the plaintiffs must prove falsity only when the defamatory statement involves a matter of public concern, the requirement will apply in most cases involving the mass media. Courts usually conclude that if a statement appears in a newspaper or a news broadcast, it involves a matter of public concern.

Injury

Under traditional libel law, courts presumed that obviously defamatory statements had injured the plaintiff. The plaintiff did not have to produce any evidence showing that she or he had suffered injury to reputation, monetary loss or emotional suffering. The Supreme Court said in 1974 that this presumption of injury was incompatible with the First Amendment. Since then libel plaintiffs have had to prove "actual injury" in order to recover damages from publishers who negligently made defamatory statements. Actual injury includes more than provable monetary loss. Evidence of damage to reputation, humiliation and mental anguish also count.

A libel suit over an anthology of humorous stories illustrates the importance of the injury issue. In 1976 the Macmillan Publishing Co. released an anthology of women's humor. One of the pieces parodied the 1955 book "Eloise," which depicted a 6-year-old girl who lived in New York City's Plaza Hotel. One of the characters in the book was "Mr. Salomone," the hotel manager. The 1976 parody, titled "Eloise Returns," portrayed Eloise as a 26-year-old woman with loose morals. The first drawing showed Eloise scrawling graffiti on a restroom wall, including this sentence: "Mr. Salomone was a child molester!!" The Salomone character was not fictional. The real manager of the Plaza Hotel in 1955 was Alphonse Salomone, who by 1977 was a senior vice president in the Hilton Hotels Corp. He sued for libel, but a New York appellate court ruled against him because he was unable to produce any evidence that his reputation had suffered. Salomone had claimed mental anguish, but the court said state law allowed compensation for mental anguish only when it was coupled with injury to reputation (Salomone v. Macmillan Publishing Co., 429 N.Y.S.2d 441 [1980]).

Sometimes the plaintiff does not have to prove injury. If the defendant published the defamatory statement with actual malice (which will be explained in the next section), then the courts can presume injury. Publications that do not involve a matter of public concern are another exception.

Fault

The most crucial issue in modern libel cases is fault. "Fault," in libel law, refers to the state of mind of the person responsible for the allegedly defamatory statement: Was the statement made intentionally, recklessly or negligently? Before 1964, many states said publishers of defamatory statements would have to pay damages even if they had taken every reasonable step to ensure the accuracy of the story. Starting in 1964, the U.S. Supreme Court changed that in the case of New York Times v. Sullivan (376 U.S. 254) and changed it further in its 1974 Gertz v. Robert Welch, Inc. (418 U.S. 323) decision. Now plaintiffs must prove some level of fault. The level of fault a plaintiff needs to prove depends on whether the plaintiff is (1) a public official or public figure or (2) a private individual.

Public officials and public figures must prove that the statement was published with the knowledge that it was false or with reckless disregard for whether it was false. This is called "actual malice," a term that causes confusion since many people think it means ill will. The attitude of the defendant toward the plaintiff is not an issue. All that matters is whether the defendant knew the statement was false or had a high degree of awareness of the statement's probable falsity when it was published. Proving this can be difficult, since the plaintiff must produce evidence about the defendant's state of mind.

Private individuals do not have such a heavy burden of proof; in most states they have to prove only that the defendant acted with negligence. Negligence involves doing something a reasonable and prudent person would not do, or failing to do something a reasonable and prudent person would do in the same situation. In a libel case, an error such as failing to check public records, misspelling or confusing names or accidentally transposing dates or figures might be considered negligence.

The difference between actual malice and negligence is sometimes confusing, but two cases may clarify the distinction:

Chris Gatto, a reporter for the Belleville Post in New Jersey, rewrote a story from a larger paper about an investigation of problems with the New Jersey School Board Association's insurance group. Lawrence Schwartz, a local attorney, represented the school board association in the investigation. Unfortunately, Gatto's understanding of the case was weak and his story was confused. When the story reached Post editor Joseph Cammelieri, Gatto was out of town on another assignment. Cammelieri had to figure out the story on his own and incorrectly concluded that the focus of the investigation was Schwartz—specifically, whether the $353,851 Schwartz had received from the association in legal fees was excessive. Cammelieri later said: "I was confused. So in my confusion, I saw a local person; and I assumed that oh, this local person must be the primary focus of the story and I was trying to simplify it." Schwartz sued for libel. The New Jersey courts said he was a public figure and had to prove actual malice. But the most he could prove was that Gatto and Cammelieri had been negligent. Gatto should have checked his facts more carefully, and Cammelieri should not have assumed Schwartz was the focus of the story. But there was no evidence that either had the high degree of awareness of probable falsity required to prove actual malice (Schwartz v. Worrall Publications, Inc., 20 Media L. Rptr. 1661 [N.J. Super. Ct. App. Div. 1992]).

The result was quite different in a West Virginia case. Charleston attorney Ray Hinerman sued the Charleston Daily Gazette for libel over an editorial about a worker's compensation case. Hinerman had helped a client win a worker's compensation award, but then the client failed to pay Hinerman's bill. The attorney sued the client and eventually won a judgment giving Hinerman 100 percent of the client's benefits until the overdue bill was paid. The Daily Gazette's editorial said Hinerman would get "every penny . . . $12,000" of the worker's compensation award as payment for one day's work. The editorial did not mention that payments to the worker would resume once Hinerman's bill was paid. Hinerman sued and won. The West Virginia Supreme Court, in upholding a $375,000 judgment in Hinerman's favor, said the evidence supported the conclusion that Daily Gazette editors knew the editorial was false or knew enough to have serious doubts about its truth. For one thing, the Daily Gazette's news story about the same case had correctly stated that Hinerman would receive the worker's compensation payments only until his bill was paid. Also, before writing the editorial, James Haught, the editorial page editor, had sent a reporter to the court to double-check the accuracy of the story. The Supreme Court said that because the news story was correct and because Haught had double-checked the court records, the Daily Gazette must have known the editorial was incorrect. The West Virginia high court also noted that Haught had had strong misgivings about the appropriateness of the editorial and that the publisher of the Daily Gazette had long crusaded against loose ethics in the legal profession. That crusade, the court said, might have encouraged newspaper executives to publish an editorial about which they entertained serious doubts (Hinerman v. Daily Gazette, 423 S.E.2d 560 [W.Va. 1992]).

Actual malice is difficult to prove. Simple mistakes in handling a story are not enough. Nor is evidence that the defendant bore ill will toward the plaintiff. But the U.S. Supreme Court has said actual malice can be found in cases where the defendant:

- Knew facts that would call the story into question;

- Refused to examine evidence that would prove or disprove a charge;

- Relied on an inherently unbelievable source;

- Published an improbable story without investigation; or

- Simply fabricated the story.

Public Officials, Public Figures and Private Individuals

The most important decision in many libel cases is whether the plaintiff is a public official or public figure. That decision determines whether the plaintiff will have to prove actual malice and what damages he or she can recover. A public official or public figure must prove actual malice to win any damages, actual or punitive. A private individual need prove only negligence to recover actual damages but would have to prove actual malice to win punitive damages. The U.S. Supreme Court has provided only hazy guidelines for distinguishing public officials and public figures from private individuals. The guidelines have left a good deal of room for states to expand or contract those categories.

The more clearly defined category is that of public official. The Supreme Court has said public officials must hold some government position. The category of public officials includes not only elected officials, such as U.S. senators, state legislators and city council members, but also appointed officials and government employees. Even unpaid government officials, such as members of a local planning and zoning commission, are public officials for purposes of libel law. Just being on the government payroll does not make a person a public official, however. The person also must have or appear to have substantial authority over governmental affairs. A low-ranking worker in the city sanitation department or a secretary in the city attorney's office probably would not be a public official. Also, to be considered a public official, the employee must hold a position important enough that the public would have an interest in his or her qualifications even in the absence of a specific news event or controversy (Rosenblatt v. Baer, 383 U.S. 75 [1966]).

A gray area exists between government leaders, like mayors, who are clearly public officials, and minor employees, like city file clerks, who are not. Whether people in the gray area are public officials may depend on how the courts in a given state have interpreted the law. Public school principals and teachers clearly are government employees, but they are not always considered public officials for libel purposes. The Vermont Supreme Court ruled that an elementary school principal was a public official because that person supervised and evaluated employees and because education is important to the public (Palmer v. Bennington School District, 20 Media L. Rptr. 1640 [Vt. 1992]). The Georgia Supreme Court, however, found a high school principal was not a public official because that person played no part in general policy making (Ellerbee v. Mills, 20 Media L. Rptr. 2095 [Ga. 1992]). Similarly, some states have found classroom teachers to be public officials, while others have said they are not. Most courts have found law enforcement officers and others who make decisions that affect the rights, liberty, health and safety of the public to be public officials.

Does a person who is a public official have to prove actual malice only with regard to published statements about her or his official conduct? The Supreme Court has said no. Anything that touches upon that person's fitness to hold that office or position is fair game (Monitor Patriot Co. v. Roy, 401 U.S. 265 [1971]). Nevertheless, one can imagine a defamatory statement that would be completely irrelevant to the plaintiff's status as a public official. In that case, the plaintiff might not have to prove actual malice. Presumably, the range of information that bears upon a person's fitness for office increases as that person rises in government. A news story about a person in government should make clear that person's status as a public official and how the information in the story bears on her or his official conduct. News organizations should weigh carefully any defamatory information about a public official that lacks relevance to the person's qualifications or fitness for office, not only because it might provoke a libel suit but also because it might have little news value.

Identifying public figures is even more difficult than identifying public officials. A judge in one libel case complained, "Defining public figures is much like trying to nail a jellyfish to the wall." Part of the problem is the vagueness with which the U.S. Supreme Court has defined the term "public figure" and part is the court's reluctance to impose any uniformity on the states.

After it decided that public officials would have to prove actual malice, the Supreme Court recognized that certain people who did not hold official government positions nevertheless exercised great influence over public affairs and public opinion. The court decided that these public figures also should have to prove actual malice, but the justices tried to define "public figure" in a way that would keep the category small. The Supreme Court in the Gertz decision identified three types of public figures: (1) involuntary, (2) general-purpose and (3) limited-purpose. The court said the essence of public-figure status is that a person has voluntarily assumed some special prominence or role in society; therefore, the category of involuntary public figure must necessarily be very small, almost to the point of being nonexistent. The other two categories are somewhat larger.

The general-purpose public figure, the Supreme Court said, has such persuasive power and influence as to be a public figure for all occasions. Celebrities from the entertainment and sports industries, such as David Letterman, Whitney Houston, Arnold Schwartzenegger, Meryl Streep, Michael Jordan and Joe Montana, would probably fit this definition. So would people from other walks of life who have become unusually prominent—people like Katharine Graham, Ralph Nader, the Rev. Jerry Falwell and Bill Gates. The Supreme Court said this category, too, must be small because few people attain such widespread notoriety.

The largest category of public figures consists of those who hold that status for the limited purpose of commenting on some particular topic or issue. These public figures have thrust themselves to the forefront of a controversy in order to affect its resolution. People who organize an abortion-rights march or who lead an effort to persuade a school board to change the curriculum in history classes or who argue publicly for passage of a state bottle-deposit law would be examples of limited-purpose public figures.

The Supreme Court has left the definitions of "public figure" so vague that lower courts have had trouble applying them. Some court decisions seem to contradict one another. For example, one court said a life insurance company had become a public figure through its advertising and public relations efforts dealing with the health-care funding controversy (National Life Insurance Co. v. Phillips Publishing, Inc., 20 Media L. Rptr. 1393 [D. Md. 1992]). Another court said neither of two corporations engaged in competitive and comparative advertising focusing on the cost and quality of their health insurance programs was a public figure (U.S. Healthcare v. Blue Cross of Greater Philadelphia, 17 Media L. Rptr. 1681 [3rd Cir. 1990]).

Trying to decide who is a public figure provides uncertain protection from a libel suit. A better approach is to remember who is not a public figure. The U.S. Supreme Court has said that people involved in civil court cases, criminal suspects and defendants, individuals and businesses who receive money from the government, and lawyers representing people in court are not automatically public figures. The court has said that such people have not necessarily stepped forward to influence the resolution of a public controversy.

Harcourt Brace & Company

Major Defenses to Libel Suits

The difficulty plaintiffs have in proving actual malice has become the major defense for media organizations in libel cases. There are some older defenses available, and they can be important in some cases. Of these older defenses, the main ones are (1) truth, (2) qualified privilege and (3) fair comment and criticism.

Truth

The use of truth as a defense arose when courts presumed defamatory statements were false. Now, plaintiffs must prove falsity; but proving a statement true can still defeat a libel claim.

Proving truth does not mean proving a news report accurate in every detail. Most courts require only proof of substantial truth or of the sting or the gist of the charge. If a news story reports that a person has been charged with embezzling $100,000 but in fact only $75,000 was taken, that person could not win a libel suit, because the sting of the story—being charged with embezzlement—is true. For the same reason, courts usually excuse errors involving technicalities. The Michigan Supreme Court ruled that a newspaper story that said a man had been "charged" with the sexual assault of a baby sitter was substantially true even though the man was not formally charged at his arraignment. Police had arrested the man on that charge, but prosecutors dropped it at arraignment. The court said that although the news story had misused a technical legal term, the error was not serious enough to support a libel suit (Rouch v. Enquirer & News, 20 Media L. Rptr. 2265 [Mich. 1992]).

If a news story misuses a technical term to create a substantially false and defamatory impression, then courts will not consider the story true. A Minnesota appeals court upheld a $676,000 damage award to a Duluth street maintenance supervisor over a series of stories and editorials in a local newspaper. The stories and editorials said the supervisor had arranged to have the clay road in front of his home paved. In fact, the street was not paved but repaired with asphalt shavings. The difference is that paving an unpaved road is a major improvement, for which the adjacent property owners would have to pay. Repairing a road with asphalt shavings is routine maintenance, and homeowners do not pay any of the costs. The difference, the Minnesota appeals court said, is substantial enough to create the false and defamatory impression that the supervisor had misused his office (LeDoux v. Northwest Publishing, Inc., 521 N.W.2d 59 [Minn. Ct. App. 1994]).

Crucial omissions can defeat the defense of truth even if every fact in a news report is accurate. A Memphis newspaper reported that Ruth Nichols had been shot in the arm by another woman. The story said, "Officers said the incident took place Thursday night after the suspect arrived at the Nichols home and found her husband there with Mrs. Nichols." That was true, but the story failed to mention that Ruth Nichols' husband and two other people also were present. Nichols successfully sued for libel, saying that the omission created the false and defamatory impression that she was having an affair with the other woman's husband (Memphis Publishing Co. v. Nichols, 4 Media L. Rptr. 1573 [Tenn. 1978]).

The defense of truth does not extend to the accurate republication of defamatory charges made by other people. A news organization that reports a defamatory statement a bank president makes about a competitor cannot escape liability by proving that it accurately quoted the bank president. The news organization is responsible for proving that the underlying statement was true, not merely that it had quoted the source accurately. There are some exceptions to this rule, the main one being the qualified privilege that news organizations have to report on official proceedings and documents.

Qualified Privilege

The law recognizes certain occasions when people need absolute protection from libel suits. People called to testify in court, for example, cannot be sued for defamation because of what they say on the witness stand. And members of legislative bodies, such as the U.S. Congress and state legislatures, cannot be sued over remarks they make in the course of their official duties. News organizations enjoy a similar, although qualified, privilege to report on what happens in courtrooms and legislative chambers and what is said in official documents. So a news reporter covering a trial cannot be sued for reporting false and defamatory statements made by a witness so long as the reporter's story is full, fair and accurate.

A reporter for the Lamar (Mo.) Democrat covered a meeting of the Golden City, Mo., council at which the members discussed the fitness of the town's chief of police and its only patrolman. The council also heard comments from citizens, including one person who said his 16-year-old daughter had been "knocked up" by the patrolman. That comment appeared later on the front page of the Democrat, and the patrolman sued for libel. The Missouri Court of Appeals said newspapers have a privilege to report on public meetings about matters of public concern so long as the reports are fair and accurate, and this one was (Shafer v. Lamar Publishing Co., 7 Media L. Rptr. 2049 [Mo. Ct. App. 1981]).

Under the qualified privilege defense, the Lamar Democrat was not responsible for proving that the deputy in fact had gotten a 16-year-old girl pregnant; it was responsible only for showing that it had accurately reported what was said at the city council meeting. If the report inaccurately states what happened at an official meeting or what was said in an official document, the privilege may be lost. So when a broadcast news report said an attorney had been found guilty of conspiring to help a client evade the federal income tax, when in fact the attorney had been acquitted, the station could not claim that it had made a fair and accurate report of an official proceeding (Western Broadcasting v. Wright, 14 Media L. Rptr. 1286 [Ga. Ct. App. 1987]).

Journalists have this qualified privilege when reporting on such governmental proceedings as court hearings, administrative agency meetings and legislative sessions at all levels of government from town council to U.S. Congress. In most states, the privilege extends to official documents, such as police reports, health inspection reports, depositions, official government correspondence and grand jury transcripts. In some states, the privilege also applies to reports of nongovernmental meetings open to the public for discussion of matters of public concern.

Reporters should be wary of statements public officials make outside the scope of their official duties. These statements are rarely privileged and must be treated with the same care a reporter would give to a defamatory charge made by an ordinary citizen. Some examples of statements that fall outside the scope of an official's duties and are not protected by privilege are statements made by a legislative committee chairperson about matters not investigated by the committee, not-for-attribution statements made by a prosecutor or a police officer, and comments made by school board members when no quorum is present.

Fair Comment and Criticism

Everyone has the right to an opinion, even an opinion that might injure another person. The fair comment and criticism defense evolved in the late 19th and early 20th centuries to protect from libel suits expressions of opinion about matters of legitimate public interest. The defense applied only if the opinions were based on true facts, were the sincere opinions of the speakers and were not motivated solely by ill will.

The U.S. Supreme Court seemed to expand the opinion defense in 1974. The court, in deciding the Gertz v. Robert Welch, Inc., libel case, made the passing remark that there is "no such thing as a false idea." Many lawyers and judges took that as creating a nearly complete defense for any statement that could reasonably be classified as an opinion. So lower courts developed elaborate tests for distinguishing statements of fact from statements of opinion.

The Supreme Court threw this area of libel law into disarray in 1990 when it declared in Milkovich v. Lorain Journal (497 U.S. 1 [1990]) that a sports writer's opinion column could be the basis for a libel suit. The court said opinions enjoy no special protection from libel suits. Chief Justice William Rehnquist, who wrote the majority opinion in Milkovich, said existing principles of libel law provide sufficient protection for expressions of opinion. Rehnquist said an editorial, column, letter to the editor or other expression of opinion can be libelous if it says something about a person that can be proved false and defamatory.

Many legal scholars worried that the Milkovich decision would expose all manner of opinions to libel litigation. To some extent, that has happened; but it appears that courts are analyzing such cases in a manner similar to that used before the Milkovich case. Now, however, instead of talking about whether a statement is fact or opinion, courts talk about whether a statement can be proved false. The result, in many instances, is the same, but a crucial question remains: How much emphasis should be given to the context in which a defamatory statement appeared?

A case involving a book review published in The New York Times provides a good look at how the opinion defense works in the wake of the Milkovich decision. Dan Moldea, an investigative reporter, wrote "Interference," a book that describes organized crime's influence on professional football. Gerald Eskenazi reviewed the book for The New York Times and concluded that the book contained "too much sloppy journalism." Moldea thought the remark libeled him and sued. A federal district court granted The Times' motion to dismiss the case. Moldea appealed to the U.S. Court of Appeals for the District of Columbia Circuit. The appeals court issued two opinions in the case, the second dramatically reversing the first.

The first time the court of appeals considered Moldea's case, it ruled that the statement about "sloppy journalism" was sufficiently factual that a jury could decide whether it was true. Furthermore, the court said the Milkovich decision prevented it from attaching much weight to the fact that the statement appeared in a book review.

A short time later, the appeals court reconsidered its ruling and concluded that the Supreme Court had not intended to prevent courts from considering context in libel cases. Context had been irrelevant in the Milkovich case, the appeals court said, but when it is relevant, context helps indicate whether readers will understand a statement as factual. The court said in the context of a book review the accusation of sloppy journalism was exactly the kind of thing a reader would interpret as opinion and not as something that could be proved true or false (Moldea v. New York Times, 22 Media L. Rptr. 1673 [D.C. Cir. 1994]).

Retractions

Most states have retraction statutes that limit damages or prevent libel suits in cases where a full, prompt and prominent retraction has been published. The statutes vary greatly in their terms, and the Supreme Court has made some of them obsolete with more than 30 years of opinions recognizing constitutional limitations on libel actions. Some obsolete statutes say a libel plaintiff can recover only actual damages where a publisher had a reasonable basis for honestly believing the original story was true and had issued a retraction. Such a law does no more to protect the media than the Supreme Court's 1974 Gertz opinion.

Other retraction statutes can be more helpful. Some states prohibit a plaintiff from recovering punitive damages where a retraction has been published; others say a plaintiff cannot seek punitive damages unless she or he has first requested a retraction. And a few statutes require a person to seek a retraction before filing a libel suit.

A retraction ordinarily is not a defense to a libel suit. A news organization may still be sued, even if it publishes a full, prompt and prominent retraction. But a retraction will lessen damages, even in states that do not have retraction statutes. Also, publication of a retraction can be evidence of good faith and an absence of ill will. In many cases, the person who has been defamed will settle for the retraction and not sue.

Some state retraction statutes specify when, where and how a retraction should be published. If you are ever asked to publish a retraction, check your state laws to make sure you publish an adequate one.

In 1993 the National Conference of Commissioners on Uniform State Laws proposed a uniform correction or clarification act that would harmonize the state laws and provide an alternative to costly and confusing libel suits. The proposed statute would limit the damages a libel plaintiff can recover to provable economic loss when the defendant publishes a retraction. The defendant would benefit from having a cap placed on damage awards, and the plaintiff would benefit from prompt vindication of her or his reputation and reimbursement for economic loss.

Harcourt Brace & Company

Only two states quickly considered this statute: North Dakota and New Mexico. North Dakota adopted it; New Mexico rejected it.

Avoiding Libel Suits

No checklist or set of steps can guarantee that a news organization will never be sued for libel. Some news organizations have checked stories and found evidence for every potentially defamatory statement but still have been sued. Usually, the conscientious news organization will win, but the cost of defending against the libel suit can be daunting. Nevertheless, there are some things journalists can do to protect themselves and their employers. Neil Rosini, an attorney and author of "The Practical Guide to Libel Law," offers 12 steps news organizations can take to limit the danger of libel suits.

WHEN TO STOP CHECKING FACTS AND GO WITH THE STORY

By **Neil J. Rosini**
From The IRE Journal

Judging from recent Supreme Court cases, when should a writer, or a writer's fact-checker, stop checking facts and publish a story? The answer seems to be: at the point where judges and juries would conclude that editors, producers and reporters had expunged all "serious doubt" from their minds. As the cases demonstrate, the actual malice test may be stretched or narrowed in meaning, like a biblical text, to suit an interpreter's purpose. Nevertheless, there are practical steps which can be taken to limit liability, as the Supreme Court decisions have shown:

1. Evaluate each source; form an opinion regarding his, her or its veracity.
2. Ask the person who is the subject of the defamatory statement whenever possible whether the statement is true. Even when the subject denies everything, if he or she fails to furnish specific facts contradicting the allegations so as to cause any reasonable person to conduct further inquiry, actual malice may not be proved.
3. If there is more than one party to a particular event, ask more than one party what happened. In other words, interview the people who are most likely to know the truth.
4. If the interviewees have documents or (particularly) tape recordings, ask for them and pay attention to them. Compare them carefully to what the interviewees say.
5. If there are limitations on the credibility of sources, state them in the report.
6. If a publication is not hot news, your investigation must be more thorough, commensurate with the additional time you have to do it.
7. Employ a system of editorial review, establish internal policies and follow them.
8. Bring an attitude of open-mindedness to your work; avoid muckraking with preconceived conclusions.
9. Employers should use reputable reporters.
10. Be sure to ask sources the key questions; do not fail to ask a question when you expect an answer that is inconsistent with your thesis.
11. Be rigorous in your choice of language. Say no more than you can directly support. Avoid conclusions, inferences or interpretations that lack direct support.
12. Don't ever publish a potentially defamatory statement if you doubt its truth.

(Neil J. Rosini is a partner in Franklin, Weinrib, Rudell & Vassallo, New York City, and author of *The Practical Guide to Libel Law*.)

PRIVACY

The right to sue a news organization that has invaded one's privacy is less than 100 years old. Already, lawsuits over various forms of invasion of privacy have become a major concern to media organizations because people are worrying more about their privacy.

The law recognizes four kinds of invasion of privacy: (1) intrusion on a person's seclusion or solitude; (2) giving publicity to private facts; (3) placing a person in a false light; and (4) appropriating a person's name or likeness for one's own benefit. The last of these is primarily a concern for advertisers, although news and advertising messages could be the basis for a lawsuit over any of the four forms of privacy. The status of these four forms of invasion of privacy varies from state to state. Some states have recognized them in statutes; in others, court decisions have recognized privacy rights even in the absence of specific statutes. Some states do not recognize all four forms. Nebraska, for example, does not recognize a right to sue for giving publicity to private facts, and Texas does not recognize false-light actions.

Intrusion

Intentionally intruding on the solitude or seclusion of another in a manner that would be highly offensive to a reasonable person is the essence of a lawsuit for intrusion. Ordinary news-gathering techniques do not constitute intrusion. Gathering information about a person by examining public records and interviewing friends, relatives, enemies and associates is perfectly legal, even if the subject of your investigation would prefer that you not do so. Nor are you intruding on a person's solitude or seclusion by requesting an interview. To commit intrusion, you would have to invade some area in which the person had a reasonable expectation of privacy.

Intrusion cases deal with a number of news-gathering techniques and issues. Some deal with news gathering in private or semiprivate places, and others deal with news gathering in public places.

News reporters must have permission to enter private property. Going into a person's home without consent would be a clear case of intrusion. It also would be grounds for a trespass action. It is possible to invade another person's privacy without physically entering that person's property, for example by using electronic eavesdropping devices, tapping a telephone line, looking into a bedroom window with binoculars or using a powerful telephoto lens to take pictures of people inside their homes. Even if some newsworthy event is happening on private property, a journalist may not enter without the owner's or legal occupant's permission.

A similar limitation applies to privately owned places that invite the public to enter, such as restaurants, shops, malls and other places of business. Because the right of privacy belongs only to people, a business or a corporation cannot sue for intrusion if a news reporter enters its premises without permission. It can sue for trespass or press criminal trespass charges, however. Also, individual patrons may sue for intrusion in some instances. An Iowa woman sued a television station that filmed her while she was dining in a restaurant. Although the Iowa Supreme Court did not say whether the woman's privacy had been violated, it did say that restaurant patrons may be able to sue depending on where they were seated in the restaurant and what they were doing at the time (Stessman v. American Black Hawk Broadcasting Co., 416 N.W.2d 685 [Iowa 1987]).

A narrow exception to the permission requirement arises when a police officer or firefighter invites a journalist to enter private property. Courts have recognized that police and other emergency officials commonly allow news reporters and photographers to enter the scene of a crime, fire, accident or other newsworthy incident. The commonness of this practice, a Florida court said in one case, establishes implied consent by property owners to allow news reporters access to their property at the invitation of police. This implied consent vanishes if the owner or occupant of the property objects.

Harcourt Brace & Company

Television "reality programs" that show actual drug busts or other police actions test the limits of police authority to invite reporters to accompany them on private property. Some courts have said police exceed their authority when they invite reporters to accompany them on raids. News organizations that accept these invitations may be liable for intrusion or trespass. Recently a federal judge said CBS News could be held liable for invasion of privacy because it sent a camera crew along with Secret Service agents on a raid of an apartment. The Secret Service agents were looking for evidence of credit card fraud, which they did not find. Their raid on the apartment of Tawa Ayeni was photographed by a CBS crew in spite of Ayeni's objections (Ayeni v. CBS, 848 F. Supp. 362 [E.D.N.Y. 1994]). CBS and Ayeni eventually reached a settlement, the terms of which were not disclosed. The law in this area is still developing, but judges who have considered such cases seem to view invitations to reporters and photographers to accompany police on raids as an effort to intimidate suspects. Intimidation is not an issue when reporters are invited to inspect the scene *after* a crime or disaster.

While the right of reporters to enter private property is limited, fewer restrictions apply to gathering information in public places. A photographer who takes a picture of a couple kissing passionately in a public park has not intruded on their privacy. What the photographer recorded could have been seen by anybody who happened to be in the park. Thus, the couple had no reasonable expectation of privacy. Neither does the right of privacy extend to things that happen on private property but that can be seen or heard from a public street or sidewalk. You probably have seen television news reports showing reporters who have staked out the home or business of someone in the news. The reporters are free to do so, as long as they stay on public streets and sidewalks. They are free to report anything they see or hear without such things as telephoto lenses or powerful microphones.

Nevertheless, there are limits to what reporters can do even in public places. A classic case involved Ronald Galella and Jacqueline Kennedy Onassis. Galella was a freelance photographer who specialized in photographing Onassis in the 1960s and early 1970s. He aggressively followed Onassis and her children. He once used a motorboat to approach Onassis while she was swimming, coming so close that she feared she would be struck by a propeller. On another occasion, Galella jumped from behind a wall in New York City's Central Park to photograph John F. Kennedy Jr. on his bicycle. Galella so startled Kennedy that he lost control of the bike. Because of these and many other instances, Onassis persuaded a court that Galella's zealous shadowing and surveillance were an invasion of her privacy (Galella v. Onassis, 353 F.Supp. 196 [S.D.N.Y. 1972]).

In both public and private places, the use of hidden microphones and hidden cameras is a difficult legal and ethical issue. It is legal in most states to record a conversation so long as one party to that conversation has consented. That means you may legally record your conversations with sources without informing them. Twelve states—California, Delaware, Florida, Illinois, Maryland, Massachusetts, Michigan, Montana, New Hampshire, Oregon, Pennsylvania and Washington—require the consent of all parties to the recording of a conversation. In all states, the ethical practice is always to ask your sources for permission to record conversations. If the sources refuse, you should refrain from recording, even if it may be legal to do so. In addition, a different 12 states—Alabama, California, Delaware, Georgia, Hawaii, Kansas, Maine, Michigan, Minnesota, New Hampshire, South Dakota and Utah—prohibit the use of hidden cameras.

Reporters have defended the use of hidden microphones and cameras as the best and, occasionally, the only way to get some stories. Nevertheless, this practice is distasteful to many readers and viewers and may be contributing to the general disgust the public feels toward news organizations and journalists.

Giving Publicity to Private Facts

Everybody has secrets, and most people would be upset if their secrets were made public. Giving publicity to private facts presents the greatest potential for conflict with the First Amendment because an unfavorable judgment may punish truthful publications. A person who sues for this form of invasion of privacy must prove that:

- Publicity has been given to a private matter;
- The matter publicized would be highly offensive to a reasonable person; and
- There is no legitimate public interest in the information.

The information must be truly private. Publicizing facts that appear in public records but are not generally known cannot be the basis for a lawsuit. Property tax information is a matter of public record in most states. If a news organization publishes a list of the most valuable homes in the community, who owns them and how much the owners pay in property taxes, the people on that list cannot sue for invasion of privacy. Even if the information is not on a public record but is merely known to a large number of people, publicizing it does not invade that person's privacy. In the 1970s, a San Francisco man named Oliver Sipple saved the life of President Gerald Ford by disrupting an assassination attempt. A newspaper column later revealed that Sipple was gay, and he sued for invasion of privacy. The courts ruled that Sipple's homosexuality was already so widely known in the San Francisco gay community that he could not sue (Sipple v. Chronicle Publishing Co., 10 Media L. Rptr. 1690 [Cal. Ct. App. 1984]).

The information that is publicized must also be highly offensive to a reasonable person. By requiring that the information be "highly offensive," the law eliminates those pieces of information that may be only embarrassing. The "reasonable person" standard is imprecise, but it asks juries to judge this issue not by what would be offensive to the most sensitive or insensitive individual but by what the reasonable person would find highly offensive. Not surprisingly, many of the cases involve sex or nudity. For example, a Florida woman was abducted by her estranged husband and forced to strip while he held her hostage in an apartment. The crisis ended when the husband shot himself. Police rushed in, grabbed the woman and rushed her out of the apartment, leaving her time only to grab a tea towel. The local newspaper published a photograph of her being escorted to a police car and clutching the towel to her front. The woman sued, saying the photograph invaded her privacy, but a Florida appeals court ruled that the picture was not offensive enough to support a lawsuit. The photo, the court said, showed little more than could have been seen had the woman been wearing a bikini on a public beach (Cape Publications Inc. v. Bridges, 423 So.2d 426 [Fla. Dist. Ct. App. 1982]).

Even if the matter publicized is highly offensive to a reasonable person, the plaintiff still must prove that there is no legitimate public interest in the information. The U.S. Supreme Court has said, in effect, that where the subject matter is of legitimate public concern, the First Amendment sharply limits what penalties may be imposed on publications. The Supreme Court has faced the issue in cases involving publication of the names of rape victims. In one case, a Georgia television station used the name of a teen-age girl who had been raped and murdered. The girl's family sued under a state law prohibiting the publication of the names of rape victims. The Supreme Court ruled in favor of the television station, saying that the girl's name had been included on a public record. By placing that information in a public record, the state must have concluded that the girl's name was a matter of public interest. Therefore, the Constitution protected the right of the television station to broadcast it (Cox Broadcasting Co. v. Cohn, 420 U.S. 469 [1975]).

The First Amendment prohibits punishing the publication of truthful information obtained in a legal manner, the Supreme Court has said, unless doing so is essential to achieving a compelling state interest. This limitation applies to civil as well as criminal penalties. The difficulty of meeting this standard has led some states to question the constitutionality of their laws forbidding the publication of the names of rape victims. The Florida Supreme Court found that state's law unconstitutional. The court said the law was defective because it automatically imposed liability without regard to the circumstances of the case and because it applied only to publication in the mass media (Florida v. Globe Communications Corp., 23 Media L. Rptr. 1116 [Fla. 1994]).

Harcourt Brace & Company

The public interest in information is broad, and courts generally have interpreted this requirement in a way favorable to the news media. The public interest is broader in people who are public figures—movie stars, sports heroes and important political figures—but it may also include private individuals who have been caught up in newsworthy events. Moreover, the public interest extends beyond the event or situation that brought the person to public notice and includes other aspects of the subject's life and information about her or his relatives. But there is a line. Courts have said that the public interest does not extend to a morbid and sensational prying into private affairs with which the reasonable person would say he or she had no concern.

False Light

A false-light invasion of privacy lawsuit is similar in many respects to a libel suit. In fact, a person often may sue for either or both on the same set of facts. The major difference between them is that a libel suit redresses injury to a person's reputation, whereas a false-light suit protects a person's interest in being let alone. A false-light suit requires that publicity place a person in a false light and that the false light be highly offensive to a reasonable person. If a magazine used a photograph of an honest hitchhiker to illustrate an article about hitchhikers who rob motorists, then the hitchhiker could sue for both false light and libel. Not only was the hitchhiker portrayed in a false light, that person was, in effect, accused of criminal conduct. If, however, a newspaper portrays as a great hero a person who assisted in the rescue of a drowning swimmer when in fact that person's role had been minor, then the newspaper may be sued only for false light. Falsely portraying a person as a hero will not injure that person's reputation, although a reasonable person would find it offensive to have her or his role in a serious event deliberately fictionalized and distorted.

This photograph demonstrates the dangers of fictionalization. The original cutline accurately described its content, explaining that, "When parents reach old age, they and their children (like this 98-year-old man and his daughter) sometimes experienced sharp role reversal as children take care of their parents." However, the woman shown in the picture sued the magazine that later used the photograph to illustrate an article about Alzheimer's disease.

Because false light is so similar to libel, the U.S. Supreme Court has ruled that false-light plaintiffs, like libel plaintiffs, must prove actual malice. The court imposed that requirement in a 1960s false-light case, Time Inc. v. Hill (385 U.S. 374 [1967]). The court left unresolved the question of who must prove actual malice in false-light cases. Must all false-light plaintiffs prove actual malice or only public figures, as in libel cases? Some states have adopted a negligence standard for private individuals, but until the Supreme Court speaks no one can be sure what standard the First Amendment requires.

Appropriation

Anyone who appropriates the name or likeness of another for his or her own use or benefit may be sued for invasion of privacy. This was the first form of invasion of privacy to be recognized by the law. The most common form of appropriation is the use of a person's name or likeness for commercial purposes, as in an advertisement or television commercial.

A recent case of appropriation involved a promotional calendar for the profit-making corporation running the Choices Women's Medical Center in New York City. The calendar used photographs of people prominent in the women's movement and in women's medicine to illustrate each month. One photograph showed a woman physician whose consent the company had not obtained. She sued for appropriation and won. The court ruled that the calendar's purpose was to stimulate client referrals to the clinic and that the use of the physician's name and photograph was directly connected to that purpose (Beverley v. Choices Women's Medical Center, 19 Media L. Rptr. 1724 [N.Y. 1991]).

The use of a person's name or likeness in a news story is not considered appropriation, even though it may benefit the newspaper, magazine or broadcast by attracting readers, viewers and advertisers. The use of the name or likeness must have some reasonably direct connection to a news event, but courts have been lenient in deciding both what is a reasonable connection and what constitutes a newsworthy matter. A case involving actress Ann-Margret illustrates how broadly courts have construed newsworthiness. A magazine called High Society, which specializes in photographs of naked women, obtained a photo of Ann-Margret performing a nude scene for one of her movies. The magazine ran the photo in a section called "Celebrity Skin," and Ann-Margret sued for appropriation. A federal court ruled in favor of the magazine, saying information about entertainment, such as Ann-Margret's decision to perform a nude scene, is newsworthy (Ann-Margret v. High Society, 6 Media L. Rptr. 1774 [S.D.N.Y. 1980]).

The exemption from appropriation lawsuits for news publications and broadcasts extends to advertisements promoting them. A news interview program can use the name and likeness of a person who will be profiled in a future broadcast in advertisements promoting that broadcast. However, the advertisement must not suggest that the person is endorsing that program or station. Nor can a broadcast or publication infringe on a performer's right to make money from his or her act. The U.S. Supreme Court upheld a judgment against an Ohio television station that broadcast a human cannonball's act in its entirety. The court said the television station had infringed on the performer's right of publicity (Zacchini v. Scripps-Howard, 433 U.S. 562 [1977]).

The idea of a right of publicity is very similar to that of appropriation. To the extent that the two can be distinguished, the right of publicity protects more than just a person's name or likeness; it extends to other distinctive attributes of a person's identity, such as voice or appearance. Usually, the people who sue for violation of their right of publicity are celebrities and performers who have invested considerable time and talent in developing distinctive personalities or unusual performances. Most right-of-publicity lawsuits arise from advertisements that employ unknown actors who look like or sound like celebrities or that use other devices to conjure up images of celebrities. Because celebrities can get lots of money for advertisements and product endorsements, they often win large damage awards from advertisers who try to use celebrities' personalities without paying them.

Harcourt Brace & Company

NEWS GATHERING

The First Amendment expressly protects the right to speak and to publish, but it says nothing about the right to gather information. The Supreme Court has recognized that freedom of the press means very little if there is no right to gather information, but what rights news reporters have to information are largely defined by a hodgepodge of state and federal statutes and court opinions. This section covers three news-gathering issues: access to nonjudicial proceedings and records, access to judicial proceedings and confidentiality for sources and information.

Access to Nonjudicial Proceedings and Records

News Scenes

News happens in all kinds of places; some of them are not generally accessible to the public. News reporters have no greater right of access to news scenes than do ordinary citizens, but officials may extend access privileges to reporters as they see fit.

Journalists frequently cover accidents, fires, crimes and natural disasters, and in all cases, the photographers and reporters want to get as close to the action as possible. At the same time, police, rescue workers, firefighters and other authorities need to control such scenes to protect lives and property. The desire of the authorities to manage crisis scenes efficiently sometimes conflicts with the desire of journalists to gather information. When the conflicts reach the courts, judges usually side with the authorities. A photographer for a Milwaukee television station was convicted of disorderly conduct for refusing to obey a police officer's orders to leave the restricted area around the site of an airplane crash. The Wisconsin Supreme Court affirmed the conviction, saying the photographer's refusal to obey the order, combined with his continued penetration into a nonpublic area, was conduct that could provoke a disorder. The court said that although airplane crashes may be news, journalists cannot demand special access to them to get photographs and information (Oak Creek v. Ah King, 16 Media L. Rptr. 1273 [Wis. 1989]).

Police and other authorities sometimes go too far in trying to protect a crisis scene or provide security for government officials. Occasionally, authorities try to prevent photographers from taking pictures or reporters from gathering information. Some officers have gone so far as to confiscate cameras and film. Others have given favored news organizations access to news while denying it to others. Courts are more likely to rule in favor of news reporters and photographers who are not violating any lawful order and are not interfering with police and other authorities. California even has a law that says people, such as reporters and photographers, whose jobs require them to view emergency or disaster scenes should be allowed to do so. And if a public official discriminates among reporters on an impermissible basis, such as the reporter's race or gender or the editorial position of the news organization, the official may be sued for violating the civil rights of those denied access.

Access to Records and Meetings

The federal government and all state governments have laws that help reporters gain access to government records. The main federal law is the Freedom of Information Act (FOIA). This law, passed in 1966 and amended several times since, opens to public inspection all records held by agencies of the federal executive branch. The law *exempts* from disclosure nine categories of records:

1. Classified information.
2. Information related solely to internal personnel rules and practices.
3. Information exempted by other statutes.
4. Trade secrets and confidential commercial information.

Harcourt Brace & Company

5. Inter-agency and intra-agency memoranda that would reveal decision-making processes.
6. Information that would be a clearly unwarranted invasion of personal privacy.
7. Law enforcement investigative files the disclosure of which would or could cause certain harms.
8. Information about financial institutions.
9. Geological and geophysical information such as maps showing the locations of oil and mineral deposits.

The FOIA says federal agencies are supposed to release nonexempt information in response to any written request that reasonably identifies the records. Furthermore, the agency is supposed to respond within 10 working days. Actually getting the information, however, may take much longer. Most agencies have backlogs of requests for information, yet they devote relatively few resources to answering them. So it may take reporters many months or years to get the information they want. Nevertheless, the law remains an effective tool. Some reporters have used it to gather crucial information for important stories.

Two other federal statutes, the Government in the Sunshine Act and the Federal Advisory Committee Act, promote access to meetings. The Sunshine Act opens to the public the meetings of federal agencies that are led by boards or commissions having two or more members. The law exempts several categories of meetings, and many federal agencies do not formally meet to do their business. Instead, members do much of their work by circulating documents among themselves. The Federal Advisory Committee Act applies to the plethora of advisory committees appointed by the president and Congress to study various issues. Again, exemptions allow many of their deliberations to occur in secret.

All states and the District of Columbia have laws opening government records and meetings to the public and the press. The terms of these statutes, and their effectiveness, vary considerably. Some laws are very broad and have few exemptions. Others exempt dozens of kinds of records or meetings or have other qualifications that limit access. Usually, these laws apply to local governments, like cities, counties and school boards, as well as to state agencies. Because the state laws affect so many levels of government, many reporters use them almost daily.

Access to Judicial Proceedings

Freedom of the press is only one of many rights the Constitution guarantees to people in the United States. The right of a person accused of a crime to have a trial by an impartial jury of his or her peers is another constitutional right. These two rights appear to conflict when news organizations publish information that may influence potential jurors. Some authorities have labeled this problem "free press vs. fair trial," suggesting that one right must be sacrificed to the other. Fortunately, most judges, including those on the U.S. Supreme Court, have not phrased the problem so starkly. Rather, they have said the judge presiding over a trial must protect both the right of a defendant to a fair trial and the freedom of the press.

American courts have long recognized the power of news coverage to prejudice juries, but the problem has come into sharp focus only as the public has become concerned about the power of large media organizations and as the courts have moved to protect the civil rights of criminal defendants. In 1966, the Supreme Court said trial judges must protect judicial proceedings when there is a reasonable likelihood that news coverage may prejudice the trial. The court did not say what a judge may do *to* media organizations. Rather, it focused on steps a judge could take that would protect the trial without interfering with the news media. Among other things, the Supreme Court said, trial judges can sequester jurors, move trials to new locations if publicity becomes too intense, delay a trial and limit the kinds of statements prosecutors and defense attorneys may make to the press about a pending trial.

Although the Supreme Court said nothing about restraining what journalists say about court proceedings, soon judges started issuing "gag" orders, which prohibited reporters from publishing certain information even when that information came out in open court. The Supreme Court declared this kind of limitation on the press a prior restraint (Nebraska Press Association v. Stuart, 427 U.S. 539 [1976]). It is unconstitutional unless:

- A defendant's trial may be prejudiced by news coverage;

- No alternative to a prior restraint would protect the trial; and

- A prior restraint would be effective in preventing prejudice.

Some trial judges have dealt with prejudicial news coverage by denying journalists access to certain information. The easiest way to do this is by closing the courtroom door. The Supreme Court seemed to endorse that approach, at least in some situations, in a 1979 decision. Just a year later, the court revisited the issue and declared that the press and the public have a First Amendment right to attend trials. The Supreme Court has elaborated on this right of access through several decisions. As it now stands, the press and the public have a qualified First Amendment right to attend judicial proceedings to which there is a history of public access and at which the presence of the public benefits the process. There is a long history of public access to trials, for example, and having the public present helps the trial process by encouraging witnesses to be truthful and by serving as a check on the conduct of the police, the prosecutor and the judge. Similar concerns argue for public access to pretrial hearings, preliminary hearings and jury selection.

Courts may abridge the right of the press and the public to attend judicial proceedings when:

- There is a substantial likelihood of prejudice to the case;

- Closure of the courtroom would prevent the prejudice; and

- There are no alternatives to closure.

This is a very difficult standard to meet, because it requires the court to find facts establishing all these conditions. Occasionally, courts satisfy the burden. More often, they do not (Press-Enterprise v. Superior Court, 478 U.S. 1 [1986]).

The right of the press and the public to attend juvenile court hearings, family courts, divorce courts and some other judicial proceedings often is more restricted. The Supreme Court has not specifically ruled on access to these, but many states allow public attendance only at the discretion of the judge or where the judge finds that it serves a substantial or compelling interest.

The problems with gag orders and court closures became so severe in the 1970s that some state press and bar groups collaborated to write guidelines for dealing with each other during trials. The guidelines were supposed to be voluntary, but they were also supposed to protect the interests of news organizations and of criminal defendants. The bar-press guidelines vary from state to state, but common provisions are outlined in a sidebar on Page 514.

Protecting Confidential Sources and Information

For almost as long as reporters have written news, they have used confidential sources. And reporters routinely promise to protect the identities of those sources. Reporters know that they depend on confidential sources for some of their best stories and that they will get those stories only if sources trust them to protect their identities.

Sometimes law enforcement officials, grand juries, courts, legislative bodies or administrative agencies demand the names of a reporter's confidential sources or other information the

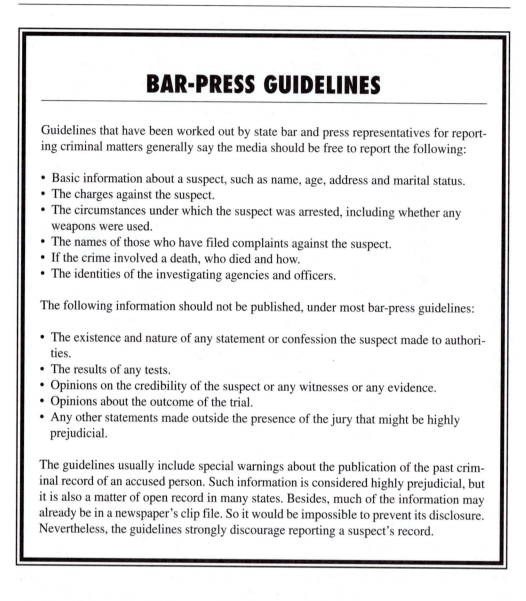

BAR-PRESS GUIDELINES

Guidelines that have been worked out by state bar and press representatives for reporting criminal matters generally say the media should be free to report the following:

- Basic information about a suspect, such as name, age, address and marital status.
- The charges against the suspect.
- The circumstances under which the suspect was arrested, including whether any weapons were used.
- The names of those who have filed complaints against the suspect.
- If the crime involved a death, who died and how.
- The identities of the investigating agencies and officers.

The following information should not be published, under most bar-press guidelines:

- The existence and nature of any statement or confession the suspect made to authorities.
- The results of any tests.
- Opinions on the credibility of the suspect or any witnesses or any evidence.
- Opinions about the outcome of the trial.
- Any other statements made outside the presence of the jury that might be highly prejudicial.

The guidelines usually include special warnings about the publication of the past criminal record of an accused person. Such information is considered highly prejudicial, but it is also a matter of open record in many states. Besides, much of the information may already be in a newspaper's clip file. So it would be impossible to prevent its disclosure. Nevertheless, the guidelines strongly discourage reporting a suspect's record.

reporter wants to protect. The lawyers and judges want this information because they think it is relevant to some criminal or civil court case. In such cases, reporters may receive subpoenas ordering them to appear and testify before some official body. The subpoena may also direct them to bring notes, photographs, tapes and other materials they may have collected in the process of gathering news. A person who fails to comply with a subpoena can be cited for contempt of court and sent to jail or fined or both.

Subpoenas are a common problem for news reporters. The Reporters Committee for Freedom of the Press conducted a five-year study, involving three surveys of media organizations, to discover the extent of the problem. The committee's final survey found that more than half of the responding news organizations had been subpoenaed. More than 80 percent of the broadcast stations had received subpoenas, often for unbroadcast video or audio tape (outtakes) as well as for tape that had aired. Newspapers were less likely to receive subpoenas, but when they did, the subpoenas often demanded confidential information or sources.

Reporters have had mixed success resisting subpoenas in the effort to protect their sources and to prevent interference with their news gathering. The U.S. Supreme Court in the Branzburg v. Hayes (408 U.S. 665 [1972]) case rejected the idea that the First Amendment gives journalists

Harcourt Brace & Company

any special protection from being subpoenaed to testify before grand juries. The court said although news gathering enjoys some constitutional protection, every citizen has a duty to provide relevant information to a grand jury. Some justices disagreed with the Branzburg decision. The dissents and the ambiguity of the majority opinion opened the door for courts in 16 states to recognize a limited privilege for reporters to protect confidential sources or information or both. The extent of this privilege varies greatly, but usually it allows reporters to protect confidential sources *except* where the information is essential to a case, can be obtained in no other way and would serve a compelling governmental interest.

Another 29 states and the District of Columbia have shield laws that specifically guarantee a journalist's right to protect confidential sources or information. Again, the laws vary in the level of protection they offer. What is protected in one state may not be in another. Some state laws let journalists protect both sources and unpublished information. Others limit the protection to confidential sources. Also, some states grant reporters a nearly absolute privilege to refuse to testify, while others qualify the privilege. However, even in states that recognize an absolute privilege, journalists are required to provide information vital for securing a criminal defendant's constitutional right to a fair trial. Also, journalists usually can be compelled to testify about information that has been published or events they witnessed personally.

CHECKLISTS

Elements of a Libel Suit

1. **Defamation:** A communication is defamatory when it lowers the plaintiff in the estimation of the community and deters others from associating or doing business with him or her.
2. **Identification:** A reasonable reader or viewer would conclude that the defamatory statement was "of and concerning" the plaintiff.
3. **Publication:** At least one person other than the publisher and the plaintiff saw or heard the defamatory statement.
4. **Injury:** The defamatory statement injured the plaintiff financially or through loss of reputation, mental anguish or humiliation. (Not required if the plaintiff proves the statement was made with actual malice.)
5. **Falsity:** If the defamatory statement is about a matter of public concern, the plaintiff must prove it false.
6. **Fault:** If the plaintiff is a public official or public figure, he or she must prove actual malice—that is, that the defendant knew the defamatory statement was false or had a high degree of awareness of its probable falsity. If the plaintiff is a private individual, he or she must prove that the defendant published the statement negligently.

Public Officials and Public Figures

1. A **public official** is someone who has or appears to the public to have substantial control over the conduct of public affairs and who holds a position important enough that the public has an independent interest in his or her qualifications.
2. A **general-purpose public figure** is someone who has such persuasive power and influence as to be a public figure for all occasions.
3. A **limited-purpose public figure** is someone who has thrust himself or herself to the forefront of a public controversy in order to affect its resolution.

Harcourt Brace & Company

Libel Defenses

1. **Truth:** A defendant can win a libel suit by proving that the sting or gist of the defamatory statement is true.
2. **Qualified privilege:** Journalists may report defamatory statements made in official proceedings or documents so long as their reports are full, fair and accurate.
3. **Fair comment and criticism:** Statements about matters of public interest that cannot be proved false or do not appear to state facts about the plaintiff are protected.

Privacy

1. A lawsuit for **intrusion** is possible when one party intentionally intrudes on another's seclusion or solitude in a manner that would be highly offensive to a reasonable person. This would include eavesdropping, electronic surveillance or photographing someone using a high-power telephoto lens.
2. A lawsuit for **publicity to private facts** requires proof that the facts were private, that their disclosure would be highly offensive to a reasonable person and that the information was of no legitimate public concern.
3. A plaintiff in a **false-light** lawsuit must show that the false light would be highly offensive to a reasonable person and was published with knowledge that the story was false or with reckless disregard for whether it was false.
4. Using another person's name or likeness for one's benefit without that person's permission may be an unlawful **appropriation** of that person's identity. Use of a person's name or likeness in connection with a news story is exempt.

News Gathering

1. The U.S. Supreme Court has said the First Amendment affords some protection to news gathering, but generally, reporters have the same right of access to places and information as ordinary citizens.
2. Some federal laws, mainly the Freedom of Information Act, require the federal executive branch to disclose information, with some exceptions.
3. State laws regarding open meetings and open records provide access to information about government at the state and local levels.
4. Judges presiding at trials must protect both freedom of the press and the right of the parties to a fair trial.
5. Judges can impose prior restraints on news reporters only if evidence shows there is a substantial probability of prejudice to the trial, no alternative to a prior restraint would protect the trial, and the prior restraint would prevent prejudice.
6. The press and the public have a First Amendment right to attend court proceedings when there is a history of public access to that type of proceeding and when public observation benefits the proceeding.
7. When the press and public have a First Amendment right to attend a court proceeding, judges can close the courtroom only if the evidence shows there is a substantial probability of prejudice to the trial, closure would prevent the prejudice, and alternatives to closure would not be effective.
8. The Supreme Court recognizes no First Amendment right for reporters to refuse to testify about confidential sources and information.
9. Some state and federal courts recognize a limited privilege for reporters to withhold confidential information and sources.

10. Twenty-nine states and the District of Columbia have shield laws that provide some degree of protection for confidential sources or information. The laws differ greatly as to who and what is protected and under what circumstances.

SUGGESTED READINGS

Adler, Renata. *Reckless Disregard: Westmoreland v. CBS et al.; Sharon v. Time*. New York: Knopf, 1986.

Bezanson, Randall P., Gilbert Cranberg, and John Soloski. *Libel Law and the Press: Myth and Reality*. New York: The Free Press, 1987.

Gillmor, Donald M. *Power, Publicity, and the Abuse of Libel Law*. New York: Oxford University Press, 1992.

Hixon, Richard F. *Privacy in a Public Society: Human Rights in Conflict*. New York: Oxford University Press, 1987.

Hopkins, W. Wat. *Actual Malice: Twenty-Five Years After Times v. Sullivan*. New York: Praeger, 1989.

Kaufman, Henry R., ed. *Libel Defense Resource Center 50-State Survey 1992–93*. New York: Libel Defense Resource Center, 1993.

Lewis, Anthony. *Make No Law: The Sullivan Case and the First Amendment*. New York: Random House, 1991.

Littlewood, Thomas B. *Coals of Fire: The Alton Telegraph Libel Case*. Carbondale, IL: Southern Illinois University Press, 1988.

Powe, Lucas A., Jr. *The Fourth Estate and the Constitution: Freedom of the Press in America*. Berkeley, CA: University of California Press, 1991.

Sanford, Bruce W. *Libel and Privacy*, 2nd ed. Englewood Cliffs, NJ: Prentice-Hall Law & Business, 1985, 1993.

Smolla, Rodney A. *Law of Defamation*. Deerfield, IL: Clark Boardman Callaghan, 1986, 1994.

———. *Suing the Press: Libel, the Media and Power*. New York: Oxford University Press, 1986.

Spence, Gerry. *Trial by Fire: The True Story of a Woman's Ordeal at the Hands of the Law*. New York: Morrow, 1986.

Name _____ Class _____ Date _____

E X E R C I S E   1

LIBEL

INSTRUCTIONS: Decide which of the following sentences and paragraphs are potentially libelous. Place a "D" in the space preceding each statement that is dangerous for the media, and an "S" in the space preceding each statement that is safe.

1. _____ The police officers said they shot and wounded Ira Andrews, a 41-year-old auto mechanic, because he was rushing toward them with a knife.

2. _____ Testifying during the second day of his trial, Mrs. Andrea Cross said her husband, Lee, never intended to embezzle the $70,000, but that a secretary, Allison O'Hara, persuaded him that their actions were legal. Her husband thought they were borrowing the money, she said, and that they would double it by investing in real estate.

3. _____ A 72-year-old woman, Kelli Kasandra of 9847 Eastbrook Lane, has been charged with attempting to pass a counterfeit $20 bill. A convenience store clerk called the police shortly after 8 a.m. today and said that she had received "a suspicious-looking bill." The clerk added that she had written down the license number of a car leaving the store. The police confirmed the fact that the $20 bill was counterfeit and arrested Mrs. Kasandra at her home about an hour later.

4. _____ Margaret Dwyer said a thief, a boy about 14, grabbed her purse as she was walking to her car in a parking lot behind Memorial Hospital. The boy punched her in the face, apparently because she began to scream and refused to let go of her purse. She said he was blond, wore glasses, weighed about 120 pounds and was about 5 feet 6 inches tall.

5. _____ Police said the victim, Catherine White of 4218 Bell Ave., was too intoxicated to be able to describe her assailant.

6. _____ "I've never lived in a city where the officials are so corrupt," Joyce Andrews, a Cleveland developer, complained. "If you don't contribute to their campaigns, they won't do anything for you or even talk to you. You have to buy their support."

7. _____ The political scientist said that Americans seem unable to elect a competent president. "Look at who they've elected," she said. "I'm convinced that Lyndon Johnson was a liar, Nixon was a crook, Carter was incompetent, and Reagan was the worst of all: too lazy and senile to be even a mediocre president."

8. _____ The newspaper's restaurant reviewer complained: "I've had poor service before, but nothing this incompetent. The service at The Heritage Inn wasn't just slow; it was awful. When she finally did get to us, the waitress didn't seem to know what was on the menu. Then she brought us the wrong drinks. When we finally got our food, it was cold and tasteless. I wouldn't even feed it to my dog. In fact, my dog wouldn't eat it. The stuff didn't even smell good."

9. _____ Police Chief Barry Kopperud said: "We've been after Guiterman for years. He's the biggest drug dealer in the city, but it took months to gather the evidence and infiltrate his operations. His arrest last night was the result of good police work, and we've got the evidence to send him away for 20 or 30 years."

10. _____ A police officer in your city, George Ruiz, today filed a $100,000 personal injury suit against Albert Tifton, charging that Tifton punched him in the nose last month while the police were responding to a call about a domestic dispute at Tifton's home. "It's the third time I've been hit this year," Ruiz said. "I'm tired of being used as a punching bag by these criminals, and I'm doing what I can to stop it."

11. _____ There was an emergency meeting of about 100 angry parents at the Wisconsin Avenue branch of the YMCA at 8 p.m. yesterday, with its director, Marty Willging, presiding. Willging said he called the meeting to calm the parents' fears and to respond to rumors. A parent asked whether it was true that the YMCA's janitor had been dismissed for molesting several boys. Willging responded that there had been some unfortunate incidents and the janitor had been discharged, but some of the allegations were exaggerated. When asked whether the police had been called in, Willging answered that they had, and that their investigation is continuing. He assured the parents that the YMCA will see that the matter is resolved appropriately.

EXERCISE 2

COMMUNICATIONS LAW

LIBEL

INSTRUCTIONS: Write an essay analyzing whether the news organization in the following situation can be sued successfully for libel. Consider all the elements of a libel case and how likely the plaintiff would be to prove each. Consider also whether the plaintiff is a public official, public figure or private individual. Finally, consider what defenses the news organization might use.

When Local 1313 of the Municipal Employees Union and the Beacon City Council negotiated a new labor contract for the city's employees last year, the union was represented by Sam Fong, its chief negotiator. The Beacon negotiations were stressful and stormy, with accusations of bad-faith bargaining made by both sides. At one point, the union threatened to strike if its demands were not met.

As the strike deadline approached, Hilda Jackson, reporter for the Beacon Daily Light, prepared a story that profiled Fong and described the union's negotiating strategy. Jackson talked to a number of people familiar with Fong and the way he conducted labor negotiations.

Jackson's story included the comments of Paula Williams, a city councilwoman, who said during a council meeting: "Fong is a first-rate bastard. That S.O.B. is trying to extort a fortune from the city. If we give him what he wants, we'll be broke, and if we don't, he'll shut down the city with a strike."

Another of Jackson's sources is Ben Davis, a union member with a grudge against Fong and a history of alcoholism. Davis said Fong had promised to keep union members informed about negotiations and to get their advice and guidance, but instead he had kept the members in the dark. Davis also said he suspected that union money had been used to hire prostitutes for union officials. He said a union bookkeeper had information that could confirm his story, but Jackson did not talk to him. Nevertheless, she included Davis' allegations in her story.

Jackson also reported that Fong had been convicted of automobile theft when he was 19 and had spent five years in a state penitentiary. Because Jackson failed to read the entire record of the case, her report was incorrect. Fong had served only 18 months of his five-year sentence and was placed on parole because of his good behavior.

Immediately after Jackson's story was published, Fong's wife sued him for divorce, alleging adultery and citing the allegation that union officials had engaged prostitutes as an instance of adultery. National union leaders also commenced an investigation of how Fong was spending his expense account money. The national union concluded that the charges of misuse of union money were groundless, but it dismissed Fong anyway for having failed to disclose his conviction for auto theft when he applied for his job.

EXERCISE 3

COMMUNICATIONS LAW

LIBEL

INSTRUCTIONS: Write an essay analyzing whether the news organization in this situation can be sued successfully for libel. Consider all the elements of a libel case and how likely the plaintiffs would be to prove each. Consider also whether each plaintiff is a public official, public figure or private individual. Finally, consider what defenses the news organization might use.

U.S. policy toward the Central American country of Costa Grande, where there is a civil war, has been the subject of extensive debate in Congress, a key issue in some congressional elections and a major news story for some months. As part of its coverage of the topic, the Continental Broadcasting Co.'s Nightly News program has investigated and broadcast a story alleging that three people, including a prominent federal official, were involved in sending arms and supplies to rebels in Costa Grande in violation of U.S. law.

One was Russell Starr, a retired Army general, who is considered an expert on Central American insurgency movements. He is president of an organization that has promoted the cause of the Costa Grande rebels. He has written newspaper and magazine pieces about the justness of the rebels' cause and has defended them on television talk shows. The second figure is Ronda Vernon, who recently became the third wealthiest person in the country when she inherited the fortune her father earned in the computer software business. Vernon rarely appears in public and never comments on political matters, but through various trust funds that she and her family control, she has donated millions of dollars to controversial groups, including the Costa Grande rebels. The last key figure in the Nightly News piece is Sean Grady, assistant secretary of state for Central American affairs, the member of the administration with primary responsibility for formulating and carrying out U.S. policy in that region.

The Nightly News story said that Starr had used dummy corporations and numbered Swiss bank accounts to channel money from his organization to the purchase of arms and supplies for the rebels. Several men involved in the illegal arms trade, all convicted felons, told reporters about Starr's financial arrangements. The information from the arms dealers was corroborated for the most part with information from several reliable staff members of congressional committees. The congressional staffers were familiar with classified information on Starr's dealings. Starr denied any wrongdoing and steered reporters to sources who would back him up. But the Nightly News reporters ignored Starr's sources because none had any inside knowledge.

The Nightly News said that Vernon had contributed $3 million to Starr's organization in full knowledge that some of the money was being sent illegally to the Costa Grande rebels. This part of the story was based on interviews with various people who had helped manage some of the Vernon family trust funds and on financial statements. Because of a reporter's arithmetic error, however, the Nightly News exaggerated the size of Vernon's contributions to the Costa Grande rebels by $700,000.

As for Grady, the news broadcast said he had used his official position in order to persuade federal agencies to ignore the trio's illegal activities. Nightly News' only source for this was another State Department official, who is known to covet Grady's job. The official said he learned about Grady's efforts to obstruct any federal investigation of Starr and Vernon when a glitch in the telephone system enabled him to overhear a conversation between Grady and an FBI agent. The network's reporters failed to check with the Federal Bureau of Investigation to find out whether any of its agents had even tried to investigate the flow of arms and cash to the Costa Grande rebels.

Starr, Vernon and Grady all sued the network for libel.

Harcourt Brace & Company

E X E R C I S E 4

COMMUNICATIONS LAW

PRIVACY

INSTRUCTIONS: Write an essay analyzing whether the news organization in this situation can be sued successfully for invasion of privacy. Consider all four forms of invasion of privacy and decide whether the plaintiff would be able to prove any of them.

Jasmine Lynd is a model-turned-actress who has appeared on the covers of many fashion magazines and in several major motion pictures. She attended a reception at the governor's mansion and stayed late for a private cocktail with the governor. The next day, Lynd reported to the police that the governor had raped her. The incident drew intense coverage from the press, including the Weekly Intelligencer, a tabloid newspaper sold mainly in supermarkets. In the past, Lynd had angered Intelligencer editors by refusing requests for interviews and threatening libel suits. One editor told the reporters covering the case, "This is our chance to pay her back."

Lynd would not talk to Intelligencer reporters, so they spoke to a number of her friends and acquaintances. One friend described Lynd's high school career, saying that she had been a "party girl" who had barely passed her courses and had frequently been in trouble with school authorities. Another source mentioned that Lynd had overcome, with great effort, a severe stuttering problem as a teen-ager.

Other Intelligencer reporters examined court records and learned that Lynd had three arrests for speeding and one for drunken driving. Other records showed that her husband had divorced her because she had been unfaithful. Her ex-husband said in an interview with reporters that he had discovered Lynd's infidelity when she gave him a venereal disease she had picked up from her lover, a professional wrestler. The wrestler told reporters that Lynd had an irrational fear of food preservatives, chewed her fingernails compulsively, and always slept in the nude. Lynd has denied none of these statements.

The divorce records also provided reporters with information about Lynd's finances, including the fact that she had purchased a controlling interest in a television production business and several pieces of commercial real estate, all of which more than tripled in value in only two years. One of Lynd's former friends, a woman who had known her in high school but had not seen her for 15 years, said that Lynd never made a business investment without consulting the famous astrologer Wesley Wilson. Wilson denied that Lynd was one of his clients, but the Intelligencer published the assertion anyway.

The Intelligencer's editors dispatched two teams of photographers to get photos for the story. One team followed Lynd wherever she went—work, shopping, social events—constantly snapping photos. On one occasion, trying to get a photo of her driving on the freeway, they maneuvered their car so close to hers that she swerved to avoid them and grazed a safety railing. Another team of photographers stationed themselves at the side of a highway on a hill overlooking Lynd's expensive home. From that location, the photographers used powerful telephoto lenses to get pictures of Lynd sunbathing and swimming in her back yard (which is surrounded by a high privacy fence).

Even though Lynd had not talked to reporters since she charged the governor with rape, the Intelligencer promoted its story about her with an advertisement in several newspapers saying, "Meet Jasmine Lynd. Find out what Lynd told the Intelligencer that she would tell no one else. You can depend on the Intelligencer—just as Lynd does—to deliver the truth!"

Lynd has filed a lawsuit alleging that the Weekly Intelligencer has invaded her privacy by placing her in a false light, giving publicity to private facts, intruding upon her solitude and seclusion and appropriating her name and likeness.

Harcourt Brace & Company

CHAPTER 21

ETHICS

If the press is truly free, it follows that it will not always be "responsible," and anything that tends to enforce its "responsibility" necessarily makes it less than free.

(Tom Wicker of *The New York Times*)

Almost every decision that a journalist makes is value-laden, a judgment call: which story is more important to report, whom to interview, what questions to ask, what angle to take, whom to quote, which side to present first, how long to make the story, where to place the story in a newspaper or broadcast, and so forth. Different decisions bring different results. In addition, some decisions involve weighty issues such as fairness and balance. All decisions affect others.

Journalists examine their actions on the basis of common and personal standards. They think about organization, industry and society norms. They are familiar with the need to balance the scales of business—making a profit—and conscience. Most journalists try to work ethically, which means acting and thinking morally. To be moral means to distinguish between right and wrong.

This chapter should increase your understanding about ethical issues, aid in your development of ethical guidelines and practices, and help you justify your decisions and actions.

MEDIA CREDIBILITY

No matter what journalists and their editors decide, some audience members are likely to criticize their decision. Audiences have a wide range of complaints: the media have become too big, powerful, arrogant and insensitive; the media are too critical and report too much bad news; the media are too sensational and more interested in their profits than in serving the public.

Although some criticisms are justified, media credibility is important to maintain for two main reasons. First, media organizations are a business; they sell audience numbers to advertisers. Thus, to succeed as a business, media need audiences—consumers for products—in order to attract advertisers, who support the media financially. Once audiences begin to doubt the credibility of a particular news organization, they will change the channel or stop buying that newspaper. When audiences turn away, advertisers do the same. Then the media organization's budget shrinks, which often means even poorer news coverage. The downward spiral usually continues until that news organization is no longer in business.

Second, people depend on media for their information. In the old days, people rarely traveled outside their community and received most of their information through word of mouth. Today, when people want information, they usually read a newspaper or listen to broadcast news. Modern news organizations give the same information to thousands of people. Often, people make important decisions on the basis of information obtained from news media. These are the central reasons it is important for media to be credible.

ETHICAL DECISION MAKING

When a story is wrong or unethical, people usually berate the organization, which in turn reprimands or dismisses the reporter or editor responsible for it.

Guiding Questions

A journalist can ask several questions when facing an ethical dilemma. Two of the most important are:

- Whom does it hurt?

- Whom does it help?

Many news stories do hurt someone or some group. Weighing the hurt against the benefits, and justifying that hurt, can make the right decision apparent. If the story hurts several people and helps several hundred, then the story is most likely important. Perhaps a physician has been accused of misdiagnosing patients' symptoms, errors which have led to incorrect surgeries. The story might embarrass the physician's family and clinic co-owners, but would help many patients and potential patients.

A retired journalist and professor, H. Eugene Goodwin, told his reporters and students to ask themselves six additional questions while making an ethical decision:

1. What do we usually do in cases like this? (What is the news organization's policy on this type of situation, and is it a good policy?)
2. Are there better alternatives? (Harmful results often can be avoided or eased by trying something different.)
3. Can I look myself in the mirror tomorrow? (You must think about how you feel, and if you can live with your decision.)
4. Can I justify this to family, friends and the public? (If we know we have to explain our decisions to the public—in an editor's column, for example—then we might be more careful about our decisions.)
5. What principles or values can I apply? (Some overlying principles, such as truth, justice or fairness, will take priority over others.)
6. Does this decision fit the kind of journalism I believe in and the way people should treat one another? (Our judgments should correspond with the way we believe the media ought to be and the way people in a civilized society ought to behave.)*

Macro and Micro Issues

Journalists wrestling with ethical decisions should identify a story's macro and micro issues. The macro issue is the main objective or reason for using the story. Micro issues tend to be less significant, but important. Too often journalists get caught up in micro issues and forget a story's real objective—the macro issue.

For example, Michigan police began receiving complaints from motorists. A popular rest stop was becoming a hangout for homosexual men, who were sexually accosting travelers in the

---

* H. Eugene Goodwin, *Groping for Ethics in Journalism,* 2nd ed. Ames, IA: Iowa State University Press, 1987, pp. 24–25.

A furniture store owner in St. Louis, Ron Olshwanger, received the Pulitzer Prize for spot news photography for his photo showing a firefighter giving mouth-to-mouth resuscitation to a child pulled from a burning building.

men's toilet. The police planned a sting operation to videotape the troublemakers in action. The police were able to identify and arrest some suspects.

A local newspaper wanted to publish the story. Editors discussed printing the names of the accused. Many had wives, children and colleagues who knew nothing of their homosexuality nor of their criminal actions. Editors realized that publicity could ruin reputations, marriages and careers. One man was a scout leader and another was in a seminary.

Some micro issues included: (1) placement—a story placed on an inside page is less damaging to the accused than a story on the front page; (2) space—a short story is not as noticeable as

Harcourt Brace & Company

a longer one; and (3) graphics and visuals—the type and number of illustrations, if any, can set a tone.

The editors revisited the macro issue: making the rest stop safe for community members and travelers. Once the macro issue was identified, the micro issues were resolved more easily. The newspaper printed the story on Page 1 with a list of names of the accused.

Journalists discuss ethical issues among themselves. Sometimes the answer to an ethical question becomes apparent as a reporter explains it to others or asks for input from co-workers with more experience.

ETHICS ISSUES

The public questions the techniques some journalists use to obtain the news. Rude, aggressive reporters seem willing to do anything to get a story: invade people's privacy, invent details and interview the victims of crimes and accidents while they are still in shock. In the past, reporters slanted some stories and invented others. Some reporters stole pictures from the homes of people involved in the news. Other reporters impersonated police officers or accepted expensive gifts from people they wrote about.

Despite the public's criticisms, the fact is that journalists in general are acting more ethically and professionally than ever before. They are better educated and better paid. They are also doing more to raise their ethical standards.

Today's journalists generally agree that it is unethical to fabricate a story or to accept anything of value from a source. Other issues are more complex because they involve conflicting values. A journalist may want to report an important story, but fear that it would intrude on an individual's privacy. Or a journalist may want to publish an important document, but hesitate because a source stole the document or because a federal official insists that it is a "state secret."

Unfortunately, other problems compound the public's criticisms of the press. Journalists want to report stories that the public needs to know, not just stories that the public wants to read. Journalists feel an obligation to inform the public about every important event occurring in their communities. Many Americans, however, worry about the stories' effects. They want journalists to be more sensitive and to suppress stories that are unpleasant or sensational or likely to harm people involved in the news.

Journalists reject the notion that they have a responsibility to suppress any stories. Katharine Graham, former publisher of The Washington Post, explained:

> To say the press ought to suppress some news if we deem it too bad or too unsettling is to make the press into the censor or the nursemaid of a weak and immature society. We cannot serve ourselves and our heritage by running away from our troubles. . . . National security does not rest on national ignorance. This is hardly the faith of a free people.

Each ethical situation is unique, and journalists must consider each individually, trying to balance the conflicting values or to decide which value is most important. While covering one story, journalists may decide to protect an individual's privacy. While covering another story, journalists may decide that the community's need to know is more important than protecting a source's identity. Regardless of what they decide, it is impossible for journalists to convince every person that they made the right decision. Thus, some criticisms are inevitable.

OBJECTIVITY

Objectivity has two meanings: absence of bias, and accuracy. Everyone has biases and opinions. Journalists' biases can greatly affect a story. Biases often subtly influence which story is picked over another, who is interviewed, what types of questions are asked, the angle a story takes and how it is organized and presented. For instance, it might be difficult for a journalist who is pro-choice to write an objective story about a new federal bill limiting abortions. To avoid the problem, journalists avoid topics about which they are strongly opinionated. They may unintentionally interview only sources who share their opinions. Journalists aware of their prejudices may go too far in the opposite direction in their efforts to present an objective story. This still results in a one-sided story.

Journalists let their editors know when they cannot cover a subject objectively. The editor will then assign the story to another reporter.

Objectivity also means being accurate. However, objective facts without context can create inaccurate impressions. Journalists who report that a married female mayor often ate lunch and worked late with a male staffer may lead audiences to assume that mischief is afoot. Even if the journalists' statements are accurate, the story needs background information or context to help audiences correctly interpret the facts. In reality, the mayor may be working overtime with a staffer assigned to research an important budget issue the city council will vote on the following week.

REPORTING OR EXPLOITING GRIEF

A national public opinion survey found that 47 percent of the country's adults believe the media do not care about the people they report on. An even greater number—73 percent—believe the media have no regard for people's privacy. The public is especially critical of the media's coverage of death and grief: of photographs of and interviews with grieving relatives. Some journalists insist that such interviews are necessary because they are the only way reporters can confirm important facts, learn more about the victims and obtain the survivors' stories.

Anantha Babbili and Tommy Thomason, professors at Texas Christian University, studied an example of the problem. When the space shuttle Challenger exploded, television cameras focused on the parents of Christa McAuliffe, the first civilian teacher to participate in the space program. Journalists wanted to record the parents' proud reaction to the launch. Instead, they recorded the parents' horror as they watched their daughter die. Babbili and Thomason wondered:

> Is the reaction of a mother to her daughter's tragic death of such public importance? The Constitution certainly implies that the public has a right to know. But do we have a right to intrude upon private sorrow of private individuals—even if they happen to be related to public figures? Was the constant replaying of those seconds of grief really necessary?

Interviewing Victims

Few journalists are psychologists. They may not realize that many disaster victims and their family members are in shock for several days after an event.

Reporters often harm a news organization's reputation when scrambling to get an early interview. Sometimes victims in shock inadvertently twist facts. Or, they may want to please the reporter by answering questions, even if they are not certain of the accuracy of the details they supply. Victims often complain after a story is used. The person may have been in shock at the time of the interview and unable to recall even talking to a reporter. Victims often recant their stories or accuse reporters of making up the interview.

Many journalists have found they obtain a more accurate and complete story if they wait several days to interview victims. Hard news stories can be written immediately after an event, with follow-up stories later.

A five-year-old boy drowned while swimming in Bakersfield, Calif., and this controversial photograph shows a rescue worker trying to console the victim's mother and siblings. The victim's father is on his knees. Robert Bentley, managing editor of The Bakersfield Californian, said: "I ran the picture because it was a powerful photograph, and it was news, and I'm a newsman." The picture also appeared in other newspapers, from Salt Lake City to Boston and Tampa.

The Californian received more than 400 telephone calls and 500 letters. A bomb threat forced employees to evacuate their office, and 80 readers canceled their subscriptions. People complained that the photograph showed a callous disrespect for the victim, and that it invaded the family's privacy at a moment of grief and shock. Bentley apologized, admitting that he had made a mistake. Photographer John Harte disagreed. "The picture should have run," Harte said. "It was a very good picture. This was an area where there have been a lot of drownings, and the photograph will have long-term benefits in making people aware of water safety and swimming safety."

VICTIMS' RIGHTS

The National Victim Center prepared this set of guidelines to help the victims of violent crime deal with the media. The center was formerly called the Sunny Von Bulow National Victim Advocacy Center.

As a journalist, you may disagree with some of the guidelines. They are likely to make your work as a journalist more difficult. The guidelines, however, reflect a growing concern about the victims of violent crime. The guidelines also reflect concern about journalists' treatment (or, in some cases, mistreatment) of victims.

1. **You have the right to say "no" to an interview.** Never feel that because you have unwillingly been involved in an incident of public interest, you must personally

Harcourt Brace & Company

share the details and/or your feelings with the general public. If you decide that you want the public to be aware of how traumatic and unfair your victimization was, you do not automatically have to give up your right to privacy. By knowing and requesting respect for your rights, you can be heard and yet not violated.

2. **You have the right to select the spokesperson or advocate of your choice.** Selecting one spokesperson—especially in multiple-victim cases—eliminates confusion and contradictory statements. You also have the right to expect the media to respect your selection of a spokesperson or advocate.

3. **You have the right to select the time and location for media interviews.** Remember, the media are governed by deadlines. However, nobody should be subjected to a reporter arriving unannounced at the home of a victim. When you are traumatized, your home becomes your refuge. If you wish to protect the privacy of your home, select another location such as a church, meeting hall, office setting, etc. It helps if you are familiar and comfortable with the surroundings.

4. **You have the right to request a specific reporter.** As a consumer of daily news, each of us identifies with or respects a reporter whom we may never have met. We often form personal opinions about reporters whom we feel are thorough, sensitive, compassionate and objective. If a newspaper, radio station or television station contacts you for an interview, don't hesitate to request the reporter you feel will provide accurate and fair coverage of your story.

5. **You have the right to refuse an interview with a specific reporter even though you have granted interviews to other reporters.** You may feel that certain reporters are callous, insensitive, uncaring or judgmental. It is your right to avoid these journalists at all costs. By refusing to speak to such reporters you may help them recognize their shortcomings in reporting victim-related stories. However, recognize that the reporters may write the story regardless of your participation.

6. **You have the right to say "no" to an interview even though you have previously granted interviews.** It's important to recognize that victims often ride an "emotional roller coaster." You may be able one day to talk with a reporter, and be physically or emotionally unable to do so the next. Victims should never feel "obliged" to grant interviews under any circumstances.

7. **You have the right to release a written statement through a spokesperson in lieu of an interview.** There may be times when you are emotionally incapable of speaking with the media, but you still wish to express your point of view. Writing and distributing your statement through a spokesperson allows you to express your views without personally granting interviews.

8. **You have the right to exclude children from interviews.** Children already suffering from the trauma of crime are often retraumatized by exposure to the media. Children often lack the means to verbalize their emotions and may be misinterpreted by both the media and the public. You have a responsibility to protect the interests of children at all costs!

9. **You have the right to refrain from answering any questions with which you are uncomfortable or that you feel are inappropriate.** You should never feel you have to answer a question just because it's been asked.

10. **You have the right to know in advance what direction the story about your victimization is going to take.** You have the right to know what questions reporters

(continued on next page)

will ask you, along with the right to veto any questions. This places you in a partnership with the reporter who is covering the story.

11. **You have the right to ask for review of your quotations in a story prior to publication.** Articles are reviewed and revised by editors who have neither seen nor spoken to you. All too often, victims' statements and the intended impact of their remarks are misinterpreted or inaccurate. To protect your interests and the message you wish to convey, you have the right to request a review of direct quotations attributed to you in the story.

12. **You have the right to avoid a press conference atmosphere and speak to only one reporter at a time.** At a time when you are in a state of shock, a press conference atmosphere with numerous reporters can be confusing and emotionally draining. If a press conference is absolutely unavoidable, you have the right to select one reporter to ask questions for the majority present.

13. **You have the right to demand a retraction when inaccurate information is reported.** All news media have methods of correcting inaccurate reporting or errors in stories. Use these means to correct any aspect of media coverage which you feel is inaccurate.

14. **You have a right to ask that offensive photographs or visuals be omitted from airing or publication.** If you feel that graphic photographs or visuals are not the best representation of you or your loved one, you have the right to ask that they not be used.

15. **You have the right to conduct a television interview using a silhouette or a newspaper interview without having your photograph taken.** There are many ways for reporters to project your physical image without using your photograph or film footage of you, therefore protecting your identity.

16. **You have the right to completely give your side of the story related to your victimization.** If you feel that a reporter is not asking questions which need to be addressed, you have the right to give a personal statement. And if the alleged or convicted offender grants interviews which are inaccurate, you have the right to publicly express your point of view.

17. **You have the right to refrain from answering reporters' questions during trial.** If there is any chance of jeopardizing your case by interacting with the media during judicial proceedings, you have the right to remain silent.

18. **You have the right to file a formal complaint against a reporter.** A reporter's superior would appreciate knowing when his or her employee's behavior is unethical, inappropriate or abusive. By reporting such behavior, you will also protect the next unsuspecting victim who might fall prey to such offensive reporters or tactics.

19. **You have the right to grieve in privacy.** Grief is a highly personal experience. If you do not wish to share it publicly, you have the right to ask reporters to remove themselves during times of grief.

20. **You have the right to suggest training about media and victims for print and electronic media in your community.** Resources are available to educate media professionals about victims, how to deal with victims, and how to refrain from traumatizing victims. You will be suggesting a greatly needed public service to benefit not only victims and survivors, but all members of the community who interact with the media.

21. **You have the right at all times to be treated with dignity and respect by the media.**

Harcourt Brace & Company

The News Story as a Second Wound

Frequently, a news story inflicts a second injury on victims and family members who lived through a disaster and experience it again when seeing the story on television or in a newspaper. For example, a young man was beaten, raped and dismembered, and his body parts were strewn along a deserted road. Journalists might have described the tragedy in detail and used sensational photographs of the scene. The result could have been painful for the victim's family. Instead, editors omitted sensational details and published only what the public needed to know. Even non-sensational stories may cause further pain to a victim or family.

Journalists debate the use of a 30-second close-up of a mother struggling to keep her composure or a brother crying. Is the close-up the only way to convey the depth of emotion in a story? Journalists discuss the purpose of the story, what the public needs to know and alternate ways to portray the emotion. They also weigh the crucial questions: Who will be hurt and who will be helped?

VISUALS: WHAT IS NEWSWORTHY? WHAT IS SENSATIONAL?

Editors will run a photograph or videotape because it seems important and helps tell a story. People upset by the editors' decisions accuse them of acting sensationally and of being more interested in selling papers than in helping people in distress. Critics assume journalists use that type

Many editors thought this photograph said much more than words could convey about the circumstances of American soldiers in Somalia. Readers could interpret for themselves the various pictures depicting the dead American's body condition, the Somalians' facial expressions and body language, and one participant's obscene gesture, not pictured here. Some readers were outraged that their newspaper printed the photograph. However, many editors cropped the photo in various ways to soften the shock it could produce. Almost all editors exercised some ethical restraint because the original photo showed the American soldier stripped completely nude as his body was dragged through the streets.

Would you publish these photographs in a daily newspaper? Does it matter that the man was a state official convicted of bribery, and killed himself during a press conference? Some newspapers used these photographs, but not a fourth taken after the official fired a single shot into his mouth.

Harcourt Brace & Company

of visual for shock effect. Critics are also concerned about a visual's effects: about whether the footage is too unpleasant, tasteless and upsetting.

Some editors feel cornered. Should they shield the public from unpleasantness or educate them? Most newspapers and television news programs used a photograph of a dead American soldier being dragged by ropes through the streets of Mogadishu in Somalia. Viewers were shocked. The soldier's body and the laughing faces of Somalians told a horrifying story. Because the soldier was not identified, hundreds of parents and wives were worried that the soldier was their relative, or at least that their son or husband might be next. The purpose of the photo, editors said, was to help describe this country's peacekeeping presence in Somalia. Many editors contended that words did not convey the situation as well as this photograph did.

Journalists in Pennsylvania faced a similar dilemma. The state treasurer, R. Budd Dwyer, shot and killed himself during a press conference. Dwyer, 47, had been convicted in a bribery scandal and faced up to 55 years in prison. He began the press conference by insisting that he was innocent and by accusing other government officials of conspiring against him. Near the end of a rambling 30-minute account, Dwyer began to also attack the press. Then he opened a manila envelope, pulled out a gun and fired one shot into his mouth. The entire episode—from the moment Dwyer pulled out the gun until he shot himself—took only 21 seconds. There were about 35 witnesses, primarily reporters and photographers.

WHTM-TV in Harrisburg broadcast the entire videotape, and so did two stations in Pittsburgh. Some parents complained that their children saw the suicide before anyone was able to change channels. Newscasters responded that the media should not sugarcoat reality. Another journalist explained: "The feeling was, this was a major news event and it was at a public press conference. It captures the horror of the story in terms everyone can understand and see. Pictures are part of the story." Stations elsewhere generally edited or discarded the videotape. Their edited versions showed Dwyer holding the gun, but not putting it into his mouth and pulling the trigger.

A California paper, the San Jose Mercury News, asked its readers "to grapple with some of the same questions editors face daily." Two of its questions involved controversial photographs. Readers were asked whether they would have used a photograph taken after a devastating earthquake. The photograph showed a woman, her legs horribly shattered, in agony as rescuers pulled her from the wreckage of a building.

Sometimes a photograph can have more impact than words. This image reflected the reality of a natural disaster's effect on humanity. About 74 percent of the San Jose (Calif.) Mercury News journalists said they would run this photo of a woman pulled from earthquake rubble, while 52 percent of their readers agreed.

Some editors who ran this photograph thought the image taught a lesson in a way words could not: This is what can happen when a youth tries to climb a six-foot iron fence with spikes on top. Twenty-six percent of the San Jose (Calif.) Mercury News journalists said they would publish the photo, and 23 percent of their readers agreed. (The boy survived the piercing.)

The second photograph was a close-up of a 15-year-old boy who had lost his footing while trying to climb a six-foot fence. As the boy fell, an iron fence post pierced his face. The boy hung from the fence, still conscious, and the picture captured his agony "as rescue teams used cutting torches to free him." Editors who printed the photograph called it "compelling" and "spellbinding." Those who rejected the photograph called it "gruesome," "grotesque" and "ghastly."

Seventy-four percent of the reporters and editors at the Mercury News, but only 52 percent of their readers, said that they would publish the photograph showing the injured woman being pulled out of the wreckage. Why? John Connell, the paper's religion and ethics editor, explained, "The earthquake was a horrible event, and no matter how unpleasant the image, they say the newspaper must mirror that reality. And this photo was one that made the whole story human."

There was more agreement between journalists and readers about the photograph of the impaled boy. Only 26 percent of the newspaper's reporters and editors, and 23 percent of their readers, said they would publish it.

News organizations must keep in touch with the public's attitudes. Journalists who see a lot of violence and unhappiness cannot assume that they know what the public will find acceptable.

INVASIONS OF PRIVACY

The media sometimes intrude on the privacy of individuals. They usually have a legal right to intrude, but do they have the moral or ethical right?

News organizations report the important events occurring in their communities, typically including every birth, engagement, marriage, divorce and bankruptcy. When people die, newspapers publish their obituaries, and some news accounts include everyone's age and cause of death. Many Americans consider the publicity embarrassing. They do not want anyone to know their age, nor that they are bankrupt or divorced. People are also embarrassed when the media publish the cause of a relative's death, especially when the cause is suicide or an illness with a social stigma, like AIDS.

Private Individuals

Some events are more obviously newsworthy than others. People who become involved in major lawsuits, crimes and accidents, even unintentionally, may expect to be mentioned in news stories about them.

Other decisions are more difficult. News organizations usually do not identify juvenile delinquents. But if several teen-agers are arrested and charged with committing a series of rapes and burglaries that terrorized a neighborhood, editors may feel a need to identify the teen-agers, and perhaps their parents as well. Editors may decide that their obligation to calm people's fears by informing the neighborhood about the arrests outweighs their normal obligation to protect the teen-agers and their families; the number of people that will be helped is larger than the number that will be hurt.

Some citizens become involved in the news by accident. Do they have the same right to privacy as the average citizen? Arthur Ashe was a public figure for many years, winning Wimbledon and other major tennis tournaments. When a USA Today editor learned that Ashe had AIDS, he wanted to print the story immediately. When he informed Ashe he was going to use the story, the retired tennis star gave a press conference first, telling the world about his condition. He had contracted the virus through a blood transfusion. Many people criticized the paper for violating Ashe's privacy. They insisted Ashe was no longer a public figure and should be allowed to die privately; certainly, he had no obligation to tell the public about his health. The USA Today editor countered that the story would help other people understand AIDS if the newspaper published a story about someone, such as the widely respected Arthur Ashe, who had the virus.

Public Figures

Journalists are often criticized for their treatment of government officials and other public figures. Journalists argue that the public's right to know outweighs a government official's or public figure's right to privacy. Most Americans seem to agree that journalists should expose government officials who abuse their power or who have personal problems, such as alcoholism, that affect their work.

But does the public have a right to know about a public official's private affairs, such as adultery? Some people say adultery does not affect a politician's public decision making. Other critics argue that if a politician breaks a solemn promise, such as a wedding vow, then promises to his or her constituency may also be meaningless. These critics say the public has a right to know about the character of the person who represents them.

Journalists become involved in controversies after overhearing—and reporting—remarks that were not meant for publication. Their victims are outraged and accuse journalists of invading their privacy and acting unfairly and unethically. Journalists respond that the remarks are newsworthy: that they reveal the speakers' true feelings, character and behavior. Some journalists add that public officials should be more careful to avoid saying anything in public that they would be ashamed to see in print.

When former President Ronald Reagan joked about bombing the Soviet Union, journalists reported the story. Reagan told the joke just before a radio broadcast, and it was accidentally

Harcourt Brace & Company

transmitted to a pressroom. During Jesse Jackson's 1992 campaign for the presidency, journalists also overheard—and reported—derogatory remarks he made about Jews.

Politicians charge that the press has gone too far. They wonder if the public really benefits from its scrutiny of public officials. Journalists respond that, unlike private citizens, politicians voluntarily place themselves in the public spotlight. They seek attention. In addition, most public figures should be role models for the citizenry they govern.

DECIDING WHEN TO NAME NAMES

Normally, journalists want to identify fully everyone mentioned in their stories. Most news organizations have adopted policies requiring their reporters and editors to do so. But some stories present especially thorny problems: stories about juveniles, rape victims, homosexuals, and prostitutes and their clients, for example. Because each situation is different, reporters and editors may want to examine them individually.

Juveniles

Traditionally, teen-agers who are under 18 and are accused or convicted of a crime have been shielded from public exposure because they supposedly do not understand what they did or the consequences of their crimes. In most cases, journalists do not publicize juveniles' names. The main exception occurs when juveniles have been tried in adult court. Authorities make the determination to try juveniles as adults for several reasons:

- The juveniles have been accused of a highly serious crime that children do not usually commit.

- The juveniles have been accused of understanding the severity of the crime and committing it anyway.

- The juveniles have a felony record and have not learned law-abiding behavior from previous forms of punishment reserved for juveniles.

Authorities then treat the teen-ager as they would an adult accused of the same crime, and so do journalists.

Victims of Sexual Assault

Most news organizations withhold the names of rape victims. Editors explain that a stigma is attached to rape and that the victims have already suffered enough. Editors do not want to add to the victims' suffering. Also, victims might be more reluctant to report rapes to the police if they thought their names would be revealed to the public.

Critics respond that the media have adopted a dual standard: They identify people charged with rape, but not their accusers. Critics add that the policy is an old-fashioned and paternalistic means of protecting women (the victims of most sexual assaults). They contend that rape should be treated like any other crime.

Increasingly, some victims want to be identified; they want to discuss the crime and help other victims. They feel that being open about rape will destigmatize the crime and correct the impression that it is somehow the victim's fault. Editors generally do not name a victim unless the victim wants to be identified.

Harcourt Brace & Company

Additional Cases

Journalists do not report anyone's sexual orientation unless it is central to a story. Journalists in doubt ask their standard questions: Whom does it hurt, and whom does it help? If announcing someone's sexual habits hurts one person but helps no one, then doing so is unnecessary.

Today, an entire neighborhood may become concerned when prostitutes begin doing business there. In some cities, coalitions of merchants, homeowners and government officials have organized to combat the problem. They encourage the police to make more arrests, and they encourage newspapers to publish the names of both prostitutes and their "johns," or customers.

The objective or macro issue is community service—to rid the community of an unsavory business that also attracts drug dealers. The macro issue is also a matter of fairness, since news organizations were practicing a form of discrimination when they identified prostitutes (mostly women) and shielded customers (mostly men). Both, after all, were breaking the law.

DECEIT: WHEN IS IT JUSTIFIED?

Journalists want everyone to believe in and trust them. But to obtain some stories, journalists feel compelled to lie or misrepresent themselves. Occasionally, there seems to be no alternative. The stories may be important, and helpful to thousands of people. They may, for example, expose crime or a government official's abuse of power.

Anonymity

Many journalists insist that anonymity is essential to their work. In some situations they may not lie about their identities, but simply fail to reveal them. Restaurant reviewers would be ineffective if everyone knew their identities. Restaurant owners, anxious to obtain more favorable publicity, would cater to the reviewers, offering them special meals and special service. As a result, the reviewers would be unable to describe the meals served to the average customer.

Other journalists may want to shop anonymously at a store whose employees have been accused of misleading customers. Or reporters may want to visit a fortune teller or attend a protest rally. If protesters realized several reporters were present, they might either act more cautiously or perform for the reporters, behaving more angrily or violently to ensure that they got into the news. Protesters might also harass or attack reporters who identified themselves.

Misrepresentation

Depending on their needs in gathering information, journalists sometimes lie about their identities. They may pose as patients while gathering information about a mental hospital. Or they may pretend to be laborers while writing about migrant workers' exposure to the chemicals sprayed on farm crops.

The Milwaukee Journal had long covered routine stories about the area's schools. Its metropolitan editor, Patrick Graham, wanted to get closer to the students: to learn "what they're thinking, what they're saying, what their likes and dislikes are, what their cherished aspirations might be." Graham also hoped to learn: "What do they really think about drugs and alcohol? About sex? About going to college? About what they'll be doing or want to do after school?" Reporter Vivian S. Toy agreed to enroll in a suburban high school. Toy, who was 25 but looked much younger, explained: "There's a natural wariness of any adult. I couldn't have broken through

Harcourt Brace & Company

that." A suburban school board gave the Journal permission to go undercover, provided the school's principal and teachers were notified. Later, while writing her story, Toy felt ethically obliged to conceal the identities of the individual students to whom she had talked.

A Chicago paper lost a Pulitzer Prize because other journalists objected to its use of a more elaborate disguise. To expose corruption in the city, the Chicago Sun-Times bought a tavern, which it renamed, appropriately, the Mirage Bar. With the help of the Better Government Association, the Sun-Times used the bar to photograph and tape-record city inspectors who, in return for payoffs, ignored the bar's violations of city health and safety standards. A panel nominated the Sun-Times for a Pulitzer Prize. Benjamin C. Bradlee, then executive editor of The Washington Post, served on a board that selected that year's prize winners, and Bradlee opposed the Sun-Times' nomination. Bradlee and other critics charged that the Sun-Times had created the story and that its reporters had become participants in it. These critics acknowledged the need to expose the city's corruption, but insisted that the Sun-Times did not have to buy a bar to obtain the story.

Typically, editors allow their reporters to use a disguise only when a story is important and there is no other safe way to obtain it. In addition, journalists think about the macro issue and about whom the story helps. While writing their stories, reporters are expected to admit their use of deception and to explain why it was necessary. Reporters are also expected to call everyone criticized in their stories and give them an opportunity to respond.

An Ombudsman's Report

CASE STUDY NO. 2

By **Henry McNulty**
Former Reader Representative
The Hartford (Conn.) Courant

Ask an editor whether newspapers ought to expose racial discrimination in the community, and the answer doubtless will be yes. Will the answer be the same if reporters must lie to uncover the discrimination?

That was the dilemma facing me last May when, as The Hartford Courant's reader representative, I examined a package of stories reporting racial bias among some Hartford-area real estate firms. The central question was: In this case, did the end justify the means?

For years, many of us at the paper had suspected that black people and white people are not treated the same when they look for homes. On May 21, The Courant provided the evidence. In some cases, real estate agents gave blacks tougher financial scrutiny than they did whites. Other times, blacks were "steered" to towns that already have significant minority populations.

Courant reporters had shown up at various real estate agencies apparently looking for a house. Two black and two white "testers" appeared to be nearly identical in every financial and personal detail—except race. They followed testing guidelines in a manual approved by state and federal fair-housing agencies. When they were with real estate agents, the reporters used altered names and provided other false information that masked their identities.

The investigation was meticulously prepared, carefully written and clearly presented. Immediately after it appeared, Connecticut's governor ordered a statewide investigation of real estate discrimination. This led many Courant editors to argue that the reporters' deception had been worth it.

With regret, I disagreed, and I said as much in my June 4 column. We had to lie to get the story, and for me, that was a fatal flaw. I don't think a news story, however important, can be based on deception.

It was not an easy conclusion to reach. There's a long history of reporters disguising themselves to root out corruption. And this investigation struck a strong blow for justice and equality.

But I can't think of a case in which such deception would be justified. Even when the goals are noble, as these certainly were, and even when the results are positive for the community, I think journalists must not lie.

The Courant's policy states: "We do not misrepresent ourselves" in pursuing a story. But that's quickly followed by the statement that, "From time to time, legitimate stories in the public interest might involve a conflict with (this policy)."

The escape clause essentially means we have a policy that permits deception. It flatly prohibits only casual or willy-nilly misrepresentation—but it lets us lie to get a story whenever we think we should. The real estate probe wasn't even an exception to the rules, since an exception is already built in.

To our credit, the testing procedure and the newspaper's policy were explained in a sidebar headed "How, Why the Test Was Done." At least we didn't hide the deception.

Saying, "Journalists shouldn't lie" opens up a host of questions. What about restaurant reviewers who pretend to be ordinary customers when in fact they intend to report on their dining experience? Aren't they misrepresenting themselves, too?

Perhaps. But there are many facets to the question of deceiving sources, and I feel each case must be examined closely. I make a distinction, for example, between actively giving a false name and passively letting someone assume a reporter is just an average consumer. Admittedly, not everyone is willing to make that distinction.

Could we have done the real estate story without telling lies? Maybe, but it would have been an arduous task. Executive Editor Michael E. Waller, who approved the project, thinks it would have been more difficult than that.

"To have an outside group . . . do the testing would still have posed problems," he said. "They would have had to misrepresent themselves—and I see little ethical difference between us misrepresenting ourselves and asking someone else to do it for us.

"Asking real home buyers . . . to be the testers posed, in my mind, insurmountable problems. The first would be finding the people to fit the test criteria and getting them to do it simultaneously and in a timely manner. The second would be keeping any reasonable control of accuracy, and assurance that they faithfully would follow all the testing guidelines."

He's probably right. So I say, with deep regret, that we couldn't—and so, we shouldn't—have done this investigation, despite its social importance.

After my column appeared, a handful of readers called me to support my position. For the most part, I had no way of knowing whether they had any stake in matters involving real estate, although one caller was a former Realtor. Another caller said he had just finished a course in journalism ethics at a local college, and a third amazed me by identifying himself as an investigative reporter at a competing newspaper!

There was moderate reaction inside the newspaper. A couple of reporters agreed with me; most didn't, saying that our deception was benign in comparison to the illegal activity we disclosed.

Credibility is our most important asset. And if we deceive people in order to do our job, we've compromised that credibility before a word is written.

Using Tape Recorders and Video Cameras

Journalists are reluctant to make secret recordings of their conversations, since the tactic may seem devious and unfair. Journalists also fear that, if sources learn that reporters secretly record some conversations, they may become more hesitant to speak candidly or refuse to speak at all.

Journalists use tape recorders to protect themselves in case they are accused of lying. Reporters fear that sources may claim the reporters had misquoted them or even fabricated the entire interview. Some sources honestly forget what they said. Others are shocked by how awful their statements appear in print. To defend themselves, they claim that the statements attributed to them are inaccurate.

If journalists record their interviews, however, they can prove their stories are accurate. They can also protect themselves more easily in libel suits. In the rare cases when journalists do record a conversation, most try to do so openly, with their sources' permission.

The reasons for hiding tape recorders are different from those for using video cameras. Audio recordings provide a means of getting complete information from someone. Audio recordings usually begin and end with the journalist.

Hiding a video camera, however, presents a different ethical situation. Video cameras also record people's faces, clothing and actions. These tapes often end up on television. Using a video

A photographer practiced for a month before secretly taking this picture of Ruth Snyder as she was electrocuted for murdering her husband. This photo appeared in a sensational tabloid, the New York Daily News. A mask was placed over Snyder's head after she was strapped into Sing Sing's electric chair on the night of Jan. 12, 1928. To avoid detection, the photographer—who posed as a reporter—tied a miniature camera to one ankle. He lifted his pants cuff to snap one photo as the first jolt of electricity surged through Snyder's body, and to snap another photo at the second jolt.

Harcourt Brace & Company

recorder without permission has greater ramifications than using a tape recorder. It is even less acceptable—though neither action is encouraged—to hide a video recorder in a private home than in a public place because the news organization could be sued for invasion of privacy.

RUMORS: GOSSIP OR NEWS?

Journalists are supposed to publish facts, but are often tempted to publish rumors. If everyone in their community seems to be talking about a rumor, journalists may want to report it. Yet some rumors are impossible to verify and, by discussing a rumor, journalists may encourage its repetition. News stories may explain that the rumor is "unconfirmed," but audience members may fail to notice or remember that disclaimer.

Some rumors are little more than gossip. They may insist that a celebrity is gay, getting divorced or dying of AIDS. Or they may wrongly relate that a celebrity has died. One rumor insisted that the governor of New York had had a facelift (a charge he vigorously denied). Even when such stories can be verified, they may not be newsworthy.

A book published after President Ronald Reagan left office reported that his wife, Nancy Reagan, had enjoyed long lunches in the White House with Frank Sinatra. Moreover, the book implied that Sinatra and Mrs. Reagan enjoyed more than just lunch with each other. Tens of thousands of people bought the book, and some discussed it with friends. Most of the nation's news media then reported the gossip. News stories added that journalists were unable to confirm the details. News stories also criticized the author's investigative techniques. Still, all the stories helped publicize the book, thus increasing its sales—and spreading the gossip.

Some rumors concern topics that might affect an entire community. They may claim that a new building is unsafe, that a local business is owned by the Mafia or that a major employer plans to move. Journalists will investigate the rumors, and generally report only those that they find are true.

MAYOR IS ALIVE, WELL AND ANGRY AT TV STATIONS FOR REPORTING RUMOR

By **Louis Mleczko and Corey Williams**
The Detroit News

The mayor's office on Sunday criticized as irresponsible TV reports on unsubstantiated rumors that Mayor Coleman A. Young had died.

WDIV-TV (Channel 4) led its 11 p.m. Saturday newscast with the rumor-denial story. WXYZ-TV (Channel 7) carried a similar story in its first segment Saturday night.

"It's incredible that anyone would put that on the air," Bob Berg, Young's press secretary, said Sunday. And to put an end to rumors once and for all, he added: "I just spoke with the mayor, and he's fine."

Some stations heard the rumor but refused to air it. Fred Brown, assistant director of news and programming for WWJ-AM (950), said, "We got tons of calls and had three reporters working on it, but we didn't broadcast anything because it wasn't true."

(continued on next page)

Harcourt Brace & Company

WKBD-TV (Channel 50) and WJBK-TV (Channel 2) also held off.

Young, who was unavailable for comment Sunday, is used to people spreading rumors, said Sharon McPhail, who is expected to announce her own candidacy for mayor in January.

"There have been so many persistent rumors (about the mayor's health) all through the years," said City Council President Maryann Mahaffey.

Dennis Archer, who recently announced his candidacy for mayor, called the rumors "regrettable."

"It causes a lot of tremendous emotions to occur, especially if you happen to care a great deal about the person," Archer said.

"I made a telephone call to someone who I know shares the same opinion of the mayor, and who is closer to him than I. This person had already heard about the rumor, checked it out and determined it was false."

Mickey McCanham, an assignment editor at Channel 4, said his staff "went into the drill" Saturday after the station logged phone calls from viewers who had heard Young was dead.

Said McCanham in explaining why his station went on the air with the rumor: "If he does die, it's the story of the year."

McPhail said one of the mayor's ap-pointees told her at about 9 p.m. Saturday that Young had died.

"This person had a lot of detail and it really scared me," she said. "I was told within a half-hour that it was not true. Then I got another call after that with even more detail. I didn't know what to believe. Why would anybody start such a rumor?"

At Channel 7, similar rumors flooded the station's newsroom late Saturday afternoon, according to Glenn Bar, weekend producer.

"People were calling in from Greektown restaurants saying they heard about the mayor's death, and one woman called after hearing the rumor at a church service," Bar said.

Bar said, "We felt comfortable about airing the rumors because they were 'the talk of the town.'"

Mort Meisner, news director at Channel 2, cited the station's obligation not to "rip the viewers off."

"I think it's highly irresponsible to report rumors," Meisner said.

"That is why a lot of people hate the media."

Channel 50's Doug Mckenzie, weekend assignment editor, also wasn't impressed with the rationale for airing the rumor story.

"Personally, I felt it wasn't fair to the mayor or to the city to run with just rumors," Mckenzie said. "Why bother?"

DO JOURNALISTS ENCOURAGE TERRORISM?

Terrorists usually want publicity and have learned to create news so compelling that news organizations are unable to ignore it. The terrorists provide genuine drama: hijackings, demands, deadlines and the threat of mass murder. They can add to the drama by moving from one place to another and by releasing or murdering hostages.

To attract even more publicity, terrorists conduct press conferences. Some allow journalists to photograph and interview their captives. Others make videotapes of their captives, typically showing the hostages pleading for their lives, reading the terrorists' demands and warning that they will be killed if the demands are not met.

Critics insist that the media do not just cover the terrorists; they encourage them. They believe that if the media ignored terrorists, they would become discouraged and abandon their acts of violence. Former British Prime Minister Margaret Thatcher urged journalists to stop covering terrorists, to starve them of "the oxygen of publicity." The critics want journalists to adopt a voluntary code that would limit coverage of terrorists. But that may be impossible. No one seems

Harcourt Brace & Company

able to develop a code acceptable to thousands of journalists in dozens of countries. It also seems impossible to develop guidelines that would cover every possible situation.

Moreover, most journalists are reluctant to accept guidelines that would limit their freedom to cover an important story. Journalists add that Americans have a right to know what is happening in the world, and that a news blackout might result in rumors about the terrorists' activities that were more frightening than the truth. Journalists also fear that, if the terrorists were ignored, some would escalate their violence. Instead of hijacking one plane, they might hijack two or three. Instead of using a small bomb to kill a single individual, they might use a larger bomb to kill hundreds. Eventually, the media would be forced to cover them.

DOES BEING A JOURNALIST CONFLICT WITH BEING A CITIZEN?

While working for the news media, some journalists find their jobs occasionally conflict with their responsibilities as citizens. Some journalists feel they are citizens first; others believe their primary responsibility is to report the news. To do so, they may have to set aside rights and responsibilities that conflict with their work. When journalists photograph or video people drowning, falling to their deaths or fleeing from fire, the public wonders why the journalists failed to lay down their cameras and help the victims.

Reporters are reluctant to become involved in the stories they cover. They feel that it is their job to record happenings, not to participate in them. They want to remain neutral bystanders, not preventing, encouraging or changing a story. This attitude puzzles and sometimes outrages citizens, who believe that journalists—as citizens—should help people in distress, cooperate with the police and support the government.

Witnessing Crimes and Interviewing Criminals

Reporters occasionally learn about a crime that is soon to be committed. They might either go to the police or watch the crime and interview the criminal.

NBC was criticized after it broadcast an interview with a suspected terrorist, Abul Abbas. Three countries were looking for Abbas after the hijacking of a ship and the murder of an American tourist. NBC agreed to conceal his location; doing so seemed to be the only way to persuade him to talk. During the interview, Abbas said the Palestinians considered the United States, not Israel, their chief enemy. Abbas then threatened to conduct his next terrorist operation in the United States. An official at the State Department called NBC's decision "reprehensible," charging that the network had become an accomplice to terror. Another government official complained that the publicity NBC gave Abbas "encourages the terrorist activities we're all seeking to deter."

The Chicago Tribune called NBC's story "an abysmal disgrace to journalism." An editorial written by Tribune editor James D. Squires argued that Abbas' location was the only new and important element of the story, yet NBC had agreed to keep his location a secret. Squires added that if the Tribune could find Abbas it would accept his offer for an interview, then tell the government his location.

Other journalists also criticized NBC, but were even more critical of the Chicago Tribune's idea of betraying Abbas. They feared that, if a news organization broke its word with Abbas, other sources would become more suspicious of journalists and more reluctant to talk with them. Sources in other countries might also feel freer to harm journalists, especially if they seemed to be cooperating with their governments.

Harcourt Brace & Company

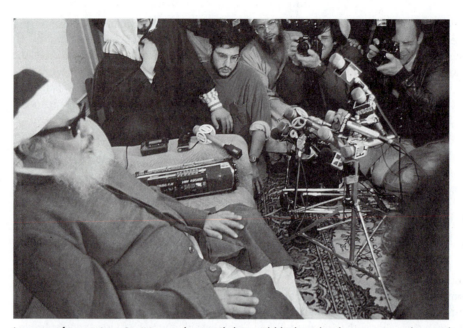

In a press conference in Jersey City, N.J., accused terrorist Sheik Omar Abdel-Rahman denied any connection to the six Muslims suspected in the Feb. 26, 1993, bombing of the World Trade Center in New York City. The blast killed six people and injured more than 1,000. The sheik had been tried and acquitted on several previous charges of inspiring the Islamic fundamentalist violence that has plagued Egypt and challenged Egyptian President Hosni Mubarak's secular rule.

CONFLICTS OF INTEREST

After years of confusion and contradictory standards, there seems to be a growing consensus about what constitutes a conflict of interest. A conflict of interest exists when journalists are influenced by outside interests.

"Freebies"—Accepting Gifts

Most journalists agree that it is unethical to accept money or anything else of value from the people they write about. Gifts could bias a reporter's story. An editor at The Washington Post has explained that: "On some newspapers (this one included), the acceptance of a bribe—for that is what it is—is a firing offense."

In the past, reporters readily accepted gifts, considering "freebies" to be fringe benefits. They received free tickets to many of the attractions in their communities. Each Christmas, a political reporter might receive a carload of gifts from officials in city hall. After writing about a jewelry store, a reporter might receive a watch from the store's owner.

Most news organizations now prohibit their reporters and editors from accepting anything of value. Other news organizations allow their journalists to accept items worth only a few dollars: a cup of coffee or a souvenir T-shirt, for example. Some news organizations also allow their journalists to accept free tickets to sports events, plays and movies that they are covering. However, news organizations generally prohibit their journalists from calling a press agent to ask for the tickets.

"Junkets"—Accepting Trips

Free trips, called "junkets," once were also common. Fashion writers were invited to New York, and television critics to Hollywood, with all their expenses paid. Sportswriters might accompany their local teams to games in distant cities, with the teams paying all the writers' expenses.

Harcourt Brace & Company

Journalists who accepted gifts insisted that they could not be corrupted because they were trained to remain objective. They also explained that most gifts were small tokens of appreciation for their work. They added that they would be less willing to accept the gifts if they were better paid and could afford to buy the items for themselves. Journalists who accepted junkets also insisted that the main issue was the public's right to know. Smaller newspapers and broadcasting stations could not afford to send their reporters to distant cities, and the junkets helped them obtain stories that would otherwise be inaccessible.

Walt Disney World invited thousands of journalists to fly to Orlando in 1986 to celebrate its 15th anniversary and, supposedly, to celebrate the 200th anniversary of the U.S. Constitution. Each journalist was allowed to bring one guest.

More than 5,000 people accepted Disney's invitation. Some were disc jockeys or worked in management, advertising or promotion. They flew to Orlando from all 50 states and were joined by several hundred Canadians, about 200 Europeans and 20 Japanese.

The junket cost about $7.5 million, but Disney contributed only $1.5 million. Seventeen airlines offered their services free or at reduced rates. Hotels donated 5,000 rooms and free breakfasts. The state of Florida and several local groups, all established to promote tourism, contributed an additional $350,000 apiece. They spent $600,000 on a single party in downtown Orlando. The visiting journalists were also treated to a concert and a fireworks display, and had Disney's Magic Kingdom to themselves for an entire evening.

The Disney organization insisted that there were no strings attached: that the journalists were not under any obligation to give the theme park any favorable publicity. Moreover, Disney said it offered the journalists three options:

- They could accept the free trip;

- They could pay $150 a day to cover a portion of their expenses; or

- They could accept Disney's invitation but pay the entire cost of their travel, food and lodging.

A writer for The Orlando Sentinel responded that: "This generosity is no better than a bribe to get puffy coverage, and the so-called journalists who accept it are a disgrace." A second critic complained that Disney "exposed dramatically the seamy side of the journalism profession." Disney's offer seemed to prove "that a great deal of favorable publicity is, without question, for sale by a significant percentage of the country's media."

Even the critics overlooked a more fundamental issue: Was the party newsworthy? Was Disney's 15th anniversary important enough to justify coverage by 5,000 media employees? Or did the recipients use Disney's anniversary as an excuse to accept a free vacation in Florida?

Disney obviously wanted publicity—and it got it. A Disney representative called it "the biggest marketing project we have ever undertaken." Within three months, Disney estimated that it had received $9 million worth of free publicity. Disney publicists collected a two-foot stack of press clippings. Television stations broadcast 186 live reports during the extravaganza, and radio stations provided 1,000 hours of live coverage. Even major networks covered the story. Both ABC's "Good Morning America" and NBC's "Today" broadcast live from Disney World.

Participating in the News

Increasingly, news organizations prohibit reporters from engaging in outside work and activities that might conflict with their objectivity. Editors explain that reporters' first obligation should be to their primary employer, and they assert that reporters continue to represent their employers even after they leave work for the day.

Editors generally agree that reporters and members of their families should not hold any public office, either elected or appointed. Most editors also agree that reporters should not serve as party officials or help with anyone's election campaign. Editors want to avoid even the appearance of a conflict. There might not be a direct conflict if a business writer ran for city council; a business writer might never cover the city council. But the public might suspect that other writers would slant the news in favor of their colleague's campaign.

In some cases, journalists' activities create an appearance of bias. A reporter for Florida's Vero Beach Press-Journal was fired after she sent letters and small copper coat hangers to all 160 members of the state Legislature. The legislators were meeting in a special session to consider the adoption of tougher abortion laws.

The reporter, Vicky Hendley, said her job as a reporter should not require her to give up her involvement in a cause she believed in. Also, she had been covering education for two years and said the abortion issue never came up on that beat.

Darryl Hicks, the newspaper's general manager, said Hendley was fired not because of her beliefs about abortion, but because she had violated company policy. In addition to writing the letters, Hendley had given interviews to other papers. "In all those she was clearly identified as a reporter for the Press-Journal," Hicks said. "We were drawn into it right away—clearly a conflict."

Free-Lancing

Journalists at most news organizations are free to accept other types of second jobs, provided that they do not create any conflicts. Typically, reporters and photographers can work as free-lancers, but cannot sell their work to their employers' competitors, such as other media in the same market.

Similarly, newspapers may allow their journalists to teach at a community college, but not to serve as scorekeepers at the games they cover. As scorekeepers, the writers would become part of the stories they were covering. Their decisions might be controversial and might determine the outcome of some games. Thus, the writers would have to report on their own actions. Similarly, newspapers might tell a sports editor to stop serving as the host of a local radio program and to avoid appearing on local television programs, especially for pay. The newspapers want sports editors to give important news stories to their readers, not to television viewers.

Pillow Talk and Cronyism

Increasingly, journalists face a newer conflict: their spouses' employment or position. To avoid the conflict, editors rarely allow reporters to cover any story in which their spouse is involved.

Another problem, called "hobnobbery journalism," arises when journalists become good friends with their sources. After becoming friends, journalists cannot easily criticize their sources. Politics presents an even greater problem; journalists are supposed to be watchdogs, not friends, of politicians.

CENSORING ADVERTISEMENTS

Many Americans oppose censorship of any type, and journalists are especially vigilant in their efforts to combat it. Yet news organizations regularly censor the advertisements submitted to them. They clearly have the legal right to do so. Courts have consistently ruled that the First Amendment gives editors the right to reject any advertisement they dislike, regardless of the reason.

For almost 200 years, newspapers published virtually every advertisement submitted to them. Editors rarely felt responsible for the content of advertisements. Rather, the editors' philosophy was one of *Caveat emptor:* "Let the buyer beware."

During the 1800s, newspapers in both the North and the South published advertisements for slaves, prostitutes and quack medicines. Some medicines contained enough alcohol to inebriate the people using them. Others contained so much heroin, opium and morphine that the people using them became addicts. Even the "soothing syrups" sold for babies were spiked with drugs; some babies may have died of overdoses.

A single medicine might be advertised as the cure for dozens of ailments, including headaches, tuberculosis, malaria, poison ivy, ulcers, varicose veins, cancer, syphilis, hay fever and diarrhea. People felt better after taking some of the medicines, but only because they contained narcotics or alcohol.

During the late 1800s, a few periodicals began to protect their readers from fraudulent advertising. When Cyrus H. K. Curtis took over the Saturday Evening Post in 1897, he began to reject advertisements for liquor and patent medicines. During the early 20th century, the St. Louis Post-Dispatch was a leader in the campaign to clean up newspapers' advertising columns. The newspaper lost thousands of dollars in revenue, but its publisher never objected.

Most editors now reject advertisements that seem distasteful or that promote products that seem illegal, immoral or harmful. The editors want to act ethically. Some explain that they have always felt responsible for the content of their news columns, routinely deleting anything that seemed tasteless, inaccurate, unfair, libelous or obscene. Now, the editors say, they are accepting a similar responsibility for the content of their advertising columns. Many readers agree with the editors' decisions. Others accuse them of censorship.

More than 100 daily newspapers reject advertisements for alcoholic beverages, especially hard liquor. Other dailies reject advertisements for X-rated movies, sexual aids, mail order goods, hair restorers and fortune tellers. Most dailies reject advertisements for abortion services and handguns. Many also reject advertisements for massage parlors and escort services, which in some cities have been fronts for male and female prostitution.

New issues are constantly arising. Some newspapers, concerned about their readers' health and safety, no longer accept advertisements for "happy hours" during which drinks are cheap or free. Bars usually advertise the "happy hours" during the late afternoon and evening, when people begin to drive home after work. Editors fear that the advertisements will contribute to heavy drinking and drunken driving.

Newspapers are also troubled by advertisements for babies. Typically, the advertisements promise to pay $10,000 or more for "a white newborn." Because of contraceptives and legal abortions, and because many unmarried mothers keep their babies, few healthy white infants are available for adoption. Couples who are unwilling to spend several years working with a conventional adoption agency may place an ad in a newspaper's classified advertising columns. To persuade pregnant women to put their babies up for adoption, couples promise to give babies loving and secure homes. In addition, they promise to pay the mothers thousands of dollars. Many newspapers have no standard policy for handling these ads. Some newspapers publish them, but others do not.

CODES OF ETHICS

Every major organization in the field of journalism has adopted a code of ethics. These organizations encourage their members to voluntarily adhere to the guidelines. They also serve as models that individual organizations follow when setting their own policies. There is little evidence the national codes are effective, mainly because they are seldom enforced. Some organizations have adopted a code merely for self-protection: to convince the public that they are doing a good job of regulating themselves and that government regulation is unnecessary. However, many local news organizations or individual media do enforce their ethics policies.

The American Society of Newspaper Editors (ASNE) adopted one of the industry's first codes, the Canons of Journalism, in 1923. The Canons did not prohibit anything; rather, they told newspaper editors what they should do. Among other things, they declared that newspapers should act responsibly: that they should be truthful, sincere, impartial, decent and fair. The Canons were so vague that even the most sincere journalists might disagree about their meaning.

Another group, the Society of Professional Journalists (SPJ), continues to debate its code at every annual conference. Its code declares that journalists must seek the truth and that they have a responsibility to "perform with intelligence, objectivity, accuracy and fairness." The code adds that journalists should accept "nothing of value" because gifts and special favors might compromise their integrity. The code also recommends that journalists avoid second jobs and political involvement that might cause a conflict of interest.

Some reporters complain that the codes infringe on their freedom and that, as citizens, they have a responsibility to become involved in their communities. Reporters also complain of a double standard. The codes limit their freedom, yet many editors and publishers continue to do as they please, heading charities and serving on the boards of local schools and businesses. Similarly, a publisher can write editorials that endorse various politicians, but his or her reporters may be forbidden to sign petitions, march in rallies or provide any other help for a politician's campaign.

The professional standards in journalism are improving. Journalists are becoming better educated, more responsible and more ethical. But it is difficult for them to convince the public of that fact. Journalists are forced to make too many controversial decisions, and the decisions are more complex than most people imagine. Also, journalists and their audiences often disagree about which stories the media should report and about how those stories should be presented to the public. Journalists are reluctant to suppress any stories. Critics, however, worry about the effects stories have on the people involved, and on other readers and viewers.

Journalists are adopting codes of ethics to eliminate the most obvious abuses, especially conflicts of interest. But the codes cannot solve every problem. There are too many problems, and the problems are too diverse. Thus, decisions will always vary from one newspaper to another—and that may be one of our system's greatest strengths. Every journalist is free to decide what is right or wrong, ethical or unethical. Inevitably, some journalists will be mistaken. But any effort to change the system—to force every journalist to conform to a predetermined standard—would limit the media's diversity and freedom. It would also limit Americans' access to information.

Harcourt Brace & Company

Society of Professional Journalists

CODE OF ETHICS

The SOCIETY of Professional Journalists believes the duty of journalists is to serve the truth.

We BELIEVE the agencies of mass communication are carriers of public discussion and information, acting on their Constitutional mandate and freedom to learn and report the facts.

We BELIEVE in public enlightenment as the forerunner of justice, and in our Constitutional role to seek the truth as part of the public's right to know the truth.

We BELIEVE those responsibilities carry obligations that require journalists to perform with intelligence, objectivity, accuracy, and fairness.

To these ends, we declare acceptance of the standards of practice here set forth:

I. RESPONSIBILITY

The public's right to know of events of public importance and interest is the overriding mission of the mass media. The purpose of distributing news and enlightened opinion is to serve the general welfare. Journalists who use their professional status as representatives of the public for selfish or other unworthy motives violate a high trust.

II. FREEDOM OF THE PRESS

Freedom of the press is to be guarded as an inalienable right of people in a free society. It carries with it the freedom and the responsibility to discuss, question, and challenge actions and utterances of our government and of our public and private institutions. Journalists uphold the right to speak unpopular opinions and the privilege to agree with the majority.

III. ETHICS

Journalists must be free of obligation to any interest other than the public's right to know the truth.

1. Gifts, favors, free travel, special treatment or privileges can compromise the integrity of journalists and their employers. Nothing of value should be accepted.

2. Secondary employment, political involvement, holding public office, and service in community organizations should be avoided if it compromises the integrity of journalists and their employers. Journalists and their employers should conduct their personal lives in a manner that protects them from conflict of interest, real or apparent. Their responsibilities to the public are paramount. That is the nature of their profession.

3. So-called news communications from private sources should not be published or broadcast without substantiation of their claims to news values.

4. Journalists will seek news that serves the public interest, despite the obstacles. They will make constant efforts to assure that the public's business is conducted in public and that public records are open to public inspection.

5. Journalists acknowledge the newsman's ethic of protecting confidential sources of information.

6. Plagiarism is dishonest and unacceptable.

IV. ACCURACY AND OBJECTIVITY

Good faith with the public is the foundation of all worthy journalism.

1. Truth is our ultimate goal.

2. Objectivity in reporting the news is another goal that serves as the mark of an experienced professional. It is a standard of performance toward which we strive. We honor those who achieve it.

3. There is no excuse for inaccuracies or lack of thoroughness.

(continued on next page)

4. Newspaper headlines should be fully warranted by the contents of the articles they accompany. Photographs and telecasts should give an accurate picture of an event and not highlight an incident out of context.

5. Sound practice makes clear distinction between news reports and expressions of opinion. News reports should be free of opinion or bias and represent all sides of an issue.

6. Partisanship in editorial comment that knowingly departs from the truth violates the spirit of American journalism.

7. Journalists recognize their responsibility for offering informed analysis, comment, and editorial opinion on public events and issues. They accept the obligation to present such material by individuals whose competence, experience, and judgment qualify them for it.

8. Special articles or presentations devoted to advocacy or the writer's own conclusions and interpretations should be labeled as such.

V. FAIR PLAY

Journalists at all times will show respect for the dignity, privacy rights, and well-being of people encountered in the course of gathering and presenting the news.

1. The news media should not communicate unofficial charges affecting reputation or moral character without giving the accused a chance to reply.

2. The news media must guard against invading a person's right to privacy.

3. The media should not pander to morbid curiosity about details of vice and crime.

4. It is the duty of news media to make prompt and complete correction of their errors.

5. Journalists should be accountable to the public for their reports and the public should be encouraged to voice its grievances against the media. Open dialogue with our readers, viewers, and listeners should be fostered.

VI. MUTUAL TRUST

Adherence to this code is intended to preserve and strengthen the bond of mutual trust and respect between American journalists and the American people.

The Society shall—by programs of education and other means—encourage individual journalists to adhere to these tenets, and shall encourage journalistic publications and broadcasters to recognize their responsibility to frame codes of ethics in concert with their employees to serve as guidelines in furthering these goals.

CODE OF ETHICS
(Adopted 1926; revised 1973, 1984, 1987)

SUGGESTED READINGS

Alexander, Alison, and Jarice Hanson. *Taking Sides*, 2nd ed. Guilford, CT: Dushkin, 1993.

Black, Jay, Bob Steele and Ralph Barney. *Doing Ethics in Journalism: a Handbook with Case Studies.* Greencastle, IN: Sigma Delta Chi Foundation and The Society of Professional Journalists, 1993.

Christians, Clifford G., John P. Ferre and Mark P. Fackler. *Good News: Social Ethics and the Press.* New York: Oxford University Press, 1993.

Christians, Clifford G., Kim B. Rotzoll and Mark Fackler. *Media Ethics: Cases and Moral Reasoning,* 3rd ed. White Plains, NY: Longman, 1991.

Goodwin, H. Eugene, and Ron F. Smith. *Groping for Ethics in Journalism,* 3rd ed. Ames, IA: Iowa State University Press, 1994.

Conrad, Charles, ed. *Ethical News.* Norwood, NJ: Ablex, 1993.

Day, Louis A. *Ethics in Media Communications: Cases and Controversies.* Belmont, CA: Wadsworth, 1991.

Fink, Conrad C. *Media Ethics.* Boston: Allyn & Bacon, 1995.

Knowlton, Steven R., and Patrick R. Parsons, eds. *The Journalist's Moral Compass.* Westport, CN: Praeger, 1994.

Moore, Roy L. *Mass Communication Law and Ethics.* Hillsdale, NJ: Erlbaum, 1994.

EXERCISE 1

ETHICS

DISCUSSION QUESTIONS

1. A student at your college has accused another student of raping her at his apartment. He lives in an apartment complex popular with students. The victim has asked that her name be omitted from news stories. You, the editor, have agreed. The accused has also asked that his name be omitted until the end of the trial. What do you do?

2. A man has called your television station threatening to set himself on fire to protest recent welfare cutbacks. Do you notify the police? Do you send reporters to cover the event? Will the protester ignite himself without the publicity? Do you interfere with events by helping the man?

3. Your news organization has received several calls one hour before deadline charging your city's mayor with having another husband and children in a different state. The caller says he is also notifying other media. What do you do? If the charge is true, then other media will get the scoop. Do you hurry to get it before deadline?

4. If you served on the board that awards Pulitzer Prizes, would you have given a prize to the Sun-Times for its exposure of corruption in Chicago? Or would you have objected to the Sun-Times' purchase of a tavern to obtain the story?

5. Imagine that you worked as the news director at a Pennsylvania television station on the day the corrupt state treasurer, R. Budd Dwyer, shot and killed himself during a press conference. If one of your photographers returned with a 21-second videotape of Dwyer's suicide, what would you do with it?

6. The Newspaper Guild, a union that represents thousands of newspeople, has endorsed candidates in several presidential elections. Do you agree with its policy? Why or why not? If newspaper owners can endorse candidates on their editorial pages, why shouldn't reporters be able to endorse candidates through their unions?

7. Normally, the newspaper you edit avoids pictures showing grief. But imagine that a driver was killed during a stock car race at your county fair. More than 10,000 people saw the crash, and your photographer snapped a picture showing the driver's wife, holding his hand and crying as his body was cut from the wreckage. It is not a bloody scene, but much of the driver's body and face can be seen. Would you publish the picture? Why?

8. Your police reporter has learned that a prominent minister has been charged with shoplifting, a crime you normally report. The police reveal that it is the minister's third arrest during the last year, but charges were dropped by the stores. The minister has learned that your reporter is working on the story. He calls and warns you that, if you publish the story, he will be forced to kill himself. How would you handle the situation?

9. Reread the list of rights prepared by the National Victim Center (see Page 528), then discuss the list with your classmates. Do you agree with the center's guidelines? Also, how will the guidelines affect you as a reporter—or as a consumer of the media?

10. If you were a journalist and Disney World offered you and a companion a free trip to Orlando for its 30th anniversary, would you accept? Why or why not?

E X E R C I S E   2

ETHICS

SETTING YOUR NEWS ORGANIZATION'S POLICIES (WHAT WOULD YOU PERMIT?)

1. As the editor of a daily newspaper, you have been asked to write a code of ethics for your reporters. You want to be fair, but you also want to prevent any conflicts that might affect your staff's coverage of the news or that might harm your paper's credibility. Would you allow:

   A. Your science writer to date the mayor?

   B. Your science writer to run for the city council?

   C. Any of your reporters to sign a petition urging the mayor to resign?

   D. Your opinion editors to write an editorial endorsing the mayor's campaign for re-election?

   E. Your political reporter to volunteer her time each Saturday to help supervise a fund drive for the Salvation Army?

   F. Your political reporter to volunteer her time each Saturday to write news releases for the Salvation Army?

   G. Your political reporter to accept $500 for occasional appearances as a panelist on a Sunday-morning television program on public affairs?

2. Normally, your newspaper reports every birth, death, divorce and bankruptcy in your community. You also identify everyone charged with drunken driving, and your obituaries include everyone's age and cause of death. You rarely approve any exceptions to the policies. You want to protect your paper's reputation and avoid charges of favoritism. As editor, would you agree to help any of these people?

   A. A 74-year-old woman mails you a letter explaining that she is dying of cancer and does not want you to report her age in her obituary. Her friends think she is 65. She is embarrassed by the matter and does not want them to know that she lied.

   B. A man's family calls and asks you not to report the cause of his death: cirrhosis of the liver. They admit that he was an alcoholic but see no reason to inform the community of that fact.

   C. A local couple with four children asks you not to report their marriage. Their children have always thought that they were married, and the news that they are finally getting married would upset and embarrass everyone in the family.

   D. A minister charged with drunken driving pleads that he is innocent, that he was taking a prescription drug that made him dizzy. He insists that, in three or four days, breath and urinalysis tests conducted by the police will prove his innocence. Normally, you report everyone's arrest at the time of their apprehension, and later report the outcome of each case.

3. Assume that you are the news director for a local TV station and that a reporter on your staff receives a tip that your city airport's security system is defective. Moreover, airport officials know about the problem and have failed to correct it. How would you respond

if the reporter proposed walking through several airport checkpoints with a toy (but real-looking) pistol in her purse?

A. Would you approve her plan?

B. Would you approve her plan, but instruct her to notify the police and other appropriate law enforcement agencies beforehand?

C. Would you order the reporter to abandon the idea and to obtain the story through more conventional means?

4. Robbers entered a local jewelry store just before 9 a.m. today, shot one clerk and seized seven hostages. Police have surrounded the store and cordoned off the entire block. As the news director at a local television station, it is your biggest story in years. Would you instruct your staff to:

A. Call and interview the hostages' relatives?

B. Call the store and try to interview the robbers?

C. Televise the confrontation live from across the street?

D. If the robbers requested it, agree to let your leading newscaster serve as an intermediary between them and the police?

E. In return for the robbers' promise to surrender and to release all seven hostages, agree to let them appear on the air—live and unedited—for three minutes after their surrender?

5. The police have shot a 15-year-old boy who broke into a liquor store. Police officers responding to a silent alarm surrounded the store and ordered the intruder to come out. At the time, they did not know his age. The intruder fired a .22-caliber pistol at the officers. They returned the fire, killing him. As a reporter, which of the following details would you include in your story?

A. The boy was an Eagle Scout, the highest rank in scouting.

B. Other teen-agers—the boy's friends—say he was often drunk and may have been an alcoholic; however, the boy's parents deny it.

C. The boy had committed dozens of other crimes, starting when he was 8, and had spent three years in a home for delinquents.

D. The boy's parents are separated but not divorced. He lived with his mother and her boyfriend.

E. The boy's father is unemployed and an admitted alcoholic, fired from at least a dozen jobs. Relatives say he rarely saw his son.

F. An uncle had sexually molested the boy.

E X E R C I S E   3

ETHICS

WHAT'S YOUR DECISION?
(SOLVING THE MEDIA'S ETHICAL DILEMMAS)

1. Imagine that you are a political reporter for your local daily and, while at a Saturday-night party given at a friend's home, you see your mayor and overhear him listening to and telling jokes that degrade women. You are attending the party as a guest, and the mayor does not know you are there (or that anyone can overhear the group he is with). What would you do?

   A. Not publish a story about the jokes.

   B. Not publish a story about the jokes, but warn the mayor that, in the future, you will feel obligated to report that type of story. Then, to prevent additional conflicts, immediately sever all your social contacts with the mayor and other sources.

   C. Publish a story about the jokes but attribute them to a "city official," without identifying the mayor.

   D. Instruct a reporter to call other participants in the conversation and to get the story from them.

   E. Inform the mayor that you overheard the jokes and feel obligated to report them. Then ask the mayor to respond, and include his response in your story, even if he insists that you are mistaken or lying.

   F. Decide on another alternative.

2. Late Saturday morning, an aide for the Democratic candidate for mayor gave your political reporter evidence proving that the Republican candidate has been treated twice for an addiction to cocaine. In return for the evidence, your political reporter promised never to reveal its source. The election is next Tuesday, and it is only a half hour before your Saturday deadline: too late to find and question the Republican candidate. Moreover, you do not publish a Sunday edition. As editor, what would you do?

   A. Ignore the story as unfair and a political smear.

   B. Because of its importance, publish the story immediately. Then, on Monday, publish a second story reporting the Republican's response.

   C. Publish the story immediately, but overrule your political reporter and identify its source, so your readers understand that it is a political smear.

   D. Wait until Monday—the day before the election—and then report both the charges and the Republican's response in the same story.

   E. Publish the story immediately, but in a column on your editorial page identify and denounce its source, pointing out that he seemed to have deliberately waited until the last minute so the Republican would not have time to respond.

   F. Decide on another alternative.

3. Normally, your TV station never reports suicides. As editor, you consider suicides a personal and private matter. Moreover, you are reluctant to add to a family's grief and

embarrassment. But during the past year, three teen-agers—all high school students in your community—have killed themselves. Last night, a fourth teen-ager, a well-known athlete, shot himself. There were no witnesses. What would you do?

A. Ignore the fourth suicide, just as you ignored the first three.

B. Assign a reporter to write a story about the problem of teen-age suicides and to mention the four local deaths, but without using any of the teen-agers' names.

C. Report the story as fully as possible, but identify only the latest victim, the prominent athlete.

D. Call the teen-agers' parents and ask for their permission to report the story as a warning to other parents and teen-agers. Then write a story about the problem and identify only the teen-agers whose parents cooperate with you.

E. Report the story as fully as possible, identifying all four victims.

F. Decide on another alternative.

4. As a reporter/photographer, you are invited inside a welfare office seized by its clients. The protesters want you to report their grievances and encourage you to interview and photograph everyone there. As you leave, police who surrounded the building ask you how many people are inside, whether they are armed and whether they seem likely to use their weapons. What would you do?

A. Decline to answer any of their questions.

B. Tell the police that you cannot answer their questions, but that your story and photographs will appear in the next morning's paper.

C. Give the police only the information that you plan to publish in the next morning's paper.

D. Answer all the officers' questions.

E. Answer all the officers' questions and give them copies of all your pictures.

F. Decide on another alternative.

5. As a reporter, you regularly cover an environmentalist group in your city. Frustrated by their past failures, the environmentalists are becoming more militant. You discover that they plan to kidnap the 7-year-old daughter of a local developer. They intend to hold the girl hostage until her father agrees to stop polluting a river. You have covered the environmentalists for years, and they have confided in you because you have never betrayed their trust. What would you do?

A. Say nothing.

B. Warn the environmentalists that, because a child's life is in danger, you cannot remain silent. You will have to notify the police if they do not change their plans.

C. Call the developer and warn him that his family is in danger, but without identifying the kidnappers.

D. Call the police and inform them that someone plans to kidnap the girl, but without identifying the kidnappers.

E. Call the police and tell them everything you know.

F. Decide on another alternative.

Harcourt Brace & Company

☆☆☆☆☆

CHAPTER 22

CAREERS IN JOURNALISM

. . . most of mankind seem to stand guard over us, ready to pounce down upon us at the slightest aberration of memory, the smallest error of detail, the minutest possible mistake or misstatement of fact. They do not seem to understand that the most ardent desire of the honest journalist is to be right.

(Charles T. Congdon in "Reminiscences Of A Journalist," 1880)

Some students decide to major in journalism because the curriculum prepares them for specific jobs. Other students select journalism because they like to write and believe journalism is an important profession that provides an opportunity to serve the public. Students also explain that they enjoy working with people, that the media are interesting and that journalism is a creative field.

There are more than enough journalism students to replace every reporter and editor employed by the nation's daily and weekly newspapers. The numbers are deceiving, however. The term "journalism" includes more than just newspaper work. It also includes magazines, advertising, public relations, broadcasting and photography, and many students seek jobs in those fields.

In fact, students should approach the job market with a broad perspective. Specialty magazines have proliferated at an amazing rate. Electronic journalism, another growing area, is more than just radio and television. It includes news on demand through databases, online services and other information outlets.

One professor explains: "Journalism continues to attract a number of young people who see such education as an excellent preparation for other endeavors, and it is simply not correct to assume that all persons majoring in journalism are going to seek media-related positions upon graduation." Some new graduates enter the military, become teachers or seek jobs in sales or management. Others go on to graduate or law school. At the University of Iowa, 16 percent of new law students had been English, journalism or communication studies majors. "Journalists have the strength in writing, the information-gathering skills and they have learned the strategy of objectivity," said one Iowa journalism professor.

Each year, Lee B. Becker of Ohio State University studies the nation's journalism students. His most recent study revealed that 22.8 percent are majoring in broadcasting, 14.2 percent in newspaper reporting and editing (news/editorial), 13.8 percent in public relations, 13 percent in advertising, 8.1 percent in journalism and 2.7 percent in mass communication. Other students major in a combination of advertising and public relations. Still others major in photojournalism or magazine, film or agricultural journalism.

Thirty years ago, most students graduating with degrees in journalism were men. Today, 61 percent are women.

WHAT JOB APPLICANTS ARE MOST WANTED?

Newspaper editors and television station news managers generally want the same qualities in applicants. They want applicants who are intelligent and well-informed and who have a sense of the news. Both also want talented writers: good grammarians who can spell and write clearly and accurately. Unfortunately, these also tend to be the qualities that many job applicants lack.

Harcourt Brace & Company

557

Of course, not all jobs have the same requirements. Broadcast journalists who want to be in front of a camera as reporters or anchors, for instance, must have adequate "looks." They must also have good delivery skills; their voices cannot be too monotone or somber. Appearance and vocal delivery are much less important in newspaper work.

The television and newspaper industries both seek applicants who are honest, curious, aggressive, self-starting and dedicated. The best applicants are also clearly committed to careers in journalism, willing to sacrifice and likely to stay in their jobs for several years. Editors and news directors look for applicants who show a long-term interest in journalism. They want applicants who have worked for student media outlets and who have sacrificed to obtain some additional experience, possibly in a summer internship.

When he was the executive editor of The Washington Post, Benjamin Bradlee said he looked first for energy, for commitment to the news business and for a willingness to take work home. After that, he looked for knowledge, ability and judgment. Retired editor Pat Murphy said he wished more of today's reporters reflected the characteristics of those of an earlier era. They should have "imagination, energy, a flair for risks, a passion for long hours and demanding deadlines, and that indefinable 'nose for news.'"

Editors and news directors complain many applicants are unfamiliar with city and county governments; cannot cope with deadline pressures; and lack an adequate general background in economics, history, literature, philosophy and science.

WHO ACTUALLY GETS NEWS JOBS?

According to a recent survey, 75 percent of all newcomers to the field come directly from college journalism programs. Many newspapers, however, prefer to hire reporters from other newspapers because those reporters have already been trained; they are experienced, productive professionals. Hiring policies also reflect two other major trends. First, news organizations rarely hire people without a college degree—82 percent of all U.S. journalists have one. Newsmagazines (95.1 percent) and news services (94.7 percent) are most likely to require a degree, followed by daily newspapers (84.3), television (83.2), weekly newspapers (77) and radio (59).

Second, applicants who studied journalism in college are more likely to be hired. Daily newspapers are most likely to employ journalism majors (48.8 percent), followed by news services (38.2), weekly newspapers (33.9), newsmagazines (22.4), radio (22) and television (20.2).

Many daily newspapers are hiring more specialists, so editors are impressed by new graduates who have developed an interest or expertise in some area of specialization. Partly for that reason, many of the students who major in journalism minor in another field. Editors at smaller newspapers often hire applicants who can operate a 35mm camera and develop their own film, so they can double as photographers. Editors also look for good copy editors. Most newspapers pay copy editors more than reporters and are more likely to promote copy editors. Nevertheless, there seems to be a persistent and widespread shortage of copy editors, so it may be easier for journalism graduates to obtain jobs as copy editors than as reporters.

Employing More Women

News organizations continue to lag behind other industries in the percentage of women they employ and promote. Of the people employed by newspapers, about 39 percent are women, compared to 58 percent of the total U.S. civilian work force. Thirty-five percent of journalists in television and 31 percent in radio are women. While women hold 43 percent of managerial positions nationwide, they hold 15.5 percent at television stations and 26.3 percent at radio stations.

Harcourt Brace & Company

At newspapers, women hold 28 percent of the positions as executives and managers. The performance of newspapers in this regard is improving, however, while in broadcasting there seems to have been a leveling off since 1990.

Employing More Minority-Group Members

The industry has been urged by internal and external groups to employ more members of minority groups. The goal by the year 2000 is that newspaper staffs will have the same percentage of racial and ethnic minorities as the U.S. population. Over the past several years, progress has been made in minority hiring, but few interim goals have been met. Recent surveys found 45 percent of the nation's daily newspapers still do not employ a single minority professional in their newsrooms.

African, Hispanic, Asian and other American minority-group members make up 20 percent of the U.S. population and 22 percent of the work force, but 18 percent of newspaper industry employees and only 10.5 percent of the people employed in newsrooms. Minorities compose 7.7 percent of newsroom supervisors, 10 percent of copy editors, 11.4 percent of reporters and 13.1 percent of photographers and artists. Over a five-year span, this distribution has remained fairly stable.

Minorities make up 18.5 percent of the television news work force—the highest it's ever been, according to surveys by the Radio Television News Directors Association. In radio, minorities account for 12.3 percent of the news work force; little progress has been made over the past 20 years. As with newspapers, minorities in broadcast news, both television and radio, are concentrated in the larger markets. Minority journalists direct 9 percent of the television and 7 percent of the radio news operations.

College journalism programs also try to attract more minorities. Ten percent of their most recent graduates were blacks, 4.1 percent Hispanics, 2 percent Asians and 1.3 percent other minorities.

What difference does it make whether women and minorities are offered more and better opportunities in journalism? David Lawrence, an executive with the Knight-Ridder newspapers, explained in a recent speech: "My vision is both moral and practical: Moral in the sense that what is proposed in the hiring, advancement and retention of minorities and women is simply a matter of being fair. Practical in the sense that what is proposed is absolutely crucial to the future of our business."

Lawrence added that people bring different perspectives to their work, and "no matter how progressive and sensitive and thoughtful, a newspaper staff and management predominantly male and white cannot fully serve a genuinely diverse readership and a genuinely diverse nation. . . . Ultimately, the very best and most successful newspapers in our business will be those reflecting the full rainbow of human experiences."

Recently, some news organizations have included homosexuals in their diversity efforts, guaranteeing them equal treatment. Problems remain for this and all other minorities—biases, stereotypes, unfair criticisms and harassment—despite improvement.

FINDING A JOB

William Ruehlman, author of "Stalking the Feature Story," tells of one of his first attempts at finding a newspaper job. He arrived in town a couple of days ahead of his scheduled interview, wrote three feature stories and submitted them to the paper as free-lance pieces. The day he went in for the interview, the paper had already published one of his stories. He got the job.

That technique will not work every time, but with an ever-tightening job market, applicants have to look for ways to make an impression. The first half of the 1990s was a difficult period for journalism graduates. There was a serious recession, advertising revenue declined and some newspapers imposed a freeze on hiring. Others laid off some of their employees and encouraged older employees to retire early without the intent of replacing them. Some newspapers have gone out of business. The total number of journalists at daily newspapers declined from an all-time high of 56,900 in 1990 to 53,700 in 1994.

A recent national survey found that most journalism graduates obtained a job within six to eight months of graduation. Seventy-seven percent of bachelor's degree recipients had either a part-time (14.1 percent) or full-time (62.9 percent) job, although only about half obtained a job in the communication field. Another 7.4 percent continued their schooling. The unemployment rate among journalism graduates was 15.6 percent. Only 26.8 percent of the graduates with a news/editorial specialization found work at a newspaper or news service. The percentages were even lower for broadcast, public relations and advertising graduates. News/editorial graduates, however, are unusually successful at obtaining jobs in other media fields, generally because of their writing skills.

Most journalism students obtain some experience while still in school. They start by working for campus publications. Later, they may free-lance or work part-time for a local paper. Internships are even more valuable, enabling students to acquire more professional experience and to become better acquainted with the editors who hire a paper's regular staff members. Such experience provides a variety of benefits: It demonstrates a student's commitment to journalism, improves professional skills and provides the "clips" or "tapes" students need to obtain jobs when they graduate. Nearly three-fourths of the journalism graduates who find media-related jobs have worked somewhere as interns.

Internships

A newspaper editor explains the value of internships as follows: "It's just not enough to have a degree. We look for someone who has interned, worked for the school newspaper and who has a pile of clips so we don't have to play journalism school." Another news executive adds: "Somehow, some way, the real gutsy students will find a summer newspaper job. We are impressed with them. They show us that they are actively pursuing a journalism career. And they can offer us something other than a journalism degree—experience."

The media employ thousands of interns every summer. Most internships are sponsored by individual newspapers, magazines, news services and radio and television stations. Applicants for internships tend to concentrate on a few prestigious media. Typically, The Washington Post receives thousands of applications for the dozen or so internships it offers each summer. Other big dailies receive hundreds of applications. Students are more likely to obtain internships with their hometown newspapers or with smaller newspapers or radio or television stations in their area. To obtain internships, students should get an early start and, in case they are rejected by one medium, should apply at several. Large media often set an early application deadline, as early as November or December for the following summer's internships. Most schools encourage their students to obtain internships, and some require them to.

Many newspaper editors expect interns to work for nothing. Some exploit interns, using them as free labor, often to replace vacationing employees. Better internships include formal training programs: orientation sessions, seminars with news executives, and regular reporting and editing duties. They also pay students the same salaries that beginning staff reporters receive. Editors may provide internships because they feel an obligation to support journalism education or because they want to help students get ahead in the field. Editors also use internships to observe talented young journalists whom they might want to employ.

Harcourt Brace & Company

Seeking a First Job

New graduates looking for their first permanent jobs should set realistic goals for themselves. Most metropolitan newspapers and radio and television stations do not hire beginners, but look for people with several years of solid professional experience. Those that do hire beginners may assign them rather menial tasks.

New graduates should write to weekly newspapers or small dailies or radio and television stations in small markets, because they receive fewer applications and are more likely to accept applicants with less experience. They should also consider jobs at newsletters, each of which focuses on a specific topic such as criminal justice, oil spills or aerospace. Many newsletter writers consider their work the purest form of journalism because their employers accept little or no advertising and thus are not pressured to change their coverage of certain subjects.

Jobs at smaller news operations often provide better experience, because they offer reporters and editors a variety of assignments and greater responsibilities. Graduates who want to work in a metropolitan area are more likely to find jobs there after they have obtained some experience in the smaller markets.

Graduates seeking jobs should consult Editor & Publisher, Broadcasting & Cable, and Electronic Media—all weekly magazines that publish help-wanted advertisements. Information about newsletters can be obtained from the Newsletter Publishers Association.

The Job Interview

If your cover letter, resumé and clips impress an editor, you may be invited for an interview, which is a critical step in obtaining most jobs. When you appear for an interview, bring evidence of your commitment and experience, such as additional copies of your clips or other samples of your work.

An applicant's appearance is important. Some authorities say an applicant's first four minutes are crucial to making a good and lasting impression. Every applicant should be well-groomed: neat, clean and properly dressed. Applicants should be neither overdressed nor underdressed. For women, a coordinated jacket and skirt or a simple daytime dress with low-heeled shoes is most appropriate; makeup, if any, should be applied discreetly. Men should wear a dark suit or jacket and tie with slacks (no jeans) and well-polished shoes (no sneakers or running shoes).

During a typical interview, you are likely to meet several members of a news organization's staff, including its managing editor or station manager and the head of the department you would work for, such as the city, suburban, sports or photo editor. Besides looking your best, you will want to: be honest; exude confidence; be consistent; be positive; use the person's name and speak in a relaxed yet assertive voice.

The editors will want to learn more about you: your strengths, personality, interests and intelligence. Are you prepared? Can you answer the editors' questions—and ask intelligent questions yourself?

Editors will want to know about your expectations and understanding of journalism. Are you realistic about the salary you might be offered, and do you understand you may have to work evenings, weekends and holidays? If you want to be a columnist, editorial writer or Washington correspondent, do you realize it may take many years to achieve that goal? If you want to be a foreign correspondent, have you learned several foreign languages?

These are the types of questions editors are likely to ask:

- Tell me about yourself.

- What books and magazines have you read during the last month or two?

- Why do you want to be a journalist?

- Why should I hire you?

- What are your short- and long-range goals?

- What are your principal strengths and weaknesses?

- Why do you want to work here? What is it that you like about this particular company?

- What would you like to know about us, this newspaper and the company that owns it?

- Why do you want to leave your present job?

With one exception, none of these questions has a right or wrong answer. Employers look for answers that provide some evidence of applicants' commitment, intelligence and initiative. The final question is the tricky one. Few employers like applicants who criticize their current or former employers.

Interviewers are also impressed by applicants who ask good questions: questions that are thoughtful and informed. You may want to ask about your probable hours, salary, assignment or opportunities for advancement. Or you might ask:

- Exactly what would I do here?

- Who would edit my stories, and how much feedback would I receive about them?

- Who would evaluate my work, and how?

- Can I meet the editor I would work for?

- Can I talk with other reporters?

After the interview, write a letter thanking the editors and expressing a continued interest in the job. If you are not hired immediately, continue to write to the editors every few months, submitting fresh clips or other samples of your work.

If you are offered a job, be certain you understand the offer. Is it a full-time position? Will you start on probation? If so, how long will you remain on probation, and will your salary increase when you complete your probation? Also, will you be expected to own a car? If so, will your employer pay your mileage and other expenses?

To save money, some newspapers give college graduates jobs as correspondents, freelancers, clerks, trainees, interns or part-time employees. Typically, these positions pay less than other jobs on newspapers' staffs—and do not include medical insurance, paid vacations and other benefits.

Job Testing

Increasingly, news organizations test applicants for jobs on their staffs. Some also test current employees who want a promotion. The tests range from simple typing exams to more elaborate tests of an applicant's personality, mental ability, management skills and knowledge of current events. News organizations everywhere are also testing applicants for drugs. Almost all daily newspapers that give entry-level tests want to learn more about applicants' ability to spell and knowledge of grammar and punctuation. Most also test writing ability, and others check reporting and copy-editing skills. To test their writing skills, applicants often are given some rough notes, then asked to write a news story summarizing the information.

A growing number of major dailies asks applicants to complete tryouts: spending one to several days working in their newsrooms so editors can see how they handle everyday assignments.

Editors may try out three or four applicants before deciding which one will get the job. Generally, one in four newspapers uses tryouts. Very large dailies (those with circulations of more than 100,000) seem most likely to use tryouts.

CONDITIONS ON THE JOB

Job Satisfaction

What keeps journalists on the job? Many explain that they find their jobs varied, creative, important and challenging. Perhaps more than anyone else, journalists witness a kaleidoscope of the life within their communities: the good and the bad, the joyous and the tragic, the significant and the mundane. They are admitted everywhere and meet everyone. And, wherever they go, journalists share some of the power and prestige of the institutions they represent.

From a broader, more philosophical perspective, journalists represent the public when they cover a story. By providing citizens with the information they need to be well informed, journalists perform a vital function within a democratic society.

In addition, newspaper jobs give journalists an opportunity to write. And writing a good story—selecting the important facts, the correct words, the proper organization—is a highly creative process. It is also challenging. Within a few minutes, journalists may have to summarize a complex topic in a clear, accurate story that will interest the public. Within hours, even minutes, the story may be read, heard or seen by thousands of people.

Studies have found journalists also like their jobs because they like their colleagues and have opportunities to learn something new every day, acquire new skills and play a role in improving their communities.

Starting Salaries

Generally, people with better educations earn higher salaries. There are exceptions, however. Many jobs that seem to require roughly comparable intellectual skills offer much different salaries. And the best workers do not always receive the highest salaries.

Most markets have two or three television stations and several radio stations, so there can be keen competition among broadcast journalists. In contrast, most cities now have only one daily newspaper, so papers are less competitive than ever before. Some news executives may think they do not have to pay competitive salaries as a result. Some newsroom employees are represented by The Guild, a labor union of reporters, copy editors, artists and photographers. Salaries at those news organizations are controlled by contracts negotiated with the union.

Many new reporters double their salaries in five years, especially if they move to larger markets. News organizations often hire their new reporters on a probationary basis, then raise their salaries when they complete the probationary period satisfactorily. Also, many young journalists receive rapid promotions.

The median income for full-time journalists is $31,297. By profession, the median incomes are: $66,071 (newsmagazines), $43,696 (news services), $35,180 (daily newspapers), $25,625 (television), $20,865 (weekly newspapers) and $20,357 (radio).

Newsroom Organization and Procedure

Most journalism graduates who go to work for newspapers begin as reporters. As new reporters, they may spend the first several weeks in their offices, completing a variety of minor assignments:

answering telephones, writing obituaries, researching information, learning to operate equipment and rewriting news releases. Such work enables newcomers to become better acquainted with their employers' policies, and it enables supervisors to evaluate their work more closely. Or, to become better acquainted with a city, newcomers may follow experienced reporters on their beats. Or they may begin work in a suburban bureau. Many believe the police beat requires less expertise than other areas, so it is often assigned to the newest and least experienced reporter.

More experienced reporters are assigned beats, often a specific building such as the city hall, county courthouse or federal building. Other beats involve broader topics rather than a geographical location. The most common of those beats are business, education and religion. Larger news organizations establish dozens of more specialized beats, ranging from agriculture to art, from medicine to consumer affairs. This system promotes efficiency, because reporters become experts on the topics they cover and are able to cultivate important sources of information. Reporters often remain on the same beats for years, become well-acquainted with their sources and obtain information from them more easily than they could from strangers.

Each beat involves a topic that is especially newsworthy or a location where news is likely to arise or be reported. When a serious problem that merits news coverage arises, citizens often report it to one of the government offices regularly visited by reporters: police stations, firehouses or city hall.

On a typical day, the reporter assigned to cover, say, the city hall for a medium-sized morning daily, will begin work at about 9 a.m. and may write minor stories left from the previous day, scan other newspapers published in the area, rewrite minor news releases or study issues in the news. The reporter is likely to confer with an editor about major stories expected to arise that day, then go to the city hall at about 10 a.m. During the next hour or two, the reporter will stop in all the major offices in the city hall, especially those of the mayor, council members, city clerk, city treasurer and city attorney. The mayor or city manager is the most newsworthy individual in most communities and may meet with reporters in his or her office at a specified time every day to disseminate information about current developments (and to generate favorable publicity for himself or herself and the policies he or she favors).

The city hall reporter will return to the newsroom and quickly write all the day's stories. Other reporters, meanwhile, will begin gathering information from their respective beats. A few reporters may not even begin work until 3 or 4 p.m. Morning newspapers with multiple editions may have a 7 or 8 p.m. deadline for their first edition. The deadline for their final edition may be as late as 10 or 11 p.m. After that, stories must still be edited and printed, and the newspapers transported to subscribers' homes by 5 or 6 a.m.

Afternoon newspapers are becoming less popular than morning newspapers. Their reporters and copy editors typically work in shifts beginning at 7 a.m., and their first deadline may be as early as 10 or 11 a.m. so the final product can arrive at subscribers' doorsteps by 3 or 4 p.m.

Some experienced writers are given jobs as general assignment reporters, and they cover stories that arise outside the regular beats. The stories are more varied, often unexpected and often highly important. At newspapers, reporters compete for a number of other assignments, including jobs as columnists and as feature and editorial writers. These jobs are likely to be given to a newspaper's most experienced writers. Likewise, at television stations a novice's ultimate goal might be the anchor's chair or the post of executive producer or station manager. Some news organizations also hire correspondents to work in their state capitals and Washington, D.C. The number of such jobs is limited, and they too are given to experienced professionals.

Because they enjoy the work, some journalists remain reporters until they retire. Other journalists at newspapers become copy editors. Most copy editors check the stories written by reporters, write headlines for those stories and help arrange the stories on a page. Copy editors, like videographers and film editors at television stations, tend to be anonymous; they receive few bylines or credits and spend most of their time working at a desk behind the scenes. Jobs as copy editors are often more plentiful and harder to fill than jobs as newspaper reporters because the positions require an excellent command of the English language. This behind-the-scenes experience is essential for people seeking promotions.

Harcourt Brace & Company

The managing editor at most newspapers supervises a paper's day-to-day operations. Editors are responsible for budgets, policies, long-range planning and, at many smaller newspapers, writing their papers' editorials (larger dailies employ specialists to write their editorials).

Several subeditors supervise the various departments in newsrooms and report to the managing editor. Many of those appointments are given to people who have learned the necessary editing skills by working as copy editors. They include the following:

- City or metropolitan editor (the most important of a newspaper's subeditors), who is responsible for the coverage of local news and supervises the staff of reporters;

- News or wire editor, who reviews stories transmitted by news services, decides which stories to use and edits them;

- Sports editor, who oversees sports coverage at the local and national levels;

- Business editor, who tracks local businesses, real estate, manufacturing and labor, as well as state and national economic issues; and

- Features editor, who may handle a variety of stories, including those dealing with entertainment, fashion, religion and the arts.

If the paper publishes a Sunday edition, a series of editors could be responsible for that day's publication. Large dailies employ many subeditors, and each of them may have several assistants.

The publisher, who is the chief executive in a newspaper office, supervises the work of all the paper's major divisions, including the advertising, circulation and production departments. In the past, many publishers owned their own papers. Today, most publishers are appointed by groups that own the papers.

The Electronic Revolution in Newsrooms

During the past 35 years, an electronic revolution has transformed the way news stories are written, edited and published. Previously, reporters wrote their stories on typewriters, then used pencils to correct them. After proofreading a story, reporters pasted all its pages into one long strip, so none of the pages could be misplaced. Then reporters placed the story in a basket or impaled it on a sharp metal spike on their editor's desk. Editors used pencils to edit the story. Then typesetters operating Linotype machines used molten lead to set the story in type, line by line, and proofreaders checked the type for errors. Other skilled workers arranged the lead type in page forms and used those forms to make heavy metal plates that fit onto a newspaper's printing press.

Today, no typewriters, typesetters, proofreaders or printers are to be found in most newspaper buildings. Reporters type their stories on computers. Some reporters take portable computers with them to a courthouse, to meetings or to athletic events so they can file their stories more quickly using a modem and telephone lines. They no longer have to return to the office to write and transmit the story.

Working at another computer, an editor can correct and trim the story; a copy editor uses a computer to write a headline for the story; a page designer uses another computer to place stories, illustrations and advertisements together on a page. Once the page is completed, other employees photograph the entire page and make a lightweight printing plate from the negative.

Electronic systems save millions of dollars in production costs, primarily because they eliminate the need for printers and other skilled workers. News stories are typed only once, by reporters. Thirty-five years ago, The Washington Post employed more than 500 printers, and The New York Times employed about 800. Imagine how much money each of those newspapers saved by eliminating most of those positions, along with all the corresponding machinery, space, power and supplies.

Harcourt Brace & Company

Many reporters use laptop computers to write their stories and telephone lines to transmit those stories to their offices, whether across town or across the country.

The new systems are also faster and more accurate. A good Linotype operator could cast six to eight lines of type a minute. Keypunch operators who replaced them could punch a tape that enabled Linotypes to set 14 lines a minute. The newer machines type hundreds of lines a minute. Moreover, because stories no longer have to be retyped by production workers after being typed and edited by journalists, they contain fewer errors.

Because of their speed, the new systems enable editors to get more late-breaking stories into their newspapers—and give journalists more control over their papers' production processes.

FREE-LANCE WRITING

College students often dream of becoming free-lance writers. As free-lancers, the students imagine, they will be able to set their own hours, write only about topics that interest them, pursue those topics in greater depth, sell their stories to prestigious national magazines and live comfortably on their earnings.

Some journalists supplement their incomes by writing for other publications, but free-lancing is more difficult than most people realize. It's been estimated that 25,000 Americans call themselves free-lance writers, but only a few hundred earn a living at it. Most free-lancers hold another job or depend on a spouse's income. To supplement their incomes, some free-lancers write speeches and books or work part-time in public relations.

Harcourt Brace & Company

Why is it so difficult to make a living from free-lance work? Many of the big magazines that once bought articles from free-lancers have folded. They have been replaced by smaller, special-interest magazines that pay much lower rates. Other magazines no longer accept any articles from free-lancers, instead relying exclusively on full-time staff writers.

The competition among free-lancers is intense. Major publications receive hundreds of manuscripts for every one they accept. Even the best-written manuscripts may be rejected because they are inappropriate for a particular magazine or because the magazine has already accepted or published another article about the same topic or has received a similar article from a more famous writer whose byline will generate higher sales.

Free-lancers may spend days, weeks or even months working on an article, only to have it rejected by a dozen editors. Even if an article is accepted, it may be severely edited, or the free-lancer may be asked to rewrite it.

Free-lancers complain that magazines pay too little and too late. After submitting an article, a free-lancer may have to wait several months until it is accepted. The free-lancer may then be told that the magazine pays "on publication," which means the free-lancer will not receive any income from the article until it is published months later.

Hundreds of magazines pay by the word: often 5 to 10 cents for each word they publish. Other magazines pay a flat fee, often less than $100 per article. Relatively few magazines pay more than $500 an article. There are exceptions: Good Housekeeping pays a minimum of $1,500 for a 1,500 to 2,500-word article; Playboy pays a minimum of $3,000 for articles of 3,000 to 5,000 words, and Harper's magazine pays 50 cents to $1 a word for articles of 4,000 to 6,000 words. Some major publications also pay a "kill fee," usually about 25 percent of their normal rate, for articles they ask free-lancers to write but then decide not to publish.

Free-lancers must provide and equip their own offices. A few large magazines pay some of their expenses, but most magazines do not. Travel is expensive, and telephone, postage, computer and supply bills can total thousands of dollars a year. Many magazines prefer articles that are accompanied by illustrations, so successful free-lancers may also have to be skilled photographers—which involves spending even more money for cameras, film and developing costs. Moreover, free-lancers receive no fringe benefits: no medical or life insurance, no paid vacations, no pensions. On the plus side, many income tax deductions are allowed for their expenses.

Few literary agents are willing to take on beginning free-lancers as clients. Typically, the Scott Meredith Literary Agency in New York has advised potential clients, "If you are selling fiction or articles regularly to major national magazines, or have sold a book or screenplay or teleplay to a major publisher or producer within the last year, we'll be happy to discuss handling your output on the standard commission basis of 10 percent on all American sales and 20 percent on British and all foreign sales." If you are a beginner, however, you may have to pay an agent to handle your articles. Again, the Scott Meredith Agency has explained, "As recompense for working with beginners or newer writers until you begin to earn your keep through sales, our fee, which should accompany material, is $100 minimum charge per magazine story or article under 5,000 words."

Most literary agents prefer to handle book authors. After spending two or three days selling a book proposal to a publisher, the agents may collect 10 percent of a $50,000 fee. With a free-lancer's article, they may work two or three days, then collect 10 percent of a $3,000 fee.

Despite all these problems, free-lance writing can be an enjoyable hobby or part-time pursuit. It provides another outlet for people who like to write and enables them to supplement their incomes from other jobs. However, beginners are most likely to sell their articles to smaller, less prestigious publications. Those publications may not pay as much as Harper's or Playboy, but they receive fewer manuscripts and are much less demanding. Aside from a typewriter or computer, a successful free-lancer's indispensable tool is a book titled "Writer's Market." This guide, updated annually, lists thousands of markets for free-lance writers and describes the types of articles that each publication wants to buy and the fees it pays.

Harcourt Brace & Company

SUGGESTED READINGS

Arnett, Peter. *Live from the Battlefield: From Vietnam to Baghdad, 35 Years in the World's War Zones.* New York: Simon & Schuster, 1994.

Beasley, Maurine H., and Sheila J. Gibbons. *Taking Their Place: A Documentary History of Women and Journalism.* Washington, DC: American University Press, 1993.

Creedon, Pamela J., ed. *Women in Mass Communication: Challenging Gender Values,* 2nd ed. Newbury Park, CA: Sage, 1993.

Kuralt, Charles. *A Life on the Road.* New York: Ivy Books, 1991.

Mills, Kay. *A Place in the News: From the Women's Pages to the Front Page.* New York: Columbia University Press, 1990.

Reston, James. *Deadline: A Memoir.* New York: Random House, 1991.

Ricchiardi, Sherry, and Virginia Young. *Women on Deadline: A Collection of America's Best.* Ames, IA: Iowa State University Press, 1991.

Robertson, Nan. *The Girls in the Balcony: Women, Men and the New York Times.* New York: Random House, 1992.

Safer, Morley. *Flashbacks: On Returning to Vietnam.* New York: Random House, 1990.

Squires, James D. *Read All About It! The Corporate Takeover of America's Newspapers.* New York: Random House, 1993.

Weaver, David H., and G. Cleveland Wilhoit. *The American Journalist: A Portrait of U.S. News People and Their Work,* 2nd ed. Bloomington, IN: Indiana University Press, 1991.

Wilson, Clint C. *Black Journalists in Paradox: Historical Perspectives and Current Dilemmas.* Westport, CT: Greenwood Press, 1991.

Wolseley, Roland E. *The Black Press, U.S.A.,* 2nd ed. Ames, IA: Iowa State University Press, 1990.

———. *A Gallery of Black Journalists.* Nashville, TN: Winston-Derek, 1994.

Zinsser, William. *Speaking of Journalism: 12 Writers and Editors Talk About Their Work.* New York: HarperCollins, 1994.

CAREER AND SCHOLARSHIP INFORMATION

For more information about careers in journalism, write to the Dow Jones Newspaper Fund, P.O. Box 300, Princeton, NJ 08540. The Dow Jones Newspaper Fund is a foundation that encourages young people to consider careers in journalism. Its program includes awards, scholarships, internships, workshops and career information. Each year, the Newspaper Fund lists millions of dollars in scholarships available to journalism and communications majors.

Harcourt Brace & Company

CITY DIRECTORY

Like other city directories, this directory lists only the names of adults (people 18 and older) who live in your community. The directory does not list children under the age of 18, nor adults who live in other cities. Also, city directories (like telephone books) are published only once a year. Thus, they may not list people who moved to your community within the past year. When it conflicts with information presented in the exercises, always assume that the information in this directory is correct and the exercises are mistaken. You will be expected to correct the exercises' errors. If a name in an exercise is not listed in the directory, assume that the name is used correctly.

As you check the names of people involved in news stories, also check their addresses and occupations, since they may also be erroneous. Sources often make errors while supplying that information to police and other authorities. Also, a person's identity may add to a story's newsworthiness. You will find, for example, that some of the people involved in stories are prominent government officials.

Finally, assume that the people listed as university professors teach at your school.

SECTION I: DIRECTORY OF CITY OFFICIALS

Belmonte, William. Member, City Council
Brennan, Rosemary. Director, City Library
Cycler, Alice. Member, City Council
Datolli, Sabrina. Mayor
DeBecker, David. Member, School Board
Drolshagen, Todd. Director, Code Enforcement Board
Farci, Allen. City Attorney
Ferguson, Tony. City Treasurer
Gandolf, Sandra. Member, City Council
Graham, Cathleen, M.D. Director, City Health Department
Hernandez, Ramon. District Attorney
Hubbard, Gary. Superintendent of Schools
Kopperud, Barry. Police Chief
Lieber, Mimi. Member, School Board
Lo, Roger. Member, City Council
Lu, Judie. Member, School Board

Maceda, Diana. Member, School Board
Nemechek, Anna. Member, School Board
Nyad, Carole. Member, City Council
Nyez, Jose. Member, School Board
Onn, Tom. Director, City Housing Authority
Plambeck, Emil. Superintendent, City Park Commission
Ramirez, Luis. Member, City Council
Stoudnaur, Marlene, M.D. Medical Examiner
Sullivan, Tony. Fire Chief
Tribitt, Jane. Member, School Board
Tuschak, Joseph. Member, City Council
Vacante, Umberto. Member, School Board

SECTION II: DIRECTORY OF COUNTY OFFICIALS

Alvarez, Harold. County Administrator
Chenn, Anne. Member, County Commission
Dawkins, Kerwin. Director, Public Works
Dawkins, Valerie. Member, County Commission
DiCesari, Gus. Sheriff
Ellis, Faith. Member, County Commission
Gardez, Jose. Member, County Commission
Grauman, Roland. Member, County Commission
Hedricks, Donald. Assistant County Attorney
Laybourne, Raymond. Member, County Commission
McNally, Ronald. County Attorney
Morsberger, Diedre. Supervisor of Elections
Shenuski, Anita. Member, County Commission
Sindelair, Vernon. County Treasurer
Smith, Ronald. County Clerk
Wehr, Helen. Assistant County Attorney

SECTION III: JUDGES

Municipal Court

Hall, Marci   Kocembra, Edward

Circuit Court

Johnson, Edwin   Ostreicher, Marlene
Kaeppler, JoAnn   Pfaff, Randall
Levine, Bryce R.   Picott, Marilyn
McGregor, Samuel   Stricklan, Julian

Harcourt Brace & Company

SECTION IV: ABBREVIATIONS

acct	accountant	drgc	drug abuse counselor
admn	administration	econ	economist
adv	advertising	ele	elementary
agcy	agency	electn	electrician
agt	agent	emp	employee
appr	apprentice	eng	engineer
apt	apartment	est	estate
archt	architect	exec	executive
asmbl	assembler	facty	factory
assn	association	fed	federal
asst	assistant	ff	firefighter
athom	at home	formn	foreman
attnd	attendant	gdnr	gardener
atty	attorney	govt	government
aud	auditor	h	homeowner
av	avenue	hairdrsr	hairdresser
bkpr	bookkeeper	hosp	hospital
bldr	builder	hwy	highway
blvd	boulevard	inc	incorporated
brklyr	bricklayer	ins	insurance
bros	brothers	insp	inspector
capt	captain	jr	junior
carp	carpenter	jtr	janitor
cash	cashier	jwlr	jeweler
cc	community college	la	lane
ch	church	lab	laborer
chem	chemist	librn	librarian
chiro	chiropractor	lt	lieutenant
cir	circle/circuit	lwyr	lawyer
clk	clerk	mach	machinist
clns	cleaners	mech	mechanic
co	company	med	medical
colm	council member	mfg	manufacturing
com	commissioner	mgr	manager
const	construction	min	minister
cpl	corporal	mkt	market
crs	cruise consultant	mstr	master
ct	court	mtce	maintenance
ctr	center	muncp	municipal
cty	county	mus	musician
custd	custodian	nat	national
dent	dental/dentist	ofc	office
dep	deputy	ofer	officer
dept	department	opr	operator
det	detective	optn	optician
dir	director	pcpl	principal
dispr	dispatcher	pers	personnel
dist	district	pharm	pharmacist
dr	drive/driver	photog	photographer

phys	physician	slsr	sales representative
pl	place	soc	social
plmb	plumber	sq	square
pntr	painter	sr	senior
po	post office	st	street
polof	police officer	stat	station
pres	president	studt	student
prof	professor	supm	supermarket
pst	postal	supt	superintendent
pub	public	supvr	supervisor
r	resident/roomer	tech	technician
rd	road	techr	teacher
recpt	receptionist	tel	telephone
rel	relations	ter	terrace
rep	representative	treas	treasurer
repr	repairer	univ	university
rept	reporter	USA	U.S. Army
restr	restaurant	USAF	U.S. Air Force
retd	retired	USM	U.S. Marines
Rev	reverend	USN	U.S. Navy
sav	savings	vet	veterinarian
sch	school	vp	vice president
sec	secretary	watr	waiter
secy	security	watrs	waitress
sen	senator	wdr	welder
serv	service	wid	widow
sgt	sergeant	widr	widower
slsp	salesperson	wkr	worker

SECTION V: SAMPLE ENTRIES

Hurley Carl J & Mary; printer Weisz Printing Co & ofc sec Roosevelt Ele Sch
  1   2   3   4   5   6

            h 140 Kings Point Dr
            7   8

Hurley Ralph studt r 140 Kings Point Dr
    9   10 11   12

 1 = Family name
 2 = Names of spouses in alphabetical order
 3 = First listed spouse's occupation
 4 = First spouse's employer
 5 = Second listed spouse's occupation
 6 = Second spouse's employer
 7 = Homeowner
 8 = Home address
 9 = Name of roomer or renter 18 years of age or older
10 = Roomer/renter's occupation
11 = Resident or roomer
12 = Address

SECTION VI: ENTRIES

Aaron Betsy retd r410 Hillcrest St Apt 302

Abare Ann recpt Chavez Bros Chevrolet h855 Tichnor Way

Abbondanzio Anthony & Deborah; brklyr Wagnor Bros & athom h473 Geele Av

Abdondanzio Denise pub rel rep Haile Associates r3218 Holbrook Av Apt 832

Acevede Miguel atty h812 Bell Av

Acevede Esther & Louis; both retd h8484 Highland Dr

Adcock George & Lydia; mgr Blackhawk Hotel & soc wkr Catholic Social Services h141 N
    Cortez Av

Adler Sandra & Stuart; athom & min Ch of Christ r1847 Oakland Blvd

Adles Dora & John; athom & rep Bach & Co h1218 S 23rd St

Ahl Thomas C facty wkr Vallrath Plastics r2634 6th St Apt 382

Ahrons Tommy managing editor The Daily Courier h1097 Leeway Dr

Ahsonn Jeffrey R & Teresa; both retd h49 Groveland Av

Albertson Wanda pers dir Vallrath Plastics h529 Adirondack Av

Alicea Carlos cty emp h2930 Leisure Dr

Allen Christopher prof Pierce CC h1810 Collins Av

Allen James D & Margie; mach opr Collins Industries & atty h28 Rio Grande Rd

Allen Michael mech Allison Ford r410 Hillcrest St Apt 82

Allersen Alice & Thomas; athom & acct Mercy Hosp h418 Meridan Av

Alvarez Harold & Tina M; cty administrator & techr Washington Ele Sch r854 Maury Rd
    Apt 11B

Alvarez Jose cpl state hwy patrol h1982 Elmwood Dr

Alvarez Thomas studt r854 Maury Rd Apt 11B

Amanpor Effie & Elton; athom & technical writer Wirtz Electronics h823 E Pierce Av

Anchall Mildred dir Sunnyview Retirement Home r2202 8th Av Apt 382

Andrews Ira auto mech Allison Ford h561 Tichnor Way

Andrews Paula wid aud Blackhawk Hotel h4030 New Orleans Av

Aneesa Ahmad univ prof h1184 3rd Av

Aneja David & Tracy; sgt sheriff's dept & carp h488 Tulip Dr

Ansell Herman clk Blackhawk Hotel r2814 Ambassador Dr Apt 61

Antonucci William plmb Rittman Engineering Co r107 Hillside Dr Apt B

Arico James K pntr Kalina Painting & Decorating r9950 Turf Way Apt 703C

Baille Maggy wdr Halstini Mfg h810 N Ontario Av

Baliet Karen & Thomas; adv exec Baliet & Associates & pres Republican Bldrs h1440
    Walters Av

Ball James studt r1012 Cortez Av Apt 870

Barber Herbert & Irene; vp Denny's Restr Group & athom h2440 College Dr

Barlow Janet & Raymond; hairdrsr Lynn's Styling & dir United Way h2868 Moor St

Barlow Janie & Wesley r977 4th St Apt 2

Barlow Kevin polof r3363 Andover Dr

Barlow Robert A mech Allison Ford r112 Hope Cir

Barsch Margaret & Michael; athom & sgt police dept h2489 Hazel La

Barton Eileen owner/mgr Barton Sch of Dance h1012 Treasure Dr

Basa Shannon optn r6718 Fox Creek Dr Apt 1010

Baugh Marcia state consumer advocate h350 Meridan Av

Bealle Denise univ prof h1018 Cortez Av

Beasley Ralph pntr Kalina Painting & Decorating r810 Howard St

Beaumont Edward & Hazel; pst wkr & athom h7240 N Ontario Av

Beaumont Roger studt r7240 N Ontario Av

Becker Maurine & Ricky; athom & publisher The Daily Courier h1521 Cole Rd

Belcuor Christine & Paul; watrs Holiday House Restr & librn h497 Fern Creek Dr

Belmonte Lucy & William; mus & archt Belmonte & Associates & city colm h177 Andover Dr

Berg Mildred univ prof h984 Elmwood Dr

Biagi Allison polof r2634 6th St Apt 906B

Biegel Franklin custd Filko Furniture r782 12th Av

Blackfoot Jason & Veronica Dawn; archt & atty h2045 Wendover Av

Blanchfield Elaine owner/mgr Elaine's Jewelry r780 Cole Rd Apt 282

Bledsoe Edward & Rosalie; photog The Daily Courier & athom h833 Meridan Av

Blohm Kevin cook North Point Inn r5604 Woodland St

Bolanker Timothy studt r854 Murray Rd Apt 107B

Boyette Willis A jtr Barton Sch of Dance r2121 Biarritz Dr

Boyssie Betty & Lee; bkpr Allstate Ins & polof h1407 3rd Av

Brame Don city emp h3402 Virginia Av

Brennan Rosemary dir City Library h1775 Nair Dr

Brookes Oliver & Sunni; univ prof & technical writer Halstini Mfg h5402 Andover Dr

Brown Howard slsp Prudential Ins Co h2745 Collins Av

Bulnes Karen atty sch board h43 Princeton Pl

Burke Lynn & Randy; athom & capt USA h412 Wilson Av

Burmeister Abraham & Esther; pres First Nat Bank & athom h4439 Harding Av

Burmester Herman A & Sally; const wkr Rittman Eng Co & athom h1412 S 23rd St

Burnes Todd polof r1502 Matador Dr Apt 203

Burnes Tyrone min United Methodist Ch r8430 Wilson Av

Butler Irene & Max; athom & courier First Nat Bank r444 Jamestown Dr

Cain Fred & Irma; mus & athom r427 Hidden La

Cantrell Michael pres/mgr Mr. Muscles r410 South St

Capiello Ann studt r8210 University Blvd Apt 311

Carey John priest St. John Vianney Catholic Ch r2020 Oak Ridge Rd

Carey Myron univ prof h641 N Highland Dr

Carigg Craig & Susan; min Allen Chapel AME Ch & athom h453 Twisting Pine Cir

Carigg James R studt r453 Twisting Pine Cir

Carson Frank & Janice; serv formn Allison Ford & athom h2197 Marcel Av

Carter Deborah counselor Lovell Psychiatric Assn r550 Oak Parkway Apt 821

Caruna Alyce min Howell Presbyterian Ch h423 Charrow La

Carvel Reba techr Colonial Ele Sch r1883 Hope Ter

Casio David & Getta; atty r711 N 31st St Apt 220

Caspinwall Andrew r416 Wilson Av

Caspinwall Nadine phys h416 Wilson Av

Cessarini Maxine & Richard M; univ prof & phys r4184 Cypress Av

Charlton John city ff r3158 Virginia Av

Cheesbro Marilyn asst pub defender r1010 Eastview Rd Apt 3

Cheng Beverly exec dir State Restr Assn h643 Wymore Rd

Chenn Anne & Steven; cty com & lt fire dept r91 Melrose Av

Chevez Larry det police dept h4747 Collins Rd

Chmielewski Albert nurse Mercy Hosp r2814 Ambassador Dr Apt 82

Chuey Karen & William J; slsp Allison Ford & clk police dept r5710 Michigan Av

Cisneroes Andrew & Lillian; min Redeemer Lutheran Ch & athom r818 Bell Av

Claunch Amy clk Annie's Auto Parts r2418 Seasons Crt Apt B

Clayton Amy univ pres r820 Twisting Pine Cir

Cohen Abraham & Estelle; asst dir computer serv city sch system & pub rel rep Evans Pub Rel Group r1903 Conway Rd

Collin Ronald const wkr Wagnor Development Corp r2814 Ambassador Dr Apt 47D

Conaho Henry & Jeanne; supvr sales ERA Realty & pres Lake CC h820 Hope Ter

Correia Bobby & Dawn; supvr Delta Airlines h9542 Holbrook Dr

Cortez Manual & Nina; polof & bkpr North Point Inn r1242 Alton Rd

Cosby Minnie agt Watson Realty r487 Jamestown Dr

Courhesne Adolph & Gloria; mech Fridley Volkswagen & athom h1186 N Highland Av

Cowles Stephen jtr VFW Post 40 h8217 Cypress Av

Cross Andrea & Lee; chiro & city acct h2 Virginia Av

Cross Dina & Raymond E; athom & pst wkr r101 Charow La

Cruz Jena atty r48 DeLaney Av

Cullinan Charles A & Susan; both sheriff's dep r848 Rio Grande Rd

Cullinan Kyle polof h615 Pennsylvania Av

Curtis Sarah sr vp SunBank r663 Harding Av

Cycler Alice & Richard; city colm & atty r7842 Toucan Dr

Daigel Annette hairdrsr Anne's Beauty Salon r431 E Central Blvd

DaRoza Sue & Terry; studt & clk Jiffy Food Store r410 University Blvd Apt 80

Datolli Roger & Sabrina; retd & mayor r845 Conway Rd

Dawkins Agnes & Kerwin; athom & dir cty Dept of PubWorks r2203 Coble Dr

Dawkins Ronald & Valerie; brklyr & cty com r1005 Stratmore Dr

Dawson Shirley wid techr Colonial Ele Sch h492 Melrose Av

Deacosti Amy studt r3254 Virginia Av

Deacosti Michael & Peggy; pres Deacosti's Restr & hostess h3254 Virginia Av

Deboare Ann & Jack R; dir emp rel Rittman Industries & mgr Lucky's Supm r1415 Idaho Av

DeCastro Wilma techr Kennedy High Sch h3277 Pine Av

Dees Karen studt r410 University Blvd Apt 52

DeLoy Joseph R phys r280 Lancaster Rd Apt 110

Desaur Roland studt r700 Classics St

DeVitini Brenda & Ronald; asst min Redeemer Lutheran Ch & mach Rittman Industries r313 Coble Dr

DeWitt Tony studt r2230 Cortez Av Apt 828

Deyo Ashley & Ralph; graphic designer & dent r2814 Ambassador Dr Apt 7

DeZinno Marc & Nancy; asmbl Vallrath Industries & athom h205 Rockingham Ct

Diaz Diane & Richard; author & nurse St. Nicholas Hosp h1978 Holcroft Av

Diaz Enrique & Lisa; atty & pst wkr r3224 Mt Semonar Av

DiCesari Gus & Henrietta; cty sheriff & athom h980 Atlantic Av

Dillan Martha atty Westinghouse Corp h702 S Kirkmann Av

DiLorrento Allison univ prof h666 Texas Av

DiLorrento Anthony exec dir State Press Assn r7800 West Av Apt 477

Dolmovich Sandra M clk Dayton-Hudson h714 N 23rd St

Dow Tammy sgt police dept r2208 17th Av

Dowdell Laura & Thaddeus; clk & jwlr Dowdell Jewelry h620 Lexon Av

Drolshagen Illse & Todd; athom & dir city Code Enforcement Board h2406 Alabama Av

Dwyer Margaret studt r2047 Princeton Av Apt 405

Dysart Troy studt r724 Aloma Av Apt 24F

Edwards Traci R psychiatrist h3303 Lake Dr

Einhorn Doris & Robert; athom & univ phys h8320 Meadowdale Rd

Eisen Priscilla phys r1118 Bumby Av Apt 204

Ellam Dorothy R & Roger A; techr Madison Ele Sch & landscape contractor r2481 Santana Blvd

Ellerbe Robert widr pres Ellerbe's Boats h3213 Hidalgo Dr

Eulon Harley & Martha; jtr St. Nicholas Hosp & athom h410 E 3rd St

Evans Mark & Trish W; cty soc wkr & owner/mgr Evans Pub Rel Group h4232 Stewart Av

Evans Nikki & Timothy; loan ofer First Fed Sav & Loan & mgr Allstate Ins r806 Apple La

Farci Allen widr city atty h818 Texas Av

Favata Celia J wid h9930 Bumby Av

Ferguson Marcia & Tony; vet & city treas h96 West Av

Ferrell Fannie & Melvin; atty & pcpl Kennedy High Sch h2384 West Av

Firmett Rene J serv stat attnd Bert's Shell Stat r4474 Colyer Rd

Flavel Vernon J dr Becker Express h827 Pigeon Rd

Forlenza Henry custd Kmart r4620 Alabama Av Apt 22

Forsythe Scott cpl sheriff's dept h1414 S 14th Av

Foucault Carmen wid techr Aloma Ele Sch h1452 Penham Av

Fowler Barbara K & Fritz; polof & owner Fowler Allstate h88 Eastbrook Av

Fowler Joel studt r2006 Hillcrest St

Franklin Allen sgt USA r840 Apollo Dr Apt 322

Friedmann Leo asst dist atty r2814 Ambassador Dr Apt C2

Fusner Charles tech h89 Peachtree Dr

Gable Frances & Jay; athom & truck dr Becker Express h1701 Woodcrest Dr

Gandolf Sandra wid city colm h8 Hillcrest Av

Gant Diana univ prof h810 Village La

Gardepe Ellen serv mgr Derek Chevrolet h210 Lake Dr

Garland Charlotte & Chester; athom & city health insp h2008 N 21st St

Garner Cheryl & David; athom & emp City Recreation Dept r2814 Ambassador Dr Apt 88

Gianangeli David gdnr r48 Stempel Apt 53D

Giangelli Marlene P pres Pestfree Inc h214 Lake Dr

Gill Todd watr Fred's Steakhouse r1893 14th Av

Goetz Beryl dent & writer h1010 McLeod Rd

Golay Evelyn & Thomas A; cash & owner/mgr Tom's Liquors h1203 Texas Av

Goree Linda exec dir cty Girl Scout Council r2202 8th Av Apt 302

Gould Darlene & Savilla; athom & slsp Anchor Realty Co h4178 N 11th Av

Graham Cathleen & Ross R; dir City Health Dept & phys h710 Harding Av

Grauman Alice & Samuel; athom & min First Covenant Ch r610 Eisen Av

Grauman Roland & Tina; cty com & asst supt for pub education r3417 Charnow La

Green Joel atty h604 Michigan Av

Greenhouse Irwin & Trina; administrator Mercy Hosp & athom h9575 Holbrook Dr

Griffin Marlene det police dept h3130 Joyce Dr

Guarino Anne chiro r4100 Conway Rd Apt 611

Guarino Belva retd r84 Lakeland Av

Guarino Gerhard chiro h1813 Texas Av

Guarino Tony A techr Colonial High Sch h6139 Eastland Dr

Guerin Anita & Ronald E; athom & city ff r1045 Eastvue Rd

Guitterman Daniel bartender Jim's Lounge r550 Oak Park Way Apt 7

Gulas Gail & William J; studt & phys h3405 Virginia Av

Guyer Joseph & Rita; artist & athom h4043 S 28th St

Guzmann Trina mgr Sports Unlimited r2032 Turf Way Apt 230

Haile Jeffrey polof r2634 6th St Apt 847

Hall Marci muncp ct judge h34 Magee Ct

Halso Beverly & Jeff; pres Halso Pub Rel & vet r879 Tichnor Way

Hamill Kimberly mgr Albertson's supm h811 N Cortez Av

Hamill Margaret studt r811 N Cortez Av

Hammar Margaret J secy ofer Macy's Dept Store h1181 6th St

Hana Edward & Jena; min Unity Ch of Christianity & athom h134 Eisen Av

Hana Kyle custd Unity Ch of Christianity r134 Eisen Av

Hanson Lydia atty r880 6th St

Hanson Myron widr retd h880 6th St

Hariss Jerry R & Jewel; asst mgr House of Pancakes & athom h2245 Broadway Av

Harmon Rhonda watrs Red Lobster r816 Westwinds Dr Apt 8

Harnish Cheryl & David; supvr sales Cargell Corp & state sen h288 Hillcrest St

Haselfe Jennifer & Richard; athom & pres Haselfe Development Corp h554 Beloit Av

Haserott Mildred wid ticket agt Greyhound Lines r411 Wisconsin Av

Haskell Thomas widr lt fire dept h2482 Elmwood Dr

Hattaway Willie widr retd r411 Wisconsin Av

Hedricks Donald asst cty atty r4320 Elsie Dr Apt 884

Hemphall Loretta dir secy State Alliance Businesspeople h429 Conway Rd

Henderson Diane & Leon; athom & sheriff's dep h902 Patty Way

Hennigen Maggy polof r550 Oak Park Way Apt A3

Henricks Florence techr Risser Ele Sch h423 Marble Rd

Herdon Joyce atty h310 Mill Av

Hermann Andrew J & Jennifer; acct & teller First Nat Bank h1888 Hope Ter

Hernandez Ramon dist atty h84 Lake Cir

Herrin Raymond W univ prof h410 Park Av

Herwarthe Gregory L & Ruth; pres Knight Realty & asst mgr Harrington & Co Investments h4410 Baltimore Av

Heslinn Allison & Burt; clk Kmart & slsr Prudential Bache h8197 Locke Av

Heslinn Dorothy L mgr Mr. Grocer r8197 Locke Av

Higginbotham Gladies Anne mgr Secy Fed Bank h1886 Hope Ter

Hilten Randall J & Virginia; lt fire dept & athom h915 Baxter Dr

Hoequist Thomas owner/pres The Jewelry Shoppe h2418 Collins Av

Hoffmann Vivian wid clk Quik Shoppe h711 Meadow Creek Dr

Hoffsinger Nora wid retd r411 Wisconsin Av

Holland George & Tanaka; dr Greyhound Lines & athom h4368 Normandy Dr

Holland Keith studt r410 University Av Apt 11

Holland Maryanne adv exec Wilson Associates h947 Greenbrier Dr

Holman Evelyn & Leonard; athom & phys h4366 Normandy Dr

Holten Liz owner Holten Doughnuts h9512 Forest Grove

Holtzclaw Norma J wid slsp ERA Realty h739 West Av

Horan Roger sheriff's dep r118 Hillside Dr Apt C3

Howard Sarah polof h812 Bell Av

Howe Lynn studt r410 University Av Apt 318

Howland Ruth & Terry; owner Blackhawk Hotel & secy ofer Memorial Hospital h1808 Gladsden Blvd

Hubbard Gary & Peggy; supt of schs & athom h384 Hillcrest St

Hyde Marie & Roger; asst sch supt & slsp Ross Chevrolet h1381 Lakeview Dr

Iacobi Neil atty r6214 Maldren Av

Innis Alvin & Sarah; lt police dept & athom h1305 Atlantic Blvd

Jabil Stephen dr Becker Express r800 Crestbrook Loop Apt 314

Jacbos Martha mgr Mom's Donuts r1889 32nd St

Jaco Milan & Robyn; dir Blood Bank & athom h2202 S 8th St

Jacobs Bill & Carol; sgt police dept & dispr Yellow Cab h2481 Lakeside La

Janviere Jeanne techr Colonial Ele Sch r1883 Hope Ter

Jeffreys Michael dir Humane Society h2781 Collins Av

Jimenez Edwin C mgr Quik Shoppe r3611 31st St

Joanakatt Cathy asst dir We Care h2442 Collins Av

Johnson Edwin & Susan; cir ct judge & athom h148 West Av

Johnson Karen asst supt sch dist h2344 S 11th St

Johnson Marc const wkr r2643 Pioneer Rd

Jones Danny & Margaret; min Metro Life Ch & athom h1152 Darlington Av

Jones Lucinda & Samuel; athom & lt USM h4851 Edmee Cir

Jones Robyn & Sean; med tech Mercy Hosp & capt USN h4216 Winford Cir

Kaeppler JoAnn cir ct judge h2192 West Av

Kaeppler Lori & Ronald; athom & sgt USM h9540 Holbrook Dr

Kalani Andrew mgr Kalani Bros Bakery h2481 Kaley Way

Kalani Charles pres Kalani Bros Bakery h2481 Kaley Way

Kasandra Kelli retd r9847 Eastbrook La

Kasparov Linda univ dietitian r9103 Lake St

Keegan Patrick Jr fed atty h505 Walnut Dr

Keel Sally & Timothy; asmbl Cargell Corp & barber Plaza Barber Shop h1413 Griesi Dr

Kehole Marvin mtce wkr Cargell Corp r182 W Broadway Av

Kernan Russell mach Vallrath Industries r168 Lake St

Kindstrom Sarah watrs Steak & Ale h4828 N Vine St

Kirkmann James dr Yellow Cab r816 Westwinds Dr Apt 202

Knapp Erik A cook Frisch's Restr r2314 N 11th St

Kocembra Edward & Heather; muncp ct judge & athom h388 31st St

Koche Ellen Jane atty Neighborhood Law Ofc h4214 Azalea Ct

Kopez Frank & Lisa; cty mech & athom h1067 Eastland Av

Kopp Suzanne wid retd r4200 S 11th St Quality Trailer Ct

Kopperud Barry widr chief of police h458 Kaley Way

Kostyn Elizabeth & Ralph E; athom & asst supt for ele education city schs h284 Erie Av

Krueger Melody & William; athom & pres Aladdin Paints h48 Michigan Av

Kubic Marilyn & Ralph; both techrs North High Sch h1452 N 3rd St

Kunze Lauren & Robert; athom & mach Vallrath Industries r94 Jamestown Dr Apt 318

LaCette Cecil serv stat attnd r2814 Ambassador Dr Apt 61

Lasiter Harriet & James; athom & techr Roosevelt Ele Sch r374 Walnut Dr

Layous Michael E studt r212 N Wisconsin Av

LeClair George cir ct judge h501 Mont Clair Blvd

Lee Fred owner/cook Kona Village h1181 24th St

Leforge Ted dent h537 Peterson Pl

Leidigh Floyd & Rose; const wkr Rittman Engineering Co & athom h1812 Dickins Av

Levin Ida mgr Mr. Waterbeds h8521 Shady Glen Dr

Levine Bryce R & Trina; cir ct judge & athom h8521 Shady Glen Dr

Lewis Jacquelin & Jonnie; watrs Holiday House & insptr Vallrath Industries h1840 Maldren Av

Linn Eddy & Marie; sgt police dept & athom h6287 Airport Blvd

Linn Ronald studt r6287 Airport Blvd

Lo Joan & Roger; athom & city colm h1993 Collins Av

Logass Jeffrey econ Larco Corp h81 Venetian Way

Lowdes Enrico & Sandra; dir Regional Medical Center & athom h77 Maldren Av

Lowrie Catrina phys Regional Med Ctr r118 Hillside Dr Apt 74

Lowrie Cynthia studt r118 Hillside Dr Apt 74

Lozando Marie clinical dir Mercy Hosp r234 E Markham Dr Apt 4

Lucas Frank cpl hwy patrol h2417 Country Club Dr

Lydin Charles R mgr LaCorte Printing Co h888 Melrose Av

Macbos Martha dir of nursing Mercy Hosp h1889 32nd St

Macco Alan mus r503 29th St

Madea Ramon exec dir Bon Voyage Travel Agcy r118 Hillside Dr Apt 606

Mahew Arthur mgr Fische's Bowling Alley h1918 Pacific Rd

Majorce Albert & Monica; archt & athom h2882 Ambassador Dr

Marcheese Harvey O & Joyce; min & organist Faith Baptist Ch h1481 Cole Rd

Mariston Saundra watrs Freddy's Inn h822 Kentucky Av

Matros Margo univ prof r410 University Av Apt 818

McCartney Mildred wrk Holten Doughnuts h1212 Alexandrea St

McCauley Melvin & Veronica; truck dr Becker Express & athom h540 Osceola Blvd

McDonald Herbert J & Rosalie; owner/mgr Tastee Popcorn & athom h1842 Hazel La

McDowell William pntr h1429 Highland Dr

McEwen Lonnie & Victoria; techr Washington Jr High Sch & athom h1024 Nancy Cir

McFarland Charlotte nursing supvr Sand Lake Hosp h1090 Timberline Trail

McFerren Patrick J widr U.S. postmaster h1227 Baldwin Dr

McFerren Patti const wkr Rittmann Engineering Co r816 Westwinds Dr Apt 3

McGorwann Karen cc prof r4320 Elsie Dr Apt 6

McGowen Bill & Rosalind; const wkr Rittmann Engineering Co & maid Hyatt Hotel h4842 S Conway Rd

McGowin William sheriff's dep h4224 N 21st St

McGrath Sunni jtr Washington Ele Sch h109 19th St

McGregor Carol & Samuel; mgr trainee Albertson's Supm & cir ct judge h1501 Southwest Ct

McIntry Eugene & Irene; pres McIntry Realty & athom h2552 Post Rd

Meir Sharon pers dir Vallrath Industries r810 Kalani St Apt 2

Mejian Colette pcpl Risser Ele Sch h415 Ivanhoe Blvd

Merrit Jacob & June; eng WTMC-TV & athom h301 Wymore Rd

Meyer Robert & Sonia M; sgt USAF & credit mgr Sears h811 Moor St

Miehee Margaret & Richard; athom & asst U.S. postmaster h1190 Euclid Av

Millan Timothy cook Grande Hotel r1112 Huron Av

Miller Sharon optn LensCrafters h2827 Norwell Av

Minh Stephen retd r410 Hillcrest St Apt 842

Moravchek Albert & Dorothy; city ff & clk police dept h4187 N 14th St

Moronesi Donna slsr Adler Real Estate h623 N 5th St

Morrell Cathy & Wayne; athom & mgr Bon Voyage Travel Agency h382 Arlington Cir

Morsberger Diedre cty supvr elections h898 Hemlock Dr

Muldaur Eddy studt r660 S Conway Rd

Murhana Thomas lab Cargell Corp r40 W Hillier Av

Murphy Joseph & Kathleen; dir research Collins Industries & athom h114 Conway Rd

Murray Blair & Patricia; mgr Beneficial Finance & athom h1748 N 3rd St

Murray Harold & Marty; atty & curriculum resource techr h1801 Hillcrest St

Neely Myron A det police dept h1048 Jennings Rd

Nego Alan polof r1840 Wymore Rd Apt 10

Nemnich Harlan & Helen Marie; electr & retd h1331 Mt Vernon Blvd

Nicholls Cheryl fed emp h1287 Belgard Av

Noffsinger Nora wid retd r411 Wisconsin Av

Noonan Jack widr det police dept h5928 Jody Way

Nouse Sharon pilot Aerial Promotions Inc r4740 Valley View La

Novarro Paula colm h41 Pine Way

Novogreski Harry R & Melba; mach Keller Plastics & athom h2891 Morris Av

Nunez Carolynn & Roger; athom & eng Kelle-Baldwin Corp h2820 Norwell Av

Nunziata Carmen h1410 1st Av

Nyad Carole city colm h850 Sutter Loop

Nyer JoAnne sec Washington Ele Sch r550 Oak Park Way Apt 264

Nyez Diana studt r550 Oak Park Way Apt 264

O'Hara Allison city sec r4729 Texas Av

Oldaker George polof r2117 Wisconsin Av Apt 488

Oldaker Thomas polof r2117 Wisconsin Av Apt 488

Oliver Franklin R & Jeannette; exec Gill Assoc Inc Pub Rel & athom h1121 Elm Blvd

Onn Esther & Tom C; athom & dir City Housing Authority h3869 Jefferson Av

Ortiz Lynn & Randy; athom & brklyr HomeRite Builders r816 Westwinds Dr Apt 78

Ortson Martha & Thomas J; athom & vp Secy First Fed Bank h810 N 14th St

Ostreicher Marlene wid cir ct judge h449 Ferncreek Cir

Paddock Cynthia & Thomas C; credit mgr Belks Dept Store & mach Cargell Corp h1736 Hinkley Rd

Palomino Molly & Ralph R; athom & vp Genesco Inc h374 Douglas Rd

Patzell Bruce & MaryAnne; carp & athom h915 Bishop Dr

Patzell Larry studt r915 Bishop Dr

Paynick Nina & Stanley; techr Washington Ele Sch & owner Paynick's Carpets h901 2nd St

Peerson Marc univ prof h4851 Edmee Cir

Perakiss Ethel & Michael; athom & atty h876 Collins Av

Percy John atty h1037 2nd St

Perez Jason const wkr Wagnor Development Corp r2414 Skan Ct

Perez Joseph & Vicki; city emp & lt police dept h2414 Skan Ct

Petchski Pearl asst cash Morrison's Cafeteria r411 Wisconsin Av

Peters Frederick & Rene C; pharm Kmart & pres Humane Society h484 Sugar Ridge Ct

Peterson Sara wid h1671 Drexel Av

Pfaff Randall cir ct judge h2134 Oak Ridge Rd

Phillips Teresa M clk The Jewelry Shoppe r800 Crestbrook Loop Apt 228

Picardo Marie nurse r510 Concord St Apt 48

Picott Marilyn cir ct judge h901 2nd St

Piloto Claire & Kenneth T; interior decorator & atty Piloto & Herndon h1472 Bayview Rd

Pinccus Jennifer atty Piloto & Herndon r2021 Dyan Way Unit 2

Pinckney Samuel & Terese; retd & athom h976 Grand Av

Pinero Jim Timmons dvlpr Pinero Developers h2411 Windsong Dr

Ping Dorothy & Louis; athom & plmb Lou's Plumbing h348 Conroy Rd

Plambeck Dolly & Emil; athom & supt City Park Com h6391 Norris Av

Porej Irvin vp for loans First Fed Sav & Loan h112 Anzio St

Povacz Julius city paramedic r210 E King Av Apt 4

Proppes Richard E asst mgr Safeway Supm h1012 2nd St

Pryor Lynne R const wkr Rittmann Engineering Co r2634 6th St Apt 45

Rafelsin Louis lt police dept h934 Old Tree Rd

Ramirez Harriet & Luis; dent asst & city colm h982 Euclid Av

Randolph James const wkr Rittman Engineering Co r654 Harrison St

Ray Elizabeth & William David; both retd h112 Riverfront Dr

Reeves Charlton E & Polly; state health ofer & athom h658 Lennox Av

Reimer Maurice & Mildred; acct & athom h2529 Barbados Av

Richards Patricia r42 Tusca Trail

Richardson Inez & Thomas E; athom & polof h5421 Jennings Rd

Richbourg Bud & Kathleen; owner/mgr Buddy's Lounge & athom h1014 Turkey Hollow

Richter Robyn Anne retd h42 Tusca Trail

Riggs Gladies Ann wid retd r1080 Harvard Rd Apt 4

Rivera Hector phys Medi-First Clinc r800 Crestbrook Loop Apt 38

Rivera Maxwell tech h11 Calico Crt

Robbitzsch John W psychiatrist h1014 Bear Creek Cir

Roehl Cecil & Esther; polof & athom h1228 Euclid Av

Romaine Gerri & Nickolas H; athom & wdr h2876 Post Av

Romansaik Michael const wkr Wagnor Development Corp r118 Hillside Dr Apt 8

Rudnike Harold & Martha; athom & sales mgr Vallrath Industries h4825 N Vine St

Ruffenbach Laura univ prof h6741 Waxwing La

Ruiz George & Lila; polof & athom h263 9th St

Ruiz Guillermo & Harriet; asst cty med examiner & dir pub affairs Regional Med Ctr h4718 Bell Av

Rybinski Kim owner Kim's Pets r2634 6th St Apt 710

Salcido Martha & Tony; athom & city ff h10 Exeter Ct

Saleeby Henry widr retd r84 Sunnyvale Rd

Saleeby Claire & John; athom & lt colonel USA h626 N 3rd St
Saleeby Olivida & Wesley; both retd h1916 Elizabeth La
Sanchez Gumersinda hairdrsr Lillian's Beauty Salon h173 Burgasse Rd
Satava Kenneth widr techr Kennedy High Sch h2204 Marcel Av
Saterwaitte Benjamin widr retd h307 E King Blvd
Sawyer Claire min Christian Redeemer Ch h7400 Southland Blvd
Sawyer Betty & Harley; athom & techr Kennedy High Sch r2032 Turf Way Apt 512
Schifini Destiny vp SunBank h3620 Timber Ter
Schipper Michele studt r4100 Conway Rd Apt 814
Schweitzer Ralph city building insp r816 Westwinds Dr Apt 160
Scott Kerry & Nancy; slsp Kohlerware & athom h4189 Hazel St
Scott Milan & Nancy; techr Kennedy High Sch & techr Wilson Ele Sch h20 Magee Ct
Shadgott Carol & Frank D; athom & phys h8472 Chestnut Dr
Sharp Lynita L clk Jiffy Foods r5836 Bolling Dr
Shattuck Christina & Dennis A; mgr Perkins Restr & emp city garage h532 3rd St
Shearer Ethel cocktail watrs Melody Lounge r408 Kasper Av Apt 718
Shenuski Anita & Frederic; cty com & dist mgr IRS h1230 Embree Cir
Shepard Frank & Helen; techr & rept h107 Eastbrook Av
Shepard Linn Marie studt r854 Murray Rd Apt 107B
Sheppard Ronald lt fire dept r2024 Vincent Rd Apt 1020
Shisenauntt Arthur & Lillian; secy consultant & pharm Walgreen h1243 Washington Av
Shoemaker JoAnn techr Colonial High Sch r6139 Eastland Dr
Silverbach Daniel G & Jill; polof & athom h3166 Wayne Av
Simmens Karen dist dir Greenpeace r708 E Lisa La
Simmons Rachel & Wayne; athom & slsp Prudential Ins h708 E Lisa La
Sindelair Elaine & Vernon; athom & cty treas h4164 Mandar Dr
Skinner Dorothy & Roger; clk typist Lawton Bros & polof h2080 Washington Av
Skurow Melvin widr carp h4138 Hennessy Ct
Slater Carolyn & David; athom & chiro h8443 Turkey Hollow
Smith Grady r8213 Peach St
Smith Linda M & Ronald; studt & cty clk h1814 N 3rd St
Smitkins Marlene & Myron; athom & mach Kohlarware h417 Huron Av
Smythe Asa A & Carol; cty emp & athom h4280 Timber Trail
Smythe Terry studt r4280 Timber Trail
Snow Dale & Terri; athom & nurse Mercy Hosp h4381 Hazel St
Snowdin Elizabeth clk state employment ofc h952 Kasper Av
Snyder Christina dir pub rel Mercy Hosp h711 Broadway Av
Sodergreen Karl & Lillian; phys & athom h788 Timber Trail
Sota Mimi dir Drug Abuse Unit Mercy Hosp h655 Brickell Dr
Stevens Julie Ann mus h624 N 3rd St
Stockdale George & Lillian; capt USM & athom h472 Bolling Dr
Stoudnaur John & Marlene; mgr Rexall Drugs & city med examiner h1350 41st St
Stovall Iris wid mgr Quikke Clns h7204 Southland Blvd
Straitten Karen & Walter; athom & cty building insptr r4450 Richmond Rd
Stricklan Julian cir ct judge h4268 Wayne Av
Sulenti Allen D studt r800 Crestbrook Loop Apt 1010
Sullivan Tony widr fire chief h863 Benchwood Ct
Svec Wallace A mech Allison Ford r4320 Elsie Dr Apt 1
Svendson Lillian & Wayne; athom & city paramedic h814 Washington Av
Swaugger Charlotte & Samuel; cc prof & rept The Daily Courier h4987 Huron Dr
Sweers Daniel & Karen; fed emp & det police dept h108 Eastbrook Av
Tai Wendy housekeeper Hilton Hotel r84 Chestnut Dr
Talbertsen Sarah A artist h3214 Riverview Dr

Harcourt Brace & Company

Taylor Fredric C r4828 N Vine St

Taylor Marsha L mgr McDonald's h2012 Lincoln Av

Temple Roger polof r2032 Turf Way Apt 818

Thistell Dirk & Mildred R; eng Rittman Industries & counselor Roosevelt High Sch h528
    Kennedy Blvd

Thomas Joseph techr Kennedy High Sch r2848 Santa Av Apt 2

Thompsen Yvonne studt r1012 University Av Apt 812

Tifton Albert & Marsha; capt fire dept & athom r2814 Ambassador Dr Apt 417

Tijoriwalli Cathy owner Cathy's Sandwiches r1320 S Embree Cir

Tiller Ida & Julius; athom & polof h539 Sheridan Blvd

Tilman Marion & Randall C; athom & city health insptr h818 N 41st St

Tontenote Eldred L & Lisa; mech Ace AutoBody & athom r2634 6th St Apt 17

Totmann Gloria & Marvin; dent asst & secy guard Brinks h1818 4th St

Tribitt Jane mgr Colonial Apts r1040 Colonial Way Apt 101

Tuschak Arlene & Joseph; master electn & city colm h2094 Byron Av

Ungarient James R & Margaret; both attys The Law Office h7314 Byron Av

Uosis Bobbie & Michael; both retd h4772 E Harrison Av

Vacante Mary & Umberto; athom & technical writer Lockheed Martin h3202 Joyce St

Vacanti Carlos & Carol; polof & athom h4910 Magee Ct

Valderama Lynn dir secy JCPenney h1020 Lincoln Av

Van Atti Joseph & Trina; city ff & athom h960 Stratmore Dr

Van Den Shuck Margaret pub serv rep Allstate Ins h7663 Robinhood Dr

VanPelt Audrey W & James; min First United Methodist Ch & serv mgr Lane Toyota h420
    N Wilkes Rd

Vasquez Guillermo & Miranda; dir State Dept of Corrections & athom h2801 Norwell Av

Veit Helen Lynn min First Covenant Ch h184 Nelson Av

Verdugo Maureen pcpl Kennedy High Sch r816 Westwinds Dr Apt 482

Verkler LeeAnn univ prof r800 Crestbrook Loop Apt 10A

Vermell Cathy S dr Yellow Cab r1010 Vermont Av

Vorholt Andrew A owner/mgr Hallmark Cards h10 E Lake Rd

Wagnor Kristine & Timothy Sr; athom & owner/mgr Tim's Coffee Shop r418 N Wilkes Rd

Ward Frances & Jon H; athom & sgt/recruiter USA r3113 DeLaney Av

Ward Lonnie D mtce wkr Colonial Apts r2814 Ambassador Dr Apt 22

Warniky Clara & Wayne; mgr Hertz Rent A Car & polof h418 N Wilkes Rd

Washington Bruce R atty David Casio & Associates r1104 Esplada Av Apt 19

Waundry James R & Lisa; mgr 2-Hour Clns & athom h5310 Stratmore Dr

Weber Nancy techr Washington Ele Sch h44 E Princeton St

Wehr Helen asst cty atty h1298 Vermont Av

Wei Albert sgt police dept h964 Jody Way

Weinstein Jeanette techr Colonial High Sch h6139 Eastland Dr

Weiskoph Herman asst min John Calvin Presbyterian Ch h4817 Twin Lakes Blvd

Wentilla Lorrie & Reid R; athom & pres Keele-Baldwin Corp h640 Clayton Av

West Billy L asst min John Calvin Presbyterian Ch h452 Central Blvd

Whidden Bonnie sec cty fair h2913 Oak La

White Katherine mgr Blackhawk Hotel h4218 Bell Av

Whitlock Randall vp Wagnor Development Corp h504 Sutter Loop

Wiess Robert A wkr Belks Moving & Storage r2032 Turf Way Apt 338

Wilke James & Laura; sgt police dept & sheriff's dep h2420 Highland Av

Willging Judy & Jurgen; athom & owner/mgr Choice Video Rentals h2204 S 8th St

Willging Marty & Tessie; dir YMCA & athom h1808 Gadsden Blvd

Williams Jon R tech K107 Radio r814 Harding Av

Williams Patricia J retd h1338 Biarritz Dr

Williams Phyllis nurse Lovell Psychiatric Assn r1220 Jasper Av Apt 56

Wong Phyllis & Steven I; mgr Sears & athom h441 S 28th St
Woods Amy dir State Federation of Independent Businesses h640 Sherwood Dr
Wymann Barbara & Paul; athom & mech Lane Toyota h2020 Lorry La
Yamer Frank studt r118 Hillside Dr Apt 1020
Yapenco Nancy & Thomas; athom & writer h4941 Pine St
Younge Rachel techr Kennedy High Sch r3361 Bolling Dr
Zarrinfair Lois retd r411 Wisconsin Av
Zerwinn Sarah h2021 Dyan Way
Zito Allen and Linda; archt Zito Associates & marketing dir Blood Bank h818 Jamestown
    Dr
Zito Nancy & Robert; athom & pharm Kmart h328 Winford Cir
Zozulla Wesley polof h5219 Ranch Rd
Zumbaddo Carlos general mgr cty fair h1902 White Av

Harcourt Brace & Company

THE ASSOCIATED PRESS STYLEBOOK

The following pages summarize the most commonly used rules in The Associated Press Stylebook and Libel Manual. Section and subsection numbers have been added. These selected rules have been reprinted with the permission of The Associated Press. Most newspapers in the United States—both dailies and weeklies—follow the rules it recommends.

Complete copies of The Associated Press Stylebook and Libel Manual can be ordered from most bookstores.

SECTION 1: ABBREVIATIONS

1.1 COMPANY. Abbreviate and capitalize *company, corporation, incorporated, limited* and *brothers* when used after the name of a corporate entity. *Gateway Inc. builds computers.* Do not capitalize or abbreviate when used by themselves: *She works for the company.*

1.2 DEGREES. Generally avoid abbreviations for academic degrees. Use instead a phrase such as: *John Jones, who has a doctorate in psychology.* Use an apostrophe in *bachelor's degree, a master's,* etc. Use abbreviations such as *B.A., M.A., LL.D.* and *Ph.D.* only when the need to identify many individuals by degree on first reference would make the preferred form cumbersome.

1.3 DO NOT ABBREVIATE: *assistant, association, attorney, building, district, government, president, professor, superintendent* or the days of the week, or use the ampersand (&) in place of *and* in news stories.

1.4 INITIALS. Use the initials of organizations and government agencies that are widely recognized: *NATO, PTA, CIA, FBI* (no periods). The first time you mention other organizations, use their full names. On second reference, use their abbreviations or acronyms only if they would be clear or familiar to most readers.

1.5 JUNIOR/SENIOR. Abbreviate and capitalize *junior* and *senior* after an individual's name: *John Jones Jr.* (no comma).

1.6 MPH/MPG. The abbreviation *mph* (no periods) is acceptable in all references for miles per hour. The abbreviation *mpg* (miles per gallon) is acceptable only on second reference.

1.7 STATES. Do not use postal abbreviations for states. Eight states are never abbreviated: *Alaska, Hawaii, Idaho, Iowa, Maine, Ohio, Texas* and *Utah*. Abbreviations for other states

584

include: *Ala., Ariz., Ark., Calif., Colo., Conn., Del., Fla., Ga., Ill., Ind., Kan., Ky., La., Md., Mass., Mich., Minn., Miss., Mo., Mont., Neb., Nev., N.H., N.J., N.M., N.Y., N.C., N.D., Okla., Ore., Pa., R.I., S.C., S.D., Tenn., Vt., Va., Wash., W. Va., Wis.* and *Wyo.*

1.8 TITLES. Abbreviate the following titles when used before a full name outside direct quotations: *Dr., Gov., Lt. Gov., Sen., the Rev.* and certain military titles such as: *Pfc., Cpl., Sgt., 1st Lt., Capt., Maj., Lt. Col., Col., Gen., Cmdr.* and *Adm.,* among others. Spell out all except *Dr.* when used before a name in direct quotations.

1.9 U.N./U.S. Spell out *United Nations* and *United States* when used as nouns. Use *U.N.* and *U.S.* (no space between initials) only as adjectives.

SECTION 2: ADDRESSES

2.1 ADDRESSES. Always use figures for an address number: *9 Morningside Circle.*

2.2 DIRECTIONS. Abbreviate compass points used to indicate directional ends of a street or quadrants of a city in a numbered address: *562 W. 43rd St., 600 K St. N.W.* Do not abbreviate if the number is omitted: *East 42nd Street.*

2.3 STREETS. Spell out and capitalize *First* through *Ninth* when used as street names; use figures with two letters for *10th* and above: *7 Fifth Ave., 100 21st St.* Use the abbreviations *Ave., Blvd.* and *St.* only with a numbered address: *1600 Pennsylvania Ave.* Spell them out and capitalize when part of a formal street name without a number: *Pennsylvania Avenue.* All similar words (*alley, drive, road, terrace,* etc.) are always spelled out.

SECTION 3: CAPITALIZATION

In general, avoid unnecessary capitals. Use a capital letter only if you can justify it by one of the principles listed here.

3.1 ACADEMIC DEPARTMENTS. When mentioning an academic department, use lowercase except for words that are proper nouns or adjectives: *the department of history, the department of English, the English department.*

3.2 AWARDS/EVENTS/HOLIDAYS/WARS. Capitalize awards (*Medal of Honor, Nobel Prize*), historic events (*Camp David Peace Treaty*), periods (*the Great Depression, Prohibition*), holidays (*Christmas Eve, Mother's Day*) and wars (*the Civil War, Persian Gulf War*).

3.3 BIBLE/GOD. Use *Bible* (no quotation marks) and *God* but lowercase pronouns referring to the deity (*he, his, thee*).

3.4 BRAND NAMES. Capitalize brand names: *Buick, Ford, Mustang.* Lowercase generic terms: *a car.* Use brand names only if they are essential to a story.

3.5 BUILDINGS/ROOMS. Capitalize the proper names of buildings, including the word *building* if it is an integral part of the proper name: *the Empire State Building.* Also capitalize the names of specially designated rooms: *Blue Room, Oval Office.* Use figures [for room numbers] and capitalize *room* when used with a figure: *Room 2, Room 211.*

3.6 CAPITOL. Capitalize *U.S. Capitol* and *the Capitol* when referring to the building in Washington, D.C., or to state capitols.

3.7 CONGRESS. Capitalize *U.S. Congress* and *Congress* when referring to the U.S. Senate and House of Representatives. Lowercase when used as a synonym for *convention.*

Lowercase *congressional* unless it is part of a proper name: *congressional salaries, the Congressional Record.*

3.8 CONSTITUTION. Capitalize references to the *U.S. Constitution,* with or without the *U.S.* modifier. Lowercase *constitutional* in all uses. Also capitalize *Bill of Rights, First Amendment* (and all other amendments to the Constitution).

3.9 DIRECTIONS/REGIONS. In general, lowercase *north, south, northeast,* etc., when they indicate a compass direction; capitalize when they designate geographical regions: *the Atlantic Coast states, Deep South, Sun Belt, Midwest. He drove west. The cold front is moving east. The North was victorious. She has a Southern accent.*

3.10 DO NOT CAPITALIZE. *administration, first lady, first family, government, presidential, presidency, priest,* seasons of the year (*summer, fall, winter, spring*), and years in school (*freshman, sophomore, junior, senior*).

Also lowercase the common-noun elements of all names in plural uses: *the Democratic and Republican parties, Main and State streets, lakes Erie and Ontario.*

3.11 EARTH. Generally lowercase *earth;* capitalize when used as the proper name of the planet.

3.12 GOVERNMENT. Capitalize *city, county, state* and *federal* when part of a formal name: *Dade County, the Federal Trade Commission.* Retain capitalization for the name of a specific body when the proper noun is not needed: *the County Commission.* Generally, lowercase elsewhere.

Also capitalize *city council, city hall, courthouse, legislature, assembly,* etc., when part of a proper name: *the Boston City Council.* Retain capitalization if the reference is to a specific city council, city hall, etc., but the context does not require the specific name: *The City Council met last night.*

3.13 HIGHWAYS. Use these forms, as appropriate in the context, for highways identified by number: *U.S. Highway 1, U.S. Route 1, Route 1, Illinois 34, Illinois Route 34, State Route 34, Route 34, Interstate Highway 495, Interstate 495.* On second reference only for Interstate: *I-495.* When a letter is appended to a number, capitalize it but do not use a hyphen: *Route 1A.*

3.14 MILITARY. Capitalize names of the U.S. armed forces: *the U.S. Army, the Navy, Marine regulations.* Use lowercase for the forces of other nations.

3.15 NATIONALITIES/RACE. Capitalize the proper names of nationalities, races, tribes, etc.: *Arab, Caucasian, Eskimo.* However, lowercase *black, white, mulatto.* Do not use the word *colored.* In the United States, the word is considered derogatory.

3.16 PLURALS. To form the plural of a number, add *s* (no apostrophe). To form the plural of a single letter, add *'s.* To form the plural of multiple letters, add only *s: 1920s. Mind your p's and q's. She knows her ABCs.*

3.17 POLITICAL PARTIES. Capitalize both the name of a political party and the word *party: the Democratic Party.* Also capitalize *Communist, Conservative, Republican, Socialist,* etc., when they refer to a specific party or to individuals who are members of it. Lowercase when they refer to a political philosophy. After a name, use this short form, set off by commas: *D-Minn., R-Ore., Sen. Hubert Humphrey, D-Minn., said. . . .*

3.18 PROPER NOUNS. Capitalize proper nouns that constitute the unique identification for a specific person, place or thing: *the River Raisin.* Lowercase common nouns when they stand alone in subsequent references: *the party, the river, the street.*

3.19 SATAN. Capitalize *Satan* but lowercase *devil* and *satanic.*

3.20 TITLES. Capitalize formal titles, including academic titles, when used immediately before a name: *President, Chairman, Professor; former President Jimmy Carter.* Lowercase formal titles used after a name, alone or in constructions that set them off from a name by commas. Use lowercase at all times for terms that are job descriptions rather than formal titles: *astronaut John Glenn, movie star Tom Hanks, peanut farmer Jimmy Carter.*

SECTION 4: NUMERALS

For general purposes, spell out whole numbers below 10, use figures for 10 and above. Exceptions: Figures are used for all ages, betting odds, dates, dimensions, percentages, speeds and times. Also, spell out a number at the beginning of a sentence, except for a calendar year. Avoid beginning a sentence with a large number or a calendar year.

4.1 AGES. Use figures for all ages. Hyphenate ages expressed as adjectives before a noun or as substitutes for a noun: *a 5-year-old boy,* but *the boy is 5 years old. The boy, 7, has a sister, 10. The woman is in her 30s* (no apostrophe).

4.2 CENTS. Spell out the word *cents* and lowercase, using numerals for amounts less than a dollar: *5 cents, 12 cents.* Use the $ sign and decimal system for larger amounts: *$1.01.*

4.3 DECADES/CENTURY. Use Arabic figures to indicate decades of history. Use an apostrophe to indicate numbers that are left out; show the plural by adding the letter *s: the 1890s, the '90s, the Gay '90s, the mid-1930s.* Lowercase *century* and spell out numbers less than 10: *the first century, the 20th century.*

4.4 DOLLARS. Lowercase dollars. Use figures and the $ sign in all except casual references or amounts without a figure: *The book cost $4. Dollars are flowing overseas.* For amounts of more than $1 million, use the $ sign and numerals up to two decimal places: *He is worth $4.35 million. He proposed a $300 million budget.*

4.5 ELECTION RETURNS. For election returns, use the word *to* (not a hyphen) in separating different totals listed together: *Bill Clinton defeated George Bush 40,287,292 to 39,145,157.* For results that involve fewer than 1,000 votes on each side, use a hyphen: *The House voted 230-205* or *a 230-205 vote.*

4.6 FRACTIONS. Spell out amounts less than one, using hyphens between the words: *two-thirds, four-fifths, seven-sixteenths.* For precise amounts larger than one, convert to decimals whenever practical: *1.25, 3.5.*

4.7 MEASUREMENTS. Use figures and spell out *inches, feet, yards,* etc. Hyphenate adjectival forms before nouns: *He is 5 feet 6 inches tall* or *the 5-foot-6-inch man. The rug is 9 feet by 12 feet* or *the 9-by-12-foot rug.*

4.8 MILLION/BILLION. Do not go beyond two decimals: *7.51 million people, $2.56 billion.* Decimals are preferred where practical: *1.5 million,* not *1½ million.*

Do not drop the word *million* or *billion* in the first figure of a range: *He is worth from $2 million to $4 million,* not *$2 to $4 million,* unless you really mean $2.

4.9 NUMBER. Use *No.* as the abbreviation for *number* in conjunction with a figure to indicate position or rank: *No. 1 woman, No. 3 choice.*

4.10 ODDS. Use figures and a hyphen for betting odds: *The odds were 5-4. He won despite 3-2 odds against him.*

4.11 PERCENTAGES. Use figures: *1 percent, 2.56 percent.* For amounts less than 1 percent, precede the decimal point with a zero: *The cost of living rose 0.6 percent.* The word *percent* should be spelled out; never use the symbol %.

4.12 RATIOS. Use figures and a hyphen for ratios: *The ratio was 2-to-1, a ratio of 2-to-1, 2-1 ratio.*

4.13 SCORES. Use figures for all scores, placing a hyphen between the totals of the winning and losing teams: *The Reds defeated the Red Sox 4-1. The Giants scored a 12-6 victory over the Cardinals. The golfer had a 5 on the last hole but finished with a 2-under-par score.*

4.14 TEMPERATURES. Use figures for all temperatures except *zero.* Use a word, not a minus sign, to indicate temperatures below zero and spell out *degrees: minus 10 degrees.*

SECTION 5: PUNCTUATION

5.1 COMMA/AGE. An individual's age is set off by commas: *Phil Taylor, 11, is here.*

5.2 COMMA/CITY-STATE. Place a comma between the city and the state name, and another comma after the state name, unless the state name ends a sentence: *He was traveling from Nashville, Tenn., to Albuquerque, N.M.*

5.3 COMMA/HOMETOWN. Use a comma to set off an individual's hometown when it is placed in apposition to a name: *Mary Richards, Minneapolis, and Maude Findlay, Tuckahoe, N.Y., were there.* However, the use of the word *of* without a comma between the individual's name and the city name is generally preferable: *Mary Richards of Minneapolis and Maude Findlay of Tuckahoe, N.Y., were there.*

5.4 COMMA/QUOTATION. Use a comma to introduce a complete, one-sentence quotation within a paragraph: *Wallace said, "She spent six months in Argentina."* Do not use a comma at the start of an indirect or partial quotation: *The water was "cold as ice" before the sun came out, the lifeguard said.* Always place commas and periods inside quotation marks. *"The journey must end," she said. "We cannot go on."*

5.5 COMMA/SERIES. Use commas to separate elements in a series, but do not put a comma before the conjunction in a simple series: *The flag is red, white and blue. He would nominate Tom, Dick or Harry.*

5.6 COLON. The most frequent use of a colon is at the end of a sentence to introduce lists, tabulations, texts, etc: *There were three considerations: expense, time and feasibility.* Use a colon to introduce direct quotations longer than one sentence within a paragraph and to end all paragraphs that introduce a paragraph of quoted material.

5.7 POSSESSIVES. Appendix C contains the rules for forming possessives.

5.8 SEMICOLON. Use semicolons [instead of commas] to separate elements of a series when individual segments contain material that also must be set off by commas: *He leaves three daughters, Jane Smith of Wichita, Kan., Mary Smith of Denver and Susan Kingsbury of Boston; a son, John Smith of Chicago; and a sister, Martha Warren of Omaha, Neb.* Note that the semicolon is used before the final *and* in such a series.

SECTION 6: PREFERRED SPELLINGS

Adviser
Afterward (not *afterwards*)
All right (never *alright*)
Ax (not *axe*)
Baby-sit, baby-sitting, baby sitter
Backward (not *backwards*)
Damage (for destruction; *damages* for a court award)
Employee (not *employe*)
Forward (not *forwards*)
Goodbye
Gray (not *grey*)
Kidnapping
Likable (not *likeable*)
Percent (one word, spelled out)
Teen, teen-ager (n.), teen-age (adj.) (Do not use *teen-aged*.)
Vice president (no hyphen)
Whiskey

SECTION 7: TIME

Use figures except for *noon* and *midnight*. Do not put a *12* in front of them. Use a colon to separate hours from minutes: *11:15 a.m., 1:45 p.m., 3:30 p.m.* Avoid such redundancies as *10 a.m. this morning* or *10 p.m. Monday night*. Use *10 a.m. today* or *10 p.m. Monday*. The hour is placed before the day; *a.m.* and *p.m.* are lowercase, with periods.

7.1 DAYS. Use the words *today, this morning, tonight,* etc., in direct quotes, in stories intended for publication in afternoon newspapers on the day in question, and in phrases that do not refer to a specific day: *Customs today are different from those of a century ago.* Use the day of the week in stories intended for publication in morning newspapers and in stories filed for use in either publishing cycle. Use *yesterday* and *tomorrow* only in direct quotations and in phrases that do not refer to a specific day.

7.2 DAYS/DATES. Use *Monday, Tuesday,* etc., for days of the week within seven days before or after the current date. Use the month and a figure for dates beyond this range. Avoid such redundancies as *last Tuesday* or *next Tuesday.*

7.3 MONTHS. Capitalize the names of the months in all uses. When a month is used with a specific date, abbreviate only: *Jan., Feb., Aug., Sept., Oct., Nov.* and *Dec. Jan. 2 was the coldest day of the month. His birthday is June 26.* Spell out when using alone, or with a year alone.

   When a phrase lists only a month and a year, do not separate the year with commas. *January 1978 was a cold month.* When a phrase refers to a month, day and year, set off the year with commas: *Feb. 14, 1976, was the target date.* Do not use *st, nd, rd* or *th* after the Arabic number in a date.

SECTION 8: TITLES

Formal titles that appear directly before a name are capitalized and abbreviated, when appropriate: *the Rev. Jesse Jackson.* If the title comes after a name or is alone, then it should be lowercase and spelled out: *The president issued a statement. Pope John Paul II gave his blessing.* Do not repeat a title the second time you use a person's name: *Sheriff Sam Smith arrested the driver. Smith did not give details of the arrest.* Some titles, such as *mayor, sheriff* and *president,* have no abbreviations.

8.1 BOY/GIRL. The terms *boy* and *girl* are applicable until the age of 18. Use *man, woman, young man* or *young woman* afterward.

8.2 COMPOSITIONS. Capitalize the principal words in titles of books, movies, operas, plays, poems, songs, television programs, lectures, speeches and works of art. Put quotation marks around the names of all such works: *Tom Clancy wrote "The Hunt for Red October."* Do not underline the titles of any of these works.

8.3 CONGRESSMAN. Use *congressman* and *congresswoman* only in references to specific members of the U.S. House of Representatives. Use *representative* if the gender is unknown or when referring to more than one member of the House.

8.4 COURTESY TITLES. In general, do not use the courtesy titles *Miss, Mr., Mrs.* or *Ms.* on any reference. Instead, use the first and last names and middle initial the first time you refer to a person. Mention of a woman's or man's marital status should not be made unless it is clearly pertinent to the story.

   For a married woman, the preferred form on first reference is to identify her by her own first name and the last name she uses, which could be her spouse's or her maiden name: *Susan Smith.* Use *Mrs.* on the first reference only if a woman requests that her husband's first name be used or if her own first name cannot be determined: *Mrs. John Smith.*

On the second reference, use only the last name of a man or woman, unless the courtesy title is needed to distinguish between the two in the same story. On first reference to couples, both first names should be used: *John and Mary Smith.*

8.5 INITIALS. In general, use middle initials. Particular care should be taken to include middle initials in stories where they help identify a specific individual. Examples include casualty lists and stories naming the accused in a crime.

Use periods and no space when an individual uses initials instead of a first name: *O.J. Simpson.* Do not give a name with a single initial (*O. Simpson*) unless it is the individual's preference or the first name cannot be learned.

8.6 MAGAZINES. Capitalize magazine titles but do not place in quotes or italics. Lowercase *magazine* if it is not part of the publication's formal title: *Newsweek magazine.*

8.7 NEWSPAPERS. Capitalize *the* in a newspaper's name if that is the way the publication prefers to be known. If the location is needed but is not part of the official name, use parentheses: *The Huntsville (Ala.) Times.* Do not underline or add quote marks.

8.8 REFERENCE WORKS. Capitalize, but do not use quotation marks around, the proper names of books that are primarily catalogs of reference material: *The Reader's Guide.* These rules also apply to almanacs (*the Farmers' Almanac*), directories (*the Columbus City Directory*), dictionaries (*Webster's New World Dictionary*), handbooks (*the News & Record Employee Handbook*) and encyclopedias (*the Encyclopedia Britannica*).

8.9 REVEREND. When using the title *Rev.* before a name, precede it with the word *the.*

SECTION 9: WORDS

9.1 INJURIES. Injuries are *suffered* or *sustained,* not *received.*

9.2 INNOCENT/NOT GUILTY. Use *innocent* rather than *not guilty* in describing a jury's verdict to guard against the word *not* being dropped inadvertently.

9.3 MASS. It is *celebrated,* not *said.* Always capitalize when referring to the ceremony, but lowercase any preceding adjectives: *high Mass, low Mass, requiem Mass.*

9.4 NOUNS/VERBS. Nouns that denote a unit take singular verbs and pronouns: *class, committee, family, group, herd, jury, team. The committee is meeting to set its agenda. The jury reached its verdict.* When used in the sense of two people, the word *couple* takes plural verbs and pronouns: *The couple were married Saturday.*

9.5 PERSON/PEOPLE. Use *person* when speaking of an individual. The word *people* [not *persons*] is preferred in all plural uses. *Some rich people pay little in taxes. There were 17 people in the room.*

9.6 RAISED/REARED. Only humans may be *reared.* Any living thing, including humans, may be *raised.*

9.7 REALTOR. The term *real estate agent* is preferred. Use *Realtor* only if the individual is a member of the National Association of Realtors.

9.8 WORDS TO AVOID. Do not use the following words in news stories: *kids, irregardless, ladies* (as a synonym for *women*), *cop* (except in quoted matter) or *entitled* (when you mean *titled*).

Harcourt Brace & Company

RULES FOR FORMING POSSESSIVES

1. If the word, whether singular or plural, does not already end in the letter *s,* add an apostrophe and *s* to form the possessive. For example:

SINGULAR	man	child	person
SINGULAR POSSESSIVE	man's	child's	person's
PLURAL	men	children	people
PLURAL POSSESSIVE	men's	children's	people's

2. If the word already ends in the letter *s,* add only an apostrophe to form the possessive. Note that this rule also applies to proper nouns, such as a person's name:

SINGULAR	fraternity	lady	Ralph	Smith
SINGULAR POSSESSIVE	fraternity's	lady's	Ralph's	Smith's
PLURAL	fraternities	ladies	Ralphs*	Smiths**
PLURAL POSSESSIVE	fraternities'	ladies'	Ralphs'	Smiths'

   *Refers to two different people whose first name is Ralph.
   **Refers to two different people whose last name is Smith.

3. If a term is hyphenated, add an apostrophe and the letter *s* to the last word only:

SINGULAR	mother-in-law	She is my mother-in-law.
SINGULAR POSSESSIVE	mother-in-law's	It is my mother-in-law's car.
PLURAL	mothers-in-law	The program featured mothers-in-law.
PLURAL POSSESSIVE	mothers-in-law's	The mothers-in-law's cars were damaged by vandals.

4. If an object is owned by two or more people, add an apostrophe and the letter *s* to the latter name only:

   Mary and Fred's entry won a prize.
   My mother and father's home was destroyed by fire.

5. If the objects are not jointly owned—if you are describing separate objects owned or possessed by different people—add an apostrophe and the letter *s* to both nouns:

> Mary's and Fred's entries won prizes.
> My mother's and my father's luggage was lost.

6. Indefinite pronouns such as *everyone* follow the same rules. However, personal pronouns have special forms that never use an apostrophe. The personal pronouns include such words as: *his, mine, ours, theirs, whose* and *yours.*

7. Generally, avoid using an apostrophe and the letter *s* to show possession by inanimate objects. Instead, try to rewrite the passage, either dropping the apostrophe and the letter *s* or converting the passage to an *of* phrase:

> WRONG: the table's leg
> RIGHT: the table leg OR the leg of the table

> WRONG: the book's chapter
> RIGHT: the book chapter OR the chapter of the book

8. When mentioning the name of an organization, group or geographical location, always use the common or preferred and official spelling. Some of the names use the possessive case but others, such as *Pikes Peak,* do not.

9. The word *it's,* spelled with an apostrophe, is a contraction of *it is.* The possessive form, *its,* does *not* contain an apostrophe:

> WRONG: Its higher than I thought.
> RIGHT: It's higher than I thought OR It is higher than I thought.

> WRONG: It's height scares me.
> RIGHT: Its height scares me.

Harcourt Brace & Company

ANSWER KEYS FOR SELECTED EXERCISES

CHAPTER 1: THE BASICS: FORMAT, SPELLING AND AP STYLE

Exercise 7

1. The consultant was given $125,000 on February 7th, 1996 in austin texas.

2. The temperature feyll to –14 after a blizzzard struck Denver colorado in december 1992.

3. Tom Becker, a black born in the south during the 1950s was elected Mayor of the City.

4. a senior who will graduate next Spring said, "history and english are my favorite subjects."

5. Susan Woo, age eleven, is five ft tall and weighs eighty-seven lbs.

6. the caddccident Occurred on Interstate 80, about twelve miles West of Reno Nevada.
   accident *12*

7. Atty. Martha Dilla, formerly lived at 4062 South Eastland DRIVE and works for the Westinghouse corporation (Caution: See the city directory. Dillan's name is misspelled.)
   Corp.

8. the company's president said her firm will provide more than $100,000,000 dollars to develop an electric car able to travel sixty miles per hour.
   million

9. The youth a high school sophomore, said the temperature in Idaho often falls below 0 during the Winter.

10. 50 women who met yesterday morning at 11 am said there children are entitled to use the new park on Vallrath Avenue.
    their

11. The 5-member city council wants to canvass the town's voters to determine whether a large group favors the establishment of a Civic Orchestra.

12. Mrs. Marie Hyde, Asst. Supt. for Public Education for the City, said the 16-year-old girls were raised in athens georgia.

13. The woman earned her bachelors degree from the university of Kentucky and her masters degree from Indiana University during the 1960s.

14. The suspects were arrested at 1602 North Highland Avenue, 64 East Wilshire Drive, and 3492 3rd Street.

15. Chris Repanski, of pocatello idaho will enroll in the college as a Sophomore next fall and hopes to become an Attorney.

16. The man, who is in his mid 30s, joined the F.B.I. after Recieving a Ph.D. doctorate in Computer Science.

17. The Reverand Andrew Cisneros estimated that ⅓ of his parishioners contribute at least five per cent of their annual income to the church's general revenue fund. (Caution: See the city directory, Cisneroes name is misspelled.)

18. The police arrested four youths driving North on Michigan Ave, minutes after the restaurant was robbed of $1640.83 last Friday.

19. the bill of rights was added to the united states constitution during the eighteenth century.

20. Since the 1960s, Marty Whitedeer has lived in five States: Ws, Ken, Mass, N.Y., & Ca.

CHAPTER 2: NEWSWRITING STYLE

Quiz

1. She was in a quick hurry and warned that, in the future, she will seek out textbooks that are sexist and demand that they be totally banned.

2. As it now stands, three separate members of the committee said they will try to prevent the city from closing down the park during the winter months.

3. His convertible was totally destroyed and, in order to obtain the money necessary to buy a new car, he now plans to ask a personal friend for a loan to help him along.

4. After police found the lifeless body, the medical doctor conducted an autopsy to determine the cause of death and concluded that the youth had been strangled to death.

5. In the past, he often met up with the students at the computer lab and, because of their future potential, invited them to attend the convention.
6. Based upon her previous experience as an architect, she warned the committee members that constructing the new hospital facility will be pretty expensive and suggested that they step in and seek out more donors.
7. The two men were hunting in a wooded forest a total of 12 miles away from the nearest hospital in the region when both suffered severe bodily injuries.
8. Based upon several studies conducted in the past, he firmly believes that, when first started next year, the two programs should be very selective, similar in nature and conducted only in the morning hours.

Exercise 5

NOTE: Several of the sentences in this exercise can be rewritten many different ways. Thus, the sentences shown here are suggested or model answers—not the only possible answers.

SECTION I: REMAINING OBJECTIVE

1. The 15th annual Pre-Law Day is scheduled for Nov. 3 at the Student Center.
2. The woman told the crowd that she favors abortions. (Are the woman's youth and beauty relevant to the story? In the same circumstances, would you mention a man's youth and beauty? If not, delete both comments. You may want to discuss this problem with your instructor and classmates.)
3. The principal scheduled a banquet to celebrate the school's 10th anniversary.
4. The audience interrupted his speech 17 times with applause.
5. The author suggested that it does not matter whether children begin to read before they are 10 years old.

SECTION II: AVOID REDUNDANT PHRASES

1. facts
2. close
3. bodies
4. dropped
5. began
6. gifts
7. to
8. innovation
9. history
10. revert
11. here
12. tracked
13. unique
14. winter
15. child

SECTION III: AVOIDING WORDY PHRASES

1. stopped
2. ignored
3. because
4. before
5. soon
6. near
7. possesses
8. investigated
9. considered
10. married

SECTION IV: AVOIDING UNNECESSARY WORDS

1. The city council voted to sue the builders.
2. A pickup truck collided with a car.
3. The sign may be installed later this month.
4. The police found only an empty box, not a bomb.
5. Police found that the assailants had kicked him in the head and neck.

SECTION V: TESTING ALL YOUR SKILLS

1. He lost his right eye.
2. The debt was smaller then.
3. He called the president inconsistent and unrealistic.
4. The politician thanked his supporters.
5. The article will examine the problems of migrant workers.
6. Before reaching the age of 18, a child will see 20,000 acts of violence on television. (CAUTION: Avoid using the masculine "he" when you are referring to any or every child, both male and female.)
7. Participants in the workshop agree that the governor should decide how to spend the funds.
8. The conference revealed that Israelis dislike the agreement.
9. Lydia Hanson is an expert on criminal law. (Are the woman's parentage, age and marital status relevant to her expertise in criminal law? If not, delete them. Use her name, not just her father's; it is listed in the city directory. Also, why would a woman not look like an expert? You may want to discuss the sentence with your instructor and classmates.)
10. Co-workers planned a party for the day of the librarian's retirement and gave her a trip to Paris.
11. Mike and Peggy Deacosti and their two children, Mark and Amy, served as the hosts.
12. Ellen Gardepe's book about auto mechanics became a best seller.

CHAPTER 3: WORDS

Exercise 6

NOTE: Several of the sentences in this exercise can be rewritten many different ways. Thus, the sentences shown here are suggested or model answers—not the only possible answers. You can divide the longer, more complicated sentences into several shorter, simpler sentences.

SECTION I

1. The club president said he plans to quit.
2. She said the student will not graduate soon.
3. The mayor said the city's financial situation is good. OR: The mayor praised the city's financial condition.
4. The bank vice president said she is missing $43,000.
5. The exercise trail is designed for adults serious about getting physically fit.

SECTION II

1. The governor wants to raise teachers' salaries. (NOTE: The word "teachers'" is a plural possessive.)
2. A boy, about 16, snatched the woman's purse.
3. Other people use the bike path as an exercise track.
4. Their lawsuit complains that the bottle contained an insect.
5. Church officials estimate that the chapel will cost $320,000.

SECTION III

1. His girlfriend, Saundra Mariston, 33, is a waitress at Freddy's Inn, 410 Lakemont Ave., and he was charged with shooting her in the throat. OR: He was charged with shooting his girl-friend, Saundra Mariston, in the throat. Mariston, 33, is a waitress at Freddy's Inn, 410 Lakemont Ave. (CAUTION: See the city directory. Mariston's name was misspelled.)
2. Her high school sweetheart, David Garner, works as a tennis instructor, and she married him in Greenville, N.C., on Jan. 3, 1985.
3. During a speech at the church Sunday evening, she begged her parents and other adults to donate money for the handicapped children's medical care. (CAUTION: Should reporters use the word "crippled"? You may want to discuss this issue with your instructor and class-mates.)
4. The good Samaritan was driving a Honda Civic, and witnesses described him as a white male, about 35 years old and 5 feet, 8 inches tall, with black hair, brown eyes and a bandage on his forehead. (NOTE: The word "Samaritan" should be capitalized.)
5. She said the students most likely to drop out of high school have failed two or more sub-jects, are often absent, have discipline problems, and show signs of low self-esteem, loneli-ness or stress.

SECTION IV

1. He said it is a good book.
2. The city attorney said the plan is illegal.
3. The teacher is not clear. OR: The teacher cannot communicate effectively. OR: The teacher is hard to understand.
4. The council chair voted against the proposal. (CAUTION: Avoid the word "chairman"—a word that excludes women.)
5. The new program will provide medical services for the poor.
6. The youths did not intend to tell their parents how they obtained the money.
7. The report stated that people of all ages can enjoy water skiing.
8. Participants in the workshop agree that the nurses should receive a raise of 15 to 20 percent.

SECTION V: AVOIDING JOURNALESE

1. She incurred $30,000 in medical expenses. OR: Her medical expenses total $30,000.
2. He approved spending $26,000 for a car.
3. The program is designed to help high school students.
4. The new building will cost about $6 million.
5. Three council members opposed the proposal.

SECTION VI: AVOIDING JARGON

1. He wants to show teachers how to use computers in their classrooms.
2. The university president said he will ask private individuals or organizations for money to build the cafeteria.
3. Teresa Phillips, who also uses the name Marie Phillips, testified that she entered the store and helped the defendant steal some jewelry on about the 9th of last month.
   SPELLING ERROR: The name Teresa (not Teresea) is misspelled.
4. Brown's lawsuit charges that he was injured in the auto accident.

Harcourt Brace & Company

Exercise 7

1. He <u>advised</u> the city to adopt the ordinance.
2. The concept was <u>too</u> <u>elusive</u> to <u>ensure</u> success.
3. Its rules were altered, but the <u>effects</u> were minor.
4. The <u>blond's</u> <u>fiancée</u> said <u>their</u> new home was <u>burglarized</u>.
5. <u>Whose</u> statue was <u>lying</u> near <u>your</u> construction <u>site</u>?
6. Rather than dissenting, he agreed to study their <u>advice</u>.
7. The <u>alumni</u>, all men, said the dissent became <u>too</u> violent.
8. He censured the <u>aides'</u> behavior and ignored their <u>dissent</u>.
9. A prison <u>trusty</u> said <u>it's</u> two miles <u>farther</u> down the road.
10. The council was <u>confident</u> that <u>its</u> advice would <u>ensure</u> success. OR: The <u>counsel</u> was <u>confident</u> that the advice would <u>ensure</u> success. (CAUTION: Avoid assuming that everyone in a position of authority is a male. Thus, avoid using the masculine "his.")
11. The data <u>were</u> placed in <u>envelopes</u> and sent to all the news <u>media</u>.
12. The <u>governor's</u> two <u>aides</u> were given offices in the <u>Capitol</u>.
13. The man was <u>hanged</u> because he <u>incited</u> a riot <u>that</u> caused three deaths.
14. The portrait hung in his <u>brother-in-law's</u> office in the state <u>Capitol</u>.
15. Six of the <u>school's</u> <u>alumni</u> said <u>their</u> <u>children's</u> curriculum should be altered.
16. The <u>principal</u> is liable to lose his <u>students'</u> respect if he blocks their proposal.
17. The <u>phenomena</u> were unusual and affected their <u>son-in-law's</u> <u>role</u> in the family. OR: The phenomenon <u>was</u> unusual. . . .
18. The board is composed of seven <u>alumni</u> rather than seven students or teachers.
19. He <u>cited</u> three precedents and implied that the <u>council's</u> decision could be altered.
20. Thomas Alvarez, a tall <u>blond</u> from California, said the <u>government's</u> data <u>are</u> false.
21. The <u>counselor</u> was <u>confident</u> of victory but said his <u>role</u> in the matter was minor.
22. The church <u>altar</u> lay on its side, less than a dozen feet from the broken <u>statues</u>.
23. His insight, conscience and high principles ensured an excellent performance.
24. The <u>school's</u> <u>principal</u> threatened <u>to</u> <u>censor</u> the newspaper if it tries to publish an article <u>advising</u> students on how to obtain an abortion.
25. Merchants, fearing that they would lose thousands of dollars, complained that the <u>government's</u> criteria <u>are</u> <u>too</u> difficult to implement.

CHAPTER 8: QUOTATIONS AND ATTRIBUTION

Exercise 3

1. "Our goal is peace," the president said. (Use a comma, not a period, before the attribution and place the punctuation mark inside the quotation mark. Transpose the attribution's wording so the subject appears before the verb. Avoid using "claimed" as a word of attribution.)
2. Benjamin Franklin said, "Death takes no bribes." (Use a comma, not a colon, before the one-sentence quotation. Because it is a complete sentence, capitalize the first word of the quotation. Place the final period inside the quotation mark.)
3. She said her son calls her literary endeavors "mom's writing thing." (Condense the attribution and place the period inside the quotation mark. Normally, you do not need a comma before a partial quote.)
4. He is a scuba diver and pilot. He also enjoys skydiving and explains, "I like challenge, something exciting." (Clearly attribute the direct quotation.)

Harcourt Brace & Company

5. The Mideast crisis is likely to last indefinitely, the president said. (The quotation can be paraphrased more clearly and simply. Place the paraphrase before the attribution.)

6. "Freedom of the press is not merely freedom to publish the news," columnist Jack Anderson said during a speech last night. "It is also freedom to gather the news. We cannot publish what we cannot gather." (Place the attribution near the beginning, not end, of a long quotation, and attribute a direct quotation only once. The attribution should be preceded by a comma, not a period. Quotation marks do not have to be placed around every sentence in a continuing quotation. Use the normal word order in the attribution.)

7. "I think that America has become too athletic," Jesse Owens said. "From Little League to the pro leagues, sports are no longer recreation. They are big business, and they're drudgery." (The attribution "expressed the opinion that" is wordy. Do not place quotation marks around every sentence in a continuing quotation. If it remains at the beginning of the quotation, the attribution should be followed by a colon. Attribute a continuing direct quotation only once.)

8. The man smiled and said: "It's a great deal for me. I expect to double my money." (Because the quotation contains more than one sentence, "said" should be followed by a colon, not a comma. Do not use "smiled" as a word of attribution. Place quotation marks at the beginning and end of the direct quotation, not at the beginning and end of every sentence. Attribute a continuing direct quotation only once.)

9. The woman said she likes her job as a newspaper reporter and explained: "I'm not paid much, but the work is important. And it's varied and exciting. Also, I like seeing my byline in the paper." (Reporters should stress their source's answer to a question, not the question. Attribute a continuing quote only once. Avoid "grinned" as a word of attribution. The attribution "responded by saying" is wordy.)

10. The librarian said the new building will cost about $4.6 million. (The attribution can be condensed, and, by paraphrasing, you can simplify the quotation. Also, virtually all the news published in newspapers is given to reporters. You do not have to mention that routine detail in every story.)

11. "Thousands of the poor in the United States die every year of diseases we can easily cure," the professor said. "It's a crime, but no one ever is punished for their deaths." (Use the normal word order: "the professor said." Place the attribution at the beginning or end of a sentence or at a natural break in a sentence. Attribute a direct quotation only once, and place quotation marks at the beginning and end of the quotation, not at the beginning and end of every sentence.)

12. Thomas said students should never be spanked. He explained that, "A young boy or girl who gets spanked in front of peers becomes embarrassed and the object of ridicule." (Clearly attribute the direct quotation. The city directory reveals that Thomas is a male. Thus, in this case, use of the masculine "he" is correct. Do not, however, assume that every public figure or other source is a male.)

13. The lawyer said: "He ripped the life-sustaining respirator tubes from his throat three times in an effort to die. He is simply a man who rejects medical treatment regardless of the consequences. He wants to die and has a constitutional right to do so." (Because the quotation includes more than one sentence, use a colon, not a comma, after "said." Attribute a direct quotation only once.)

14. Bobby Knight, the basketball coach at Indiana University, said: "Everyone has the will to win. Few have the will to prepare. It is the preparation that counts." (Use a colon, not a comma, after "said," because the quotation includes more than one sentence. Attribute a continuing quotation only once. Place quotation marks at the beginning and end of a direct quotation, not at the beginning and end of every sentence.)

15. She said the federal government must do more to help cities support and retrain the chronically unemployed. (Condense the attribution and avoid orphan quotes—quotation marks placed around one or two words.)

Harcourt Brace & Company

COMMON WRITING ERRORS

The Writing and Editing Committee of the Associated Press Managing Editors Association prepared this list of common newswriting errors, arranged alphabetically. The list has been edited and condensed for this book.

1. **Affect, effect.** Generally, *affect* is the verb; *effect* is the noun. "The letter did not *affect* the outcome." "The letter had significant *effect*." But *effect* is also a verb meaning to bring about. Thus: "It is almost impossible to *effect* change."

2. **Afterward, afterwards.** Use *afterward.*
   The same rule applies to *toward* and *towards.* Use *toward.*

3. **All right.** That's the way to spell it. *Alright* is not acceptable in standard usage.

4. **Allude, elude.** You *allude* to (or mention) a book. You *elude* (or escape) a pursuer.

5. **Annual.** Do not use "first" with it. If it's the first time, it cannot be annual.

6. **Averse, adverse.** If you do not like something, you are *averse* (or opposed) to it. *Adverse* is an adjective: *adverse* (bad) weather, *adverse* conditions.

7. **Block, bloc.** A *bloc* is a coalition of people or a group with the same purpose or goal. Do not call it a *block,* which has some 40 dictionary definitions.

8. **Compose, comprise.** Remember that the parts *compose* the whole, while *comprise* means to include or embrace. *Comprise* in the sense of compose or constitute is regarded as poor usage. Water is *composed* (not *comprised*) of hydrogen and oxygen.

9. **Demolish, destroy.** They both mean to do away with completely. You cannot partially demolish or destroy something, nor is there any need to say *totally destroyed.*

10. **Different from.** Things and people are different *from* each other. Do not write that they are different *than* each other.

11. **Drown.** Do not say someone *was drowned* unless an assailant held the victim's head under water. Just say the victim *drowned.*

12. **Due to, owing to, because of.** We prefer the last.
    WRONG: The game was canceled *due to* rain.
    STILTED: *Owing to* rain, the game was canceled.
    RIGHT: The game was canceled *because of* rain.

13. **Either.** It means one or the other, not both.
    WRONG: There were lions on *either* side of the door.
    RIGHT: There were lions on *each* side of the door.

14. **Funeral service.** A redundant expression. A funeral *is* a service.

15. **Head up.** People do not *head up* committees. They *head* them.

16. **Imply, infer.** The speaker *implies*; the hearer *infers*.

17. **In advance of, prior to.** Use *before*; it sounds more natural.

18. **It's, its.** *Its* is the possessive; *it's* is the contraction of *it is.*
    WRONG: What is *it's* name.
    RIGHT: What is *its* name? *Its* name is Fido.
    RIGHT: *It's* the first time she scored tonight.
    RIGHT: *It's* my coat.

19. **Lay, lie.** *Lay* is the action word; *lie* is the state of being.
    WRONG: The body will *lay* in state until Wednesday.
    RIGHT: The body will *lie* in state until Wednesday.
    RIGHT: The prosecutor tried to *lay* the blame on him.
    However, the past tense of *lie* is *lay.*
    RIGHT: The body *lay* in state from Tuesday until Wednesday.
    WRONG: The body *laid* in state from Tuesday until Wednesday.
    The past participle and the plain past tense of *lay* is *laid.*
    RIGHT: She *laid* the pencil on the pad.
    RIGHT: She *had laid* the pencil on the pad.
    RIGHT: The hen *laid* the egg.

20. **Less, fewer.** If you can separate items in the quantities being compared, use *fewer.* If not, use *less.*
    WRONG: The Rams are inferior to the Vikings because they have *less* good linemen.
    RIGHT: The Rams are inferior to the Vikings because they have *fewer* good linemen.
    RIGHT: The Rams are inferior to the Vikings because they have *less* experience.

21. **Like, as.** Do not use *like* for *as* or *as if.* In general, use *like* to compare with nouns and pronouns; use *as* when comparing with phrases and clauses that contain a verb.
    WRONG: Jim blocks the linebacker *like* he should.
    RIGHT: Jim blocks the linebacker *as* he should.
    RIGHT: Jim blocks *like* a pro.

22. **Marshall, marshal.** Generally, the first form is correct only when the word is a proper noun: *Susan Marshall.* The second form is the verb form: She will *marshal* her forces. The second form is also the one to use for a title: *fire marshal* Cynthia Anderson, *Field Marshal* Erwin Rommel.

23. **Mean, average, median.** Use *mean* as synonymous with *average.* Both words refer to the sum of all components divided by the number of components. The *median* is the number that has as many components above it as below it.

24. **Nouns.** There is a trend toward using nouns as verbs. Resist it. *Host, headquarters* and *author,* for instance, are nouns, even though a dictionary may say they can be used as verbs. If you do so, you will come up with a monstrosity like: *"Headquartered at her country home, Allison Doe hosted a party to celebrate the books she authored."*

25. **Over, more than.** They are not interchangeable. *Over* refers to spatial relationships: The plane flew *over* the city. *More than* is used with figures: *More than* 1,000 fans were in the crowd.

26. **Parallel construction.** Thoughts in series in the same sentence require parallel construction.
    WRONG: The union demanded *an increase* of 10 percent in wages and *to cut* the work week to 35 hours.
    RIGHT: The union demanded *an increase* of 10 percent in wages and *a reduction* in the work week to 35 hours.

27. **Peddle, pedal.** When selling something, you *peddle* it. When riding a bicycle or similar form of locomotion, you *pedal* it.

28. **Principle, principal.** A guiding rule or basic truth is a *principle.* The first, dominant or leading thing is *principal. Principle* is a noun; *principal* may be a noun or an adjective.
    RIGHT: It's the *principle* of the thing.
    RIGHT: Liberty and justice are two *principles* on which our nation is founded.
    RIGHT: Hitting and fielding are the *principal* activities in baseball.
    RIGHT: Jessica Jamieson is the school *principal.*

Harcourt Brace & Company

29. **Redundancies.** Avoid the following redundant expressions:
    Easter Sunday. Make it *Easter.*
    Incumbent representative. Use *representative.*
    Owns her own home. Make it *owns her home.*
    The company will close down. Use *The company will close.*
    Jones, Smith, Johnson and Reid were all convicted. Use *Jones, Smith, Johnson and Reid were convicted.*
    Jewish rabbi. Just *rabbi.*
    8 p.m. tonight. All you need is *8 tonight* or *8 p.m. today.*
    Both Reid and Jones were denied pardons. Use *Reid and Jones were denied pardons.*
    I am currently tired. Just *I am tired.*
    Autopsy to determine the cause of death. Just *autopsy.*

30. **Refute.** The word connotes success in argument and almost always implies editorial judgment.
    WRONG: Father Bury *refuted* the arguments of the pro-abortion faction.
    RIGHT: Father Bury *responded to* the arguments of the pro-abortion faction.

31. **Reluctant, reticent.** If someone does not want to act, that person is *reluctant.* If someone does not want to speak, that person is *reticent.*

32. **Say, said.** The most serviceable words in the journalist's language are the forms of the verb *to say.* Let a person *say* something, rather than *declare* or *admit* or *point out.* Never let a person *grin, smile, frown* or *giggle* a quote.

33. **Slang.** Do not try to use "with-it" slang. Usually a term is on the way out by the time we get it in print.

34. **Temperatures.** They may get higher or lower, but they do not get warmer or colder.
    WRONG: Temperatures are expected to warm up Friday.
    RIGHT: Temperatures are expected to rise Friday.

35. **That, which.** *That* tends to restrict the reader's thought and direct it the way you want it to go; *which* is nonrestrictive, introducing a bit of subsidiary information. For instance:
    RESTRICTIVE: The lawnmower that is in the garage needs sharpening. (Meaning: We have more than one lawnmower. The one in the garage needs sharpening.)
    NONRESTRICTIVE: The lawnmower, which is in the garage, needs sharpening. (Meaning: Our lawnmower needs sharpening. It's in the garage.)
    RESTRICTIVE: The statue that graces our entry hall is on loan from the museum. (Meaning: Out of all the statues around here, the one in the entry hall is on loan.)
    NONRESTRICTIVE: The statue, which graces our entry hall, is on loan. (Meaning: Our statue is on loan. It happens to be in the entry hall.)
    Note that *which* clauses take commas, signaling they are not essential to the meaning of the sentence.

36. **Under way, not underway.** But do not say something *got under way.* Say it *started* or *began.*

37. **Unique.** Something that is unique is the only one of its kind. It cannot be *very unique* or *quite unique* or *somewhat unique* or *rather unique.* Do not use it unless you really mean unique.

38. **Up.** Do not use *up* as a verb.
    WRONG: The manager said he would *up* the price next week.
    RIGHT: The manager said he would *raise* the price next week.

39. **Who, whom.** A tough one, but generally you are safe to use *whom* to refer to someone who has been the object of an action. *Who* is the word when somebody has been the actor.
    RIGHT: A 19-year-old woman, to *whom* the room was rented, left the window open.
    RIGHT: A 19-year-old woman, *who* rented the room, left the window open.

CREDITS

Harcourt Brace & Company

INDEX ☆☆☆☆☆

Harcourt Brace & Company

Harcourt Brace & Company